Penguin Books

MORRISON OF PEKING

Cyril Pearl is one of Australia's best known journalists, authors and literary provocateurs. He has been editor of the *Sunday Telegraph, A.M.* and the *Sunday Mirror.* He has a penchant for exploring and demolishing social myths and has published a number of books on contentious aspects of Australian history and society, including *Our Yesterdays, The Girl With The Swansdown Seat* and *Wild Men of Sydney.* Mr. Pearl's most recently published book is *Dublin in Bloomtime.* He is a regular contributor to several Australian newspapers and journals.

When he is not writing, Cyril Pearl is discussing and dispensing Australian wines.

Cyril Pearl

Morrison of Peking

Penguin Books

Penguin Books Ltd, Harmondsworth,
Middlesex, England
Penguin Books Australia Ltd, Ringwood,
Victoria, Australia

First published by Angus and Robertson Ltd
1967
Published in Penguin Books 1970
Copyright © Cyril Pearl, 1967

Printed in Singapore for
Penguin Books Australia Ltd,
by Times Printers Sdn Bhd

PREFACE

ONE OF the main streets in Peking used to be called "Morrison Street". Today it is called "Former Morrison Street". It was named for an adventurous Australian who went to Peking in 1897 as correspondent for *The Times* of London. He became a world authority on China, played a gallant part in the defence of the legations during the Boxer rising, and in 1912 became political adviser to Yuan Shih-k'ai, first president of the Chinese Republic. Because Yuan's memory is execrated by contemporary Chinese historians, Morrison Street has received its discreditable prefix, and Morrison's name is otherwise forgotten. But China never had a more ardent or more disinterested champion than this incorruptible Australian.

Before he settled in Peking, Morrison had wandered in many places. He had sailed before the mast on a blackbirding vessel in the Pacific; walked across Australia from north to south, alone and unarmed; led an exploring party into wild New Guinea; and made his way on foot and horse from Shanghai to Burma. Before he died he had travelled through every province in China except Tibet. A latterday Elizabethan who never quite grew up, he was infected with the raging Imperialism of the nineties, that curious conspiracy of rogues and idealists, poets and entrepreneurs, prophets and profit-seekers, which he saw romantically as a crusade. He was flattered to meet the poet of Imperialism, Rudyard Kipling, and one of its crudest practitioners, Dr Jamieson; he believed with its high-priests, Curzon, Chamberlain, Milner, and Rhodes that Britain had a historic, if not a divine mission to redeem the world. A few quotations revive the flavour of this belief: Curzon dedicated his book on the Far East to "all those who believed that Great Britain, under providence was the greatest Instrument for good the world had seen". Chamberlain declared that it was Britain's duty to enlarge the Empire and thus carry British justice and British law to millions who "lived in ignorance". Milner could never understand why these millions failed to realize that Britain's benevolent paternalism was imposed on them for their own good. Rhodes, "the Loyola of Empire", was convinced that the British Empire was "the divine instrument of future revelation" and wanted to create a Secret Society of the Elect to serve it. These men were not hypocrites. As Violet Markham, who stayed with Morrison in Peking in 1913, and admired him greatly, wrote thirty years later: "England's mission as a benevolent ruling power . . . was accepted with enthusiasm by many people, myself included . . . there was nothing unworthy in the vision as we saw it. Its fault lay in its shortness of range, and its failure to reckon with a host of psychological factors."

The most potent, of course, and one that has since been written, re-written, and underscored in blood, was the fact that non-European races, the "lesser breeds", however ignorant, "would rather govern themselves badly, corruptly even, than be governed by an alien administration". Morrison could not perceive this. Though he developed a great contempt for Britain's rulers, he never doubted the validity of British rule. But his love for Britain was sometimes difficult to reconcile with his love for China, and his love for China always difficult to reconcile with the corruption of its élite. He became adept at "double-think", passionately justifying British ways to the Chinese, and Chinese ways to the British. He also tried, in vain, to warn his fellow Australians of the growing menace of Japan.

He was a dying and disillusioned man when the tragedy of Versailles was enacted, and it is impossible to say how he would have adjusted himself to what he regarded as the gross betrayal of China by the Western powers, or to the regimented China of today. But he never doubted the destiny of the Chinese people, and his belief in their future greatness is one of the recurring themes in the diaries which he kept assiduously almost till the last day of his life, and on which this biography is largely based: diaries, still unpublished, which illuminate not only the complex history of China over many critical years, but also the complex character of the man who wrote them. Few have revealed themselves with equal honesty, warts, weaknesses and all.

Morrison of Peking

CHAPTER ONE

[I]

GEORGE ERNEST MORRISON, a man of quenchless curiosity about other people, was curiously uninterested in his own origins. When he was a world-famous newspaper correspondent, the confidant of statesmen and diplomats, and political adviser to China's first President, a distant and pompous kinsman in New Zealand, who was gathering material for the Clan Morrison Society in Edinburgh, asked Morrison about his ancestry. "To tell the truth I know very little about the earlier history of my family," he replied. "All I know is this, my grandfather—I do not even know his Christian name—was a grieve on a farm belonging to Gordon Cumming, the father of the lion hunter, at Altyre, that he himself possessed a small farm at Edinkillie. . . . I have been to the ancestral home of Edinkillie, which is close to Forres, and inspected the two cows and five sheep which the domain carried but was not inspired with curiosity to enquire whence my ancestors had come.

"The Rev. James Morrison used to enquire into such matters, and I fancy I can recollect that he had made the discovery (which caused him great satisfaction) that we were descended from an illegitimate son of a King of Norway. His researches further disclosed the interesting fact (which caused him less satisfaction) that one of his ancestors had got into trouble over a little question regarding the ownership of a sheep, the possession of which he was unable to explain to the satisfaction of a harsh gentleman in the judgment seat. The activities of this sheep fancier I believe ended somewhat abruptly."

Morrison ended this brief essay in genealogy by suggesting that his kinsman consult the Edinkillie Church register, though he pointed out that "in that part of the world a very considerable number of the alliances—some 16 percent I believe—take place without the knowledge of the church."

The Morrisons were certainly of Scandinavian origin. The home of the clan was the Island of Lewis, the most northerly of the Outer

Hebrides, and its badge was a piece of driftwood. According to clan tradition, its founder was a shipwrecked traveller who was cast ashore clinging to driftwood. One of his descendants, Hugh Morrison, became hereditary Deemster of Lewis. Another, the Rev. Kenneth Morrison, had a daughter who married the great-grandfather of Lord Macauley. Many crossed to the north of Scotland. George Ernest Morrison's grandfather, whose Christian name he professed not to know, was Donald Morrison, who was born in Morayshire in 1790 and married in 1815. A country merchant, and an elder of the Church of Scotland, he successfully combined piety and shopkeeping, retiring "with a modest competence" to end his days in the parish of Edinkillie, on the banks of the Findhorn, one of the most beautiful parts of Scotland. Donald had eight sons and two daughters. The eldest son, James, was the first Free Church minister of Urquhart after the Disruption, the founder of the Free Church at Edinkillie, and for fifty years Clerk of the Presbytery. Five other brothers distinguished themselves as teachers: Donald was Rector of Glasgow Academy for nearly half a century; Thomas was Rector of Glasgow Free Church Training College; Alexander, who had been Rector of the Hamilton Academy, went to Australia in 1857 to become principal of Scotch College in Melbourne, a position he held till his death in 1903. He was followed soon after by Robert, who was a master at Scotch College till his retirement in 1904, and, in 1858, by George, who founded Geelong College on Corio Bay, forty miles south of Melbourne, and was its principal, and later its proprietor, till his death in 1898.

[II]

From Dollar Clackinaman, in April 1858, George, who was twenty-eight, wrote to his brother Alexander in Melbourne:

My dear Sandy—

My last letter would have apprised you that you may soon expect my long proboscis to darken the portals of your Australian scene—a continuous run of bad luck in the mother country has induced me to emigrate and see if Fortune will smile more propitiously in the Antipodes. . . . You may have some idea of the work and the ineffable drudgery of teaching figuring for six weary monotonous hours. . . . I never liked my present post and was only too glad that your glowing description of Antipodal Scholastic prosperity gave me a good ground for desiring to emigrate.

But he assured dear Sandy that he would not in any way be an encumbrance to him, nor would he accept a situation "in any institution that may be in any way a rival to you". What he had in mind was to start with his brother Robert "some venture school", or to try his luck not in Melbourne but in some other towns that were rising in importance.

2

The letter presented a budget of local news and some comment on English politics. Lord Palmerston had lost the Prime Ministership and the Indian Mutiny was in its eleventh month:

> Poor old Pam has been kicked from power. The old cock showed fight to the very last and died with the old harness of abuse on his back . . . the country at large takes very little interest in politics or at all events cares very little who is at the head of affairs. We heard today that Lucknow was taken and that the rebellion is now fairly crushed. What an ambitious nation we are to be sure. In four years Russia has been humbled, the Persians defeated . . . Canton taken and the Chinese drubbed and an extensive mutiny quelled.

About the same time, George wrote to his brother Robert:

> Whether it is my bad luck in the profession hitherto that has given me a disgust of teaching I cannot say; but for my own part I would prefer almost any other trade even that of standing behind a counter and bowing and scraping with feigned obsequiousness to supercilious customers.

Despite this disgust, when he arrived in Melbourne at the end of 1858, George became mathematics master at Scotch College and, after six months, headmaster of Flinders National School, Geelong. The discovery of gold in Victoria in 1851 had transformed the colony. In a few chaotic years Melbourne had evolved from a ramshackle village of huts and tents and mud into a city of stone buildings, elaborate hotels, paved streets, gas-lighting, and suburban railways. In this feverish expansion, education was not neglected. A national education system was established, and dozens of church and private schools were opened, not only in Melbourne, but in the goldfield towns of Ballarat and Bendigo, and in Geelong, a busy port on the golden road to the diggings. In the early days of the gold rush it had progressed so rapidly that many believed it would become the capital of Victoria. After less than two years at the National School, George Morrison, in 1861, established his own school, The Geelong College. It occupied a building of eighteen rooms in Skene Street that had originally been the Hotel Garni, and later, as Knowle House, had been in turn the "Geelong Grammar School" and "Mrs Boyce's Establishment for Young Ladies". Principal Morrison commended his school eloquently: "Everything is done to promote the health and happiness of the boarders. They have sea bathing every morning, and are always accompanied by the principal or one of the resident masters. . . . Each boarder has a separate bed."

Before he left Scotland, Morrison had become engaged to a Yorkshire girl, Rebecca Greenwood, whose family had settled in Haworth about 1680. Miss Greenwood went to Australia before Morrison, in a clipper ship that took 140 days from Gravesend to Melbourne. They were married in Melbourne in 1859, and at Knowle House, on 4th February

1862, Mrs Morrison had her second child and first son. He was christened George Ernest Morrison. Mrs Morrison subsequently had four more sons and two more daughters.

"My father had a distinguished University career. He had an unusual memory, was an excellent shot, and in many respects was the best mimic I have ever known," George Ernest Morrison wrote in some unfinished "Reminiscences" in 1912. This is the only reference to his father in the huge collection of autobiographical material that he amassed, and it is impossible to escape the conclusion that, though passionately devoted to his mother throughout his life—and she outlived him—George Ernest Morrison had little sympathy with his father. But old Geelong boys of the early sixties used to tell of the pride headmaster Morrison had in his eldest boy; according to a historian of the college, G. McLeod Redmond, a pride that was manifested rather curiously:

> He used to bring the little fellow round the schoolrooms. Sometimes he would shut the door and George Ernest would be left outside. All would listen eagerly as he cried "Open! Open." Then there would be a tiny kick at the panels and a baby voice would call "Open, old George." The father would be delighted, and the door would be opened. The boy would be placed on the mantelpiece, and the stern Principal of the College would back away, saying "Look at me." When a good distance off, he would shout "Jump" and George Ernest, with implicit confidence, would spring boldly off the mantelpiece, to be caught in his father's arms.

Morrison's father, known as "the Doctor", was described by Redmond as a "tall, square, slight but powerful figure in a frock coat, and carrying a silk hat, a chalk-box and a stout cane". His head was broad, wide-browed, wide-eyed, and heavily whiskered. He wore heavy creaking shoes. A nephew, Dr W. A. Morrison, of Melbourne, remembered him as "an impressive figure of a man, upstanding, readily aggressive and forthright, and probably a formidable wielder of the disciplinary cane or tawse. He was reputedly a first-class mathematician, and all his sons were taught to play chess at an early age. . . . It was a fine sight at breakfast when he would add salt, butter and milk to his porridge and stir and stir the mixture with wholehearted vigour."

[III]

George Ernest Morrison remained at Geelong College till he was eighteen. "We may not have been hard students, but we lived healthy, happy lives, giving more time to outdoor play than to study," he recalled in the "Reminiscences". Despite the menace of the principal's omnipresent cane, the pupils seemed to enjoy remarkable freedom. In one of his schoolday diaries, young Morrison records without comment how the boarders warned a new resi-

4

dent master, Mr J. E. Martin, that "in consequence of his not having had a bath since his arrival they would see he had one next day". And "next day, four of the biggest boys laid hold of him and succeeded notwithstanding his struggles, in which he bent the head of the bed, in carrying him in triumph, headfirst, down the stairs. He was yelling like a bull all the time." Mr Martin, Morrison noted, when deposited in the bath, was "one mass of grease and filth and his legs were covered with a thin cake of mud which he declared was hair." He was threatened with another bath in a fortnight if he failed to take one voluntarily.

Morrison was an all-round athlete. In 1877 he rowed in a clinker four in Victoria's first interschool match, against Hawthorn Grammar. He weighed 10 stone 8 lb and was described as "the best oar in the boat 'when he liked'." In 1878 he won the Geelong College Cup for running and played in a school team against the second Australian Eleven to play in England. His diary records glumly that he made one off "Demon" Spofforth before he was bowled by Boyle. Spofforth, the greatest bowler of his time, perhaps of all times, had rocked England that year by taking six wickets for four runs in twenty-three balls against the M.C.C., led by Dr Grace.

Early in 1878, when he was sixteen, Morrison began what he called "a rum sort of diary", a practice which he continued with few interruptions till the last days of his life. His school diaries are largely devoted to sport, but there are candid descriptions of boys and masters ("Jerry is a big-headed overgrown boy. From want of exercise his eyes are bunged up with fat while his face is covered with bunches of headless excrescences") and entries that reveal a catholic interest in world, as well as local, affairs. The birth of another daughter to the Duchess of Edinburgh is recorded with the annotation: "What is still better, our little cow was happily delivered of a little daughter on Thursday." An event in October 1878 that has become enshrined in Australian folklore is economically reported: "There has been a terrible tragedy enacted near Mansfield 20 miles or so from where Uncle Arthur is. Four men, two of them brothers Kelly, have turned bushrangers and murdered 3 bobbies. A reward of £200 each has been offered for them. They will not be easily captured." (It was an accurate forecast. The Kelly Gang—Ned and Dan Kelly, Joe Byrne, and Steve Hart—evaded capture for two years.) Next day, there was domestic drama: "Annie the housemaid has left. She was drunk on Saturday, Sunday and today." That year, too, the Melbourne Cup had its drama. "There were 90,000 people present. . . . Chester looked like winning when it ran against a fence. On this, a fat gentleman had an epileptic fit." When Hector MacCommon, a former captain of the Scotch College Cricket Club and one of Victoria's most promising cricketers, was caught stealing money from members of the Melbourne Cricket Club, Morrison commented tolerantly: "I am very sorry for him. He no doubt got into the clutches of some prostitute and she has come down on him." Sometimes an entry suggests that Morrison was not attuned to the Calvinist faith of his forebears: "Sunday. To Hell. I mean to Church morn

5

and even." Another entry reads: "Thursday. Lovely. Victor Emmanuel the late King of Italy left 95 illegitimate children." The diaries also record great quantities of poetry, from Shakespeare to Oliver Wendell Holmes.

Each year the Morrisons spent the Christmas holidays at Queenscliff, a fashionable watering-place that had grown around a fishing-village three miles from the entrance to Port Phillip Bay. Queenscliff in the late seventies had a fixed population of about a thousand, which was more than doubled during the holiday season. Here Morrison developed three enthusiasms that he retained throughout his life: walking, hunting, and collecting. When he was sixteen, he got up at a quarter to four one morning to walk from Geelong to Queenscliff, twenty-one miles away, and back. The outward trip took him five and a half hours, including a stop at the Wallington, a public-house nine and a half miles out, for a shandy-gaff. At Queenscliff he had a bath and half an hour's rest, and set off a little before midday for home. "Forty-two miles in 12¼ hours," he noted in his diary. "I put my feet in hot water and felt pretty tired."

At fifteen, as at fifty-five, Morrison was an ardent hunter, methodically recording each day's bag. A typical day in 1877 yielded ten rabbits, fifteen native bears, three opossums, one bandicoot, and six hawks. (The native bear, or koala, is now almost extinct in Victoria.) There was an abundance of game in the grass and samphire-covered sandhills near Queenscliff: rabbits, gannets, black duck, teal, snipe, quail, bronze-winged pigeons, parrots, and wattle-birds. "My tastes were those of a nomad," Morrison recalled in middle age. "I loved books of travel. I loved to travel alone." At sixteen he read H. M. Stanley's *Conassie and Magdala*, and noted: "I greatly admire Stanley." Two years later he compiled a book about Australian exploration which he dedicated to "Henry Moreland Stanley . . . the greatest traveller of this or any other age / The most extraordinary man / and the man / For whom before all others in this world / I admire the most. . . ." In the preface he wrote:

> In this book I intend to write out information concerning everything about travel which I may happen to glean. More especially do I intend to devote myself to the great explorers of Australia. I shall first write out short condensed accounts taken from their own works and this completed I shall join them together in a connected narrative to which I shall give the grandiloquent title of Exploration in Australia by George Ernest Morrison. I may here remark in parenthesis that it is my fixed determination to do something great "some day."

Like most schoolboys, Morrison collected stamps, but at Queenscliff he also made a collection of shells that he sold to an itinerant dealer called Flatyre—better known as "Old Flatarse"—for £30, a considerable sum in those days. It was this collecting instinct that in adult life led Morrison to assemble the famous Chinese library that he sold to a Japanese baron for £35,000.

Forrester's Hall in Learmonth Street was the administrative, social, and cultural centre of Queenscliff; it served as Court House, Council

Chamber, State School, Concert and Lecture Hall, Skating Rink, and Ball Room. At a concert one night where Morrison and his mates banged the forms with waddies and stones till their favourite songs were encored ("Nancy Leigh", "Poor Old Robinson Crusoe, weren't he a fool to do so", "Julia, she were so werry peculiar", "Tell him I love him yet") he noted that one of the singers, Little Jordan, was "a little nut, 5 ft 2½ in. in height, weighs 8 st. 2 lb, and wears 6½ gloves and 4 boots". Watching Miss Charlotte Jordan "going through the complicated evolutions of the Quadrille," he noted that "she was fitted up in rare style, white dress, blue-bowed boots, six button gloves, bare breast, and a knock-me-down fringe, three inches long". At sixteen Morrison had developed a perceptive diarist's eye, a vivid power of description, and a scientific passion for detail. His eye was constantly focused on the social scene, particularly on the girl components of it.

He describes himself objectively:

Then there is Ernest Morrison. He is 5 ft 10 in high and weighs over 10 st and a half. He has fair hair, blue eyes, no whiskers and few eyebrows. His complexion isn't bad, his head is long and his profile good. He isn't by any means goodlooking and I am sure doesn't think so. His expression of countenance isn't very cheerful owing to the way he has been brought up and his nature is excitable though he isn't bad-tempered. But when he does lose his temper he has great difficulty in finding it again. He is pretty good at everything, takes lots of exercise, doesn't smoke, and drinks but little, so is always in good condition. He is very bashful and hasn't got good manners, but will improve at everything being only sixteen.

The constable, E. D. Hall, was a man "of beer-barrel proportions. He always gives me the idea that he has sent his paunch on ahead and is vainly trying to catch up with it."

Morrison's room at Geelong College was decorated with two dozen woodcuts from the *Illustrated London News*. It was a period of burgeoning imperialism, when artists and war correspondents succeeded in investing every Empire occasion—however trivial or dubious—with an aura of romance, piety, and derring-do: the extermination of a few Ashanti warriors, the expulsion of an Afghan amir, the homage of a Bechuana chieftain or two. . . .

One day in 1879 a master at Geelong College told Morrison that Archibald Forbes, the correspondent of the London *Daily News*, was allowed £5000 expenses for his services in the Turko-Russian war and received a present of £2000 when he got home. Morrison had already thought of becoming a correspondent. A year before, on the road to Queenscliff, he and his father "had a yarn about my future prospects". It was agreed that Morrison was to go to Edinburgh to study medicine. "I haven't given up hope of becoming a Special Correspondent," he wrote in his diary, "though of course I cannot become it. I would like to be a surgeon and then most certainly I would go to the war, that is if war happened to be at the time I was finished."

Meanwhile, Morrison explored life enthusiastically. There were frequent visits, for cricket or football, to "Marvellous Melbourne", a brash and booming city, its arteries pulsing with gold from the seemingly inexhaustible mines of Ballarat and Bendigo. In Melbourne he would stay with Uncle Alexander, at Scotch College, opposite the Treasury Gardens and agreeably convenient to the Melbourne Cricket Ground and the Melbourne Football Ground. But Melbourne was also proud of its culture and its churches. Some Sundays Morrison would go to the Presbyterian Church in the morning, and in the evening attend the Catholic service at St Francis', or the Anglican at St Paul's. On one visit he went to the Theatre Royal and saw actor-manager George Rignold, a magnificent Henry IV, ride his white horse down a stage on which a cast of 200 was deployed. "I think it was the most beautiful sight I have ever seen," Morrison wrote. But equally beautiful was a newly acquired picture at the National Gallery, Edwin Long's "Esther". "You could look at her all day and as she returns your glance you could easily fall in love with her. Oh, that face haunts me still," wrote the seventeen-year-old Morrison.

A few weeks afterwards Morrison visited the Geelong jail. He was disappointed at the gallows, though his host told him grisly stories of bungled executions in which the victim's head had been inadvertently pulled off, or in which the hangman had to leap from the scaffold to assist the process of strangulation by tugging sweatfully at the subject's legs. Morrison had a long talk with the current hangman and flagellator, Mr Gately, "who had despatched no less than 71 criminals". Gately was "a horrible looking wretch, 5 ft 10 in high, very broadshouldered with a brutal head, a face deeply pockmarked, a mouth big enough for two men and an appetite big enough for ten". Morrison was told by the cognoscenti that it was "much more trying to the nerves to see a man flagellated than hanged". The cat consisted of three wire thongs on a stockwhip handle, and at each stroke it cut away some flesh "so that when the flogging is finished the back resembles a lump of raw beef". Morrison recalled the horrors of Australia's penal system when, fifteen years later, he was able to compare it with the cruelty of the Chinese.

[IV]

On 30th December 1879, Morrison wrote in his diary:

This morning having made all preparations beforehand I started on a walk to while away my holidays to I don't know exactly where but at anyrate as far around the coast as practicable. All necessaries are carried in a canvas knapsack on my back, for defence a tomahawk is in my belt, whilst cooking utensils in the shape of two billies suspended by straps dangle behind.

Packed in the billies were writing materials, matches, lead pencils, a penknife, flannel and calico bandages, five pairs of socks, two toothbrushes, and a box of toothpowder. In the knapsack were two loaves of bread, a leg of roast mutton, half a pound of salt, quarter of a pound of pepper, and eight lemons. Morrison wore serge trousers, a thick woollen guernsey, his cricketing coat and shirt, strong boots, leggings, "as a protection against snakes" and, "at Mama's earnest solicitation" a sun shade which fitted into his cap and protected the back of the head. He must have appreciated Mama's foresight when, a few days later, he encountered shade temperatures of up to 115 degrees. In a chamois bag he carried £6 14s. 6d. in sovereigns, notes, and silver.

Though he told no one at home, he had resolved to walk to Adelaide, a distance round the coast of 652 miles. Letters and telegrams kept his mother informed of his progress. Some days, despite a blistering summer sun, he covered thirty-five miles. One day he was without water from 7.30 a.m. till 5 p.m. "No incident marked the journey," he wrote years later. "It was only a walking tour." In fact it was a remarkable achievement for an inexperienced youth. Much of the route lay through rugged and unsettled country. Beyond Cape Otway, as a writer in the *Picturesque Atlas of Australasia*, explained in 1884, the country inland was still imperfectly explored "owing to the difficulties it presents, for it is in places so heavily timbered, and there is such a mass of underwood to obstruct the tourist, that the most adventurous lover of the picturesque is baffled in his efforts to penetrate it".

Morrison's route lay through the Otway, Curdies' Inlet, Belfast (now Port Fairy), Portland, Cape Bridgewater, Gambierton, Millicent, Kingston, Coolatoo, Wellington, and Strathalbyn. Each day he wrote up his diary assiduously. At Curdies' Inlet he saw on the beach "the wreck of the *Young Australia*, once the *Carl*, of Dr Murray, Mount and Morris and South Seas Islanders kidnapping notoriety". At Nirrandi he lunched with Mr William Irvine, "a genius, a poet, painter and phrenologist, and the inventor of a new system of phonetic spelling". Mr Irvine told Morrison that he was a teetotaller and had a keen sense of the ridiculous. He would make a good parson or merchant as he had a good business head and was of sedentary inclinations, but there was no use his trying to be a doctor as he had neither courage, energy, endurance, determination, nor self-esteem. In the immemorial history of quackery, there can never have been a prognosis more unsound, though Morrison's "keen sense of the ridiculous" might have appreciated the tribute to his teetotalism when, some days later, he made this entry in his diary: "I drank too much whisky got damned well screwed and during the night nearly spewed my guts out."

Morrison reached Adelaide on Saturday, 14th February 1880, just before noon, and in time to see Jarvis play at the Oval. He had walked altogether 752 miles in forty-six days. Two days later, when he was resting at the house of a friend, Dr Gardiner, he wrote to his mother:

9

To show how a young fellow like me can get on in the world, when I was in Victoria I was offered £1 a week to do binding. A week or so ago I was offered 25/- a week to follow sheep. Tomorrow if I chose I could work my way in the barque *Montez*, Captain Bruss, to Western Australia, unload there for three weeks and then go to Christchurch in New Zealand. I was sorely tempted you can imagine with the offer. . . . I suppose you feel a load off your mind in knowing that I have accomplished what I resolved to but as I said before I am not half satisfied and am now game for the Northern Territory. . . .

He did not tell his mother that, "fired with a desire to see foreign countries", he had tried to ship as a seaman on board a sailing-ship bound for South America. Unsuccessful, he returned to Melbourne by steamer. Before he left Adelaide he had a brief experience of "mixing in grand society": "Tea and coffee at all hours. I wear a white cotton Northern Territory military suit of Gavin Gardiner's with nothing underneath also stylish grey belltopper of the Drs. and carry a gold-headed cane. Gavin being much shorter than me the breeches just reach to the top of the boots."

[V]

One day in April 1879, Morrison went to the University of Melbourne and matriculated, "that is, I signed a declaration promising to adhere to the rules, etc.". After this he called at a city hotel to pay his respects to the visiting English pugilist Jem Mace, the last bare-knuckle champion of the world and the father of scientific boxing in Australia. Eleven months later Morrison bought a gown and trencher for £3 and began his medical course. His diary for 1st May 1880 has a brief entry: "Saw first dead body. Old Man. Opera House. Grand Duchess of Gerolstein." He studied Latin and Greek, chemistry, mineralogy, and natural philosophy, some days working for twelve hours. His spare time on Saturdays and Sundays he spent on Melbourne's Albert Park Lagoon, learning to handle a canoe, for he had decided on another expedition: to paddle down the Murray, from Wodonga in Victoria to the sea in South Australia. The Murray, Australia's longest river, rises on the slopes of the Snowy Mountains in New South Wales, and flows 1609 miles.

Morrison had made his début in journalism by selling the diary of his walk to Adelaide for seven guineas to the *Leader*, a weekly paper published from the office of Melbourne's most popular morning paper, the *Age*. With this money and £10 earned by preparing the vocabulary of a Latin grammar written by Uncle Alexander, he bought a clinker-built cedar canoe, fourteen feet long, twenty-eight inches broad, with an arched deck, and upcurving bow and stern, like a whaleboat. A cork-filled canvas tubing went right around the deck. The paddle, eight and a half feet long, weighed nearly fifty ounces. The mast, when not in use, was carried on deck, and the little lug sail and the yard boom were stowed under the after deck. With practice, Morrison was able not only to stand up in the canoe and paddle but to balance himself standing on the rounded deck. On 30th November 1880 he left Melbourne by train with his canoe. Painted on the bows in gold letters was *The Stanley*. "My wish is that it may as successfully go down the Murray as his party descended the Congo," he wrote in his diary. "Of course, I can make no new discovery in it but I can see the noblest of Australian rivers and one of the finest rivers in the world in a way never before tried and as I shall be by myself I shall have the maximum of excitement, and as my canoe is so frail I shall have to exercise the greatest care." Certainly no one before had tried to explore so much of the Murray by canoe, though in 1853 Francis Cadell, a Scottish sea captain, had navigated a canvas canoe from Swan Hill to Wellington, where the Murray flows into Lake Alexandrina —a distance of about 875 miles. Morrison's equipment included 100 cartridges, cocoa, essence, biscuits, a small bottle of chlorodyne, and a flask of brandy. Before crossing the bridge into Victoria from Albury to Wodonga he bought a bottle of colonial wine for one shilling. The customs officer did not think it worth while to claim duty on the brandy. From Wodonga, with the Australian ensign fluttering at the peak of the lug sail, Morrison began his journey to the sea. It was easy to live off the country: there was abundance of bird life, pelicans by the hundreds, mountain duck, wood duck, teal, blue crane, black and white crane, ibis, great black shags, snake-necked divers, peewits, snipe, tarn, plover and waterhen, as well as wild pigs, kangaroos, rabbits, wild cattle, iguanas, snakes, and porcupines. And lonely station managers were happy to offer him hospitality.

"At Echuca," the local paper reported, "several gentlemen assembled at the boatshed to wish him *bon voyage*, and a pair-oared and four-oared crew accompanied the *voyageur* as far as the Wharapilla Station. The rowers here bade him farewell, giving three hearty cheers for the adventurous young colonial. . . . The scorching sun of the Murray Valley had been severely felt, as the oarsman is very much burnt, his neck and arms being covered with blisters. At Wentworth, Mr Morrison intends to deliver a lecture, in which he will relate his experiences in his river cruise."

At Murray Downs, near Swan Hill, Morrison walked out to Mr Officer's ostrich farm, established in 1875, and "for the first time in my life, saw these magnificent birds". At Narong one of Henry Miller's boundary riders gave him a grateful meal, and Morrison noted that Miller —who was known as "Money" Miller—had one block in Victoria, Kulkine station, of more than three million acres, with a river frontage to the Murray of 212 miles. It took Morrison seven days to pass it. "From boundary fence to boundary fence is 100 miles, yet the run is such a wretched one that . . . shearing accounts for only 30,000 sheep, one hundredth of a sheep to the acre," he commented. Morrison had Christmas dinner with the man in charge of the mail stables at Loungara, a "fine-looking fellow" called William Shoebridge, who "had fought through the

Crimean war and the Indian Mutiny, was at the taking of Peking, was thrice recommended for the Victoria Cross, taught Valentine Baker the goose-step and now received a pension for his meritorious services in the field". Morrison was "extremely anxious to bring home, as a trophy, an aboriginal skeleton, or part thereof". Near Euston he was told that a well-known black called Bryant was buried in the neighbourhood. With the help of a friend he found the bark gunyah erected over Bryant's grave, and after sweatfully excavating a hole six feet long, two feet broad, and four feet deep, found the bark that shielded the remains. "To make a long story short," he wrote, "we were entirely successful and bore off in triumph the complete skeleton enclosed in a black mass of corruption. I carried the skull over 750 miles and it is now bleaching on the sands of the Murray mouth. 'Alas poor Yorick!' We were very tired after our work. The temperature at 4 p.m., in a cool shade, was 106 Fahrenheit."

At Moorna, a property of 384,000 acres, carrying 70,000 sheep and 1000 head of large stock, Morrison was told that the station received an average of four tramps daily: "These 'Murrumbidgee whalers', as they are termed, each receive a pannikin of flour, some tea, and perhaps a little meat," he noted. "The life must possess some strange fascination, judging from the number of men who are content to drag out their existence, loafing from station to station, ostensibly looking for work but invariably finding an excuse for refusing the work offered them."

Morrison reached Goolwa, across the lake from Wellington, at the end of January 1881. Here he got a tow from a gig to the point of Mundoo Island, from where he set sail up the arm of the sea known as the Coorong, to a coaching stage, Cockatoo Wells. It was sixty-one miles up the Coorong, which at places was two and a half miles broad, and lashed by a terrific gale. Waves foamed round sharp reefs and his canoe was half full of water as the seas washed over it. But he arrived safely with his store of provisions intact—seven eggs, a small piece of corned beef, a loaf of bread, and three bottles of water. The shanty-keeper at Cockatoo Wells was a man who had spent some years in Spain. "His stories thrilled my imagination," Morrison recalled, "and for years I looked forward to the day when I might repeat his experiences."

Morrison had travelled 1555 miles when he reached Wood's Well. He sent his canoe by coach to Kingston, from where it was shipped to Melbourne. He then walked back to Geelong, a distance of only 347 miles. "This was quite a successful journey for the account published week by week in the Melbourne Leader more than paid its expenses. I feel however that the journey was more interesting and less tedious than the account thereof," he wrote in his "Reminiscences". His editor, Mr G. A. Syme, brother of the proprietor of the Age, David Syme, agreed with Morrison. Before the narrative was finished he repeatedly assured the author that everyone was tired of it. It was wearisome, he said, and monotonous. Few people would agree with these judgments today. The series of articles, published under the title "Down the Murray in a Canoe" by "G.E.M., Melbourne University", give a vivid and instructive account of Australian outback life in the 1880s, and their publication certainly revived Morrison's interest in journalism as a profession. It was not long before another event made him think more seriously of this. In March 1882 he was failed in his second professional examination, Materia Medica. He did not accept the verdict with equanimity. He sat up till 3 a.m. going over his paper, demanded an interview with his examiner, Dr Williams, and discussed the paper, question by question, with him, claiming that Williams did not know his subject. Then, from Geelong College, he sent a characteristically vigorous account of the interview to the Chancellor, the Vice-Chancellor, and Members of the University Council. It read, in part: "Gentlemen: An unfortunate medical student plucked in his 2nd year and thus compelled abruptly to leave the University, I ask in all humility if it is unreasonable that I should feel dissatisfied at being rejected by an examiner who had not first read the textbook prescribed by the University authorities."

Dr Williams had told him that he had done a shocking paper, had failed to obtain twenty-five per cent of the marks, and had answered only one question satisfactorily. Morrison pointed out emphatically that many of his rejected answers had been taken from Garrod's *London Dispensatory*.

Dr Williams read without comment till he came to "Mercurials are not so largely used in syphilis as formerly owing to the terrible sequelae". He threw the paper down on the table, shrugged his shoulders, distorted his features with an appalling grimace, and stammered "Lord have mercy on my soul, man. Don't you know that mercury is as much a specific in syphilis as quinine is in ague!" But a reference to Garrod showed him my authority.

"I seek no redress," Morrison's manifesto concluded, "indeed Dr Williams taunts me with having none as rather than now let me through he would resign as a lecturer!"

Years later he added a footnote: "That I was unjustly plucked, I have no shadow of doubt, but I bear no grudge—on the contrary, his error was one of the fortunate episodes of my life." On the other hand, in his only published book, *An Australian in China* (1895), Morrison suggests that the plucking was not entirely unjust:

In the examination for the Second-year Medicine, hoping the more to impress the Professors, I entered my name for honours—and they rejected me at the preliminary pass. It seems that in an examination in Materia Medica, I had among other trifling lapses prescribed a dose of Oleum Crotonis of "one half to two drachms *carefully increased*." I confess that I had never heard of the wretched stuff: the question was taken from far on in the text book and, unfortunately, my reading had not extended quite so far. When a deputation from my family waited upon the examiner to ascertain the cause of my misadventure, the only satisfaction we got was the obliging assurance "that you might as well let a mad dog loose in Collins Street" as allow me to become a doctor. [Collins Street is the haven of Melbourne's best-known doctors.] And then the examiner produced my prescription. But I thought I saw a faint chance of escape. I pointed a nervous finger to the two words "carefully increased," and pleaded that that indication of caution ought to save me. "Save *you* it might," he shouted with unnecessary vehemence: "but, God bless my soul, man, it would not save your patient." The examiner was a man intemperate of speech; so I left the University. It was a severe blow to the University, but the University survived.

CHAPTER TWO

[I]

AT CURDIES' INLET, as he tramped round the Victorian coast, Morrison had seen the rotting timbers of the brig *Carl*. Eight years before, when Morrison was a boy of ten, her owner, Dr James Patrick Murray, had been on trial for murder. Even in an age of remarkable rogues, when there was often a perverse association between piety and villainy, Murray was a unique monster. A licentiate of the Royal College of Surgeons in Ireland, and a resident physician in Invercargill, New Zealand, and in Melbourne, he had been a member of the party led by Alfred William Howitt in 1861 to search for the explorers Burke and Wills, and in 1865 was medical officer and second-in-command of an expedition that searched for traces of the explorer Leichhardt, who vanished with his entire party on a trans-continental expedition in 1848. Dr Murray was described as a man "of good address, with some pretensions to culture and given to religious exercises". His practice of medicine, like his practice of religion, was unconventional; as a staff member of the Victorian Benevolent Association, he used to give his patients generous doses of morphia so as to keep them somnolent for a few days while he took a holiday. From this minor infraction of the Hippocratic code, he graduated, within a few years, to mass murder. Early in 1871 he bought the 256-ton brig *Carl*, omitting the formality of paying for her, and in June sailed from Port Phillip for Fiji with six passengers. He quarrelled with two of them and set them ashore, protesting, on the island of Tanna in the southern New Hebrides, where they were soon eaten. Murray then sailed to the Solomon Islands in search of native labour for sale in Fiji.

[II]

The traffic in islanders for plantation work in Fiji, Samoa, and Queensland was pioneered by another godly man, Robert Towns, an English collier boy who commanded a brig at the age of twenty, and sailed his own vessel to Australia some fourteen years later. He settled in Sydney in 1842, married a sister of William Charles Wentworth, and became a wealthy merchant, with big squatting interests in Queensland, and a fleet of ships trading in bêche-de-mer and sandalwood. He gave a handsome pulpit to St Andrew's Cathedral, Sydney, and his name is perpetuated in the Queensland port of Townsville. When the American Civil War cut off supplies of American cotton, Towns planted cotton on the Logan River, forty miles from Brisbane, and after trying unsuccessfully to import cheap Indian labour, in 1865 sent his schooner, the *Don Juan*, to stock up with islanders from the New Hebrides. The *Don Juan* was commanded by Henry Ross Lewin, a tough sandalwooder and beachcomber who had a station on Tanna. He had been a seaman in the Royal Navy, serving on the China coast in 1840 during the Opium War.

Apologists for Captain Towns say he really believed that the islanders would benefit spiritually from the influence of Christianity, just as the cotton-growers would benefit materially from a supply of plantation workers at ten shillings a month. Mr Lewin was illiterate, but Captain Towns addressed a scholarly circular "to any missionary into whose hands this may come", soliciting his aid in obtaining islanders. "I . . . will do more towards civilizing the natives in one year than you can possibly in ten," Towns wrote. A few years later Lewin dictated a letter to a Brisbane paper describing the great benefits that the recruiting trade had conferred on the natives only a few days before he was charged with criminally assaulting a Tanna girl who had been dragged naked onto his boat. Lewin, not surprisingly, was acquitted, and continued his work of uplifting the heathen until he was killed, and presumably eaten, by some ungrateful inhabitants of Tanna who did not want to be uplifted.

Thomas Dunbabin, answering the question, "How far did the cannibal isles profit by the Christianizing and civilizing influences to which they were subjected in Queensland?", quotes some "curious evidence" given by Charles Eden, who in the seventies employed twenty kanakas on his sugar plantation on the Murray River, near Cardwell. Mr Eden tells how the favourite Sunday occupation of the Tanna men was hunting the local aborigines. On one of these excursions they drove ten aboriginal men into a waterhole, and drove them out by harpooning them with a shear-blade fixed to a long pole. One by one the blacks were prodded to the edge of the waterhole, and then killed. "If they were not all eaten," Mr Dunbabin comments dryly, "it was only because the supply of meat was too large to be consumed." Mr Eden did not object to these healthy Sabbath diversions, though Mrs Eden seems to have been a little critical when the Tanna men returned one Sunday evening with a dead cassowary and a live black boy of six or seven. The Tanna head man explained how they had destroyed a party of aborigines but kept the boy so that he could be roasted as a Sunday supper treat for their mistress. Mrs Eden fastidiously refused the *plat du jour*, and the boy's life was spared.

By September 1866, Towns had imported 315 kanakas—a generic name for the islanders—only seven of whom were returned within the promised period of twelve months. Other entrepreneurs were soon attracted to the trade. In 1867 the *King Oscar*, a barque of 248 tons, was chartered by two Queensland statesmen—Mr W. D. White, M.L.C., and Mr Graham Mylne, M.L.A. It sailed under the missionary banner of Ross Lewin and returned with 270 kanakas, who were quickly sold for £9 a head. Mr Lewin, in his Christianizing role, had found it necessary to shoot a number of unco-operative natives and to burn their village and crops. But the success of his venture greatly stimulated "blackbirding", as the business was called, and the interest shown in this unlawful trade by Queensland's respected law-makers made its suppression difficult. Among other successful backbirders was a firm of which the Premier of Queensland, the Hon. Robert Ramsay Mackenzie, was a partner.

When the cotton boom burst, Captain Towns lost interest in blackbirding, but Lewin made it a full-time occupation. In April 1867 he advertised in Brisbane that he would supply "Sugar Planters, Cotton Growers, and Others" with "the best and most serviceable natives to be had among the islands at £7 a man". By the end of the sixties the trade in islanders had become extensive and notorious. The British Government had early expressed its belief that the recruiting of islanders was likely to be associated with violence, deceit, and crime. The most serious abuses occurred beyond the jurisdiction of the Queensland Government, and British naval commanders sent to the Pacific to report on the traffic advised the Colonial Office that Imperial rather than Colonial action was necessary to suppress it.

Despite this, the Colonial Office in 1868 approved a Queensland Act which attempted to control the traffic. It obliged dealers to enter into heavy bonds before being granted licences to import natives: it fixed wages at a minimum of £6 a year and laid down a minimum scale of rations. Natives were supposed to understand clearly the terms of their employment, to embark of their own free will, and to be returned to their home islands when their three years' contract expired. The Act was quite ineffectual. Within a year British officials advised their Government that attempts to control what had now become known as "the slave traffic" had failed. In 1870 a Select Committee of the Queensland Legislative Assembly pretended to inquire into the operations of the Act. One witness, Mr Robert Short, gave damning evidence which was suppressed on the grounds that it was not based on personal experience. Mr Short had a more plausible explanation. The majority of the committee, he said, were either employers of Polynesian labour or known advocates of the system. By then, increasing demand for native labour had raised the price in Queensland to £12 a head, and outrages by blackbirders increased. They were matched by native outrages. It had become customary to pay natives partly in inferior rifles and ammunition, and these were at times used against the slavers. Despite many recommendations, this arms traffic was not suppressed till 1884. In 1878 planters protested that a proposed ban was "interference".

Early in 1871 the first Anglican Bishop of Melanesia, Bishop John Coleridge Patteson, vigorously condemned the "deception and violence" practised by the recruiters, and called for Imperial legislation "to put an end to this miserable state of affairs". He told Captain Palmer, of H.M.S. *Rosario*, how some recruiters painted their ships white to resemble his mission schooner, the *Southern Cross*, and sent ashore a crew member dressed as a missionary to tell the natives that the Bishop had broken his leg and wanted to see them. "More than one cargo was secured in this atrocious manner," the Bishop said.

On 27th September 1872 he landed with his colleague the Rev. Mr Atkins, on Nukapu Island, in the Santa Cruz group, where, a few days before, one of these spurious bishops had lured a number of men on board a blackbirding ship. Some of the remaining natives received the genuine churchmen with poisoned arrows and clubbed the bishop to death. Patteson had many friends among British parliamentarians, and his murder led to renewed demands that the British Government suppress the slave traffic. A Kidnapping Act, passed the same year, made it a felony to remove a native without his consent, and five fast schooners were sent to patrol the islands. Within a year some offenders were convicted and received heavy sentences. But once more the limitations of the Act soon became apparent. A trader had only to change his flag—legally or illegally —to evade British jurisdiction, and as the Act recognized native sovereignty in the islands, effective control on land was impossible.

[III]

Dr Murray, having disposed of his two intransigent passengers, stocked up with seventy islanders from Tanna and continued his voyage to Bougainville, where he kidnapped eighty very fierce savages by sinking their canoes with pieces of pig-iron and small cannon dropped on ropes from the *Carl*. An attempt by one of the *Carl's* passengers, Mr Mount, to lure them aboard by the less troublesome fake missionary trick had failed. The Bougainville natives resented their captivity and tried to set fire to the ship by lighting coconut fibre. A conflict took place between them and the less aggressive Tanna natives, and Dr Murray gave orders to fire at them indiscriminately. He and some of his shipmates assembled on deck, and Mr Mount obligingly turned a bulls-eye lantern on the screaming natives, while Dr Murray brightened the proceedings by singing "Marching Through Georgia". Later Dr Murray and another passenger bored holes in the bulkhead and continued firing throughout the night. The cook then served coffee, and Dr Murray read prayers. At least seventy natives were killed, and thirty-five who were seriously wounded were heaved overboard with the dead.

After a second voyage, when Murray believed that his captain was trying to poison him, he turned Queen's evidence on his accomplices, two of whom were sentenced to death but not executed. Murray and Mount were later charged in Melbourne with murder, found guilty of manslaughter, and sentenced to fifteen years' penal servitude. But even this generous sentence was not carried out. It was upset on appeal on the grounds that there was no such sentence as penal servitude in Victoria. By the time the Privy Council had reversed the decision, Murray and Mount had left Victoria.

[IV]

The Queensland sugar industry expanded rapidly in the early eighties, and with it the demand for native labour. It was still believed that white men could not work in the tropics. Scores of Australian vessels—schooners, barques, brigantines, and brigs—engaged in blackbirding. They went armed and equipped, says Mr James Cowan, "like privateers, or like the man-stealers of the old Middle Passage of infamous slave-trade memory. Some mounted guns on their decks. All the crews were armed with rifles and revolvers." And all the old techniques of recruiting were employed once more, from deceit and enticement to kidnapping and murder. The government agents employed to prevent these abuses either abetted or ignored them. They were, as Morrison afterwards wrote, a poorly paid, poor type of official, often brutal as well as corrupt. Typical, perhaps, was Mr W. A. McMurdo, government agent on the schooner *Stanley*, whose master, Captain Joseph Davies, was charged in Adelaide in February 1884 with kidnapping two Lachlan Islands natives whose village he had burned. Mr McMurdo, in his log for March-April 1883, laconically if ungrammatically recorded another unfortunate incident. He had caught some of his kanaka passengers stealing biscuits: "I then thrashed the whole six . . . and laid it on well this time. . . . They can stand pain wonderfully and their skins are thick, only breathing a little." When one of them died next day, Mr McMurdo observed: "I must have greatly overrated their powers of endurance. I had asked Connell [a seaman] to make a proper 'cat' as there was no hold upon the other—three tails of spun-yarn; he made one of five, done up hard with strips of lead let into the strands, and had just finished it when the man *died* (horror!)." Next day two other natives died.

[V]

While traders, plantation-owners, and interested politicians continued to defend the blackbirding traffic, it was bitterly attacked by humanitarians, liberal politicians, and missionaries. One of its most vehement critics was the Rev. John G. Paton, who had a Presbyterian mission on the New Hebrides. In speeches, sermons, and letters to newspapers he repeatedly denounced the traffic as "a criminal agency for the extermination or moral ruin of the South Sea Islanders".

Disgusted at his failure in medicine, and more than ever determined to become a journalist, Morrison saw an opportunity to nourish his

19

ambition by investigating the controversial kanaka traffic at close range. He called on David Syme, the proprietor of the Melbourne *Age*, and outlined a plan to ship as a seaman on a blackbirding vessel. Syme, an uncompromising Scot who had rejected his Calvinist faith, told Morrison that a truthful report on the traffic would be welcome, because no one believed "that old liar Paton". The *Age* was then a radical, hard-hitting, and influential paper, claiming a circulation of 50,430 copies, "more than five times that of any other daily newspaper in Victoria". On its staff was a future Prime Minister of Australia, Alfred Deakin.

Both his father and mother tried to dissuade Morrison from this venture. He wrote to his mother from Scotch College, Melbourne, on 20th March 1882:

> I am not taking a hasty step. . . . In no other way can I see any hope for furthering my wish to become a newspaper correspondent and only as a newspaper correspondent can I expect to distinguish myself above the common herd. . . . In spite of all that is said to the contrary it is the noblest in my opinion of all the professions and as energy, courage, temperance and truthfulness are necessary to its success, to this fact must be ascribed the high positions occupied by journalists all over the world. . . . If my letters from Queensland are of sufficient merit, Mr Syme will print and I will be paid for them at the rate of one pound a column.

In a second letter he wrote:

> I go to Queensland to commence the apprenticeship of a profession in which I earnestly hope some day to make my mark. . . . You ask me not to run into unnecessary danger—my whole life has been a combat against a natural shrinking from the most trifling approach to danger.

Morrison left Melbourne by the steamer *Leura* on 3rd April 1882, and landed in Sydney after an exceptionally rough passage of ninety-nine hours. The *Leura* encountered one of the worst storms on record, and a report circulated in Sydney that she had foundered. Her survival does not seem to have been due to skilful seamanship. Early on the morning of the last day the captain decided that they were thirty miles north of Sydney and directed his course accordingly. When the storm broke, it was found that they were 110 miles south of Sydney, heading back to Melbourne.

From Brisbane, Morrison embarked on the *Lady Bowen*, a slow old paddle steamer, for Rockhampton. The *Lady Bowen* left Brisbane six hours later with a half-drunken captain, and was delayed a few more hours when it stuck in the river. From Rockhampton, he sailed in a new steamer, the *Ranelagh*, for Port Mackay, the main centre of the Queensland sugar industry, and of the blackbirding trade. Of 11,059 islanders brought to Queensland between 1881 and 1883, 4426 went to Mackay. It was in Mackay that a young woman named Mrs Charles Armstrong, who was to become famous under the name of Madame Melba, began her career as a singer.

Here, after many rejections, Morrison shipped as an ordinary seaman—at one shilling a month—on the 119-ton brigantine *Lavinia*, which was recruiting a fresh batch of natives and taking back eighty-eight who had completed their three years' contract in Queensland or were too sick to be worth keeping. Among them were seven women. One, Morrison noted, "though her lips were rather thick, bore a striking resemblance to the Princess of Wales", the future Queen Alexandra.

The *Lavinia* sailed for the New Hebrides on 1st June 1882. Months later Morrison wrote to his mother, who was constantly warning him against the evils of loose speech, drink, and bad companionship:

> I went on board a cripple having severely sprained my two knees so that I could with great difficulty and pain crawl up to my meals. I slept in the hold with the Kanakas and received no harm from the foul air generated there indeed it was better to put up with discomfort for I then could keep myself aloof from the sailors. I rowed in the recruiting agent's boat crew with the Kanakas an uncommon thing for a white man and rather risky. In this way I was enabled to see the natives on their own islands, to speak with them and to undergo what excitement there was in avoiding reefs and breakers and being in the middle of armed savages who could if they liked have taken boat and crew without trouble. I am come back from the voyage stronger and better than ever I was in my life. I wouldn't care to tell anyone else but my mother that nearly all the reading I did on board was confined to Milton and the New Testament and I honestly feel changed much for the better by the reading.
>
> In my account of the island voyage I shall only give my own experience. I shall be careful not to try and describe the scenery for I have not the ability and any sentence which I might think *grand* I shall following the advice of Dr Johnson score out.

Dr Robert McBurney, the health officer for Mackay, was also part-owner of the *Lavinia*. In his convenient dual role he arranged for eighteen sick islanders to be included in the home-going batch. The first night out, a sickly little boy of about fourteen, with "a withered little frame", died and was thrown overboard. "I felt very sad for this homeless Malo boy, and indignant that any health officer could be heartless enough to allow that he was in a safe state to make the long voyage . . ." Morrison wrote in his dispatch to the *Leader*. A few days later two other kanaka passengers died, both from dysentery. "They were reduced to the last stage of weakness before they ever came on board, but I suppose the health officer expected the sea voyage to do them good," Morrison wrote. "In the middle of the night I was awakened by hearing the officer of the watch call out 'Pass the dead Api boy up on deck quick!' so I got up. The body was roughly sewn in canvas, a rice bag of stones was made fast to his feet, and two of his countrymen in silence dropped him overboard."

Morrison's attitude towards the sick islanders is a curious mixture of sympathy and cynicism. He is still, obviously, the undergraduate, with a pawky, ponderous medical student's humour:

The Islander that caused the most amusement was a gaunt Albino from Lakono, with a horrible skin disease. His neck was as if it had been dusted with fish scales; his body was covered with a black eruption of spots. He was always scratching himself, the itching must have been well nigh insupportable, as his skin from head to foot was peeling off in great flakes. . . .

With malicious intent I often approached him with a pannikin in one hand and my *fidus Achates*, the castor oil bottle, in the other. But there was a noisome stench about him that, to again quote poetry —for what is more suggestive of poetry than castor oil?—"settled his hash," so far as regards the hope of his being cured by me. I have read that if you give a live fish snuff his scales will fly off. I thought of preparing for scurvy an inhalation of burnt paper, hopeful that it might relieve him of the muscular exertion of scratching himself every minute of the twenty-four hours by depriving him of his epidermis whole.

There was a sickly Aoba woman

moving across the deck on her hand and left heel, the right leg being carried forward like a bowsprit. She was suffering from a diseased foot, more than half of the sole having rotted away. The woman was in a shocking state of filth and disease, yet she had been landed in Queensland only ten months before healthy and active.

Morrison treated her with linseed poultices and a strong bluestone lotion, and she "got much better".

Not so an Aoba boy, a nice lad, who was ill with violent dysentery. I gave him a stiff dose of castor oil and chlorodyne. Two days later I repeated the dose, adding ostentatiously, as the captain was standing by, a little sulphate of zinc, to show him that my knowledge of *materia medica* was practically unlimited. "The value of this prescription," I remarked to the captain, "is self-evident. The chlorodyne seeks to bind him up internally, the castor oil wrestles with the chlorodyne, when the zinc sulphate steps in, intent on dislodging them both. The dysentery, disgusted with the angry contention, makes haste to quit." It turned out as I expected partly. The dysentery took its departure, but, worse luck, so did the boy. . . .

It was my forenoon watch, and about eleven o'clock it was reported to the mate that he was dead, so a sennit was made fast round his neck and another round his ankles, and he was hauled out of the hold. The mate was greatly excited, and told Joe to sew him up at once and chuck him over. But I suggested that it might be more humane to first wait till the boy was dead. I observed a slight heaving of the chest, and on uncovering his face, he slowly opened his eyes, showing the death film upon them. The rope round his neck nearly strangled him. Shame to tell, that boy was roughly laid in the weather scuppers, and there, in sight of all on board, he gasped in his death throes for four hours. I was below when he was thrown overboard, so can merely say that the opinion was freely expressed in the forecastle that the man was not dead even then.

Morrison was kept busy dosing the sick, steering, and writing the notes on which his articles were later based:

Our Manners

If you were told to hurry up with the grease-pot, you understood that someone was waiting for the butter. If you were requested to shy along the shoeleather you at once cast about for the saltmeat and if you were politely told that it was inadvisable to detain the dry chuck and tar all night, you knew that there was a mouth watering for bread and molasses.

He found steering "exhilarating fun", especially at night, and when the skipper was lighthearted: "He then jaunts up and down the poop, his trousers hitched up to his armpits, and suddenly trills out this charming verse . . .

> *For we live in unitigh,*
> *And Beelzebub is nigh,*
> *So it's come and join the Hallelujah band."*

Morrison made a detailed study of the arms trade which the Queensland Government was reluctant to suppress. He found that there were seventy-three men on board the *Lavinia* "well enough to carry a musket". These were armed with 78 Sniders, 6 Spencers, 29 Enfields, 47 muskets, 9 shot guns, and two revolvers, and had between them 1861lb. of powder, and 9300 rounds of ammunition. "Even the ladies were armed. Mrs M'Lean, the old witch we had left at Lakona, having a Snider and a musket, 14lb. of powder, and 100 Snider cartridges." He estimated that the seventy-three kanakas had spent on offensive weapons £730, or £10 a head out of the £18 each had earned for his three years' labour:

Now we can see what a great loss would be caused to tradespeople were the Queensland Government to prohibit the sale of firearms and ammunitions to the Kanakas. There are over 4000 Kanakas in that district alone of which the port we sail from is the town, where they spend all their money. Let this prohibition be enforced, and over £13,300 will be annually diverted into a different channel.

The *Lavinia* cruised through the New Hebrides and the Banks group, from Vanua Lava on the north, to Futuna on the south, and, with seventy-six recruits in her hold, made a rapid run home. She reached Port Mackay on 8th September 1882, just 100 days after her departure. The boys fetched £16 a head, a very good price.

[VI]

Morrison's account of the voyage appeared in the *Leader* in six weekly instalments. They were headed "A Cruise in a Queensland Slaver, by a Medical Student". Apart from his account of the treatment of the sick natives, he was not very critical of the slave trade. The articles were written in a bantering, would-be humorous style which softens much of his criticism.

As the *Leader* commented editorially:

> The papers . . . give a glimpse of the better side of the Queensland labour trade, but there is another side. . . . It is neither more nor less than a slave trade encrusted with the horrors to put down which the naval force and treasure of the mother country have been spent for many years. We know from independent sources that the natives are often obtained . . . by force or fraud. . . . Besides this, we find that even those who complete their time of servitude and are despatched 'home' find quite a different kind of destiny. Ship captains only seek to get rid of them, and take no pains to land them on the particular island from which they came. . . . The *Rhoderick Dhu* recently landed a number of returning Kanakas at Paama, where they were straightaway killed and eaten. The *Helena* since then discharged some of her freight at Apii, where their end was just as summary. The men who, knowing this fact, cast them upon these coasts, are unquestionably guilty of murder.

[VII]

Ten days after arriving back in Port Mackay, Morrison took steerage passage in the steamer *Ranelagh* for Cooktown. Once again he found sea travel on the Australian coast hazardous. The *Ranelagh*, crowded with miners going to the gold rush at the Palmer River, on the Gulf of Carpentaria, left at midnight. Morrison, who had been up all the previous night finishing his report for the *Leader*, found an empty berth and turned in. Some hours later he heard a noise that sounded like the chain running out of the hawser pipe. It only half awakened him: "I thought we had come to anchor in Bowen. . . . Suddenly, I was awakened by a loud voice calling me, 'Hey, mate, are you going to stay there all night—with the ship on the rocks and orders out for everyone to come aft!' " He looked out and saw that the water was over the cabin floor. The ship was slowly sinking. He ran quickly up on deck and could see the land quite close. "I knew that if the worst came to the worst, I could swim ashore. I came back to the cabin, put all my things together, and brought them on deck. When I left the cabin the water was well above my knees, but there was no danger, and no need for excitement."

Next morning they were taken ashore. This was only the *Ranelagh*'s third voyage, and the second time she had been wrecked. "It has been a tame wreck, one of the tamest on record," Morrison told his mother.

From Bowen, Morrison took another steamer to Cooktown, where he found cheap accommodation in a public house kept by a lady "affectionately known to her fellow townsmen as 'Everybody's Annie'". While he was in Cooktown the missionary schooner *Ellangowan* came in, with two well-known missionaries aboard, the Rev. W. G. Lawes and the Rev. James Chalmers.

The *Ellengowan* belonged to the London Missionary Society. In it, Messrs Lawes and Chalmers had during the seventies made several expeditions to unkown New Guinea, ascending the Baxter and Fly rivers and exploring the coast from Port Moresby to Milne Bay. Morrison, who was now determined to make his long-dreamed-of walk across Australia, starting at Normanton, wrote to the Rev. Mr. Chalmers, and asked if he could work his passage to Port Moresby, where their mission was, to Thursday Island, and so to Normanton. His letter was obviously composed with an eye on the reverend gentlemen:

I have reason to believe I am a very good helmsman. I do not of course ask for any pay. I do not mind how rough the accommodation may be. I will willingly sleep on deck. . . . You of course understand that I travel as rough and cheap as possible because I can't forget that it is my father's and not my own money I am spending and beside enjoyment is all the more satisfactory the more hard worked one has been to attain it. I am a total abstainer and don't smoke.

Morrison's offer to work his passage on the *Ellengowan* was accepted. He berthed with the men, kept watch, and regularly took his trick at the wheel. From Port Moresby he accompanied Mr Chalmers in the mission boat as far as Aroba and, returning to Port Moresby, went on a bird-shooting party with the naturalist, Andrew Goldie, who had been sent to New Guinea by a firm of London nurserymen. After some "delightful days" with Goldie he returned to the mission station and took passage in a Chinese junk, the *Wong Hing*, bound for Cooktown with the season's catch of bêche-de-mer, or trepang, a sea-slug which, slightly smoked, is prized by Chinese as a delicacy.

It was another eccentric voyage. The captain, a Cantonese, was the only man on board "who knew the bow from the stern or could tie a knot or wield the tiller". The others, twelve Chinese, two New Guinea boys, a Raratonga woman, and a Maltese half-caste, were concerned only with smoking the bêche-de-mer. The voyage from Port Moresby to Cooktown took twenty-three days. Sixteen days out, off Borrow Head, with Cooktown 108 miles dead to windward, Morrison found time to write to a cousin in Port Mackay, Elisabeth Carter:

Apple of my heye (Lizzie)
Having proved myself triumphantly to be the most intolerable un-mitigated wit-befogged ass that ever trembled at a Melbourne Univer-

sity examination I received so many polite hints to try something else that at last I was really compelled nolens volens to clear out from Melbourne in order to save the family from further disgrace. . . . I have been knocking about ever since and am now a dull moping hard-worked outcast from civilization. Instead of having the proud letters M.B. Ch.M., after my name I shall I fear have to content myself with the more humble O.S., ordinary seaman. I am now on board a small and believe me not over-safe junk. . . . I am weak and thin from insufficient food, dry bread and rice with occasional feeds of fish.

His brother Alick was "the personification of success". He was "the incarnation of failure".

The captain of the *Wong Hing* was no more skilled in navigation than the captain of the *Leura*. At one stage of the twenty-three days' sailing he reckoned he was eighty miles south of Cooktown when he was 120 miles north of the port.

[VIII]

After a brief look at the Torres Strait pearl fishery Morrison visited Thursday Island, where he stayed with the police magistrate, Henry Chester, the virtual ruler of the island. Mr Chester had a beautiful garden in which the prisoners worked, and Morrison noted that the magistrate's sentences were apt to vary with the season and the condition of his garden. Morrison then took a steamer down the Gulf of Carpentaria to Normanton, "a quiet little bush township 55 miles up the Norman River", and the centre for the Etheridge and Palmer goldfields. Its population, which once reached 2000, has dwindled today to about 500. He arrived in Normanton on 19th December 1882, and at once prepared for the journey he had long contemplated, a walk across Australia from north to south. In his notebook he wrote:

For a long time I have wished to cross Australia. It was lying in bed at Port Mackay with two crippled knees so frail that they could not support my weakened frame across the room that I resolved to cross Australia on foot. It was hearing on all hands of the long stages between stations and the impossibility of travelling without at least two horses that decided me to go alone. It was the reports told me by everyone of the danger to be incurred from the blacks especially unless the traveller showed a rifle and revolver that promoted me in the decision to go entirely alone. Fever I had to fear as well as floods. Quinine would be required to combat the former a telescope was necessary to forewarn me of the latter. My telescope was stolen from me in Cooktown, my quinine by accident was thrown away at Thursday Island. Of all things a compass would be absolutely useful yet mine was utterly destroyed in New Guinea. What could I argue from these but that fever would pass me unharming, floods would never endanger my life nor would I ever be in a situation where I could find no escape but by the use of the compass?

He also set down useful hints for the transcontinental walker:

Drink well before starting. Drink only at long intervals.

Soap the inside of the stockings before setting out making a thick lather all over. A raw egg broken into a boot before putting it on greatly softens the leather.

Thirst is a fever of the palate. Excite the saliva—moisten with olive oil.

"Every hour was precious, for the rainy season was close at hand, the sky already threatening," he recalled in his "Reminiscences". But, as always, he found time to write to his mother. He had been "rather tickled", he said, by a letter from David Syme, asking him for a fuller account of the effects of missionary effort, on the one hand, in promoting the civilization of the kanakas, and the effect of the labour traffic on the other: "I don't know what the dull head of Syme means by this. . . . I should say generally that the primary effect of missionary civilizing was to make the natives lying, fawning, cringing, deceitful and as bad as possible. . . ."

At Normanton's general store he bought a rough swagman's outfit—a panama hat, heavy boots, corduroys, an oil cloth and blanket, a billy and a quart pot, and on the evening of 19th December started on his walk. The distance was 2043 miles. "Roughly speaking," he wrote, "it was my intention to follow the route taken 21 years before by the Burke and Wills expedition, that most disastrous of all Australian expeditions."

Robert O'Hara Burke, an amiable but incompetent Irish ex-soldier and police inspector, and William John Wills, a cultivated young Englishman, set out from Melbourne on 20th August 1860 to cross Australia from south to north. Their expedition, the most elaborate in Australian history, consisted of fifteen men, twenty-five camels, twenty-three horses, waggons, and twenty-one tons of equipment, including four gallons of brandy for the men and sixty gallons of rum for the camels. It ended in tragedy. Burke and Wills almost reached the Gulf of Carpentaria, at a point near the mouth of the Norman River, on 11th February 1861, but perished after returning to their base at Cooper's Creek. Five other members of the party died. The expedition was bedevilled by lack of water, lack of food, scurvy, ophthalmia, flies and ants, and extremes of temperature. Certainly there had been pastoral settlement along part of the trail since then, but Morrison's was still an extraordinary walk for a young man to undertake, alone and unarmed.

The citizens of Normanton did not encourage Morrison:

. . . people professed to think me mad. The rainy season was impending, and many signs, including the comet, pointed to its being earlier than usual. "How reckless," said one: "so insane," put in another:

"it's suicide," added a third. The elderly landlady of the hotel grew eloquent as to the dangers which awaited me. She was no cur, she assured me, but she wouldn't be game to tackle such a walk.

Even today, searing heat, blinding sandstorms, and shortage of water make it perilous to travel in Australia's dead centre. In January 1964 a family of five who abandoned their broken-down car on the Birdsville Track, north of Cooper's Creek, died of thirst and exposure. And when the rains come, rivers that have been dry clay beds become raging torrents, in places many miles wide.

Rain began to fall as Morrison made his first camp along the road to Cloncurry, not far from where Burke and Wills had made their northern-most Camp CXIX, beside the Bynoe River, on a rainy Sunday in February, twenty-one years before.

> On Friday evening, the 2nd December, the sky was clear for the first time, and starting at once I was 30 miles on my way before it came on to rain again. . . . This long stage is much dreaded by the carriers. It lies through country lightly timbered with the gutta-percha tree, the stunted bastard box, and the cooliebar, a district said to swarm with blacks, and annually subject to inundation. When I was half-way through, there came on a violent tempest of wind and rain. The track became a bog and the knapsack got so soddened with water that I groaned under its weight. It was not safe to rest. The accounts I had heard of the track made me tremble to sit down, so I wearily struggled on through water and mud up to my knees. . . .

Morrison pushed on to Cloncurry, methodically recording each day's walk in his diary and collecting material for a newspaper article:

> The wretched blacks are shot without mercy. One night I was at a station, whose owner is said to have shot more blacks than any two men in Queensland, when the mailman came in and reported he had seen a black prowling about the stockyard.

Loading his rifle, the station owner at once sallied out, but came in an hour later "quite disappointed" that it was too dark to follow the tracks of the black. Sometimes, of course, the wretched blacks, like the wretched kanakas, hit back. Ten days after Morrison crossed the McKinley ranges, though he was unaware of it, blacks in the district killed a police inspector and wounded four troopers.

From Cloncurry, Morrison set out for Winton, a township founded in the late seventies. A kindly Cloncurry publican drew a diagram to guide him to a hut on the M'Kinlay River, 104 miles distant. Morrison preserved the map as a cartographic curiosity:

> A distance of 9 miles was made to appear twice as long as one of 22 miles, a trifling inaccuracy which caused me unnecessary anxiety and torture. The first night I could not sleep from fear that I had taken the wrong turning. In the morning I started to go 35 miles without

knowing whether there was water on the track, or even water where I was making to. My waterbag holds two quarts and a half, but the day was so hot—the thermometer registered 130 degrees in the shade of the hut I refer to—that by midday, although I had hardly wet my mouth, the water was all evaporated.

Still I kept moving, but at half-past four I just knocked up. It came upon me most suddenly. Without any warning I was seized with an irresistible desire to throw off all my clothes. I camped under a tree. The anxiety of mind, for it was but a chance if water was within 13 miles of me, added to my torments. All through the night I lay naked on my back, my tongue contracted to a point, my body hot and feverish, my brain reeling.

Leaving the M'Kinlay River, and steering diagonally over its first sandy billabong, Morrison made for the McKinley ranges where the Diamantina has its source. He was two days without food, and suffered much from thirst.

The heat was something fearful, there was an entire absence of animal life, a faintly marked track which turned and twisted to every point of the compass and continually ran out, and no water. . . . The only excitement that sustained me in my weakness was the fear of the blacks—the wild kalkadoons who are so greatly feared in the hills.

Morrison followed the Diamantina for 113 miles, to its junction with the Western at Elderslie, a highly improved run of 30,000 square miles, owned by Sir Samuel Wilson. Here was "immense activity":

Two or three years hence they intend having 300,000 sheep at Elderslie. . . . Fencing, tank sinking and building were proceeding with marvellous activity: wages are very high; any unskilled man can earn 30/- or 35/- a week; he will be well fed, as a vegetable garden is now an essential part of a large Queensland station. I was out of the country where men are content to exist on salt beef and damper.

Exiles from England's stately homes were to be found in the most remote parts of Australia. Morrison noted that a son of Hugh Childers (who had been an inspector of schools in Melbourne, and had recently replaced Gladstone as Chancellor of the Exchequer) was dam-sinking on Elderslie, and that a nephew of the Grand Old Man, Robert Gladstone, was cattle-droving to Port Darwin. A year or so before, Cecil Charles Balfour, a gifted but wayward brother of Arthur James Balfour, and a nephew of the Marquess of Salisbury, had died of drink in Australia, where he had been banished after forging a cheque.

Morrison's route now lay past several other sheep runs, to the Thomson River. The day after crossing the Thomson, Morrison was overtaken by an old gentleman on horseback whose companionship he found so agreeable that they travelled together for seventy-five miles:

29

He was a toothless darkie, a native of the Gold Coast of Africa, a cook by profession and one of the kindest, most considerate men it has been my lot to meet with. . . . He would stint himself of water if the day were hot that I might have the more. And this is how we fell out. We had to go one day 25 miles carrying water. Though parched with thirst he would not take his share. Not to be outdone I also refused any water, and being annoyed I vowed we must part.

Before parting, Morrison noted that his companion's name was John Smith, and that he was the first black man ever seen in Iceland, having been taken there as a boy on a Dutch man-of-war that was taking Prince Henry of the Netherlands round the world.

At every opportunity Morrison sent back a letter to his mother. On 28th January, near Winton, 579 miles from Normanton, he wrote:

You must think it a mad idea this wish of mine to cross Australia on foot—it has been on my mind for many months indeed it is not too much to say that my primary object in coming to Queensland was to do this walk. The experience I have gained in former trips has been of great value to me. Mine is no feat—*no feat of endurance*—only a pleasant excursion. I am as free as a lark. On my back I carry a warm blanket, a large oilcloth, a light Ashantee hammock, 4 pairs of socks, white duck trousers, a pair of shoes, 3 handkerchiefs, 2 shirts, suit of pyjamas, two or three books, soap, toothbrush, a billy, a quart pot and pannikin and a waterbag and tucker. I wear heavy boots and thick stockings, tweed trousers, shirt and cabbage-tree hat.

In my belt is a sheath knife and compass. I buy my tucker as I go along and at every station I come to I buy my rations and then camp out. There is plenty of water all along the track and instead of as formerly sweating to get to a place to get something to eat I camp as soon as hungry and live as happy as the day is long.

For breakfast I usually have two quarts of tea, half a Johnny cake, and occasionally a pint of American [dried] apples. About 11, I camp and make myself a cup of cocoa. At dinner I usually have three courses *viz*: beef-tea, beef, potatoes and stewed apples, besides tea of course. And supper is about the same. When I get to a town people come to look at me as if I were a gorilla. If people croak to you about the dangers of my walk treat them with the same comtempt that I would. Wink your left eye and say my son's no fool and I guess knows what he's about.

The reference to the compass, like the reference to water along the track, may have been put in to reassure his mother. In 1913, Morrison wrote to a friend in London: "I vividly remember that on starting on my journey . . . I lost my compass and I came across without one."

In the article he wrote later Morrison amplified his culinary intelligence:

I spread the oilcloth, and having lit a fire put on my salt beef to boil in the billy. By the time it was done, and the quart of tea made, I had a Johnny cake or flapjack ready for cooking on the raked out coals. The former differ only in size, and are distinct from a damper in that they are cooked on the hot embers, whereas a damper is baked on the hot ashes with hot embers outside. No wood that I have seen can equal the Gidya for giving the very ash and ember most valuble to us. A Johnny cake made with baking powder is a most delicious scone— the very best baking powder is Eno's fruit salt. . . . Soda is an excellent baking powder; the Johnny cake becomes a beautiful yellow, so that you can imagine you are eating bread made with milk, butter and eggs. At the stores—every station has its store—flour was 9d to 1/- a pound, rice 1/-, [preserved] apples and potatoes 1/6, and meat, though most stations do not charge for it, was 3d to 6d a pound for salt beef.

Morrison reached Cooper's Creek, "the most interesting river in Australia", on 15th February. It was at Cooper's Creek that Burke and Wills had established the depot towards which they struggled back from the Gulf of Carpentaria to die. It took them sixty-seven days to reach the deserted depot, days during which, as Alan Moorehead puts it in his splendid reconstruction of the tragedy, *Cooper's Creek*, they "crawled over the enormous landscape like wet insects". They, like Morrison, encountered incessant rains, cyclonic storms, and enervating humidity. Morrison reached Cooper's Creek fifteen miles below the junction of the Thomson river and the Barcoo, and about 200 miles above the site of the depot. From Cloncurry he had deviated westward from the route of Burke and Wills. It had taken him fifty-five days to walk from the Gulf. As he waded across the creek he paused halfway

> to admire the glorious reaches of the river opened up above and below me, and the high banks crowned with magnificent timber. Every description of wild fowl floated idly on the unruffled surface of the current, and it was idleness which reigned supreme over the encampment of blacks in the timber on the opposite bank. I was so delighted with seeing Cooper's Creek at last that, despite an empty tucker bag, I must need camp for the night on its margin.

Four days after leaving Cooper's Creek, Morrison wrote to his mother that he was "rapidly increasing in size" and could promise "with tolerable certainty to be dining at the College on the 26th April". He then had 1119 miles to go. Three days later, approaching Thargomindah, he was caught by more torrential rains. For fifteen miles he did not see land, and was so often in water up to his armpits that he travelled with nothing on but a shirt. For 350 miles he waded nearly as much as he walked:

> It rained for 76 hours at one stretch. In five days nine inches and 30 points fell. . . . The whole country into Thargomindah was become a vast series of swamps and flooded creeks. Buckling to it, every danger

vanished at my approach. Wading through swamps and swimming creeks with long distances to carry food, I yet experienced no fatigue; the dash of excitement kept it away. Where the swamp extended for miles it was but natural that in threading my way among the trees, with no guide but the sun, and water often to my breast, I should wander from the track, but a wide cast on dry ground would as surely discover it to me. When the water was in motion, centipedes in hundreds and an occasional snake constantly floated across the path in unpleasant proximity. . . .

He wrote to his mother on Sunday, 25th February:

. . . On Friday I got a late start and travelling slowly I was overtaken by another swagman about sundown. We saw that we were to have a wet night so we built a bough humpy, shared my provisions, lit a roaring fire and resolved to grin it out. Such heavy rains fell all through the night that we had to wade next day 15 miles. All the creeks were running, the country was a perfect swamp and I walked with nothing but a shirt on. The fierce wind and rain beating against my naked skin made me colder than I have been for many months. I may be delayed here a week as I could not go 5 miles a day over this country as it is now, and the next house is 40 miles ahead.

A new sheep station is being formed here . . . and two of the men have been lost since Friday morning and everyone is afraid that they will perish from cold and hunger. It is impossible to track them and few bushmen can make a line across country in such dark gloomy weather as this. A little over a fortnight ago a poor hawker perished up here from thirst—it is either a famine or a feast. . . . I have finished the thousand miles and am better and stronger than at any period of the walk. Had I carried as light a swag all through as I do now I should be 200 miles ahead of this by the time. . . . This is written on two leaves of my notebook with vile ink and viler pen. All my note paper is destroyed. I have really nothing to say. . . .

At Thargomindah, Morrison crossed the Bulloo River, a mile wide, in a boat, and a "deep wade" put him on the track to Hungerford. By this time he had trained himself to do with very little water; he could walk twenty-five miles without wetting his lips.

The rains continued. The Paroo River, on the border of Queensland and New South Wales, was "not less than half a mile wide". You could not see the opposite bank till quite close to it, and Morrison was warned that the river bed was thickly timbered with the Ypunyah. But he walked "slap in", and crossed without difficulty. Over the river was Hungerford. The boundary between the two States passes through the centre of the town, and Morrison noted that the hotel was in Queensland, where the license fee was less, and the store in New South Wales, where there was free-trade.

In crossing the Paroo, 20 miles below Hungerford, I waded in a careless way into the stream, with my heavy swag on my back. Gradually it got deeper; it came over my waist; it reached my breast, my chin then was in the water; the next moment I went out of my depth altogether. The current in among the lignum bushes was very strong, and being impeded with my swag and boots I was a long time floundering about before I could get into my depth again. The experience was of use to me. I stripped and found a passage among the trees; then, returning for my things, I swam over with them in comfort.

Not till I was 100 miles below Hungerford did I overtake the flood waters of the Paroo and wade through the last of the swamps.

Between Hungerford and Wilcannia lay a "wretched country of clay pans and sand ridges . . . uninteresting scrub . . . vast flats of salt-bush, and occasional stretches of barren hills". It seemed "the very incarnation of dreary desolation":

These days were very lonely. Weak and fagged, and badly in need of a spell, I could not rest till I was in Wilcannia. I got in an hour after the telegraph had closed on Easter Monday; it was Wednesday before I had the means of buying any food. With no money in my pocket, and camped on the flat below the hospital, where those vagrants who have knocked down their cheques in the hells of this town rest till recuperated enough to start away with their swag, my experience of Wilcannia was not a cheerful one. Another young fellow was in a similar predicament to myself, but he knew a Chinese cook at one of the hotels, and twice sponged a supper. On the second evening another of us camped there was put in the lockup and got a fortnight. Another had been living on this flat for months; no one knew how he lived; he hadn't a sixpence.

Before he left on the seventy-mile track to Mount Manaro station, Morrison, with money telegraphed from Geelong, gave an *al fresco* feed to all the tramps and vagabonds. The way now meandered through "vast clay flats of salt-bush and mallee, interspersed with sedges of mulga, boree, leopard woods and sandalwood". The walking was heavy, and water scarce. But from Ivanhoe there were public-houses every ten or twelve miles. The landlady of one of them posed in Melbourne society as a squatter's wife. Locally, Morrison noted, she was known as "the scrub Turkey".

It was now less arduous country, and Morrison travelled rapidly through Hay and Deniliquin to Echuca, where he had stopped on his canoe trip two years before. Echuca is in Victoria, and Morrison was moved by native pride. "It was a perfect picnic," he wrote:

Instead of immense tracts of country owned by one man, and given up to sheep, there was a succession of beautiful little farms, each with its haystack, its neat little cottage, its substantial fence, and its scene of vigorous activity. . . . Certainly, I thought, my colony may be the smallest, but it is the healthiest and most beautiful of them all.

He reached Melbourne "in perfect condition" on 21st April, in good time for his dinner appointment at Geelong College on the 26th. David Syme asked him to write an account of the walk, and paid him £4 10s. for an article of 6000 words that occupied four and a half columns of close print. As a last word, Morrison said that he had come 1700 miles through the interior of Australia without seeing a kangaroo. And he added modestly:

> My only objection to writing this account of my walk was a natural one. If it had never been written many people might think I had done something wonderful. They will read this and see that any one who cared to take the trouble and give up four months of his time could have done the walk more quickly than I did, more easily, and with less discomfort to himself.

Many years later he wrote, "If nothing else, my walk proved how great had been the progress of colonization in the interior . . . since the Burke and Wills party met with disaster."

Morrison's transcontinental ramble of 2043 miles in 123 days received curiously little attention from the Australian Press. But a Victorian country paper, the Inglewood *Advertiser*, invoked the memory of Burke and Wills, a giant statue of whom had been erected in the heart of Melbourne's fashionable Collins Street:

> If the bronze Burke and Wills . . . could have seen young Morrison trudging home with his swag upon his back, would they not have been rather astonished? A solitary footman, with no help beyond a strong will and wonderful powers of endurance, had accomplished the task which brought such disaster on the grand cavalcade of horses and camels. . . . Alone, unarmed . . . for four months, this gallant youngster, day by day, through flood and fire, had won his weary way. To what good? cries some Collins Street dandy, with slim waist and spindle legs. To what good? Why, to show that in the hardy Australian native's veins there flows the same blood that sent Cook to traverse, in his cockle-shell, the great and unknown Southern Seas; that sent Livingstone to the source of the Nile, and Franklin to the thin-ribbed ice that guards "the arctic Zone."

And an equally erudite writer in the *Leader* said it was "a very hopeful sign that the colony had been able to produce already so fine a specimen as Mr George Ernest Morrison" whose "quiet self-reliance, dauntless courage and invincible determination" provided "a splendid foundation for a national character". His daring achievement was compared to Leander's swim across the Hellespont and Captain Webb's swim across the Channel:

> It has been alleged that Australians have a tendency to blow. In young Morrison this characteristic is conspicuous by its absence. He tells his story with the simplicity of a Swift or Defoe. And what a

34

strange story it is! The romantic episode in which he and his black-fellow traveller vied with each other in self-sacrifice in the thirsty desert brings to mind the curiously parallel and pathetic incident in Sir Samuel Baker's *Cast up by the Sea*.

More austerely, *The Times* in London observed:

A man who ventures in this country alone and unarmed must be possessed of no small amount of hardihood. Mr Morrison's feat commands the admiration of all interested in exploration, and must be set down as one of the most remarkable of pedestrian achievements.

[IX]

Morrison's final article on the kanaka traffic had appeared in the *Leader* in December 1882, while he was on his way to Normanton. When he got back to Melbourne he found the traffic was still being discussed. The Rev. John Paton, now living in Melbourne, had again attacked it vehemently. He had been supported by another missionary, the Rev. Thomas Neilson, who said that during his sixteen years on Tanna he had known dozens of young islanders trained "under the British flag and by British subjects" to a career "of bloodshed and crime" as kidnappers. "If Mr Paton and those who share his views are correct in only half their assertions," the *Age* commented" . . . we must either bring about a change or sweep the entire system away as an accursed thing."

From Geelong College, two weeks after his return, Morrison wrote a letter of 2700 words to the *Age* which went far beyond his articles in its denunciation of the "Queensland slave trade". He was convinced, he said, that the "slave captains" did not encourage kidnapping "except under very exceptional circumstances". Most kanakas were obtained by a simple and effective technique of false pretences:

When a schooner arrives at an island its two whaleboats are at once sent ashore for recruits. In one is the recruiting agent paid by the owners of the vessel to get boys, in the other is the Government agent paid by the Government of Queensland to see that the boys are obtained fairly. . . . The boats pull in to the shore, and while the recruiting agent's boat backs into the beach, the one in which is the Government agent keeps 50 yards or more away, so as to cover in case of an attack. Then the bargaining commences. At every island there are beachcombers, cunning natives, who have been carefully trained to decoy boys off to the schooner. The recruiting agent quickly engages in conversation with one of these, and enters into a compact by which the beachcomber undertakes to sneak off a certain number of boys, his success to be substantially rewarded. He is given a present to cheer him on his task, and the boats put back to the schooner. Nothing further is done until a smoke is seen on the beach —a preconcerted signal. . . . The moment the smoke becomes visible we jump into the boat and pull for it with all our might. The recruiter urges us by promises of grog if there in time. Perhaps while we are rowing over the water the natives—friends of the boys—opposed to their going, are running along the beach to intercept them. The boat must be there first even though the recruiter has to fire on these friends to compel them to cease running. Just as the keel grates on the sand the boys, who all this time have been waving us to come quick, step into the boat and are pulled leisurely off to the schooner. Most of the boys are recruited in this way. They have not keen kidnapped, they have come of their own free will deceived by the lies the beachcomber has been bribed to tell them, and the Government agent assists in the deception. . . .

No native could leave the schooner once he was recruited. If he tried to escape by jumping overboard

the watch will vie with each other in the sport of shooting him. So that in this traffic in flesh, encouraged by the Queensland Government and fostered by the Imperial Government, a native, if he attempt to regain the liberty of which he has been fraudulently deprived, is to be shot like a dog, and the sailor who held the rifle that slaughtered him is to be honoured on the schooner as a hero.

On some sugar plantations, Morrison wrote, the kanakas were treated kindly, on others "most shockingly". They were kicked, beaten, "terrorized with the stockwhip". At one of Queensland's finest plantations the owner showed his guest with pride "a terrible prickly hedge, through which he compelled a naked Kanaka to pass under fear of braining him with a tomahawk". This man was known in the trade as responsible for "one of the most awful massacres in the slave trade".

Righteous-minded men favour this labor traffic so long as they make money out of it, but surely they cannot justify the recruiting of women. . . . A nice, pretty chaste girl leaves for Queensland, and a year or two later she is sent to her home an ugly, wrinkled, diseased hag. It is the diseases brought back by the women that are depopulating the islands, no less than the taking away of the men. . . . When a number of women are recruited by a vessel the ship becomes a brothel. . . . The Government agent, you will say, is on the schooner to protect the women. But the Government agents, I can testify from personal knowledge, connive at every misdeed. . . .

Morrison told the story of Remnestelesa, a "bright, pretty and happy" woman from Vanua Lava, who with her husband was recruited by the *Lavinia*:

A sailor conceived an unholy passion for her, and thrashed her husband every day until he was compelled in self-defence to forfeit his wife's honour. That sailor communicated a disease to the poor girl, a disease which she will carry to her grave.

Next day the *Age* devoted its first leader to an endorsement of Morrison's letter, which was of "transcendent interest, not because the facts told in it are new, but because the writer, an educated young man of high character, witnessed them with his own eyes". The leader, almost certainly written by David Syme, said it was noteworthy that Morrison, "no closet philanthropist . . . but a practical man . . . was not roused to protest against the atrocities . . . when he first returned from the islands". His letter therefore was not an outburst of passionate indignation. (Morrison's reticence in his articles was puzzling as well as noteworthy, and was later invoked to discredit him.) The leader ended apocalyptically:

> When we read the descriptions of the floating hells . . . we are tempted to wonder that fires of heaven do not consume ship and crew. But it is not in this tumultuous manner that God's vengeance executes itself. We shall multiply sugar plantations, keep irreproachable Sabbaths, and boast of our imports and exports for scores of years before the thunderbolt falls. When it comes it will be inexorable.

A few readers of the *Age* supported Morrison. One, who signed himself "Mallicola", said he had taken labour to almost every market, and his experience coincided exactly with that of Mr Morrison: "He tells a plain, unvarnished tale . . . in fact, he lets the trade down softly." The Rev. Paton, congratulating the *Age* and Mr Morrison "in the interests of humanity", pointed out that "the sad traffic" had carried off about a third of the population of the New Hebrides group and of many other islands. In a personal letter Mr Paton thanked Morrison with all his heart for his "excellent and swiping letter" and prayed that our Lord Jesus would bless and reward him. But Melbourne in May 1883 was much more concerned with the "Sunday Question" than with the slave question. A decision of the trustees of the Picture Gallery and the Public Library to open these institutions on Sunday had fired a tremendous explosion of puritan protest. There were endless meetings, deputations, petitions, and sermons, though the Sabbatarians could not decide whether the supporters of culture on Sundays were atheists or Papists.

"The ways of the Victorian clergy are certainly very wonderful," said the *Age*:

> Who has ever heard a clergyman denounce the greed of house owners, which has led them to convert whole streets of our populous city into rookeries and clusters of brothels? . . . Take again the Queensland traffic in human flesh. The true character of it has been notorious for years, but where do we read of a Presbyterian synod waiting upon a premier of Queensland to stop it? . . . Is there not a tacit understanding, incomparably better observed than any written law, which constrains the clergy to keep silence when all matter in which vested interests of property are concerned? . . . But how magnificently do the clergy avenge themselves on sin when it has no balance in the bank.

As the organ of the "vested interests", Melbourne's other morning paper, the conservative *Argus*, found it necessary to discredit not only Morrison's attack on the labour traffic but also his walk across Australia:

For some time past the accredited exponent of radical opinion in Melbourne has devoted a good deal of pains to the task of showing that Queensland sanctions a wholesale system of murder and man-stealing under the guise of the Polynesian labour traffic. To prove its assertions it relies chiefly on the authority of a young gentleman who has recently acquired some transient notoriety by performing the curious and purposeless feat of walking as a swagman from Carpentaria to Melbourne and who had previously gratified his love of adventure by taking some trips to the South Seas in labour vessels. This amazing pedestrian recently published a horrifying story of murder and violence, which he presented as a series of facts, that had come within his personal knowledge or under his own observation. It would, of course, strike every reader of his letters that, if his allegations were true, he should have sworn an information of murder or kidnapping against the offenders ... and that by omitting to do so, he made himself an accessory to all the crimes he witnessed. But so obvious a reflection did not apparently occur to the radical writer. ...

To which the *Age* replied:

If Mr Morrison had not been a native of the soil, or if instead of humping his swag like a common bushman, or roughing it in a Queensland labour boat like a still more common sailor, he had sauntered Europe round with recommendations from Sir William Mitchell in his pocket, or had been presented at Court by that distinguished nobleman, the Duke of Manchester, there would have been scarcely anything too polite to say of his prowess. ...

In London the secretary of the Aborigines Protection Society, Mr Chesson, sent a copy of Morrison's letter to the Secretary of State for the Colonies, the Earl of Derby, a distinguished statesman who had defected from Conservatism to Liberalism, and his Lordship politely advised the Governor of Queensland, Sir Anthony Musgrave, that he would be glad to receive a report on the subject. By appropriate bureaucratic processes the Inspector of Pacific Islanders, Mr A. R. Macdonald, and the Police Magistrate at Mackay, Mr W. R. Goodall, were instructed to inquire into Mr Morrison's charges. The inquiry, held at Mackay on 1st June 1883, had little more value as a judicial process than the trial of the Queen of Hearts in *Alice in Wonderland*. The man who had made the charges was not present, and the only witnesses were the men involved, and a few bewildered and no doubt intimidated natives, testifying through a native interpreter.

Nearly all of Morrison's charges were categorically denied, and some of the witnesses defended themselves by attacking him. Able seaman Frank Whitford said that "Morrison used frequently to long for a woman, but was afraid to touch one—like a hungry man looking at a tart"; Able seaman Cooper said, "I have often heard him say he would like to have a woman himself, but that he was afraid to attempt it"; and Captain Smith, whom Morrison had described as the "little brutal skipper", said that at Cape Lisburn, Santo, Morrison had attempted to drag a woman into the bush, and only by threats was induced to return to the boat. Able seaman James Gerard, known as Joe, admitted having connection with one of the Vanua Lava women, but denied laying hands on her husband Manlip, and was not sure whether he had paid him five shillings for the loan of his wife. Manlip, through an interpreter, gave his own account of the transaction.

> One fellow sailor man been take my Mary and had connection with her; his name Joe; he paid five shillings; Joe one fellow been take him; Joe says he want him Mary; I told Joe suppose you give me five shillings I give you my Mary; Joe did not fight or hit me; no other man been take my Mary; Joe only took my Mary one time. . . . Joe did not make my Mary sick; my Mary is not sick now.

Dr Robert McBurney, as health officer rather than as part owner of the *Lavinia*, testified that neither Manlip nor his Mary "at present nor at any past period have . . . apparently suffered from any venereal disease". He also explained that he was always in favour of sending sick islanders back to their homes, and had he not done so he did not think any of the eighteen or twenty—he was vague about the number—sick "returns" would have survived. He did not explain the mysterious therapy of curing a number of sick natives by cramming them for a long sea voyage into a tiny hold, where, according to Morrison, the atmosphere was so pestilential that, no matter how cold it was on deck, the moment he turned in he was "bathed in a horrible sickly sweat" as if he had a "malignant fever". On only one point did all the witnesses not agree; Captain Smith swore that he had never heard of the song about "Beelzebub being nigh", and three seamen swore they had never heard the captain sing it, but a fourth, apparently inadequately briefed, swore that he had heard the captain singing it.

Mr Macdonald ended his report on a remarkably eloquent note:

> We dismiss Mr Morrison with the hope that, ere his restless vanity again urges him to sally forth from the classic precincts of the Scotch College, Geelong, in quest of a fresh budget of horrors . . . he may have learned to discriminate between the loveliness of truth and the hatefulness of falsehood, and that he may pause to consider whether the ephemeral notoriety of a newspaper scribbler is not dearly earned by the indelible stigma of infamy attached to the character of a slanderer and a liar.

Magistrate Goodall entirely concurred, and Queensland's Colonial Secretary and Premier, Samuel Griffith, had the honour to forward a copy of the report to the Governor, Sir Anthony Musgrave, observing that "no facts were elicited corroborating in the slightest degree the serious allegations of Mr Morrison", and adding the improper comment that Morrison was "a very young man, who does not bear a high reputation, and whose narratives need to be received with much caution". Sir Anthony had the honour to forward a copy of Mr Griffith's letter, and a copy of the Mackay Report, to the Earl of Derby, regretting very much that he was "unable quite to agree" with Mr Griffith that none of Morrison's accusations had been corroborated: "The evidence is that of witnesses more or less implicated in the offences charged, and simple denial . . . by no means amounts to disproof; while a good deal that is distinctly admitted is not inconsistent with Mr Morrison's narrative." As for Morrison's character, Sir Anthony directed his Lordship's attention to "two remarkable leading articles in the Melbourne *Age*" in which Morrison had been described as "not an interested or untrustworthy observer".

Morrison himself, about to leave Melbourne for Edinburgh with a New Guinea spearhead in his abdomen, wrote a spirited letter to Mr Griffith, which the *Age* published:

> Sir—I observe . . . that you have been pleased to describe me as a "very young man who does not bear a high reputation". I need hardly say that, were you not shielded by Parliamentary privilege, I should compel you to retract your words or you should have to answer for your libel in a court of justice. . . . But your cowardly attack upon me is not likely to achieve the end you had in view. At an early date I am leaving for England to continue at a home university my medical studies begun at the Melbourne University, and I shall then have an opportunity of laying before the Right Honorable the Secretary of State for the Colonies well-authenticated vouchers as to my character. . . . The Colonial Secretary will doubtless be able to discriminate between the value of statements made by a disinterested witness, whose veracity can be vouched for, and a person like yourself, whose policy is to suppress all the facts connected with the "odious traffic in human flesh", and whose character, moreover, may be estimated by the fact that he has selected to preside over the deliberations of the Assembly, of whose honour he should be the jealous custodian, an individual who has twice been brought under the purview of the criminal law.

There was a sting in the peroration. The Speaker in Queensland's House of Assembly, William Henry Groom, had come to Australia as a convict with two convictions—a disability which did not prevent his also becoming Mayor of Toowoomba nine times and the member for Darling Downs in the Federal Parliament.

CHAPTER THREE

[I]

THE GREAT island of New Guinea, "like a vast bird hovering over the continent of Australia", was in 1883 the largest unexplored and unwanted region in the world. *It was the last unknown. Only the fringe / Was nervous to the touch of voyagers*, wrote the American poet, Karl Shapiro, who was stationed in New Guinea during World War II. Missionaries and naturalists had explored a little of the coast, and attempted to penetrate inland. In 1879 a young Italian naturalist, Luigi Maria D'Albertis, steamed up the Fly River some 580 miles, in a nine-ton launch lent by the Government of New South Wales. But as the Melbourne *Argus* said four years later: "The streams are untraversed, the mountains unscaled, the forests and plains of the interior are unvisited. Romance and mystery, dispelled from most other portions of the habitable globe, still linger about New Guinea."

During the seventies the Australian colonies had become increasingly aware of New Guinea's proximity and importance. Disturbing rumours of French, Russian, Italian, and German designs on unclaimed New Guinea—the Dutch had held the southern coast since 1828—reached Australia from time to time. In 1874-5, Great Britain rejected several Australian appeals that, in her own and Australia's interests, she should annex eastern New Guinea. Lord Derby's attitude was expressed in his often-repeated statement that the empire had "too many blacks already".

The New Guinea question came to a head in 1882, with fresh reports of a German colonization plan, but again the Colonial Office showed a polite indifference to Australia's fears—partly because of Britain's reluctance to offend Germany, partly because she did not want to bear the cost of annexation, partly because of her suspicion that Queensland wanted to make New Guinea safe for blackbirders. The Premier of Queensland, Sir Thomas McIlwraith, an aggressive, unscrupulous entrepreneur with a zeal for empire-building, national and personal, who was said to be endowed "with all the vulgar forces of the Glasgow school", reacted forcefully and vulgarly. While the Colonial Office shilly-shallied, McIlwraith ordered the Thursday Island police magistrate, Henry Chester, to take formal possession of "all that portion of New Guinea ... lying between the 141st and 155th meridians of east latitude, in the name and on behalf of Her Gracious Majesty Queen Victoria, her heirs and successors".

Without Her Gracious Majesty's knowledge or approval, Mr Chester raised the Union Jack at Port Moresby on 4th April 1883, in the presence of the white population of three, and a few bewildered natives, to one of whom he presented a commemorative red felt hat. "The annexation of New Guinea, coming upon the almost criminal neglect of the Imperial Government, has found favour throughout the continent," said the Geelong *Advertiser*, on the very day that Morrison finished his transcontinental walk. But it did not find favour in Britain. When Lord Derby learned of the annexation—by courtesy of Reuter's News Service, which sent him a copy of a message from its Brisbane correspondent—he was inclined to accept it grudgingly, rather than bicker with the troublesome Colonies, but the Prime Minister, Mr Gladstone, an old-fashioned anti-imperialist, was not convinced of the "necessity or propriety" of Queensland's action, which was also opposed by the Aborigines Protection Society, on the grounds that Queensland, with its notorious slave trade, was unfit to govern a native people. Mr Gladstone agreed with this when, on 2nd July, he told the House of Commons that Cabinet was not prepared to recognize the annexation, which was illegal and unjustified. Derby made a similar statement to the Lords, adding the suggestion that if the Australian colonies desired an extension of territory they should federate, as singly they would be unable to undertake the task. "The Ministry have decided, if not exactly to snub the Australians, at least to check their ambitious ardour by the timely application of a little cold water ..." said the *Saturday Review*, approvingly.

The Colonials did not appreciate the cold-water treatment. There was general indignation at Britain's action. Fifty-seven public meetings were held throughout Australia in 1883, all insisting that British rule in New Guinea was essential to Australia's security. As the *Leader* said on 16th June:

> We cannot afford to let the islands of the Pacific pass into the hands of dangerous neighbours; and it is not only the European powers who can be dangerous to us. Settlements of Chinamen or Malays will infallibly be formed. .... If Chinamen enter in, they will be the outpost of a possible Chinese invasion.

In Victoria the New Guinea Question had displaced even the Sunday Observance Question as the topic of the day, and Morrison saw another opportunity for a special correspondent. He let it be known that he was prepared to lead an expedition into unknown New Guinea:

> My desire was communicated to Mr Syme, and took his fancy. The result was that I undertook to return to New Guinea, with the grandiloquent title of "Special Commissioner of the Melbourne *Age*,"

but without any pay, and without the remotest prospect of obtaining any. I was young and inexperienced and ardent. I cared nothing for money. I had a firm belief in my own future. I could not believe in the possibility of failure, and against the advice of my friends, I accepted a responsibility for which I was unfitted.

Swiftly and secretly he prepared for the expedition. He tried to insure his life, but no company in Victoria would issue a policy. A Geelong chemist made him up a medicine chest, "a marvel of compactness", that included not only instruments, scales, bandages, and ointments, but a galvanic battery. On the advice of the Government Astronomer, Mr L. J. Ellery, he bought two Waltham watches instead of a chronometer, a fact which the Waltham Watch Company advertised proudly when Morrison's departure was announced.

At the end of May, Mr J. C. Syme wrote to Morrison urging him to hasten his departure: "If the *Argus* people once know definitely you are going they will be certain to try and get up an expedition of their own," he wrote. The *Argus* people soon learned of Morrison's plans, and hastily organized a rival expedition under the leadership of an ambiguous adventurer whom it presented as "Captain William Armit, a Fellow of the London Linnean Society . . . a former officer of the Queensland Native Police, an accomplished writer, and a gentleman specially qualified for such an hazardous enterprise". In a letter to his mother Morrison described Armit as "a drunken scamp", twice discharged from the Queensland service for misbehaviour, and "a bullying, boastful, lying, man of 35, with no more claims to the title of Captain than I have to General".

New Guinea now became the prize in a contest between two rival newspapers.

Morrison left Melbourne by train on 6th June and was interviewed on his arrival in Sydney. He told the *Sydney Morning Herald* that he was going "a short distance inland from Port Moresby to see what prospects there would be of forming a mission station in connexion with the Presbyterian Church of Victoria".

Two weeks later David Syme telegraphed him at Cooktown: DO NOT STUDY ECONOMY IN MEN OR EQUIPMENT FOR PERSONAL SAFETY AND SUCCESS WIRE IF ANYTHING REQUIRED SYDNEY MORNING HERALD SHARING EXPENSES. Encouraged by Syme's unexpected telegram, Morrison overdrew his account by £150 and laid in £100 worth of additional stores. In the complete catalogue that he sent his mother in a letter from Lizard Island he lists 6lb. soap, files, saws, axes, soldering irons, and photographic apparatus including a ruby lamp with 6lb. of candles and 37 dozen plates. Food included 400lb. salt, 200lb. sugar, 450lb. meat, one side bacon, 6 tins extract of meat, 6 bottles pickles, 60lb. tea, 8 tins coffee, 12 tins milk, 1 doz. Lea and Perrins sauce, 250lb. flour, 6 tins baking powder, 42lb. oatmeal, 30lb. maizemeal, 40lb. apples, and 1 dozen tins Huntly & Palmer biscuits.

"Trade", for the conciliation and civilization of the natives, included

44½ dozen knives, 14 dozen tomahawks, 50 dozen fishhooks, 3 dozen bead necklets, 128lb. beads, 1 gross necklets, 3 dozen lockets, 2 dozen mouth-organs, 5 dozen "jawharps", 4 dozen whistles, 2 gross mirrors, 5 dozen magnifying-glasses, about 100 yards print, 100 yards turkey red, 5 dozen pipes and 120 pounds of "trade" or inferior tobacco. (Tobacco, introduced by the missionaries, was the most effective weapon in their evangelizing armoury. When the Board of the London Missionary Society expressed doubts about the ethics of conversion by nicotine, the Rev. Lawes told them tersely, "If we dispensed with the use of it, the expenses of this Mission would be increased at least twelve-fold. We should have to give a tomahawk which costs a shilling where we now give tobacco which costs a penny." Each teacher in the mission used about 120 pounds of tobacco a year.)

Apart from "trade" tobacco, Morrison's stores included 12lb. of "good tobacco" for consumption by the white men of the expedition. Other items were fireworks, medicines, books, and writing material. The stores, weighing four tons, were loaded on board a two-masted, five-ton lugger which Morrison chartered for £80—"a large sum," he wrote to his mother, "but I would pay double that to be in New Guinea before the *Argus* expedition." The lugger was commanded by a former Boston whaler, Captain J. W. Bolles.

In Cooktown, Morrison engaged two white men, John Wheeler Lyons and Edmund Snow, and two natives, a man from Tanna named Lively and a Malay named Cheerful. Lyons was a tall, wiry man of twenty-six, an experienced prospector, reputedly one of the best bushmen in Queensland, who gave up a job at £12 a month, with everything found to accompany Morrison. He and Snow were both to receive £7 a month and the natives each £4 a month. Snow was a typical "wandering digger" in his late forties, who had tramped with pick and shovel through many parts of Australia and taken part in the unsuccessful gold rush behind Port Moresby in 1878. "I should have picked my men with care," Morrison afterwards wrote, "but I was anxious to commence the important work with which I had been entrusted. The men I had engaged . . . were with one exception, curious customers." The exception was Lyons.

"Captain" Armit enlisted an equally dubious team. It included "Professor" William Denton, whose academic title was as questionable a his leader's military title, and his two sons. Denton, a former grocer assistant from Durham, England, had lived in America, where he edite a paper, practised psychometry, and once debated with a future Presiden of the United States, James Garfield, on the origin of man. In Melbourn he was known as a writer and lecturer on Methodism, geology, spiritual ism, mesmerism, temperance, and evolution. Armit left Cooktown on 20t June, and reached Port Moresby on 10th July, three days behind Morri son. "In the race to supply the public with news of New Guinea, it pleasant to notice that Morrison has been the first of the 'specials' to ge there, landing in that darkest of lands on the 7th of July," the *Leade* announced on 21st July. And it added optimistically, "Whether we are to annex New Guinea or not, we shall now know all about what we should gain in one case or lose in the other."

[II]

Morrison had a "wretched passage" from Cooktown to Port Moresby. The lugger was "patched together in a disgraceful way. The deck was not caulked, and the seams of the top streaks and round the combings let water in by the bucketful." Eleven days out from Cooktown, about sundown, they sighted New Guinea, and in the morning ran in through a howling gale, not knowing whether Port Moresby was to windward or leeward. It was dark when they reached an anchorage, and they could not land till the following morning. The stores had all been damaged by sea water, "the sugar resembling the original juice".

Morrison found the port little changed since his previous visit, but there was visible sign of the abortive annexation. The Union Jack now waved before one of the largest and finest of several new houses, this being "the seat of royalty, the palace of Bor Vagi, the great chief of Motu, who now sports an old suit of missionary's pyjamas". In the afternoon Morrison went to church and saw a missionary pour about a pint and a half of water on the mop of a savage, who "laughed and seemed to enjoy it—for visions of tobacco rose before him". Morrison did not approve. In his dispatch to the *Age* he wrote:

> I think the missionaries do wrong to pander to the taste of the natives for tobacco. . . . The missionaries give the natives tobacco, not because it does them good but because it does you good to see their heartfelt gratitude. . . . Their fondness for the fragrant weed seems to amount to a passion. There is scarcely any sacrifice they will not make to obtain a supply.

He did not mention the 120 pounds of inferior tobacco in his own stores.

Morrison spent sixteen days making his final preparations. He ran into trouble from the start. The two natives proved unsatisfactory—one was a drug addict and the other a drunkard—and were replaced by two Australian aborigines. The two missionaries, Messrs Lawes and Chalmers, were equally troublesome. Morrison was soon involved in a bitter and unChristian argument with them over the ownership of fifteen horses that were running free about the mission. Ten had been brought over by the diggers in the gold rush of 1878; five were young brumbies which Morrison and Lyons broke in. The missionaries claimed them all. Morrison resolved the dispute rather arbitrarily by announcing that, as there was no law in New Guinea, he proposed to take the horses in spite of the missionaries. "By my arrival, I simply euchre Armit," he wrote to his mother, ". . . the horses he counted on will be hobbled and belonging to me before

45

he can get here." As for the missionaries: "The behaviour of Mr Lawes causes me the greatest disgust. It is charitable to assume that he is half-witted. St George [another missionary] is over here on a visit chiefly I think to aid in drinking the missionary spirits. He is usually drunk for he can't stand as much as Mr Chalmers."

Morrison left Port Moresby on 11th July, planning to cross the island to Dyke Acland Bay, on the north coast, 100 miles away. "I shall be away months perhaps a year or over", he telegraphed his mother, by way of Cooktown. "Everything promises success apprehend no danger. . . ." But he did not underestimate his task. "It is evident that the difficulties of travelling in this country are not trifling," he wrote to the *Age*:

> I do not know if any of your readers have ever been in a mangrove swamp. Nothing can exceed the toilsomeness of endeavouring to penetrate such country. It is a serious matter to lose your way in one of these labyrinthine thickets, for the sunlight is often completely shut out, and as you go stumbling along in a most oppressive atmosphere—now plunging in an unexpected slime, through missing your foothold on the tortuous twigs, and now narrowly escaping impalement from a projecting bough, you feel a good deal like a rat in a cage. . . . In some places these giant mangroves, closely packed, rise in a dark mass of foliage to a height of 70 feet.

Beyond the malarial swamps of mangroves, cane, and floating grasses, a much more formidable obstacle lay in Morrison's path, the majestic Owen Stanley mountains, a series of jungle-covered peaks, rising from eleven to thirteen thousand feet, their summits lost in mist.

"Lianas, creepers, rattan and lawyer vine form thick webs among the trees, shutting out sunlight and impeding human travel," wrote Stephen Winsor Reed in 1943. "Ferns, begonias, mosses and orchids grow underfoot or attach themselves to trees and vines. In the swampland country a thick layer of oozy, decaying vegetation offers the poorest imaginable support for travel on foot." Sixty-four years before, D'Albertis had written: "It is easier to ascend the highest peaks of the European alps with an alpenstock than to cross an ordinary hill in New Guinea."

Morrison had an inauspicious start, which he reported in another telegram to his mother:

> . . . HORSE RAN ABOUT SMASHED PACKS STARTED AGAIN WORTHLESS YOUNG ENTIRE RUSHED MARE SHOT IT DRUNKEN MISSIONARIES EXAGGERATED TRIFLING ACT OF NECESSITY INTO DASTARDLY CRIME THEY HAD NO CLAIM TO ENTIRE MISSIONARIES BEHAVED DISGRACEFULLY THREATENING TO SET NATIVES ON ME HAVE NOW GOT HORSES MISSIONARIES BEING SATISFIED WITH DELAYING ME ONE WEEK. . . . DONT BE AFRAID I DO ANYTHING ILLEGAL WITH HORSES.

On 24th July they set out again. The expedition now consisted of three white men, two aboriginal boys, and eleven Motu carriers. Travelling north-east from Port Moresby towards the Goldie River, Morrison had covered only fifteen miles in three days, when he had trouble with Ned, who was in charge of the horses. "The old digger who swore to go with me to death gave in at the end of 15 miles from the start," Morrison wrote. The party returned to Port Moresby and Ned was replaced by the only available white man, Frank Wilkinson, who was acting as cook in Port Moresby's one store. But—Frank was "a worthless half-witted new chum, who became a constant source of danger to us": "Our party was very weak. . . . The two black boys could never be taught to fire a gun. . . . Lyons gave unqualified satisfaction, but when I went forward to prospect the track I was never certain but that I might find the camp wrecked on my return."

When Morrison came back to camp one day he found the black boys drying some damp cartridges on hot cinders, while "the new chum" lay close alongside watching. "As might have been foreseen," Morrison later wrote, "my journey ended in disaster." There was constant trouble with the natives:

They saw the weakness of our party, and took advantage of it. . . . Our camp was always more or less surrounded by natives, waiting an opportunity to make a raid. . . . In spite of all our vigilance we had axes and tomahawks stolen, and a native sneaked off in open daylight with one large red blanket. We awoke one morning to find our tea stolen. . . . Our only safety lay in conciliating the chiefs by a liberal distribution of gifts.

Morrison seemed incapable of seeing the natives' point of view. It may have been irritating to lose a tomahawk, a blanket, or a tin of tea, but, on his own account, these cannibals and headhunters, who had never enjoyed the blessings of baptism or bad tobacco, behaved with admirable restraint:

. . . crowds of men were in the habit of coming with spears, clubs and shields, and motioning us to go back. They would also run with their spears and pretend to discharge them at us. On one occasion, a man brought a shield down to our camp, laid it at our feet, signed to us that it would be to our advantage to go back, and immediately ran away.

As the Sydney *Bulletin*, a strident organ of Australian nationalism and a bitter opponent of imperialism, later said of the natives:

They discovered, pushing his way among them, a mysterious stranger, of alien race and suspicious motives. He came uninvited and undesired. These savages showed wonderful—we may say unheard of—forbearance. The numerous population of each district resorted to every means short of actual violence to induce the intruder to turn back. We scarcely see what the most civilized society could have done that would have been more decent and praiseworthy.

The party struggled on for thirty-eight days, hacking its way through tangles of liana and lawyer vines, till it reached the foot of the dividing range:

> As we got further inland, the country became densely populated, and the natives increased in boldness. One came quietly down to where three of us were packing the last horse, picked up a tomahawk, and darted for the scrub. I could have shot him easily but instead of doing this, one of the party chased him, caught him, punched his head and let him go, though the savage had turned round half-way and flung the tomahawk at his pursuer. We decided next time to use the gun. The opportunity came on 2nd October. On that day I went out with four natives to cut the track, all the others but the new chum being sick with fever. I gave the natives a valuable scrub knife. . . . As we proceeded with our work the natives increased in number till 4 had become 40, most of them carrying spears. . . . One of them suddenly seized the knife and bolted with it. This stealing was getting a farce, so I waited until the man had got such a distance that a shot could not inflict much injury, and I then gave him one charge in the back.

Morrison's purpose, he said, was to show the natives, "without doing serious injury to any of their number", that he would no longer submit to the thievery which threatened to put an end to the exploration. When he fired, the native rolled over. Morrison went along the track; when he got close, the native rose to his feet and walked away through the scrub. Morrison went back to camp, three miles away, and told Lyons, who was very ill with fever, that he felt like a murderer. They passed an uneasy night:

> The forest was brightly illuminated by huge fires which had been lighted by the natives on the hills everywhere around us, and within the glare, the forms of the savages, all in full war trim, could be seen constantly moving about. Some of them were so close to us that we could observe the white paint with which they had besmeared their faces, and in the night, as in the day, additional members of the tribe continued to come up, each wearing his charm, and carrying three or more long spears, a club, and a shield. . . . We determined to make an early start in the morning.

Next day, as Morrison loaded up, warriors with heavy bundles of spears gathered in crowds, and the long grass "fairly bristled with spears". Lyons was scarcely able to walk. Morrison was leading his horse a little in advance of the others, climbing a steep spur densely covered with scrub. The top was clothed with long grass as high as the top of his head. He was making his way quietly through the grass when he was struck violently by two spears thrown almost simultaneously. One penetrated his stomach just under the chest, the other entered the hollow of his right eye and struck the bottom of the bridge of his nose:

At the moment I was struck, I was raising my foot to step up a bank, a couple of feet in height, and instinctively, as the spear sped towards me, I threw my head back, overbalanced, and fell to the ground. Had it not been for this, I should undoubtedly have been killed, for if instead of yielding with the spear and falling beneath the elevation of its range before it struck me, my head had offered a firm resistance to the weapon, it must have pierced through my skull. As soon as I fell, I pulled out the spear, which still hung from a corner of my eye, and directly I did so, a torrent of blood rushed from my nose. I rose and picked up my rifle which had fallen from my hand, and discharged it in the direction from which the spears had come. . . . I was overcome by a feeling of faintness, and had just lain down again when Lyons, alarmed by the report of my gun, came running up. I was reeking in blood.

Morrison gave two accounts of the attack in his reports to the *Age*, one written from hospital in Cooktown. But the most vivid came from the untrained pen of Lyons. Writing to Mrs Morrison of her "kind and generous son" and his "noble behaviour", he said:

We were going alright and were not much more than a mile from place where we intended to camp going up a very steep scrubby hill when suddenly I heard a piercing scream after which a shot was fired then your son called out Jack. I rushed up saw your son stretched on his back covered with blood from head to foot with spear in corner of eye and another in his body, I have seen a good few spear wounds in my time but never saw two in one man so close to vital parts and not to prove fatal. The first words he uttered were "Oh my poor dear Mother the trouble I have caused you." He also said "What will Mr Syme say at my failure." He hurt his leg very much for in falling his leg must have doubled under him so must have contracted some of the sinews—could not touch it without paining him very much.

I quickly made up my mind to unpack all the horses leave the trade and only take your son's instruments and most valuable things. Your son told me to be sure and take the Bible and Testament also Watch you had made him a present of. He was very anxious about these. Then he started vomiting large clots of blood. The other man the whole time I was unloading horses seemed frightened to death lent me no assistance whatever but wanted me to go and leave everything. However I unloaded the horses I don't know how for I was very bad with fever . . . I was thinking all the time which would be best way to take your son down to Port. I knew he must be very weak from loss of blood in fact I was thinking whether he would be able to sit a horse for he was very bad—To go back the way we had come would be madness, I determined to cut across country and

49

strike old track 30 miles from here. At last he made a start but he had to get off on top of hill to vomit more blood. After little while we went a little further and gave him a drink of nice cold water. Drinking it I thought he would have died he suffered such awful pain in stomach. We kept going though very slowly. We fell in with five natives at sundown and I got them to carry him a short distance in his blanket. The black boys had lost the other blanket so all your son had on that night was a blanket but no covering. I had to shift him from side to side about every ten minutes he could get no rest whichever way he lay but he bore it very bravely without complaint. Next day we made a good stage, then I had to leave him in charge of Frank while I went to find and cut track. I was away two days and when I came back your son told me that Frank would not go to get him his blanket that was on his horse tied up about 100 yards away so he laid there in the bitter cold all the night. He could not walk himself ... I had the fever and your poor son was as ill as ill could be—He eat nothing for 8 days and getting like a shadow but he kept up bravely all the time. I never saw a better fellow to endure hardships, such a fine temper never complaining though how he managed to sit a horse was something wonderful for at places it was like going up and coming down side of house that steep—one side of his face got paralysed his eye he could not close I can assure you he suffered very much. His chief anxiety seemed to be thinking what Mr Syme would say at his turning back. I tried to cheer him up by telling him he had risked his life in the service of Mr Syme and he could expect no more from anyone. I have written to Mr Syme and told him main points of trip up till the time they attacked us ... I should say that Mr Syme ought to give him great credit for what he has done. . . . Anyway he had the satisfaction of going 25 miles further than any white man and that over country that has never been reported on. ... If the party had been a large one your son would have done what he had undertaken to do. That was the only fault he made in taking too small a party. None but a very large party will ever penetrate far inland in New Guinea. . . .

I have no doubt at some future time he will make a brilliant name for himself.

I know he will make very light of this to you and I think it nothing but right that a mother should know what her son has gone through.

[A party of fourteen white men, eleven Malays, and a New Guinea interpreter, organized by the Geographical Society of Australasia, tried to explore New Guinea in 1885. More than £4500 was spent in preparations, and the supply of trade included four and a half dozen cricket and boating caps and four dozen fancy garters. The expedition spent four months in New Guinea, but despite a generous distribution of haberdashery, achieved little.]

A clinical account of Morrison's injuries appeared in the *Edinburgh Medical Journal* in October 1884. It was written by Mr George Mackay, House Surgeon of the Royal Infirmary, Edinburgh, and President of the Royal Medical Society. "One spear," he writes, "entered at the side of the nose about ¼ inch below the inner canthus of the right eye; the other pierced the abdominal wall about 2½ inches above the umbilicus, and 1 inch to the left of the middle line." The spears were about twelve feet long, made of wood sharpened only at the point. "Rising to his feet he pulled out the spears. That in the abdomen came away much more readily than that in the face. . . . Towards evening he became unconscious and remembers nothing more of that night."

4th Oct. Rode all day in great pain. . . . Once while sitting in the saddle he had a sensation in his left leg as though a "nerve had been drawn out like a bow string, and suddenly let go". He says he heard it distinctly, and that it was accompanied by a "galvanic shock" down the leg. He felt dazed all day. He ate nothing. Had great thirst but found that if he drank water it set up griping. No shelter at night.

5th. His mouth broke out, and was very sore both inside and on the lips. He had to lie down most of the day, while his men were cutting a track through the forest. The weather was very cold and damp, and he had neither blanket nor sheets. He ate nothing.

6th. The lower part of his belly to the left was swollen and yellow and walking was painful. The wound in the abdomen was closed up, but the horse falling with him the wound opened and pus began to trickle down. Stooped very much; same shocks; mouth very sore. For nourishment ½ pint coffee, ¼ pint Liebig, 3 little fancy biscuits. No shelter.

7th. Pus still trickling. Had to walk 3 miles because horse knocked up. . . . Some coffee and a little Liebig.

8th. Pus stopped trickling, and wound closed. Left side of his face benumbed and paralysed . . . complete loss of power over left eyelid. Left eye protruding. Ate nothing. Drank plenty of water. Rained all night.

9th. Left leg becoming fixed in flexed position. Face bad. Very hard work this day. Took ½ pint coffee and a few wet biscuits.

10th. Shot a duck, and had a pint of soup.

11th. Shot six ducks and had giblet stew. Left leg almost useless. . . .

15th. Carried into Port Moresby.

[IV]

Morrison remained in Port Moresby for a fortnight. The numbness in his left cheek continued, and he did not regain power of the eyelid. His leg was so shrunk up and contracted that he could scarcely walk. He took forty or fifty minims of laudanum every other night to induce sleep. On the night before leaving, the pain in his thigh was so acute that he took 100 minims, and finished his supply. He was very thin. His normal weight was over 11 stone. In Port Moresby, he weighed 7 stone 2 lb.

From Port Moresby, Morrison sailed in a small bêche-de-mer schooner, the *Pride of the Logan*, for Cooktown. At the end of the first week, anchored under the lee of a mangrove swamp, he developed fever and ague, which continued more or less severely every other day till after he got back to Geelong. The journey from Port Moresby to Cooktown took twenty days. Just before reaching Queensland, Morrison's mouth healed up and he found he could close his left eyelid. In Cooktown he saw a German doctor who tried to straighten his leg by kneeling on it. He spent seven days in hospital in Cooktown before catching the steamer *Warrego* for Sydney. Five days out from Cooktown, he blew a splinter of wood about ¾ inch long out of his nose.

"I do not care to dwell upon these disagreeable months . . ." Morrison wrote in his "Reminiscences", "and I have destroyed every paper that I had in connection with my journey and endeavoured to efface from my memory, all recollections of it. . . . My voyage back to Melbourne, defeated and wounded, was the most disagreeable experience of a lifetime. It seemed to me as though I had been lamed for life."

In Geelong, Morrison saw his family doctor who treated his fever with quinine and gave him borax to snuff up his nose. The homely therapy was not effective. Morrison blew another splinter out of his right nostril, and continued to suffer from intermittent fever, and though anxious to complete his journal was quite unfit to do so. Syme was not to be put off. He sent a reporter, Mr Stephens, down to Geelong with instructions to wait till the whole account of Morrison's journey was finished. Ultimately the *Age* received nine long articles which Morrison titled "My Failure in New Guinea". "The exigencies of the newspaper required a less modest title," he wrote later. "I had no copy to speak of. . . . Very ill at the time, I am only partly responsible for the series. . . ."

After a few weeks in which his condition got worse Morrison consulted Australia's leading surgeon, Mr T. N. Fitzgerald, who lanced his buttock twice and removed from his right nostril a splinter which was impinging on the spine, being wedged in between the first and second cervical vertebrae. Considerable force had to be used in pulling it out, and the operation, performed without chloroform, was a very painful one. The splinter which had been in 169 days was a tapering piece of wood about 2 inches long by ½ inch in diameter at its thickest part. The other spear point remained in his body. Fitzgerald would not operate on it, and suggested that Morrison be put in the hands of the celebrated John Chiene, Professor of Surgery at the University of Edinburgh. Fitzgerald was going to England on the R.M.S. *Mirzapore*, and Morrison sailed with him on 27th March. He suffered greatly from severe rigors, and the day after the ship left Colombo, Fitzgerald, having detected the presence of a foreign body by a probe in the left buttock, put Morrison under chloroform, cut into the buttock, and finding a sinus leading into the pelvis, came to a large sac of pus in which fragments of splinter were collected. He wanted to make an abdominal incision, but was deterred by an epidemic of scarlet fever on board, and by lack of antiseptics. Morrison was in bed six days, and became a great favourite with the young women passengers, who decorated his cabin and brought him gifts. He arrived at Gravesend on 14th May.

Fitzgerald would accept no fee, but before he left Melbourne, Morrison had raised with David Syme the matter of his medical expenses. Syme replied through his manager, K. D. Bennet, that he was not refusing to pay any expenses, "but we cannot be expected to pay an indefinite account". A second letter from Bennet was equally sympathetic:

> Mr Syme requests me to ask you what further expenses you want the firm to defray. You must bear in mind that already your expenses have far excelled the limit to which you pledged yourself and that we have gained nothing whatever from the Expedition one way or another, and that in fact the Expedition has not only been a pecuniary loss to us, but the source of serious annoyance and vexation.

When this letter reached him, Morrison was in the Royal Infirmary, Edinburgh, also suffering a little annoyance and vexation.

[V]

"Captain" Armit's expedition had been no more successful than Morrison's. Leaving Port Moresby on 14th July with fifty native carriers, Armit went in a north-easterly direction to Sogeri, which he made his headquarters.

In his first dispatch to the *Argus* he wrote: "These Papuans are no more savages than we are. . . . My love of botany, and a habit I have of sticking specimens in my hat when on the march, seems to have endeared me to them. I reciprocate the feeling. . . . I am actually beginning to love these Papuans—so much belied and yet so good."

By 17th August, Armit had reached a point which he claimed was about 120 miles ESE. from Port Moresby, and sixty miles from the nearest point on the coast. Here the party was attacked by fever, and at the end of August the expedition was abandoned. "Professor" Denton died on the way back. In his last sickness he refused all nourishment because of a theory that food stimulated the progress of disease. The rest of the party reached Port Moresby on 3rd September. Armit's claim to have penetrated 120 miles inland, and Morrison's to have gone twenty-five miles farther into the interior than any other white man, were both disputed by the Rev. Chalmers, who declared that he himself had reached the farthest point, forty miles inland from Port Moresby. According to Messrs. Lawes and Chalmers, who seemed to have a proprietary interest in New Guinea exploration, Armit had penetrated no farther than thirty-nine miles in a straight line from Port Moresby, and Morrison, thirty-five miles. But the missionaries were not reliable witnesses. Writing to a Sydney newspaper in 1888, Sir Edward Strickland, president of the Royal Geographical Society of Australasia, denounced them both for the "deplorable looseness" and "absurdity" of the accounts of their travels, and their "melancholy ignorance" of the geography of New Guinea.

Both Armit and Morrison were criticized by Mr Hugh Hastings Romilly, Deputy Commissioner for the Western Pacific, in a report dated 20th November 1883:

> The two so-called exploring expeditions have done no good. One of them has unfortunately done much harm. It is worthy of notice that the accounts of their doings . . . are very inaccurate. Mr Morrison, a boy of 21 . . . reached a point probably 15, certainly not more than 22, miles from the coast, though he asserts it must have been nearly 100 miles from the sea. . . . Mr Armit . . . reached a spot 40 miles from the coast, which had previously been visited by Mr and Mrs Lawes. These private expeditions, led by men of no experience, will do much harm if any more should be organized.

The *Bulletin* was even more uncharitable towards Morrison. Identifying him with the hated cause of imperialism, it devoted a page to a sardonic inquest on his misadventures, and another page to a series of cartoons ridiculing them. "When MR MORRISON introduced capital punishment, so did the savages, and not before it," it said. "Thus MR MORRISON was the first savage in the affair." And it drew a political moral:

> The imaginative persons of Jingo proclivities, who have begun to gabble about the necessity of annexation should discover in MR MORRISON'S narrative—notwithstanding its MUNCHAUSEN-like episodes of starvation—sufficient reason for suspending their excited clatter. . . . It becomes clear that, although the mere farce of hoisting a flag and firing a salute will hurt nobody and do nobody any benefit, any steps to take active possession of New Guinea must lead to a bitter and bloody conflict.

In spite of the *Bulletin*, Britain on 6th November 1884 proclaimed a protectorate over south-east New Guinea. She had been spurred into action because Germany had taken possession of north-east New Guinea. The Union Jack was again hoisted at Port Moresby, this time by the commander of the Australian naval station, Commodore J. E. Erskine, who adorned the ceremony with a display of electric lights on his flagship H.M.S. *Nelson*, rockets, speeches, salutes, the presentation to a native chief of a walking-stick with a two-shilling piece screwed into the top, and a generous distribution of trade tobacco. The commodore is reported to have said to a group of natives who were relaxing after a feast of human flesh, "Queen Victoria doesn't like her children to do that sort of thing." Among them was Queen Koloka of Naara, who, however, called herself Queen Victoria's sister. It is doubtful whether Victoria would have approved her buxom sister's ceremonial costume: a short grass skirt and a trade necklace.

Morrison arrived in London, lame and suffering severely, on 14th May 1884, and was admitted to St George's Hospital for treatment. A week later he entered the Royal Infirmary, Edinburgh, where Professor Chiene examined him, probing the sinus deeply. Chiene could feel no foreign body, and determined to wait and see the effect of simple rest, but when an intense burning pain in Morrison's left thigh got worse, with great abdominal tenderness, he decided to operate. His decision was supported by another distinguished surgeon, Mr Joseph Bell, whose powers of deduction had so impressed a young student called Arthur Conan Doyle a few years before that he inspired the character of Mr Sherlock Holmes.

On 1st July, Chiene, assisted by Bell, and with sixteen other surgeons watching, made the incision that Fitzgerald had wanted to make on board ship, and with some difficulty withdrew from the iliacus muscle, where it was firmly embedded, a tapering fragment of wood 3 inches long, and from $\frac{3}{8}$ to $\frac{1}{4}$ of an inch in diameter. A countryman of Morrison's, Dr F. Lidell, who assisted as instrument clerk, said, "I well remember the look of surprise and satisfaction when, having carefully manipulated a long pair of forceps in the depths of the wound, Chiene extracted . . . the head of the spear."

The fragment is preserved in the museum of the medical school at Edinburgh University. Morrison wrote to his mother: "It was about the size of your second finger. . . . I was extremely fortunate I came home here when I did for who in Victoria could have removed it?. . . . An account of this very remarkable case will appear in the *Edinburgh Medical Journal*. . . ."

In his "Reminiscences" Morrison recalled that a year after the operation Chiene gave a dinner in honour of Morrison's recovery, and expressed his intention of sending Morrison's parents a model of the spearhead in gold:

> It was very pleasant for me to hear this, and I wrote to my parents in Australia telling them of the gift that would soon reach them. But the gift was never sent. In 1895, I was again in Edinburgh . . . and it was pleasant for me again to meet the Professor to whom I owe so much. He then said to me, "Man, I have long intended to send your father a model of the spearhead in *silver*." I again wrote to my parents, telling them that they were shortly to receive this valuable souvenir. But the model was never sent. Some years later, when I met the cautious professor a third time, I was disappointed that he did not offer to send me a model in bronze.

Morrison was in the Infirmary for eighty days. When he left for the country on 7th August his leg was no longer bent, although he walked with a slightly rolling gait. By the end of the year his health was so much better that on 6th January 1885 he was able to resume his medical course. He took lodgings at 6 Marchmont Road, Edinburgh. A fellow-student, T. J. Henry, also an Australian, recalled him at the university:

In mentioning men, he invariably mentioned their full names, Christian and surname. This was in line with his passion for precision in all things. He was a non-smoker and an abstainer. A healthy contempt for sartorial conventions was a characteristic. At that time we suffered under the tyranny of the prim fashions of the Victorian era and he who did not wear the stiff-fronted shirt, high collar, and full cuffs prescribed, was liable to be classed with socialists, artists, poets and other undesirables. Morrison courageously defied this prejudice, and affected a soft shirt, with limp turn-down collar, a suit of inconspicuously patterned tweed, loosely cut.

"There is no question but that I worked hard," Morrison wrote in his "Reminiscences", "I was anxious to finish my course as soon as possible, and travel round the world." He took little interest in sport, either as participant or as spectator, but it is apparent from some of the letters he kept that he had time for girls, if not for games.

"I regret to hear that the Woman incident still lies heavy on your breast," another student, W. S. Newton, writes to him. "Remember your late experience of the lady who wants your address and keep clear of the wiles of the charmer opposite. As your landlady is exzematous, I need not warn you against her."

The life of Edinburgh medical students in the eighties followed a traditional pattern. Newton reported on a students' ball:

Tonight, or rather tomorrow, for it is to begin at 12, will be a grand and affecting farewell from the students to the ballet girls, said farewell to take shape of a grand ball, tickets to men 10/- each, females free, drinks and feed found, bar champagne. Under these circumstances I suppose it will resolve itself into a drunken riot. . . . Some of the ballet girls are sure to fight, there was a big fight, I hear, amongst them the other night. It began by one telling a rival charmer that she was little better than a prostitute, the rival fair replied that at least she could "thank her gawd" she had never slept with 4 men in one night. Thereupon they tore each other, and a free fight ensued. Both these ladies are to be present tonight, besides other inflammable material. . . .

The report continued next day:

Saturday . . . Ballet did not quarrel consumed its superfluous energy in putting away liquor which, being gratis, was swallowed by them literally in *floods*. One helplessly paralytic drunk lay on floor with rest sprinkling her with brandy and soda, perhaps as a "pick-me-up". Committee got mostly drunk and quarrelled fearfully. Out of the wreck I have 3 bottles of cham. Dresses of ballet were pictures. Mostly horribly ugly with an enormous amount of adipose tissue, and evidently all were proud of these personal charms, else the display of mammae even unto the nipples in one case—would not have been so great. Greville and I got home about 8 o'clock. . . . Does the girl opposite "go it"?

Two medical students who shared Morrison's sexual confidences, J. C. Hutton and J. W. Dungate, were to remain his lifelong friends.

From Corrie, a primitive and "tipsy", but pretty little village of thirty-five cottages on the isle of Arran, Hutton in August 1885 counselled Morrison on the technique of rustic love-making. He described an "Arcadian afternoon":

> Today I have been nutting with my landlady's daughters—We manage it this way. I run after the eldest daughter aet. 18, a buxom wench—she runs away—I catch her and drag her to a nut tree—I place her hands on a bough and tell her to swing on it or pull it down as low as possible—I then place a hand on the bough and my disengaged arm round the lassie's waist and thus I give the advantage of 14 stone to pulling down the branch. The others then pick of the nuts whilst I take my pleasure in clasping Flora . . . as tight as I can. In about one minute both Flora's hands give way she slips on the ground and I slip my hand from the bough the other one remaining in its *original* position around Flora's waist— and I find myself on the ground beside Flora. Tableau d'amour and curtain falls. Only to give rise again to show another similar scene and yet another. . . . I hope you have ceased that charming waste of time *legitimate love making*. Give me the illicit still where the love elixir is brewed perhaps not with the same refined flavour but where the strength is strong and lusty and enflames one's ardour to heroic pitch with the additional quality that it doesn't pay any legal duties.

Two years later, Hutton, who then had a junior post in a Liverpool hospital, wrote to Morrison:

> Please do not make me envious again. Three in one night. On landing after a voyage to Montreal I treated myself to a couple of ladies in one evening but three in one night—it's positively too greedy. How the Lord must watch over you to give you three. . . . I really think that every week that a man doesn't have his lassie is an insult to Human Nature.

When Morrison was involved with a "little courtesan" or "strumpet", Hutton advised him to come down to Liverpool. "In a week or two or a month you will get a ship and you are out of the way."

Morrison had another diversion, less demanding. He collected glossy studio portraits of the faculty, which he annotated with brutal frankness. Alexander Russell Simpson, Professor of Midwifery, was "a pious fraud". Thomas Grainger Stewart, Professor of Medicine and Queen's Physician for Scotland, "a man universally distrusted. The most unpopular teacher in Edinburgh." On the other hand, Sir John Wyllie, lecturer in Medicine, was "the best physician in Scotland".

[VII]

Morrison graduated on 1st August 1887, having in two years and six months passed the preliminary, first, second, and final examinations. His examiner gave him a generous testimonial: "His knowledge of Medicine and Surgery is extensive and accurate, his abilities are great. . . . Besides being well versed in his professional work, he is a widely read and cultured man. . . . I know few whom I can more highly recommend, and few whose success in life I look upon as more certain." And John Chiene wrote as a "sincere friend":

My dear Morrison

I first made your acquaintance in the students' ward two years ago when you suffered from the effects of a spear wound. . . . You were then working for your first professional and you have now graduated. . . . This gives the best evidence of your capability, perserverence, and energy. . . . You go from here with knowledge and power for your future work.

A few days after his graduation, with testimonials and diploma in his bag, £15 in his pocket, and a "bona fide emigrant's" certificate, Morrison sailed as an intermediate passenger on the S.S. *Hibernia* for St John's, Newfoundland. The fare was £6. Three other men shared his cabin. One, a Glasgow manufacturer of pork sausages, confidentially explained to Morrison how one pound of pork, blended with knowledge, could flavour forty pounds of anonymous meat. Applying this expertise, he made an income of £700 a year.

From St Johns, Morrison went to Philadelphia, in time to participate in the celebration of the Centennial Anniversary of the adoption of the American Constitution. He saw General Phil Sheridan riding at the head of the troops, heard President Cleveland deliver a stirring address, and Marion Crawford's Commemoration Hymn sung in Constitution Hall. Then he wandered aimlessly about the town. He thought of walking to San Francisco, but one day, strolling along the river, he saw a steamer unloading bananas from Jamaica, and decided at once that he ought to go to Jamaica, which he pictured as a small island that could be crossed in a day's walk. After beating the agent down from $50 to $30, he booked a passage, but forgot to ask to which part of Jamaica the steamer was going. He found himself landed in St Ann's Bay, on the north of the island, when his destination was Kingston, on the south. By this time he had little money left, and when he had paid for a passage to Ewarton he was almost penniless. In Kingston he took a room in a boarding house and tried without success to find employment as a doctor. He spent his last money on a train to Ewarton and walked on through the night. Next morning he called on a doctor in the neighbourhood, Dr Frank Rand, who told him there was no possibility of his getting a job. Rand advised Morrison to leave Jamaica, and lent him enough money to see more of it. With this money Morrison walked from Falmouth round the coast to Montego

Bay, and then crossed back over the island to the Black River, and finally to Porus. From here he took the train back to Kingston. "Travelling as I did," he wrote in the "Reminiscences", "a 'walk-foot bucra', I excited the derision of the niggers and still more of my white countrymen. A white man walking in Jamaica, they said, was an 'insult to the Almighty'."

In Kingston he found he could get a job either at the Panama Canal or on the Costa Rica Railways, if he could speak Spanish. "It may seem ridiculous," he wrote, "but I detected in this the hand of providence directing me to go to Spain, and I remembered the intercourse I had had at the Cockatoo Wells in South Australia, with the shanty keeper who had lived in Spain and whose stories of that country of ancient glory had fascinated my imagination. I determined to go to Spain." But Spain was a long way from Kingston, "immensely far for a man whose pockets were empty". Again, help was given him. The editor of the *Colonial Standard*, a namesake of Morrison's, give him a little money, and the Kingston agent of the Atlas Steamship Co., Captain W. Peploe Forwood, offered him a free passage back to New York, shipping him as an assistant purser. On the Atlas steamer *Alps* he sat on a chair with his heels on the rail, keeping tally of the oranges and bananas brought on board at Morant Bay and Port Antonio.

He arrived in New York on 4th November 1887 with $7.13 in his pocket. It was bitterly cold and he was dressed for the tropics. He took a room at 203 West 19th Street, Mrs Davis proprietress, at $2 a week, payable in advance. The room was at the top of the building, and very cold. Morrison tried to warm it by keeping the gas burning, but Mrs Davis told him sharply that lodgers at $2 a week were expected to put their light out at 9 o'clock. He continued to shiver as he tramped round New York in search of a job. He applied for many without success. Among them was the post of warder at $30 a month at the New York Hospital in 15th Street. A "motley crew" waited in the ante-room to be questioned by the secretary on their qualifications. When Morrison's turn came, he showed his testimonials. "How do I know these haven't been written by yourself?" asked the secretary. Morrison replied that had they been, they would have been more flattering. The secretary said, "You would have to obtain the guarantee of some reputable citizen of New York that the testimonials were genuine and while you were doing that I could obtain 100 men competent to fill the post."

Piece by piece, Morrison pawned his things to buy food, beginning reluctantly with his cardigan jacket, the only piece of warm clothing he possessed. He asked the pawnbroker, Mr Simpson, of 171 Bowery, for $5 on this, but had to accept 75 cents. Then he lived for several days on his small surgical instrument case, taking one proper meal only every second day: ten cents' worth of pork and potatoes at Beefsteak John's in the Bowery. After twenty-four days of semi-starvation Morrison met a man named Junner M. Croll, who inspected his credentials and arranged for him to get a passage to Glasgow for $30, to be paid on arrival.

On his last evening in New York, Morrison went round the dime shows of the Bowery—which included a man with two mouths and a man with no arms who could thread a needle with his toes—and had a long talk with the Tichborne Claimant, Arthur Orton, who still insisted that he was Sir Roger Charles Doughty Tichborne, Bart. Sir Roger was mixing and swallowing drinks as manager of a saloon called Cassidy's Shades in Chatham Square—a sleazy neighbourhood between the Bowery and Chinatown. He was in "an elevated condition" and told Morrison he would soon return to England to renew his claim, backed by Miss Georgiana Baring, a cousin of Lord Northbrook, who was putting up £100,000 to restore him to his domain. "It was amusing to hear this overfed bullock tossing about thousands with such cheerfulness," Morrison wrote to his mother.

[VIII]

Back in Edinburgh, Morrison set about getting a job in Spain. To see Spain had become an obsession with him. One day he learned that Dr J. S. Mackay, Senior Medical Officer of the Rio Tinto Co., was in Edinburgh. Morrison called on him, produced his well-worn credentials, and told Mackay of his desire to go to Spain. Mackay promised to do what he could, but was suddenly recalled to the mines, and Morrison, again penniless, took a locum-tenency in Skye for three weeks. When he returned to Edinburgh, Captain David Gray, of the *Eclipse*, a famous Arctic whaler, sailing from Peterhead, offered him the post of ship's surgeon. But Morrison, unable to escape his obsession with Spain, refused the offer. He also refused the job of ship's surgeon on a steamer trading to the West Coast of Africa. He was temped to accept this, when he received a telegram ALRIGHT BUY SPANISH GRAMMAR MACKAY. It was followed by a monitory letter:

> Go up to London . . . and call upon Mr Mathieson at Lombard Street. . . . Say that you will come out for £20 per month. . . . Of course, you will have a house and horse . . . expenses, fare by sea. Do not mention you have had fever. Keep clear of religious topics. And drop your "isms". Have your certificates with you and tell him all about the Labour traffic etc. . . . P.S. Do not let your Socialism be roused by being in Lombard Street.

Mr Hugh Mathieson, of Mathieson & Co., agents for Rio Tinto, was described by Morrison as a "pietistical Presbyterian elder". In appointing Morrison as assistant surgeon to the Rio Tinto mines on six months' probation, he said he was confident Morrison would not only perform his duties well but also "could help bring the word of Grace to the heathen in Rio Tinto". Morrison arrived at Huelva, the port for the mines, on 8th May 1888. "Don't stay there longer than is necessary to get a good smattering of the lingo," Hutton wrote to him, "then wend your way to other climes. Your life will be such as I would like to lead—that educated poetical adventuring which you indulge in." In June, Morrison wrote to his mother, "I am becoming a very great surgeon indeed and amputate limbs with a sang froid which is wonderful."

Three months later Mackay resigned and Morrison became Chief Medical Officer at a salary of £400 a year, in charge of a staff of eight Spanish and three British doctors who served 9500 workmen and their families. The company's wage bill was £450,000 a year. "Nothing of interest marked my time in Rio Tinto," he wrote. "It was a god-forsaken spot." There was not a blade of vegetation to be seen. The country was desert-like, devastated for miles around by sulphur fumes from the mine.

Despite Mr Mathieson's exhortation, Morrison's missionary endeavours seem to have been limited to one heathen, a Spanish girl called Pepita who fell passionately in love with him. His relations with his employers, particularly with the manager, Mr William Rich, were not harmonious. There were many disputes, such as when Morrison complained that the gait of his horse, Liebre, was not to his taste, and Rich replied that it was a hopeless task to supply every member of the staff with an animal that suited him. Finally Morrison received a letter from Rich which he could not stomach, and on 7th August 1889 he resigned. "I was thankful to leave Rio Tinto," he wrote:

> The immediate cause of my resignation was this: As head of the medical service, I had discovered an extensive series of frauds in the druggist department involving several thousands of pounds. On sending the Company a report on this fraud, I received an astonishing letter ... expressing the gravest disapproval of the directors at the unbecoming language in which my report was couched. I resigned two hours after getting the letter. It appears that the frauds I discovered were insignificant compared with other frauds that soon after came to light, of which even some of the directors who had admonished me had not been guiltless.

[IX]

When he left Rio Tinto, Morrison drew up a balance-sheet, the first of many that he was to compile with great precision throughout his life. He was owed £65 4s. 6d., he had furniture worth £4 13s., £187 2s. 11d. in the bank, £7 12s. 2½d. in his pocket, and in his valise an authorization, seldom granted to foreigners, to practise medicine in Spain, a bundle of love letters from Pepita, written in purple ink, and a silk dance programme which showed he had danced a waltz and a polka with her, and sat out the Circassian circle, the mazurka, the Sir Roger de Coverley, and the quadrille. "Pepita appears to be very much affected, poor girl, at your going away," a colleague of Morrison's at the mines reported. She continued to pour out her heart in ardent letters:

Today I am little more calm because I see that you love me very much, and believe me that today I end up by being mad with joy and satisfaction with your precious letter. I have always loved you very much but I love you very much more life of mine. Your departure has aroused in me a love and a passion so that I do not leave off thinking of you for a moment. . . . I am not content nor satisfied if I am not at your side. . . . You tell me in your letter it is not so hopeless. . . . but I cannot calm the grief that I suffer today. . . . Never forget me, my dearest. . . . you are my joy, my consolation, my life. . . . I am blind with love and do not think of other thing except to give you pleasure. . . .

From Rio Tinto, Morrison went to Jerez and Cadiz, where he saw the trials of a submarine invented by a young Spanish engineer named Isaac Peral:

All Spain went mad about the discovery. Pictures were seen in every shop in the Peninsula, depicting the *Peral* restoring to Spain her ancient naval glory. Every town in Spain . . . gave the name Peral to one of its streets. . . . An immense crowd mounted the ramparts of Cadiz to witness the triumph. At the trials no proof was given that the vessel could move underwater. The Spaniards were quickly disillusioned.

Unable to find employment, Morrison, through his friend Newton, spent £4 10s. on an advertisement in ten London and provincial papers, including the *Lancet*, the *Country Gentleman*, and the *Manchester Examiner*, offering his services as a travelling companion to an invalid. "There is . . . I am sorry to say, no reply—absolutely none," Newton reported. "I can only pity the British travelling invalid public—and hope they will all die." Medical graduates were not much in demand; a contemporary advertisement in the *Lancet* for Clinical Assistants reads: "Remuneration is limited to residence and rations."

In December, Morrison was in Tangiers. He went into a chemist's shop to buy some glycerine. The chemist was very busy and explained in a high-pitched falsetto voice that he was leaving for Fez next morning. Morrison said he had often wished to see Fez. "Then come with me, sir," said the chemist, introducing himself as Nicholas Dassoy. "You shall have a mule and we shall go first to Wazan, to see the son of the Sherif who is ill, and then to Fez. I shall present you to the Sultan. I have bedding and pack-mules and everything needful. It won't cost you anything. Nothing. Nothing. Nothing." Dassoy had a strange history. His father was Greek, and his mother Italian, but he claimed British nationality because he had been born on a ship flying the British flag in New York Harbour. He spoke eighteen languages and was famed as a doctor throughout Morocco. He had been Sir James Paget's favourite pupil at Gray's, where he took his degree of Bachelor of Arts, and had been wounded in the Franco-Prussian war. "His chief surgical work," Morrison wrote, "may be emphatically described as repairing the ruptured anuses of the buggered."

Early next morning Morrison packed a holdall with a few clean things, his telescope, his pocket instrument case, and £3 15s. in English money, and the party, which included a soldier of the Sultan's bodyguard, a Jewish servant, and five Moors, set out. Before leaving, Morrison was presented to the Sherif of Wazan, an ugly mulatto. "Sherifs are as common as Colonels in America or Captains in Queensland," Morrison noted. But the Sherif of Wazan was an uncommon specimen. As the spiritual head of the Mohammedan church in Morocco, his person was so sacred that his subjects would try to kiss his foot as he passed on horseback; failing this, they would fall to the ground and kiss the imprint made by the horse. His many wives had included an Englishwoman, Miss Keane, whose father had been Governor of Horsemonger Gaol. The Sherif had recently been cured of a long illness by Dassoy, who was now on his way to treat the Sherif's son, also a holy man. When they reached Wazan, Dassoy invited Morrison to take over the case. Morrison reported on it to his mother. The patient, who had not been out of his house for four months, was an effeminate man of thirty-five suffering from a huge abscess in the loin and thigh. Dassoy washed him, for he was "fearfully dirty", and Morrison opened the abscess and removed 22 ounces of extravasated blood: "His relief was great and instantaneous. It is such a ridiculously small thing to us that you will be amused to hear the whole town now knows of the improvement in the saint and the whole town is in jubilation."

Morrison and Dassoy celebrated Christmas in the Palace with a tin of Cambridge sausages from their stores, and so much port wine that Morrison had to sleep off its effects. From Wazan they rode to Fez, where he noted that the lost books of Livy were said to be preserved, and venereal diseases were inconceivably common: "Hemmorrhoids are the commonest non-venereal diseases which afflict the suffering ladies of the harem. Their life is sedentary and voluptuous . . . they habitually overfeed . . . everything conduces to that unladylike complaint—piles."

In Fez, Morrison met the English Commander-in-Chief of the Emperor's army, Henry de Vere Maclean, who told him that on one occasion when the Sherif was in Morocco city, twelve sons were born to him in one day. "This is probably a lie," Morrison wrote. But the report set him thinking:

It is said that a minute record is kept of all the births in the family of the Sultan. If such be the case, the Emperor owes a duty to science to publish this record since hardly anything is known of the possible fertilizing power of man. The late Victor Emanuel left 95 illegitimate children besides his lawfully begotten. Sir Samuel Baker mentions that at the time of his visit to Mamrasi, this potentate was blessed with 125 sons and daughters. And Trotter estimates that the Sultan must have at least 100 children per annum.

Maclean also mentioned some of his experiences as a mercenary. Rebel prisoners were offered the choice of serving the Sultan or having their heads cut off. Maclean had seen eleven rebels one after the other choose decapitation. A soldier would draw a sharp curved knife across the throat, sever the muscles at the back of the throat, twist the head around to separate it from the upper cervical vertebra, and pitch it into a sack. As the Sultan paid for each head, there was a strong temptation to fill the sack with the heads of innocent non-combatants.

Morrison noted with equal interest that Mrs Maclean measured eighty-five inches round the buttocks.

For the next few months he wandered again through Spain. He told his mother that Madrid was a magnificent city "and licks Geelong into a cocked hat". In Madrid he boarded for 3s. 7d. a day, including morning chocolate, went to the Prado during the day, the Teatro Laro at night, drank coffee, bought lottery tickets, and visited a few gay houses. When he got back to London his money was running out, and an Edinburgh friend, Edward Jacob, then working in Paris, suggested Morrison join him: "I don't think there's a cheaper town than Paris in Europe . . . cost of living would not exceed six francs a day." (A franc was worth 9½d. sterling.) Morrison took Jacob's advice. Before leaving London he had three shirts refitted and reversed at a cost of three shillings each by the Capital and Labour Clothing Association—"The Largest Firm of Manufacturing Clothiers in the World"—of Tottenham Court Road, whose trade-mark depicted a refined hand labelled "Capital", emerging from a neatly cuffed sleeve, clasping a rugged hand labelled "Labour", emerging from a carelessly rolled-up sleeve.

"I went to Paris to study at the Salpêtrière under Professor Charcot," Morrison wrote later, tongue in cheek: "Unfortunately the only day that I went to the hospital, Charcot was not there, but I can truthfully assert that I did go to Paris to study at the Salpêtrière."

With the assistance of a grisette named Noelle who not only betrayed him for a waiter but misspelt his name, Morrison soon spent what remained of his savings. In August 1890 he applied, unsuccessfully, for the job of medical officer to the British North Borneo Company. At the end of the year, when he returned to Australia after an absence of five years and eight months, he had only seven francs, and owed £63 for his passage money.

[X]

Back home, Morrison found nothing to do. For a few months he loafed around Victoria, but his mother's keen eye read an advertisement for a resident surgeon at the Ballarat and District Base hospital, and on 21st April 1891 he was given the appointment, at a salary of £31 3s. 4d. a calendar month. "This was in some ways the most coveted hospital appointment in Australia," he wrote, "for the city is interesting, the climate glorious, and the pay was generous." The hospital, established in 1855 during the gold rush, was administered by a rather heterogeneous committee of laymen, elected by public vote:

> In giving me the appointment the Committee paid attention to other factors than mere medical knowledge. On paying my visits before the appointment was made, I called first on the most aggressive member . . . Mr George Smith, a market-gardener, who had been in his time a handy man with his fists. "Weren't you the young man who walked across Australia?" Mr Smith asked. "We all admired that plucky feat. I don't think we will go far wrong if we appoint you." . . . And when I was appointed, the Press notices, while generously referring to my going to Paris to study at the Salpêtrière, laid special stress upon the circumstance that I had carried my swag across the continent of Australia.

Morrison was soon at loggerheads with the committee. The hospital was bankrupt, with an overdraft of £3290, and the committee insisted on retrenchments, which Morrison resisted. He would not compromise the efficiency of the hospital by reducing the nursing staff, though he agreed to a five per cent cut in salaries and a cut of £24 a year in the annual budget for fish and poultry. (The cost of feeding 108 patients and 48 staff was 6¼d. per head per day.) He also displeased members of the committee by isolating typhoid cases. The Ballarat *Courier* congratulated him: "Anxious and sympathetic friends of patients have doubtless felt aggrieved at their rigid exclusion from the typhoid ward, but the Resident Surgeon, Dr G. E. Morrison, and his very able and successful staff of nurses, can confidently appeal to the results of that policy fully to justify it."

A war of words developed between the committee and their resident surgeon, which an obdurate Morrison, in signed and anonymous letters, carried into the columns of the Ballarat Press. The conflict went on from February 1892, when the committee gave Morrison notice of removal, till 21st April 1893, when he agreed to leave. "What a loss I was to Ballarat, and what a vast amount of suffering I alleviated when I was there with Mist. Cop., Mist. Lax., Mist. Ammon., Mist. Sod—really I forgot what mists they were!" he wrote to a former colleague, John Anderson, in 1911. "I remember I wrote countless thousands of times, 'Rep. Mist.'" Anderson's reply recalled their time together, when Benevolent Society patients were called "Beneveyes", and Chinese patients "mowlahs" or "chows":

> Yes, those were the days—when one never knew what day a chow had to be helped downstairs with his pigtail—or whether a fellow was to have his pyjamas ripped to pieces in a holy Tommy Burns scruff on the bottom landing. . . . I often think of Harry Salmon's endeavouring to "tap" an old "Benevey's" vesica in No 1, and he and

Leach couldn't make out why—with a gallon of fluid in him—none would rise through the tube, until as he walked down the ward scratching his head and like the captain's immortal parrot—wondering what-the-devil was he to do next—I had noticed his trocar had never entered and watching a chance gave the thing an extra jab (permiscuously like) that might have transfixed the old fellow to the mattress—to the great relief of the Surgeon Major as much as to the Benevey.

CHAPTER FOUR

[I]

ONCE MORE out of work, Morrison decided to try his luck in the Far East
—that part of the world which to an Australian is neither far nor east.
Refusing the post of surgeon on a China steamer, he took passage to Hong
Kong and then to the Philippines, hoping, because of his knowledge of
Spanish, and his Spanish authorization to practice, to get a job there. Unsuccessful, he returned to Hong Kong and went up the coast to Tientsin.
He found it economical to travel as a Chinese missionary, in Chinese dress,
with pigtail and slippers. In this guise he presented himself to the China
Inland Mission House in Peking. "You will be delighted to hear what a
blessed time I am having with the Missionaries," he wrote to his mother on
15th September 1893:

> To-day, for instance. Called 7. Breakfast 7.30. prodigiously long
> grace then prayers, including psalms, bible-reading and prayer for
> 20 minutes. Then to hospital. Address by Doctor to outpatients kneel-
> ing down in outpatients' room among a lot of dirty Chinamen. Then
> lunch with grace and then a special prayer for one of the seven mis-
> sionary divisions of China. Then afternoon tea with grace and special
> prayer for the conversion of all Unitarians. Then to dinner with Doc-
> tor—grace, and in the evening, music, hymns, etc., a most blessed
> conversation concerning the conversion of a sea captain by the Doc-
> tor's sister and then family prayers. Then home or would have had
> more. Total 10 hours, having sung 26 hymns, 25 being out of tune,
> have had prayers 17 times and have put in gracious word for Heathen
> of all lands and of every colour. I am making up for lost time with a
> vengeance.

From this salvational orgy Morrison moved on to Peking, where, concealed in the London Mission chapel with two other Australians, he saw
the Emperor of China and his cortège pass down the road on his return
from the Summer Palace—one of the rare occasions upon which the
Emperor had been seen by strangers, Morrison noted. After a few days in

Peking, he returned to Shanghai, where he pawned his boots, hat, and socks for two thousand cash—about two shillings ("interest 3% per month, sold if not redeemed within fourteen months") and crossed over to Japan. Again he failed to find employment. "I was really hard up in Japan," he recalled. "In Kobe when I sold my telescope for $12, I truthfully wrote to a friend in Australia telling him that I had come round from Yokohama on my shirt studs, that I was at present living on my telescope, and that I hoped to return to Shanghai on my surgical instrument case. And that happened. . . ."

From the Seamen's Refuge in Kobe, where he spent most of his time, he wrote to his mother:

> Japan has been a very costly experience to me and when I arrive in Shanghai I will hardly have anything. I could raise a good many dollars on my books which I have picked up for a trifle, but I am not going to do that and I really am afraid that I will have to telegraph home for money from Shanghai. £30 will, I think be enough for me.

Methodically, he recorded that he had been "taken in" by "1. English vice-consul. 2. English shipping office. 3. Japanese bank-teller. 4. Japanese guide. 5. Yokohama hotel keeper", besides having his handkerchief and his umbrella stolen.

He arrived in Shanghai with fifteen shillings. His mother telegraphed him £40, which he changed into $362. Acknowledging it, he wrote: "I always pay my debts and I will of course return with 5% interest every penny of the money spent on me. . . ."

In Kobe, Morrison had conceived the idea of crossing Western China, the Shan States, and the Kachlin Hills, to Burma. "The journey was, of course, in no sense one of exploration," he wrote, adding with his characteristic half-contrived, half-genuine understatement:

> It consisted simply of a voyage of 1500 miles up the Yangtze River, followed by a quiet though extended journey up another 1500 miles along the great overland highway into Burma, taken by one who spoke no Chinese, who had no interpreter or companion, who was unarmed, but who trusted implicitly in the good faith of the Chinese.

In fact much of the journey was through a part of China at that time almost unknown to Europeans, and believed to be very anti-foreign.

On 11th February 1894, Morrison left Shanghai by steamer, again dressed as a Chinese. He had found that the traveller who "put his pride in his pocket and a pigtail down his back need pay only one-fourth of what it would cost him . . . in European dress." Ten days later he reached Ichang, the most inland port on the Yangtze accessible by steamer. From here to Chungking, a distance of 412 miles, the Yangtze for a great part of its course was a series of rapids. At Ichang he chartered a *wupan*, a frail craft twenty-eight feet long and drawing only eight inches, whose captain, with a crew of four, contracted to land him in Chungking in fifteen days, for £2 16s. There were anxious moments in the great Yangtze gorges, but Chungking was reached on the promised day; the fastest journey on record up the perilous rapids. Five days later Morrison started his land journey to Suifu, 230 miles west of Chungking. He hired two coolies to carry his things, paying one 4s. 10d., the other 5s. 7d., for the seven-day journey. They would not go beyond Suifu. The way was mountainous and little trodden, and they feared robbers would come down and stab them. Morrison engaged new coolies and pressed on to the walled city of Chaotong, in Yunnan province, 290 miles distant.

In Chaotong, which had been devastated by plague and famine, he was told that the previous year at least 3000 children, mostly girls, had been sold to slave-dealers and "carried like poultry in baskets to the capital". Normally the price of girls was one tael (about three shillings) for every year of their age, but in time of famine girls of any age fetched no more than six shillings. In this district infanticide, too, was common. Dead, and often living, infants were thrown out on the common where they could be seen any morning, gnawed by dogs.

Morrison noted other facets of civilization in Chaotong. He was shown a spot near the west gate where a few days before a woman taken in adultery was done to death in a cage before a crowd of spectators who witnessed her agony for three days. On the gate itself a murderer and robber had been nailed with red-hot nails through his wrists, and then exposed in turn at each of the three other gates, till he died four days later. In the published account of his journey Morrison wrote:

> No people are more cruel in their punishments than the Chinese, and obviously the reason is that the sensory nervous system of a Chinese is either blunted or of arrested development. Can anyone doubt this who witnesses the stoicism with which a Chinaman can endure physical pain . . . and the indifference with which he contemplates the suffering of lower animals, and the infliction of tortures on higher?

The belief that the Chinese are relatively insensitive to pain has often been proclaimed by Europeans, sometimes to justify their own brutality. When General Burgevine, of the Ever-Victorious Army, in 1863 blew Taiping rebels from the guns—a picturesque mode of execution perfected by the British during the Indian Mutiny—Mr Andrew Wilson, editor of the *China Mail*, reassured his readers that "what might be exquisite torture to the nervous vascular system" was something "much less to the obtuse-nerved" Chinese. Mr George Lanning, a Shanghai schoolmaster, writing of China in 1912, suggested that this insensibility, which, like Morrison, he took for granted, might be due to a vegetable diet; surely a powerful argument for vegetarianism.

But Morrison recalled that his own countrymen could also contemplate with indifference abominable cruelties:

> I question if the cruelties practised in the Chinese gaols, allowing for the blunted nerve sensibility of the Chinaman, are less endurable than

the condition of things existing in English prisons so recently as when Charles Reade wrote *It is Never Too Late to Mend*. . . . And it cannot admit, I think, of question, that there are no cruelties practised in Chinese gaols greater, even if there are any equal, to the awful and degraded brutality with which the England of our fathers treated her convicts. . . .

Morrison's route from Chaotong lay through Tongchan to Yunnan. In Tongchan he again looked on the face of famine. Descending a picturesque valley from the flower-girdled Temple to the God of Literature, he was shown two common burial pits:

With famine in the city, with people dying at that very hour of starvation, there was no lack of dead, and both pits were filled to within a few feet of the surface. Bodies are thrown in here without covering, and hawks and crows strip them of their flesh, a mode of treating the dead grateful to the Parsee, but inexpressibly hateful to the Chinese, whose poverty must be overwhelming when he can be found to permit it. Pigtails were lying carelessly about and skulls separated from the trunk. Human bones gnawed by dogs were to be picked up in numbers in the long grass. . . . Many, too, were the bones of dead children; for poor children are not buried, but are thrown outside the wall, sometimes before they are dead.

Morrison found the people "cowed and crushed". Like countless generations before them, and many after them, they had seen "the horrors of rebellion and civil war, of battle, murder and sudden death, of devastation by the sword, famine, ruin and misery":

In the open, uncultivated fields women are searching for weeds and herbs to save them from starvation till the ingathering of the winter harvest. The children were pitiful to see. It is rare for Australians to see children dying of hunger. These poor creatures, with their pinched faces and fleshless bones, were like the patient with typhoid fever, who has long been hovering between life and death.

Yet nowhere in the famine district was Morrison solicited for either food or money. The people, dressed in rags that scarcely held together, were friendly and charming, their courtesy and kindliness a "constant delight".

From Yunnan, one of the most important cities in China, which Marco Polo visited in 1283, to Bhamo, on the Irrawaddy in British Burma, was "a difficult journey of thirty-three stages over a mountainous road". Morrison bought a little white pony in Yunnan City for £3 6s., and partly riding, partly walking, reached Bhamo exactly a hundred days after leaving Shanghai. Bhamo is 1520 land miles from Chungking, and Chungking about the same distance from Shanghai. The entire journey, Morrison calculated, had cost less than £30 sterling, including his Chinese outfit. "Had I travelled economically," he wrote, "I estimate that the journey need not have cost me more than £14."

As he farewelled it on the Irrawaddy, Morrison saw China as a place of great beauty, hideous poverty, and widespread corruption. He was at once appalled by the indifference of the Chinese to life and suffering and charmed by their courtesy and friendliness. He thought that the evils of opium-smoking had been greatly exaggerated by the missionaries and that the missionaries were, on the whole, meddlesome and futile. His dislike of them is an often recurring theme, though he sometimes conceals it with ponderous irony: "Among the most comfortable residences in Hankow are the quarters of the missionaries and it is but right that the missionaries should be separated as far as possible from all discomfort—missionaries who are sacrificing all for China and are prepared to undergo any reasonable hardship to bring enlightenment to this land of Darkness."

This enlightenment, he noted, was sometimes obscured by the great diversity of Christian sects, and their rather un-Christian hostility to one another. The principal bone of contention was the "Term Question"— each of the sects, to the bewilderment of the heathen, insisting on its particular Chinese term for God. It was also hard to explain to a people dedicated to ancestor-worship the words of Christ: "If any man come to Me and hate not his father, he cannot be My disciple." Despite these difficulties, converts were sometimes made, though many were said to be mere "Rice Christians" who accepted the faith in return for a ration of rice. Of the missionaries generally, Morrison wrote: "Expressed succinctly, their harvest may be described as amounting to a fraction more than two Chinamen per missionary per annum. If, however, the paid ordained and unordained native helpers be added . . . you find that the aggregate body converts nine-tenths of a Chinaman per worker per annum."

In the province of Yunnan he asked the question: "In a population of from five to seven millions of friendly and peaceable people, eighteen missionaries in eight years . . . have converted eleven Chinese, how long then will it take to convert the remainder?"

Five years before the Boxer uprising, in which anti-missionary feeling played an important part, Morrison wrote:

China may be a barbarous country: many missionaries have said so . . . but let us for a moment look at the facts. During the last 23 years foreigners of every nationality and every degree of temperament, from the mildest to the most fanatical, have penetrated to every nook and cranny of the empire. . . . But all the foreigners who have been killed can be numbered on the fingers of one hand, and in the majority of these cases it can hardly be denied that it was the indiscretion of the white man which was the inciting cause of the murder. In the same time how many hundreds of unoffending Chinese have been murdered in civilized foreign countries?

[II]

From Bhamo, with the congratulations of the garrison ringing in his ears, Morrison went by river-boat to Mandalay, by train to Rangoon, and by steamer to Calcutta. The night after his arrival he was stricken with inter-mittent fever, and a few days later nearly died. His slow recovery was illuminated by the solicitude of a nurse named Mary Joplin. In the first draft of his book he wrote:

> My nurse was a Eurasian dark of complexion but most fair to look upon. It did my heart good to watch the animation of her beautiful features, it inspired me with enthusiasm to witness the charming grace and noiseless celerity of her movements. Quinine I took from her hands in a cracked medicine glass and smacked my lips after it with greater unction than ever did Jupiter when Nectar was brought to him by Hebe in a golden goblet.

Fortunately for Morrison's reputation, in the published text this in-congruously purple paragraph was bleached to a few pallid lines. Nor did he mention that when he went to a French settlement in the hills to con-valesce his Hebe accompanied him in a much more agreeable role than as an adroit dispenser of hydrochlorate of quinine.

When he was well enough to travel Morrison shipped as surgeon on the steamership *Port Melbourne*, bound for Auckland, New Zealand. Five days out from Calcutta, a full ash-bucket fell on the head of a Lascar sea-man, splitting his skull from frontal bone to occiput. Morrison treated this successfully, and was given by the grateful captain a free passage to Sydney. He reached Geelong at the end of November 1894, to find several letters from Mary Joplin awaiting him. In one she wrote:

> Darling—I received both your loving letters . . . Darling I promised to give 10 R's for the Holy Souls but I have not been able to do so as I have been out of work all this month. . . . Will you dear one give the Rs 10 to some priest in Australia as the promises I made were more in fact all on your account and myself. *Darling give it God will bless you for it.*—and do get married to some good girl of your own station in life who in safety can be at your side and care for you. *I love you* but us living together will be a sinful life and when we will be dying death would taunt us much, do not be angry sweet one darling . . . but if I were to live with you I would be unhappy . . . those few short days so enjoyed in the little home along the river bring me one un-happy thought of sin. . . .

Theodore Fink, a benevolent if unscrupulous Melbourne lawyer with newspaper and literary interests, tried to get Morrison appointed to the staff of the *Argus*. "It is impossible," the editor, Edward Cunningham, told Fink, explaining, with sublime imperception, "he cannot write up to our standard." The distinguished editor was later given a doctorate of let-ters and a knighthood, for his services to Australian journalism. Soon after, Morrison faced two alternatives; he could return to medical practice in Ballarat at a salary of £1000 a year or go to England as a ship's surgeon and arrive in London with £30 and the manuscript account of his journey across China. He consulted Fink, who advised him to take the risk and go to England. But he had already made up his mind. "There was never any doubt as to the decision," he wrote later. "The craze of travel had bitten me. I had never seriously contemplated the discomforts of medical practice." He shipped as surgeon on the *Warrego*, paying £10 for his passage. There were no passengers, and he had plenty of time to complete his manuscript.

[III]

Morrison arrived in London on 15th February 1895. He took a room in Burton Crescent at 6s. 6d. a week, lived austerely, and tried to find a publisher. He had acquired an impressive collection of polite rejections when Douglas Sladen, a prolific if undistinguished writer who had lived in Australia, induced Horace Cox of *The Field* to buy the manuscript outright for £75, "a sum with which I was well content," Morrison wrote. While waiting for the book to be published he worked in the British Museum on a thesis for his doctorate. The subject was *Hereditary Transmission of Various Malformations and Abnormalities*. The thesis was accepted, and on 1st August he graduated in Edinburgh.

An Australian in China, being the narrative of a quiet journey across China to Burma was dedicated gratefully to John Chiene, "who gave me back the power of locomotion". It was enthusiastically reviewed. *The Times*, the *North British Daily Mail*, and the *Aberdeen Free Press* said it was "lively"; the *Saturday Review* and the *Athenaeum*, "very entertaining"; the *St James Gazette*, "fascinating"; the *Lancet*, "delightful"; the *Liverpool Daily Post*, "thoroughly enjoyable"; the *Morning Advertiser*, "most original" and the *Whitehall Review*, "most readable". The *Saturday Review* found the book fascinating, but could not explain why. All the reviewers seem to have been charmed by Morrison's informal, personal style. Morrison sent a copy to Mr Gladstone, who, without reading it, wrote courteously, if not very grammatically: "The great importance of the subject of your work combined with the remarkable nature of your feat (as I estimate it) you have achieved . . . invests the book with a very high interest."

In a long review the Melbourne *Age* said: "Christianity was introduced in its early days by adapting it to the creeds and modes of thought existing at the time among the Gentiles. But the missionaries in China seem to have gone on exactly the opposite tack, and most of the enmity and angry contempt with which they are regarded . . . must be attributed to this cause."

This so displeased the Bishop of Ballarat that he wrote six letters to the Melbourne *Argus* denouncing Morrison and his works. Morrison, in his reply, said:

> The opinion was forced on me that when 41 different Protestant mission bodies are working . . . with little harmony and often at complete variance . . . mission work must be seriously retarded. . . .

73

Without having read my book the Bishop says bluntly that he does not believe me. Yet he has "no imputation whatever to make against my veracity." His method reminds me of that American senator "who would not say Mr John P. Binn was a covetous person, but who was prepared to wager a five dollar bill that if you baited a mousetrap with a threepenny bit and stuck it within six inches of his mouth, you'd catch his soul."

His Grace wrote Morrison a sharp personal letter rebuking him for his "improper" and "offensive" remarks.

[IV]

Throughout these months Morrison tried to get a job on a newspaper. There was trouble in Venezuela and Cuba, and he thought that his knowledge of Spanish and his experience of travel would commend him as a correspondent. But from every editor he received the stereotyped reply that the staff was complete. Mr Cooper, of the *Scotsman*, and Sir Henry Norman, of the *Daily Chronicle*, advised him to try *The Times*, but Morrison was too abashed by the transcendent repute of The Thunderer even to write for an interview. He was, says the *History of the Times*, "apparently more afraid of Printing House Square than of the New Guinea jungle". It was through Sir William Gowers that he was introduced to the paper he was to serve with such distinction. Gowers, a great authority on nervous diseases, had read with interest Morrison's remarks on the blunted nerve sensibility of the Chinese. He invited Morrison to call, and introduced him to Sir Henry Howarth, author of a *History of the Mongols*. To them Morrison confided his wish to join a newspaper. At the Athenaeum Club, Gowers spoke to the editor of *The Times*, George Buckle, whose physician he was, about Morrison. As a result Morrison, to his profound astonishment, on Tuesday 22nd October received a letter from the manager of *The Times*, Moberly Bell, asking him to call at the office on the following Wednesday, Thursday, or Friday:

When I received the letter I was worth considerably less than one sovereign. Every day, therefore, was of importance, and I proposed calling on Wednesday, but confiding my intention to Thomas Watters, a retired British Consul General from the Chinese service . . . he said to me, "That would be bad policy. They will think you are too eager. Better go on Thursday." So I went on Thursday.

Morrison presented himself at Printing House Square, "dressed", says the *History of the Times*, "in a manner more appropriate to King's Cross than to the City", and was ushered into the office of the manager. As Morrison recalled the interview:

Mr Bell said to me, "I don't know where I heard of you but I have read your book. Would you care to go to Peking as our correspondent?"

74

I said, "I will have to think over the matter." "If you went, what salary would you require?"

I told him that in my two previous appointments I had been paid the equivalent of £400 a year. He replied, "You will have at least that." Then he said: "But why do you hesitate to go?"

I said, "Because for some time past I have been studying the subject of Siam and French Indo-China. Relations between England and France regarding Siam have been critical. My hope was that I might be sent there as a correspondent." He said, "Compared with China, Siam is of minor importance to us. Will you come and dine with us quietly one evening?"

"I am in an embarrassment," I said, "because I have no dress clothes. I was hard up," I added hastily, "and I sold them."

This made him laugh. He said "Never mind about your dress clothes, but come and dine with us." I agreed to.

Among other things he said to me was: "Have you read the articles by our Special Correspondent who has lately been in China?" I had read them. There were the articles by Mr Valentine Chirol which were afterwards republished in a book *The Far Eastern Question*. He said "If you come to dinner you will meet the author of those letters."

Chirol, who was assistant to Sir Donald Mackenzie Wallace, head of the Foreign Department of *The Times*, had returned from a tour of the Far East convinced that a Russo-French combination had displaced Britain as a dominant power in China. A week or so before Morrison received Bell's invitation to dine, the *Saturday Review*, commenting on Chirol's articles, lamented:

It seems only the other day that the influence of England in China was greater than that of any other country, perhaps indeed greater than that of all other countries combined. But a year ago the power of the purse was ours; we had the undivided power of the Imperial Maritime Customs, which afforded China the only revenue upon which she could raise money, and this revenue was in main due to British trade and British administration. And behind the power of the purse, we had also the power of the sword. In 1842, and again in 1860, we had proved our strength. . . . Now everything was changed.

[V]

Morrison went to dinner at 98 Portland Place and met not only Chirol but Buckle, W. F. Moneypenny, who was Buckle's assistant, and the Colonial Editor, Flora Shaw (later Lady Lugard). "This was the turning point in my career," Morrison wrote. In the galaxy of Printing House Square talent, the host, Charles Frederick Moberly Bell, was the outstanding personality. Bell, then forty-eight, was more than the manager of *The Times*; he was the force that was keeping it from disintegration. He was born in Egypt, the son of an English merchant in Alexandria, and had been Egyptian correspondent of *The Times* for many years when the proprietor, Arthur Walter, summoned him to London to take charge of a paper that was bankrupt. A heavily built man with a big head, strong acquiline features, and a short moustache, he radiated energy, enthusiasm, and hospitality. He had a peculiar sense of humour; when he lost an entire ankle bone in an accident he had it set in the top of his walking-stick so that as he limped along he could say that his bone still supported him. As a former correspondent, he was interested in news, and had a big say in staff appointments and foreign policy. The editor, George Earle Buckle, was described by a colleague, Leopold Amery, as a "vast, burly man, with a fine red beard and a laugh that shook Printing House Square". A barrister of Lincoln's Inn, and a Fellow of All Souls, he had become assistant editor of *The Times* in 1880, at the age of twenty-five, and editor four years later. "He had given himself heart and soul to *The Times*," says Amery, "and his conception of what it should stand for in accuracy, good English, dignity and fair-mindedness." Very different in temperament was Valentine Chirol, a slight, neat, nervous man with a pointed reddish beard and restless blue eyes. He had left the Foreign Office in 1876 after four years' service, in circumstances that he never discussed. He turned to journalism, and joined *The Times* as Berlin correspondent in 1892. It was difficult to get on with him. "Chronic ill-health, and acute self-consciousness rendered him extremely sensitive . . . and apt to take offence without cause," says the *History of the Times*.

Bell and the head of the Foreign Department in effect dictated the foreign policy of *The Times*. "It was an illogical set-up," says Amery. But no more illogical than the fact that Bell, as manager, had no say in the production of the paper, which was conducted as a separate business by two members of the Walter family, and that Buckle, as editor, had little or no control of the staff. Behind its august façade, and despite its thunderous voice, *The Times* was disorganized and debilitated. But Morrison did not suspect this when he sat around Moberly Bell's great dinner table, an awe-struck boy from the bush, listening to some of the most distinguished journalists in England. "I dined in a friendly way with G. E. Buckle . . . and other famous people who treated me well," he wrote to his mother. "Don't think I am boasting when I tell you that one man said I was a 'delightfully modest man.' . . . Mrs Moberly Bell said my book was a fascinating story."

Morrison had his wish. A few days later it was arranged that he should go to Indo-China and Siam on six months' probation, "to carefully report upon the political, financial and commercial prospects of Siam". His mission was to be confidential. He was to travel as an Australian doctor with business interests in the Far East, "and as long as possible," Bell instructed him, "to maintain this character and appear to have no connection with *The Times*." Even the Foreign Office, which gave him introductions to British diplomatic representatives in Asia, did not know of this connection. It was not the first time that *The Times* had employed a secret correspondent.

Relations between France and England had been tense since July 1893, when the French fleet forced the passage of the Menan, and France, despite British protests, took over a large part of eastern Siam, nearly doubling her possessions in Indo-China. The French Colonial Party, with Russian approval, was mapping out an Empire of Indo-China that would stretch from the Russian border in Asia to the British border in India. France was steadily encroaching upon Siamese territory to the west of the Mekong, which she had accepted as her boundary, and upon British territory in the Shan State of Kiang Tung, east of the river. "The idea," wrote Holt S. Hallett in the *Saturday Review* of 7th September 1895, "is to effect a *rapprochement* with Russia in Asia, the whole of the Chinese dominions, which contain about one-fourth of the inhabitants of the world, being divided between the two Powers." But the immediate rivalry between France and England was, in Victor Purcell's phrase, "a race to Yunnan", a race to penetrate Chinese markets "from behind".

[VI]

Morrison left England in November, equipped, as he told his mother proudly, with "a nice Kodak . . . good dress clothes and letters of introduction that would surprise you". He reached Saigon two days before Christmas, and sent his first report on 28th December. It did not flatter the French administration. He described the French functionaries as "fat, wheezy middle-aged gentlemen, sipping absinthe, and perspiring even with the effort of speech, as they mopped their close-cropped heads and double chins. They were not only inefficient but corrupt." It was an assessment very similar to George Curzon's, who in 1893 wrote of them as "shuffling little stubble-bearded Frenchmen of the most unattractive type, superficial and indolent".

Morrison was convinced that France was planning to annex all Siam. He urged Britain to preserve Siamese independence because British interests, particularly in Singapore, would suffer if France were not checked. He did not know that the Foreign Office was already negotiating a compromise settlement with France. On 3rd December, while Morrison was crossing the Indian Ocean, the Prime Minister, Lord Salisbury, wrote to Curzon, then Under-Secretary of State for Foreign Affairs: "If no agreement is come to, France will swallow up Siam in ten years, and I greatly doubt the English being disposed to run any risk in its defence." The agreement, signed on 15th January 1895, a day or two before Morrison reached Bangkok, guaranteed the integrity of the central portion of Siam, conceded France a free hand in east Siam, recognized British and French spheres of influence east and west of guaranteed areas, and divided commercial privileges in the provinces of Yunnan and Szechwan, the richest provinces in China. It also rectified the boundaries of Burma and Indo-

China—partly at China's expense, of course. Morrison's dispatches, written while the settlement was under discussion, were widely read, especially in Paris, where, says the *History of the Times*, they were "known to have had important reactions".

As the guest of the British chargé d'affaires in Bangkok, Maurice de Bunsen, Morrison wrote to his mother;

> . . . I am here with letters of introduction from the India Office, the Foreign Office, the Colonial Office, from Scott, the Former Minister, and many others. Sir Thomas Sanderson, the right-hand man of Lord Salisbury, actually wrote privately to Mr de Bunsen about me. I have been treated everywhere with the greatest attention by the Royal Princess and the Siamese authorities. I did the work I was asked to do whether satisfactory or not remains to be seen. I am now going a little into the North to see things. . . . I have at last got my chance and if successful you will hear of me, if unsuccessful I am no worse off than I was before. Guard strict silence about this mission of mine.

From Bangkok, Morrison set out up the valley of the Mekong for Yunnan City, where two years before he had bought his white pony. He journeyed to Korat, partly on the unfinished railway, partly on horseback, and struck north-west across Siam, travelling on bullock cart, on horseback, on foot, and by elephant, into Burma. At Keng Tung he had passport trouble. A British subject crossing from Burma to China needed a passport written in Chinese. No one in Keng Tung could write Chinese, so the British Commissioner fabricated an impressive document in English, Shan and Lu, which Morrison put in the biggest envelope he could find and stamped with "a magnificent official-looking seal"—the lid of a Van Houten's cocoa tin. Thus equipped, he set off for the frontier, accompanied by a Chinese half-caste, seven coolies, and two ponies. Again he was unarmed. The Chinese frontier official, despite the Van Houten seal, wished to detain him till a superior officer at Saumao was consulted. Morrison gave the official a cake of a "much advertised soap" to treat a skin affection of the neck and at once received a letter authorizing him to proceed. "It was not my fault," Morrison wrote, "that his letter somewhat imaginatively described its bearer as a 'Chao Sala, a Prince Doctor specially sent by the Queen of England at the urgent entreaty of the Viceroy of Yunnan to save the sick and dying.' "

A few days before reaching Yunnan City, Morrison was plundered by brigands and lost his medicine chest with the rest of his kit. Soon after, he became seriously ill with what he believed to be a form of bubonic plague. Without medicine or medical help, he thought he might drive out the sickness by profuse perspiration. He had a big fire lit in the long flat brick stove of a Chinese house, and lay down on the hot bricks till his skin was scorched and blistered. "It was something like the old compurgation by fire," he said, "but I came out of the ordeal triumphantly, and it is probably the most original cure I ever effected."

After convalescing in Yunnan City for some weeks, Morrison went south-east to the treaty port of Mengtzu, the most distant from Peking of the Maritime Customs Stations then operating. On 1st October he started westwards along the base of the Yunnan plateau for Saumao, following mountain paths not previously visited by a European, through a tangle of jungle, ravines, and watercourses. From Saumao, which he reached on 31st October, he travelled south to Mong Hsing, the small state which had so severely strained the relations of England and France, and which, by the agreement of 15th January, Britain had handed over to France. The town of Mong Hsing, a "paltry village of 160 native wooden houses", was the chief town of a "jungle-covered malarious district, scantily peopled by an enfeebled race steeped in opium" but abounding in tigers and leeches. Contemplating its unusual charms, Morrison recalled how possession of Mong Hsing once nearly involved England and France in war. "Truly the quarrels of nations have often strange origins," he reflected.

Morrison crossed the Mekong at Chieng Lap and travelled southwards to the Siamese border. At Chieng Mai he sold his horses and, engaging a native boat, floated down the Menan to Raheng and Bangkok. It was almost exactly a year since he had set out to go "a little into the North". At Bangkok, to his great surprise, he was met by Valentine Chirol, who, before taking over the Foreign Department from Wallace, was touring the world reorganizing the services of *The Times* and appointing new correspondents. Morrison felt that his work had been "of little advantage to the paper", but was soon reassured. Among the messages that Chirol brought from Printing House Square was an instruction to Morrison to go at once to Peking as permanent correspondent. His work had been appreciated not only by *The Times* but by the Foreign Office. On 14th November 1896 the Under-Secretary for Foreign Affairs, Sir Thomas Sanderson, had written to Moberly Bell: "We are greatly indebted to Mr Morrison for the information which he has forwarded. Have you any idea how I should address to him my acknowledgement?"

When Chirol returned to London he gave his new Peking correspondent a briefing:

> For our purpose, the incidents and adventures of travel must always be merely subsidiary to the general information and enlightenment we require for the furtherance of British interests and of an Imperial policy. In one word, what you seem to me to lack in some measure is a sense of perspective. You must try and focus your lens to our eyes, remembering always that we are a very long way off and only want to look through the big end of the telescope. Picturesque details should be the garniture, not the foundation of your work. . . . Condense as much as possible, giving us a maximum of information and instruction in a minimum of space.

CHAPTER FIVE

[I]

THE CHINA that was to be Morrison's home for the rest of his life was weak, badly governed, and corrupt, a fossilized society indifferent alike to progress within its frontiers and to the dim world of barbarians beyond. Recurring crop failures, flood, and drought brought death and misery to millions of its people; celestially remote from them was the Court, living a fantastic charade in its closely guarded, resplendent palaces. Kuang Hsu, the Manchu Emperor, had assumed titular power in 1889, at the age of twenty-two. As the "Son of Heaven", the "Supreme Ruler", the "August Lofty One", the "Solitary Man", the "Buddha of the Present Day", and the "Lord of Ten Thousand Years", he was the object of profound reverence and worship; but the real ruler of the Empire was his Heaven-Blessed, All-Nourishing, Perfect, Worshipful, Exalted, Illustrious aunt, the sixty-one-year-old Empress Dowager Tz'u Hsi, known also as Yehonala and the "Old Buddha". Beginning her career as a beautiful, tomboyish concubine of the third rank, one of twenty-eight Manchu recruits to the harem of the Emperor Hsien Feng, she had become, at the age of twenty-six, an absolute monarch of enormous power. Murder, intrigue, and betrayal punctuated her progress, but the authors of *China Under the Empress Dowager*, J. O. P. Bland and Edmund Backhouse, say approvingly, "It is not recorded that she ever took life from sheer cruelty or love of killing":

> When she sent a man to death, it was because he stood between her and the full and safe gratification of her love of power. . . . Among the effete classical scholars, the fat-paunched Falstaffs, the opium sots, doddering fatalists and corrupt parasites of the Imperial Court, she seems indeed to have been . . . a cast back to the virility and energy that won China for her sturdy ancestors. . . . To get something of her atmosphere and perspective we must go back to the early days of the Tudors. In a country where merciless officials and torture are part of the long-accepted order of things, no more stress was laid on her numerous acts of cold-blooded tyranny than . . . was laid on the beheading of the Earls at the close of the 15th century.

In fact the Court of Peking closely resembled a European court of the Middle Ages. The life of the Imperial Palace, says a historian, was "one of profound learning and crass stupidity, of infantile gaiety and sudden tragedy, of flashing fortunes and swift dooms". The Empress, who liked appearing in pageants as Kwang-Yin, the Goddess of Mercy, was above the law which she herself made. A few days after issuing a decree prohibiting corporal punishment, she had a troublesome reformer flogged to death. Her successor, Lung Yu, was no less capricious. When an eminent actor was playing before her, she found his performance lacked enthusiasm, and ordered him to receive forty strokes of the whip before being expelled from the Court.

Peter Fleming says of Yehonala: "Her public life was paved with ceremony, and roofed with superstition. Of her private life we know little, save that she was fond of amateur theatricals, water-picnics, and pugs." She was also fond of clocks (I have inspected her considerable collection in the Imperial Palace), of eggs poached in gravy, and of money. When she died in 1908 her private fortune was estimated at about £16 million sterling. This figure is speculative, but during the Sino-Japanese war of 1894-5 she consulted Guy Hillier, manager of the Hong Kong and Shanghai Bank in Peking, about remitting to London a nest-egg of £8,250,000 in gold and silver bullion. China's disastrous defeat in this war was largely due to the fact that Yehonala had spent most of the naval appropriations on her fairy-tale Summer Palace. The cost of maintaining her Court with its vast population of parasites, headed by the ambiguous Chief Eunuch, Li Lien-ying, was about £6,500,000 a year. Li Lien-ying was a very much magnified John Brown. He enjoyed a remarkable intimacy with his Celestial Mistress, influenced her greatly, and rewarded himself richly by relentless "squeeze", selling official posts for as much as £40,000. He had millions of pounds invested in pawnshops and money-lending establishments.

Eunuchs, most of whom did a brisk trade in appointments and ceremonies, occupied an envied position at Court, where they often attained high rank and power. They were treated with great discretion: because they resented allusion to their deficiency, a teapot with a missing handle, or a tailless dog, could not be mentioned in their presence. Most were natives of Chihli, a province so famous for their manufacture that all good-quality eunuchs were supposed to come from it. The lost parts, known as the "precious", were treasured in hermetically sealed pots and had to be produced by the ambitious young eunuch seeking promotion.

Eunuchs had adorned the Imperial Court for thousands of years. Their survival into the twentieth century was as anachronistic as the survival of slavery, torture, and a criminal code as brutal as it was arbitrary. A wife who struck her husband was punished with a hundred blows of the bamboo on the buttocks; a husband could assault his wife with impunity so long as he did not inflict a cutting wound. A man sentenced to flogging could save his skin by paying five ounces of silver; an officer above the fourth rank sentenced to strangulation could save his neck by paying 12,000 ounces. Anyone using a road on which the Imperial retinue was passing suffered death by strangulation. More overt acts against the Throne were punished by the lingering death of many cuts; the culprit was tied to a cross, and gashes were made on his body "varying in number according to the disposition of the judge", before his head was mercifully cut off. All male relatives above the age of sixteen of a man convicted of treason were beheaded.

[II]

Morrison took up residence in Peking on 15th March 1897. "That first summer I recall with shuddering," he wrote later. "Everything was in darkness." A friend tried to light his way; it was easy to extract information about the Far East, he said. If he wished to cable the latest intelligence on, say, Manchuria, he would call in his No. 1 boy. They would have a talk in pidgin:

"What belong very bad business in Manchuria?" The boy would say: "I no savvy." His friend would then say: "What for you no savvy Russia belong very bad Manchuria." The boy would say: "Please, Master, suppose belong angly, all lite." And that evening a telegram would be sent for the enlightenment of the world to the following effect: "In a confidential conversation which I had this afternoon with a high Chinese authority, whose name I am not at liberty to mention, he spoke with indignation of the aggressive attitude assumed by Russia to Manchuria."

This was scarcely the Morrison method, and despite the prevailing darkness he got to work right away. Albert Edmonds, the correspondent of the *Pall Mall Gazette*, recalled his arrival in Peking:

The next day he devoted himself to his first communication. There was a reception at the Russian Embassy that night to which we were all invited. Morrison would not come. He was too keen on his first dispatch. He sent me a note to the Embassy. "Come round and see me when the show is over. I am damned miserable." I dropped in to find him immersed in his manuscript doubtful as to whether to send it or not. He asked me to give him my frank opinion on it. I read it and found it to be a perfect diagnosis of the then troubled condition of China, masterly in its phrasing, luminous in its broad conception of the general situation. I said to him, "Moberly Bell will be delighted. It's great stuff." This was the first of the long series of brilliant contributions which made Morrison the most far-seeing foreign correspondent of his day and generation.

[III]

From the beginning, Morrison wrote, he received "help and encouragement" from the recently appointed British Minister at the Manchu Court,

Sir Claude MacDonald. Sir Claude, an elongated man of forty-five, with a long nose, reproachful eyes, and long, lovingly waxed thin moustaches, had fought in Egypt and the Sudan, been Consul-General at Zanzibar, Commissioner of the Oil Rivers Protectorate, and gunnery instructor at Hong Kong. It was a training which, though varied, was perhaps inadequate for one of the most important and difficult posts in the diplomatic service. "Everyone denounced the appointment," Morrison wrote. "He was attacked as imperfectly educated . . . weak, flippant and garrulous . . . the type of military officer rolled out a mile at a time and then lopped off in six foot lengths." Morrison himself would have endorsed this popular estimate, though he wrote, in a manuscript intended for publication: "such were the criticisms levelled against a British officer of singular charm of manner who had not sought the post thrust on him by Lord Salisbury, and who quickly inspired to an unusual degree the confidence of his famous chief." A note in Morrison's diary was less flattering: "When Admiral Bruce asked Sir Thomas Sanderson . . . the secret of MacDonald, 'Don't you know?' said Sanderson, 'I thought everyone knew that Salisbury believes MacDonald has in his possession evidence to prove that Lord Salisbury and Jack the Ripper are the same person.'"

Another friend whom Morrison soon made in Peking was Sir Robert Hart, a much-decorated sixty-two-year-old Ulsterman, perhaps the most important figure of his time in Sino-foreign relations. As Inspector-General of the Imperial Maritime Customs of China, he wielded enormous power. This vast and complex organization, which Hart had directed since 1863, and of which he was the virtual creator, controlled the Customs services of all China, and collected about one third of the Manchu Government's revenue: it employed nearly a thousand foreigners, of whom more than half were British, and about 4500 Chinese. Though a servant of the Manchus, Hart had been honoured by Queen Victoria with two orders of knighthood and a baronetcy, while the Chinese had conferred on him in turn the Red Button, the Peacock's Feather, the Double Dragon, and even a Patent of Ancestral Nobility. He was constantly consulted by the Tsungli Yamen, the Chinese equivalent of the Foreign Office—which Morrison described as "the most cumbrous body that ever mismanaged the affairs of a nation"—and was, in effect its principal adviser. At the same time, as *The Times* wrote of him in 1900: "For a quarter of a century, at least the final instructions given successively to every British Minister on his appointment to Peking might be summed up in half-a-dozen words: 'When in doubt, consult Sir Robert Hart'."

His position was ambiguous. British critics accused him of being pro-Chinese; Chinese critics, of being pro-British. He had lived so long in China—he had gone out as a student interpreter in 1854, and made only two brief visits to England since—that *The Times* thought "he was perhaps too much accustomed to look at China mainly through Chinese spectacles". Yet to many Chinese the fact that he had been decorated by the British Crown proved conclusively that his true function was to further Western penetration of China. A contemporary historian, Victor

Purcell, favours this view. He describes the Imperial Maritime Customs as "an outstanding instrument for indirect foreign political control of China". Certainly Sir Robert had a genuine love for the Chinese, blended with a curious admiration for the Empress Dowager, and his administration, unlike any of their own, was efficient and incorrupt. In Peking's social life he played a conspicuous part. His position, said *The Times*, was "socially, as well as politically, unique". In the constant squabbles between diplomats his Customs compound was recognized as neutral ground. He was an accomplished host and a passionate music-lover. He had organized a band of twenty Chinese, Portuguese, and Filipinos, known as "I.G.'s Own", whose weekly concerts in the compound gardens were an appreciated feature of Peking's social life during the cool season. As a man, Morrison found he had "limitless capacity for work, considerable ambition, and love of power".

[IV]

On 30th March 1900, Mr Joseph Walton, M.P., recently returned from a fact-finding and tea-drinking mission to China, spread a large map in the Tea Room of the House of Commons and invited the Hon. Members to inspect it: the map illustrated a speech which he had that day delivered on the neglect by Lord Salisbury's administration of British commercial and political interests in China. Having regard to the fact that out of a total Chinese foreign trade of £70 million in 1899, the share of the British Empire was £43 million, and that, in Mr Walton's opinion, the great Empire of China, "with its four hundred millions of industrious trading people, its greater fertility of soil, and its enormous mineral resources", was commercially more important to the British nation than India, Britain's failure to pursue a firm and definite policy in China was "disastrous".

Mr Walton was typical of many Englishmen in the City, for whom China was a melon of infinite proportions to be sliced eternally to their greater profit. That it was also an ancient civilization, and still a sovereign power, however mismanaged, never seemed to have occurred to them. In the counting-houses of E.C.1 no distinction was made between the Confucian scholar and the coolie labourer; both were inhabitants of an outlandish country upon whom Britain was conferring the inestimable benefits of British trade—whether they liked it or not. As Colonel Francis Younghusband, of Lhasa fame, declared in a letter to *The Times* during the siege of the legations: "The earth is too small, the portion of it they occupy is too big and rich, and the intercourse of nations is now too intimate, to permit the Chinese keeping China to themselves. . . ."

The English attitude—or the attitude of some influential Englishmen, for it is impossible to know what the general public feels about foreign policy, even if it is aware of it—towards China at this period is summed up with engaging naivety by Leopold Amery, in his book *My Political Life*. Amery, who was in charge of the Foreign Department of *The Times* from October 1900 till June 1901, writes:

> For some 50 years we had been active in opening up an Empire hitherto sealed up from the outer world. At Hong Kong we had built up ... one of the world's most flourishing transit ports. At Shanghai we had, without actual annexation, created what was, in effect, another flourishing British colony dominating the whole trade of central China. Her Majesty's ships patrolled some 1600 miles of China's great waterway, the Yangtze. ... A tottering Empire had been saved from destruction at the time of the Taiping Revolution by the courage and energy of "Chinese" Gordon. Another Englishman, Sir Robert Hart, had organized a great British financial service, the Chinese Maritime Customs, which was the mainstay of China's central finance. ... All this seemed part of the natural order of things. ... We were well content that it should endure. But if the feeble control of the Manchu dynasty should break down entirely ... then presumably we might have to take on greater responsibilities, particularly in the Yangtze Valley, either through the great provincial Viceroys, or even more directly. No one was clamouring to see Queen Victoria Empress of China, as well as of India. But no one, at the time of the Diamond Jubilee, would have dismissed the idea as inconceivable. ...

This is how an intelligent Englishman interpreted his country's role in nineteenth-century China. But an intelligent Chinese might have put it rather differently:

For some fifty years Britain (and other powers who followed her example) had been active in *carving* up the Chinese Empire. At Hong Kong, Britain had taken from China, at the point of a gun, a strategically important island, and added to it, by diplomatic pressure, the leasehold of 355 square miles of Chinese territory. At Shanghai (and elsewhere) Britain had robbed the Chinese of their fiscal independence, forcing on them tariffs that allowed foreign imports to flood the country at the cost of native industries. Her Majesty's ships patrolled the Yangtze (and other rivers) to protect British interests which had driven Chinese ships from the waterways without any compensation to their owners. A tottering Empire had been saved from destruction (partly) by "Chinese" Gordon because Britain was prepared to support any dynasty, however unpopular and corrupt, rather than suffer injury to her commercial interests. Sir Robert Hart had organized a great British financial service which was, in effect, a powerful instrument for the indirect foreign domination of China. ...

None of these facts would be disputed by a historian today. Yet Morrison, despite his intimate knowledge of Chinese affairs and his deep-rooted affection for the Chinese people, seems to have been so bemused by his Imperialist faith that he never perceived them.

Peking with its two million people was, according to a writer of the time, a city of "marvels, dilapidation and dirt". Within the buttressed walls of the Tartar City, forty feet high, fifty feet broad at the base, and wide enough at the top for four teams of horses to be driven abreast, were the pink- and yellow-tiled walls of the Imperial City, which in turn enclosed the red battlements of the Forbidden City, a sprawling, walled congeries of gardens, courts, lakes, pavilions, pagodas, and buildings, the most important of which was the Winter Palace. An unauthorized person passing through any of the gates of the Forbidden City was punished with a flogging of a hundred strokes. If imprudently he strayed into the Imperial apartments, the penalty was death by strangulation. The Tartar Wall, with its crenellated parapet, was a favoured promenade among Europeans, the one place where you could escape the dirt and smells of the narrow crowded streets. There was no sanitation in Peking, and, with the exception of Legation Street, the streets were unpaved, ankle deep in dust or mud. The nine gates that led into the Tartar City were closed and barred each night at sundown. South of the Tartar Wall, surrounded by another wall, was the Chinese City.

One of the first things Morrison noted when he arrived in Peking was the self-imposed isolation of the diplomats. Surrounded by their own nationals, they lived in a diplomatic vacuum, completely detached from the Chinese. The eleven legations were grouped in an enclave about three-quarters of a mile square, bounded on three sides by Peking's towering walls. They had their own shops, their banks, their hotel, their chapels, their club, their theatre, their sports-grounds. Perhaps the most dedicated exponents of this splendid isolation were the British. In a little transplanted world, they allayed their nostalgia with dinners and dancing, gossip and golf, happily ignorant of the customs or language or feelings of the people they lived among. Though China has perhaps the most exquisite food of any nation, the British exiles clung tenaciously to their native fare; Morrison attended a British banquet one torrid night in June to celebrate Queen Victoria's Diamond Jubilee. The guests were fortified with Jubilee Soup, Oyster Patties, Roast Beef, Macaroni, Boiled Ham, Tongue in Jelly, Roast Lamb, Spring Chicken, Plum Pudding, Citron Ice Cream, and Cheese, before they sang vociferously:

> Thou Who for threescore years
> In Sunshine, cloud and tears,
> Has kept our Queen.
> Still be her guide and stay
> Through life's uncertain way,
> Till dawns the perfect day,
> God save the Queen.

Not surprisingly, there were raised eyebrows among the diplomats when Morrison found himself a house in a Chinese quarter, some distance from the enclave. He described his establishment to his mother:

> I live in a Chinese house which I have converted into a European one. I am alone with my books on China, cut off by dirty streets from the rest of the foreign community. I have a cart and horse and driver £2. a month. A No. 1 Boy—£1. a month. No. 1. Cook—£1. a month. No. 2 cook—12/- a month, but he is paid by the No. 1 cook. A coolie at 14/- a month, two horses and two grooms, together at £3. a month. No. 2 groom is paid by No. 1 groom.

Life in Peking may have had its disabilities, but shortage of servants was not one of them.

[VI]

As soon as he was settled, Morrison set out on a journey to Siberia "to inspect the course of the railway and report upon its possibilities". He went by boat to Vladivostok, part of Russia's great grab of Chinese territory in 1858, and travelled over the main line, then on to the verge of completion, to Iman, where he embarked on a river steamer to Khabarovsk. The Russians received him "correctly if not cordially". He had a look at the quarters of the 1200 convicts who had been working on the railway, and reported favourably on their conditions. From Khabarovsk he went by crowded steamer more than one thousand miles up the Amur as far as Stretensk, the limit of steam navigation. He had been round three sides of Manchuria by river. Leaving Stretensk in a tarantass, he drove eastwards as far as Nerchinski Zavod and southwards through country "as treeless as the plains of Australia" across the Chinese border to Hailar, in Mongolia, a village of 2000 men, no women, and vast supplies of *samshu*, "that fiery spirit which is Chinese vodka". Here he exchanged his tarantass for a light and springy high-wheeled Mongol cart in which he drove across the steppes and through the forests of the Khingan mountains to Tsitsihar in the Nonni valley. Russian engineers and Russian guards were everywhere. The guards "marched through the town with an air of possession" which greatly impressed the Chinese while the engineers, "big bearded men", were reverenced for their age, the Chinese "being apt to estimate years by the length of a beard". The Chinese soldiers were armed with "old Tower muskets bought . . . in the belief that they were the weapons with which England won the battle of Waterloo".

At Tsitsihar, Morrison acquired a heavy springless Peking cart in which he drove along the banks of the Nonni to Petua, and crossed to Kirin, the capital of Kirin province. There was still uncertainty as to the route the Trans-Siberian railway was to follow, but every Russian engineer of authority whom Morrison met spoke of Port Arthur as the hoped-for terminus. With this knowledge, Morrison made his way back to Vladivostok and cabled *The Times* that a preliminary survey for the projected railway was about to be made to Port Arthur:

> Fearing, however, that the words "Port Arthur" would not be permitted to pass over the wire, I wrote instead its Chinese name "lu Hsuan Kao." But the name was unfamiliar; it was printed as "lu Ksuan kan" and was unintelligible. No attention was given to the announcement, and in view of what happened shortly afterwards, this was unfortunate.

The telegram was supplemented with a long report which Morrison posted from Vladivostok on 22nd November. In it he said that Russia intended her railway to go "farther and farther to the south, so as to loop on to Russian territory an ever-increasing area of Manchuria". The Russians, he added, spoke with "unconcealed derision" of Japan's pretensions, but "the importance of Japan in relation to the future of Manchuria cannot be disregarded". A few days later Morrison went by steamer to Chefoo, where the British consul told him that the Germans had seized Kiaochow, in Shantung province. "A new chapter of far Eastern history had opened," he wrote. Though it is true that the seizure of Kiaochow was one of the causes of the Boxer uprising three years later, it was just another chapter in the long and shameful record of the vivisection of China by the European powers. But the events that led up to it are worth recapitulating as a typical case history of this international butchery.

Germany, with commercial interests in China second only to Britain's, had for a long time been pressing China to grant her a naval station. The most favoured site was Kiaochow. Early in October 1897 the German Minister in Peking, Baron von Hayking, a worthy *protégé* of Bismarck, called at Kiaochow in the cruiser *Prince Heinrich*. Under pretence of examining the ship's hull, divers were sent down to inspect the harbour. Satisfied that Kiaochow was suitable, von Hayking went on to Hankow to continue negotiations. But he was happily saved the tedium of a long diplomatic parley; on 1st November two German Roman Catholic priests in Shantung were murdered by armed Chinese; simple robbers according to some historians, members of a secret society according to others. The Kaiser responded enthusiastically: "I am firmly determined to . . . demonstrate through our use of sternness and, if necessary, of the most brutal ruthlessness towards the Chinese, that the German Emperor cannot be trifled with," he declared. And "Hundreds of thousands of Chinese will quiver when they feel the iron fist of Germany heavy on their necks." Admiral von Diedrichs was ordered to occupy Kiaochow immediately. When the German marines landed on 14th November the Chinese garrison was quite unaware of their intention. Soldiers turned their old-fashioned jackets inside out to conceal their military character and carried the luggage of the Germans ashore to earn a few cents. At the price of two priests Germany had acquired a ninety-nine-year lease of the finest harbour on the coast of China, together with exclusive railway rights, mining rights, and preferential employment rights throughout Shantung, a province larger in population and area than England. She also exacted, according to time-honoured precedent, an indemnity for her military expenses.

"The blood of martyrs is a seed that sometimes yields a strange harvest," reflected Henry Cockburn, then Chinese Secretary of the British Legation.

[VII]

While China was being sliced up bit by bit, and the ultimate disappearance of the Empire was taken for granted by many observers, the idea began to spread among enlightened Chinese that the assimilation of Western ideas, and the reform of China's cumbrous, archaic, and corrupt administration offered her only hope of survival. Of those who advocated reform, the most eminent was a brilliant Cantonese scholar named K'ang Yu-wei, whose writings greatly impressed the Emperor himself. About him gathered a group of enthusiastic supporters, including Chang Yin-huan, the best-known Cantonese in China, who as a member of the Tsungli Yamen had represented China at Queen Victoria's Diamond Jubilee in 1897 and been invested with the G.C.M.G. K'ang Yu-wei six times memorialized the Emperor, urging reforms. Japan supported him, Russia supported the reactionaries, and England remained indifferent.

Reform societies sprang up in many parts of the Empire. The Imperial Tutor, Weng Tung-ho, himself an outstanding scholar and a man of great influence, introduced K'ang Yu-wei to the Emperor. "The results," wrote Henry Cockburn, "were speedily seen in a shower of Imperial Decrees by which the Emperor feverishly strove to effect, in the space of a few weeks, a vast number of radical changes, administrative, financial, educational, military and industrial. . . ." The Empress Dowager at first accepted these reforms, though she brought about the dismissal of Weng Tung-ho, and when the Emperor began abolishing sinecures she joined forces with the court reactionaries to get rid of him and his dangerous experiments.

By the middle of September 1898 the Emperor realized that for his own safety, as well as for the sake of reform, the Empress must be locked up and her faithful supporter—some said her girlhood lover—Jung Lu, executed. Jung Lu, recently appointed Viceroy of Chihli, was commander-in-chief of the imperial forces, but the most powerful man in Chihli was Yuan Shih-k'ai, the creator and commander of the only well-equipped, well-trained army in China. He had shown sympathy with the reform movement, and, trusting in his loyalty, the Emperor instructed him to carry out the coup. But Yuan betrayed the plot to Jung Lu, who hastened to the Summer Palace and informed the Empress Dowager. At dawn on 21st September the Emperor was seized by guards and eunuchs and put under palace arrest on an island in the lake of the Forbidden City. K'ang Yu-wei escaped on a British steamer with a price on his head, dead or alive, and passed into exile. His brother and five other young reformers—"The Six Gentlemen", as they have been called ever since—were swiftly decapitated, without even pretence of a trial, and countless officials were dismissed and punished or exiled to the remote north-west. The so-called "Hundred Days" were over. Chang Yin-huan, arrested and falsely charged, was banished for life to the New Western Dominion. Morrison and a number of other English stalwarts, including Hugh Grosvenor, of the British Legation, offered to rescue him and bring him into the sanctuary of the legation. They claimed, with dubious authority, that they had the right to protect a man whom Queen Victoria had created a Grand Commander of St Michael and St George. The offer was disclosed to Sir Chentung Liang, the confidential secretary of the Tsungli Yamen, who conveyed it to his master, but Chang replied that it was not his desire to interfere with the course of "Imperial Justice". Two years later he was put to death with great barbarity in his place of exile.

But if British derring-do was unable to save Chang, British diplomacy probably saved the imprisoned Emperor. Sir Claude MacDonald warned the Empress Dowager that his and other governments would "view with extreme disfavour" the execution of her nephew. Despite this, there were widespread rumours that he had been put to death, and the diplomatic body suggested that he should be inspected by a foreign physician "to knock the bottom out of all these Shanghai rumours", as Sir Claude MacDonald put it. Morrison was greatly disappointed when a French physician, Dr Dethève, the only medical man attached to a foreign legation at that time, was chosen for the historic examination, rather than himself, "the senior doctor in Peking". But Sir Claude took the view that, as correspondent of *The Times*, Morrison was "out of court". Dr Dethève visited the palace-prison and announced after an appropriate inspection that the Emperor was alive.

The Empress proclaimed her second regency. One by one, the reform decrees were rescinded. The sinecures were restored, and Yuan Shih-k'ai was richly rewarded for what Dr Jerome Ch'en calls "his kiss of death on the cheek of the Hundred Days reform". From a safe retreat K'ang Yu-wei sent forth fierce denunciations of both Yuan and the Empress. He denounced her comprehensively, in private and public life, accusing her of illicit relations with a "spurious eunuch" and of savage despotism. "Of her minions, he impeached no one more passionately than Yuan Shih-k'ai, charging him with perfidy to the young Emperor whose person he was in duty and honour bound to support," Morrison reported, adding: "His views prevailed for many years. But this judgment of Yuan has been reversed by History." This judgment of Morrison's has in turn been reversed by History. It was based on a written account which Yuan gave him years later, of the events of the "Hundred Days". In it, Yuan said that when he was given an order, allegedly from the Emperor, to seize the Empress and execute Jung Lu, he objected that it was written in black, not vermilion, ink, and therefore was not an Imperial Order. He insisted on a Vermilion Order, and would not act till he got one. Meanwhile, the reactionaries had been kept informed of the plot:

> When he called on Jung Lu, after an audience with the Emperor who made no reference to the "sound plan of action," Jung said "You have come for my head. You had better confess all, because a man who was here just before you came, has told me everything." Yuan answered, "What you have heard is but the plot of a few political schemers. His Majesty the Emperor said nothing to me about such a plan, and he is innocent of such intrigue."
>
> Next morning, 21st September, Jung Lu called on Yuan and said, "Lately friends from Peking have repeatedly informed me of the reformers' minutest movements. Their daring is astounding. We must rescue the Emperor from their clutches."
>
> In the evening, he sent for Yuan and told him that the plot had been exposed in Peking. On dismissing Yuan, he pointed to the teacup and said "You can drink—there is no poison in the tea."

Morrison, with a naivety hard to reconcile with his usual political acuity, never questioned Yuan's blatant exercise in apologetics.

In the midst of these stirring events, during which foreign guards were brought up from Tientsin to protect the legations—not since 1860 had foreign troops marched into Peking—Charles William de la Poer Beresford, better known as Lord Charles Beresford, then an unemployed rear-Admiral, also arrived in Peking. Lord Charles's career in the Navy had been brilliant, and he was no less distinguished as the playboy companion of the pleasure-loving Duke of Edinburgh, whom, uniquely, he was privileged to call "Darling Matilda". His qualifications for his mission to China were less evident: he had been sent by the Associated Chambers of Commerce of Great Britain to inquire into the position and prospects of British trade. He returned with a gloomy view of both, impressed by Russia's growing power in the Far East, and convinced that China, under the decadent and ineffectual rule of the Empress Dowager, was rapidly breaking up. But during his stay he thought of a bold scheme to get rid of the indestructible old lady. After inspecting Yuan Shih-k'ai's efficient army he suggested in picturesque language that Yuan should tie her in a blanket and hold her suspended above a well in the palace. A mandate decreeing her retirement would be produced and she would be told that if she refused to sign it she would be lowered into the damp and darkness until she changed her mind. So pleased was the admiral with his idea that he telegraphed the British Prime Minister, Lord Salisbury, asking to be allowed to accompany Yuan's forces when they marched on Peking and took over the government. Yuan, he explained, would then rule China under the orders of Sir Claude MacDonald, and in the interests of all— not forgetting, it is to be assumed, the Associated Chambers of Commerce of Great Britain. Lord Salisbury's reply was unsympathetic. "The idea would have been attractive at the beginning of the century," it read, "but any attempt to take over the Government of China in defiance of the vast mass of the Chinese and all the European powers would be too exhausting a task for England." Sir Claude, forwarding this dispatch to Lord Charles, added a terse annotation: "Better stick to Trade and Commerce."

[VIII]

Morrison noted with interest how closely Japan was associated with the abortive Reform movement. K'ang Yu-wei had advocated an alliance with Japan, the adoption of Japanese reforms, and the reorganization of China's Army and Navy by Japan. Each of the "Six Gentlemen" had been on terms of intimacy with the Japanese, and the Marquis Ito, who was in Peking during the crisis, had been received in audience by the Emperor only a day before the Empress Dowager struck. Although travelling unofficially, he was received with unusual attention by the Chinese. Morrison had a long talk with him, the gist of which he reported to Chirol on 20th September:

> He despairs of reform in China, there is no statesman, no man willing to take responsibility, no man standing out boldly and conspicuously before his fellows. Edicts decreeing reforms are being issued by the Emperor in profusion but they are never acted upon. An imperial ordinance that the officials shall be virtuous, upright, and incorruptible, cannot transform men who are hopelessly corrupt with the corruption carried to them by hereditary transmission through hundreds of generations. China must increase her revenue. She can do so only by improving the means of communication, by building railways. She can do so by decreasing or abolishing the expenditure now amounting to some £3,000,000 sterling per annum absorbed by the vast hordes of Manchu retainers dependent on the Court. To do this most easily and effectively the removal of the Court from Peking would be wise. No reform of the court is possible as long as the Emperor remains in Peking. At the reformation in Japan the court was removed from Kyoto to Tokyo. Russia would probably concur in the removal of the court because the vast cosmopolitan interest centred in Peking as the capital would then be transferred and the movement of Russia southward be less liable to be thwarted.

Morrison ventured to suggest that on the other hand it was to the paramount interest of Russia that the court should remain in Peking, that the Manchu dynasty should increase in power in China. As long as Peking was the capital, Russia, holding Manchuria, the traditional home of the dynasty, must acquire an increasing voice in the councils of the Emperor and an increasing influence through the reigning class.

The Marquis continued:

> China must have an army and viewing the hopeless corruption of the people, the army must be foreign drilled and foreign officered, and

this must be done by officers from England and Japan. Events must bring closer together England, Japan and China. Russian aggression, where is it to end? Before it was an ice-free port on the coast of Northern Korea, now it is a port on the extremity of the Liaotung peninsula, some hundreds of miles further south. No one can foresee where it is going to end. All is dark. . . . Already England has recognized the right of Russia to impose the conditions upon which a railway shall be built north of the Great Wall. Where is it going to end? . . .

"What the object of the visit may be," Morrison commented, "had not yet become known."

[IX]

The year 1898 closed with Russia feverishly consolidating her power in Manchuria. Railway construction, Morrison wrote, was being pressed forward with "unexampled rapidity". No less than 140,000 of the finest labourers in the world were working overtime on the track. England had recognized that Russia's "special interests" extended at least as far south as the Great Wall, and had defined, though less explicitly, her own sphere of influence in the Yangtze Valley. It seemed to Morrison that the policy of the Open Door, though the British Government clung to it hopefully, was becoming difficult to maintain and that "events were sending to a clearer definition of Spheres of Influence", with rights within these spheres of "interposition if not of exclusion". In Peking, Russia was supporting the reactionaries. Officials who had shown any sympathy with reform were everywhere dismissed:

> In the Tsungli Yamen, the notorious Prince Ch'ing was President and with him were associated five of the most incompetent old fossils that were ever entrusted with the foreign affairs of a country. Their chief recommendation in the sight of the Empress Dowager was their complete ignorance of foreign affairs. While above all was the Old Buddha . . . plotting schemes for the extermination of the foreigner. . . .

Morrison saw the old year out on the flagship of the British Squadron in Hong Kong, the guest of Vice-Admiral Sir Edward Seymour. Two other admirals were in Hong Kong at the same time—Lord Charles Beresford, returning to England, dispirited at the rejection of his stratagem to end the Manchu dynasty, and Prince Henry of Prussia, returning to Germany elated at having propagated the gospel of the Kaiser's "anointed person". Morrison was on his way to Siam to report on its progress since his last visit, and to refute "misleading and mischievous reports" in the French papers that England was considering the exchange of her interests in Siam for concessions on the west coast of Africa; and that the Siamese were incapable of governing themselves.

It was a great delight to me to return. I had first seen Siam when after fierce international rivalry, breathing time had been given to the country. The King, crushed and brutally humiliated by the French occupation . . . remained some time in retirement. But he had pulled himself together and with the loyal assistance of his brothers had set himself the task of reorganizing the administration of the country. . . . He engaged the services of selected foreign experts and . . . wise above the oriental, he listened to their advice. That capriciousness of appointment so conspicuous in China was absent. . . . The King and his brothers . . . had been free from the degrading influence of Eunuchs.

The world had been kept ignorant of the true state of affairs in Siam after "two astonishing years": its financial and legal reforms, its improvements in communications, education, and sanitation. The Treasury, under the control of an English expert, Mr Alfred Mitchell-Innes, had one million pounds in reserve, and Morrison was gratified to note how closely Englishmen were identified with Siam's rehabilitation. He arrived in Bangkok on 23rd January 1899, and a week later telegraphed *The Times* a succint report on these developments, followed by a comprehensive mailed survey. One of the King's brothers, Prince Damrong, gave him every assistance, and the King himself received Morrison warmly. "Welcome to my Kingdom," he said. "There is no one more welcome than you." *The Times* endorsed Morrison's conclusions and, "in two striking leaders, altered the opinion of England with regard to Siam". Drawing attention to the "remarkable telegram" from its correspondent, *The Times* reminded its readers that only three years before "the decadence of Siam seemed to have reached a pitch which constituted a danger to her European neighbours . . . the collapse of the Kingdom appeared to be at hand."

His work in Bangkok completed, Morrison hurried back to Peking, arriving just in time to be an eye-witness of the first appearance of Italy at the crowded vivisectionists' table. On the ship he wrote to his mother: "Did you see my portrait in *Black and White*? I am told it was in conjunction with the Empress and Sir Robert Hart. How curious it is that my portrait should be considered worthy of insertion." In an article by Alexis Krausse that appeared in the English illustrated weekly *Black and White* on 17th December 1898 Morrison was described as one of "four Britons who play a very marked part" in the affairs of China. The others were Sir Robert Hart, Sir Claude MacDonald, and the railway engineer, Mr C. W. Kinder. Krausse commented on "the regularity with which Morrison had beaten not only his competitors, but also governmental sources of information".

[X]

For more than half a century China had submitted to a humiliating and apparently endless series of demands by the Western barbarians. But early in 1899 she had a minor but unprecedented victory in resisting yet another

94

claim. Italy, for the sake of pride as much as profit, demanded the lease of Sanman Bay in Chekiang, with the usual accompanying parcel of preferential mining and railway rights. Britain had promised her diplomatic support, and Morrison received instructions as to the course he was to follow in a laconic, and no doubt to the Chinese post-office enigmatic, telegram: MORRISON PEKING REMEMBER MACARONI FRIENDSHIP TIMES. "The situation was one which called for a high exhibition of tact and urbanity," he wrote. But the mission was entrusted to Signor de Martino, the Italian Minister to Peking, a highly strung, excitable and superstitious man, much dependent on omens and portents. He had represented Italy in Japan and Brazil, where he had refused one day to sign an important convention because, on the way to the Foreign Office, he had encountered a squint-eyed man. In Japan he had formed an attachment with a Japanese woman who accompanied him to China. While he was conducting his negotiations in Peking she remained in Tientsin. "Her husband, I suspect," wrote Morrison, "gave friendly assistance to the Japanese who throughout . . . were more than usually well informed."

In presenting Italy's demands, de Martino encountered semantic difficulties. None of the Ministers of the Yamen could recognize the name of the bay which Italy demanded, and Morrison, in his account of de Martino's dispatch, said that the Chinese characters for the words "European Concert" were those used commonly for theatrical performances:

> Astonishment filled the Chinese when they received the Italian demands. Wholly ignorant of the place of Italy among the great Powers, they had some vague impression that it was a minor state whose troops had been defeated by some black barbarians in Africa. They discussed the dispatch . . . and then accepted the suggestion of one of their wiseacres that the most friendly act they could do to save the face of the Minister . . . was to send it back to him.

Signor de Martino was "frantic and furious". Apart from the obduracy of the Chinese in resisting Italy's demands, he had to cope with the demands of his mistress in distant Tientsin. To make things worse, the 13th of March fell in the midst of the crisis. He would conduct no business on the 13th, which he would not even name: to avert the evil eye, he always referred to it as "the day of the fox". In a state of wild excitement, and without authority from his Government, he served an ultimatum on Peking and sent Italian warships to the Yellow Sea to make an intimidatory demonstration. Britain at once withdrew her support, China ignored the ultimatum, and de Martino was recalled to Italy in disgrace. But as Dr Arthur H. Smith, a knowledgeable American missionary, wrote: "The results to China were, perhaps, more serious than if the Italian demands had been acceded to." For the Empress Dowager became convinced that the barbarians could be resisted, and even expelled from the Middle Kingdom, and the stage was being set for the disaster of the Boxer uprising.

Almost exactly a year after his arrival in Peking, Morrison became the centre of a diplomatic cyclone. On the evening of 5th March 1898 he received a note from W. M. Pethick, an accomplished American scholar who for more than twenty years was private secretary to Li Hung-chang, China's elder statesman, and a member of the Tsungli Yamen, asking if it were convenient for Morrison to come and see him. Pethick was living in the Temple of Worthies, which Li always occupied when he was in Peking. Morrison found Pethick walking up and down the room in a state of "surpressed agitation". He asked if Morrison were prepared to do a service to China by publishing, without disclosing the source, a telegram which Li Hung-chang had instructed him to send to Prince Oukhtomsky in St Petersburg. It contained a brief summary of peremptory demands which Russia had just served in China; the surrender of all sovereign rights over Port Arthur and Tailienwan on the same conditions as had been granted to Germany in the case of Kiaochow—a lease for ninety-nine years with a neutral zone fifty kilometres wide surrounding the concession, etc. Pethick did not tell Morrison, and perhaps did not know, that Li Hung-chang and Chang Yin-huan, also a member of the Tsungli Yamen, had each been offered a bribe of 500,000 taels—about £62,500—by the Russian chargé d'affaires in Peking, Pavlov, to obtain this concession. Li Hung-chang's telegram to St Petersburg, in which he begged the Prince to persuade the Tsar to withdraw the demands, was probably a manoeuvre to protect himself should there be any suspicion of his role in the negotiations.

Morrison agreed to send *The Times* the text of Li's telegram. He amplified it by saying that Russia had threatened to move troops into Manchuria if China did not comply with the demands within a stipulated period of five days. This interpolation was safe because Morrison knew Russian troops had already moved in. He had mentioned them in his detailed report on Manchuria, which by happy chance was published in *The Times* on the same day as his telegram, 7th March. Before sending the telegram, since the matter was of national importance, Morrison told Sir Claude MacDonald of his intention, but he could not disclose the source of his information. Sir Claude, wrote Morrison, cautiously replied to an urgent inquiry from the Foreign Office that there was "no indication of anything in the shape of an ultimatum, nor . . . had any time limit been given for a reply".

The telegram caused an immense sensation, in Europe as well as England. An Anglo-German loan to China, the first of many, was being offered for public subscription in London. Chirol wired Morrison agitatedly: FOREIGN OFFICE SUGGESTS YOUR INFORMATION THROUGHOUT PROBABLY MANDARIN PROMPTED BY RUSSIAN LEGATION PURPOSE HAMPER BRITISH NEGOTIATIONS . . . YOUR TELEGRAM NEARLY WRECKED LOAN CREATING FINANCIAL PANIC. To which Morrison replied, not entirely honestly: FOREIGN OFFICE

UNJUST KNOW NO MANDARIN WORTH TRUSTING ALWAYS OBTAIN CORROBORA-
TION BEFORE TELEGRAPHING.

He was, in fact, risking his reputation on the truth of an uncorrobor-
ated report. Two days after its publication the banker Guy Hillier wrote
to him saying he had "high authority" for declaring Morrison was mistaken, and begging him in the interests of the loan to modify the message.
Sir Robert Hart still more strongly assured Morrison he was mistaken:
Sir Chentung Liang had convinced him that no threat had been made by
the Russians, only a "friendly proposal". Sir Robert begged Morrison, if
he wished to avoid wrecking his career at the outset, to withdraw the
message. "When I left him," Morrison recalled, "I walked up and down
outside the garden wall for a few minutes, thinking the matter over, and
then I walked to the telegraph office and wired: 'The Chinese Government, while admitting that it has received Russian demands, denies that
they are pressing or in the nature of an ultimatum. Despite this, I repeat
the correctness of my message . . .'."

The Foreign Office, more concerned with the fate of the loan than
with the fate of Manchuria, continued its bland denials, but the loan
was a failure, and on 25th March *The Times* published a telegram from
Morrison saying that China had agreed to all the demands. That evening
George Curzon, Under-Secretary of State for Foreign Affairs, told the
House the Government had no confirmation of the "rumours" *The
Times* described the situation as a "time of exasperating doubt and per-
plexity". No one was more perplexed than Curzon himself. As representative of the Foreign Office in the House, he had to echo in his speeches an
optimism about events in the Far East which he did not share. As the
History of the Times says, "His position was one of extreme difficulty":

> The public . . . saw with far keener insight than the Government the
> trend of events . . . and developed what Mr Balfour described later as
> "an almost irritable anxiety" on the subject. Curzon's own estimate of
> the position coincided with that of the public rather than with that of
> the Government. . . . The difficulty of the position was increased by
> the reticence of the Government and the enterprise of the Press.

It is questionable whether "the public" was very much concerned
about the future of British commerce in China, or had much insight into
what was happening there, but the enterprise of the Press, particularly of
The Times, was certainly a constant irritation to the Government, and
the obscurantism of the Government a constant embarrassment to Curzon.
"We never had and we have not (now) any policy towards China," he
wrote to his successor, St John Brodrick, on 3rd May 1899. "No one
knows this better than you or I who have successively had to conjure up
make-believes. But of course, the supreme lesson of the F.O. is that there
is no determined policy about anything."

On 27th March the Port Arthur convention, giving Russia everything she had demanded, was signed in Peking. When the House met, two

97

days later, Mr J. Dillon (Mayo E.) put a question to the Under-Secretary of State for Foreign Affairs: "I beg to ask . . . if he can explain how it is that *The Times* correspondent in Peking has been able on several occasions recently to publish facts of the utmost public importance several days before the Foreign Office had obtained any information in reference to them?"

Curzon and Morrison had, in fact, identical views on the ineptness of the Foreign Office, but Curzon was a loyal spokesman and, perhaps a little goaded by Mr Dillon's taunt, made a reply in which he coined an often-quoted phrase: "I am not quite sure that this question should not be addressed to the editor of *The Times* than to me. At the same time, I think the explanation asked for is not far to seek. It is the business of Her Majesty's representatives abroad to report to us the facts of which they have official cognizance, and to obtain confirmation of them before they telegraph. . . . I hesitate to say what the functions of the modern journalists may be, but I imagine that they do not exclude the intelligent anticipation of facts even before they occur, and in this somewhat unequal competition, I think the House will see that the journalist, whose main duty is speed, is likely sometime to get the advantage of the diplomatist, whose main concern is accuracy."

The Times sprang to the defence of its correspondent, "with the passion of a furious partisan", Curzon wrote to Lord Salisbury, adding: "Some mild chaff in which I indulged in a spirit of subdued compliment to its Peking correspondent, brought it down on me with the tread of an elephant."

Britain, having decided that Port Arthur was not worth a war, consoled herself by acquiring Weihaiwei, on the opposite side of the Gulf of Chihli. Japan, though bitter at the seizure of coveted territory by one of the powers that had forced her to surrender it only three years before, was not yet ready to challenge Russia. She consoled herself by extracting concessions in Fukien province. France found consolation in acquiring a naval station at Kwangchouwan, on the southern Chinese coast, and this, according to the inviolable rules of the balance-of-power game, led to Britain acquiring more territory on the mainland opposite Hong Kong. If the venerable Ex-Viceroy, Li Hung-chang, had any qualms about his complicity in the continuing vivisection of his homeland, he had the consolation of his 500,000 taels. Besides, it was not the first time he had engaged in such transactions. He had no inhibitions about either taking or giving bribes. He had received a handsome *douceur* from Russia in 1896 for his part in obtaining concessions for the Chinese Eastern Railway, and the following year had offered the indignant Morrison a bribe to advocate in *The Times* a doubling of import dues. "The crafty old man is failing," Morrison wrote to Bell, a little prematurely. Li Hung-chang was not only the Grand Old Man of China; he was also one of its greediest old men. He had big interests in shipping, mining, banking, and telegraphs, and owned all the big stores and money-brokerage firms in Nanking and Shanghai.

When Morrison interviewed the seventy-seven-year-old statesman some months later, Li blew his nose into a mug, a ritual which Morrison found "very disgusting", and questioned him closely about Anglo-Russian relations. Li told of his audience with Queen Victoria, whose legs like his own, were weak, and praised her "clever face". He then asked Morrison, "What salary does *The Times* give you?" "It is really so insignificant that I am ashamed to mention it," Morrison replied. "It must be more than mine, 240 taels (£30) a year for being Grand Secretary of State," said Li ingenuously.

Though removed from the Tsungli Yamen, Li retained his post as Grand Secretary till he was given the "much coveted and lucrative" post of Commissioner of Yellow River, to devise measures against flooding. Commenting on the appointment, Morrison recalled a "classic passage" by George Wingrove Cooks:

> The life and state papers of a Chinese Statesman abound in the finest sentiments and foulest deeds. He cuts off ten thousand heads and cites a passage from Mencius about the sanctity of human life. He pockets the money given to him to repair an embankment and thus inundates a province: and he deplores the land lost to the cultivator of the soil.

[XII]

In August, Morrison decided to take a brief holiday in England and Australia. Before leaving, he made a quick visit to Korea. In Seoul he asked Count Hayashi if important events were pending in the Far East, reminding the Count that *The Times* and he himself were "ever friendly" to Japan. Hayashi replied that as far as he knew there was nothing to detain Morrison in China. Thus reassured, Morrison returned to Peking. On the ferry launch a woman passenger called excitedly to the captain, "Stop the launch quick. There is a poor coolie fallen overboard." The captain was not perturbed. "Maskee [no matter]," he said. "He have pay fare."

Early in September, Morrison left Shanghai for England, with a sheaf of introductions from Henry Bax-Ironside, then head of the British legation at Peking. At Hong Kong he had tiffin with Captain Hadworth Lambton of H.M.S. *Powerful*, who gave him an introduction to Curzon which read: "My dear George—This is Dr Morrison . . . whose intelligent anticipation of facts used to make you sit up in the Foreign Office." In the *China Mail* he read a eulogistic leading article about himself:

> . . . From Siberia to Siam, from Shanghai to Yunnan, from Korea to Burma, and from Canton to Peking, Dr Morrison is known personally to all the Foreign residents, who have learned to respect him and the great work he is accomplishing for British interests in the Far East. For it is an open secret that, without in any way subordinating the interests of the influential journal he represents so ably . . . Dr Morrison has been guided by higher considerations than the desire to administer journalistic shocks to an apathetic public. . . . Thanks to

him, there is no journal in the world better informed on Chinese affairs, of the undercurrent that passes for politics in Peking, of the machinations of the Foreign diplomatic representatives and the schemes that have drawn so many speculators and adventurers to the Chinese capital during the past three years. His success as a newspaper correspondent has been phenomenal—he bids fair to become, if he is not already, the greatest living authority on Modern China— we have become so accustomed to have an able and unfettered critic at Peking, a kind of unofficial attaché, that we have come to regard Dr Morrison as one of the institutions of Peking official life.

[XIII]

Morrison reached Marseilles at the end of October, and with a shipmate, the travel-writer Henry Savage Landor, made the traditional round of the brothels near the Old Port. His experience in one, the Maison Rebekah, he recorded in Spanish, following the principle established by Pepys that sex is more respectable in a foreign language. Two days later, in Paris, he was "stricken down, paralysed, with the news yelled at a thousand street corners" of British reverses in South Africa. "In honour of the glorious news," he noted bitterly, "the office of *La Patrie* is hung with the flags of the Transvaal and the Orange Free State." He was even more embittered when, passing through Paris again in December, he found a "foul press" directed against Queen Victoria. "Foul and filthy," he wrote in his diary, "a wretched race." And: "On every pair of English legs doth walk three Frenchmen."

London was a flattering, but often boring, round of lunches, dinners, receptions, and interviews. His first call was *The Times* office, where he met the proprietor, Arthur Walter, the fourth of the Walter dynasty, and his "fine handsome wife". Walter treated him with "much distinction":

> Among other compliments, he said "I need hardly say you've been a most tremendous success. You have done what no other man, we believe, in the world could have done. Your telegrams carry tremendous weight in the City. If you were to telegraph a flat lie, it would be believed because it came from you. Salisbury was furious with you. 'Newspaper rumour', he stigmatized it, when it was proved to be literally true."

Morrison was invited for a weekend to Bear Wood, Walter's vast Gothic mansion near Wokingham, where members of *The Times* staff were frequently entertained with what Leopold Amery called a "kindly, yet somewhat formal" hospitality. Morrison's assessment of it in later days was less charitable. He recorded his first visit tersely:

> *November 5.* Caught 4.45 train for Wokingham. Miserable day. Spent £21.15.0., plus 8/- plus £1 . . . for clothes plus ticket 9/- return etc., all to spend one months' salary in getting an outfit to take

me to Arthur Walter's, the amiable philistine who spoils me. Carriage at the station, two horses. Fine park, magnificent house. Splendid picture gallery where I was received by Mrs Walter, a majestic queenly woman, very sympathetic and regal. I told the story of Li's question "How much are you paid by *The Times*?" and my reply. . . . Scarcely polite, but apropos. Mrs Walter looked rather queer. Much style. A pokey bedroom, No. 2 well furnished.

Having tipped the footman four shillings, the "paunchy butler" six shillings, and a coachman four shillings, Morrison returned to London early next morning. "Poor breakfast and arrived very hungry," he recorded.

This note of disillusion with the stately hostesses of England was to recur many times in his diaries. A few days after the inadequate breakfast at Bear Wood he was the guest of Lady Warrington. "Infernal bad dinner, cooking atrocious," he wrote. "And the company was obnoxiously dull." He was seated between Miss Hilton Price ("mannish with side chops and moustache") and her mother, who "conversed upon frozen mutton". Equally unattractive was an "infernally dull and infernally slow" dinner party to meet the Crown Prince of Siam. The guests included Lady Westbury ("old cat with great hair and acid tongue") and Lady Ashburton, who not only ate salt by moistening her finger and dipping it in the salt cellar, but had dirty nails. Morrison estimated from evidence that she had not washed her hands since Jubilee Year, 1887.

At the Author's Club, Morrison met Lord Garnet Wolseley, hero of most of England's "little wars" of the second half of the nineteenth century, and a veteran of Crimea and the Indian Mutiny, then Commander-in-Chief of the forces. His repute was such that the phrase "All Sir Garnet" was the popular equivalent of "all correct", but Morrison did not find him very acute in military prognosis. Wolseley had served in China in 1860, and claimed to be an authority on the Far East, but when Morrison told him that war between Russia and Japan seemed imminent, Wolseley replied firmly: "Then Japan will go to the wall." When Morrison reported this to his colleagues, Chirol said: "I am glad Wolseley said this because he is always wrong." Buckle's comment was: "Wolseley never makes a speech without saying something he ought not to have said."

Morrison could learn nothing from Sir William Everett, A.A.G. in the Intelligence Department of the War Office, but left him imbued with Morrison's belief "1. That war was inevitable. 2. That Japan would be victorious. 3. That England should not interfere, but 4. That England in her own interests should incite Japan to take early action." He repeated this to Herbert de Reuter, of Reuter's news agency, "a Jew with an accent, but with a marvellous knowledge and insight", but de Reuter, despite his insight, placed no confidence in rumours of conflict between Russia and Japan, or even of strained relations between them. He was more interested in the enormous cost of the Transvaal war service, of which he spoke "ruefully"; runners, £40 apiece, telegrams, four shillings a word. However, he was "very complimentary" to Morrison.

Lord Rosebery invited Morrison to call on him at 38 Berkeley Square. Rosebery, who was Foreign Secretary from 1892 to 1894, had surrendered the Prime Ministership in 1895 and the leadership of the Liberal Party a year later. He was taller than Morrison had expected: "very grey with a weak, ill-formed mouth and somewhat prominent upper teeth—the same kind of mouth as Oscar Wilde's". Morrison added a cryptic footnote: "Name closely associated with that of Oscar. Viscount Drumlanrig elder brother of Lord Alfred Douglas was his private secretary and committed suicide. He fainted when report brought him of punishment of Oscar".

"You were in Peking during stirring times," said Rosebery. "You have a very effective news service."

"I have none," Morrison replied. "I never did, as was implied in the papers, forestall the Government. Always I told Sir Claude MacDonald anything important I happened to hear. The difference was he did not believe things which I credited."

"But one would have thought he would soon discover that your information must be credited. I should have been extremely annoyed if I had been in the Foreign Office not to have been better informed."

Morrison said that occasionally he was better informed than the legation because he had mixed among the Chinese, whereas at the English Legation there was no intercourse whatever with the Chinese.

"That is very extraordinary," said Rosebery. "Why is that?"

"It is one of the traditions of the service," said Morrison.

"Then the sooner the tradition is forgotten the better."

Rosebery turned to reports of friction between Russia and Japan. He could not understand why Japan should choose such a time when "her chief, if not her only friend" was engaged in serious trouble in South Africa. Yet it was obvious, he reflected, that if Japan were to act she must not delay until Russia had completed her railway. "I think it would not be inadvisable to draw closer to Japan, to make an alliance with Japan even," he said. "To continue the friendly action and encouragement given by us—for which action how they attacked me when we refused to join the other Powers in the Liaotung peninsula."

(Japan, after crushingly defeating China in the war of 1894-5, had seized the Liaotung peninsula, with the strategically important harbour of Kiaochow, but had been forced to disgorge it by the combined pressure of Russia, France, and Germany, whose motives, it is scarcely necessary to say, were not entirely unselfish. Britain remained aloof.) Morrison's diary comment on Rosebery's complacent remark was: "Note this: Thus the act of laissez-faire and muddle-headedness is now to be interpreted and we are to take credit to ourselves for great political foresight."

Morrison stayed at Queen Anne Mansions with Chirol, but dined frequently with Moberly Bell in Portland Place, where he met his boyhood idol, Sir Henry Stanley ("lion-headed and white-haired"), St John

Brodrick, ("very deaf but seemed honest") and many other eminent people. These dinners were his most enjoyable experiences in London. Conversation was brisk and uninhibited. At one Buckle said, "Kitchener is a boor, no table manners," and Chirol quoted Winston Churchill as saying, "My father was War Minister before he was thirty-seven. Before I am thirty-seven I will be War Minister. There is then time for me to get my knife into Kitchener." At another Bell recalled an unfortunately punctuated *Times* poster which read:

> PRINCE HENRY OF BATTENBERG
> WHO WOULD NOT DIE FOR ENGLAND

and told stories of Rudyard Kipling and the Poet Laureate, William Austin:

> An agent had sent *The Times* a poem at Fleet Time (the naval review at Spithead on the occasion of the Queen's second Jubilee, 1897). Breathing war and thunder, bellicose to a degree, urging this great fleet to action. The poem was unsuitable for a peaceful time. Moberly Bell saw Rudyard, said that the price was nothing, he would willingly pay ten times more, etc., but the poem was unsuitable. Rudyard agreed. He threw it in the fire and sent the *Recessional* instead. He would accept no pay for this. All his later contributions had been gratis. Bell had met Austin today who showed him "a little thing I threw off coming down from Oxford." He announced his verses thus: "The Bard will sing tonight."

Morrison had a long talk with Lily May, wife of the brilliant black-and-white artist, Phil May. She told him that May got £105 for twelve sketches, two days' work, for the *Daily Chronicle*. "He makes any amount of money, but is very improvident, and drinking, has an Ally Sloper nose," Morrison wrote.

Among the many fellow-Australians whom Morrison met were the writers Morley Roberts and Guy Boothby. Morrison visited Boothby, a nineteenth-century precursor of Edgar Wallace in popularity and fecundity, at Hampton. "Guy dictates into a phonograph," Morrison noted. "Has three novels going at the same time. Has turned out 14,000 words in one day."

[XIV]

Morrison left England on 2nd December 1899, paying £70 for a first-class passage to Melbourne. Moberly Bell farewelled him with a pleasing valediction: "I cannot guarantee it, but you may count upon having £100 a month." Despite this, it was a "damned miserable trip". With no one to talk to, Morrison consoled himself by writing innumerable letters. The first day at sea he wrote dispiritedly in his diary of his London experiences:

Being on *The Times* I am always treated as a superior person of much gravity of demeanor and solidity of account. Thus when my friend, Lionel James, invited me to the play he took me *not* to a sprightly extravaganza but to a solid and depressing tragedy *King John*. At dinner at Mrs Bell's I am not seated next to a beautifully-bosomed woman of lax morality like Mrs Carl Meyer, but I am stationed gravely between her husband and a grim old duchess long past the climacteric called St Albans. Thus when Guy Boothby invited me to spend the Sunday with him in the country, he added, "I am delighted you can come. Usually some actors and actresses come to see me on Sunday. Some are coming on Sunday, but I'll write and tell them not." "For God's sake" I said impressively, "don't do that. I'd rather they came than not." He praised complacently my good nature. The actresses, however, did not come, but I had two members of the stock exchange instead! When I went behind the scenes, I am not introduced to the beautiful Irene Vanbrugh, but am gravely presented to the elderly manager, John Hare.

Morrison broke his journey at Calcutta to make a pilgrimage to Assam, a five days' steamer trip, to see Mary Joplin. (He afterwards told *The Times* that he had gone there to study new methods of tea cultivation.) Mary was out of work, had no money and was very unhappy. He gave her 150 rupees (about £10 12s.) and some handkerchiefs, and ordered professional cards and circulars for her to distribute among doctors and chemists. He also left £10 with an English friend to be paid her in instalments. "Thus she is fairly well provided for the winter," he wrote in his diary. "She has in hand 50 or 60 rupees."

He was at sea for Christmas, "the dullest and stupidest Christmas spent for many years". He amused himself by tabulating his whereabouts on twenty previous Christmases:

'98 Hongkong	'88 Rio Tinto
'97 Peking	'87 Edinburgh
'96 North Siam	'86 Edinburgh
'95 Saigon	'85 Dumfrieshire
'94 Sea on *Warrego*	'84 Dumfrieshire
'93 Kyoto, Japan	'83 Corryule, near Geelong
'92 Ballarat	'82 Walk across Australia
'91 Ballarat	'81 Corryule, near Geelong
'90 Geelong	'80 Canoe down Murray
'89 Wazan, Morocco	'79 Queenscliff

In a similar statistical mood, Morrison compiled a list of his assets at 31st December 1899. The total value was £1249 10s. of which his house and furniture in Peking represented £250, and his 2500 books, £250. He had £600 in a London bank and £10 in Peking. Again like Pepys, Morrison made a practice of setting down what he owned at the end of each year.

"Dr Morrison stepped ashore from the *Ville de la Ciotat* yesterday with a rifle under one arm and a breech-loading gun under the other," reported the Melbourne *Age* on 4th January 1900. It was an uncomfortable home-coming. Melbourne was limp under a heatwave; the *Argus* reported that ten people had died of "heat apoplexy" the day before, when the shade temperature reached 105.2 degrees. Morrison told the *Age* reporter that Russia was not a grave menace to British interests in the Far East, though Japan viewed with alarm her growing strength. But Japan was infinitely stronger, and her strength was increasing by leaps and bounds. To England, Japan had always been, and was then, a sincere friend. To a reporter from the *Argus* Morrison said that Great Britain's sound and satisfactory position in China was in a very large measure attributable to the admirable skill with which Sir Claude MacDonald performed his duties. In his diary he added the gloss: "Very stupid interview and many errors, but glori-fied MacDonald, which was all I wished—political necessity, quite insin-cere, though personally attached to man."

Morrison's ship called at Thursday Island, which he found "more a Japanese settlement than a British colony". Queensland was the only Australian colony which, by treaty, had admitted Japanese artisans and labourers. There were 3100 Japanese on the island and in the fishing fleets.

Morrison returned to Peking by way of Japan and Korea. In Japan he met many statesmen and diplomats and discussed approvingly with Hayashi Tadasu, later Japanese Minister in London, the proposed Anglo-Japanese alliance. He also talked of the developing tension between Japan and Russia over Korea, and the possibility of its leading to war. Unlike most of his countrymen, he wanted Japan to fight Russia because he wanted to see Manchuria freed by the Japanese from Russian control. He desired this so strongly that he became an ardent warmonger, as his diary repeatedly shows.

From Keijo, the capital of Korea, he sent off a long telegram about Russia's acquisition of a naval base at Masampo, on the southern tip of Korea, menacingly close to Japan. Russia had sought this base for years, but had always been frustrated by Japan. On 16th March 1900, a few days before Morrison's arrival, she had forced the issue. A Russian squad-ron anchored at Chemulpo, thirty miles away, and the Admiral talked so persuasively to the King of Korea that two days later Russia was granted the rights to a coaling-station and naval hospital at Masampo. In his tele-gram Morrison reported that Japan viewed the "stand and deliver" attitude of Russia with "increasing distrust".

[XVI]

Every foreign correspondent suffers from the malaise of isolation. Too close to the events he records, and convinced of the primary importance of his beat, he resents any interference with his copy, whether the interference is dictated by space or by policy. Morrison, early in his Peking assignment, began to brood over the way Chirol handled his dispatches, sometimes cutting, sometimes amending them. His resentment was to grow with the years into an intemperate hatred of his chief. Chirol, on the other hand, early complained of the growing bitterness of Morrison's comments on Britain's fumbling foreign policy. Morrison was furious when his telegram from Korea ("costing a very considerable sum of money") was cut down to make room for a report from Paris on the opening of a recreation hall for the use of jockeys in Chantilly. "Nothing could show better the entire lack of interest in anything to do with China," he grumbled in his diary.

Leaving Chefoo on 31st March, Morrison was in his cabin aboard the *Tokyo Maru*, reading a Maupassant novel before going to sleep, when the steamer crashed on the rocks in the straits of Pechili. There was great confusion. The Korean passengers rushed the boats, and Morrison remained with the captain on the ship, which was firmly aground, till they were rescued in the morning by a passing vessel. Morrison's second shipwreck inspired an elegaic verse from his ribald friend Dr J. L. Molyneux, surgeon of the Maritime Customs at Chefoo:

> *Escaped the perils of ten thousand poxes*
> *He came to grief on them there blasted rock'ses*

CHAPTER SIX

[I]

THERE WAS plenty of gossip awaiting Morrison when he reached Peking on 4th April 1900. Pethick told him that Li Hung-chang was "revelling in the spoils of Canton", and that the Empress had received from him "with much weeping and recrimination" the irritating news that 6000 military uniforms were being made in Hong Kong to the order of K'ang Yu-wei, each with characters saying: "Destroy Manchu Dynasty". But of greater interest to Morrison was the news that the Brooks murder case had been "settled satisfactorily" and that the Boxers were "ceasing agitation". This was the first mention of Boxers in Morrison's diary.

On 31st December 1899 a young British missionary, the Rev. S. M. Brooks, was decapitated in Shantung, a province where anti-foreign feeling was intense. His murderers were members of a secret society whose name, literally, meant "the Fists of Righteous Harmony". The English term "Boxers" was coined by missionaries and first appeared in print in October 1899, but the movement dated back at least to the eighteenth century. It was one of the innumerable associations that had sprung up among the Chinese masses from earliest times: secret societies which, by ritual, incantation, and magic, promised a better life to an ignorant, oppressed, and impoverished people. Many factors contributed to the revival of a very active Boxer movement in 1898. China's financial position was desperate. The extravagances of the Manchu Court, the cost of the Sino-Japanese War, with the huge indemnity imposed after her defeat, had brought her to bankruptcy. Her resources were being mortgaged to meet ever-growing foreign debts, and foreign penetration was increasing rapidly. Railways were spreading out, to the great misgiving of a people who saw tracks and cuttings desecrating the graves of their ancestors; and, as Peter Fleming says, "The foreign businessmen who negotiated the concessions were often boors; the overseers who supervised the work were often bullies."

As hated as the railway engineers were the missionaries, particularly the Roman Catholic missionaries, who had demanded, and been granted, far-reaching civil powers. By a decree of 15th March 1899, Roman Catholic bishops were given the rank and dignity of viceroys and governors, with their ceremonial trappings—the mandarin's button, the retinue of attendants, the umbrella of honour, the salute of cannon on arrival or departure; while even ordinary priests were ranked with magistrates. A conference of Anglican bishops in Shanghai viewed "with alarm" the "rapidly growing interference of . . . Roman Catholic priests with the provincial and local government of China", but Protestant missionaries, though theoretically without secular power, were often as dictatorial, and no more sympathetic towards the people whose country they had invaded. They would erect a tall spire on a site which, according to Chinese belief, should not be disturbed by a building, lest the *feng shui*, the spirits of wind and water, be offended. As a Chinese writer put it: "Their disturbance by a church spire is considered as much a grievance as the erection of a hideous tannery beside Westminster Abbey would be."

Anti-foreign feeling was as strong in South China as in the north, but in Shantung an army reform had created bands of unemployed soldiers, desperate for food, and a poor harvest had been followed by famine and widespread floods. Hundreds of thousands of people were hungry, homeless, and ripe for action. In this febrile atmosphere the Boxer movement erupted violently. Anti-foreign and therefore anti-Christian, it was directed not only against the "Primary Devils", the missionaries, but also the "Secondary Devils", the native Christian converts: and, at one stage, partly against the Manchu dynasty. But by 1900 the movement had allied itself with, and was supported by, the Throne. Exactly when and why this change took place has been the subject of a patient study by Victor Purcell, *The Boxer Uprising*. As he points out, to call the uprising a rebellion is absurd; the Boxers were supporting the Manchu Government, even to the point of killing members of another society that was anti-dynastic.

The murderers of Mr Brooks were tried in the presence of a British official, and executed, the Tsungli Yamen expressing appropriate regret. But, as Morrison's diary for April and May shows, the Boxers were far from "ceasing agitation":

April 17 . . . the danger of the Boxers is increasing. The danger is *scarcity of rain* which is attributed to the disturbance of the *feng shui* by foreigners. If rains come, the Boxers will soon disappear.

April 26 . . . Saw Squiers [First Secretary of the American Legation]. Anti-foreign literature is being sold in the streets. There has been some serious Boxer fighting near Paotingfu, with an alarming account of a "battle" written by a missionary, Ewing, there.

May 16 . . . According to my boy, 8,000,000 men are to descend from Heaven and exterminate the foreigners. . . . Then the rain will come. . . . F. Huberty James [a professor of English in the Imperial Chinese University]: "The movement may become serious especially if a leader can be found". . . . Many stories of pillaging. . . .

May 18 . . . Much agitation still about Boxers. I said to Sir Claude, "The first shower and the movement expires." Yesterday some rain fell. Just my luck I wire in the morning the alarming Boxer movement and in the afternoon rain falls. *Boxers.* French priests report 61 men, women and children suffered death at Kaolo . . . midway between Peking and Paotingfu. Also trouble at Anshsien, from which people are fleeing by train into Peking. Some burned alive. The whole village of Kaolo is destroyed.

The same day, a London Mission chapel about forty miles from Peking was burnt to the ground, and the next day Bishop Favier, the Vicar-Apostolic of Peking, sent an alarming message to the French Minister, M. Pichon. He reported on the casualties inflicted by the Boxers, the damage they had done, and the thousands of refugees who were fleeing from them. Their *known* intention, he said, was to attack the churches first, then the legations. "For us, in our cathedral, the date of the attack has actually been fixed." His cathedral, the Peitang, had within the walls of its compound an orphanage, a convent, a dispensary, several schools, a printing-press, a chapel, and a museum, as well as the Bishop's house, with its stores, stables, and other buildings. It was about two miles to the northwest of the legations. The Bishop's message finished with an urgent plea for forty or fifty sailors "to protect our lives and property".

"Saw Pichon," Morrison recorded on 21st May. "Very amiable, thinks Favier an alarmist." Sir Claude MacDonald was equally sceptical: "I confess that little has come to my knowledge," he wrote to the Foreign Office, "to confirm the gloomy anticipations of the French Father." Nor did his Chinese Secretary, Henry Cockburn, take a serious view. "I agree with him," Morrison wrote, "that we cannot feel this peril in the air." Yet "all knives and swords have doubled in value. Shops are working day and night to supply the demand."

The following day, Sir Claude told Morrison that a meeting of the diplomatic body had just been held which had called upon the Chinese Government to suppress the Boxers and the anti-foreign propaganda, otherwise the legations would again be compelled to bring guards to Peking. On 23rd May, Morrison noted in his diary that the movement had "the cognisance and approval of the Government, as shown by them drilling in the grounds of Imperial barracks and royal princes. . . ."

As a religious sect, the Boxers underwent a fantastic training of incantations and gymnastics which they believed made them invulnerable. Morrison recorded that when a boy of sixteen was practising this ritual he bared his chest to M. August Chamot, the Swiss proprietor of the Hotel de Pekin, saying, "The foreign bullet may strike me here, but it will not hurt me." The sceptical hotelier let out and kicked the boy, who fled "as from the wrath to come". (Yuan Shih-k'ai, as Governor of Shantung, made a more definite test of the Boxers' invulnerability. His firing squad experimented on and killed a number of them without difficulty.)

Morrison and Pethick on 24th May witnessed a Boxer at his prostrations, repeating his prayers and his gymnastics: "He pretends to receive a spirit from Heaven and in a trance slashes the air with sword and knife. He is impervious not only to the foreign bullet and the foreign sword, but the foreign poison . . . with which the foreigner is infecting the native wells."

That night Morrison attended a dinner at the British Legation to celebrate Queen Victoria's eighty-first—and last—birthday. There were fifty guests, and each lady took in two men. Morrison and Sir Robert Hart were taken in by the hostess, Lady MacDonald. Dinner was served in a small theatre. Champagne flowed, toasts were exchanged, and after dinner there was dancing on the decorated tennis court, to the music of "I.G.'s Own". The threat of the Boxers seemed remote.

Yet that very day there had been a massacre of missionaries and railway engineers at Hsiang Hsien, eighty miles from Peking, and on 28th May, Morrison had much to record:

> Early this morning, a man hobbled into my house very foot-sore. He had escaped from the Paotingfu railway from Ch'anghsintien. [The junction of the Tientsin-Peking with the line which was to link Peking and Hankow was at Fengtai, about 15 miles south of Peking, and Ch'anghsintien was the headquarters of the construction staff.] The railway had been destroyed, the station [Fengtai] besieged and the engineers besieged in their houses. . . . Reports from Chocow are very bad, terrorization and massacre forcing Christians to abjure their faith and burn incense, selling the prettier girls into prostitution.

Morrison, with two companions, rode out across the racecourse to Fengtai:

> As we approached the black smoke was rising and the whole countryside was afoot, streaming towards the station. The engine sheds were on fire . . . and the villagers from all around were looting. We could do nothing, though we should have shot a Chinaman who threatened us with swords and swore to cut our throats. It will always be a regret to me that I did not kill this man. Crowds of threatening people were standing by the temple near the racecourse.

Morrison's companions returned to Peking, but he rode on to give the alarm to Mrs Squiers and her guest, an American girl named Polly Condit Smith, who were summering in a converted temple in the Western Hills. Miss Smith, under her married name of Mary Hooker, later described his arrival in her book *Behind the Scenes in Peking*:

> Our position now was critical. Not a foreign man on the place to protect us; a quantity of badly frightened Chinese servants to reassure; three children and ourselves to make plans for. We did what women always have to do—we waited; and our reward came when we saw down in the valley a dusty figure ambling along on a dusty Chinese pony, crossing from the direction of Fengtai. . . . It was Dr

Morrison. On hearing early in the day of the mob at Fengtai, and the burning of the place, he promptly started in that direction . . . to ascertain if the wild rumours circulating in Peking were truths. Finding the worst corroborated, he started on his return trip to Peking, hot haste for the cable office, when he became oppressed with the startling remembrance that we were at the temple and probably alone and unprotected. So, instead of returning to Peking, he promptly came to us. . . . He was studying a possible defence of our balcony when Mr Squiers arrived post-haste, bringing with him a Russian Cossack, whom he had borrowed from the Russian Minister. Plans were now made to defend the place from attack or incendiaries during the night. . . . Sentry work of the most careful sort continued all night, as well as the packing up of our clothes and valuables. At 6 a.m. we were en route for Peking, an enormous caravan—most of us in Chinese carts, some riding ponies, mules or donkeys, the 40 servants placing themselves wherever they could. The three protectors, heavily armed, rode by us.

While Morrison was playing knight-errant in the Western Hills the diplomats met again and were persuaded by Sir Claude MacDonald to bring up the legation guards at once. The Tsungli Yamen was asked for formal permission and, after at first refusing, agreed on condition that no legation should have more than thirty men. Sir Claude spoke very plainly to the six members of the Yamen. . . . "They were a damned lot of fools. He told them at once to tell Prince Ch'ing, who is at the Summer Palace with the Empress Dowager, that the troops are coming tomorrow, and if there is any obstruction, they will come in ten times greater force." M. Pichon had already ordered up his guards; the other powers ignored the Yamen's limit, and by 3rd June 426 officers and men, American, British, French, Italian, Japanese, and Russian, from warships anchored off Tientsin, had arrived in Peking. Morrison recorded without comment, and Miss Polly Condit Smith with pride, that the first to march up Legation Street were fifty-six United States Marines. Victor Purcell, sixty-three years later, wrote: "It is at least arguable that the bringing up of the guards added fuel to the fire of anti-foreignism and thus endangered the very individuals it aimed to protect." It also made the dispatch of reinforcements necessary, "and to secure their retreat, the Taku forts had to be taken, which in its turn led to war".

Sir Claude MacDonald himself was now "very much alarmed". On 2nd June he asked Morrison "not to belittle the alarming reports": "The British Government was indifferent, he said. He had received only three telegrams. 1. A European concert we think, is advisable. 2. Keep in the background, let the initiative come from the others. 3. Do not hesitate to land men for the protection of nationals." This was not very positive advice to a not-over-intelligent minister facing an unprecedented situation. But he was soon to be swept up in the swift tide of events. Next day the murder of two British missionaries was reported forty miles south of

Peking: anti-foreign feeling was rising everywhere; the railway to Tientsin was cut; the British Consul at Tientsin on his own initiative telegraphed Lord Salisbury for strong reinforcements, and the ministers in Peking telegraphed their respective governments asking for their naval officers to take concerted measures to defend the legations.

On 4th June, when Henry Cockburn went to the Tsungli Yamen to discuss the fate of the two missionaries, he found, in the midst of his address, that one member was fast asleep. He got up and left. "There you have China," he said to Morrison. "What are you to make of such people? The Empress Dowager is giving a theatrical performance while the country is in serious stress and strife."

The Empress Dowager was not only playing at theatricals in her fabulous Summer Palace; she was playing, on a much wider stage, a role of tortuous duplicity: issuing, on the one hand, cloudy edicts condemning the Boxers and, on the other, edicts absolving and encouraging them. As her complicity with the Boxers became apparent, the fears of the Europeans increased, and when on 8th June the grandstand and stables of the Peking racecourse were burnt—a caddish and calamitous affront to English sensibility—Sir Claude MacDonald reported that this had brought home "more vividly" than any previous incident "to the minds of all Europeans in Peking, a sense of the perilous position in which they stood". Next morning, in response to his urgent appeal, Admiral Sir Edward Seymour, a veteran of the Crimean War, left Tientsin with a mixed force of 500 men. Four other trains, carrying 1376 troops, followed soon after. All expected to be in Peking that night. It was more than two months before they arrived.

On the afternoon of 11th June several parties of Europeans went out by cart or on horseback to meet Seymour's forces at the station. Among them, in bowler hat and tailcoat, was the Chancellor of the Japanese Legation, Mr Sugiyama. At the main gate of the Chinese City he was dragged from his cart by Chinese soldiers and hacked to pieces. His heart was cut out and sent as a trophy to the general whose men had committed the murder. Other outrages followed.

On 13th June the German Minister, Baron von Ketteler, armed with a walking-stick, captured a Boxer, "a mere boy", Morrison noted, in Legation Street. "The boy in full uniform was sharpening his sword on his sole. He had yellow phylacteries inscribed 'This is good for eight foreigners.'"

Later that day "the Boxers came down in force from the north of the city, and the burning of foreign buildings began". Morrison's diary has a passage that reflects the mounting excitement:

13 June—Attack of Boxers. Cries of Boxer incantations.
　　　Passing the French Legation I found all on guard. "The Boxers are coming." Then rush home. . . . Kept watch all night. . . .
　　　Awful cries in the west part of the city all through the night. The roar of the murdered. Rapine and massacre.

Morrison's diary, normally a model of order and clarity, from now on becomes more and more confused and fragmentary: notes are jotted down haphazardly, at odd angles, in margins and blank spaces, out of sequence, and sometimes abbreviated to the point of obscurity. But he continues to record in detail the momentous events of the passing days— except where he himself figures importantly in them. Thus, on 15th June, the laconic entries "My suggestion to search Prince Su's house, which we did. . . . We rescue several hundred and bring them back" are unintelligible without amplification. This is supplied by many historians of the Boxer crisis; among them, Dr A. H. Smith, the Rev. Roland Allen—acting chaplain to the British Legation—and Henry Savage Landor.

At two in the afternoon [writes Savage Landor] Dr Morrison, who has a nobler heart than many of the selfish refugees, on hearing that many Christian converts were still at the mercy of the Boxers near Nan-tang church, applied to Sir Claude MacDonald for guards to rescue them. Twenty British were given him, and were joined by a force of Germans and Americans. Morrison guided them to the spot, and it will ever be a bright spot in the record of the doctor's life that he was the means of saving from atrocious tortures and death over a hundred helpless Chinese.

Mr Allen takes up the story:

Dr Morrison returned with a large convoy of Roman Catholic Christians and brought the most ghastly stories of the state of affairs. . . . He said it was the most horrible sight he had ever seen. They found the Boxers going about from house to house cutting down every Christian they could find and the place was running with blood. The rescue party marched through the streets, calling upon the Christians to come out and join them, and many did so. Among them many were wounded and some were sick. They were escorted over to the East City and placed in Prince Su's palace, commonly called "The Fu" by the care of Dr Morrison and Mr Huberty James, and there tended with the utmost care by these two men, assisted by a few volunteers.

Prince Su's palace, in its high-walled ornamental grounds, flanked the British Legation to the east, across a street and a canal. At Morrison's suggestion, the palace and grounds were searched by a party that included Huberty James and himself, and it was arranged with Prince Su that the rescued native Christians should shelter there. "Prince Su was most suave," Polly Condit Smith noted in her diary. "He vacated the same day, leaving all his treasure and half of his harem. Thanks are due to Dr Morrison."

Another eye-witness, B. Lenox Simpson ("Putnam Weale"), praising Morrison's "energy and resolution", described how all that afternoon hundreds of converts were pouring into the Fu, "laden with their pots and pans, their beds and their bundles of rice".

When the siege of Peking began, the Fu held nearly 2000 refugees. Mr Allen continues:

By rescuing these people and placing them in the Fu, Dr Morrison did signal service to the besieged. In the first place he provided a large number of coolies, whose labour was invaluable in the building of the barricades which formed so marked a characteristic of the later stage of the siege. Secondly, he opened the way for the Protestant missionaries to insist on the right to bring in their Christians, whereby we gained an equally valuable accession of useful workmen. This right had up to this date been steadily refused by the foreign Ministers. . . . Thirdly, in occupying the Fu he seized a most valuable strategic position, from a military point of view, since the artificial hills in the grounds of that place overlooked the east wall of the British Legation and covered the back of the Spanish, Japanese, and French Legations. When the legations were attacked by the Imperial troops the importance of this position was fully realized.

Next morning Morrison took part in another expedition which he described succinctly:

16 June—Up early very much refreshed. Had a chit from Sir Claude MacDonald asking, will I go out? Captain Wray, 20 British, 10 Americans and 5 Japanese with an officer and Captain Shiba [Japanese military attaché]. Damned poor not knowing his own mind. We made a raid on a temple 30 yards from the Austrian outpost; the Austrians coming up afterwards. 45 killed—butchered. Christian captives with hands tied being immolated while actually massacring, 5 already dead. Rescued 3. One accidentally killed. All boxers killed; one only dared to face us. I killed myself at least 6. Back tired having paraded city and witnessed devastation in many places.

If his diary entries were chaotic, Morrison's telegrams to *The Times* continued to give a clear picture of the worsening situation. But on 13th June the telegraph line that ran north through Russian territory was cut. This was the last link between Peking and the outside world; the wires to Tientsin had been pulled down three days before. Morrison, however, managed to get a final telegram carried by special messenger to Tientsin —at a cost of twenty taels, he noted methodically—which was published in London on 18th June. It was dated 14th June, two days later than the last diplomatic dispatches to get through, and read:

A serious anti-foreign outbreak took place last night when some of the finest buildings in the eastern part of the city were burnt and hundreds of native Christians and servants employed by foreigners were massacred within two miles of the Imperial Palace. It was an anxious night for all foreigners who were collected under the protection of the foreign guards. The Boxers burned the Roman Catholic east cathedral, the large buildings of the London mission, and the American Board of Missions, and also all the buildings in the eastern part of the city occupied by the foreign employees of the Maritime Customs. If the troops reinforcing the foreign guards fail to arrive today further riots are expected. It is believed that no European has been injured.

That day Admiral Seymour's forces were precariously strung out along the railway line. The leading train, carrying the admiral, was only halfway to Peking; the others straggled behind. They were under constant attack, and ammunition was running out. On 18th June, to avoid encirclement, Seymour decided to fall back on Tientsin. With him was the twenty-nine-year-old David Beatty, who in a private letter described the operation as "the maddest, wildest rottenest scheme that could emanate from the brain of any man".

There was now danger of Tientsin being cut off before Seymour could fight his way back, and the foreign powers decided to occupy "provisionally, by consent or force", the Taku forts at the mouth of the North River on which Tientsin is situated. In the legations at Peking nothing was known of these happenings, but on the afternoon of 19th June each of the eleven ministers and Sir Robert Hart received from the Tsungli Yamen a large scarlet envelope containing an ultimatum. It said that the allied fleets had threatened to bombard the Taku forts. As this was equivalent to a declaration of war, the ministers were notified that unless they quit Peking within twenty-four hours their protection could not be guaranteed. If they did they were promised safe conduct to Tientsin. In fact, the Allied fleets, after a few hours' bombardment, had already occupied the forts on 17th June.

A meeting of ministers was quickly convened by the doyen of the diplomatic body, the Spanish Minister, Señor Cologan. There was a spirited debate. At first the majority accepted Baron von Ketteler's vehemently expressed view that it would be suicidal to accept the Yamen's offer of protection. Others, led by the French and American ministers, were in favour of accepting it. Morrison afterwards reported in *The Times* the "profound astonishment" everywhere expressed that M. Pichon, as "Protecteur des Missions Catholiques en Chine", and "so humane a man as Mr Conger", the American Minister, could have advocated a course of action that meant "the immediate abandonment to massacre of the thousands of native Christians who had trusted the foreigner and believed in his good faith". But, after long discussion, the views of Pichon and Conger prevailed. Just before midnight an answer signed by Cologan was sent back to the Yamen: the ministers were ready to leave Peking, but not within the short space of twenty-four hours. They intimated that they knew nothing of what had happened at Taku, and requested an interview with the Yamen the following morning, to discuss transport, provisions, and protection.

Morrison was disgusted. "Conger to his everlasting dishonour has asked for 100 carts," he wrote in his diary. "As he said to me 'the Chinese have guaranteed us safe conduct'."

"If you place confidence in Chinese guarantee, why do you have your legation guards here?" Morrison asked pertinently. "Did they [the Chinese] not promise to protect you?"

To Cologan he said: "The Chinese will be massacred to a man."

Cologan shrugged. "That does not regard us," he said. But it greatly "regarded" Morrison:

> A more disgraceful determination I never heard of. I went home and could not look my servant in the face. "So European man all run away?" "Who speakee that fool pidgin?" I went back to the Legation, argued and remonstrated. Sir Claude wavered.

Polly Condit Smith writes of the ministers "moving about from one legation to another, arguing, talking, always talking . . . it looked very much as if we were all to start out to our deaths the following morning":

> At one time Dr Morrison took the floor, he being the spokesman for the vast crowd of intelligent individuals—engineers, bankers, trades-people and missionaries, who one and all were in favour of waiting until Seymour . . . arrived. He looked the ministers square in the eyes and said: "If you men vote to leave Peking tomorrow, the deaths of every man, woman and child in this huge unprotected convoy will be on your heads, and your names will go down to history, and be known for ever as the wickedest, weakest and most pusillanimous cowards who have ever lived."

Early next morning Morrison was at the United States Legation. "Well doctor," said Conger, "how do you feel this morning?"

"I feel ashamed to be a white man," Morrison replied heatedly. "Of all the inhuman, barbarous pusillanimous decrees I have ever heard of, the decision of the eleven ministers yesterday is the worst."

Conger repeated his argument that the Government had offered them safe conduct to Tientsin, and Morrison repeated his rejoinder: "Why have you got the marines here if you trust the Government?"

"Well, doctor, I don't agree with you," said Conger.

"But the world will agree with me," said Morrison.

"Much I care of the opinion of the world," said Conger. He thought Morrison meant the *New York World*.

Pethick agreed with Morrison that a column two miles long proceeding to Tientsin would be very vulnerable. He distrusted the good faith of the Chinese, and thought it all might be a "plant" arranged for their massacre. And where would they get food, water, and transport?

All the ministers were up early that morning, anxiously awaiting an answer from the Yamen. By half-past nine, none had come. They decided to go on waiting; in Sir Claude MacDonald's words, "it would be undignified to go to the Yamen and sit there waiting for the Princess". But von Ketteler, "a very passionate and excitable man", did not agree. He banged his fist on the table and cried, "I will go and sit there till they do come, if I have to sit there all night!" His Chinese secretary, Herr Cordes, was to accompany him. Morrison saw them leave in their sedan chairs, hooded in scarlet and green to show their official status, and accompanied by two liveried outriders. Not many minutes later his boy burst into his office and said, "Any man speakee have makee kill German Minister." Morrison said, "Nonsense!" But it was true. Von Ketteler had been shot at point-blank range by an Imperial bannerman in full uniform. (Just before he was decapitated by German troops six months later, the murderer said reproachfully that he had been promised by his superior officers seventy taels and promotion for the job, but had received only forty taels and no promotion.) Herr Cordes was shot through both thighs and pursued by men with lances, but somehow dragged himself into the American Mission, and fell fainting at the entrance. Ill in hospital, he told his story to Morrison, concluding with these words: "I affirm that the assassination of the German Minister was deliberately planned, premeditated murder, done in obedience to the orders of high government officials. . . ."

There was now no question of leaving Peking. Von Ketteler had emphatically proved his point. During the morning the diplomatic body received a note from the Tsungli Yamen that made no mention of the murder. The Yamen regretted that it would be unsafe for the ministers to make their proposed visit, but granted them an unspecified extension of time. Despite this, at 4 p.m., precisely at the expiration of the original time-limit, heavy firing broke out, directed at the Austrian and French outposts. A French marine fell dead. An Austrian was wounded. A sergeant of the Royal Marines Light Infantry marched up to his commanding officer, Captain B. M. Strouts, and saluted:

"Firing has commenced, sir," he said.

"Thank you, Sergeant Murphy," said Captain Strouts.

The siege of the legations, and of the Roman Catholic Cathedral in the north of Peking, had begun.

[II]

More than two months later, when the siege was over, Morrison dined with Squiers and Baroness von Ketteler:

> She was very sad, talking all the time of her husband, whose death did undoubtedly save the lives of all the ministers. She confirms what I already knew, that Ketteler alone of all the ministers was opposed to the pusillanimous and yet suicidal decision come to by all his colleagues, Sir Claude among them, to leave Peking. De Giers was strongly of this opinion, and professed to believe that China in this matter acted as a civilized power—an act of war had been committed; it was the only course she could follow. Ketteler shrugged his shoulders. Pethick, who was present, said the President of Civil Appoint-

ments, Hsy Fu, had told him there was a plot to murder all the ministers that morning, and the murder of one minister only was a premature accident, deplorable from the Chinese point of view, for it prevented a general massacre.

[III]

Into the three-acre compound of the British Legation, which had a normal population of about sixty human beings, a great number of ponies and mules, a small number of sheep, and a cow, were now thronged about 900 people; the entire foreign community of Peking—except M. Chamot and his American wife, who doggedly remained in their hotel at the other side of the canal—and groups of converts, including 126 Chinese schoolgirls. The British Legation had been chosen as the key points of the defences because it was the largest and least exposed. Morrison was among the last to enter it. Soon after the first exchange of shots, the Austrian Legation, an isolated outpost, had been precipitately abandoned by its garrison. "No sufficient reason has ever been given for its abandonment," Morrison wrote when the siege was over. In his diary for 20th June he wrote: "This involved the sacrifice of all the Customs buildings. Accordingly I had to leave my house. I took my silver, my provisions etc., and went off to the British Legation. Here all the ministers were assembled. There was an immense crowd—missionaries, Catholic, who had left their flocks; Chinese nuns and crowds of Chinese, Customs people, Russian ladies, and others."

Morrison's house lay just on the other side of the Fu. Before it was destroyed he returned to it and worked "very hard" to save all his books, assisted by an eccentric Norwegian missionary, Nestergard (known as "Nearest to God") and a "very cool and brave" Chinese. They had to make many journeys, skipping hurriedly over the little bridge that crossed the canal between the legation and the Fu.

Next day Morrison watched with emotion the destruction of the greatest library in China, and the oldest in the world, the Hanlin Yuan, which stood immediately to the north of the British Legation. Some of its buildings were separated from the legation by only a few feet. A strong wind was blowing right into the legation, and the Chinese saw an opportunity to burn the foreigners out. They set fire to "the most sacred building in Peking . . . centre of all learning". To the rattle of musketry and the roar of flames, Morrison wrote:

> . . . the combustible books, the most valuable in the Empire, were thrown in a great heap into the pond round the summer house . . . a heap of debris, timber in ashes, sprinkled with torn leaves, marked the site of the great library of the Middle Kingdom. Other great libraries, the Alexandrian and in Rome, had been destroyed by the victorious invader, but what can we think of a nation that sacrifices its most sacred edifice, the pride and glory of its country and learned

men for hundreds of years, in order to be revenged upon foreigners? It was a glorious blaze. The desecration was appalling. Noble manuscripts lying untouched on the shelves for centuries were scattered, burned, stolen: tons of splendid editions were in the water hole.

To save the legation it was necessary to dismantle the remaining library buildings. An attempt was made to save the more valuable manuscripts, but few survived. Books carried away as loot were handed to Sir Claude MacDonald, who, after the débâcle of the Austrian Legation, had replaced the Austrian naval captain, von Thomann, as commander-in-chief. While the fire in the Hanlin Yuan was raging, Sir Claude sent a note to the Yamen saying that he had endeavoured to save the books and asking for officials to be sent to supervise the salvage. The note was not answered.

Morrison's indignation at the destruction of the Hanlin Yuan, and at the nation that could commit such sacrilege, is understandable. But he could record without indignation, and without criticism of the nation concerned, this episode of the defence:

> Eighteen prisoners were captured by the French in a temple near the legation. They were soldiers and a Chinese Christian gave information as to their whereabouts. Everyone of them was put to death without mercy in the French Legation, bayoneted by a French corporal to save cartridges. Questioned before death they gave much information that was obviously false. . . .

[IV]

The siege of the legations, as Hollywood has reminded us in a film of egregious absurdity, lasted fifty-five days. But the Hollywood fantasy was really no more improbable than the historical facts. During those fifty-five days a polyglot and loosely knit community which at the outset comprised 473 civilians, a garrison of 409, 2750 native Christian refugees, and some 400 native servants was besieged by Chinese forces, which, had they pressed home the attack determinedly, could quickly have overcome all resistance. The long defence perimeter was poorly fortified; the defenders were poorly armed. They had four pieces of light artillery, including a five-barrelled Nordenfelt that jammed after every four shots, and an Italian one-pounder with 120 rounds. Each national contingent had its own type of rifle, making a pool of ammunition impossible, and the best-equipped had only 300 rounds per man. The attackers, vastly superior in numbers, had no lack of small arms or ordnance. "The Chinese," writes Peter Fleming, "are estimated to have fired 3000 shells and cannon balls into the defences during the siege. There was nothing to prevent them firing a like number each day. If they had, the legations would have become untenable in no time."

Why they did not is one of the great enigmas of the siege. The other is why the lunatic attack was ever launched. As Chester Tan wrote, after studying Chinese sources, "while it is evident that the attack . . . was authorized by the Imperial Court, it is not clear why such an attack should have been made". Victor Purcell agrees with him that the motives were complex, but probably included sheer hatred of the foreigners, the desire to stimulate patriotism, fear of the legation guards, and the need to kill all witnesses of the Court's and the Boxers' misdeeds. What saved the legations was the irresolution and division of the Court. Among the Empress Dowager's advisers was a peace party as well as a war party, and their influence fluctuated as her moods swung from doubt to confidence.

Her original purpose, unquestionably, was to exterminate the foreigners in Peking and the Chinese converts. She had allied herself with the Boxers because of their claims to supernatural powers, but these proved disappointing, and when, on 13th July, Tientsin fell to the allied forces she decided to become more conciliatory. Two days later, to the bewilderment of the besieged, who knew nothing of what was happening beyond their perimeter, an unofficial truce took place that lasted nearly a fortnight and the Chinese began an extraordinary correspondence with the diplomatic body that went on till the end of the siege. During the fantastic period of the truce the Empress Dowager sent cartloads of watermelons, vegetables, ice, and flour to the people she had been trying for weeks to destroy; the garrison bought eggs and even a few rifles from the enemy; a Chinese trumpeter, formerly in Sir Robert Hart's band, whose ear had been half-severed by an irate officer, was admitted blindfolded to the British Legation to be treated by its physician, Dr Poole; sailors rowed up and down the canal on improvised rafts; and, of course, the British played cricket.

In their letters to Sir Claude MacDonald the Chinese expressed their affectionate desire to protect the legations, and repeatedly renewed the polite suggestion that the diplomats, for their own protection, should depart. They also invited the ministers to send telegrams home saying all was well. These letters, to which Sir Claude replied, temperately and equivocally, so as not to antagonize the moderates at Court, were curious enough, but even more remarkable was the correspondence between the Tsungli Yamen and Sir Robert Hart. Having killed a member of his staff, wounded two others, burnt his house with all his official and private papers, and destroyed eighteen buildings in his staff quarters, the Chinese on 22nd July wrote him a courteous letter saying it was more than a month since they had heard from him, and inquiring earnestly about his welfare. This was followed by other letters; one seeking his advice about a delicate Customs problem. Sir Robert replied to each with punctilio and, concerned about his wardrobe, threw a letter over the wall addressed to his tailor in London: "Send quickly two autumn suits and later two winter ditto with morning and evening dress, warm cape, and four pairs of boots and slippers. I have lost everything but am well. We still have an anxious fortnight to weather. Hart, Peking, 5th August 1902."

Despite the interruption of normal communications, the warm clothing arrived on 26th October.

As well as the sartorial Sir Robert, the besieged community had many picturesque members. The Italian Ministry, the Marquis di Salvago Raggi, fastidiously dressed for dinner every night though the *plat du jour* might have been a pony steak, or a ragout of magpie and sparrow. The wife of the United States Minister was a Christian Scientist; when a bullet entered a room crowded with men and women and passed within an inch of a baby's head, she declared that it was only in their "receptive minds" that the bullet existed. Throughout the siege M. Chamot and his young American wife remained in their hotel in an exposed sector of the outer defences, furiously grinding flour and baking 300 loaves a day, as shells crashed through the hotel walls. M. Pichon was the acknowledged clown of the legations. A coward and a chatterbox, he flitted about "nervously and ceaselessly" emitting portentous and gloomy statements: "Nous allons tout mourir ce soir!" "Nous *sommes perdus!*"

Another inveterate pessimist was Robert Bredon, Sir Robert Hart's deputy inspector-general and brother-in-law, known as the "Knight of the Rueful Countenance". Morrison tried to cheer him up by saying: "A siege does not occur to any individual but once in a lifetime. Our lives are marked by few landmarks. Let us, while we live, have a siege that will be recorded in history . . . a siege where half the garrison will perish by the sword and the other half be reduced to the utmost privation by starvation. . . ." Equally spirited was the rebuke administered by Señor Cologan to the Dutch Minister, M. Knobel, who wanted to send an appeasing note to the Tsungli Yamen: "We are writing a page of history. Let us not sully it."

The missionary Nestergard was a tragicomic figure. During a very important operation he appeared on the barricades in a long black cassock and a top-hat, and began to cry loudly for justice, appealing to the Norwegian royal family to clear his maligned name. He could not be silenced, and was led away, gagged and struggling, to the stables, where he continued his protestations. One day he escaped and made his way to Chinese headquarters, where his papers were examined; among them was a letter to the Russian Minister, M. de Giers, in which he apologized for indecently exposing himself to Madame de Giers. Four days later Nestergard was sent back to the legations and admitted that he had told the Chinese all he knew about the state of the defence. Some wanted him shot as a traitor; he was locked up again in the stables.

Morrison messed with the Squiers, and for a few weeks was much better off than most of the besieged. The Squiers had the best stores in the compound: preserved Californian fruits, macaroni, corned beef, tinned beans, anchovy paste, Liebig's extract of meat, and plenty of coffee. But by 25th July, Polly Condit Smith wrote, "this menu was in the dim past". The chief comfort of the Squiers mess then were the "Selzogene bottles", in which enough soda water was made to last the day. Horseflesh and rice had become the staple diet. Each day two of the 150 beautiful racing ponies remaining from the May race-meeting were brought out and shot.

"Dr Morrison is the most attractive at our impromptu mess," Polly wrote. "He works where a strong man is needed, and he is as dirty, happy and healthy a hero as one could find anywhere. . . ." Morrison was less flattering about Miss Smith, whom he described as "fat and gushing". Despite his unfailing outward courtesy, he was often brutally frank about people in his letters and notes: Sir Claude MacDonald was "weak" with "as little wisdom as judgment"; M. Pichon was "a craven-hearted cur"; the Japanese Minister, Baron Nishi, "resembled an anthropoid ape".

[V]

There were frequent unsuccessful attempts to get messages through to Tientsin. One, which Morrison made on the night of 6th July, is of particular interest because the actual document survives. It not only gives a vivid picture of the situation in the legations at that time, but, as Morrison's colleague on *The Times*, J. B. Capper, said, it shows "with how few words . . . a wealth of information can be unambiguously conveyed" by "a master of lucid and condensed telegraphy".

Morrison wrote the message on both sides of a scrap of very thin paper measuring 5 inches by less than 2¼, dipped it in oil to waterproof it, and buried it in an old dish of gruel, which was carried by a young Chinese Christian who was let down over the wall, disguised as a beggar. The boy was stopped and sent back at daybreak through the watergate. Morrison retrieved the message and pasted it in his diary. It read:

> Whoever receives this please forward it by special messenger to E. B. Drew, Esq. Commissioner of Customs Tientsin. I will defray all expenses. Mr Drew will then forward the following telegram to *The Times*, urgent, if necessary.

> *Bland Shanghai Times*
> Since January 20 been besieged by Chinese troops all communications cut isolation complete stop for ten days unable communicate even with Peitang cathedral where Monseigneur Favier priests sisters 3000 Christians in one enclosure guarded by 30 French 10 Italians their position great peril enemy encompassing fire starvation stop Enemy daily shelling British Legation which crowded all foreign ministers women children Christian refugees danger extreme position being commanded from city wall also wall Imperial city working day night desperate efforts strengthen defence barricades sandbags loopholes nightly furious fusillade all quarters bullets thousands one marine killed inside legation stop Italian Dutch Belgian Austrian legations burned French legation abandoned but retaken severely bombarded wall opposite American Legation held by 35 Americans British Rus-

sians stop princes grounds palace east British legation bravely defended by small number Japanese whom seven killed thirteen wounded British two killed also David Oliphant student interpreter of 414 men and 20 officers besieged area 2 officers killed Japanese Ando French Herbert six wounded including Halliday severely doing well 43 men killed 65 wounded civilians five killed including Wagner Frenchman son consul general six wounded stop ammunition carefully husbanded supplies insufficient great anxiety prolonged delay arrival troops we unprovided field pieces general health good Morrison Peking July sixth.

As Capper pointed out, this message is notable not only for its economy but also "for its unconscious disclosure of the strain under which Morrison himself was working—notwithstanding the coolness of his demeanour. For he made the glaring blunder of giving 20th January as the date when the siege began."

After the failure of this attempt, Pokolitov, the Russian financial agent who had arranged the bribing of Li Hung-chang in March 1898, offered $10,000 to any courier who would go and bring back word from Seymour's forces. "Liu, the Frenchman, said he would go," Morrison noted, "if the Father—the eczema-cheeked padre who eats and smokes all day would permit him to deny that he was a Christian if seized and questioned. He was forbidden; a Protestant might do it, a Catholic could not. No one could be induced to go." Morrison disapproved of this unnamed and uncompromising Father, but was full of praise for the foresight and preparedness of Bishop Favier: "How we ridiculed his attempts to purchase all available rifles and ammunition; and his frantic letters! Yet he was more than justified—more. He made no statement that was not understated." On another page of his diary Morrison scribbled: "Missionaries to blame for a good deal of the Boxer trouble."

[VI]

Early in July, Morrison with a committee inspected the Fu, where the refugees were crowded "like bugs in a rug". He found it "stinking and insanitary. . . . Children ill with scarlet fever and small-pox, with diptheria and dysentery." As he wrote this in his "Lett's Rough Diary", he may have read in the front a modest advertisement for Eno's Fruit Salts:

To PREVENT the BILE becoming TOO THICK and impure, producing a gummy, viscous, clammy stickiness or adhesiveness in the mucous membrane of the intestinal canal, FREQUENTLY the PIVOT of DIARRHOEA and DISEASE, ENO'S 'FRUIT SALT' prevents and removes diarrhoea in the early stages.

Without such a Simple Precaution
The Jeopardy of Life is Immensely Increased

[VII]

"The morning of the 16th opened with a disaster," Morrison wrote in his detailed report to *The Times* at the end of the siege. "Captain Strouts, the senior British officer, was shot while returning from the outposts in the Fu . . . and died an hour after being brought into hospital." Morrison did not mention the fact that he, too, was shot while accompanying Strouts. That night, in bed in Sir Claude MacDonald's library, he recorded the full story in his diary:

Monday July 16

This morning early, "are you on for the Fu?" It was Strouts, and raining. He had a cup of tea at the Customs Mess while I slipped on my things, and I went over to him. We crossed by the deep cutting and stone barricade to the south of the Legation and in the Fu kept well under the wall while making our way to the outpost. The wall was pitted with shot and shell. It was difficult to imagine how I could have passed it unhurt yesterday amid that hail of bullets. At the outpost there was not much change. The cutting had been made a little deeper rendering access less dangerous but I observed with alarm that no attempt had been made to heighten the barricades above that I had myself made the other day. Colonel Shiba joined us; then he and I went alone and passed from the cutting along the direction of fire a short distance, then turned up over the brow of the slope into the Japanese trench. Shots were fired at us. We were evidently within view of the barricade not 35 yards away. There we waited while Strouts came along. "Come and see the Japanese line," I said. He replied that he must go back to the Legation. "Then I will go with you," I replied, as I was bound to do, for I had accompanied him across. "And I will go too," said Shiba. We three then descended a few paces into the line of fire and we were walking forward towards the barricades when suddenly I heard some shots, how many I cannot tell, but I think three, and felt a cut in my right thigh. At the same moment, "My God," said Strouts, and he fell over into the arms of Shiba, who was on his left. Then I jumped forward and with Shiba dragged Strouts out of fire, though shots were still coming whizzing by us, and then he lay down while Shiba ran off for the surgeon. In the meantime, I tried to slip my handkerchief round his thigh and stepped out to find a twig to use as a tourniquet. But the result was no good. I could see the fracture and the bone projecting against the trousers. Then Nakagawa (the Japanese Surgeon Captain), came up and we tried to staunch the bleeding by compressing the external iliac. The body was soaking in blood but the poor fellow was conscious and asked me where I was hit. I said mine was unimportant. Then I fainted. In a little while the stretcher-bearers came up and the captain was carried away. Then I walked, but getting faint, was carried into the Legation. Then it was found that another bullet had splintered and some of the fragments struck me.

Poole cut this out and while he did so I fainted again and then vomited, the pain being intense, though I have no reason to think it was one half as great as other pain I have suffered. In the ward, Strouts was brought in. He was dying. He said nothing but by and by gave a few sobs of pain, then his breath came quietly and then he sank away into death.

The day before, Morrison had recorded many remarkable escapes among his companions—escapes "such as must occur when a small body of people are shelled and fired upon from close range": a four pounder round shot had jumped through a window where Mrs Bredon and her daughter, Juliet, were sleeping and fallen harmlessly between them; a captain, holding a bottle of vermouth, had the neck of the bottle whipped off by a bullet; a sergeant had the razor carried out of his hand while he was stropping it; a bullet had passed through Colonel Shiba's coat and another had grazed Captain Strouts's neck.

"Dr Morrison acted as lieutenant to Captain Strouts and rendered most valuable assistance," reported Sir Claude MacDonald in his dispatches. "Active, energetic and cool, he volunteered for every service of danger and was a pillar of strength when things were going badly. By his severe wound on the 16th July, his valuable services were lost to the defence for the rest of the siege."

[VIII]

On the day Morrison was wounded the people of England—or those who bought the *Daily Mail*—read a terrible story. Datelined Shanghai, and headed "The Peking Massacre", it told in harrowing detail how on the night of 6th July the Europeans, battered by heavy artillery fire, had been attacked by wave after wave of Chinese and in the morning, after a desperate stand in the British Legation, wiped out. The cable from the enterprising special correspondent ended: "Thus, standing together as the sun rose fully, the little remaining band, all Europeans, met death stubbornly. The Chinese lost heavily, but as one man fell, others advanced, and finally, overcome by overwhelming odds, every one of the Europeans remaining was put to the sword in the most atrocious manner."

Another newspaper added the picturesque gloss that the men, before being dispatched, had shot their women and children. "We can hardly dare to hope that in substance the reports of the massacre are inaccurate," Mr Brodrick told the House, and next day *The Times* added its solemn imprimatur: "The time has now come when hope must be abandoned. It would be foolish and unmanly to affect to doubt the awful truth." Nor was its own account of the tragedy lacking in first-hand observation: "The Europeans fought with calm courage to the end against overwhelming hordes of fanatical barbarians thirsting for their blood. . . . When the last cartridge was gone their hour had come. They met it like men. . . . They have died as we would have had them die, fighting to the last for the helpless women and children who were to be butchered over their dead bodies."

Morrison's name had never before been mentioned in *The Times*. But now the name of "our devoted Correspondent" was given an honoured place with those of Sir Claude MacDonald and Sir Robert Hart; in the news item, in the editorial, and on the whole page of obituaries. In the editorial *The Times* said:

> Dr Morrison has had so many hairbreadth escapes in the course of his most adventurous life of 38 years, and possessed such infinite resource in moments of emergency, that we cannot quite relinquish the hope that he may possibly have escaped in the confusion of the final slaughter. At any rate, if any European does survive it seems not unlikely to be he. His career is characteristic of one of the best types of colonial Englishmen. A wanderer in strange lands and desert places from his youth up, he had developed by wide and patient observation his remarkable natural powers of insight and of generalization. It is not for us to dwell upon the extraordinary value of the telegrams he sent to this journal in the most critical period of recent history in the Far East. They showed some of the highest gifts of statesmanship in a degree which savoured of genius.

The obituary, which occupied nearly two columns, said:

> No newspaper anxious to serve the best interests of the country has ever had a more devoted, a more fearless, and a more able servant than Dr Morrison. . . . It is not too much to say that throughout the last three critical years in China, it is to Dr Morrison that the British public has looked from day to day for the earliest and most accurate intelligence concerning events in which the interests of this country have been so largely and often, we fear, prejudicially involved. With extraordinary judgment, amounting almost to intuition, in an atmosphere which he used himself to describe as "saturated with lies", he discriminated with unfailing accuracy between what was true and what was false. With never a penny of "secret service" money at his command, his own shrewdness and resourcefulness, his untiring industry, his infinite capacity for taking pains enabled him time and again to transmit important information of which the official confirmation used only to limp in with halting steps two or three days later.

"Of the ladies," said *The Times*, "it is enough to say that in this awful hour they showed themselves worthy of their husbands. Their agony was long and cruel, but they bore it nobly, and it is done. . . . All that remains for us is to mourn and to avenge them." Kaiser Wilhelm was more emphatic in his cry for revenge. He exhorted a contingent about to embark for China in these words: "Just as the Huns a thousand years ago, under the leadership of Attila, gained a reputation by virtue of which they still live in historical tradition, so may Germany become known in such a manner in China, that no Chinese will ever again dare to look askance at a German!" But the dean of St Paul's, Robert Gregory, had a more Christian outlook. In arranging a memorial service for the victims of the massacre he took special care, as a newspaper reported, to avoid those psalms "which seem to breathe a spirit of revenge". The service was to take place on 23rd July, but was cancelled at the last moment when doubts arose about the authenticity of the *Daily Mail* report.

From the University of Liverpool, the Professor of Latin, Herbert Strong, who had taught Morrison classics in Melbourne, wrote to the *Spectator* of the appalling fate of his "old friend and pupil":

> When poor George was 16 years old he came to me and asked would I give him some advice as to the career he was to follow. He was strongly drawn to imitate Stanley and to become an explorer, but he was ready to give up everything if he could only carry out his plan. I entreated him to take his degree and to adopt a profession before starting as an explorer. . . . He was a slim, delicate-looking boy with frank and open looks . . . the most absolutely fearless fellow I have ever met.

In Geelong, Morrison's home town, flags were flown half-mast to his memory.

Arthur Adams, a young Australian war correspondent, was staying with Morrison when a copy of *The Times* arrived containing the premature obituary. "What do you think of this?" Morrison asked. "Well," said Adams, "after two columns in *The Times* and the cheers they gave you, the only decent thing they can do is double your salary."

[IX]

Morrison lay on his bed—the mattress was stuffed with straw from cases of wine—till 8th August, when he went out for the first time, in a chair carried by four coolies, to see Nestergard, who was still yowling in the stables.

It was not till 14th August, almost a month after his wounding, that Morrison was able to walk. Four days before, a messenger had got through the enemy lines with a letter from the British Commander-in-Chief in the Relief Force, General Gaselee. It read: "Strong force of Allies advancing. Twice defeated enemy. Keep up your spirits." The force, moving in four parallel columns, expected to reach Peking within a few days. On 13th August it was at the walls of the city, and the Chinese made a final effort to overwhelm the legation. "For the last two days we had to sustain a furious fusillade and bombardment, and our casualties were many," Morrison wrote. "One shell burst in Sir Claude MacDonald's bedroom."

At three o'clock on the morning of 14th August, Morrison was awakened by "the booming of guns in the east and the welcome sound of volley firing". Word flew round that the relief troops were shelling the East Gate. Morrison, with most of the defenders, hobbled on to the wall to watch the shelling. He had just finished his horse-flesh luncheon when the cry ran out "The British are coming": "The stalwart form of the general and his staff were entering by the Water Gate, followed by the 1st Regiment of Sikhs and the 7th Rajputs. They passed down Canal Street, and amid a scene of indescribable emotion marched to the British Legation. The siege had been raised."

Despite his dislike of missionaries in general, Morrison in a postscript to his report paid generous tribute to "the splendid services" of the Rev. F. D. Gamewell, of the American Episcopal Mission, who as a former engineer had been responsible for the designing and construction of the defences of the British Legation; to the Rev. Frank Norris, of the Society for the Propagation of the Gospel, who had superintended, "often under heavy fire", the construction of other defences; and to Bishop Favier, whose "wonderful foresight" had saved the Christians in the Peitang cathedral from starvation.

With these words Morrison completed what Peter Fleming calls his "lapidary account" of the siege. He posted it off in 108 sheets, comprising about 30,000 words, on 15th August, and it appeared in *The Times* on 14th and 15th October. Written for the most part in a hospital bed under conditions of extreme difficulty, it remains an eminently readable account of those memorable fifty-five days and, considering how fragmentary were the sources, a remarkably accurate one. "Gibbon could not have told the story better. It has been accepted as *the* history of that strange episode," said the *Spectator*. *The Times*, in an editorial, praised Morrison's "transparent impartiality" and added: "In one instance only has he been unjust. He has left us to learn from private sources of the manful part he himself played in the defence, and of the severe wound, which, we regret to hear, still prevents him from walking save with pain and difficulty." Morrison received a telegram from *The Times*, THANKS SPLENDID NARRATIVE, and from Arthur Walter a handwritten eight-page letter of flowery praise:

> So far as my knowledge and judgment go no other correspondent of *The Times* ever did so remarkable a piece of work as your description of the siege of Peking, and no other correspondent ever gained as completely the confidence of the Public as you have done. . . . The service you have rendered to the paper surpassed any expression of value I can use. . . . I am proud . . . to associate the paper with the great reputation you have made for yourself. . . .

London publishers, some of whom had rejected Morrison's manuscript in 1895, now beseeched him to write a book about his experiences. "We have been reading with great interest, as indeed all London has been reading, your accounts of the siege of Peking", wrote Smith Elder, inviting him to put them in a more permanent form, "and we have been recalling your book *An Australian in China*. . . ." Mr J. Everleigh Nash, a literary agent, offered £1000 in advance of royalties for British rights, and £400 advance for American rights. It was a generous offer, but Morrison does not seem to have considered it.

Morrison's diaries record not only the important events of the day; they contain always a seasoning of anecdotes and jokes, some of which suggest that his appreciation of humour did not mature equally with his other faculties. Typical of his more tolerable Boxer anecdotes are:

> Russians looting, ravaging the women in a bandboy's house, when the Chinese seized a cornet and played the Russian national anthem, and at once the soldiers jumped to their feet, and when the notes were finished, saluted and walked out.

> The Australian blue jacket floating down in a junk . . . and his altercation with the Frenchman whom he attempted to draw into the junk with his boathook; and his rage when he failed. Standing at the stern, shaking his fist: "Waterloo, you bastard! Fashoda, you sod."

> Leitch says: "I sent my servant on a message. He was robbed by a Russian, buggered by a Frenchman, killed by a German. In my dismay, I made complaint to a British officer. He looked at me, put his eye-glass into his eye, and said, 'Was he really? What a bore!!' "

But it is curious to find the world-famous correspondent carefully preserving such puerilities as:

> After Oscar Wilde's liberation, it is said the Corporation of Edinburgh passed a resolution to put barbed wire round Arthur's Seat.

> Mrs Hawkins: The Astronomer Royal took her to the Observatory where she saw the Constipation of O'Brien with all the stars sparkling in his fundament.

[XI]

Four days after Peking had been relieved, without any Germans taking part, Field-Marshal Count von Waldersee was appointed Commander-in-Chief of the International Relief Force. The Kaiser had persuaded Russia and France to accept him, though as one of the conquerors of 1870-71 the Count was not popular in France. Nor was he popular when he arrived in China six weeks later, and made up for his belatedness by his brutality and zest for loot.

"An order for a portable asbestos house for the use of Count von Waldersee during the campaign has been given by the German Government to the Calmon Asbestos and Rubber Works," *The Times* announced proudly on 23rd August. "Seven large and comfortably furnished rooms in sections, packed in cases. The order was executed and shipped within a fortnight." But the Count does not seem to have occupied this triumph of prefabrication and British enterprise. Certainly, in the spring of 1901, he was living not under asbestos but in the Imperial Palace, sharing an Imperial bed with a beautiful harlot called Tsai-Chin-hua, but not forgetting to organize looting raids under the name of "punitive expeditions".

Morrison found himself a "lovely" corner house in "Gaselee Road"—running north and south just beyond the western boundary of the enlarged British Legation—which he described as his "Klondyke". It had harboured soldiers of the Imperial army, and digging excitedly in the garden he unearthed two chests containing "gold things of much value, discovered by the said soldiers". In the orgy of looting that followed the Allied occupation of Peking, Morrison's participation was small, but apparently he had no scruples about keeping these "gold things", and when he accompanied the Allied troops on their triumphal entry through the Imperial Palace on 28th August he "succeeded in looting a beautiful piece of jade splashed with gold and carved in the form of a citron, the emblem of the fingers of Buddha". In a later note he added regretfully: "Of no value, having a blemish." But through Colonel Ducat he acquired "the finest piece of jade in Peking", which he sold to Squiers for 2000 taels.

On 17th August, Morrison wired *The Times*:

The Peitang Cathedral was relieved yesterday and Peking is now entirely under foreign control. Looting is proceeding systematically. The French and Russian flags are flying over the best portion of the Imperial domain, where it is believed that the Imperial treasure is buried. The Japanese have seized a hoard amounting according to rumour to half a million taels of silver (about £62,500). The Dowager Empress, the Emperor, Prince Tuan, and all the high officers have escaped to Tai-yueh-fu, in Shansi, whence they will proceed to Sianfu [Sian]. The *Peking Gazette* ceased to appear on 13th. There is no Government.

Characteristically, the British imposed system on the anarchy of individual theft. General Gaselee issued instructions that loot should be collected by organized search parties and auctioned under the direction of a Prize Committee of four officers. His order, dated 17th August, read:

LOOTING: the GOC is aware of the difficulty in restraining the unmilitary practice of looting in a force composed of mixed nationalities. He has now felt obliged to countenance the systematic collection of articles which may be found in unoccupied houses for the benefit of the whole force. In consideration of the temptation to which the troops have been exposed, Sir A. Gaselee directs that all punishments hitherto given for looting may be cancelled.

Colonel Scott Moncrieff superintended the auctions in the British Legation. Morrison thought he might be "better employed at his own duties".

"A spirit of revenge was abroad, the city was in disorder and half abandoned, and it may be questioned whether it was humanly possible to prevent looting in the first place, still less to stop it once it had started," writes Peter Fleming. It may have been difficult to restrain the troops, but, as Mr Fleming admits, "the highest as well as the lowest plundered" and it should not have been impossible for diplomats or their wives and officers to restrain themselves. Lady MacDonald, as a British officer put it, "devoted herself most earnestly to looting", and when Morrison dined with Sir Norman Robert Stewart in the First Brigade Mess, "all condemned the way Sir Claude and Lady MacDonald had looted . . . 185 boxes at least".

From Calcutta, George Curzon, now a peer and Viceroy of India, sent Guy Hillier £1000 "to invest in curios". Mr Squiers told Morrison he was concerned about attacks made by Stephen Bonsal in the *New York Herald* "upon the looting done by an American diplomatist in Peking". A Russian Lieutenant-General, who was rewarded with the Cross of St George for his services, left Peking with ten trunks full of looted valuables from the palaces. An English civilian who, uninvited, accompanied General Gaselee's punitive force to Paotingfu, on a borrowed horse, returned with two horses, four mules, 100 taels, and two carts laden with loot. "Every nationality accords the palm to some other in respect to the act of plundering," Count von Waldersee wrote, "but it remains the fact that each and all of them went in hot and strong for plunder." The damage done by ravage and plunder was incalculable, he said. Describing the British system of auctioning the stolen goods and dividing the prize money among officers and non-commissioned officers, he commented dryly: "Hence it is intelligible that no Englishman sees anything to be shocked at in looting."

On 24th September, Morrison wired *The Times*: "The systematic denudation of the Summer Palace by the Russians has been completed. Every article of value is packed and labelled." He described the destruction of the White Pagoda, which had been the headquarters of the Boxers, as "an unworthy act of vandalism" and sent a "scorching telegram" about the removal from the Imperial Observatory of the world-famous instruments which had been made in France and presented to the Chinese by Louis XIV. Because the observatory stood in the German sector, von Waldersee decided they were to be regarded as "German war-booty", but compromised with a French claim by dividing them between the two powers. Morrison's telegram read:

> In persuance of its regrettable policy of appropriation, the French and German generals, with the approval of Count von Waldersee, have removed from the wall of Peking the superb astronomical instruments which were originally erected by the Jesuit fathers and have been for more than two centuries one of the chief glories of Peking. They are so beautiful that even the Chinese, who wrecked every other evidence of foreigners within reach, left the instruments untouched throughout the recent outbreak. Half of them go to Berlin, though Germany has no possible claim whatever except by the appointment of Count von Waldersee, and half to Paris. This act of vandalism is deeply regrettable. . . .

Morrison considered the French the worst offenders. "Not content with looting," he wrote, "they commandeer the despoiled Chinese to carry the spoils down to the French camp." And he noted: "Dr Smith or someone has written 'The hand of God as evidenced by the siege of Peking.' A companion volume might be written on 'The Hand of Man as evidenced by the emptiness of Peking palaces.' "

All the nations went it "hot and strong" for loot, but the Russians and Germans also distinguished themselves by their savagery. Sir Claude MacDonald was told "awful stories of the cruelties done by the Russians, men murdered, women raped". Morrison lunched with a Chinese teacher who told him that his sister was ravished by Russian soldiers and in consequence seven other members of the family had committed suicide by opium, having first buried their treasure and burnt the house to the ground. "This is a common story."

Morrison repeatedly exposed the brutality of von Waldersee's men. "German expeditions continue to harass the neighbourhood of Peking, mainly in search of loot," he reported on 24th November. "Such raids are incorrectly described in German official communications as important military operations." On 27th December he was engaged "most of the day" drawing up a telegram of 503 words vigorously denouncing the wilful harshness of the Germans. Citing specific instances of their punishing without discrimination the innocent and the guilty and "pillaging systematically people who were already conquered before the Germans arrived in China", he suggested that the British forces should be separated from von Waldersee's command. This telegram enraged the Germans. Morrison was threatened with court-martial: "*The Times* . . . is represented here by a wretched scamp," wrote the indignant von Waldersee. "Mr Morrison . . . probably in true English reporter's megalomania, believes I ought to take notice of him. I am no more impressed by press attacks than by the barking of a dog." But according to Dr A. H. Smith, the attacks brought about some improvement in the behaviour of the Germans. A German war correspondent, Rudolf Zabel, conceded that Dr Morrison was "very objective, ready to expose British excesses committed by the expeditionary forces as well as those of the Germans".

Not only the Germans were displeased by Morrison's dispatches. The Spanish Minister was "furiously angry" at his account of the siege, "especially in its relation of the pusillanimity of the ministers". The Austrian Minister was equally angry because Morrison had reported the defection of the Austrian garrison, and for many years he was not admitted to the Austrian Legation. The Italian Minister repeatedly complained to the British Legation about "the difficult Morrison".

[XIII]

The wrangling over peace terms continued for months. Some of it was semantic, as when the ministers disagreed over the translation into French of the word "comply". The Japanese wished it to be *accepter*, the Germans *remplir*, and the Russians *adhérer*. When Washington instructed Edwin Conger to oppose vehemently the use of the word "irrevocable", he read the cipher message incorrectly and vehemently insisted on using it. And so on.

Much thornier was the problem of indemnities. Here each great power nobly maintained the tradition of loot which its individual representatives, diplomatic and military, had established, and piously criticized the greed of others. Dr von Mumm upbraided the Americans for their iniquitous demand. "They had only 1700 men," he said to Morrison, "and undertook to charge only the increased cost of keeping them here instead of Manila. To charge £5,000,000 was monstrous." Squiers agreed. He thought the Americans had made a "deplorable blunder". (Yet when China's total debt was finally, in some arcane fashion, fixed at £67 million America alone tried to have it reduced by more than a third.) Von Mumm also condemned the large British claim— £6,500,000 with private claims for £2 million more. The Italians claimed nearly £3 million, including £80,000 for the reconstruction of the legation, the market value of which was £5000. Morrison estimated, in a telegram to *The Times*, that England's claim, if made on the relative strength of her forces and Italy's would amount to £25 million.

On 21st July, Morrison noted that the orders of the American Secretary of State, Hay, to the new American Minister, W. W. Rockhill, all the time were "For God's sake, finish it, settle it, we are tired of it." Rockhill confessed to Morrison that the work was beyond the powers of the ministers and should be transferred to the first brains of Europe.

Mr Hiram Parkes Wilkinson, son of the Chief Justice of Her Majesty's Supreme Court for China and Korea, was appointed British Claims Commissioner. To him Morrison addressed a claim which Sir Claude MacDonald described as "flippant", but which, despite its lighthearted tone, was as seriously concerned with hard cash as the much-criticized claims of the powers. The claim was for £5804 10s. 3d., "for losses inflicted on me by Imperial and other soldiers, and Boxers, acting under the commands of their Imperial Majesties, the Emperor and Dowager Empress of China". Items included the burning of Morrison's freehold house of twenty-six rooms, "situated in the most aristocratic portion of Peking", £1500; "a valuable and irreplaceable collection of photographs, collected to illustrate a book already ordered", £515; a valuable collection of books on China, £484 10s.; valuable furniture, fittings, embroideries and curios, "the collection of many years", £417 18s. 6d., and "six Chinese costumes purchased for Phil May, Esq., an artist", £7 15s.:

> And finally being cruelly shot in the right thigh while walking in the grounds of His Highness Prince Su on June 16, 1900, such injury being inflicted by an Imperial soldier obeying the commands of their Imperial Majesties whom God preserve (till this claim is settled) such injury causing me to remain in bed till 15 August and since interfering

with my work as a correspondent and leaving a cicatrice which causes me much pain and for the shock and mental anguish which I have endured from this wound, £2625.0.0.

Your Excellency will see at once what a reasonable sum I have assessed the damages due to my property and the injuries done to my person.

[XIV]

From H. A. ("Taffy") Gwynne, Reuter's representative in South Africa, who had known Morrison in Peking, came a flattering report on the prowess of the Australian contingent—in war and peace:

> Your countrymen have been splendid. . . . They have made brother Boer run and altogether have shown themselves to be the pick of the world. I have often spoken to them of you and I always tell them the future Prime Minister of the Commonwealth will be G. E. Morrison. You have got a young shit coming to the Legation. His name is Vaughan and you have only to look at him to sum him up. Still he talks as well as any other diplomatic mechanical toy. . . . [John Charles Tudor St Andrew-Vaughan, who had been political secretary to Lord Roberts, was on his way to Peking to become 2nd Secretary.] This is a splendid country for f - - - - - g. [Gwynne's coy spelling.] The Australians have shown the way in laying down the keels of young Australians. . . .

[XV]

Morrison celebrated his thirty-ninth birthday—4th February 1901—in a mood of restlessness and dissatisfaction: "Damnably dull and sick beyond measure of being in Peking." He was worried too, about his weight—186lb, "being one stone too much".

At the beginning of May he was still unsettled and discontented, "feeling how poor is my position and how unpromising my prospects". This mood no doubt coloured his comments on some of his associates, particularly on Reginald Thomas Tower, who had succeeded Bax-Ironside as Secretary of the British Legation, and because he was very tall, very thin, and very fatuous, was known as "The Tower of Babble". One day Morrison wrote the word "Tower" in his diary, and left a blank space with this inscribed diagonally across it: "This vacant space is emblematic of the advantages an intelligent man derives from conversation with this poor pigeon-breasted diplomat." Of Tower's habit of falling asleep at formal dinners, he wrote, "People were not sorry, preferring Tower asleep to Tower orating." (Tower subsequently had a distinguished diplomatic career, serving in Siam, Bavaria, Mexico, the Argentine, Paraguay, and Danzig. He was created K.C.M.G. in 1911.)

CHAPTER SEVEN

[I]

WHILE THE aftermath of the Boxer unpleasantness was being tidied up, the Empress Dowager and her Court rested discreetly at Sian, capital of the mid-western province of Shenshi. The peace treaty was signed, after tortuous negotiations, on 7th September 1901, and on 24th October the Court began its 700-mile journey back to Peking. From Sian, on the Yellow River, to the railway terminus at Chengtingfu, a distance of about 250 miles, the Imperial party travelled in yellow sedan chairs, escorted by a huge bodyguard of cavalry, an enormous suite of officials, eunuchs, servants, and a baggage-train of some 3000 gaily flagged and caparisoned carts. It was a spectacle and a moment of history that gave Morrison unexampled scope. In his long report to *The Times* he deployed all his powers of observation, description, and sardonic comment:

> Every Manchu Prince had a retinue of horsemen varying from thirty to a hundred in number; along the frost-bound uneven tracks which serve for roads in Northern China, an unending stream of laden wagons creaked and groaned through the short winter's day, and on, guided by soldier torch-bearers, through bitter nights to the appointed stopping places. But for the Empress Dowager and the Emperor, with the Chief Eunuch and the ladies of the Court, there was easy journeying and a way literally made smooth. Throughout its entire distance the road over which the Imperial palanquins were borne had been converted into a smooth, even surface of shining clay, soft and noiseless under foot; not only had every stone been removed, but as the procession approached gangs of men were employed in brushing the surface with feather brooms. At intervals of about ten miles well-appointed rest-houses had been built, where all manner of food was prepared. The cost of this King's highway, quite useless, of course, for the ordinary traffic of the country, was stated by a native contractor to amount roughly to fifty Mexican dollars for every eight yards—say, £1000 a mile—the clay having to be carried in some places from a great distance. As an example of the lavish expenditure

of the Court, and its officials, in a land where squalor is a pervading feature, this is typical.

From Chengtingfu to Peking, the Empress, for the first time in her life, travelled by train. Four freight trains crammed with her less important possessions preceded her special train, which consisted of a locomotive and twenty-one carriages, including nine freight cars laden with servants, sedan chairs, carts, mules, etc; the Empress Dowager's and the Emperor's special carriages; special carriages of the young Empress and the Imperial Concubine; a first-class carriage for the Chief Eunuch, and two second-class carriages for the eunuchs in attendance:

> The special carriages had been prepared at great expense under instructions issued by the Director-General of Railways, Sheng [Hsuanhuai]. Those of the Empress Dowager, the Emperor, and his consort, were luxuriously furnished with costly curios and upholstered in Imperial yellow silk; each had its throne, divan and reception room. . . .

* * * * *

To the native spectators, the ladies of the Court with their eunuch attendants were as much objects of interest as the foreign railway officials; the Imperial Concubine, 'Chin' (or 'Lustrous') Kuei-fei, a lively young person of pleasing appearance, attracting much attention. This lady, gaily clad and with lavishly painted face, bestowed upon everything connected with the train an amount of attention which augurs well for the future of railway enterprise in China, running from car to car and chatting volubly with the ladies-in-waiting. All the ladies of the Court wore pearls in profusion—those of the Empress being particularly fine—and all smoked cigarettes in place of the time-honoured water-pipe. Herein again, for the optimistically inclined, may be found a harbinger of progress.

* * * * *

An incident occurred at Paotingfu which throws a strong side-light upon the Empress Dowager's character. The high Chinese officials who travelled in the first-class carriage between the Emperor's special car and that of the Empress, finding themselves somewhat pressed for space, consulted the railway officials and obtained another first-class compartment, which was accordingly added to the train. Her Majesty, immediately noticing this, called for explanations, which failed to meet with her approval. The extra carriage was removed forthwith, Yuan Shih-k'ai and his colleagues being reluctantly compelled to resume their uncomfortably crowded quarters

* * * * *

The Empress Dowager possesses in a marked degree a characteristic frequently observed in masterful natures: she is extremely superstitious. The soothsayers and astrologers of the Court at Peking enjoy no sinecure; on the other hand, more attention is paid to their advice than that which the average memorialist obtains, and the position of necromancer of the Throne is not unprofitable. On the present occasion sages-in-ordinary had fixed the auspicious hour for the Sovereign's return to Peking at 2 p.m. on January 7th. . . . To do this, as the engineer-in-chief pointed out, would entail starting from Paotingfu at 7 a.m., but the determined ruler of China was not to be put off by any such considerations. At 6 a.m. this wonderful woman arrived at the station; it was freezing hard, and the sand storm was raging violently; soldiers bearing lanterns and torches led the way for the chair-bearers, since the day had not yet dawned. . . .

* * * * *

The Empress Dowager, reverently welcomed by the Emperor, who had preceded her, as usual, entered the city, from which she had fled so ignominiously eighteen months before, at the hour named by her spiritual advisers as propitious. Present appearances at Peking, as well as the chastened tone of Imperial Edicts, indicate that the wise men were right in their choice. It may be added, in conclusion, as a sign of the times that the Empress Dowager's sleeping compartment, prepared under the direction of Sheng Hsuan-huai, was furnished with a European bed. *Per contra*, it contained also materials for opium smoking, of luxurious yet workmanlike appearance.

It is interesting to compare one of Morrison's set pieces, such as that from which these passages have been taken, with his brief notes written immediately after an event. Here are extracts from his diary entry for 29th April 1902:

This morning went along to the Chien-men to see the Return of the Court . . . waited for hours. Huge crowds of Chinese. Huge numbers of carts came. After interminable wait soldiers with band marching well, lancers on Australian horses bought from the Germans (it gave me rather a shock to see the horses with such riders. It is a plague of locusts.) Then the Emperor. Prince Su in his new yellow jacket. Temple in the N.W. corner pathway spread with yellow sand. Priests finely apparelled. Chair outside, yellow, not richly upholstered. Emperor passing out side tray with spittoon etc. Then out walking to the temple with some dignity never looking up very hollow cheeks long sad face very weak and narrow chested. Stayed inside only a moment then out and into the chair. Very simply dressed like any Chinese gentleman. Then having gone there came with great pomp the procession. . . . She came to same place but was carried inside gate small temple, room just being sufficient. Much grander chair covered with peacock feathers. She looking up went inside and prayed. Came out attendants round her she waved them back. An umbrella brought forward she waved it back. Then standing out enshrined stood alone and looked up to us. Curious sight. Well dressed

Manchu headdress. Uncoloured with missing teeth. Brave and undeterred. Unprepossessing face. Could not but admire courage a woman facing the curious crowd motley crowd of a dozen nationalities on the wall. Everyone showed respect but still there was a democratic friendliness and familiarity in her attendants that was striking. Then she got into her chair and passed on without going to the other temple where an equally large crowd of spectators on the wall awaited her. So home in the dust.

"Along the well-worn path of international jealousies," as J. O. P. Bland and Edmund Backhouse put it, "unpunished and even welcomed", the Empress returned to Peking: "Already the horrors of the siege, the insults and the arrogance of 1900, were forgotten; already the representatives of the powers were prepared, as of old, to vie with each other in attempts to purchase Chinese favour by working each against the other."

Very soon the ladies of the diplomatic corps were gratefully enjoying the hospitality of the Palace. At a reception in the Pavilion of Tranquil Longevity, Señora Cologan, as the wife of the doyen of the corps, presented a flowery address to "welcome her Imperial Majesty back to her beautiful Capital". At another reception Mrs Conger, the wife of the American Minister, and her Japanese friend, Mrs Nehada, lay down side by side on the Empress's bed. The Emperor placed his hand on one lady's bosom, and a young eunuch raised the skirt of another. The Empress passed round American cigarettes and said she would like to have given each guest a puppy but the Boxers had killed them all. However, she gave each child $100. It was all very nice.

[II]

Among the student interpreter recruits to Sir Robert Hart's establishment in 1902 was Willard Straight, a tall blond twenty-two-year-old American "with an eager mind, a talent for drawing, and a lively taste for good company". At Cornell, from which he had graduated the year before, he had been greatly influenced by the Professor of History, Henry Morse Stephens, an Anglo-Indian by descent, with a great love of Asian culture. Stephens persuaded Straight to abandon his idea of becoming an architect and accept the appointment in Peking. Here he was quickly befriended by Morrison, for whom he formed a warm regard.

Morrison, who was now thinking of writing a book titled *The Experiences of a Times Correspondent in the Far East*, commissioned Straight to make drawings from photographs to illustrate it. "He talked much of himself as he works", Straight wrote in his diary. "Regretted he could not write—it was very difficult for him. Hard for him to accomplish anything, he said. . . . It seems almost too good to be true that I should be working with such a man. The only thing I fear is that one who is such a tireless worker will never have time to do this outside work, and for this reason the book will never be written."

The fear was well founded. The book was never written, though nine years later Morrison began—but did not finish—a book of reminiscenses.

Straight, greatly impressed by Morrison's "immense political influence" and background knowledge ("more even than the I.G. himself") set down his impressions of Morrison at the age of forty:

> He is a most charming man to meet—in appearance, stocky, with sloping shoulders and big head, though a short neck supports it. His features are very pleasant indeed, regular and clean-cut, eyes blue-grey and twinkling, and a strange wandering smile plays about the corners of his mouth. His hair is never brushed or at least, if it is, never looks it. He has a happy faculty of getting acquainted with every one, and what is more to the point, finding out all about them without telling anything about himself. . . .

One night in October 1902, Straight had dinner with John Otway Percy Bland, Irish author and journalist, and later co-author of *China Under the Empress Dowager*, who had joined the Imperial Customs Service in 1883 and been Sir Robert Hart's private secretary for two years, resigning in 1896 to become Secretary to the Municipality for the Foreign Settlements in Shanghai. From 1897 to 1907, he represented *The Times* in Shanghai. The ingenuous Straight was shaken by the table talk. His heart shrivelled within him, he wrote, as he heard "tale after tale of the rogueries of American officials in the East, of the bribery, of a consul and a group of missionaries, such things of Americans, of the great, the proud home of the Eagle, such rotten corruption by the representatives of one's native land, was enough to make me wish for an absolute despotism that the stable might be cleansed."

Morrison was equally disturbed by the corruption of the Chinese. On the second anniversary of the Boxer uprising—an anniversary celebrated by a Siege Dinner in the Peking Club, at which the dishes included *Shell Fish*, *Filet de Cheval à la Commissariat Mule*, *Mine de glace internationale*, and *Barricades de gelie*—he wrote:

> What hope is there for China? None at all. Is there any improvement? None at all. No attempt at reform. The officials in power now are as stiffnecked and reactionary as those that brought about the Boxer convulsion. Sheng the most enlightened is the most obstructive of all. He plays only for his own hand. Let the country go hang provided he makes money! [Sheng Hsuan-huai, the economic and commercial lieutenant of Li Hung-chang, had amassed a huge fortune through his control of railways, telegraphs, and shipping.]

But however profound his inner disillusion, Morrison's dispatches to *The Times* never revealed it. He continued to express an optimism about China which he did not feel, and which Chirol did not share. Chirol continued to alter his dispatches, and the gulf between the two widened from day to day. Morrison was particularly angry about the emasculation of a dispatch dated 26th February 1902. In his diary that day he wrote: "Sent a stirring telegram *re* Germans in Shantung which I hope to Heaven may arouse attention in England to the folly of directing our attention to Manchuria to the exclusion of other provinces. . . ."

Morrison discussed the text with the Acting Chinese Secretary, Charles William Campbell, who agreed that the Germans were evidently "going to play for all it's worth the murder of Ketteler". Morrison argued that if Britain could stop the Germans in Shantung she would get some credit from the Chinese and perhaps the compensation of a railway to the Yangtze. But when the telegram appeared he could not recognize it. "I feel acutely and bitterly hurt and chagrined," he wrote. "God forgive me!" From Chirol came a letter explaining why the message had been toned down. *The Times* had to walk warily. The danger of some combined action on the Continent was more acute than it had ever been. Till the South African war was over, Britain had to cut her coat according to the cloth, etc.

Morrison's repute is well shown by a telegram he received on 2nd February 1902 from Major Alfred Wingate, head of the British Intelligence Department in North China, then stationed in Tienstin:

> THERE IS A MAN HERE WHO STATES HE HAS IMPORTANT INFORMATION ABOUT FAR EASTERN AFFAIRS TO COMMUNICATE WE ARE UNABLE TO JUDGE ITS VALUE STOP YOU ARE IN A POSITION TO DO SO STOP GENERAL CREAGH WILL BE GLAD IF YOU CAN COME HERE MONDAY AND WILL PUT YOU UP WIRE REPLY.

General Moore O'Creagh was a Victoria Cross veteran of the Afghan War of 1879-80 who had taken part in the China Expedition two years before. Morrison was always willing to help British Intelligence, though he had a very unflattering opinion of it. When Captain A. W. Brewster, the United States military attaché, called on him in November 1902 he described his visitor as "a man almost dull and stupid enough to be a member of the British Intelligence Service". He was little more complimentary about Sir Ernest Satow, successor to Sir Claude MacDonald (who had become British Minister in Japan), a distinguished Oriental scholar who had spent much of his life in diplomatic posts in the Far East. To Morrison, in splenetic mood, he was a "selfish old dryasdust who uses me and gives me nothing in return but frequent bad dinners. . . ."

On the boat to Port Arthur in August he met a very voluble French champagne salesman who told him that the Russian Customs at Vladivostok had seized all his English books—Darwin, Spencer, Morley and Carlyle—and that the Tsar was a confirmed onanist whose Polish mistress complained that he had never touched her in twenty-five years. In the Hotel de France, the proprietress, a Frenchwoman, came into Morrison's room in the morning and offered herself for one rouble. "Much cheaper than the Americans," she said, "because I do not drink."

Throughout the year Morrison's health had been poor. In December he received permission from *The Times* to take a holiday in Australia. Before he left, Major George Fielding Menzies, a nephew of Burke, the Australian explorer, wrote to him from Tientsin: "Bless you for all your kindness. . . . I always feel that I owe much of the interest you take in me to the memory of my uncle. My endeavour shall be to prove worthy of that interest. . . . Please raise your hat for me, to the tall statue of Burke, and express your hope that his nephew may one day do some action worthy of his uncle." Menzies, who had been on the staff of the China Expeditionary Force in 1900, was then serving in the Chinese Army, at the request of Yuan Shih-k'ai. Morrison regarded him as "a maddening bore" and rated him high in the table he drew up of China's most lethal bores. "No wonder my nose bleeds when Menzies is in the house," he wrote.

Morrison arrived in Sydney Harbour early on the morning of 22nd January 1903, to face a tiresome barrage of reporters and photographers. At breakfast next day A. B. ("Banjo") Paterson, the Australian war correspondent and poet, who had just become editor of the *Evening News*, called with the news from England, privately cabled, that the foreign situation was "critical". But more critical to Morrison was the situation with a beautiful German woman who had been one of Germany's most distinguished actresses and was married to a prosperous but rather stolid German merchant in Sydney. Her earlier relations with Morrison are obscure, but apparently they had been lovers, ("for years she was my *intimate* friend," Morrison wrote in 1911) and soon found opportunities to resume the old intimacy, despite her "silly, half-witted husband", as Morrison ungenerously described him. Morrison took a room at the Metropole Hotel, and for two successive days entertained her in it, cabalistically recording their reunion thus:

> 22 January   X X X
> 9.30 a.m.
> 11.30 a.m.
> 6 p.m.
>
> 23 January   X X
> 11.30 a.m.
> 3 p.m.

Morrison's appetite for scandal was well flattered by his Australian hosts. In Victoria he spent a night at Government Cottage, Macedon, as the guest of the Governor, Sir George Clarke (later Lord Sydenham), an old soldier and defence authority. Macedon is about forty miles from Melbourne, and Sir George complained about having to live so far away: "It is a political job," he explained. The Premier of Victoria, the Hon. William McCulloch, rented the cottage for the Government from the owner, Richard Wagner, who was McCulloch's son-in-law. "A better and more convenient Government House could have been got nearer Melbourne for £200 per annum less," said His Excellency, gloomily. He told

Morrison that the prestige of *The Times* in Australia was immense and urged them to send out a correspondent. Buckle, he said, was "very parochial and narrow to a degree". Sir George, Morrison noted, was "a thick-set man of considerable ability, though a poor speaker". Lady Clarke was a "white-haired, majestic, with a gubernatorial smile displaying long white teeth".

Madame Melba was singing triumphantly in her native town, and Morrison was told by another of his hosts, R. S. Smythe, whose son, Carlyle, was a music and dramatic critic, that she was "a really bad woman":

> Her earnings princely but her extravagance knows no bounds. Since she landed in Australia, she made £30,000. She is exploiting little Miss Clarke, the Governor's daughter. Miss Clarke goes behind the scenes is received by Melba who sends her carriage to the station. Yet Melba drinks and uses foul language and at her table permits a ribald conversation that would shock any decent woman. The Governor ought not to let his daughter be on terms with Melba.

In Sydney he heard "always the same story—the corruption of our public men, especially Barton who ought never to have been Premier". The Rt Hon. Sir Edmund Barton, G.C.M.G., P.C., K.C., and M.A., was then Australia's first Prime Minister. He appears in later editions of *Who's Who* also as a recipient of the Order of the Rising Sun, a freeman of the City of Edinburgh, Hon. D.C.L.(Oxon.), Hon. L.L.D.(Cantab. and Edin.), Fellow of the Senate of University of Sydney, and Senior Puisne Judge, High Court of Australia. To Morrison, Barton was described by an eminent Sydney citizen, Norman Pope, of Farmer's, as "a drunkard, and a man of low life who never pays his debts". Another distinguished states-man, Sir George Reid, was always in financial difficulties because he had to maintain two establishments: his wife was in Sydney, his mistress and her son in England. One of the most brilliant politicians in the colony, Bernhard Ringrose Wise, a former president of the Oxford union, was "so crooked that he can get no credit anywhere". And drunkenness in public life was almost as common as corruption.

Morrison turned from the squalor and venality of Sydney politics to renew his acquaintance with an intellectual and civilized Australian, Alfred Deakin, then Attorney-General in boozy Barton's Government. Deakin, who was "very pleasant and complimentary", said the year 1903 would possibly be fraught with peril for the Empire, and for that reason the British Government was anxious to send Kitchener quickly to India so that he might be prepared in the event of trouble with Russia.

At the end of his Australian diary Morrison made a few random notes on the Australian scene. There was a shop adjoining Melbourne's Federal Palace Hotel where portmanteaux were hired for the night to intending "visitors". The commonest phrase in Australia was "Well, I don't mind if I do." When the Duke of York—the future George V—was paraded through Sydney at the inauguration of the Commonwealth, "no enthusi-asm could be roused for the little bandy-legged sickly Prince".

The Anglo-Japanese agreement, which Morrison had discussed sympathetically with Hayashi Tadasu two years before, was signed on 30th January 1902. Born of a common fear of Russia, it bound Great Britain and Japan to support each other in the event of a third power joining in any war in which either was engaged, and piously affirmed the independence of China and Korea. In effect, it assured Japan a free hand with which to fight Russia, and acknowledged her pre-eminence in Korea. Sir Ernest Satow, the British Minister at Peking, told Morrison that he knew nothing of the agreement till he received the text from Japan twelve days after it had been signed. "What an astonishing thing," Walter Townley, then acting chargé d'affaires, said to Morrison, "that the Anglo-Japanese treaty should have been concluded without consulting Satow or informing him!" But the antics of the British Foreign Office had long ceased to astonish Morrison. "N.B. This is the view that occurs to the Chinese," he noted. "Suppose Russia be driven forcibly out of Manchuria by Japan, a military feat which is regarded as well within Japanese power, will Japan remain in possession of the territory so occupied?" It was a prescient fear, but in spite of it Morrison was convinced that Japan should defeat Russia. His desire for war became obsessive, and he thought that Britain should encourage Japan, "knowing that a victory over Russia would enormously diminish Russian prestige in Asia and give a corresponding increase to British". But Britain was restraining Japan and urging her to resolve Russo-Japanese differences by diplomatic action. Her policy seems to have been to maintain peace for the sake of British trade. *The Times*, too, supported a policy of peace, and to his gnawing discontent Morrison's belligerence was constantly damped in Printing House Square.

Chirol wrote to Morrison in May 1903 saying that he had shown up Russian diplomacy "even more effectually perhaps than on former occasions" and that, even in official circles, no faith was put in Russian denials or assurances. But, formally, they had to be accepted unless action was to follow words. And action was out of the question. The Boer War had greatly taxed Britain's resources and—this was "extremely confidential"—Kitchener had told Chirol that he wanted two years of peace before he could confidently take the Indian army into the field.

Chirol said they must therefore do their best to prevent Japan precipitating a crisis. "I should be very sorry to give encouragement to the idea that Japan was eager for war," he wrote. He agreed with Morrison that war was inevitable and that Japan would win. But as St Augustine said when he prayed for continence, he did not want it too soon. He explained that he had written at length because he wanted Morrison to understand why his dispatches were toned down. Despite his chief's policy of pacification, Morrison continued to work for war. At every opportunity he encouraged Japan to challenge Russia, and he became a much-hated man in Russian circles.

On 28th April 1903, Townley showed Morrison a letter from Lieutenant-Colonel Charles Merewether Ducat, British military attaché in Peking, in which Ducat presented evidence that Russia was preparing for war, which she would force on Japan in the autumn, before it was too late to crush her. Townley obligingly sent the letter to the Japanese. When Henry Cockburn came for lunch at the end of July, Morrison told him that the British Government did not realize the gravity of the position. He found his guest "very nervous, weak and irresolute" and commented in his diary: "Chinese secretary paid £1200 per annum, he has never had a Chinaman in his house." And Ducat, he thought, was "hopelessly incompetent". Here are typical extracts from Morrison's diary towards the end of the year:

> *3 November 1903*—Wrote a long letter to Bland harping still on the same subject the much desired war saying if there is no war I will repine that my whole work in China has been a failure.
>
> *17 November*—Lady Susan [Townley] said: "If there is a war, it will be your doing!"
>
> *18 November*—Feel today greatest elation for war seems assured.

When the Chefoo correspondent of the *Asahi* of Osaka published a four-column interview with Morrison, "breathing war", Morrison asked his diary: "What will *The Times* think?" A few weeks later, on 28th December, after another of his dispatches had been butchered, he wrote: "There wasn't the smallest evidence that *The Times* realizes the importance of the Far Eastern crisis! No excuse for it! Will there be war? Pray God there may be!"

In August, at Weihaiwei, Morrison breakfasted with Admiral Sir Cyprian Bridge, Commander-in-Chief of the China station, on his flagship H.M.S. *Alacrity*. Sir Cyprian "seemed not to have considered the possibility" of war between Russia and Japan, and admitted he was badly informed. "What can one do in the face of such ignorance?" Morrison wrote. It is not surprising that Sir Cyprian was badly informed. On 5th February 1904, three days before the war began, Sir Claude MacDonald assured Lionel James it would never occur.

In the midst of these alarums, Morrison read *Anna Lombard*, by Victoria Cross, which he thought "the most immoral work" he had ever read (it is still banned in the Republic of Ireland); had a curious dream ("my Premiership of Australia") and learned that Tom Dayton, son of a former British Consul in Shanghai, had accepted an appointment at $200 a month as chucker-out to a syndicate of brothels outside Peking. ("His duties consist of being at hand when American and other foreign soldiers endeavour to break their way into proscribed houses.")

"You have been the true prophet," Edwin Conger said to Morrison on 6th February 1904. "We shall look to you in the future." Two days later, without bothering about the formality of declaring war, Japanese torpedoboats attacked the Russian fleet off Port Arthur, as forty years later Japanese bombers would attack the American fleet in Pearl Harbour. These were "joyful tidings" to Morrison, who could "hardly write with excitement". Though he did not know it, President Theodore Roosevelt was equally delighted. The Japanese, he said, were "playing our game". The United States, Great Britain, and Japan had a common purpose in protecting their monopoly of foreign trade in Manchuria against Russian penetration, and Roosevelt had actually thought about war with Russia, "her attitude towards all nations, including us . . . being grossly overbearing", he wrote to his son, two days after the attack on Port Arthur. A monstrous aspect of the Russo–Japanese war, which did not seem to perturb either Roosevelt or Morrison, was that it was fought on Chinese territory—the territory of a neutral and supposedly sovereign power. And neither was concerned with the cost in human lives. As Roosevelt wrote in 1902, he was not "in the least sensitive about killing any number of men if there is adequate reason."

[V]

While Chirol was discouraging Morrison's warmongering, Moberly Bell was busy preparing for war. Towards the end of 1903 he told Lionel James to be ready to go to the Far East at a moment's notice. James, the thirty-two-year-old son of an old Bengal gunner, had been special correspondent for Reuter's in the Chitral campaign, in the Malakand and Tirah campaigns, and in the Sudan. He joined *The Times* in 1899 as special correspondent in South Africa, and was attached to Lord Roberts's staff.

James sailed for the Far East, on 23rd December 1903. He travelled across the Atlantic on the *Majestic*, because the American inventor, Lee de Forrest, was on board, and James wanted to discuss with him secretly the installation of two wireless stations to cover the war: a receiving station on the China coast and a transmitter on a chartered boat. The land station was to be operated by David Fraser, a dour-looking Scot who had begun life as a bank clerk and had fought with Lumsden's horse in the Boer War. To keep rivals off the scent, Fraser travelled second-class as James's "valet".

De Forrest's "wireless machine", capable of receiving at the rate of forty to fifty words a minute, was then the most efficient of the various systems, and he agreed enthusiastically to equip the two stations for £250. By the end of February 1904, Fraser was established at the British concession of Weihaiwei, and James had chartered the fast 1200-ton steamer *Haimun* (she could do sixteen knots) for £1500 a month. She carried five European officers and a crew of forty-four Chinese and Malays. The total running cost was £2000 a month, and Moberly Bell later calculated gloomily that its new-fangled wireless messages cost *The Times* 20s. a word. For a paper struggling desperately to survive, the cost of covering the war was, as the *History of The Times* puts it, "almost unbearable". Bell had mobilized a great team of correspondents, including "experts" such as General Sir Alexander Tulloch, a veteran of the Crimea, India, China, Egypt, Spain, and Africa, who also had been military adviser to the Australian colonies, and Captain Colquhoun, of the Australian Navy.

Morrison resented his role of wet-nurse to these newcomers. "I have become a kind of exchange clerk and I will not submit to it," he wrote. But he was always amiable towards James, whom he regarded as a "good simple, hot-tempered impatient self-willed able man".

In Tokyo, the *Haimun* venture was opposed on various grounds by the American Minister, the British Minister, and *The Times* man in Tokyo, Captain Brinkley; by Major-General Ian Hamilton, India's military representative with the Japanese forces, who regarded all correspondents as a curse; by all the other correspondents, who resented James's technical advantage; and by Sir Cyprian Bridge, who thought James was committing a flagrant breach of neutrality.

Though he did not know it, Sir Cyprian was right. James, a man of great enterprise, having persuaded Bell to back his wireless scheme, persuaded the Japanese naval authorities to put on board the *Haimun* a Japanese officer who, while pretending to be his interpreter, would also be his censor, and an Intelligence officer for Admiral Togo's Grand Fleet. In short, he very improperly offered Japanese Intelligence the unqualified use of his ship in exchange for the opportunity to get scoops for his paper. It was a dangerous transaction, as James realized one day when a Russian cruiser ordered the *Haimun* to heave-to. If the Japanese officer, who was disguised as a Malay steward, had been detected, the *Haimun* would have been seized as a prize of war, and James would have faced a Russian court-martial as a spy.

The Times got very little from its bold experiment. The equipment broke down frequently, and even when it worked, Japanese censorship and restrictions reduced James to impotence. Nor did the other correspondents fare better. Bell was "dreadfully disappointed. . . . The Japs have simply bottled the news, and draw it off at their own will," he wrote to Morrison.

In an effort to break the deadlock, James asked Morrison to plead his case in Tokyo:

Morrison's name was one to conjure with in the Far East and his influence was not nugatory in Japan. . . . He . . . was the close friend, both of Sir Claude Macdonald . . . and of General Fukushima, who from our journalistic point of view was the actual Machiavel of the Japanese General Staff. Over and above the considerations, he was possessed of a sound and almost uncanny judgment and was imperturbable in debate. . . .

At the end of June, Morrison accompanied James to Tokyo, where most of the correspondents, similarly frustrated, had been idling in the bars and bordellos for six months or so; but even his prestige, judgment, and imperturbability could not prevail against the obduracy of a Japanese Army intoxicated with swift victories. As they parted at Yokohama, Morrison said: "James, you have made a great fight of it. As far as I can see you have against you the Japanese General Staff; the British Minister; all the press correspondents; Brinkley; and the Foreign Department of *The*

Times as well. Make your peace with the Almighty, because if He turns against you, you are forever damned."

The charter of the *Haimun* was surrendered, and James awaited permission to join one of the columns moving on Port Arthur. Morrison was to have landed on the Yalu with the 2nd Army Corps, but before his accreditation came through, Bell sent him back to his old China beat. James was not accredited till August, and when he reached the front he found he could transmit only fifty heavily censored words every other day. He quarrelled bitterly with the Japanese, was threatened with *gens d'armes*, returned in fury to Peking, sent an angry telegram to *The Times*, and was ordered back to London. Though Morrison could not broach the wall of Japanese censorship, his services to Japan were not forgotten. "We are much indebted to Dr Morrison, for he counselled us to go to war against Russia never doubting the result," Marshal Yamagata said to a Japanese correspondent, and when, on 2nd January 1905, the fortress of Port Arthur fell to General Nogi's forces after a five months' siege, Morrison was invited to accompany Nogi and his general staff on their triumphal entry. He rode in with Sir Ernest Satow on a borrowed pony:

> Japanese carrying Russian sick on stretchers—much humanity. Russians doing nothing of the kind but witnessing procession. . . . Past all the wrecked fleet burned and perhaps past repair a sight for French creditors a fleet destroyed by incapacity. . . . All British officers spoke contemptuously of the Russian surrender and of the trenches paved with vodka bottles . . . introduced to Nogi, Ijichi his Chief of Staff and others. All very kind speaking flattering words.

On a cool and frosty morning next day Morrison attended a thanksgiving service before an improvised shrine. Twenty caparisoned priests sat at tables in a square, with ceremonial red rice coloured by beans. Morrison sat with Nogi and his generals at a cross table: "Lunch wonderfully organized. Saki, claret, rice dishes of Japanese food, aluminium cups, cake etc. Excellent. Fireworks and rockets. Nogi on stand. Banzai which rent the air. . . . Some soldiers dressed up one fooling as a Russian officer dancing and fooling."

Morrison inspected the battlefields, listened to gossip about the correspondent Ashmead Bartlett ("discreditable, crooked, etc."), who had challenged James to a duel, and wired *The Times* a vivid account of the fall of Port Arthur, for which the Japanese thanked him warmly. In it he castigated the defenders for their cowardice, stripped them of every shred of honour, and characterized the surrender as one of the most discreditable in world history. W. T. Stead, the famous English journalist, said this telegram altered the opinion of the whole of Europe about Russia.

When he passed through Tientsin on his way home, Morrison talked to a Russian general who expressed the opinion that the war would last for two years. Morrison said: "My opinion is that the war will be over in three months. Your troops will be defeated at Mukden and then peace will be in sight. You have not a chance of victory. . . . Your Government has blundered. It ought never have entered upon this war, it should now with-draw from the consequences of its blunders as soon as possible." The general thanked Morrison for his "informations".

[VI]

Morrison may have been imperturbable in his relations with diplomats, but in his relations with women he was often as agonized as an infatuated schoolboy. Behind his assured and worldly exterior he was emotionally immature, and racked by self-doubt. When Mrs Archibald Little told him he was "very shy with women" he brooded over her remark—though he disliked her intensely—and next day wrote in his diary: "Oppressed by invincible shyness. Why is it that I can never overcome this?" (Mrs Little, wife of an old Yangtze hand, was an indomitable traveller, writer, lecturer, feminist, and philanthropist. Despite her manifold good works in two hemispheres—she founded the Anti-footbinding Society in China and sat on innumerable benevolent committees in England—Morrison referred to her always as "that awful woman" or "the detestable".)

During the most eventful months of 1904, while he was sending his masterly dispatches to *The Times*, organizing its variegated correspond-ents, and advising the Japanese on how to run their war—on 16th Febru-ary he told them it would be easy to cut the cable to Port Arthur, and two days later it was done—Morrison was involved in a tempestuous affair with an American nymphomaniac who at least seems to have succeeded in overcoming his "invincible" shyness.

May Ruth Perkins, the golden-haired daughter of a millionaire Ameri-can senator, was travelling through the Far East in company with a "chap-erone", Mrs Ragsdale, whose duties were obviously nominal. Before—and after—she met Morrison, Miss Perkins was the joint tenant of a great many beds in Japan and China. Morrison met her briefly in Peking, in December 1903, and was "immensely taken" with her. "It was a type that pleased me infinitely that excited me passionately," he noted. Months passed, and he thought of her "occasionally". In February, after the out-break of war, he was dining with Ducat in Shanhaikwan when Mrs Rags-dale and the "flashing-eyed maiden", to use Morrison's courtesy title, came into the room:

> It was a night of limpid moonlight almost as light as day. Maysie said she would like to go to the Great Wall. I offered to accompany her and Ducat when he found that he could be useful and take away Mrs R. agreed to join us. Maysie and I went together; he kept at a distance we climbed the wall sat down on the crest and then was disclosed to what I had never experienced before—a revelation that astounded me.

Fuelled by a perverse mixture of desire and indignation, the fire kindled in the February moonlight burned fiercely till the end of June, when Miss Perkins returned to the United States.

Scorning pretence, she catalogued her promiscuities with a wealth of
ogical detail. Morrison was soon told that her current lover *en chef*
one of his friends, Martin Egan, an American newspaperman stationed
`okyo, and her candour enabled him to fill three pages of his diary—
t from many shorter entries—with notes from her sexual auto-
graphy:

Aged 24 last 28 January. Accustomed as long as she can remember to
play with herself every morning even when unwell, even after passing
the night in bed with a man. Seduced by Jack Fee a doctor in the
French restaurant in San Francisco known as the Hen and Chickens
or the Poultry or some such. Pregnant. . . . Went to Washington got
out of difficulty (after abortion) . . . slept constantly with Congress-
man Gaines. . . . Four miscarriages. "Kissed" all the way over in the
Siberia after leaving Honolulu by Captain Tremaine Smith. Had for
days in succession by Martin Egan. . . . Mrs Goodnow had told her
that once she was kissed by a woman she would never wish to be
kissed by a man. Her desire now is to get a Japanese maid to accompany her back to America and to kiss her every morning. . . . In
Tientsin she was kissed by Zeppelin the Dutch consul. . . . In
Shanghai she . . . wired me *Please come Japan be good*. . . . That same
evening she met C. R. Holcomb . . . who had her 4 times in 2 hours.

The "most phenomenal fornicator she ever encountered was Linton
ford". Morrison entered up five other names "for future reference"
decided that May was the "most thoroughly immoral woman" he had
r met, "a born prostitute without desire for money or present". None-
ess she accepted from him "the following—all beautiful—a silver
rette case—a silver belt with the characters for happiness—half a dozen
roidered handkerchiefs—an ivory umbrella handle—a gold bracelet".
When she told Morrison of her nights with Holcomb he "suffered
s greater than any that have racked me since I was in Paris with Noelle
890". But he followed her whenever she beckoned, recording clini-
y how his head "as a bleeding trophy had been displayed on the point
Maysie's lance":

March 30—Came up to Peking distressed and disturbed in my mind.
What an individuality to be thrust in my path! And how as usual
it comes too late. But I am better in body and mind! . . .

May 4—Sleepless night, much brain worry, furious jealousy and every
reason. . . . My head in a whirl of excitement distraught with passion
and with blinding jealousy. The image most deeply impressed on my
brain is that of a big man trying to hypnotize the impressionable
woman.

May 5—Slept a little better but still torn with anguish and haunted
by that evil face dominating yielding weakness. What an ass I am and
what infatuation it is! No emotion seeing her body clad but hair
down and body discovered thrilling every fibre of me.

There was brief anodyne in the news of a great Japanese victory—twenty-eight Russian guns captured and three or four thousand men—but the agony continued:

June 6 ... diary neglected for 3 days and neglected because of Maysie. Why can I not remove her from my memory? It fills me with pain to think of her in the arms of Martin Egan as she will be in a day or so. ...

June 9 ... due to arrive in Kobe tomorrow. ... What is the morrow to bring forth? Where am I to meet Maysie? ... Does she still love me or care for me or am I forever excluded by the lucky Martin?—That is the problem and I am worried and restless. But will accept what is given to me.

June 10 ... Maysie was on the telephone. Martin Egan left this morning and would not return till tomorrow? Would I come down to dinner ... afterwards ... I had an interview in her room, 105, one of most staggering I have ever suffered. It ended happily or I should have perished.

One night, after a violent attack of nose-bleeding, ("it seems to attack me when I am worried") Morrison lay down and "had the curious experience of Maysie going through piles of love-letters many passionate, many truly loving ... a remarkable collection all carefully treasured and anyone sufficient to convict her of unchastity."

Of Morrison's enraptured correspondence with Maysie, only his valedictory telegram survives. Perhaps it is just as well. The telegram, dated Shimonoseki, 25th June 1904, does not exhibit that talent for telegraphic compression for which Morrison was distinguished:

MISS PERKINS GRAND HOTEL YOKOHAMA JUST STARTING FOR SHANGHAI MAY YOUR VOYAGE HOME BE ALL SUNSHINE YOUR RETURN WHILE LEAVING MANY DESOLATE IN THE ORIENT WILL SURELY MAKE GLAD THE HEARTS OF THOSE DEAR TO YOU IN OAKLANDS WHO ARE SO EAGERLY WAITING TO GIVE YOU WELCOME I TRUST THAT AMID YOUR DISTRACTIONS YOU WILL SOMETIMES FIND LEISURE TO WRITE TO ME AND WILL NOT LET ME SLIP ALTOGETHER FROM YOUR MEMORY I KNOW NOT IF FATE WILL PERMIT US TO COME TOGETHER BUT WHATEVER HAPPENS I SHALL ALWAYS TREASURE YOUR MEMORY AND GRATEFULLY RECALL THOSE HAPPY MOMENTS WE SPENT TOGETHER GOODBYE MY DEAR ERNEST.

Morrison was "much disappointed" when Maysie did not reply.

[VII]

When Chirol called on Theodore Roosevelt in Washington in October 1904 the President began a three-hour conversation—it was almost a monologue—by saying: "This war has got to be stopped and *The Times* has got to stop it." All his sympathies were with Japan, but, he told Chirol, "we don't want the Japanese to come trailing their men-of-war right across *our* ocean". Chirol reminded him gently that the Pacific contained some very large islands, such as Australia and New Zealand, that were not American.

With the fall of Mukden, Roosevelt became more and more afraid that a triumphant Japan might become "puffed up with pride and turn against us". On 6th June 1905, Morrison dined with Rockhill who told him that neither President Roosevelt nor the British Government wanted to see the unchecked supremacy of Japan. "Poor little Japs," was Morrison's diary comment. "Neither the United States nor Great Britain want them in Vladivostok." Roosevelt had started peace negotiations early in March and was surprised when Britain did not support them. After Russia's defeat at Tsushima, both belligerents agreed to discuss a settlement, and on 5th August, under Roosevelt's friendly auspices, their representatives politely shook hands aboard the U.S.S. *Mayflower* at Oyster Bay. Four days later the peace conference opened at Portsmouth, New Hampshire.

Morrison was "knocked all of a heap" by a telegram he received on 23rd June instructing him to attend the conference, which it was then thought would be held in Washington. He was very depressed by the assignment. "Could not sleep. Much worried about going. . . . Feel damned sick," he wrote in his diary, and to his mother: "The mission was quite unexpected and though a compliment to me I dislike exceedingly the going." But Satow and Rockhill assured him that his mission could do much good, and he immediately wired Bell: "Ready leave anytime." Before he left he had an interesting talk with Dr Wu Ting-fang, a Chinese graduate of Lincoln's Inn, who had represented China in Washington before returning to become a minister in China's Ministry of Foreign Affairs. Wu sought Morrison's advice about China's affairs, Rockhill having told him that Morrison had "more power than all the ministers put together". Wu drew attention to the growing power of the Viceroy in Chihli, Yuan Shih-k'ai, and asked Morrison a question that was to be answered seven years later: "Where would it lead?"

Morrison left Peking on 3rd July, farewelled at the train by the Rockhills, Colonel Bower (Commandant of the Peking Legation Guard), Colonel Aoki (the Japanese military attaché), and many others. In Tokyo he had a long talk with Sir Claude MacDonald ("garrulous, inaccurate, long-winded"). On the ship from Yokohama to Vancouver he made notes, with his usual precision, about the bad women among the passengers (Mrs Seeley, who drank her pint of wine, and had "lain with hundreds" was "under 40", 6ft 1½in, 219lb), but spent most of his time writing letters. In one he told Sir John Jordan, then British Minister in Korea, that he was going to London to urge Lansdowne, who had succeeded Salisbury as Foreign Secretary, to appoint Jordan as Minister in Peking, "and not a European diplomat ignorant of the very rudiments of the China question". Jordan, who had gone to China as a student interpreter in 1876, had been Chinese Secretary in Peking before going to Korea as Consul-General in 1896.

Morrison arrived in New York, by way of Vancouver and Montreal, on 4th August, and took a room at Holland House, 7th Avenue and 30th Street: "Eight stories up, room 10 x 16, $6 per day English style which means meals not included; Good breakfast $1. Arrived late and drive 50 cents to Holland House, 25 cents to porter for carrying my stick. . . . This marble palace where I am paying about four times what I can afford."

The other two representatives of *The Times* who were to cover the conference were George William Smalley, the Washington correspondent of *The Times*, and Sir Donald Mackenzie Wallace, Chirol's predecessor in the Foreign Department. Morrison's first call was to the Netherlands Hotel overlooking Central Park, where his two colleagues were staying. Here a letter from Bell was awaiting him. Chirol had told Bell that Morrison did not intend to return to the Far East:

> He offered me a new post the more important he thinks it will become in the service namely correspondent for the American continent. I was asked to send the code word "Returning" if I wished to return to Peking. Whether right or wrong however, I determined to wire *en clair* "Times London Chirol mistaken desire return Peking after Holiday Morrison." 10 words at 25 cents, $2.50.

Morrison was delighted with Portsmouth: "Beautiful wooded country, picturesque and balmy." But he felt "the overpowering oppression of population and the rush of automobiles". He lost his purse containing £23 8s. 3d. and subsequently found it, but did not tell the hotel manager, for a curious reason: "No one would suffer if he were honest and the searching of the boxes of the negro servants might discover thefts that would have passed unnoticed." Nelson Lloyd of the New York *Sun* took him to a brothel at 51 Walter Street, which Morrison thought "a curious evidence of civilization in a New England town". Two New York journalists said they expected him to be an elderly man with a long white beard. He was surprised to find he was so well known. "I am consulted by everyone and advise always pro-Japanese," he wrote. The German correspondent of *Lokalangeiger* reported: "Dr Morrison is influencing public opinion here as he does in Peking." He discussed the negotiations at length with both sides. Baron Komura, one of the Japanese representatives, said to him:

> We reduced our terms to the smallest possible. . . . Our Government would fall if these terms were abated. Witte says such terms are incompatible with the dignity of Russia and will never be accepted by the Russian people. But the Japanese people must also be considered, and their wishes consulted. That is the fundamental difference. The Russian people have no voice in the matter the Japanese people have a voice.

The Russian de Witte ("a man of splendid stature . . . he towered above me") agreed with Morrison that the conference was futile: "We did not know the Japanese terms. The President did not know them. Had our Government known the Japanese terms they would not have sent the mission. . . . They cannot be accepted." Morrison said he thought the war was the most foolish that had been waged for years—a curious judgment from a man who regarded himself as one of its begetters—and that Russia was in the wrong and should end it by paying an indemnity—a curious recommendation from a man who was doing his best to keep the war going:

> We spoke of the war. I told him if it continued Harbin would be isolated and Vladivostok captured. He granted it possible after enormous losses, 50,000 at Vladivostok, 150,000 in Manchuria. "Lives," I said, "are cheap in Japan. But if Harbin falls, what then?" "Our troops retire into Siberia." Can the Japanese follow them? Can they come to Moscow?" With some earnestness I reminded him that there was no place west of Harbin where an army can live, no grain for men nor fodder for horses. He said the Hingan Mountains. I said there was no grain and I reminded him of the immense mills in Harbin by which his army was being fed. And the ground of Manchuria, frozen solid hard to several feet. He agreed. He was curious to know the lines of Japanese advance. I said their objectives must be Harbin and Vladivostok. Then he spoke of the Japanese in Manchuria. They would obtain Manchuria as they had seized Korea. I disputed this expressing the opinion that Japan had everything to gain by keeping good faith with the Chinese in Manchuria. "We shall see," he said. "We shall see."

Chirol had composed his reporting team of curiously dissident elements, perhaps in the belief that objectivity would result. Smalley ("very Irish, snub-nosed") was a man of seventy-two, whom Roosevelt described as a "copper-rivetted idiot" and Morrison as a "grumpy old devil . . . impossible to work with". Morrison soon compiled his dossier:

> . . . Born in 1833. Educated Yale. Joined *Tribune* 1861, and remained till July 1895, when joined *Times*. His mother daughter of Hon A. Eastburn. Smalley married daughter of Wendell Phillips. One son very handsome, 2 do. very ugly. One married badly. Phillips believed millionaire left nothing. Sons done badly. Bad lot. Father sold library to start him. Is useless. Separated from his wife. Has unmarried daughter recently accepted post as stenographer at $15 per week to Negro Collector of Customs New York. Smalley is proud and no doubt suffers hence his viciousness of temper and spirit.

Smalley was also a "growling old club frequenter . . . associated with the Astors, Vanderbilts, and that class of millionaire", and a "tuft-hunter" who proudly displayed his invitations from "Mrs Stuyvesant, Mrs Fysh, Mrs Astor, Mrs Clarence Mackay and others."

Wallace ("a dapper Jew having complete false set uppers and lowers"), like Chirol, had been with the Foreign Office before turning to journalism. He was, Morrison wrote, "a very kind man, and an intimate friend of King Edward, of the Tsar, the German Emperor, and nearly everyone in Europe. He was extremely kind to me and we could not have been more intimate."

Smalley and Wallace had come over on the same steamer with Count de Witte, one of the two Russian representatives. Chirol thought that Wallace, who was strongly pro-Russian, and persona grata with the Russians, would balance Smalley, who was supposed to be violently anti-Russian. But when the conference began Smalley identified himself closely with the Russian viewpoint, perhaps because the Russians were more liberal with news. "I am here to get news *news*. I am not concerned with policy," he told Morrison.

Morrison was more concerned with making news than with reporting it. Just as he had worked ceaselessly for war, now he worked ceaselessly against peace. Again and again he urged on Wallace and Smalley that the war should continue. "Why should there be peace?" he asked. When Smalley said Britain wanted peace in the interests of her trade and her bankers, Morrison "questioned strongly if trade was affected and said he could find no interest whatever in China in favour of peace except among the Chinese themselves". He does not seem to have considered the views of the Chinese, on whose soil the war was being fought, and who had no reason to welcome Japanese overlordship in Manchuria. He hoped the negotiations would be unsuccessful and wanted *The Times*, with the help of Wallace and Smalley, to shape its policy to assist in the failure. "They thought me bloodthirsty," he records ingenuously.

The chief obstacle to a settlement was Japan's demand for an indemnity. Another was her claim to the island of Sakhalin, off Siberia. The wrangling continued through August, and Roosevelt feared that the conference would collapse. Morrison's diary records his satisfaction at this possibility:

> *11 August*—So excited with everything that I cannot compose myself. But to my great joy there is every hope that the conference will fail. . . . Russia will not accept the terms of peace and if Japan will not modify them the conference must close. . . . I am delighted.

> *23 August*—There is no hope of peace. Smalley saw de Witte, he said: "We will not pay a kopeck. We will not pay in any form. A woman may change her dress, but is still a woman," he said, speaking of the suggestion to change the term indemnity into redemption of territory. Smalley in his telegram altered this to a soldier changing his uniform.

> *26 August*—Conference with correspondents. To all I express my unabated confidence in the failure of the conference.

But three days later Onishi, a Japanese correspondent, burst excitedly into Morrison's bathroom: "Peace is concluded," he cried. "Envoys are in accord on all points!" Unexpectedly, Komura had agreed to a compromise suggested by Roosevelt: Russia would pay no indemnity, but half of

Sakhalin would go to Japan. Both powers agreed to evacuate Manchuria, except the territory affected by the lease of Kwantung, on the Liaotung peninsula, where Japan took over Russia's concessions; Japan also became suzerain in Korea. "The news fairly made me stagger," Morrison wrote. "It is a complete surrender. Poor Onishi was on the point of crying."

Before he left Portsmouth on 31st August, Morrison had lunch with Nelson Page, the novelist:

> Among guests was Assistant-Secretary of State Peirce who was suffering from alcoholic tremor and is dull heavy sodden man tremendously important and the most copious leak of all Government officials. He holds his post not because he is competent to fill it but because he is a brother-in-law of Henry Cabot Lodge. His father was a famous mathematician and a man of great academic distinction.

Another distinguished visitor in Portsmouth for the conference was the humorist Irvin Cobb, then on the staff of the *Sun*. Cobb apparently took his role of funny man seriously. Morrison was told that when he was returning through the cemetery one evening he was seen to stop, make a gesture of grief, put a handkerchief to his eyes and sob: "Poor fellow," he said, pointing to a tombstone. "I knew him well. I had a running acquaintance with him for years." On the tombstone was "Sacred to the memory of J. T. Clapp."

[IX]

Back in New York, Morrison booked in at the Park Avenue Hotel ("$5 a day") and sent Roosevelt an introduction which Rockhill had given him. Waiting for a reply, he browsed among bookshops, looked at the Pierpont Morgan collection of China in the Metropolitan Museum, inspected the "wonderful $2,000,000 house" of multi-millionaire Schwab, and made a sentimental journey to pawnbroker Simpson's and Beefsteak John's in the Bowery. Next day came the reply: the President would see him "briefly" at 3 p.m. on Monday. "How long is briefly?" Morrison asked his diary.

After breakfast on Labour Day, 4th September, he boarded the 34th Street ferry dressed in light tweeds, though he had been advised to put on a frock coat and top-hat. He was met by Hamilton King, First Secretary, and his one-armed brother, editor of the *Sun*, who had designed the machines for making Gillette razor blades. They, too, had an appointment with the President. After a good lunch in Oyster Bay the three drove through the woods to Safanwo Hill, with a splendid view of Long Island Sound. Two secret-service men were under a tree opposite Roosevelt's two-storied country cottage, and under other trees were displayed horns of big game that he had shot. The visitors were shown into a large trophy room—"polished floor with skins of bears . . . and heads and antlers"—and Morrison noticed among the books "the highly ornamental Album sent by the Empress Dowager containing her portrait". On a sofa was young Kermit Roosevelt, "a nice clean-looking sun-burned lad" to whom Hamilton King gave a small ivory elephant. The President came in soon after. He was shorter than Morrison had expected, "very powerful vigorous with energy incarnate". He was dressed in corded holland with leggings. He greeted his visitors and said in a hearty voice, "Bully that peace, wasn't it?" He asked Hamilton King to accompany him and walked out. When Morrison was ushered into his office Roosevelt said:

> I'm always glad to meet an Englishman and still more glad to meet an Australian. . . . You are working out in Australia many problems that have previously confronted us. . . . But what I don't like to see is the power of the labour party. I don't like to see a cleavage like that between the political parties, should be vertical through the different layers not a separation of the different layers by a horizontal stratum.

He illustrated his point with a forcible gesture and went on: "I don't like to see your diminishing rate of population increase, the decrease in your birthrate. It is a problem we have here also. And the growth of your city population . . . some 40% of the population of the whole state in a capital city." But Morrison had not come to talk about Australia, and he was relieved when the President swung off to the Far East:

> We spoke of the Peace. He thought it was well and that Japan was wise to give up the indemnity. He argued it £.s.d. If the war had continued there would have been greatly increased expenditure and the certainty that Russia would not have been able to pay an indemnity. I could not get the Japanese to see this. I pressed them but they would not give way. Till 48 hours before giving way I was doubtful of success. You see I was not trammelled by precedent. Precedents are good in their way, but you may get enmeshed in them.

Morrison "saw clearly" from the conversation that Roosevelt had brought much greater pressure on Japan than he had suspected. "And the greater seemed the injustice in view . . . of his knowledge that Russia could for purposes of peace . . . pay the indemnity."

Roosevelt did not seem to show either sympathy or even good feeling for the Chinese. He doubted if China would ever govern Manchuria. "I had intended returning to China the balance of the Boxer money," he said. "The amount was largely in excess. But this boycott is not pleasing and I may not return it. Taft [U.S. Secretary of War] is over there now. Perhaps they are throwing bricks at him."

Roosevelt said he would like to see Japan enforce a kind of Monroe doctrine in Eastern Asia ("not of course in the Philippines"). England could return Weihaiwei. It was no good to her.

> Then we spoke of many things. Of Wolseley he spoke contemptuously, especially of his ignorance in his book on Lee, written when he was Commander-in-Chief. It was wrong, unpardonably . . . he would

attribute to the South what had happened to the North, and so on. He had a high opinion of Lee and had his grandson at the White House. . . . Wolseley wrote with astonishing ignorance. . . . I said all Wolseley's work was like that. He said he had a Commander-in-Chief Miles who did the same sort of fool work. He never feared Russia and could never understand why Englishmen were so apprehensive of Russia . . . there was never a Russian naval contractor yet who could not be bought or a naval overseer who could not accept money not to see. With the Japanese it was just the other way.

As Morrison was leaving, the President drew his attention to an excellent portrait of Lincoln, taken two years before his Presidency, that hung near the door.

New York was as "hot as hell". Morrison had violent diarrhoea, and felt "damned lonely and miserable" despite Moberly Bell's flattering letters, and the attentions of several American magnates. He called on General Hubbard ("worth $30,000,000 or $40,000,000"), president of the International Banking Company, and vice-president Jim Fearon ("looks as if he drank overmuch") in their "magnificent marble offices" at 80 Wall Street. Fearon told Morrison that America was "simply rotten with money"; he could only get 1¾ per cent; he was "tremendously interested in China" and discussed China's offer to buy back the concession for the Canton-Hankow railway, which had been granted to the American-China Development Company in 1898. He showed Morrison a letter from General J. A. Whittier, president of the company, urging that the offer be rejected. This represented the view of the King of the Belgians, who held 2800 of the 6000 shares, the other 3200 being held equally between the International Banking Company and Pierpont Morgan. China had offered $6,750,000 in gold for the concession, representing a clear profit of $3,200,000, which Morgan wanted to accept. Next day Fearon took Morrison to dinner at the Metropolitan Club to meet Whittier ("a bad egg") and Clarence Gary. Morrison told them that America ought not to allow China to redeem the railway, that it would be a blow to foreigners and that the railway in that case would never be built. Whittier and Gary both agreed, and Whittier said it was most important that Morrison should speak to Morgan. But the meeting did not take place, and China's offer was accepted.

Another of Morrison's hosts was the millionaire Robert Sterling Clarke, who introduced him at an extravagant dinner to a man called Irving, "a bull-headed nephew of Washington Irving and great grandson of Fenimore Cooper—the dullest and most unintellectual of men—a bounder". It was a period when elaborate brothels still enjoyed the patronage of wealthy men-about-town, and after a theatre Clarke took his guests to a swell sporting-house that Morrison found "dull as well as vile". Morrison left in disgust and walked home. "A rotten misspent evening" was his summing-up.

Before he left for England, where he had arranged to have a brief holiday, Morrison got a letter from Susan Townley, whose husband had been transferred to Washington: "If you get a chance in England remember that my husband's ambition is to go back to Peking when Sir Ernest leaves," she wrote. "Do say that he is the man for the place and that the people there want him, *if* you think so, but for Heaven's sake don't quote me." On the day before he sailed he wrote a long letter to his mother:

> The papers have praised my work in Portsmouth saying it was the only redeeming feature of *The Times* work here. I shall strongly recommend that Smalley be removed from his post. . . . I shall stay in England and the Continent a month or so. . . . I am anxious to meet the German Emperor who thinks I am the "most formidable enemy that Germany has in the Far East.". . .

His ticket on the *Oceanic* cost $105. He was gratified when the hotel knocked $1 a day off his bill because of the "infernal racket" made by some machine drilling for foundations opposite. He gave $1 each to the porter and the chambermaid, "not a cash" to anyone else, and paid $4 to get his eight packages to the steamer. He sailed on 5th September.

[X]

London in the autumn of 1905 was a goldmine of gossip, social and political, and Morrison worked both lodes assiduously. He arrived on 13th September, bought a hat, and drove to Printing House Square, where Bell received him warmly, congratulated him on his Portsmouth work, and agreed that Smalley was a "disagreeable brute". Later Bell told him that telegrams from the Far East in 1904 had cost £9800. Morrison's next call was at the offices of the *Standard*, in Shoe Lane, where his old Peking friend, "Taffy" Gwynne, now occupied the editorial chair. Here was rich "pay dirt" indeed. Gwynne, who gave his hobbies in *Who's Who* as "all outdoor games and exercises", also took much of his exercise indoors and in bed. He was one of London's most notable lechers—a distinction which never failed to fascinate Morrison—and a dedicated scandalmonger. Before long he had told Morrison how Lady Swettenham, wife of Sir Frank Swettenham, former Governor of Straits Settlement, had tried to "lie with him" and was discussing Arthur Pearson's "bad clap". They spoke of the "rottenness of society", of "the unchastity even of unmarried women"— on which Gwynne could discourse with authority—and "of the rotten example set by the King". They agreed that his Majesty King Edward VII, then a corpulent debauchee of sixty-four was "a miserable specimen". Edward's widely discussed intimacy with Mrs George Keppel was linked with another Edwardian scandal—the lively traffic in honours. According to Gwynne, one of the principal pedlars of Coronets, Stars, and Garters was Edward's friend, Sir Thomas Lipton, the millionaire Irish grocer, whose vast tea and rubber estates compensated for his unfortunate lack of ancestors and aitches. Arthur Pearson, the Wookey clergyman's son who founded a newspaper empire, had explained the procedure to Gwynne:

> Pearson told him that Lipton invited him to dinner and then after wine with some nervousness asked him if he would not like a baronetcy. Harmsworth had one. [Alfred Harmsworth, a rival newspaper monarch, received a baronetage in 1904, and became Baron Northcliffe of the Isle of Thanet the following year.] Pearson said, of course he would for it was a recognition of which to be proud. The King has many private charities he [Lipton] said tentatively. It gives him much satisfaction if contribution is made to them. The long and short of it was this:—The baronetcy would be given if Pearson would give £25,000 to the private charities of the King!—for Mrs George Keppel doubtless. Wernher, of Wernher Beit & Co. bought his baronetcy for £37,500, having to pay 50% extra because of being a foreigner.

General Browne, home from Peking, came to breakfast and said the King was a "damned bad lot" who had no religion but was always attending divine service, and Lady St Helier ("wizened witchlike with grey hair") added to the dossier when Morrison accepted her invitation to call at 79 Harley Street:

> The public are beginning to know about the King. His debts his disreputable associates his wealthy Jew money-lenders. She said that when the Queen died the King had debts of between 2 and 3 millions. Instead of coming frankly to the people and making a clean breast of it, he feared doing so. Had he said he was filling the actual Kingship without its emoluments parliament would gladly have paid off the amount. Hicks Beach who was then Chancellor (and is spending tonight at Lady Jeune's) himself told Lady Jeune that he would recommend payment by the State. We spoke of the purchase of office and of the scandalous barony of Harmsworth following so soon upon his baronetage.

Lady St Helier, wife of the Advocate-General, was one of those energetic Edwardian women who played an important part behind the political scenes. She was reputed to exert great influence at the War Office, through Field-Marshal Sir Evelyn Wood.

Edward VII was discussed with equal irreverence by Valentine Chirol, at whose rooms in Queen Anne Mansions Morrison met Leo Maxe, editor of the *National Review*, and J. L. Garvin, editor of *The Outlook* ("all brilliant and singularly attractive men"):

> Chirol began by expressing his despisal of the King—such an *unmitigated blackguard*. When he went to Paris in order to bring about, his deluded subjects believe, the *Entente Cordiale*, he really went to dally with Mrs George Keppel at a house especially rented for the purpose by Sir Ernest Cassel. And look at his associates! said Chirol, and Maxe agreed.

Chirol's estimate of the King as diplomat was endorsed by Dr (later Sir Starr) Jameson, the Kimberley doctor who in 1895 led the ill-considered raid into the Transvaal and was rewarded with the Prime Ministership of Cape Colony. "The King is an ass," he said. "By reason of being called the peacemaker he will grow convinced that he did make peace just as his distinguished ancestor George IV believed he had commanded at Waterloo." These were heretical views in 1905. Not till 1912, two years after the King's death, were they publicly expressed in a memoir written by Sir Sidney Lee for the *Dictionary of National Biography*; it revealed Edward as a "superficial mediocrity" who had played little or no part in the creation of the *Entente*.

"What a Royal Family (with capitals) it is!" wrote Morrison. "The King and Mrs George Keppel, also the Jews Cassel and Sassoon and the baker, Sir Thomas Lipton" (whose religion he did not disclose). Morrison's disenchantment with the British monarchy did not affect his faith in British Imperialism. One of his heroes was the practical imperialist, Dr Jameson; the other, the poet laureate of imperialism, Rudyard Kipling. Gwynne told Morrison that "the death of Jameson would be a national misfortune and that Kipling considered him to be "the greatest man he has ever met". Someone also told Morrison that "Dr Jim" was a "great ram".

Morrison's bowl of happiness gushed over on the day ("one of the most interesting . . . of my lifetime") he went with Gwynne and Jameson to visit Kipling in Sussex:

> At Heathfield station there was waiting for us the motor of Kipling and in this we were rushed out to his residence. An old stone house the modern part of which is dated 1634 and the old part is 13th century. Beautiful grounds with splendid oaks—lawns—ornamental pond with boat. Kipling came to the gate to meet us. And then his wife came from the garden, a very pretty clever energetic little woman. One dark daughter, one dark complexioned son. Rudyard very cordial and pleasant. Constant wit. Such brilliance such lighting flashes I had never before experienced.

Kipling's conversation ranged from criticism of the peace conference ("Teddy had done a bad day's work") to praise of "Jacky" Fisher, then First Sea Lord. There was also talk about Mrs Wale Dace, "a strumpet who interviewed the King at Marienbad about Mrs Cullinan of the great diamond. . . ."

Roosevelt and his part in the Portsmouth conference were much discussed in London. Chirol thought the President had been unjust to Japan in putting pressure on her to give way, and said, in confidence, "it was Japan who approached Roosevelt and asked him to bring about peace". Morrison underlined this in his diary, adding: "This explains a good deal." Lord Lansdowne, when Morrison called on him at the Foreign Office, confirmed it. "The President certainly informed me that it was Japan who approached him to bring about the conference," he said. (Mackenzie King told Morrison in 1909 that the Japanese had asked Roosevelt to return the letter in which Japan had asked him to intervene, and that Roosevelt had refused, though promising to treat it as confidential. Roosevelt had told this to King.)

Chirol told Morrison that "William and Teddy"—Kaiser Wilhelm and President Roosevelt—were undoubtedly very intimate. "William does influence Teddy. Both are strenuous, energetic, and masterful. "John Morley, dining with Morrison and Bell at Buckle's, said he had stayed a week with Roosevelt just after his election and was impressed by "his fire, his energy, his loftiness of ideal":

> Buckle said it was a pity William had such influence on Roosevelt. Morley thought not. Bell said telegrams had passed between them which, if published, would astonish the world. "You rule one hemisphere, I can rule the other," said Roosevelt in one. . . . Morley said Roosevelt received a telegram every day from the Emperor, but said of it contemptuously, "Another telegram from Kaiser Wilhelm," as I, he added laughing, might say "Another telegram from whom shall I say, Lord Knollys [King Edward's private secretary]."

The lodes of gossip were inexhaustible. Lady Brownrigg told Morrison that Sir Frank Swettenham had a questionable reputation in money matters, and that Lady Swettenham was a nymphomaniac. Sir Schomberg McDonnell, secretary to H.M. office of Works, told him that Sir Francis Bertie, the new British Ambassador in Paris, was an ignorant man who had never read a book since he left Eton, "his chief claim being as a retailer of lewd stories in coarse English". And an artist on the *Graphic* told him that Alma Tadema and Holman Hunt were two of the dirtiest storytellers he knew. . . .

Gertrude Bell, the intrepid traveller, mountaineer and huntress, invited him to dine at 95 Sloane Street, and talked till 11.10 p.m.: "We ranged from the Vale of Damascus to the fiscal controversy. She is very brilliant, gushes amazingly, has marvellous energy and extraordinary knowledge and she bored me to distraction. It was my fault and I say it with humility. . . ."

Gertrude thought Japan would swallow up Australia and that it would be a good thing because the Japanese were our superiors. Morrison walked home by way of Piccadilly Circus "yawning all the way".

He was not bored by Lady Dorothy Neville, "the wonderful old lady . . . with an astonishing memory", whom he took in to dinner at a glittering party given by the Moberly Bells. Among the eighteen other guests were the Duchess of St Albans; Lord Minto, who had just succeeded Curzon as Viceroy of India; Lord Cromer of Egyptian fame, and Mr Gladstone's former private secretary, Sir Algernon West. Lady Dorothy "spoke of the Georgian era, has an acid tongue, and some title to fame in the fact that she once saw Disraeli in the bath", Morrison wrote after their first meeting. She had other claims to recognition, of course. She had often entertained Edward VII when he was Prince of Wales, using as "bait" the beautiful American actress, Mrs Brown Potter, and she once ended a rarefied discussion of *haute cuisine* by exclaiming, "Oh, gimme a good blowout on tripe and onions!" When Morrison visited her in her beautiful rooms at 45 Charles Street, overlooking the garden of Lansdowne House, she told him her greatest friend was the second Duke of Wellington, "a most amusing man married to a beautiful but singularly stupid woman whom he used to ridicule". She said that the great Duke had proposed to Baroness Burdett-Coutts, "who is now spectral at 93". The Duke of Teck had also proposed to her. (The Baroness, a very wealthy philanthropist in 1881 married an American, William Ashmead Bartlett, who assumed her name.)

Morrison talked to the new Foreign Secretary, Sir Edward Grey, about the changes in China, and suggested to the new Secretary of State for India, John Morley, that India's "accursed" opium traffic with China should be gradually abolished. Curzon, who had resigned the Viceroyalty of India because of his disagreements with Kitchener, said it was important that Morrison should return to China "to guide the opinion of the world"; Sir Charles Hardinge, British Ambassador to St Petersburg, spoke "with much frankness" of Sir Claude MacDonald's "ignorance and incapacity"; and Henry Bax-Ironside, now Minister Resident at Caracas, spoke with equal frankness about his colleague Sir Henry Durand, British Ambassador to Washington, who had muddled everything in India as Foreign Secretary, "and was now quite useless in Washington".

At dinner with Sir Frank Swettenham, Morrison met a "clever and very attractive American woman, without accent", who had lived long in Paris and was one of the last to leave before the siege. She was Mrs Moreton Frewen, one of the three conquering Jerome sisters from New York; Kitty, Clare, and Leonie. The eldest, Kitty, married Lord Randolph Churchill and was the mother of Winston Churchill. The youngest, Leonie, married Sir John Leslie, and was the mother of Shane Leslie. Mrs Frewen was accompanied by her nineteen-year-old daughter, also called Clare, who smoked cigarettes and was "fleshy, fresh and animal". (Miss Frewen, as Clare Sheridan, became famous as a sculptor, painter, and journalist.) Later Morrison met Lady Randolph—who was then Mrs Cornwallis West—at the Lister-Kayes' and described her as a "hard-faced woman with dark hair, the typical woman in charge of a brothel".

Morrison called on "the dull insipid Godfrey Walter", and Lady Clarke told him that the "austere old father" had left £30,000 a year to Arthur, his eldest son, and £14,000 a year to Godfrey, the second son by the second marriage, and to his numerous other sons £600 a year. "This is just and honorable," Morrison commented sarcastically.

He took the Bells to Covent Garden to hear Melba in *Rigoletto* and *La Bohème* ("£1 1s. a seat") and noted that she was "stout matronly unbecoming but voice absolutely divine". Sir George Clarke told him that Australia had produced only two people of world-wide reputation—Morrison and Melba—and he put Morrison first.

Sir Walter Hillier, a former Chinese Secretary, then Professor of Chinese at King's College, London, thought Morrison should be the new minister in Peking, and said he was amazed at the influence Morrison had in China. He gave "a ludicrous picture" of the Chinese Legation in London. The minister, Chang, who was paid 80,000 taels (£ 10,000) a year, lived in a back room, never refused an invitation, but never asked anyone in return:

> He goes to bed at 5 a.m. rises at midday never does a stroke of work of any kind. From Saturday night till Monday he plays cards and rooks his staff. Last spring he sent away half of his people and is now pocketing their salaries. Useless is the mildest term to apply to him. ... And China it is who suffers.

Hillier suggested that Britain should get control of the Canton-Hankow railway. His brother Guy, Peking agent of the Hong Kong and Shanghai Banking Corporation, had found out that the Hong Kong Government had advanced the money with which China repurchased the concession.

Morrison received a cordial invitation from his old boss, William Rich, to dine at any convenient time, and replied "in as studiously a stinging a way as possible, 'Dear Sir—My time in England is fully occupied.' " In his diary he wrote: "This man did me much injury when I was medical officer in Rio Tinto and now because I am famous he would wish to lick my boots." But Morrison had a long memory for kindnesses as well as for injuries. In Edinburgh he called on his old landlady, Mrs Leighton, of Marchmont Road, with presents for her and her daughter Maggie: "Poor people, they were really glad to see me."

The "vitiated" air of London did not agree with Morrison. He saw a Harley Street specialist about his nose-bleeding, and took the train to Edinburgh ("first-class return 59/6 very cheap") to consult his old medical associates. Professor Wylie, Professor of Medicine at the university, examined him and found no enlargement of liver or spleen and no heart abnormality. Dr George Mackay, Edinburgh's leading oculist, pronounced his eyes "perfect". Thus reassured, he made an unhappy call on his benefactor, John Chiene: "To lunch with Chiene and walleyed wife. He lugubrious and sermonizing. She common. He eating like a hog. ... And lunch absolutely atrocious unfit for a hog. He drinking cheap claret. ... Two dishes nauseating to think of." He was still brooding over this memorable meal when he wrote to his mother two months later: "They are a pair of pigs and gave me a lunch that was absolutely revolting. It gives me nausea now to think of it." There was another "damnable lunch" at the Lister-Kayes' in London: "I passed the first course expecting something solid and when the pudding suddenly appeared I found myself stranded and hungry." To make things worse, he had to praise Lady Lister-Kaye's "drivelling book".

Himself the most careful of men with money, Morrison had a pathological hatred of meanness in others. When he attended an "infernal dull party" given by Sir Archibald and Lady Douglas, Commander-in-Chief, Portsmouth, he reported that the admiral was the "meanest man in the navy": "They pinch and squeeze and save every penny never entertain and he will best become the navy by leaving it. His predecessor Sir John Fisher was most hospitable and kept open house."

He was almost as uncomplimentary about a dinner at Moberly Bell's ("food very bad simply atrocious and badly served") though the guests were interesting: they included Mr and Mrs Joseph Chamberlain ("he extraordinarily young she remarkably fresh and attractive with the most delightful manners"); Sir Thomas Barlow, the Royal physician ("who listened respectfully while I spoke to Chamberlain as if he were a first-year student and I a President of the Royal College of Surgeons"), the Kiplings, and a "deuced attractive woman", Lady Strachey.

[XI]

On 13th January 1906, Morrison watched the posting of the election results at the National Liberal Club. The Liberals were sweeping the polls. The Conservatives, led by Arthur Balfour, but divided by Joseph Chamberlain's tariff-reform proposals, had been crushingly defeated. "Retribution indeed and I am overjoyed though I may not say so," Morrison wrote in his diary. Crossing Piccadilly Circus, he saw Buckle, "sick and downcast . . . heavily lumbering through the crowd":

> He has good reason to be cast down. Nothing could exceed the virulence and animus of *The Times* as conducted by him against the new Government. Narrow-minded, parochial, opiniated, he is a fit colleague of Arthur Walter and an entirely unfit editor of the greatest paper in the world. Entirely out of touch with liberal public opinion, he can now see the result of his handiwork and party that he has supported though evil pulverized and beginning with Balfour scattered to the winds.

Mrs Moberly Bell shared Morrison's opinion of Buckle. "I want you to become editor of *The Times*," she said. "You have the qualities which Mr Buckle lacks. You have knowledge, you know men, and have good judgment." Arthur Barry, too, thought Buckle "unworthy" of his position. "Ignorant of men and parochial, untravelled and ignorant of foreign affairs, he is not a man to guide a paper except to failure," Barry said.

Barry invited Morrison to lunch at the Savoy to meet Northcliffe ("whom Moberly Bell thinks nearly as great a liar as Lord Lonsdale"). Northcliffe "came in bustling and was very cordial". At the next table was the Sultan of Johore, and his English "wife" Nellie, for whom he had just bought the lease of 34 Park Lane. Nellie, a former Gaiety girl, had refused to live in Johore. Barry said the sultan had a privy purse of £40,000 a year and had enriched Nellie with jewels to the value of £40,000. Lady Brownrigg told Morrison that the Johore Advisory Board had resigned because of the sultan's expenditure on Nellie. Morrison later lunched with the sultan, an "ugly looking mongrel" with a stiff jaw, which Barry attributed to the Norwegian sea-captain who was his grandfather.

Morrison set himself two objectives in London, and despite the minor distractions of lunches, dinner, interviews, bookshops, and theatres, and the major disruption of another consuming love affair, achieved them. One was to have Sir John Jordan appointed to Peking; and the other to have the Order of the Garter conferred on the Emperor of Japan. He pleaded Jordan's cause eloquently to George Tyrrell, in charge of the China Department at the Foreign Office, to Lewis Mallet ("an amiable weak man with an eyeglass"), private secretary to Lord Lansdowne, and to Lansdowne himself, and quickly convinced them of Jordan's "incomparable qualifications". But the Mikado's Garter was a more difficult business. Mallet said that the King absolutely refused to give the Garter to a non-Christian. In the case of the Shah of Persia, who had bluntly asked for it, he had yielded to the persuasions of Sir Arthur Hardinge, then Assistant Under-Secretary for Foreign Affairs, but angrily announced that he would not do so again. When the Foreign Office box containing the Order arrived on the yacht *Victoria and Albert*, where the Shah was to receive it, Edward had shown the Royal displeasure by hurling the box across the cabin. Morrison pursued the matter doggedly, and Lord Lansdowne thought it could be arranged. It was. Before he left London, Morrison was told that Prince Arthur of Connaught, as Morrison had suggested, would lead a special Embassy to Tokyo with the Mikado's Garter in his baggage.

[XII]

"Dr Jim", who had rooms in Duke Street, asked Morrison to dinner and presented him to "three ladies" who enraptured him:

> Rarely has it been my good fortune to sit by three better types of English womanhood. Mrs Alfred Lyttleton, wife of the Colonial Secretary, like a peach with sweet musical voice . . . Lady Edward Cecil, sister of Leo Maxe, very handsome with a beautiful set of even teeth . . . and a delicious red tongue, and Mrs Leo, daughter of the twin brother of Sir Godfrey Lushington. . . . They were all clever unusually so. . . . Altogether my evening was one of the most enjoyable I have spent in my life—an evening of joy.

But it was with a dubious type of Hungarian womanhood that Morrison experienced his next grand passion. A few weeks after his arrival in London his friend A. P. Stokes introduced him to "the beautiful Toni—Antonia Sofia Victoria Steaffan". Morrison took her to dinner and drove her home to 16 Sutherland Place, near Queen's Road. This was the first of fifty-nine meetings—he later tabulated them with actuarial precision—in 109 days, and the beginning of an infatuation compared to which the affair with Maysie was a game of Postman's Knock. When he got back to 22 Jermyn Street he had garnered from her enough biographical material, fact or fancy, to provide a diary entry of 450 words. Here are some extracts:

Antonia born in Buda Pesth March 27 1883. Beautiful and dark. Has lost weight since she came to London. Fears consumption. Is lady well educated in Professor Krausse's Boarding School in Berlin. Bad family history. Father died 52 consumption, Mother died 38 consumption, sister 32 Emilie dying consumption, another sister Frida 26 living and healthy. Was the friend of an Indian official living in Mayfair 60 years old . . . who treated her well during 6 months. Man of great stature. . . . Left August 3 sailing from Marseilles August 4. Her life a sad one. She loved a man of her own country and of a suitable age resident in Berlin where he makes leather for jewellery cases. Under promise of marriage he seduced her. She had a miscarriage at 7 months. She was at that time in employment in the millinery department of Wertheim & Co. in the Leipzigstrasse . . . (Toni says of 800 girls in Wertheims there is probably not one virgin) and was there for 18 months rising from 50 to 95 marks per month and dinner found. The work was too hard and she resigned the post. Then she discovered the perfidy of her lover and found him involved with another girl. She was desperate and would have drowned herself, but was frustrated by her lover who divined her intention. Then she came to London having with her about £25. That spent, she seems to have had the good fortune to meet that Indian official. No wonder she is thin and emaciated. Her heart is broken and she is pining away. He tall slight with moustache forbade her to divulge his name and she has loyally kept her promise. A former mistress he had taken out with him died in India. He took her once to the Grand Hotel in Paris. . . . On one occasion when her sister was ill in Gladbach he sent her over to her bedside. When she left he gave her £50 and later sent her two or three letters and £25. For at least 2 months she had heard naught from him and fears that he may be dead. . . . He spoke French well.

For the rest of the month Morrison saw Toni nearly every day. They dined at Frascati's, at the Pall Mall Restaurant, and at Alphonse's, ran down to Brighton, visited the National Gallery and Madame Tussaud's, saw *The Blue Moon*, walked in St James's Park, and rounded off each day with a session in Morrison's Jermyn Street rooms.

A few days after the first encounter Morrison bought Toni a "muff and wrapper, £6.6.0". This was followed by a "travelling large light millboard trunk" and many other presents which, too, he carefully catalogued.

On 20th November, Morrison gave up his rooms ("crushingly overcharged") and moved to the Esplanade Hotel, Seaford. To his great disappointment, Toni could not come with him ("poor girl looked ill"), but joined him after two days. They spent five days together, Toni discreetly occupying a separate bedroom and sitting-room. Morrison then left for Paris. Again he was "shockingly overcharged—Damn them!" (Toni had good reason for not accompanying Morrison to Seaford. The day before she had married a barber named Loth, but Morrison did not learn this till eleven months later.) From Paris, Morrison went to Vienna, Berlin, and Copenhagen. In Berlin he bought Toni a trinket from Wertheim's and was "much disappointed" at not hearing from her. But when he got back to London on 8th December they had a "delightful meeting", dined at Frascati's, took dress-circle front seats at the Hippodrome, and laughed heartily at the "most amusing bioscope" of *The Christmas Cheese*.

Two days later came "bitter staggering" news:

> A very unhappy day. To say that it stunned me is truth. I sat down and wrote a reply. Ran across to the Army and Navy and bought a gold watch for £7.1.0, and forwarded it by express. She is to marry an Englishman. Bless her. She is the most honourable and true of all the girls I have ever met. True as steel. It is better to end up thus for she has her chance and it would have been cruel to have counted a few days with me as equal to loss of such opportunity.

The sympathetic Ducat, who like many of Morrison's friends—and the proprietor of the Jermyn Street rooms—took an informed interest in Morrison's love-life, dined him at the Criterion and took him to see a comedy, *The Mountain Climber*: "Bewildering coincidence. I heard the name Toni called on the stage. Amusing play. But I have no ears for anything amusing."

A "very bad night" was followed by an "infernal lunch with the putrid-smelling A. R. Colquhon, who writes for the *Morning Post*". Mr Colquhon added to Morrison's discontent by picking his teeth with his finger.

But next day, when Morrison returned home after discussing the new Cabinet with the "charming and delightful Maxes", he met Toni stepping out of the lift: "Told me her story. Of the Bank Broker, grey hair, probably 50, St James Court, Buckingham Gate. Dined and evening together. She comes again tomorrow." Morrison deposited £50 for her in the savings bank, and two days later, on 16th December, gave her £10, allegedly to go to her sister Émile's funeral, in Germany. He did not see her again that year.

Glumly, "for policy only", Morrison accepted a command invitation from Mr and Mrs Arthur Walter to spend Christmas at Bear Wood. He was in a mood of "great distress and apprehension" because of Toni's long silence: a "beautiful Christmas card with handpainted pansies" which he had sent her before leaving London had not been acknowledged:

> Is she going to leave me again and shall I receive a letter saying that we must part? I am nervous and distraught for truly I love that maid so sweet and beautiful, so tender and true. I cannot sleep. I cannot think of anything but her. After breakfast a mail, but no letter from Toni, only a letter from Buckle asking me to write at once for *The Times* on the situation in China. How can I think of the situation in China when I may have lost Toni?

The Walters' hospitality, which Morrison had experienced without enthusiasm years before, offered little consolation. "Damned dull again," he commented in his diary, and a colleague and fellow-guest, W. F. Moneypenny, then writing his life of Disraeli, concurred: "They don't find it easy to get people to come here," he said. "For both can be very rude." Mrs Walter was certainly frank. She told her guests that she hated Christmas and hoped she would never experience another as dull. "I am having a fascinating time here," Morrison wrote with ponderous irony to Lady Brownrigg on Christmas Day. Coyly, he referred to Toni as his "niece":

> The weather is also charming—fog with a slight drizzle just sufficient to make the roads pleasurably slippery. . . . It is most cheerful and exhilarating and happiness would be complete if only we could have family prayers. I feel particularly cheerful because I feared that I might have to spend Christmas in worldly joyfulness with my niece. But she is remaining in Germany. . . . We are having rollicking fun. I rise at 7 a.m. and go for a walk before breakfast. . . . Then I walk out alone. We lunch together then I go with Mrs Arthur to see her rhododendron sprouts. We have afternoon tea and then I go out alone. We dine together and discuss the Athanasian Creed and other enlivening topics. And then I come upstairs and swear quietly to myself while the three men play bridge . . . we have all been to church where I returned thanks for the beautiful Christmas gift given me by Mr & Mrs Walter. In return for the services I have rendered *The Times* and in recompense for raising the paper to a position in the Far East such as no paper ever had, I have been given a very handsome sealing-wax holder, nickel-plated, luckily secured by my hostess in a window in the Tottenham Court Road where all goods are at one price 6½d, also a small bottle of cold cream the use of which I cannot imagine. I shall give it to my niece for her complexion. . . .
> P.S. I return to London tomorrow early. . . . As early as possible. By the first train. My chief anxiety is lest I might miss it.

"All my thoughts are on Toni, and I hesitate to leave the house for long fearing that a letter or telegram may come in my absence," he wrote in his diary. "What shall I do?" Restlessly, he went to Holborn Viaduct Station and waited for the Flushing Express. It was late, and Toni was not on it. He returned to his rooms, where the manager "sympathizes with me in my loneliness and thinks Toni has not played the game". The page in Morrison's diary for 4th January is missing, but according to his tabulation of their meetings he saw her every day except one from 4th January to 25th January, when he left London. There are a few diary entries:

5 Jan.—Toni lunch, stayed an hour or two.

9 Jan.—At 6 Toni came looking as beautiful as a dream. Her courtier is 53 hair parted down centre thin hair small pointed beard, bulbous nose. . . . Initials H.H.C. and goes to office late. Is probably a bill broker. I wired Moberly Bell that I could not join him. *Join M.B. at 58 when I can spend a few days still with Toni at 22!*

11 Jan.—Another disappointment. Toni . . . could not come to the country tomorrow. Her sister objects. She was disporting a mink jacket given her yesterday by her lover at a cost of £14.14.0. She laughs when she speaks of him. But he seems in earnest. I will remain here for I cannot bear to miss even an hour of companionship.

16 Jan.—Toni came along in the afternoon, dined in my rooms. This is my only joy now to be with Toni. The more I see of her the more I admire her simplicity her truthfulness her sincerity her kindness and gentleness. Terms of praise I could exhaust in her honour. Yesterday she was with the unknown one who has honorably asked her in marriage. Her eyes twinkle when she speaks of him. She can't bear to think of him and says it is impossible that she can marry him certainly impossible that she can ever hope to love him. . . . Another lover awaits her in Munchen Gladbach, but he is a Catholic and she cannot change her religion. For she is a devout Protestant. . . .

He woke on his last morning in London, after a miserable night, "full of anguish at having to leave Toni, and dreading the parting":

Along in good time to 9 a.m. from Victoria. Just 5 minutes before train left came Toni in tears depressed and looking the picture of sadness beautiful as a dream sweet and pure if ever there were purity and sweetness in woman. She said she would be brave and we kissed good-by. It is desecration to speak of it. But why do I have to? *Why not sacrifice my position and stay one year with her one year that would be full of happiness and joy.!* I have nothing to reproach myself with. For I have treated her with the utmost generosity and trust. She has now £70 in the Savings Bank and £10 or so in her pocket and will after the return of her sister, live in a room costing £1 a week instead of the £2 that she now pays. Every present I could think would please her I have given her. She has since Oct 9th been the dominant influence in my life. And now I must leave her. When shall I see her again?

The weather matched his mood. "Arrived in England in a fog," he wrote. "Left it in a rainstorm. It poured all day." He compiled a memorial list of the presents he had given Toni: dressing-gown, dress with cloth from Timony, muff and boa, shawl, boots, gloves, trunk, small dressing-case, three brooches from Continent, gold brooch from Edinburgh, pearl cross and chain, gold watch, ring of sapphires with his initials ("T.S. from G.E.M. 24 Jan '05"), his Chinese gold sleeve-links, red coral necklace, photographs, books. Supplementing this was an account of what he had spent in England from 13th September 1905 till 25th January 1906. The total was £1387, of which the biggest item was "self—£645.10.3". It is impossible to say how much of this, or of the Army and Navy Stores bill

169

for £108 8s. 3d., represented the high cost of Toni's company. More explicit items were "Books— £486", and "Tailors— £41.3.3". Before he left London, Morrison was photographed in four positions by Elliott and Fry and, following a contemporary custom, sent copies of his portrait to friends and acquaintances in England and the United States.

[XIII]

Dispiritedly, because of Toni, but conscientiously, Morrison made his quick round of European capitals. It was not very rewarding. In Paris he saw *The Times* representative, "the Jew William Lavino", and His Britannic Majesty's representative, Sir Francis Bertie. Lavino discussed the inevitability of war between France and Germany, though Germany nursed no hatred of France. "Her enemy now is England," he said. Bertie, a "florid-faced over-eating Englishman", discussed the Far East, but his views were "so ignorant, so vulgarly expressed and so ill-considered that he wasn't worth listening to". In Vienna, Morrison saw *The Times* representative, Wickham Steed, and the Emperor of Japan's representative, Makino. Steed told him the story of the Austrian Crown Prince Rudolph, whose beautiful mistress castrated him in his sleep and whom he strangled before shooting himself. Makino said how much the Japanese were indebted to Morrison. In Berlin he saw *The Times* representative, George Saunders, and the representative of the Tsar of all the Russias, Kroupensky. Saunders told him that Bell was stupid and that Chirol had been the tool of the German Foreign Office until the "thunderclap" of the Kaiser's telegram supporting Kruger turned him against Germany. Kroupensky was too upset by news of revolution in Russia to say much. "He shed tears when reference made to the sorrows of his country." In Copenhagen, Morrison saw Princess Waldemar, whose hobby was collecting fat Buddhas; there were 400 in her boudoir. The Princess told Morrison that she had refused two thrones, Bulgaria and Norway, and congratulated him on his work in China, though she thought he was too severe on Russia.

Back in London, he met Sir John Jordan, who had just arrived, and who expressed his gratitude to Morrison for the Peking appointment. When he heard the news Walter Townley wrote to Morrison, rather too archly:

A small gaily-coloured bird has sung, doubtless with mischief intent, in my ear that you were in no small measure instrumental in persuading foolish people that Jordan would make a better Minister at Peking than I should. It was almost naughty of you to do this, though of course it was quite right of you to say so if you felt it. . . . I was awfully disappointed at first, but that feeling has quite worn off now. . . . You must not think I bear you any ill will on account of this bird story. . . .

"I did not enjoy myself [in London] and had little freedom," Morrison wrote to his mother on board ship. "Social duties claimed much of my time . . . it is astonishing how well I am known . . . the only man who as far as I know refused to meet me was Lord Rosebery who seemed embittered against all the world. I met lots of well known people; Lord Lansdowne and Sir Edward Grey, Morley, Asquith, Minto and many others. Constantly I met Sir George Clarke, who has now a position of much power in England who is consulted by the F.O. frequently. . . . Curzon was especially friendly to me. So was Sir Charles Hardinge, the new Permanent Under-secretary for Foreign Affairs." He did not mention Toni.

It was a miserable voyage. Morrison could not escape his obsession with Toni. He telegraphed her from Paris on his way to join the ship at Marseilles, wrote and telegraphed from Marseilles, and wrote from every port between Port Said and Singapore, sometimes sending three or four letters or cards at a time. Many were accompanied by gifts—"thimble, bracelet, silver toilet, silver bell, belt buckle, grass cloth, dress handkerchiefs, silk, lace", he recorded. And, never doubting anything she had said, he asked with anguish, "What will she do now?":

> Will she go to Berlin? Will she marry the enterprising broker from St James Court? . . . What a fine character. Even to me who knows her so intimately she has never betrayed the name of her prince from Rohiland. I know that he is 60 that he is very tall that he had to do with natives that he had been educated largely in France. I therefore assume that he is in the Forestry Department? But how can retain engagement in the Forestry Department at 60? I should like to know who he is. Sensually he is almost impotent but he is a kindhearted gentleman and Toni owes him a debt of gratitude for service rendered at a critical time.

He tried to resolve these harrowing problems by writing of them to Lady Brownrigg, but as soon as he finished the letter he tore it up, "feeling that it was a desecration to write of my attachment". He read all Toni's letters again—"simple badly-written almost childish but thrilling me as they did when first I received them":

> She is in all my thoughts and I am very unhappy for she will soon forget me or remember me only as an amiable friend who rescued her from an *embarras*. . . . She is so weak and easily influenced. . . . I know neither the name of her old nor the name of her new lover. But I have sufficient evidence wherewith to discover her whatever happens. . . . If necessary I shall get Dungate to come with me and we can search Munchen Gladbach. . . .

"My loneliness is increasing!" he wrote as his ship, the *Mooltan*, crawled through the Suez Canal. "What is to be the future for Toni?"

And a "powerful novel" by Filson Young, *Sands of Pleasure*, enthralled him because the heroine was a foreign girl called Toni.

Moberly Bell was on the ship as far as Port Said, and Morrison found some solace in his candid evaluations of Buckle and Arthur Walter:

> Buckle's incapacity and absence of all journalistic instinct must be a heavy cross for *The Times* to bear. . . . Arthur Walter knows nothing of accounts. He expressed surprise at the remarkable coincidence that the two sides of a balance-sheet amounted to exactly equal sums. . . . Narrow ignorant deplorable incapacity. Every quality that a man should have in his high inheritance is lacking. . . .

Bell said that with £500,000 he could make *The Times* a power in the world. The building should be rebuilt. The present building, designed by John Walter, combined the smallest comfort with the greatest waste of space:

> John Walter appears to have been a disgruntled brute more ignorant and narrow-minded than Arthur. Bell surprised me by saying that his income had not come within £1000 of his expenditure any year since he joined the management . . . in March 1891. John Walter whose knowledge of money was even inferior to that of Arthur thought that Moberly Bell should live in Grosvenor Square I judge on an income that would about cover the ground rent. I can now believe the truth that Buckle who entertains but rarely received £1500 a year only and not the £5000 given him by tradition.

As an example of Arthur Walter's methods, Bell related how the policy of *The Times* on the South African war had been formulated:

> At the commencement of the war, Arthur suddenly took into his stupid head that the war was unnecessary that our policy should be to discount its importance. Alarm seized his editorial bosom. For one day the paper hedged. Then Arthur informed Bell that he was going to see Chamberlain and would be guided by his conversation. Without telling Walter, Bell immediately dashed off to Chamberlain and . . . urged him to make a special effort to convince Walter of the necessity of the war and the need of assistance from *The Times*. Walter went and on his return wrote an elaborate memorandum in which he instructed the Editor to go even further than the Editor had contemplated.

"Thus is the chief organ in Great Britain tuned," wrote Morrison, underlining his words. "Now I can understand the Parnell case."

He had little to do with his fellow-passengers. One, a Cambridge padre who had been secretary to Conan Doyle, told him that Doyle was paid £6000 for the eight Sherlock Holmes stories published by *Harper's*, "each 3000 words, represents 5/- a word". Another was the Australian millionaire, Sir Rupert Clarke, Bart., who "bore all the evidence of alcoholic tremor" and had "a gift of mendacity almost equal to Lord Lonsdale's". He was selling horses in India, and wanted to sell his estates in Australia and get out altogether. A squat man called Fitzsimmons, who sang beautifully, spoke of the extraordinary success of Australian singers in England; Ada Crossley had the finest contralto ever given to a woman, and Amy Castles would challenge Melba.

The *Mooltan* reached Singapore on 17th February, and Morrison on a self-appointed mission took the train to Johore, where he was amiably received by the regent, "a fine old Malay of 63". Morrison explained how necessary it was for the sultan to return; his conduct was unworthy and the Colonial Office viewed with disfavour his liaison with Nellie, "his lavishing jewels on her and his flaunting her before the public". The Colonial Office, Morrison added, could not regard with favour the handing-over as a free gift to Sir Frank Swettenham of 25,000 acres of valuable rubber land. "They regarded it as little better than a bid for favour." In Bangkok, Morrison had a very cordial reception from Prince Damrong, "now the most powerful man in Siam", who was very complimentary and thanked Morrison for his deep interest in Siam. Morrison walked out backwards without knocking anything over, and was received by the King in a large drawing-room. The King spoke chiefly on China. What would happen if the Empress died? Was the Emperor strong enough to resume the reins? Particularly, he inquired after Yuan Shih-k'ai, and Morrison explained Yuan's great power and said the world judged the Emperor too harshly. In Hong Kong, Morrison brought a gold charm and gold link bracelet for Toni, and sent *The Times* a report on Siam. On 15th April he was back in Peking, where he noted "a developing city pride" and a "healthier moral sense": "Peking—Improvements: Roads—Police—Carriages and Rickshaws. Telephone service, Building of public latrines along the main roads. Prohibiting of indecent placards advertising: 'To-make-the-penis-as-if-it-were-iron pills'."

Swiftly, from a lightning round of calls and callers, Morrison picked up the threads. "China is awaking to a consciousness of her nationality," Sir Ernest Satow told him. Sir Robert Hart, too, spoke of a "newborn national spirit". Colonel Aoki, the Japanese military attaché, was sceptical. "The dragon of China is still a paper dragon," he said. But all agreed that Yuan was rapidly increasing his power, and was becoming the real force behind the throne. Morrison discussed the rise of Yuan with Wu Ting-fang: "He said trouble was coming and he was going away. He didn't want to lose his head. He has a house in Shanghai and will live there in retirement. His work is finished. He spoke of the danger of the Empress Dowager's death. Suppose the old lady died he would stand up for the Emperor and he could not fail to have trouble."

Wu Ting-fang had lately acquired the conviction that Yuan Shih-k'ai was bidding for the throne. All power was gradually passing into his hands. He controlled the best forces in China, had his own troops in Peking and in Shantung, his own nominees as Viceroys in Mukden and Nanking, and two sworn brothers on the Grand Council.

Wu Ting-fang was one of Morrison's confidants. Another was Tang

Shao-yi, who was to play a role of ever-increasing importance in the next few years. Tang Shao-yi had been a friend of Yuan Shih-k'ai since they had met in Korea in 1884, when Tang was assistant to von Molldendorf, a German who controlled the finances of the Korean Government. Yuan had been impressed by Tang's courage during an attempted coup by the pro-Japanese party, and when Yuan returned to Korea in 1885 as Commissioner of Trade, Tang accompanied him as assistant. Tang, who had been educated in the United States, remained in Korea with Yuan for ten years, till China lost her sovereignty over Korea after her defeat by Japan in 1895. When Yuan took over his army command at the end of 1895, Tang became his secretary, and when Yuan acquired control of China's railways and telegraphs, Tang again was one of his assistants.

Tang was frank about his addiction to opium. He had formerly smoked one ounce of Indian opium—twenty-four pipes—a day. One ounce of Indian had satisfied him, but two ounces of Chinese opium left his craving unsatisfied. Now that he had broken the habit, it was the height of his ambition to see opium banished in China. He thought it could be done in ten years, a view which Morrison considered utopian and ill-informed. China was smoking ten times as much native as Indian opium, and Morrison thought that China was embarrassed by England's proposals to suppress the sale of opium: "It paid them in the past to deal blows at England on account of supposed opposition to the opium trade, but now they are asked to show their sincerity and . . . suffer the diminution of income they regret their previous attitude."

The Times has rescraped all the stock arguments in support of the traffic, particularly the fact that India would lose £3 million a year if China banned Indian opium. Morrison continued to work fervently in opposition to the policy of his paper, and on 20th September 1906 the Opium Edict, which provided for a progressive reduction of the opium trade, was issued.

[XV]

Morrison suffered constantly from ill-health. His diaries for 1904-5 offer a melancholy catalogue of maladies; nose-bleeding, piles, rheumatism, gout, dyspepsia, hydrocele, orchitis. Once, when he felt "really ill", with a temperature of 100.6, he consulted two English doctors and cynically entered up in adjacent columns their diametrically opposed views about his illness and its treatment. One day he writes, "Gloomy suicidal", and another. "Solitary in this God-forsaken town; no real friends here." But to a man of his avid curiosity Peking presented one of the greatest shows on earth. There was an ever-changing parade of diplomats, entrepreneurs, concession-hunters, eccentrics, intriguers, do-gooders, and picturesquely assorted scoundrels, and a never-ending flow of gossip. Morrison kept a private Who's Who of the scoundrels, and lovingly recorded the gossip.

When the Russian Minister Pavlov fought a duel with a man whom he caught embracing Madame Pavlov, a dinner guest, Miss Sontag, gave Morrison details of a rather complex family background:

Mrs Pavlov used to reproach her husband. "Tu etais l'amant de ma mère, tu es le père de ma soeur." It was true. Her mother was one of three sisters who used to sing at the *café chantants*. The eldest sister was the mistress of Cassini, former Russian Minister in Peking, and bore him a daughter and came to Peking with him where her daughter passed as Cassini's niece and the mother as the governess. This niece Marguerite is now the bosom friend of Alice Roosevelt. The second sister is the mistress of a Jew in Paris. The youngest sister came to Peking to see her sister and bore a child to the Italian Minister, who is the present Mrs Pavlov and then became the mistress of Pavlov to whom she bore a daughter. Pavlov arrived to espouse the niece of Cassini, but instead married the cousin. . . . Alexieff the financial adviser used to sleep with his own daughter.

When the fifth Earl of Lonsdale left his house in Carlton House Terrace, his two castles, and his 175,000 acres, to visit Peking, he chartered a yacht and invited Morrison to join him in a cruise. Morrison recorded his impressions of the nobleman under the heading "The lies of Lord Lonsdale":

. . . he is a whacking liar. Was very pressing. Questioned me about the action of the Germans and was very anxious to communicate my opinion to the Emperor William. He seemed respectful and I must say I never felt before how powerful must be the influence of *The Times* when this man the friend of Emperors had to apologize for being presumptuous in inviting me to accompany him. To the Americans he tells that he discovered the Klondyke and the Yellowstone Park. To me he mentioned casually the fighting he had seen in the Western States with General Custer and Buffalo Bill. To . . . others he confided that he declined the Viceroyalty of India. To the Germans he speaks of his frequent communications with the Emperor and his having a private code. . . .

A few days later, Baron Mumm provided a footnote: "Condemned Lonsdale. Said when in Berlin the guest of the Emperor he had an orgy with women disgraced the hotel and would have been expelled . . . but the Court prevented it."

One night, as chief guest at a Mess dinner, Morrison sat next to Colonel Bower, Commandant of the Peking Legation Guard. Bower "staggered" him with a vehement castigation of Kitchener, who since 1902 had been commander-in-chief in India:

. . . a windbag, a poltroon, a man who received a wound in the hand at Suakin and cried, actually cried, who reaped all the praise and honour due to Evelyn Wood and Grenfell for the organization of the

Egyptian army. In India he has been a terrible failure. The Sepoys are nearly mutinous. His schemes are paper schemes that appear good on paper but are impracticable. His last circular sent confidentially to all commanding officers asking for the reason of the discontent in the army has put him beneath contempt. His appointments are resented by the whole service. Gubby Armstrong, Lady MacDonald's brother, a blacksheep and a man so crooked that when up for the United Services Club at Simla—I saw this myself—had 20 blackballs and 2 white, though one blackball in five is sufficient to blackball him. A man of criminal instincts whom no decent woman will have in her house is made A.A.G., the appointment having actually been created for him.

Occasionally there were nostalgic letters from old Edinburgh friends. When Dungate wrote from Pontypridd that the Welsh were "simply dirty savages" Morrison replied:

I am much pleased to hear of your high opinion of the Welsh. We had a Welsh regiment here, Royal Welch Fusiliers after the trouble and the general opinion . . . was that they were worse than the Boxers only not so courageous, bigger thieves and bigger liars, men who rob graveyards. . . . Their Colonel Bertie was given the Companionship of the Bath for meritorious services in bringing his troops into Peking without a casualty except for drink. His men took good care that there would be no casualties. . . . They're a putrid lot, worse than the Irish—the only virgin I thought I met when I was in Wales was three months in the family way. She explained to me that she could not possibly be pregnant because she had never gone with less than five men in the same day.

[XVI]

Early in October, Morrison received a letter from A. P. Stokes telling him that Toni had married the German barber, Loth. He received this cataclysmic news with extraordinary calm. To Stokes he wrote back mock-heroically:

You can well imagine the anguish that gripped my vitals when I read of my having been done in the eye by a barber! I compare it with the shock I sustained when a student in Paris enamoured of a ladylike person of no character. She disappeared for a week having gone to *la campagne avec sa mère* and I was heartbroken. Subsequently I met *mère*, of this occasion and found her to be a male, a big-girthed dago, a major-domo in the Chat Noir!

But talking aloud to his diary he confided his unshaken faith in the barber's wife:

Much however of Stokes's story is incorrect. The fat landlady tells me that Toni became Mrs Loth in November 19. She was certainly at a wedding on that day but it was not her own but that of a friend at Brixton. If she has deceived me I will bear no resentment on the contrary I will ever after be amazed at the miraculous cleverness and consistency of the deception. As a matter of interest I would almost be glad at such an exhibition of duplicity but it is altogether impossible and not to be considered seriously.

CHAPTER EIGHT

[I]

JAPAN'S SURPRISING victory over Russia had wide repercussions. In China, this question was asked: How had a small Asiatic country been able to inflict such a crushing defeat on the European colossus? The generally accepted answer was that autocracy had been defeated by constitutional government, and respectfully goaded by memorialists, including Yuan Shih-k'ai, the Empress Dowager now agreed to accept what she had opposed seven years before. Five high-ranking officials, including Duke Tsai Tse and Shao Ying, were sent on a mission abroad to study the mysteries of constitution-making. They set out from Peking in December 1905 and returned eight months later, filled with admiration for the English constitution, but not for the English monarchy. As Sir John Jordan told Morrison, King Edward did not like Chinese, and made it apparent by his reception of the commissioners. Tang Shao-yi was more explicit:

> The King would see the Duke only and for two minutes only. The door was shut in the faces of the others, literally. Shao-yi was shut out and the Minister to Belgium was directed to wait in the ante-room.

"No wonder the Commissioners have come back very anti-British, though they were given degrees at the Universities and were dined at the Guildhall," Morrison commented. A Bureau of Political Studies was set up to study the commissioner's report. Tang Shao-yi spoke "with contemptuous candour" of the thirteen old gentlemen who composed it. The president was the "opium sot", the Prince Ch'ing. One member was eighty-two, another seventy-nine. Only one had ever been abroad. None knew any foreign language. Despite these limitations, and the fact that many were deaf, they produced a report, and in September 1906 the Empress Dowager issued an edict promising the grant of a constitution. The creation of an Imperial Parliament with very limited powers was foreshadowed, as a goal to be approached circumspectly.

[II]

On the ship which brought the new secretary of the French Legation, M. Paul Claudel, to the Far East in June 1906 was a Dr Takeno, travelling to Tokyo. "Dr Takeno" was the *nom-de-voyage* of a forty-year old Cantonese, Sun Wen, better known as Dr Sun Yat-sen—or, in official Manchu reports, as Brigand Sun Yen. Dr Sun, who was educated and converted to Christianity in Hawaii, and studied medicine in Hong Kong, had been a revolutionary since 1895, when he led an unsuccessful rising in Canton. A refugee from China with a price on his head after the abortive coup, he toured Europe, collecting supporters, money, and political theories. In his wanderings he became more and more remote from the realities of life in China, and Morrison developed an enduring contempt for the vagueness of his thinking, in which a woolly, ineffectual idealism often prevailed. In Tokyo, Dr Sun formed a new revolutionary society, the Tungmenhui. On the ship he talked frankly to Claudel, who reported the conversation to Morrison:

> Sun said (which was true) that he had been to the F.O. in Paris (what was probably untrue) that he had been received by Sir Edward Grey. He had planned the rising which failed in January 1903, and was on his way to Japan to raise money for the next rising which he has promised would burst forth shortly. He spoke of having access to millions.

Some of the "millions" came from dollar notes, redeemable at ten dollars after the revolution, which were selling "like hot cakes". In August, Claudel showed Morrison a long dispatch from Sun, "the tenor of which was hare-brained, utopian and anti-foreign". But the revolutionary movement continued to gather impetus.

[III]

The last day of 1906 found Morrison on the *likin* (Customs) boat in the Siang River near the walled town of Yochow. He was on one of his periodical jaunts, this time by river and road, from Peking to Hanoi, by way of Kaifeng, Hankow, Changsha, and Kweilin.

In Changsha, Commissioner Oliver Ready ("a strong Norfolk man") author of *Life and Sport in China*, told him of "a shocking murder in the Customs compound which had haunted him for days and kept him awake at nights":

> It was the murder by the wife and mother of P. C. Yu, the chief Superintendent of Customs police and Mixed Court Magistrate in Changsha settlement, of a pretty slave girl of whose influence with Yu they were jealous. The poor girl was beaten to death suffering terribly for more than three hours her cries being heard all this time and no one venturing to interfere—it was none of their business, Yu

himself being absent. In the morning the dead body was hastily buried but the news had got about and Ready demanded an enquiry. This was denied him. The woman had died from cholera said the Magistrate. But Ready was not satisfied and he demanded more peremptorily. Again there was evasion. It was a matter, the death of a slave girl bought for a few dollars, of small importance.

But the dogged man from Norfolk had his blood up, and insisted on an inquiry. Reluctantly the *tipao*, or headman, sent along two men who raised the coffin, threw open the lid, and reported that the girl had died of opium. That was the end of the affair. "What did it matter"? Morrison wrote. "It was only the murder of a slave girl. Yet this country where this can be done—slavery eunuchs torture and a thousand cruelties and barbarities—is an aspirant—for the abolition of extra-territoriality . . . abolition . . . is a dream which will not be realized in our time. . . ."

Many other things shook Morrison on his journey: "The awful street beggars. One form haunts me yet, that of a boy naked in the cold lying on his side on the muddy flags croaking his dolorous refrain. . . ." And the torture of footbinding: "Since leaving Hankow I have not seen a single woman or girl in childhood who has not small feet. Exhortations may be issued by the Viceroy but for his own harem he prefers small-footed women. Such is the mockery of it all." At Kweilin the Rev. Frank Child, a "good clean nice-spoken Englishman", told Morrison that it was a Kwangsi custom to drink the blood and eat portion of the body, calves and heart of a brave rebel who suffered death for his crimes. At Hanoi he was pestered by rickshaw coolies asking if he desired to go to a girl's house, "and when you said no, asking if you desired a boy, and then proceeding to detail the kind of boy, Annamite or Chinese. . . . It is truly a pestilential city and it is pretty certain that the vices that degrade it were introduced by the French and are not indigenous."

His disillusion with the Chinese continued. "China is guided by more ignorant men than ever," he wrote in June 1907. There is no hope. There is not one man who knows anything about foreign affairs at all." When Lu Chuan-lin was made a member of the Grand Council, he wrote:

He is sufficiently mature verging on eighty.

He is adequately decrepit requiring two men to raise him to his feet and two others to balance him there.

Sight and hearing failed him during the Taiping rebellion (1851-65) so that he can bring an unprejudiced mind to bear upon questions of which he is ignorant.

[IV]

Morrison had another first-hand, and dispiriting, look at life in the provinces when he journeyed by ponies and mules to the city of Sian, where the Imperial Court had rested after the Boxer uprising. As he rode through the thickly populated but impoverished country he was struck by the squalor along this main route of the Empire: "No traveller could pass along here without getting the worst possible impression of China's poverty and decadence, and yet while true of this route it is not true elsewhere. It is impossible to generalize in China."

The district had been devastated first by the Taiping and then by the Mohammedan revolts: "General poverty. Monuments of former wealth and prosperity left to decay. Buildings and temples and bridges and pagodas and watchtowers all unrepaired. . . . Roads the worst in the world. . . . Women with small feet, horrible diseases among men. No benevolence no charity children sold into slavery."

In Hanchung, where girls were bred for sale, they were very cheap. "This afternoon," Morrison was told, "Mr Cho of the Money Order Office purchased a girl of 14 with natural feet for 24 taels (£3 sterling). He will keep her and bye and bye sell her for 60 or 100 taels for a concubine." In a squalid inn at Sian, with patched paper ceiling, cobweb and insect-infested walls, mud floors on which people had spat for years, a yard two feet deep in muck and mud and animal droppings, and a well with its mouth below the level of the surface drainage, Morrison brooded over the "frightful prevalence" of tuberculosis in China. "To think," he reflected, "that these people, steeped in ignorance and suffering patiently such inns and such roads, should care for a constitution." But the countryside was beautiful. The wheat was "just high enough to green the swards, as in England", and the persimmons, the chief industry, hung in festoons "in glorious red" from the branches and lit up the landscape "with rich glorious colour".

He read an *Anthology of Australian Verse* and felt "heartily homesick".

His homesickness recurred when A. E. Wearne of Reuter's said to him one day, "Why don't you go home to Australia? You're just at the age to take up political life." The suggestion set Morrison "furiously to think": "I have often thought of this and out of sympathy as I am with Chirol I think the time has come for me to think seriously whether it is good enough to continue in this post or not."

He recalled that Mackenzie King had thought he might become Prime Minister of Australia, and that Gwynne had urged him to return. And there was that "curious dream" of being Prime Minister. . . .

Lady Brownrigg urged him not to delay if he wished to enter political life. She had been "much touched" at a gift of lace that Morrison had sent for her baby daughter, and wrote a lively account of the launching of the dreadnought *Collingwood*, one of "Jacky" Fisher's controversial brainchildren, by Mrs Asquith:

> . . . a magnificent spectacle which impressed even the wooden hearts of Asquith and McKenna, the former quite emotional which he only reported to be after a good dinner [Asquith had succeded Campbell-Bannerman as Prime Minister] . . . we frankly discussed the appoint-

ment of McKenna as First Lord of the Admiralty—he asked me a tremendous number of questions and displayed in them all a profound ignorance of the affairs of the Navy. . . . Mrs Asquith . . . presented the oddest appearance. She wore a skin-tight biscuit coloured skirt, and obviously no petticoats, as there was a gale of wind blowing into the launching platform, her outline (which is angular to a degree) was visible to *all*—she started in a hat which flapped wildly on her head, and ended by having to borrow suitable headgear from Mrs Waldorf Astor—Mrs McKenna . . . looked a tangle of hair—veil—feathers—with the countenance of an animated nursery governess— her "Right Honourable" spouse must have been originally intended to perambulate the busy aisles of "Marshall and Snellgrove" if features and figure mean anything—but they were all hugely delighted with themselves—

With the introduction of a new regime in China it might be a good moment for you to give up your work there or if you are reluctant to do that I think you are fully entitled to ask for an increase in pay —surely after 12 years *The Times* would not hesitate—I suppose any other paper would give you more? If you will forgive the impertinence of my offering you advice—I should say that if you *ever* intend to abandon your present position and take up Australian politics— or English political life . . . you ought not to delay the change much longer—every year after 40 the roots strike deeper and every year makes the uprooting more difficult—sometimes more painful.

Morrison had inquired about Admiral Lambton, of the *Alacrity*. Lady Brownrigg's reply showed that the Nelson spirit, in some respects at least, had survived: "Gossip has drifted home that he has been keeping a lady on board the *Alacrity*—a foreign countess. There was talk at one time of recalling him in consequence of this breach of discipline."

[V]

Late in September 1907, Morrison was "staggered" by a letter from Moberly Bell, asking him confidentially if he would come to London as Foreign Editor of *The Times*. Bell hinted at "a good many changes" that would take place in the following six months:

. . . no single person knows that I am writing to you nor will know. After receiving this letter will you wire me any word you like beginning with Y which I shall take as Yes or any word you like beginning with N which I shall take as No or any word you like beginning with D which I shall understand as dubious. . . .

Morrison did not use Bell's ingenious code. He spent two days and much of one night considering the offer and decided he would go to England and see what it was all about. He wired Bell accordingly and left

Peking on 3rd October, arriving in London, by way of Moscow, twenty days later. He booked in at the Hotel Windsor ("room 182, double, 5/- a day and 1/6 attendance").

Bell tried to persuade Morrison to remain in London, where, he said, "new blood" was urgently needed. He gave a melancholy report on life in Printing House Square. Chirol was in a state of "hyper-excitation and exceedingly jumpy" and wanted to go away. His assistant, Gordon Browne, had recently broken down. Another editorial man, Macdougall, had retired with a nervous breakdown. "Poor Buckle" had been operated on for cancer of the tongue. Amery had serious ear trouble. No one was left. Bell thought Morrison would be a great success as Foreign Editor. If he liked he could alternate with Chirol. But Morrison was not convinced. He talked to Chirol, mentioned that his ambition was to become British Minister in Peking, and "in a guarded way" communicated part of what Bell had written to him. It was the first Chirol had heard of it. He said he had no intention of retiring, even if he could afford to, and he could not.

The malaise of *The Times* was not confined to its staff. Economically, too, it was very sick—its circulation, 38,000, was 22,000 less than it had been thirty years before. All kinds of rumours were circulating. One was that it was to close down within a month. "What is going to happen?" Morrison asked. "It is being hopelessly badly run." He got some enlightenment from Horace Everett Hooper, an enterprising New Englander who, with his partner, William Montgomery Jackson, had induced *The Times* in 1898 to reprint the ninth edition of the *Encyclopaedia Britannica*, and sell it direct to the public on the instalment plan, a publishing technique then almost unknown in England. According to Bell, Messrs Hooper and Jackson, another New Englander, had been making £110,000 a year for the past nine years. *The Times*, which sponsored and advertised the *Encyclopaedia*, received from them 70s. on each set sold, and had cleared £108,000:

> Hooper told me the story. Arthur Walter unless change effected will have to leave Bear Wood within a year. Extraordinary business incapacity. Is paid £1000 a year to manage. Two separate concerns publishing of paper and printing thereof. Former pays not a cent. Latter pays handsomely too handsomely. Hooper would call him a knave if he didn't know he was a fool. . . . Arthur is hopeless and John is vacuous. . . . Arthur owns one third *Times* and more than half the printing, Godfrey owning one quarter of the printing.

Morrison could not understand why *The Times* should be involved in book-selling and book-publishing. It ran the Times Book Club, which sold an average of 1400 books a day, and was preparing a *Times Universal History* and a new edition of the *Britannica*. Why was all this adventitious work necessary? Bell explained:

> Because of the competition of the Modern Press and the impossibility of running a paper purely as a newspaper. To be independent of

advertisers it is essential that revenue should be derived from other sources than advertisements. He gave me many instances of how advertisers will advertise only if they can have access to what will be written by the paper in which they advertise on the subject of their advertisement. Nobel offered an advertisement of £2000 per annum if he could be shown *The Times* articles, on say, "Electricity" before they were published. *Truth* attacks us because we did not advertise the E.B. in *Truth*, or rather, because we withdrew our ad. In all the papers the news columns are made subservient to the adv. columns. *The Times* is the only paper which publishes the letters adverse to the railways. All papers will publish attacks on the G.P.O. but the G.P.O. does not advertise. It is a rotten and corrupt state of things that makes one ashamed.

Morrison saw most of his old friends in London. Leo Maxe was in a mood of violent and apocalyptic despair. All was lost. There was no patriotism. In twenty years he had never known such hopelessness. And now Germany was egging on America to fight Japan and rupture the Anglo-Japanese alliance. (Maxe was a virulent, fanatical Germanophobe, "one of the two great war-lords of the English press", in the words of the English historian Wingfield-Stratford, "who led the campaign of mass suggestion against Germany". The other was Northcliffe. Maxe was read in the clubs, Northcliffe in the pubs.) Another man who disliked Germans, according to "the faithful" General Browne, was the Prince of Wales, the future George V. Browne talked "garrulously and foolishly" after too much claret at the Naval and Military Club:

> But he repeated with zest stories by Sir Kelly Kenny of the Prince of Wales and his antipathy to those "bloody buggers" of Germans! and whores in whom he included Mrs George Keppel. He hates whores— and Jews and will have none in his house . . . the latter makes something out of all the purchase price paid for titles. Her husband has £800 per annum. She has jewels that cost many thousands! Such is our modern society.

"Taffy" Gwynne urged Morrison to go back to Australia, where, he said, Morrison's future lay. He had spoken to Alfred Deakin about this when Deakin was in London at the Imperial Conference earlier in the year. "It was pleasant to hear this for it agreed with my views," Morrison wrote. A few days later he got a letter from Gwynne: "I am particularly anxious to talk to you about Australia; your true destiny is there, old chap. It wants a man and a statesman. I have some idea of the wrench it will be to you to leave China but there is a bigger career for you in Australia. . . ."

There were the inevitable social occasions. The Duchess of St Albans invited Morrison to dinner to meet Sir Henry Blake:

> . . . and damned bad table manners had her Grace, eating her food like a bosun on a limejuicer. . . . Sir Henry complained with some bitterness of the way he had been shelved—41 years public service,

governed one third of the Colonies of Great Britain and now retired without even a thankyou! Others had been given the Privy Councillorship—he nothing!

Morrison suggested to Chirol that he get Blake the Privy Councillorship, and suggested to the Chinese Minister, Lord Li Ching-fong, that he appoint Sir John McLeavy Brown as adviser. Brown, an old friend of Morrison's, who had held many diplomatic posts in the Far East and had recently been controller of Finance in Korea, was duly appointed two days later. Morrison was not impressed with the Chinese Legation at 49 Portland Place: "Old slattern woman. No doormat. Very dirty large room with seedy furniture. Other room office of bumptious Soochow man unshaven for a week with dirty sweat cloth across back of chair. . . ."

When he called on Lady Brownrigg and Lady Percy Scott he noted, characteristically: "Latter hates and despises her husband. Former amorous still and now pregnant 6 months or more for noticed twitches showing viability of foetus." (Admiral Sir Percy Scott divorced his wife in 1911.)

The President of the China Association, Richard Gundry, a former editor of the *North China Herald*, who had been correspondent of *The Times* in China from 1865 to 1878, invited Morrison to address the association. Morrison replied that he would see if he could summon sufficient courage. Gundry wrote back: "I know the feeling well. . . . The difference between a Britisher's shyness in public speaking and an American's easy approach is a psychological study." The invitation at once flattered and frightened Morrison. "I am nervous as a little girl and my heart thumps when I think I have to stand up in the great hall and talk without confusion," he wrote in his diary. He worked very hard preparing his speech, showed the text to Dungate and McLeavy Brown, read it to Mrs Hutton, repeated it to himself on a long solitary walk, and carefully tested the volume of his voice in the empty hall of the Metropole Hotel where the dinner was to be held. He was a great success. "The annual dinner of the China Association was enlivened by a brilliant speech from Dr Morrison in which he vigorously deprecated scepticism as to the sincerity of the progressive movement in China," said the *Spectator*:

> We were too apt to believe stories of alleged barbarities, and too readily forgot the gruesome fictions published in 1900 about the fate of those who were besieged in Peking, when he "had the honour of being pictorially represented as being boiled in oil in the same cauldron with his Excellency the Russian Minister." He could not too severely reprobate the point of view which regarded England for the English, Australia for the Australians, and Canada for the Canadians as loyal, laudable, patriotic aspirations, but denounced China for the Chinese as the manifestation of an anti-foreign and reactionary spirit. There was much to blame in China, but far more to praise, —the awakening of a consciousness of nationality, the spread of Western education, attempts to reorganize the Army, and the growth of the native Press, which displayed an admirable outspokenness and

courage, and unanimously supported the Government in its efforts to deal with opium evil. In conclusion, Dr Morrison strongly disputed the political wisdom of keeping the sore rankling in North China by the retention of English and Indian regiments on Chinese soil "as a perpetual reminder of the sin which China had committed seven years ago, but which she claimed she had made a sincere effort to expiate." America had certainly lost nothing in prestige by withdrawing her troops from Tientsin. Sporadic disturbances might occur in China, but nothing could now stay the progress of the people.

There was well-fed laughter from the distinguished guests, who included a generous sprinkling of knights, and representatives of the Foreign and Colonial Offices, when Morrison said:

It was natural that we, who were the most superior of all God's people, whose mission it was to pry into the internal affairs of other less favoured countries, should condemn procedure in China that would never be tolerated here. It was natural, for example, that the system of purchase of rank in China, still so common in that Empire, should be condemned by those nondescript capitalists of alien origin whose entry into their ranks was adding so greatly to the dignity and prestige of our hereditary aristocracy.

The confidence in China expressed by Morrison the after-dinner speaker was scarcely an honest expression of the views of Morrison the diarist, and at least two of his friends were critical. "I am afraid I cannot share your optimism," said Gundry. And Sir Walter Hillier wrote: "Your speech . . . carried me away but a letter from my brother Guy tonight has destroyed those pleasing visions which your eloquence . . . conjured up." Others were full of praise. Sir Ernest Satow wrote: "You said a great many things I should like to say myself, but they come better from you," and C. S. Addis, of the Hong Kong and Shanghai Bank: "You rendered a public service by your speech. . . . There was a sense of conviction and of knowledge . . . which . . . will, I am sure, create a profound impression." Gwynne described the speech as "admirable and plucky". When he returned to Peking, Morrison was told that his speech had caused a sensation there and would help to restore British prestige among the Chinese. Sir James Stewart Lockhart, H.M.'s Commissioner at Weihaiwei, wrote: "I . . . admired your pluck in telling your hosts what could not have been entirely pleasing to their self-satisfied ears, and in giving expression to what you well know will not make you popular with the white men in the Far East . . . interested you boldly advised removal of the troops."

On his second day in London, Morrison took a "taximeter" to Maggs, the booksellers, and after dinner at the Grand Grill Room ("3/6 plus 6d, quite as good as the Junior Naval and Military") went to 31 Pulteney Street, Bayswater, to see Toni. "Seemed like a trull at the gate but children were upstairs . . . probably decent," he noted. But Toni was not there. There is no other mention of her for a month. On 21st November, three days before his departure, the maid at his hotel drew Morrison's attention to a telegram on the looking-glass: "It was from Toni. I was nearly knocked over. Just WOULD YOU LIKE TO SEE ME AND WHEN TONI LOTH 24 WESTMORELAND STREET BAYSWATER; I have written to say that I will meet her tomorrow at 3 at the Marble Arch."

Next day's entries, disjointed and enigmatic, say nothing of Morrison's reaction to the elaborate fabric of lies which Toni had woven about herself:

Toni Loth—b. March 27 1874. Husband is manager of Hairdresser at 126 Queen Victoria Street is 31 years old. German and Protestant. Wanda is the niece.

Everything I gave her except the red coral necklace which is probably false is in the pawnshop.

Married about September 23 1905.

Divorced her first husband. Her child died at 7 months.

She had still the suit of clothes that I had got for her from Timony of Donegal.

There was another meeting next day at Appendrodts in Oxford Circus ("Toni . . . came more than half an hour late when in fact I was debating to go away".) They met again in Queen's Road the following day, Morrison's last in London, lunched at Frascati's, then along to Queen's Road by tube, "as in the old days". They had tea in a "horrible Italian place" opposite Knightsbridge, and dinner in an L.C.D. restaurant. McLeavy Brown and Lionel James came to the train to see Morrison off. Toni apparently had gone back to the barber.

[VI]

"The most astonishing thing today is the Reuter's telegram saying that *The Times* had become a limited liability company with Arthur Walter as Chairman and C. Arthur Pearson as Managing Director," Morrison wrote on 8th January 1908. Next day came a telegram from Paris: MORRISON PEKING SHOULD REORGANISATION INVOLVE CHANGE PLEASE REMEMBER NORTHCLIFFE RITZ PARIS. A hurricane of change had blown through Printing House Square in the six weeks since Morrison's departure. One night in December, Northcliffe had gone to a party in Berkeley Square to hear Paderewski. But his interest in the pianist had waned when a fellow guest mentioned casually that Arthur Pearson's moribund *Standard* was to be amalgamated with the not over-healthy *Times*. Northcliffe soon found out that Pearson and Arthur Walter had been discussing a marriage of the two ailing papers, but had reached no finality. To create alarm and confusion, he put a paragraph in the *Observer*, which he then owned, hinting that *The Times* had been sold to him. This appeared on 5th January. Moberly Bell knew nothing of the discussions with Pearson till the following day when he received a paragraph from Walter for insertion in *The Times*, announcing the proposed merger.

The staff of *The Times*, and Walter's partners, who, too, had not been told of the negotiations, were equally bewildered. Moberly Bell wrote bitterly to Walter: "Forgive me if I say I cannot help feeling deeply hurt at the want of confidence you have shown in one who has tried to serve you faithfully and who regarded you as a friend." Bell and Buckle both denounced the Pearson scheme as financially unsound, and while Walter, under pressure from them and his partners, was seeking an alternative scheme, Bell was approached by Northcliffe, who said he intended to buy the controlling interest in *The Times*, if possible with Bell's assistance. Northcliffe remained in the background while Bell put before a judge-in-chambers a plan by which *The Times* was reorganized as a limited liability company with Arthur Walter as chairman, Bell as managing director, and Buckle, Chirol, and Moneypenny as directors. On 16th March, Bell counted out to the judge 320 Bank of England notes of £1000 each, and Northcliffe had acquired control of the *The Times*. His hidden role was disclosed within a few weeks by W. T. Stead, but apparently Morrison knew nothing of it till early in November, when Bland told him that Lovat Fraser, formerly editor of the *Times of India*, had joined *The Times*, that Northcliffe was the proprietor, and that the outlook for the paper was "very good indeed".

Chirol later told Morrison how he had helped to save *The Times* from Pearson: "When the time was most critical he went to see Lord Lansdowne who received him in bed. 'I was with Walter at Eton. He was an ass then. I often told him so. I will tell him so again if it is any good.' He sent for Walter and this influenced him."

One of the directors of the proposed Pearson-Walter company was to be Sir Charles Tennant, who held 1/213 share in *The Times*. Chirol saw Tennant, who said that a good thing about the proposal was that it would enable them to get rid of Moberly Bell, who was "feathering his own nest and ruining the paper":

> Chirol satisfied him . . . by means of affidavits . . . that when Moberly joined the paper in 1890 it was not solvent and was overdrawn £48,000 and that in the 16 years he had earned for the paper £480,000 and that at the end he was poorer than when he began; Tennant was horrified at the way he had been misled . . . and rendered immense assistance.

[VII]

In September the Dalai Lama, accompanied by 300 lesser lamas and other Tibetan attendants, a small force of soldiers, 800 camels, and 500 horses and mules, came to China to pay his respects to the Empress Dowager, who was preparing to celebrate her seventy-third birthday. It was the first time a Tibetan ruler had visited Peking since 1652.

Morrison's interview with the Dalai Lama was disappointing. He was entertaining, when he received a note from the Foreign Office saying that the Dalai Lama would receive him at midday:

I rushed round to Sir Walter Hillier to ask him to look after my guests, rode on to Bland and thence to Rockhill to borrow a Ceremonial Scarf. And then rode hell for leather. . . . Did not have long to wait when in came Dalai Lama. Crowds of Mongols outside and kneeling in adoration, a curious sight. Could see Dalai Lama like Buddha on yellow silk-lined dais and canopy in conventional attitude of Buddha. Deeply pockmarked—receding forehead—close-cropped hair, growth not being able to shave. Prominent teeth and meeting well. Small chin. Draped in dull purple robe. Very insipid conversation. I sat down having given him Ceremonial Scarf and had it returned. Bad tea apples and nuts.

A few days later the Mongol Prince of Hanta, Chin Wang-yeh, called on Morrison by appointment. Morrison showed him his guns and books, and the prince said: "The Dalai Lama is much concerned to know if anything may betide him in Tibet in regard to the English?" Morrison assured the prince there was nothing to fear. When the Dalai Lama left Peking by special train he took with him all the thermos flasks that could be bought.

"The Emperor is suffering from constipation and the Empress Dowager from diarrhoea, so the Imperial balance is struck," Morrison wrote to Bland on 9th November. Next day he left on a shooting expedition to Kwantai, returning on 15th November to find that the Emperor and the Empress were both dead. "Mighty sick" at his "hard luck" in missing the big news, he worked hard all day "trying to retrieve my blunder".

The Emperor had been in a coma for some days. Some said he had been poisoned by Yuan Shih-k'ai. But a Cantonese doctor trained in Western medicine thought it resulted from his gluttonous appetite for women. The malaise of the Empress was easier to diagnose. At a fancy-dress picnic given in honour of the Dalai Lama she had indulged a gluttonous appetite for cream and crab-apples, exacerbating a looseness of the bowels from which she had suffered throughout the summer.

Periods of public mourning—a hundred days for the Emperor and twenty-seven months for the Empress—were proclaimed, and newspapermen in Peking avidly discussed the succession to the Imperial Throne and the future of its principal prop, Yuan Shih-k'ai. Yuan's deadly enemy, the Emperor, had conveniently died before the Empress. Had she died first, and the Emperor been restored to power, Yuan's kiss of death in 1898 would surely not have been forgotten. Yuan's relations with the Empress had remained very good. Just before her death he had presented her on her birthday with two fox-fur gowns, a chunk of calambac inlaid with precious stones, a pair of filigree and pearl phoenixes, and a piece of coral as tall as a man; a costly investment in goodwill now unfortunately lost. On her deathbed the Empress had named P'u Yi, the three-year-old son of Prince Ch'un, successor to the throne, and appointed his father Regent. Prince Ch'un, a brother of the dead puppet Emperor had, like him, no love for Yuan Shih-k'ai, nor had the other Manchu princes who now held power. Kuang Hsu's widow, Lung Yu, now became Empress Dowager.

On 4th January 1909, Morrison was about to set out for his cottage in the hills when "providentially" he was delayed. Charles Tenney, of the United States Legislation, came in excitedly with a copy of an Imperial decree, just issued, dismissing Yuan from all his offices. The text was deliberately insulting:

> Unfortunately, Yuan Shih-k'ai is now suffering from an affection of the foot, he has difficulty in walking and it is hardly possible for him to discharge his duties adequately. We command Yuan Shih-k'ai to resign his offices at once and to return to his native place to treat and to convalesce from the ailment. It is our resolution to show consideration and compassion.

It was Yuan's first intimation that there was anything wrong with his foot, but he was not to forget the imaginary malady.

Yuan feared that he might be assassinated. On the morning after the publication of the decree Tenney received a hastily scribbled note from his son, "young Yuan", asking if the gates of the legation could be kept open. Yuan himself fled to Tientsin, to the Astor House, but was persuaded to return in the evening when messengers arrived with dispatches pointing out that he would lose face if he remained, and promising him protection. Sir John Jordan had a rugged solution to his problem: "Why can't Yuan Shih-k'ai put himself at the head of 10,000 men and sweep the lot out?" he asked Morrison. But Yuan retired with dignity to a retreat near Changten which he named appropriately, The Garden for Cultivating Longevity. He was "much touched", he told his follower, Tsai Ting-kan, by the telegram of sympathy which Morrison sent him. Tsai gave "young Yuan" the *Meditations of Marcus Aurelius* so that he might accept adversity as calmly as his father had.

Despite great nose-bleeding, Morrison was up in good time on the morning of 2nd May. In his best clothes, his helmet "framed in the habiliments of woe", he walked to the diplomatic stand at the Hatamen to witness the funeral procession of the late Emperor. He was not impressed by the "wretched Manchu cavalry" on their half-starved ponies, with "illclad riders carrying bows and arrows", or by the raggedness of the bearers with broken umbrellas and tattered banners, and drafted a telegram about them which he did not send. But in November, when the Empress Dowager was buried—almost exactly a year after her death—he mailed *The Times* a "lapidary" description of the ceremony:

> The 9 November at 5 a.m. was the hour of good omen originally chosen by the Astrologers for the departure of the remains of Her late Majesty the Empress Dowager from their temporary resting place in the Forbidden City to the mausoleum prepared for her at the Eastern Hills. To meet the convenience of the foreign representatives, the hour was subsequently changed to 7 a.m.
>
> The catafalque was borne by eighty-four bearers, the largest number which can carry this unwieldy burden through the City

gates; but beyond the walls the coffin was transferred to a larger bier borne by one hundred and twenty men. In front walked the Prince Regent, the bodyguard of Manchu Princes and the members of the Grand Council, attended by the Secretariat staff. Behind rode first a smart body of troops, followed by a large number of camels whose Mongol attendants carried tent-poles and other articles for use in the erection of the 'matshed palaces,' wherein the coffin rests at night at the different stages of the four days' journey to the tombs. Behind the Mongols were borne in procession the gaudy honorific umbrellas presented to the Old Buddha on the occasion of her return from exile at Hsi-an-fu [Sian] in 1901: all these were burnt on the 16th instant when the body was finally entombed. Following the waving umbrellas came a body of Lama dignitaries, and after them a contingent from the Imperial Equipage Department bearing Manchu sacrificial vessels, Buddhist symbols and embroidered banners. Conspicuous in the *cortège* were three splendid chariots with trappings and curtains of Imperial Yellow silk, emblazoned with dragons and phoenixes and two palanquins similar to those used by the Empress Dowager on her journeys in State; these also were burned at the mausoleum. Noticeable figures in the procession were the six chief eunuchs, including the notorious Li Lien-ying and the short handsome attendant who usually accompanied the Empress's sedan chair. The spectacle, as a whole, was most impressive; no such pomp and circumstance, say the Chinese, has marked the obsequies of any Empress of China since the funeral of the Empress Wu (circa A.D. 700) of whom the annals record that hundreds of attendants were buried alive in her mausoleum. Ninety miles away, in a silent spot surrounded by virgin pine forest and backed by protecting hills, are the Eastern Tombs, towards which, for four days, the great catafalque made its way along the yellow-sanded road. There stands the mausoleum, originally built by the faithful Jung Lu for his Imperial Mistress, at a cost which stands in the government records at eight millions of taels. . . . Throughout her lifetime, and particularly of late years, Yehonala took great interest and pride in her last resting-place, visiting it at intervals and exacting the most scrupulous attention from those entrusted with its building and adornment. On one occasion, in 1897, when practically completed, she had it rebuilt because the teak pillars were not sufficiently massive. After the death of Jung Lu, Prince Ch'ing became responsible for the custody of the tomb and its precious contents—the sacrificial vessels of carved jade, the massive vases and incense burners of gold and silver, which adorn the mortuary chamber; the richly jewelled couch to receive the coffin, and the carved figures of serving maids and eunuchs who stand for ever in attendance. . . .

The cost of the late Emperor's funeral has been officially recorded, with the nice accuracy which characterizes Chinese finance, at

459,940 taels, 2 mace, 3 candareens and li. (about £57,000). As the cost of a funeral in China closely reflects the dignity of the deceased and the "face" of his or her immediate survivors, these figures become particularly interesting, when compared with the cost of the Empress Dowager's funeral, which is placed at one and a-quarter to one and a-half million taels. Rumour credited the Regent with an attempt to cut down this expenditure, which attempt he abandoned at the last moment in the fact of the displeasure of the powerful Yehonala Clan.

[VIII]

In December 1908, Sir John Jordan, whose cards had been marked *ad interim*, was confirmed as minister, though "to his great disappointment", his salary was cut from £5000 to £4500. He showed his gratitude for the appointment by inviting Morrison to share his Christmas turkey and plum pudding. A few months later P. A. Chance, who had served in the British Legation in Peking at the end of the nineties, wrote to Morrison: "I am glad to have got Jordan now. He is a good man so far as the F.O. permits anyone to be active, and if he does not accomplish much you may safely attribute it to the fact that at home the authorities don't want to hear anything about the Far East. . . ." Chance, who found life "a weary business, full of disappointments and vanished ideals", summed up the English political and social scene. Cromer was dying of cancer. (He did not die till 1917.) Joseph Chamberlain was "done for" with paralysis. (He died in 1914.) Rosebery had "buried himself with his own tongue", and: "Socially things are not well. . . . The working classes are all right, but the lower middle class, the distributors and small traders, are being ground to bits by big organizations hardly distinguishable from U.S.A. trusts." The journalistic world, too, was in trouble, because of the Harmsworths and Pearsons and their "halfpenny rags". The Japanese were steadily losing popularity, and Chance could not understand why *The Times* had backed them, or how they could ever hope to pay the money they had borrowed.

Morrison, too, was losing faith in the nation whose cause he had championed so ardently. Disquieting reports reached him from Korea, where Japanese suzerainty was inevitably hardening into sovereignty, and from Manchuria, the independence of which both Japan and Russia had publicly agreed to respect, but which by secret agreement was being divided between them. F. A. Mackenzie, of the London *Daily Mail*, who was later to write *The Tragedy of Korea*, brought back moving stories of the "indefensible" cruelties and injustices which the Japanese were inflicting on the Koreans; and in Manchuria they were behaving so brutally that the inhabitants were regretting the "good old days" of the Russian occupation. "Every offence committed by the Russians and condemned by us is repeated by the Japanese with our approval. It is a strange world," Morrison reflected. But the Japanese had added a new weapon to the armoury of conquest: prostitution. There were 8000 state-aided Japanese prostitutes in Manchuria, Morrison was told, "whose earnings were greater than those of the South Manchurian railway, 450,000 dollars a month". "It is more disgusting than the African slave trade," said Rockhill. "The most immoral traffic I have ever heard of." A candid Japanese explained that Japan used prostitutes in the way England used missionaries, as the advance guard of commercial penetration: disputes could easily occur in a brothel that might justify diplomatic intervention. Many high Chinese officials had Japanese women in their harem, including Yuan Shih-k'ai, and T'ieh-liang, a powerful army man.

Morrison's changing attitude towards Japan was reflected in his dispatches. Robert Collins, London bureau chief of Associated Press of America, wrote to him in July 1907: "In your recent telegrams I have noticed a certain tendency to prod our good friends, and your allies, the Japanese, that I am sure must irritate them." It irritated them so much that they made two rather crude attempts to win back Morrison's old allegiance. Baron Hayashi offered him a high decoration, the Third Class Rising Sun, which he refused on the spot ("as I would have refused the Grand Cordon of the Gold Peach Blossom"), and Baron Goto, the Japanese Minister for Communications, sent him "a work of the most exquisite beauty" which he returned with a flowery explanation:

> If I were in a position to send your Excellency a gift in any way commensurate in value with the picture you have sent me I would not hesitate to keep the picture hanging on my walls, but to obtain a work of art of equal value . . . is quite beyond my means. I have, therefore, no alternative but to ask your Excellency to permit me to send back the gift which you have so thoughtfully and so kindly desired to give me.
>
> Your Excellency will, I am sure, recognize that I am but doing my duty in declining to accept a gift so long as I am a correspondent of a paper, for I could never wish it even to be thought . . . that my judgment of events . . . had ever been in any way influenced by personal gifts from those whose policy I might . . . have to criticize or comment upon. . . . Ever since I came to China I have declined to receive any gift of any kind whatever or to accept passes on the train or on the steamer. . . .

What Britain felt about Japan at this time was expressed in a letter Sir Edward Grey wrote to Roosevelt in December 1906:

> I can give you no forecast of Japanese policy. They have been quite satisfactory allies; cautious and not exacting. But they are very reserved, and I do not feel that I know the working of their mind on questions outside the alliance itself. As for ourselves . . . we should detest war anywhere. This is not because we have grown weak or cowardly, but because we have had enough war for one generation. Before the Boer War, we were spoiling for a fight. We were ready to fight France about Siam, Germany about the Kruger telegram, and

Russia about everything. Any Government here, during the last 10 years of the last century, could have had war by lifting a finger. The people would have shouted for it. They had a craving for excitement and a rush of blood to the head. Now, this generation has had enough excitement, and has lost a little blood and is sane and normal. . . .

Morrison's estrangement from the Japanese was accelerated by disputes over railways in Manchuria, where Japan steadily refused to permit China to extend her own railway system. (By the treaty of Portsmouth, Japan had acquired control of the South Manchurian railway from Changchun to Port Arthur, and various subsidiary lines.) He continued to expose Japanese activities in Manchuria, and to rage when his telegrams were suppressed or modified. "Insertion of my telegram of today," he wrote, "will depend upon whether or not Chirol has been entertained at the Japanese Embassy within the last few days." In April 1909 the Japanese Ambassador in London, Kato, told Chirol that Morrison's attitude towards Japan had become "very regrettable", and Chirol replied that he was "very concerned" about it.

When the Japanese invited Chirol to visit Japan to discuss their problems, particularly the railway issue, and Morrison's embarrassing hostility, Chirol suggested that Morrison be invited too, so that he "would not be able later to raise objections to the conclusions which I reach". Kato agreed.

[IX]

"Tomorrow begins the round of visits, etc., and boredom and lies," Morrison wrote when he arrived in Tokyo. It was a busy round of official lunches and dinners, interviews and speeches, backslapping and bows. Chirol and Morrison were treated like visiting statesmen. They were entertained by the Prime Minister, Viscount Katsura, the Vice-Minister for Foreign Affairs, Ishi (the Minister, Komura, was ill) and by leading diplomats, bankers, industrialists, and editors. They had an audience with the Emperor, an unprecedented honour for journalists, though Morrison's account of it lacks appropriate humility.

Resplendent in borrowed frock-coats, hats, and gloves, he and Chirol drove to the palace in a carriage sent by the Foreign Office:

Shown into a splendid audience chamber with two great paintings—on cut velvet—of Mt Fuji. A Chamberlain came in in uniform and cocked hat who told us in reply to our enquiry that everything would be the same as in our Court. This was particularly enlightening to me who has never been to Court. However, after waiting 15 minutes we were conducted along long passages to some hall where we had to stand outside a door. Hushed voices were heard within. It was all most sepulchral. Chirol went in first and I heard voices inside hushed and solemn. Then he backed out and I stepped forward. At the entrance

I had to bow and then march forward to where a figure was standing supported by two chamberlains in uniform. In another corner were two other silent images. It was most sepulchral and grave-like and I felt as if I were being ushered into the presence of divinity. But the image before me was not godlike. A man of about the ordinary height in the most illfitting uniform ever seen, with white kid gloves. A tremulous bleary pimply face sodden it seemed to me with alcohol. He was very nervous stepped one step forward and shook me by the hand. My right hand was bare my glove being held in my gloved left hand. Then he mumbled something to the introducer who said, "His Majesty desires me to convey to you the same greeting that he has for Mr Chirol." This was double-dutch to me. I had not the remotest idea in the world what he said to Chirol. The Emperor seemed still nervous and embarrassed but I put out my hand to put him at ease and he grasped it in his flabby paw. I bowed again and disappeared backwards feeling somewhat ashamed to render so much homage to bibulous Royalty. In speech I did not even say "Eh". It will be difficult for the correspondents to manufacture an interview out of this episode. On reaching the Hall, with the pictures the Chamberlain said: "Everything has gone off very well."

The *Japan Chronicle*—an English newspaper published in Kobe— sharply criticized the practice of attempting to influence visiting journalists by flattery and lavish entertainment. "Mr Chirol and Dr Morrison . . . would be more than human if they failed to be impressed by the attentions they have received in Japan," it said. "What wonder if Mr Chirol's previous good opinion of Japan should be confirmed or that Dr Morrison should take a more favourable view in future of Japanese policy in Manchuria?" Certainly Chirol required little persuasion. After a few meetings with Japanese statesmen he sent *The Times* a cable (of which Morrison "greatly disapproved") justifying Japan's railway policy; but Morrison, who had refused a handsome Order and a valuable picture, was not to be seduced by a surfeit of saki and handshakes. As the British chargé d'affaires in Tokyo, Horace Rumbold, reported:

The Japanese made a great splash over Chirol and Morrison and were eager to explain the Japanese case in their difficulties with China. All reticence was abandoned. They knew of course that Chirol was their friend and they hoped to win Morrison over but the latter is a tough nut to crack and isn't so easily won.

"There are many references in Japanese archives to Japan's fear and suspicion of Morrison's influence in 1909," says Dr I. H. Nish, in a study of Morrison's relations with Japan.

Morrison and Chirol journeyed together through Japan, Korea, and Manchuria, to Peking. At the annual dinner of the Yokohama Foreign Board of Trade, Morrison expounded his journalistic credo:

Twelve years ago, I was sent to Peking, having had no previous journalistic work. The instructions given to me were simply that I was to tell the truth without fear or favour and during the time that I have been in the Far East, I hope that I have carried out these instructions and that I have endeavoured to allow no personal prejudice or predilection to interfere with my work or to colour any cable that I have been able to send the great journal I am serving. I feel indignant when I read in the papers that I am pro-this or anti-that country. I am an Englishman and all I think about and all that I desire to serve are the interests of my own country.

His diary provides an instructive footnote:

My flapdoodle incident. At the end of my manuscript speech I had written "and any more flapdoodle that may occur to me". This MS I gave to a Japanese forgetting I had added these words. Fortunately I stopped it in time.

Morrison's dislike of Chirol flamed into fierce hatred during their travels. "That infernal ill-natured disagreeable discourteous brute", was one of his milder descriptions of his chief. "Chirol who acted like a sneaking cur in Tokyo" was another. But hatred was at times tempered by pity for Chirol's obvious physical frailty ("he is sorely stricken and will probably commit suicide . . . he is breaking up and is not long for this world. . . . poor fellow with not many years of active life yet to be"), and though Morrison found Chirol "an extremely uncongenial companion" and had a "rooted dislike for him", he admitted his "marvellous ability" and "great experience": "I believe he knows the world better than any man living but he does not know China." Chirol's knowledge of the world provided some piquant diary entries:

Austin Henry Layard when British Ambassador at Constantinople accepted valuable presents from the Sultan including a priceless Bellini. . . . Our long eclipse in Turkey from which we are suffering was due to his perfidy and avarice.

Berlin is the European capital where sodomy finds its chief home. Saunders will send his girls to school and have no fear of their being molested in any way.—not so with the boys.

Sir Edgar Vincent, later Baron d'Abernon, amassed probably £2,000,000 when Director of the Imperial Ottoman Bank by the simple expedient of speculating with the Bank funds. If successful he pocketed the profits, if a failure he debited the Bank. He really made £3,000,000 but had to disgorge one million. But for this he would have been Chancellor of the Exchequer.

Jacky Fisher squares our corrupt old King. With reluctance the King handed over Osborne to the Nation. But Jacky contrived to get him £18,000 for it.

There was another remarkable outburst against Chirol later in the year:

> I wrote to the detestable Chirol who stands in the way of my ambition and because I can send the best telegram in the world—Putnam Weale says that . . . and because it is by telegrams that I have made my reputation and because I hate writing letters and do not write good letters he refuses to allow me wire but insists on my writing: I hate the man but I must pretend to like him and I praise and flatter him because it is expedient to do so.

It is curious that Morrison should have quoted Putnam Weale, whom he disliked as intensely as he did Chirol. On the day of this entry he referred to Weale as a "loathsome fat Jew and his whore Lady Bredon". In a moment of confidence Chirol made the enigmatic confession that he "went a mucker and resigned from the Foreign Office".

[X]

Apart from his demanding work for *The Times*, Morrison had multiform private activities. He induced the Chinese to cancel the "obnoxious" decree of 1899, giving official rank to the Catholic hierarchy, and was gratified when the president of the Wai Wu Pu (the Ministry of Foreign Affairs), Liang Tun-yen, thanked him for rendering this important service to China. He frequently gave Liang "good advice on foreign affairs" ("they are like children crying in the night"). Often he complained, and with justification, that he had spent the whole day "in the service of others". His house was a combination of transit hostel, information Bureau, and reference library. Sometimes he had as many as four uninvited guests staying with him, and he was consulted almost daily by diplomats of many nationalities. When Sir Walter Hillier, then foreign adviser to the Chinese Government, asked his advice about Japanese affairs, he grumbled in his diary: "Sir Walter . . . in complete ignorance . . . paid £5000 a year absolutely for doing nothing." But he urged the Grand Secretary, the Viceroy Na Tung ("fat and chinless") to send Sir Walter Hillier on a special embassy to Tokyo to effect an honourable settlement of China's differences with Japan, and advised the Viceroy to enlist Alfred Hippisley, Commissioner in the Imperial Customs, in China's financial service. Hippisley, he pointed out, was the author of the "open door" policy enunciated by the U.S. Secretary of State, John Hay, in his famous circular of 1899. Morrison took Chinese lessons, was indefatigable with his gun, sometimes took a two-hour walk to his cottage in the Western Hills, and devoted much time—and money—to his rapidly expanding library. His interests were catholic. He noted that "Captain Scott-Harden", who was leading a gaggle of tourists from Boston, was the Alfred Taylor who had kept the male brothel patronized by Oscar Wilde, and he patiently studied the inscriptions at the cathedral outside the Ping-tsu-men, where the German missionary, Terentius, who helped to correct the Chinese calendar, had died in 1630, and the Italian missionary Ricci, who founded the Peking Observatory, had died in 1638.

He entertained a lot, and was entertained a lot. There were many unhappy gastronomic experiences, as when the ex-Viceroy Tuan Fang gave a "shocking bad dinner" in a cold room:

> The man next to me ate like a hog, the servants hawked and spat and so did the Viceroy. It was not appetizing and I was ill. Afterwards as we sat on the sofa, I saw the servants collecting the wine according to the colour pouring the half empty glasses into the tumblers. In this way claret and port were treated as one and the same with chablis and light sherry. No doubt such mixtures would serve at another feast. . . . I came home feeling that something had disagreed with me. . . . Was very ill during the night.

Lady Hillier, too, who was painting Morrison's portrait, was an undistinguished hostess. Her lunch was "a very small meagre and cheap one, a small section of partridge a slice of bread pudding recooked and stick of celery".

[XI]

Morrison left Peking for Shanghai in January 1909 to cover the sitting of the International Opium Commission. Again he scooped the Foreign Office, and all other papers, with a "highly important" telegram of 519 words on which he worked hard for an entire day. He had long talks with two of the delegates, Lady Brownrigg's father, Sir Cecil Clementi-Smith, and the Canadian statesman and sociologist, William Mackenzie King. Sir Cecil condemned Jacky Fisher for getting rid of Lord Charles Beresford, who had strongly disapproved of Fisher's naval policy. Fisher, said Clementi-Smith, "hypnotizes the King, who . . . shelved Charlie Beresford, a much greater admiral". Sir Edward Grey had done extremely well, but he would not learn French or go abroad, and the King disliked him because he would not tell the King anything. Mackenzie King said that Roosevelt had admitted sending the United States Great White Fleet on its world cruise "to put Japan in her place".

[XII]

Colonel Bruce, of the Shanghai police, wrote to Morrison in July that Lord Kitchener, with himself "in humble attendance", would be in Peking about 14th October. Kitchener had handed over his command in Poona to Sir O'Moore Creagh, and was on tour to represent Great Britain at Japan's annual manoeuvres, and to advise Australia and New Zealand on defence. "He is a somewhat restless traveller in so far that a day or two in any place is usually sufficient to satisfy him," Bruce wrote. "But I think Peking and its treasures should suffice to keep him for a week." Morrison does not seem to have recalled Colonel Bower's rather caustic estimate of Kitchener when he replied: "I hope the Chinese will treat him with becoming dignity. He will be the greatest Englishman who has come to Peking within my knowledge."

The Chinese and Japanese, but—at Kitchener's request—not the British, welcomed him with a guard of honour. He stepped from the train, "blear-eyed, strabismus, flushed florid face", giving the impression, Morrison reported, "that he was under alcoholic influence". A later note was more charitable: "But Kitchener is a very shy man and I think the bloated look was due to morbid flushing or blushing." Kitchener had written to Sir John Jordan saying that he would like to meet "the Regent, Tang Shao-yi, and Dr Morrison". His first visit was to the Wai Wu Pu, where he was received by the Regent's brother, Prince Tsai Tao, and the President of the Ministry of War, T'ieh-liang. He noted with disapproval the squalor of the premises:

> The white-washed room . . . was not fit for an Indian Syce. And in this country where they made the most beautiful porcelain in the world! He was handed tea by a dirty waiter and in a cup marked "Forget me not Billy." He was certain that the other cup was marked "A present from Margate." At the Wai Wu Pu they took the wrong turn and found themselves in the urinal!

A second audience equally dispiriting, convinced Kitchener that China must get rid of its rulers:

> "These people must go," he said. There was no Rajah in India—not the smallest—who would have received him in such squalid undignified surroundings. . . . He and his party advanced by one door when a Chinese who by his dress seemed a servant entered unobserved by the other. He advanced . . . and before they realized where they were they discovered it was the Regent. He was painfully nervous and undignified a poor figure and spoke the silliest questions most banal. . . . It is impossible to realize that this is the ruler of the Empire! He must go, said Kitchener, gruesomely!

If Kitchener was the greatest Englishman who had come to Peking, he was also one of the most acquisitive. He had a passion for porcelain which he fed partly by purchase but preferably by scrounging. His biographer, Philip Magnus, says he spent over £1700 on art treasures in China. Morrison records that he "lifted" from Tang Shao-yi porcelain to the value of 13,000 taels, and tried to get more. "Will Kitchener give anything in return for the splendid gifts he received from the Chinese?" was Morrison's unanswered question. Jordan, knowing Kitchener's acquisitiveness, and knowing also that Tang was as poor as he was generous, told Kitchener when he was leaving that Tang was "in much reduced circumstances. . . ." It was poetic justice, perhaps, that four pieces of peach-blossom china which Kitchener gratefully accepted from the Regent, believing they were worth thousands of pounds, were condemned when he returned to London as worthless fakes. So was a Kangshi vase ornamented with fish and birds for which he paid $3000. (Two years later Morrison was told how at a reception at Mukden, Kitchener had put one peach-blossom vase into his pocket, and given another to his companion to pocket in the same way.)

Kitchener dined with Morrison, and spent a morning with him, but does not seem to have made any inroads into Morrison's collection. When he was taxed with including in his farewell speech at Poona whole passages from the speech Curzon made when leaving India, he replied, unabashed: "How could I do better than borrow from the great orator Curson?" A. E. Wearne, Reuter's representative in Peking, like Colonel Bower, was not one of his admirers:

> Wearne . . . has the utmost contempt for Kitchener as a commander in the field and speaks of the extraordinary incapacity for leadership displayed at Paardeburg. Says he drinks and has the other failing acquired by most of the Egyptian officers, a taste for buggery.

[XIII]

It had always been Morrison's wish to see every part of the Chinese Empire. He had been in seventeen of the eighteen provinces and in every province of Manchuria when, on 15th January 1910, he started on a journey through Far Western China, or the province of the New Dominion, and Russian Turkestan, to Moscow. His route lay through Sian, Suchow, and Urumchi, across the Musart Pass, to Kashgar and Tashkent. He took three Chinese servants, two ponies, and two carts, loaded with supplies that included soup, Bovril, sausages, tinned tomatoes, caviare, corned beef, marmalade, honey, and fresh salmon, and a few dozen books: among them, *The Bible in Spain*, *Hiawatha*, *Heroes and Hero Worship*, *The Light of Asia*, and the *Anthology of Australian Verse*, which again he read until he was "quite homesick and melancholy".

Once more he was appalled by the poverty, squalor, brutality, and corruption of Chinese life: "Truly Buddhism in China is terribly deteriorated. Everyone . . . keeps prostitutes and a large section of their earnings is the perquisite of the priests who farm them out. . . . China is I believe the only country in the world which deals in a slave traffic among its own people."

On the road he met prisoners "cruelly chained to heavy rods of iron like a crowbar, bound by rings of iron to the neck and to the ankle". Sometimes two prisoners were chained to the same crowbar, eight feet in length, weighing fifty catties (about 66½ lb).

For hundreds of miles, from Suchow to Kashgar, he saw the ruins of what once had been thriving towns and villages, memorials to the pitiless suppression of the Mahomedan rebellion by General Tso Tsung-t'ang, who had made a wasteland of a region that once sustained some thirty million people: "He is one of the greatest curses that have ever blighted

China. His expedition was a calamity as great as the inundation of the Yellow River. Yet he is glorified not as a scourge who reduced a whole province to a desert but as hero."

In the poor, dimly-lit mud huts and cave dwellings, where people at night sat huddled over a wick dipping in oil, Morrison reflected: "What a change in their lives when they can buy kerosene and foreign lamps. Their evenings can be spent in reading. How much ignorance in China is due to the absence of light it would be hard to say but at any rate it is an important contributing cause."

Again he encountered "excessively anti-pathetic missionaries": At Lanchow he wrote:

> Contact with them and their narrow-minded views would make any man agnostic. . . . There must be some defect in their methods seeing that a succession of missionaries have been working unceasingly for 24 years and they have in all some 20 Christians. . . . They teach an incomprehensible jargon obscuring the truths of Christianity and the teaching of Christ. They endeavour to interpret *Revelations* and *Romans* by means of diagrams which confuse the Chinese as they certainly confused me.

Scriptures were sold very cheap. The Mohammedans either resold them at double the price or used them to stuff their boot soles.

Extreme variations of temperature made travelling very unpleasant. The men drove naked to the waist in the morning but shivered even in their sheepskins when the wind rose. At times the temperature fell below zero and writing-ink froze solid. At times the scorching sun caused Morrison "real suffering", making his clothes almost too hot to touch. "And yet I used to boast that I had never seen the sun that was too hot for me!" he wrote, recalling that he had walked across Australia in the extreme of summer. His health was bad. His liver was disordered, his body often stiff with rheumatism. He had recurring attacks of nose-bleeding and lumbago. Food was inadequate. "Cannot travel without meat," he wrote. But he conscientiously sent his dispatches to *The Times*, some of them 7000 words long.

Flags were flying at half-mast as he rode into Kuldja on 18th May and learned, without regret, of the death of the "Emperor of the Great British nation", His Majesty King Edward VII.

At Urumchi, capital of the New Dominion, Morrison was warned of the hazards of the Musart Pass, "dangers by road, dangers from robbers". He reached the summit of this pass, the most important of China's western frontier trade routes, after a steep climb of thirteen miles:

> The dividing ridge is 12,000 feet above sea level. The descent down the glacier is the chief danger. Covered with debris, the surface is broken into millions of tiny tentshaped knolls . . . deep crevasses yawn on each side of the irregular and slippery track which zigzags down the glacier. The way is strewn with the skeletons of dead pack-animals.

. . . In the precipitous ice-face steps have been cut and down these the laden animals are passed singly with much care . . . neglect of the pass is cited as striking evidence of national decadence. Traders require uncommon fortitude to face its dangers, and their losses in transport animals are very great. . . .

Morrison reached Kashgar 158 days out from Peking, and three days before the schedule he had set himself. At Ulugchat, on the border of Chinese and Russian Turkestan, he found more evidence of China's decadence:

On all maps of Central Asia Ulugchat is given prominence, its name being set out in type worthy of a frontier stronghold. I examined it accordingly with some care. It is a mud fort situated in a basin on the right bank of an unbridged river, the Kizil Su, and is commanded by mountains on all sides. Inside the fort there is complete disorder. Everything is rotting. Windows are blocked with broad sun-dried bricks. There are ruined stalls, but no horses. Of the four Chinese who hold this frontier post and represent the majesty of China, two at the time of my visit were weeding in the fields, another was washing some onion-sprouts, and the fourth, clad only in a jersey and pants, was playing the banjo at a cake-stall in the street. No one was in uniform. All were ragged and unkempt. Their arms, which I saw, in one dirty room, were rusty old Tower muskets—emblems of authority, not weapons of offence. Outside the camp in four Khirgiz tents were the 15 Khirgiz who constitute the second line of defence. They are armed with similar Tower muskets cut down to carbine size and are employed as cavalry patrols. Two filthy ponds of surface water provided the garrison with water. The courageous Khirgiz drink this water unboiled and unstrained, the less courageous Chinese dare not do so.

I am no military expert, but I formed the opinion that this frontier stronghold would fall before the resolute attack of three old ladies armed with broomsticks. There could be no better illustration of the neglect which is characteristic of China's frontier policy. Other countries employ smart serviceable soldiers on their borders. China alone sends to her frontier the most wretched of her ragamuffins.

At Oshi he left behind "all things not absolutely needed, camp bedstead, camp chair, spare medicine, clothes, cooking-stove, etc." At Andijan he paid off his servants and on 12th July boarded the train for Moscow. He arrived in the capital, suffering acutely from diarrhoea and piles, five days later. It was six months and two days since he had left Peking. In the papers he read that Charles Hardinge had been appointed Viceroy of India, that the aeronaut C. S. Rolls had been killed, and that a Russo-Japanese agreement had been signed. This was the agreement by which both powers agreed to respect China's territorial integrity—while secretly dividing Manchuria between them. Japan was also about to annex Korea.

In the last of his twelve articles Morrison wrote:

Throughout my ride of 3670 miles, occupying 174 days, between the Chinese railway and the Russian railway, I met with nothing but kindness. I cannot recall a single disagreeable incident. I was entertained by native Princes, by Viceroys and Governors, and Tartar Generals. I met all manner of people from the humblest carter to the most powerful Mandarin, and by all I was treated with equal civility, friendliness, and respect. I found, as I have always found in my travels in China, that I was well treated because I belong to a country which is known to sympathize with every movement in China that has for its object the advancement of the people, the encouragement of education, and the extension of liberal ideas, of methods of truth and justice and fair dealing. To me the suggestion is preposterous that British influence is waning in China. On the contrary, I think the British prestige has never been higher than at present.

From W. W. Rockhill, now United States Ambassador to St Petersburg, came an appreciative letter, which reached Morrison in London:

... I am treasuring your articles on the journey through Turkestan. ... I hope you will bring them out fully elaborated with your usual array of facts ... in volume form. You would really be rendering a service to China as well to the rest of the world, for we all have—except you and a very few others—a most incorrect and imperfect idea of the present conditions of the Chinese Empire. The world—the official world, I mean, is getting to believe that China is once more a "quantité negligible" and is preparing to act accordingly. A new stage in the history of the Far East is just opening now with Japan a Continental Power. There must be some day a new policy adopted by the interested Powers of the West to meet this absolutely new condition. The passing away of Korea is only the beginning of the new period and before many years we will all regret that we were not in a position to stop this step being taken in violation of treaties—for it *does* violate both the Treaty of Portsmouth and your alliance treaty—both of which only recognize to Japan the right of "control" in Korea. It's all very interesting to me—though apparently nobody cares much just now, or is willing to say anything about it. ... I hope against hope the Chinese will be intelligent enough to begin putting their house in order and not be too assertive and too "rights-recovery" style. If they could only be persuaded to devote themselves exclusively to financial questions, fiscal, currency, etc., for the next ten years—what a future the country could have!!

[XIV]

"I am not, or ever shall be, the 'Chief' of *The Times*; do not interfere in the conduct of the paper," Northcliffe wrote to Wickham Steed in September 1908, six months after he had acquired control. "*The Times* is conducted entirely by Messrs Walter, Buckle, Chirol and Moneypenny, who understand the task better than I ever could." But this mood of tolerant humility did not last long. Newspaper proprietors tend to become megalomaniac with power, and Northcliffe's megalomania grew rapidly when he became overlord of Printing House Square. "As early as 1910 there had been whisperings that the Chief was not always right in his mind," says the *History of the Times*. He began to wage a war of nerves against Buckle, Bell, and Chirol, whom he variously described as the "giant tortoises", "Ye Black Friars", "the Old Gang". *The Times* was a "barnacle-covered whale" floundering on the financial rocks, and the Old Gang the barnacles, to be scraped off as soon as possible.

Morrison knew none of this when he met Northcliffe in *The Times* office in August 1910. Northcliffe asked when Morrison was going back to Peking, and he answered with heavy sarcasm, "I think there is little use of my going back seeing that I have done no work for two years," explaining that his messages were mutilated or suppressed. "What is the use of paying a man £1200 a year and keeping him at the end of a silent wire?" asked Northcliffe. He said he would never interfere with *The Times* as long as it did not support Germany or Free Trade, but Morrison was told by men on the paper that he was interfering more and more.

The Times was, in fact, one big unhappy family. "A devilish fine muddle," Morrison wrote. Arthur Walter had died in February, and John had become chairman of the company. Ralph was in charge of an economy and efficiency campaign; he had cut foreign-service costs from £62,000 to £42,000 a year and introduced such bold innovations as a typewriter in the Foreign Department, and numbered coatpegs. But the man with a big stick, which he was waving with increasing authority, was Northcliffe's intimate friend from the *Daily Mirror*, Reginald Nicholson, who in August 1909 had become assistant manager. "*The Times* resents the active interference of Lord Northcliffe," he told Morrison. Moberly Bell said that, apart from an occasional shortage of ready cash *The Times* was doing well. But others were less reassuring. Gwynne and Garvin both thought the paper was shockingly mismanaged and had lost much prestige by its paid-for supplements. Edward Grigg (later Lord Altrincham), who had joined *The Times* in 1903 as Buckle's secretary and was now in the Foreign Department, said the paper had no leader and no policy. It wobbled. Buckle had charm and suavity but no political decisions, and Ralph Walter, who was convinced he was running it, knew nothing of politics or newspapers, a judgment which Morrison endorsed after talking to Ralph:

> Ralph Walter and his views. Early telegrams no advantage in making paper sell. . . . It is the leading articles which sell the paper not news. What *The Times* wants is that people should ask themselves in the afternoons what will *The Times* say next morning.

This was not very encouraging to one of the world's most distinguished news-getters, and Morrison found little solace in the flattering words of "the pompous" John Walter: "Before it was Blowitz of *The Times*. Now it is Morrison of *The Times*." Lovat Fraser, the fastest leader-writer on *The Times* (he was paid £4 4s. for a leader), agreed with Grigg that the paper had no policy, and Wickham Steed, the Vienna correspondent, had just resigned because of the treatment he had received. "If the paper is to live again, it must be regenerated," he wrote to Morrison: "The downfall of *The Times*, as Lord Northcliffe truly said to me ... two years ago, dates from the day when the Walters went to Eton and Oxford, became gentlemen-proprietors, and allowed themselves to be bamboozled into not perceiving that they were not running the paper."

At first Morrison found Chirol "very friendly and sympathetic": "One would never realize that he has been my most bitter opponent for years and had done me harm in the Far East that has been almost irreparable." But before long Chirol was again that "disagreeable brute". Relations were not improved when Mackenzie King disclosed that he had urged Lord Gray to appoint Morrison as Minister to China, that Sir Edward Grey had approved and consulted Chirol, who opposed the idea on the grounds, apparently, that Morrison was too pro-Chinese. "Really, I presume," Morrison commented, "because I was too anti-Japanese." But Chirol was at last changing his mind about Japan. The Russo-Japanese agreement and the annexation of Korea had profoundly shaken him. He had gone to Kato in a furious state, and angrily complained that the Japanese had deceived him. Grigg told Morrison that the feeling against Japan was growing. At the defence conference, each of the representatives of Australia and Canada had declared formally that his country would never join Japan in any war against a white people.

[XV]

A few days after his arrival in London, Morrison and a friend went to the five-shilling promenade of the Empire Music Hall to see one of London's most celebrated spectacles: the Grand Parade of English and imported whores. Among the cosmopolitan *voyeurs* Morrison was surprised to encounter the seventy-seven-year-old G. W. Smalley, of New York, and "the lecherous Casenave", of Peking. Later, at the Japanese Exhibition, Morrison was "much struck" by a "beautiful maiden" seated alone near the bandstand. While he was wondering whether she was "virtuous or plying for hire" an obvious stranger answered the question by carrying her off. "It is difficult in these days to distinguish vice from fashion," Morrison reflected. "The features overlap." Hoping to see the features of the beautiful maiden again, Morrison returned to the exhibition a few days later and spent some hours vainly looking for her. But he could not escape his memories of Toni, and soon Dungate, an ever-willing pander, was sent in search of her. He traced her to 33 Sutherland Place. "Much pleased. Have written to her," Morrison recorded on 8th August. Toni was in no hurry to reply. It was not till 1st September, when Morrison was lunching at the Oxford and Cambridge Club, that to his "joy and delight" he received a telegram reading: WILL YOU MEET ME AT 3 O'CLOCK MARBLE ARCH TUBE STATION T." "Will I? Is there any force in England that could prevent me from meeting Toni?" He hurried off and found Toni "ravishingly beautiful":

> She is well-dressed and had redeemed all the presents I had given her and . . . wanted, as she told with pride, for nothing. . . . She is now living in a small house of 8 rooms £45 a year. Her husband has a business in Berlin and is also doing well here. The pimp is "jealous" of his wife to the earnings of whose forced unchastity he owes the beginnings of his prosperity. Yet he seems to treat her kindly and Toni certainly looks fresh and contented and singularly beautiful.

Next morning there was another message from Toni: "MEET ME AT 1.30 FRASCATI'S OXFORD STREET. T.":

> Punctually at the minute I was there and waited grinding my teeth until 1.55 and when I went in and had lunch. . . . I had just finished when in walked Toni. She could not come earlier and only by subterfuge was able to come at all. Beautiful she is and fairly enmeshes me.

Next day Toni, who was obviously well informed about Morrison's movements, wired him at the Chinese Legation, where he was lunching: so SORRY CANNOT COME HOPE YOU ARE VERY WELL. "How can I be well when I cannot see Toni?" he asked himself.

A few more diary entries, not entirely explicit, chronicle the end of the affair:

> *10 September*—Saturday. Dungate came to breakfast and afterwards helped me catalogue. Afterwards out bookhunting. . . . Then down to Westbourne Grove passed the nice house of Toni's and found it all open: She had said she was going to Folkstone on Monday for one week but she was not gone. On the door post is brass plate H. LOTH. She had told me that she had recently been at Munchen Gladbach. She had declared that her high colour was natural. Dungate accordingly called while I waited at Lyons. He saw Paula. Frau Loth was washing her hair. He returned and had a talk with her while I waited in the park. She refused to come out and displayed no emotion when she spoke of me. She had been hurt because I had not answered letters sent to me on my birthday or on a more anxious occasion. . . . Charmingly dressed but cheeks undoubtedly *rouged*. She had recently been 2 weeks in Hamburg and had stayed in Wiesbaden at the Hotel Nassau, the finest hotel there, and one of the finest in the world. She never once mentioned Munchen Gladbach. She said she was prosperous. Not only was business prosperous but her husband had *won a prize in a Lottery*. [Morrison added a sardonic side note: "the prize won by this ponce was probably a retired Indian civil servant of 60 or more."] In the room was my photograph, also the picture of Dante I had given her. Dungate did not press Toni to come

out. She could have come had she wished. She gave afternoon tea
with a nice service. Is she kept and by whom?—Back and we dined
at the Grand Hotel Grill Room and then a walk and home. I chastened and absorbed. All my kindness in rescuing her from life of
misery forgotten and my failure to acknowledge letters remembered.
12 September—Today I spent most of the day writing to Toni—a
letter that would have melted a heart of stone.

My new secretary had come and she translated a letter that had
come from Toni to Dungate in German—a polite letter making
friendly conventional references to the pictures I had given her. . . .
Then in the afternoon I went out and purchased after some search . . .
a beautiful diamond and pearl brooch at Harrods', a really beautiful
present costing me £11.15.0 and this with the letter I sent by special
delivery.

13 September—Beautiful afternoon at Slough with Fraser. Back and
dine at Paddington Station hotel, then home where I receive a blow
that has shaken me but is well deserved.

On my return I found the following letter from Toni written
not in eager hurry but at 5.30 today. It is the only recompense for my
sending a beautiful present costing £11.15.0, a flutter and a gamble a
coup manqué. Now mind there is no fool like a lovesick fool of 48. It
is a wrench but it is the end of a romance the pleasures of which
were often adequate compensation for the pains and humiliations.
Here it is. I am ashamed to transcribe it. But the pill must be swallowed however nauseous!

My dear Ernest,

*Thank you for your nice letter and for the beautiful present
sent me last night. I will always think of you when I am wearing it.
It gave me such a pleasure to see Dr D again after nearly four years.
He is a dear old man and very true to you. E. He praised you very
much, he simply worships you. I wonder will I ever see him again. I
do not know enough English to answer your letter as I would like to
but, Ernest I think you did not treat me in the past two years as a
real friend ought to. I very often felt inclined to write to you once
more, but how could I, you never answered one of my last letters and
I thought you did not wish to hear from me any more. With all my
heart I hope you will always be very well and happy and perhaps we
will meet again one day.*

Toni.

Morrison added a footnote to his transcription:

There's a sweet and touching and affectionate letter of *congé*. However it is better that we should not see one another again better for
my peace of mind and for my pocket—infinitely better for the latter.
It is curious how mendacious can the beautiful Hungarian be. I wonder who keeps her—someone with a deeper pocket than mine—that
is certain.

207

Three days later he sent Toni ("I the damned fool and dotard") a copy of Filson Young's the *Sands of Pleasure*, in which the chief character had her name, and, the following day, wrote to "the faithful Dungate" asking him to write to Toni in German "a translation of a letter which I enclosed to him wherein the sting was in the words 'our friend wrote to me to say he had written to you fully to explain why he had not written to you and that you had sent him in reply a few cold and unfeeling lines of formal acknowledgement.' ":

> Why am I such a fool? Why have I such an obsession? I cannot get Toni's image from my mind. All the time I am scheming to bring her back to me yet I know that it is in every way better for me that I never see her again. Yet why did she ever ask me to meet her, why did she ever ask me to lunch with her at Frascati's? To meet me, to play with me, to stir up the flames that had died to the dust and then to coldly leave me after accepting my gifts and my beautiful letters. It is all inexplicable to me. But the truth is that I am an unbalanced fool. Yet I love her more than anything on earth.

The curtain came down three weeks later. The drama of Toni, which had been played over five years in three acts—1905, 1907, 1910—ended in a diary entry of anguished brevity: "Telegram from T. Visit from Toni 2.30 to 5. Gave Toni her *congé*. Told her with brutality had burned her photograph etc."

[XVI]

Morrison's activities, as always, were protean. He wrote to S. F. Edge Ltd about supplying cars for a proposed motor service between Urumchi and China proper, "a distance of some 2000 miles through a country, largely desert, with no made road". Petroleum could be obtained near Urumchi. S. F. Edge sent back their "admirable catalogue", but did not think it worth communicating with the officials at Urumchi, as Morrison had suggested.

He called on Sir Robert Hart, who as a result of a stroke, was "exceedingly shaky and frail, shattered in mind and body", but whose sad condition evoked little sympathy: "He hopes to return in April, is still clinging to the shekels . . . wretched feeble animal he has caused infinite suffering in his time," Morrison wrote.

He read with amusement a London paper's reference to Hart's brother-in-law, Sir Robert Bredon, as a "man of mettle" who had been decorated for his valour during the Boxer uprising. "Thus is history written" was Morrison's wry annotation. "The greatest poltroon of the siege who for a long time was refused a medal, and the cuckold with the longest horns . . . in China."

He had a reunion with a genuine hero of the siege, Herbert Squiers, who had since been American Minister in Cuba and Peru. Squiers told

Morrison that he had made a lot of money and had a 400-ton steam yacht, *Invincible*, at Cowes:

> Loot. Squiers says he could have been Minister in Peking, but for the *New York Herald* story of his loot. It was a true story. He values his collection at $200,000.

Asked to recommend an editor for the *Peking and Tientsin Times*, Morrison nominated David Fraser, "40 years, a brilliant writer, a gentleman and a man of high character. . . ." Fraser, accepting the appointment at £500 a year, wrote gratefully: "You are a brick. . . . It is not a question of pay—what I want is scope to develop whatever the Almighty has put into my head . . . as a responsible writer on foreign affairs."

He sat for his portrait to Charlie Ritchie [C. E. Ritchie, B.A., Oxon., who had abandoned the Scottish Bar for art] and had another memorably bad meal as the guest of Sir Percy Bunting, the seventy-four-year-old editor of the *Contemporary Review*. He engaged a secretary to go to Peking; Miss Jennie Wark Robin, a dark, attractive, and accomplished New Zealand girl of twenty-one, whose mother was born in the small mining-town of Jericho, Victoria, Morrison's native state. Miss Robin knew French and German and had been private secretary to Lord Balfour of Burleigh. Morrison gave her £15, and booked a passage for her on the *Mongolia* for £46 8s. To Lovat Fraser he wrote: "My secretary will help me put in order all the papers and documents I have accumulated during the last 15 years. I have more than 60 foolscap volumes of diaries and notes, and if I had only your gift of literary expression, I could make a vivid and interesting history of the last few years in China."

He was interviewed at length by "An Old China Hand" for Northcliffe's *Daily Mail*, and by F. A. Mackenzie ("good-natured Jew"!) for Northcliffe's *London Magazine*. The Old China Hand wrote:

> How has this man contrived to obtain such power as mentor of the world about the Far East? Travel in outlying parts of China, and you will soon learn one of the causes. Wherever you go, you are sure to find traces of Morrison, his investigations, and his friends. Walk just outside the Legation quarter in Peking, and you come to a typical Chinese house, its outer lodge facing the street, a big courtyard within, a house on one side, a long low building on the other. . . . The long building is his library, containing probably the finest collection of books on the Far East in existence today. It is managed on a plan which reveals the man. Everything is systematized and indexed. The least fact can be ascertained at once. The clean-shaven, sturdily built Australian loves to show an appreciative visitor his books, his cuttings and his methods. Here he works; here he maintains constant correspondence with men of all nationalities throughout the Middle Kingdom. System, accuracy, constant intercourse with all classes, and a tremendous correspondence have been the foundations on which he has built up his knowledge.

MacKenzie's article was titled "China's Four Hundred Million China-men Awake"—a "curiously infelicitous title," Morrison wrote to Wickham Steed, "for the Chinese hate to be called Chinamen: there are not four hundred million, and those who have awakened are the infinitesimal number." He pretended to be disturbed by the "awful portrait" of himself that confronted him "everywhere" on the yellow cover of the magazine, but noted with satisfaction that "six tons" of the issue had been sent to Australia, and 50,000 copies to Canada.

He politely declined many invitations: to become president of the Wolverhampton Literary Society; to rewrite the article on China in *Chambers Encyclopaedia*, 16,000 words, for an "honorarium" of thirty-nine guineas; to lecture under the auspices of Mr Gerald Christy, whose notepaper proclaimed in big red letters SOLE AGENT FOR SIR ERNEST SHACKLETON AND COMMANDER PEARY, and whose other clients included the Right Rev. Bishop Welldon, Mr Joseph McCabe, and Lady Beerhohm Tree; to sell in China, for a "real good commission", the medical products of a Mr Ibberson, who accompanied his invitation with the gift of a tortoiseshell-covered knife. Mr Ibberson received the knife back with a letter that was quite as sharp: "The man who could offer a commission displays as lax a sense of morality as the man who would accept a commission."

When a Kensington estate-agent asked Morrison if a "Mrs George Morrison" was a responsible and desirable tenant for a flat, he replied playfully:

I have known the lady in question fairly intimately for a long time, in fact ever since the 4th February 1862, and I have every reason to believe that she is quite respectable. She neither drinks, smokes nor chews. . . .
P.S. I forgot to mention that the lady referred to is my mother.

With the aid of a secretary and "an overtime typewriter" he carried on an "enormous correspondence". And he noted without comment that a suggested name for Australia's new Federal capital was "Kangarooma".

[XVII]

Morrison's gossip service in London had a picturesque recruit. William Maxwell, the far-flung correspondent of the *Daily Mail*, who had recently been spying on Germany's new naval base at Borkum, introduced him to the Countess of Contardone, a "voluptuous, dyed and painted foreign-looking Englishwoman". The Countess spent much of her time in Egypt, but was a Baedeker of London scandal. Though of a distinguished diplomatic family—two of her brothers, Sir Edward and Colonel "Algy" Durand, had shared the white man's burden in India, and her half-brother, Sir Mortimer Durand, had been ambassador in three capitals—she was not troubled by diplomatic reticences. At their first meeting she told Morrison that her husband was a morphinomaniac, and that she herself, though not an addict, took morphia in large doses. His appetite whetted by these and more scabrous disclosures, Morrison called on her at 51 Rutland Gate. He described her in his diary as a "venomous woman", but listened avidly as she named the more prominent perverts in the House of Lords and spoke with "vitriolic acidity" of his old hero, the late Sir Henry M. Stanley: ". . . a bugger who took his native boy with him the first night of his wedding. . . . Stanley murderer, sodomite etc. etc."

The Countess's first husband was Jameson, who had been a member of the Stanley expedition. Bartellot, she said, was murdered with a gun given to a native by Bonney. She bombarded Morrison with *billets-doux*. "The damned frowsy-headed Countess favours me with letters and telegrams," he wrote a fortnight after the first meeting:

> She has what is vulgarly known as a "lech" for *The Times* Peking correspondent. I have no time to answer her letters. She does not seem to realize how many are my engagements and how superior are other attractions to her faded charms. Certainly she is interesting and has a gift for scandal unequalled by any of my acquaintances.

One of the superior attractions was a girl from the Army and Navy Stores named Dora, with whom Morrison began to console himself during the Toni crisis.

"How I wish you were here!" the Countess wrote when she returned to Egypt, in a letter that comprised seven sheets of coroneted lavender notepaper:

> I am drifting down the Nile . . . the golden sands on the Libyan side stretch out into the limitless horizons—in soft folds of yellow hills full of blue shadows—indeed the wind ripples the sand into tiny waves for miles—in each wave or cup you might think sapphires had been crushed. Here . . . one breathes deep and I feel when I ride into the desert I am riding into God—it intoxicates me. . . . I often think what a glory—a perfection of joy almost not to be lived thro'—would it all be, could one do it with a soul and mind really responsive to one's own. . . .

There was an abundance of gossip from other sources. Moberly Bell deplored the Queen Mother's folly in leading Mrs George Keppel to Edward VII's deathbed, with the words, "we both loved him". Sir Cecil Clementi-Smith said Sir Frank Swettenham had made a quarter of a million out of rubber. Captain Robert Muirhead Collins, Australia's representative in England, said Roosevelt's diamond pin, a cherished gift from his mother, had been stolen by his *amie* in London, "the handsome barmaid of the Alhambra upstairs". Gwynne said Balfour was a hermaphrodite. . . .

[XVIII]

When he addressed the Author's Club on "The Awakening of China" Morrison took the opportunity to contrast an awakened Australia with a somnolent England:

... judged by every test of modern progress, by the happiness of the individual, especially of the working-man, by its determination to maintain the purity of its race, by its willingness to accept universal military service . . . Australia . . . was awake. . . . England, with its unrestricted importation of alien undesirables, with its refusal to train up men to defend themselves, was slumbering and snoring, while preparations to "give us our lesson", as our enemies said, were preparing with appalling rapidity at our door.

Reminding his distinguished listeners that while they spoke of a Yellow Peril in Europe they forgot that in China there was ever-present a much more vivid peril, the European peril, he presented a balanced picture of a China recovering from the devastation of three rebellions, improving communications and education, but still tolerating a medieval penal system, torture, slavery, and footbinding. And he criticized the Foreign Office for supporting Japan's opposition to China's proposed railways in Manchuria. Halfway through his speech Morrison had the "inconceivable mortification" of having to stop while he battled with a violent attack of nose-bleeding. But he went on to acclaim, with dubious sincerity, the "high character and good work" of English missionaries in China and, apart from the Manchurian railways issue, to praise British policy in China:

"I am one of those," concluded Dr Morrison, "who have hope in the future of this great country, and I am one of those who believe that the policy followed by the British Government in its dealings with China has been at heart a good one. (Hear, hear.) We have treated the Chinese with consistent moderation and fairness. Opportunities of territorial expansion have been given to us many times during the past fifty years, but we have never availed ourselves of these opportunities. We have dealt with them fairly and squarely. (Hear, hear.) When the Chinese Government for the first time in its history made a serious effort to suppress the cultivation of the poppy, we gave the movement active support. We met their wishes in a conciliatory and reasonable spirit. We undertook to make great sacrifices. We are told that we ought to have a constructive policy in China, forgetting that China is an independent Empire. We have encouraged every movement that has made for progress. We have supported every scheme that has tended toward the improvement of the condition of the people and the increase of their wealth and happiness. We have loyally fulfilled our engagements, and all we have asked and pressed for is that Chinese on their side should fulfil their Treaty obligations as loyally as we have done." (Cheers.)

After Sir Walter Hillier had confessed that he personally preferred the sleepy old China of past years, and Sir Francis Younghusband had declared that China was not a very good neighbour in Tibet (the Dalai Lama had been deposed by a Chinese Imperial Edict on 15th February and had fled to India), Dr Bernard Hollander, as a "scientific phrenologist", paid a gracious tribute to Chinese skulls. Anyone looking at the heads of cultured Chinese, he said, must be struck with the massive brains they possessed. From the standpoint of anthropological science, therefore, great deeds might be expected from them.

Morrison's address was reported at length in the *Morning Post*, which also devoted a leading article to it, but was not mentioned in *The Times*: "Roused by the danger of foreign aggression, the Chinese have shaken off their lethargy, and are setting themselves to the task of national reorganisation," said the *Morning Post*:

> The Western World is now only realizing that the idea of the break-up of the Chinese Empire was somewhat premature. It is also beginning to wonder, not without some anxiety, what will be the end of the movement of awakening, and there is sometimes an uneasy recollection of a prophecy of Sir Robert Hart's that the day would come when the Chinese would repay with interest all the injuries and insults which they suffered at the hands of European Powers. It is easy, no doubt, to make too much of the signs of progress and development visible in China today. But it is still more foolish to ignore or sneer at the working of the new spirit in the Empire, and to pretend that the reform movement is an empty sham. Doctor Morrison, at any rate, does not hold with any such view. . . . He is confident that the Chinese people have a great future before them.

From Northcliffe came a telegram: SPEECH MOST INTERESTING CAN'T UNDERSTAND WHY THE TIMES HAS NO REFERENCE TO IT. The speech made a "big impression" on J. L. Garvin, and on the amorous Countess de Contardone, who wrote: "I can't tell you how much your talk interested me— you fairy-land person—you must find all *our* lives so dull." The fairy-land person when he received the Countess's letter was still trying to stop his nose-bleeding. "I read your address with the greatest possible interest," wrote Lord Stanhope, who was "living in hopes" that Morrison would be able to come to a weekend shooting party at Chevening, Sevenoaks. "I am indeed glad you don't think our prestige in the Far East impaired. I was afraid our deplorably weak and pro-Japanese policy must have had that effect."

Dr Douglas Gray, medical officer to the British Legation in Peking, thought Morrison's speech "fine and to the point". But his report on China was not encouraging. In a letter dated 21st October 1910 he wrote: "Things Governmentally are not going well—in spite of all this cackle of progress . . . there is really less progress and reform than there was in the day of the Empress Dowager. Every man for himself and his relatives is the order of the day. . . ." America's gesture in arranging for the balance of the Boxer indemnity to be spent on Chinese education in America was going to popularize her in China in a "far-reaching way: for every returned student looks upon the United States as God's own country. . . . The country is mad for education and it has been really surprising to note the numbers of well-educated young fellows trooping into Peking . . . all keen to get to America." But Gray was sure that China, driven by financial stress and popular demand for reform, was rapidly approaching a crisis:

> Corruption, speculation, bribery and the sale of offices continues, and the army of salaried sinecurists increases; and, with all this, there is doubt that the government finds increasing difficulty in providing for its foreign liabilities. The people will not stand it much longer. The Provisional Assembly is already making its power felt in a way which was never anticipated, and the demand for the shortening of the probationary period and the immediate establishment of a National Parliament is gathering strength before which the government is beginning to perceptibly weaken. I believe the people will get their way, it will be a bloodless revolution; and whatever mistakes they may make to begin with, I believe it is the only salvation for the country . . . the financial question overshadows everything else at the present moment, and reform in this respect cannot be hoped for from above. It can only come from the people, the enemies of the official class, who in their present temper are prepared to sweep away corruption in high quarters, and the multiplication of highly-paid sinecurists, with an unsparing hand. . . . I am in complete sympathy now with the movement for hastening on the establishment of a constitutional government; if matters are allowed to go on as they are, I think we shall soon be faced with a very much worse alternative.

Morrison summed up the English scene in a letter to Lord ffrench in Peking; ffrench was associated with Pauling's, the British contractors involved in the Manchurian railways dispute:

> So far as I can make out it will be impossible to avert war with Germany. . . . I do not see how we can suffer our naval supremacy to be challenged. Kitchener is no longer being employed. He desired the Viceroyalty of India and he was backed by both the late and the present King, but Morley so strongly opposed his appointment that he threatened to resign if it were made. Morley . . . has reduced the Viceroy to mere agent, not of the India Office, so much as of himself. . . .
>
> *The Times* has lost much credit by publication of the Japanese supplement towards which the Japanese Government contributed £10,000. . . . The British action (or inaction) in Manchuria seems wholly unjustifiable. . . . There can be no question that the feeling in this country against Japan is growing day by day. . . . The country seems richer than ever. Wealth is in evidence everywhere. . . . The country is full of German Jews, while the unrestricted immigration of aliens is so great that there are districts in London peopled by the scum of Europe who do not speak English.

Morrison's reference to "German Jews" reflects a puerile anti-Semitism which afflicted him all his life, and to which his diary bears frequent witness. At times, when he was not denouncing Chirol as a "wily Jesuit", he would label him a "damned Jew", but he never noted that his early friend and champion, Theodore Fink, was a Jew. Northcliffe suffered from the same disease, though he used to make the traditional "some-of-my-best-friends-are-Jews" disclaimer. When Morrison called on him in Paris, Northcliffe, conducting the audience from his bed in the Ritz, described "Old Moberly Bell"—who was more English than Northcliffe—as a "slippery Oriental. . . . a Jew and a Levantine Jew, the worst and the most slippery kind".

They talked of Dudley Disraeli Braham, who had joined *The Times* in 1897 and was its correspondent in St Petersburg from 1901 till 1903, when he was expelled because of his reports on the Kieshneff massacre. He was then in Peking. "Braham is another Jew," said Northcliffe. "He can never be Foreign Editor, that is impossible. I will never have a Jew in control of the Foreign Department. They can all be got at. It was a fatal blunder to send a Jew to St Petersburg. Who was responsible?" Morrison said Braham's work in the Far East was "excellent—calm, judicial and reasonable". Northcliffe then spoke uninhibitedly of *The Times*:

> It is a family party there. Buckle, Capper, Grigg, Bruce Richmond all sit together and each one takes up one department and asks only to be let alone and have no trouble. It is impossible to affix responsibility. That will have to be changed. If it cannot be changed from within, it must be changed from without. I'll simply put my men in. [J. B. Capper and Bruce Richmond were Buckle's assistants.] Would you believe it, but it was the custom until not long ago for *The Times* to be empty after going to press on Saturday morning until 5 p.m. on Sunday afternoon. I have changed that.

Morrison dined with Northcliffe and met "a little man named Lane, American, manager of the Paris edition of the *Daily Mail* and has recently written a book that has attracted much attention *The Great Illusion*, already translated into 10 languages". (Lane, who was not an American, was better known as Norman Angell, and his book, a powerful indictment of war, was subsequently translated into five more languages—Hindi, Bengali, Urdu, Marathi, and Tamil.) Northcliffe continued his disclosures. He was suffering from pancreatitis, but was confident he would get better. Arthur Walter granted his staff £1 a year pension for service. "Some earned thus £42 a year!" The whole parliamentary staff was turned into the street when Parliament was not sitting. Arthur Walter would have been in jail had he lived. He had defrauded *The Times* of £42,000 a year for five years. The Times Book Club was a millstone. With 800 members, it was losing £28,000 a year. "Is a glorified assignation house and will certainly figure in the divorce court."

Next time Morrison called at the Ritz, Northcliffe was again in bed, designing the 1911 poster for the *London Magazine*. "Are you free to-day?" he asked. "Would you like to see a duel—then we'll go and after-wards have a walk in the Bois de Boulogne." The duel was disappointing. It ended farcically when one of the contestants received a scratch on the thigh. One of the seconds told Morrison it was his 220th attendance at an affair of honour.

[XIX]

Morrison spent a few weeks in Spain, which he had last seen through a romantic haze twenty-one years before. Now he found a squalid, primi-tive, and impoverished country which compared unfavourably even with China:

> People as improvident and more backward. Villages as in China low huts similar roofs. . . . Small villages dominated by the Church out of all proportion. Often apparently large enough to hold the whole vil-lage. Country stony and bare. No conservation of water. Women are allowed no exercise. More backward than China. Education more defective than China. Habit of expectoration and exclusion of fresh air maintaining tuberculosis prevalence and acting as an efficient check upon growth of population. A decaying race? Noticeable in-ferior status of troops. No gold. Bigotry. Is not this partly account-able for their decay? Or mainly accountable? Chief industry seems to be the sale of lottery tickets and next the sales of postcards made abroad. . . . Bootcleaning is an important industry.

There was another flourishing trade, prostitution. In Barcelona, Mor-rison went to a couple of saloons "and saw the same women, I imagine, who frequented the place 21 years ago". He left, disgusted, but in Val-encia, the most prosperous city he had seen ("people well fed well clad well shod, no paupers, no begging"), he visited a Madrid lady who was "undeniably pretty and only 18". Malaga was a wretched town, "filth and squalor worse than China": "Half the population wishing to black your boots, other half begging alms. Pestered with beggars and your footsteps dogged by disreputable young scoundrels offering to show you *muchachas* of 15 years of age, 'very pretty' in 'casas particulares'."

The Museo del Prado at Madrid was "horribly badly ventilated. Pic-tures badly hung. Two attendants could not read", and the state-owned Fabrica de Tabacos, with 3200 workers and no machinery, a good example of the nation's decadence:

> An astonishing spectacle—mostly horribly old hags many of whom had been there since childhood. The air awful and oppressive the atmosphere putrid—the women spitting freely on the floor for atmos-phere increases salivation—the tobacco drippings with the tuberculous droppings all swept up and made into cigarettes. I could hardly keep

from vomiting. Children were in the factory. Women fatigued were sleeping with their heads buried in the heap of tobacco fibre. . . .

Spain medical fees ridiculously small and profession 100 years behind. Universal corruption from King downwards. Extraordinary prevalence of tubercle and syphilis.

As he journeyed across the country Morrison continued to make comparisons with China:

Corruption is universal and the system of squeezing worse than in China. No idea of sanitation. . . . Cruelty to animals is worse than China. . . . Cobble roads nearly a century behind the roads of France or Belgium, death rate owing to the ignorance of the people and absence of hygiene appalling. . . . Illegitimacy great. . . . More than half the people born out of wedlock. Newspaper press beneath contempt. Postal service as corrupt as Japan.

What is the church doing for the country? Is it helping to educate the people? Is it emptying the gaols? Is it keeping the prettiest girls from slave brothels? Is it checking a single one of the abuses which have brought the country to ruin? . . . People half-fed in the midst of abundance. . . .

"Why should there not be a revolution?" Morrison asked himself. The only hope was a republican government. But he was impressed when the British Minister, Sir Maurice de Bunsen, with whom he dined, said: "A republic requires a well-educated people. In neither Spain nor Portugal are people educated."

From Spain, Morrison made a brief visit to Vienna, where he saw the disgruntled Wickham Steed, and to Berlin. Steed said bitterly that he had no further interest in *The Times*. Moberly Bell and Chirol had both insulted him; Chirol, who, he said, had been brought up by the Jesuits, had long tried to get back into the Foreign Office. But the best position promised him was private secretary to Sir Edward Grey "or some such", at £600 a year. Chirol had hoped for a legation. E. B. Bourcier, the Balkans correspondent of *The Times*, had also been treated scandalously by Chirol, and nearly driven to suicide. "What despicable intrigues!" Morrison wrote in his diary. "What a mean-spirited cur. Jesuitical treacherous jealous is Chirol!"

It was an even more unhappy family that Morrison found when he returned to Printing House Square on Christmas Day. Lovat Fraser, who had been under caffeine treatment for dipsomania, had broken down again, and was trying hypnotism. Lionel James, "of world wide reputation", whose salary had been £600 a year, had been cut to £200 a year and so much a column. Chirol, the Jewish-Jesuit cur, had had another breakdown. Moberly Bell was known as the "dying Titan", and Lord Northcliffe was harrying them all. He told Morrison that Bell's father had intended to christen him "Miserly Bell"—a contemptible libel on a man who had impoverished himself in the service of *The Times*.

XX

In his war of nerves against the "Old Gang" Northcliffe saw in Morrison a useful ally. He invited Morrison to his rented Elizabethan mansion, Sutton Place ("very luxurious, built 1521-1526 by wealthy brewer named Weston"), and launched another slashing attack on "flabby, peace-at-any-price" Buckle, Bell the "slippery Levantine Jew", and Chirol, "very able, very opinionated, very prejudiced and as jealous as a woman—don't forget this, *he's a Jesuit*". They were all clinging to their highly paid positions, Northcliffe said, and were determined to stick it at all costs. And they were all hostile to Morrison:

> They've got you in the neck. I won't repeat what they said of you. But they want you out. They think you so soft that they can do what they like with you. You'll go back as before and they'll treat you as before. They'll shut you up. They'll put cotton-wool in your ears. For six hours I was with Bell and Buckle yesterday. These men you must beat with a big stick, it is the big stick only that makes them listen to reason. . . . I insisted that you shall go back happy and contented. I said you have rendered great services to *The Times* and to the Empire, and the proprietors of whom I am the Chief are determined that if any man has to go, it is not the Peking correspondent. . . . You can't trust these men. . . . They want to get you out, but you will not go.

Northcliffe said Morrison must insist on three things: all his telegrams to be published unless the Foreign Office specially asked for publication to be withheld; seventy-five per cent of all his letters to be published within a reasonable time, and reasons to be given when letters were not published.

Back in London, Morrison had a telephone call from a "much perturbed" Moberly Bell. Northcliffe had told Mrs Moberly Bell that Morrison had brought many charges against Chirol. "So I have involved myself in a tidy row," Morrison wrote in his diary. "What an astonishingly indiscreet man is Northcliffe. What is his game?"

Morrison found Moberly Bell "cheerful and contented, despite the mischief-making of Northcliffe", whose policy of divide and conquer had apparently been employed with some success on the *Daily Mail*. Moberly Bell's printer, an old schoolmate of Northcliffe's named Bland, had described the *Daily Mail* as "a hotbed of intrigue, everybody tale-bearing, everybody conspiring to dispossess the man above him".

At Northcliffe's suggestion Morrison sent a long letter to Moberly Bell, with a copy to Chirol, protesting strongly against the policy of the Foreign Department—"a policy which regards foreign news not from the journalistic point of view, but from the diplomatic point of view". He complained, as Wickham Steed and Bourcier had complained, of "the systematic suppression of facts when they conflict with the preconceived prejudices of Chirol". He said that his only interest was the efficiency of

The Times as a newspaper, and this had been destroyed by Chirol. And he asked whether *The Times* was to continue to reflect Chirol's view that "Japan can do no wrong; China can do no right".

Moberly Bell replied so sorrowfully that Morrison felt concern for the "poor fellow" and wired him: VERY SORRY MY LETTER UPSET YOU AND MUCH SURPRISED FOR NO SUCH INTENTION OR DESIRE. Chirol's reply was eight foolscap pages of bitter condemnation. He spoke of the exceptional consideration always shown Morrison, reproached him for the scantiness of his work, and declared that Morrison was the only correspondent of *The Times* who had been allowed one year's leave of absence on full pay.

"He considers my journey across China . . . was a private holiday of my own," Morrison wrote to Wickham Steed, enclosing a copy of the letter to Moberly Bell:

> My letter upset the office. . . . Chirol is indignant beyond measure and says he will never forgive me . . . apparently *The Times* makes a distinction between suppression of facts and non-publication of facts. Out of consideration for Chirol who is of a very sensitive temperament (by the way, nobody imagines . . . that a foreign correspondent can possess a sensitive temperament) the wish is expressed that everything will be done that can be done to meet my wishes, but I am asked to write a letter saying that in speaking of the suppression of facts I referred mainly . . . to the suppression of facts occurring within my own knowledge in reference to my own sphere. This I am quite willing to do.

To Steed he wrote:

> There seems to be a desire to send me back contented, and in many ways I am more contented than I have been for some years . . . my letter has "deeply pained V.C." but it has shaken them properly. . . . It is most important that you should have an opportunity of speaking to Lord Northcliffe. . . . I certainly hinted communicating freely with him in the future. He is a sympathetic man and inspires devotion. You need have no fear about your future position on *The Times*.

Steed telegraphed: BOURCIER JOINS IN THANKS FOR SERVICES RENDERED PAPER DURING YOUR STAY IN ENGLAND, and wrote:

> The stale breath of sham diplomacy has withered our Foreign Department for the last 10 years; and instead of being the chief informants and, as such, the leaders of the public, we have tended to become disingenuous partisans. Your gallant stand will not have been made in vain. It has strengthened the hands of colleagues who have never been able to drive things home as you have done. . . .

Moneypenny thought Morrison had gone too far, but he was just as critical of the Foreign Department for being "the mouthpiece of the Foreign Office" and for subordinating correspondents to Chirol's personal views.

When Morrison for the first time met Dudley Braham ("clean-shaven, markedly Jewish features"), who had returned from the Far East as acting Foreign Editor, Braham said the future under Northcliffe's regime was so uncertain that he hesitated to take a house on a seven-year lease: "He knows Northcliffe's peculiarities, setting men one against the other." And he repeated a now all-too-familiar lament: "There is chaos in the management and in editorial control, disorganization and unrest." Braham agreed with Morrison about many things in China and Japan. He thought that revolution was inevitable in China because the Central Government was too weak to control the Provincial Assemblies. He said the Japanese hated Morrison, and specially warned him against Honda, who had described Morrison as a "political adventurer". Describing himself as a liberal, Braham regretted that *The Times* leaders could never be read by liberals without anger. "Is only 36 years of age—able and lucky man with a great future before him!" wrote Morrison. "A brilliant journalist."

A few days later Morrison turned forty-nine. "How time is passing," he wrote. Continuing ill-health sharpened his awareness of time's transience. He was run down and depressed, and spent a day among the doctors of Harley Street. One found "hepatic congestion" and very high blood pressure, and ordered him a purely beefsteak diet, with hot water. He dined on a twelve-ounce steak, and felt better. Then he dined on two steaks, and felt better still. But the improvement was short-lived, and he was advised to take an "electric shower-bath":

> Was in the chair getting the electric bath when such was the gruesome conversation of the doctor about albuminiria, diabetes and suchlike horrible things that I went off in a faint and was so shaken that I had to rest all the morning first on the sofa in the Doctor's drawing room. . . .

Disillusioned entries follow:

> Much distrust of the doctor, doubting if he is doing me any good am nerveless uncertain worried and dispirited—largely, I fancy, climatic. The awful gloom of the climate is nearly maddening.

> Horrible, gloomy day. Dense fog. Am much in need of a change. Feel very depressed and think an hour's sunshine would do me more good than any amount of galvanic battery.

But many nights "Dora came to cheer me". She seems to have been less demanding than Toni. Morrison bought her a blouse, and a bracelet that cost £6 6s., and on 16th February 1911 said good-bye to her on Swan and Edgar's corner as he drove off to the station, *en route* for St Petersburg. Before he left he was photographed for the *Daily Mirror*, which published the picture with the caption: "Dr Morrison, *The Times* famous correspondent at Peking, who knows more of China than any other European. He had two new experiences yesterday. He had gas when a tooth was extracted and was photographed by flashlight while packing at Artillery Mansions, S.W."

Morrison's valedictory letters included one to Northcliffe:

I cannot thank you too warmly for all the kindness you and Lady Northcliffe have shown me since I came to England. I count it among the greatest privileges I have enjoyed in England, the opportunity you have given me of meeting and talking over with you our hopes and aspirations for the future of *The Times*. I will keep in touch with you and let you know from time to time how things are going. There will, I believe, in the future be no further suppression of facts that conflict with the prejudices of our foreign editor. Thanks to you I go back to China more contented than I have been for a long time past, for I know that I can always communicate with you should need arise.

And to Sir Cecil Clementi-Smith:

Things in *The Times* do not look well at all—financially, I mean. Lord Northcliffe is doing all he can to improve the paper, to remove the "raging discontent" of its staff, to raise its tone, and to release it from the unfortunate entanglements in which it was enmeshed—the Book Club and such things—before he became connected with it. Money is being spent lavishly, especially on the Canadian and American service, but I am afraid that the increase of circulation is not commensurate with the increase of expenditure. Chirol is quite unfit to be our foreign editor. . . . All of us recognize his ability, but all of us think that he is the most hopelessly unjust and jesuitical foreign editor that can be found in Great Britain. . . . Fancy our foreign service being subject to the caprice of a man who only goes to the office between the hours (and then not every day) of three and seven in the afternoon. . . . Lord Northcliffe says he is going to have two mottoes inscribed over "The Times" office—"News, like wine, improves by keeping" and the other: "All scope abandon ye who enter here."

Sir Cecil replied:

The account you give me of the state of affairs in *The Times* office is most interesting and most deplorable. As an Englishman I have always been proud of *The Times*, but it is difficult to be so any longer. . . .

[XXI]

In St Petersburg, Morrison called on the British Ambassador, Sir George Buchanan, a diplomat of thirty-eight years' experience—"a faded roué type, thin and bony with buck teeth, a hook nose and high cheekbones, a typical nincompoop, an astonishing freak to be in an Embassy, even when it is remembered what Ambassadors England does employ". Sir George created an impression of "feebleness and irresolution". But a talk with the Russian Foreign Minister, M. Sasonoff, was "deeply interesting". Morrison reported it in a letter to Lady Blake:

> He spoke with much freedom to me, especially about China. The burden of his story was, "We want to see a prosperous China, but not a strong China." He seemed to be afraid as all Russians whom I met are afraid, of Chinese immigration into Siberia, of the defenceless state of the Siberian frontier, and of the ultimate danger should that frontier still be undefended and China become a strong and aggressive power. I pointed out that for years to come China cannot be strong, that although her army had been greatly improved during the past five years, the whole available force which she now possesses, modern drilled, is certainly less than 200,000 men, an insignificant number to protect even the borders of an Empire of such vast area.

[XXII]

Before he left London, Morrison wrote in his diary, on 26th January 1911: "Alarming news from Peking of the spread of the plague, Harbin. Not bubonic but the deadly pneumonic." He was soon engaged in a conference at the Chinese Legation with McLeavy Brown, the minister (Liu), and the plague expert, Professor William Simpson, who had offered his services to China for a retaining-fee of £2000, a salary of £500 a month, an assistant, all expenses for both, and funds for laboratories and anti-toxin. Morrison advised the minister to reduce the retainer to 500 guineas.

> Simpson spoke of plague being carried by fowls and pigeons. Said that the pheasant had almost disappeared from Manchuria. He thought this very interesting. In east Anglia, he found plague in cat, rabbit, ferret, as well as the rat. Simpson speaks with experience gained in South Africa, South China and India.

Apparently Simpson would not reduce his retainer, and Dr Petrie, of the Lister Institute, was appointed, with Dr Farrar, of the Local Government Board, his assistant. Morrison travelled with them from Moscow to Harbin. Farrar, whose father was the eminent author of *Eric, or Little by Little*, was a "gassy little cocksparrow", ignorant, pretentious and loud-mouthed, and Petrie, though a very able bacteriologist, a "dull, heavy wearisome and uninteresting" conversationalist. Morrison found the train journey rather trying. The talk was mainly about plague-bearing fleas and rats, with such questions as whether a man who died after eating a plague-infected marmot had been infected by ingestion or contact. Morrison, after recording these learned discussions in pages of his diary, added some curious observations of his own: There was no reference to the rat in Defoe's *Journal of the Plague Year*, except of its destruction . . . and there were those enigmatic references to men "smitten with the emerods (Samuel, 1:5) and the "five golden emerods and five golden mice that mar the land" (Samuel, 1:6). . . .

At Harbin, Morrison was met by Dr Wu Lien-teh, an accomplished Chinese graduate of Cambridge, who was in charge of the anti-plague campaign, and together they inspected the hospitals and quarantine stations. Morrison saw the hovels in which the coolies lay "close packed naked side by side along a raised earthen platform . . . or in tiers in bunks rising from floor to roof, in an atmosphere that is simply awful". The Chinese authorities in Harbin, he reported, "showed deplorable ignorance, vacillation and mendacity as they concocted lying reports for the bewilderment of the authorities in Peking". He corrected some of these reports in dispatches which, in Dr Wu's words, "attracted universal attention" and which the *Peking Daily News* said were "in striking contrast to the wild rumours" which other correspondents had been circulating.

The Russians, particularly, for political reasons, were sending "grossly and grotesquely exaggerated" accounts, and Morrison wrote to Dr Wu suggesting that Wu should communicate the true facts directly to *The Times*:

> . . . The Russian policy has, for some considerable time past, been bent on exaggerating in the press in Europe the unsatisfactory condition of Manchuria. You no doubt know what shocking lies have been told in this connection. . . . Many of these statements I am correcting in *The Times*. . . . Can you do anything in the way I suggest? We are deeply interested in the plague; we are as much interested almost as China herself in the maintenance of the integrity of Manchuria.

The epidemic did not last long, but 67,000 people died.

[XXIII]

Morrison was back in Peking on 12th March. There had been more improvements during his fifteen months' absence. "The city is being transformed," he wrote to Lady Blake:

> Macadamized roads are being made everywhere: every important house is lit with electric light, the streets are lighted by electricity: there is an excellent telephone system: there is a postal service with a delivery eight times a day. The police force cannot be too highly praised—a well-paid, well-equipped, well-disciplined body of men. Why, I saw yesterday a sergeant of police assisting a poor wheelbarrow man, wheeling manure, whose barrow had overturned, this most humble of all coolies, to right his barrow. Could you have conceived such a thing in the past? All the ministries are now either stationed in western buildings, some of quite imposing size, or will be stationed in such buildings soon. There is a good water supply, and I

have no doubt that before long we shall have electric tramways. . . . The Chinese here are taking largely to the use of modern things. For example, there is a large trade in English bedsteads. All over the city you find rubber-tyred rickshaws. Letters are delivered by coolies riding rubber-tyred bicycles. Carriages in Peking now you can count by the thousands, and there are a few motor cars. There will soon be as many as there are in Shanghai. Building is going on all over the city. . . .

He was convinced that the country was much more prosperous, but currency reform was still the crying need, though here, too, there had been "very considerable" improvement. Coined money could now be used all over the Empire, and banknotes were everywhere current, though at varying discounts. Railway development was making real progress. The last great railway loan of £10 million for the Huan-Hupeh Szechwan railway was the most important ever signed in China, for it provided for the construction of 12,000 miles of railway, through the richest and most densely populated part of the Yangtze Valley, within three years of commencing work. There was much less friction between the powers than before: England, France, Germany, and America were working together with their "Four Nations" loans:

What we are trying to induce the Chinese to do is to build their railways by contract, the only wise way. . . . We want them to have a railway built, and when finished and paid for, to be handed over to the Chinese to do with it as they choose—as they would have a battleship built for them.

But the Navy was in a "hopelessly rotten condition":

With the exception of Prince Ch'ing, probably the most corrupt of the high officials in Peking is Prince Tsai Ch'en, the Minister of the Navy, a bloated, evil-living parasite of the worst type. He has placed what are called "courtesy orders" among the foreign powers, buying from each country which entertained him on his journey through Europe, a different ship of a different type, so that not even the bolts are interchangeable. The Navy is spoken of as a "naval museum". He has now ships of different types from England, Germany, Japan, America, Austria and Italy.

The Japanese Navy may have been more efficient, but according to the British Naval attaché in Tokyo, Sir Douglas Brownrigg, it was no less corrupt. Sir Douglas wrote to Morrison:

There are some confiding idiots who fancy that this country is run on the non-squeeze principle: all I have to say to that is that it shows them either to be absurdly credulous or lamentably ignorant! as there is not a move made of any sort or kind in the Armament or Machinery line or of course in the ship-building line generally, without very large sums of money being diverted from their intended destination!

[XXIV]

For eleven years the Austrian Legation in Peking had boycotted Morrison because he had reported the panic withdrawal of the Austrian commandant, Captain Thomann, at the beginning of the Boxer uprising. Now the British military attaché in Peking, General George Pereira, asked Morrison to meet Count Lutzow, formerly Austrian Ambassador to Rome, who was visiting Peking: "Count Lutzow is especially anxious to meet you. . . . As he said yesterday you are one of those who have the power of making peace or war, so I hope in the present emergency you will make for peace." The Count was very complimentary, and suggested a formula for ending the diplomatic impasse: "I am to write him a letter which . . . will be shown to the Emperor. I am to speak of 'Austrians shedding their blood upon a hundred fields of valour' and such like balderdash and I will do it gladly. I'll lay it on with a spade."

Morrison wielded the spade effectively, and after sending off his "ornate letter", in which he not only extolled the glorious valour of Austria's soldiery but referred to the Austrian Emperor as the most revered figure in the world, he asked at the British Legation if Austria had ever won a single victory? No one could answer the question. "Such flapdoodle to remove an eleven-year boycott!" he commented.

Morrison's relations with the other ministers were harmonious, he reported to Garnett, of the Foreign Office. The Germans were "more cordial", France was now represented by "an unusually able" minister, de Margerie, and the "intriguing" Japanese, Honda, had been replaced by Ijuin, who, Morrison commented dryly, "may be expected occasionally to tell the truth". On 15th July, Ijuin sent Morrison a copy of a new Anglo-Japanese Treaty, which had been concluded two days before. Morrison acknowledged it fulsomely:

> I desire to join my congratulations with the many you will have received on the extension of our Alliance, which is so important a factor in the maintenance of the world's peace, and in the peaceful development of our two great Empires.
>
> I thank you exceedingly for your thoughtfulness in sending me so promptly the full text of this epoch-making agreement.

"I have no new instructions and do not propose to make any notification to the Chinese on the subject," Sir John Jordan wrote to Morrison.

[XXV]

Ghosts from the past continued to stalk Morrison's letterbox. From Charleville, Queensland, came a letter from "Matt J. Langtree", whom Morrison had met on his walk across Australia: "We were both stuck up together at Hammonds on Kyabra Creek for 2 weeks. . . . you will remember how we had to light fires for the horses on account of the sandflies."

Mr Langtree, who had been a droving stockman in many parts of Australia and wanted a job in China as a stock inspector, wrote with contempt of a possible Japanese invasion of Australia: "Let the Japs have one try, they will not want another. . . . Hurrah George! Australia for Ever." Mary Joplin, who was hard up again, wrote from Calcutta: "Now let me wish you luck for the Derby and don't forget me if you are so Lucky as to win a handsome prize." And Maggie Leighton, also hard up, wrote from Edinburgh: "It is very difficult to get our rooms let. . . . Perhaps you will not take it amiss if I ask you for a little money. . . ." Morrison sent a postal order, and got a grateful acknowledgement from Mrs Leighton: "I return many thanks for I do not understand she never told me anything about it till after she had done it. . . . She had been upset with coloured men which we had to put away. . . ."

He did not forget Toni—or Dora. Soon after his return to Peking he asked the energetic Dr Dungate to tell Toni he was asking after her, and to send Dora some money to buy a present. Dungate could not find Toni's address, but carried out the other commission: "I wrote at once to La Traviata, and here is the reply from her." La Traviata's reply was addressed not to Alfredo but to "John Brown", the *nom-de-lit* apparently used by Morrison during their association:

I received your very nice present this morning through your friend Dr Dungate of course I was very much surprised to receive it, as I began to think you had quite forgotten me and Mrs Barker often talks about you and wonders how you are I need hardly tell you that I miss you very much and often wish you were in London, as you know I was fond of my *John Brown*. I shall go straight to Madam Rose and order myself a nice costume and every time I wear it will think of you not that I ever forget you as I have so many things to remind me of you the Bracelet you gave me is not in *pawn* yet and is not likely to be why don't you write to me I have looked for a letter so often we are having very nice weather here now and am looking forward for the coronation I suppose there is no such Luck as you coming for it I wish there was I am asking your Friend to forward this on to you I will now close

With Love and Kisses
from Dora.

P.S. I have forgotten to add that I thank you very much for the nice present.

There was a notable difference between Dora's sinewy prose and the lush cadences of the invitation Morrison received from the Countess de Contardone:

When will you come home again? Stop in Egypt on your way and come and stay with me—or if next summer, come to the Greek Isles and spend a few lazy days with me there.

One must every now and again go into retreat into the quiet

backwaters—to rest and regain from nature all that is constantly taken out of us by strenuous life among men and women. . . . So do spare a few days from your splendidly full life—to come and listen to Pan's reeds—and the sighs of the Lesbia dreamers flowing over the sunlit Greek waters. . . .

A few months later Morrison again wrote to Dungate about Toni: "I should like to hear of her. Rarely has anyone treated me with baser ingratitude. It was my own fault, and there is no need to repine, though I do regret the loss of that beautiful pearl pendant." But in September he wrote: "Don't trouble any more about Toni, I, of course will never write to her again." By then he had two big distractions—another revolution and another romance. Once more in his life there was a conjunction of foreign and sexual crises. The Russo-Japanese war had found him involved with Maysie. The Chinese revolution found him involved with Bessie—an Australian girl whom, month after month, he feared he had impregnated. Entries, scattered between long passages on the fall of the Manchus, chart his turbulent emotions:

27 September—Worried as I have not been for years—and with reason. I will rejoice when the next month is passed safely. . . . Why am I of such a sensitive nature?

5 October—More hopeful. Premonitory symptoms . . . Pain in the side.

6 October—Bessie . . . beautiful last night but hair dyed today unattractive. Is singularly attractive to me and has a host of admirers.

25 October—Worried and fretful because Bessie has deserted me. . . .

26 October—Bessie . . . did not speak of the end of the Dynasty. Spoke about the races tomorrow and the dress she was to wear.

7 November—Should be today—God grant it may be!

24 November—Bessie left me today the severest wrench I have suffered for many years. So bright attractive winning kind and sympathetic so sweet to look upon so exquisitely formed so natural . . . all day in a haze that fair image was ever before me that beautiful voice ringing in my ears. My God why do I lose my sense—my perverted sense of duty!

25 November—My thoughts mainly for the absent Bessie. How keenly do I miss her and her winning attractive ways her bright smile and her engaging frankness. . . . What have I done to deserve such happiness and how horribly I will suffer when such happiness is taken from me?

3 December—It is her day but nothing has yet transpired. No need for anxiety until Wednesday 6th.

7 December—Nothing yet and I am in increasing anxiety. . . .

CHAPTER NINE

[I]

THE FIRST Cabinet in China's history was formed in April 1911. "The new Cabinet is an undoubted advance towards constitutional government," Morrison wrote to Garnett in the Foreign Office. It was five years since China had been promised a constitution. Provincial Assemblies, set up two years before, had inaugurated a campaign for the immediate summoning of the National Assembly, the body that was to function until the birth of the Imperial Parliament. The National Assembly met in 1910, and China seemed to be moving steadily if unhurriedly towards a system similar to that of Japan, in which the Emperor was an absolute monarch exercising very wide powers within the limits of a constitution. But on 10th October 1911 an accidental explosion in a house in the Russian concession at Hankow sparked off the eleventh and last rising against the Manchu dynasty and ended an Empire more than 2000 years old. When police investigating the explosion searched the house they found a collection of arms and a list of men who were planning an uprising to take place a week later. Some of the conspirators were officers of the local garrison. To avoid arrest they mutinied and, against little opposition, seized the three cities of Hankow, Hanyang, and Wuchang that make up Wuhan. Next day Morrison telegraphed *The Times*: "Peking is thoroughly alarmed by the news of a revolutionary outbreak and mutiny of troops. ..." Peking had good reason for alarm. City after city in south and central China joined the rebellion. On 13th October, Morrison telegraphed: "The Manchu dynasty is in danger. The sympathies of the immense mass of educated Chinese are all with the revolutionaries. Little sympathy is expressed for the corrupt and effête Manchu dynasty with its eunuchs and other barbaric surroundings. The Court is in great anxiety and the outlook for the throne ... ominous."

Panic-stricken, the Regent, Prince Ch'un, turned to the man who had been insultingly dismissed two years and ten months before. Yuan Shih-k'ai was appointed Viceroy of Hupei and Hunan, with instructions to suppress the revolt. "The Throne must be in an extremity to appoint

Yuan Shih-k'ai and for him to accept," Morrison worte on 14th October. But Yuan was in no hurry to accept. He remembered the remarkable affection of his foot, and solemnly declared that it had not yet been cured. Meanwhile the revolutionaries had also tried to win his support by offering him the Presidency of the Republic if the revolution succeeded. Yuan let the revolutionary pot boil for nine days before he announced the conditions on which he could be induced—despite the foot—to emerge from retirement. He must be given supreme command of the armed forces, with adequate money and supplies; a responsible Government, with himself Prime Minister, must replace the existing council of princes; the revolutionaries must be pardoned. The Regent hesitated, and Yuan remained in his Garden for Cultivating Longevity, cultivating his historic foot. Finally, with the revolution spreading, the Regent gave in. Yuan's foot was miraculously cured, and on 31st October he was able to inspect his troops at the front.

Morrison, despite his concern over Bessie, worked furiously at his telegrams. He spent five days in Hankow, and between 11th October and 24th November wired *The Times* 8113 words ("equals £591.11.5½"). The only acknowledgment he received was a telegram, GRATEFUL SLIGHT REDUCTION SERVICE, but Mrs Moberly Bell wrote: "Once again you are the most read man in London." On 13th November he watched Yuan Shih-k'ai arrive in Peking by special train, with a bodyguard of "wild-looking halberdiers carrying long two-handled swords". Dr Charles Tenney, Chinese Secretary of the American Legation, was at Yuan's home—the temple in which Li Hung-chang had lived—awaiting his arrival. He handed Yuan a message from Dr Wu Ting-fang in Shanghai, who represented the revolutionaries. The message, which Dr Wu asked to be delivered to the Regent, said that if the Emperor abdicated his safety would be guaranteed and he would be adequately pensioned. Tenney told Yuan he could not take this message to the Regent. Yuan said it was nonsense. He gave Tenney to understand that he would support no policy that had for its object the removal of the dynasty.

But Yuan was interested neither in saving the throne nor in setting up a genuine republic. The "Machiavellian old Brutus", as Victor Purcell calls him, had one objective: to make himself ruler of China. He intended to use the revolution—as he had used the Sino-Japanese war of 1895, the Reform movement of 1898, and the Boxer uprising of 1900—to serve his own ends. This required adroit manipulation of the conflicting forces. The three main political groups in China, all of them opposed to the Manchu regime and to one another, were the radical revolutionaries, led by the peripatetic Sun Yat-sen—he was in Denver, Colarado, when the rebellion broke out—the reformers, or constitutional monarchists, and Yuan's followers, who were more concerned with power than with policy.

Yuan removed the immediate threat to the North by recapturing Hankow, but he did not follow up his victory, and the rebels restored the balance on 2nd December by capturing the ancient capital of Nanking.

While Nanking was still in the Government's hands Sir John Jordan spoke "very straight" to Yuan about the barbarous behaviour of his troops there. "Men were beheaded and their heads stuck outside the door. . . . if such things continued, China would estrange the good opinion of the whole world." Yuan seemed impressed, and promised to look into the matter.

On 16th November, Captain Tsai Ting-kan, of the Navy Board, called on Morrison. Tsai, a Cantonese, was an American graduate who not only spoke perfect English but wrote English verse. For many years he had been a devoted follower of Yuan Shih-k'ai, and Yuan had sent him to Wuhan to negotiate peace with the revolutionary leader, General Li Yuan-hung. He had known Li personally when Li was third engineer on a torpedo boat in a flotilla which Tsai Ting-kan commanded. He told Morrison of his reception by the revolutionaries in Wuhan:

> He was . . . given tea, and conducted into a room where he was given the seat of honour, and began a discussion with some 40 delegates. . . . What impressed him most was the youth of the delegates, who were from all the Yangtze provinces. . . . The eldest Li Yuan-hung was (Chinese counting) 48, nearly all had been in Japan and there had acquired their revolutionary ideas. . . . Tsai was asked to state his case. He said he came to endeavour to restore peace and if possible effect a compromise. He urged that a republican form of government was not adapted for this country. If each province was a state of a federated republic, what was to prevent the secession of each province in turn? . . . He urged that in the opinion of Yuan Shih-k'ai, the retention of the dynasty as a limited monarchy was the best safeguard for the preservation of the integrity of the Empire. He claimed that every reform movement demanded by the revolutionary party had been conceded. Then the delegates spoke. In turn . . . each declared emphatically that the reigning dynasty must be dethroned. "You cannot trust the word of a Manchu", was their bitter saying. . . . the only hope for the country was to sweep the curse from it. . . . The dynasty would be guaranteed pensions and protection but they must be swept into retirement. . . . The delegates unanimously declared that they stood for a United States of China, . . . a republic modelled partly on that of America, and partly on that of France, with some modifications derived from Switzerland, the President to be elected by the people and to hold office for three years.

> Tsai Ting-kan replied that a constitutional monarchy such as existed in England was the most stable of all, and the highest illustration possible of purity of administration. He spoke of the great corruption that had been known to exist in the Republic of France, and cited the Panama scandals as instances of what occurred there, and while reminding them that he had been educated in America, he described the immense corruption rampant there in all departments of public life. They asked him what instance could he give to show that a monarchy was more stable than a republic. All desired the stability

of a United China. Look what had happened, he replied, in Mexico. Remember the recent revolution. Do not forget the internecine strife occurring in the South American Republics ever since they became republics—a revolution every second or third year.

In the evening Tsai dined with the delegates. They sat together "as one family" and chatted. He argued for Yuan and a limited monarchy and admits they were in no way shaken by what he said. He said all the delegates spoke highly of Yuan Shih-k'ai and expressed their surprise that after the treatment he had been accorded by the Manchus, he should now come to their assistance. Tsai replied that Yuan would have been a coward had he not come forward when appeals were made to him to try and save the country from disruption.

After listening to Tsai for nearly an hour Morrison was forced to the conviction that Tsai himself was a republican at heart: "While defending constitutional monarchy in theory, he is as strongly anti-Manchu as the men with whom he was sent to parley." Instead of influencing them he had been impressed by the strength and sincerity of their arguments.

Tsai and Morrison discussed Yuan Shih-k'ai's difficulties. Morrison said he could not declare for the retention of the dynasty shorn of all its powers and reconcile this view with the determination of the South for a republic. What better solution could there be, Morrison asked, than that the dynasty should abdicate? But in that case would Yuan Shih-k'ai be appointed President? Tsai was not certain. Tsai spoke of China's desperate financial position. The Wai Wu Pu had no money to pay its own staff, and the Ministry of Communications would have to close down altogether. He said Yuan had spoken to him about the services Morrison had rendered to China:

Then I suggested that perhaps the foreign powers might be induced to intimate to the Manchu dynasty that they could expect no help from foreign intervention and better accept the proposals and abdicate, withdraw into honourable retirement.

Impressions left by my talk: 1. No hope of a constitutional monarchy in so far as it involves the retention of the Manchus. 2. That Tsai Ting-kan himself, the intimate confidant of Yuan, is opposed to their retention. 3. That the Throne itself is beginning to realize that its position is hopeless that it will withdraw to Jehol.

At Wuhan, Tsai had asked what part Sun Yat-sen had played in the revolution, and was told none at all. It was purely a military uprising. The revolutionaries whom Tsai met spoke with some contempt of a man who had been only a drummer of the revolution, always keeping away in order to save his own skin. They said that while some of them who had been trained in Japan were of Sun Yat-sen's party he could not be said to have taken any part in the present revolution.

A few days later Tsai Ting-kan again called on Morrison and said

Yuan Shih-k'ai would like to see him. Morrison got a carriage and presented himself at Yuan's house, where he was cordially received by Yuan's son, K'e-ting, a secretary in the Ministry of Communication. K'e-ting begged Morrison to urge his father "to cease his stubbornness and become President or even Emperor". "Not lacking in ambition is the son, but very stupid," Morrison commented.

Yuan ("much stouter than before. Bronchitic. Spoke largely in whisper") was "very cordial and complimentary". The most significant thing he said was: "If there were more pressure, perhaps the Court would leave for Jehol." Morrison came away convinced that the Court intended to leave and that Yuan was conspiring to that end: "All the people around him are Revolutionary. Tsai Ting-kan and his own son and others. . . . Young Yuan almost violently Republican and anti-Manchu but not strong in the wits." Sir John, who was acting as mediator between Yuan and the revolutionaries, agreed that Morrison had "grasped the situation".

Morrison's grasp of the situation and his intimacy with the Chinese leaders enabled him to get what Dr Jerome Ch'en calls "the scoop of the year" when on 10th January he forecast the abdication of the Manchus in a dispatch headed "A Republic by Imperial Decree". Events had moved swiftly since Tsai's visit to Wuhan.

On 30th November, after the recapture of Hanyang by the Imperialist forces, Morrison wrote to Colonel Bruce, of the Shanghai police: "To us here it seems as if the revolution . . . has collapsed. Li Yuan-hung has told our consul that he is now willing to accept the terms offered him by Yuan Shih-k'ai some time ago." Li was now prepared to accept a constitutional monarchy, but this did not suit Yuan. "It is difficult to know what Yuan has at the back of his mind," Morrison wrote. "Two of his men have gone to Hankow in order to induce the revolutionary leaders to proclaim him President of the Republic." At the back of Yuan's mind was the realization that he had to preserve the facade of a successful revolt so as to play off the revolutionaries against the Manchus. The half-hearted revolution was his highway to power. The capture of Nanking by the rebels was followed by a three-day truce, arranged by Sir John Jordan and the British Consul in Hankow, which was extended for three weeks.

In the midst of these excitements, on 8th December, Tsai Ting-kan wrote to Morrison: "Thank you for Boswell's Johnson. . . . Tang Shao-yi had his queue cut last night in Room No. 4 of the Wagon-Lits. Liang Shih-yi and others had their hairy 'pendants' hauled down probably in the same room."

The Tartar custom of wearing a queue, which Englishmen offensively called a "pigtail", had been forcibly imposed on the Chinese by the conquering Manchus in the seventeenth century. Its removal was a sign of loyalty to the revolutionary cause.

Morrison returned to Hankow on 13th December, as the guest of Yuan Shih-k'ai, in a complimentary carriage with a cook and boy provided by

Astor House. He was "fed and wined with sybaritish luxury", having apparently overcome his inhibitions about accepting largesse. In Hankow he noted: "Great loss of property, little of life. Conduct of revolutionaries model. Imperialists much raping", and came to the conclusion that the Manchus could not be retained in any form. "China is indifferent whether Yuan Shih-k'ai makes himself President or Emperor; the Manchus must go. There seems absolute unanimity about this."

Early in December the Regent, Prince Ch'un, abdicated, and was told by the Empress Dowager to keep out of politics, and Yuan Shih-k'ai was authorized to negotiate a peace with the revolutionaries. On 18th December, Tang Shao-yi, leading a delegation from Yuan, and Dr Wu Ting-fang leading the revolutionary delegates, met in the Municipal Council Building in Shanghai to discuss Dr Wu's four-point plan for peace: the abdication of the Manchus, the establishment of a Republic, a generous pension to the Emperor, relief for aged and poor Manchus.

On Christmas Day, while the negotiations were dragging on, the drummer of the revolution, Dr Sun Yat-sen, arrived in Shanghai and, as a compromise between the conflicting revolutionary factions, was elected President of the provisional Government. At his inauguration on 1st January 1912 he swore to relinquish the office of provisional President as soon as the Republic was firmly established and recognized.

"Oh! such a rag-tag and bobtail!" Alfred Pope, general manager of the Imperial Chinese Railways, wrote to Morrison when President Sun and his followers left Shanghai for Nanking:

> *No* control among them. It is impossible to recognize a cabinet of scallywags like the one put up by Dr Sun Yat-sen (most of them). . . . Do draw attention to the appointment of Tang Shou Chien, the head of the worst railway in China, a known rogue, and Minister of Communications. A bad beginning.

"Sun Yat-sen himself has created so far a favourable impression," Morrison wrote to Braham on 8th January. "How far this is due to the fact that he is believed to have brought with him vast sums of foreign money is difficult to say, the fact being, I understand, that he had not brought any money at all." But he had brought a dubious American companion, "General" Homer Lea:

> a little hunchback who if half of what is reported of him in the papers be true, must be an appalling liar. I cannot find anyone who was ever able to discover that he was at any time in the service of the Chinese, yet he declares in an interview that he organized four divisions (sic) of Chinese troops to march to Peking in 1898 in order to rescue the imprisoned Emperor after the coup d'état. His claim to the title of "General" appears to be based on the fact that when resident in Los Angeles he taught the goosestep to some Chinese laundrymen. . . .

Charles Maguire, a contractor in Nanking, believed that Sun Yat-sen was being supported by the Standard Oil Company. He wrote to Morrison on 14th January:

> . . . I want to give you some information for what it is worth. . . . That is that the Standard Oil Company have been all along and are now supplying the finances of the revolutionary party, their object being to secure the concession for the oil wells in Shansi and any other oil discovered in China. Blake of the S.O. Co. was up here a couple of days ago from Shanghai to see President Sun Yat-sen and immediately after their very long interview it was announced that the party had obtained funds to the extent of Taels, 40,000,000. . . . This is bringing the revolution down from the sentimental and patriotic to a very sordid level.
>
> You know of course that the S.O. Co. did a great deal of the financing of the revolution in Mexico which it engineered to obtain rights which it could not get under Diaz. This is mischievous money to my mind. You know also from what you observed here that the S.O. crowd are very much in with the revolutionary party. . . . It is the S.O. crowd that are booming and supporting Sun as President, though his star is on the wane among the Chinese. They support him, as a weak man suits their game. But for the S.O. I would not give Sun 6 weeks . . . in the Presidential Chair. He is a man obviously without personality, as is instanced in one case by his great intimacy and friendship for that *first class bum* "General" Homer Lea. The people are sick of him already and would do a lot to kick him out but the S.O. pulls the strings.

Dr Yen told Morrison that Wu Ting-fang, who was denouncing the corruption of the Imperialist Government, was himself very corrupt. He had made much money in the United States by smuggling coolies in as his servants, and had also made money out of the Canton-Hankow railway. Wu was a baptized Christian with two concubines.

[II]

Miss Robin, Morrison's new secretary, was welcomed by Peking's many bachelors. Morrison was delighted with her efficiency, but dismayed by her social success. "It already looks as if I were to have some trouble with the Robin," he commented a month after his return. "She is much admired." Among her many admirers was David Fraser, who six weeks after her arrival in Peking took her to the Temple of Heaven and proposed to her, but was rejected. "He outraged her sense of duty to her employer whom she could hardly leave after so short a service," Morrison commented smugly. His own interest in Miss Robin was growing. There were frequent diary references to her efficiency and charm ("a fine worker . . . very gentle and sweet in her manner and most intelligent"), and he was "disgusted" when he received a facetious letter from the "impudent and tactless" Brent, of Jardine, Mathieson and Co.:

The rumour is current in Peking that you are considering the installation of an electrically-driven fan in the office of your secretary. We would be pleased to submit quotations but before doing so, would request the following particulars:—

Age & sex of secretary.
State whether married or single.
If single,—any followers?
Has he (or she) a dog?
Is the dog healthy?
Superficial area of secretary in square inches. This indicates surface to be cooled and is ascertained by taking the cube of his or her velocity, plus size in gloves, minus length of eyelashes.
Present temperature of secretary.
Temperature desired (minimum 40 degrees below zero).
Is secretary subject to cold feet?
Is secretary subject to excessive blushing?

Should your secretary be of a talkative or sprightly disposition, we can recommend our Hot Air Fan. This type would effect a saving of 75% in cost of power required to drive same. If soulful, our Spirit Driven Fan would we feel sure, give satisfaction. Our price for a 14" desk fan is approximately $30, but on receipt of the above particulars we will submit you a firm offer.

[III]

Morrison pointed out to the Republican leaders in Shanghai that it was hopeless to expect that a leader such as Sun Yat-sen, who knew nothing about China, could obtain for the Republic early recognition from foreign powers. He said that Yuan Shih-k'ai alone could obtain their confidence. The leaders assured Morrison that Yuan would certainly be appointed first President. But would he accept the appointment? Morrison discussed this vital question in a letter to Braham dated 29th December:

He has told Sir John Jordan emphatically that he will not do so, and sent similar communications to all other foreign governments. He said that he and his ancestors have served the Manchu dynasty faithfully, and he could not go down to the future as an usurper. But suppose the Manchus themselves should desire his appointment? Their interest would be better safeguarded with him in the Presidency than with other Chinese in the Empire. . . . This seems to me the best possible solution. I do not see why it cannot be arranged that the Manchus themselves shall support his appointment. . . . This is my own idea. I have not yet had time to develop it.

This was the germ of the idea that was to produce the most remarkable event in China's long history: the creation of a republic by the edict of an Empress. On 31st December, Morrison told Tsai Ting-kan of his scheme, and Tsai said he would pass it on to Yuan Shih-k'ai. Three days later, when Morrison was very ill with influenza and severe vomiting, Tsai called to consult him "how best to bring about the abdication and after the abdication what was the procedure to follow"?

Five weeks passed before the idea was again discussed. On 5th February, Tsai told Morrison "Yuan was tickled to death at your suggestion for the establishment of a Constitutional Republic by the Throne in an Imperial edict—appealing thus to the traditions of the Empire and saving the face of the Throne and of Yuan Shih-k'ai. It is the best possible solution of the difficulty, the method by which the earliest recognition possible will be given to the Regime. For as the foreign legations are now accredited by the Court, they cannot refuse recognition of a Government delegated by the Court. The Republic will then be legally, legitimately and constitutionally established."

Later in the day Morrison had a telephone call from Tsai, who had just received a telegram from Nanking suggesting total suppression of hostilities: "The uncertain factor is Sun Yat-sen," Morrison wrote. "Will he accept? Tsai says he knows nothing of China. . . . this 'Hawaian Chinese' . . . this so-called Christian."

While Morrison was giving good advice to Yuan Shih-k'ai in Peking, another Australian newspaperman, W. H. Donald, was performing a similar service for the Republicans in Shanghai. "It is a very curious feature," Morrison wrote to Sir John Jordan, "that the foreigner most intimately connected with the revolutionary party, the man who was offered the post of private secretary to Wu Ting-fang and declined it, is the Shanghai correspondent of the *New York Herald* . . . W. H. Donald." He was in "intimate relations" with Sir Everard Fraser, the British Consul-General in Shanghai, and was Fraser's "chief source of information with regard to the revolutionary party". Donald, who was born at Lithgow, New South Wales, had worked as a journalist in Sydney before coming to China in 1902. Like Morrison, he had a great affection for the Chinese, and gave the Republicans not only advice but active military co-operation. The erudite and eloquent Republican Manifesto which Sun Yat-sen issued four days after his election as provisional President was hammered out by Donald on a battered typewriter with the aid of a bottle of bourbon.

[IV]

"We are living in the midst of excitement," Morrison wrote to Braham on 16th January. "The abdication Decree should be issued tomorrow or next day":

Yuan Shih-k'ai's confidential secretary . . . came over to tell me that the evening before Yuan Shih-k'ai had finally accepted the inevitable, and had agreed that within four days an Edict should be issued by the Empress Dowager abdicating the Throne, and deputing the succession to a republic. . . . Yuan Shih-k'ai will be instructed to carry on the government. . . . In the meantime the Court will not leave Peking, he says. I strongly urged that it should be forced to retire to Jehol. The question of the Imperial pensions is being arranged with the Princes. Yuan Shih-k'ai is prepared to pay them as much as five million taels per annum, a quite preposterous amount. . . . I have said that one million taels is ample. . . . I cited the cases of Persia and of Turkey. The pension of the ex-Shah was only £20,000 a year.

There was more excitement later in the day. Just after midday Morrison and Miss Robin were at their gate in Morrison Street, waiting to see Yuan Shih-k'ai drive by in his carriage. Yuan had been to the palace to present Cabinet's petition to the Empress Dowager, requesting her early abdication. There was a loud explosion, and a burst of smoke at the corner of the street:

At once I knew that a bomb had been thrown. A riderless horse dashed past other men riding after it then after a moment of suspense the carriage was seen coming round the corner with its escort of mounted men. It paced quickly past giving us a passing glimpse of Yuan seated. Nothing had happened to him, thank God, but another riderless horse dashed past and soldiers were seen running up the street. . . . I ran to the corner. There the telephone or telegraph wires cut by the explosion were lying in a tangle . . . soldiers and police were still at their posts but an excited crowd of soldiers were struggling at the third house from the corner . . . with the butts of their rifles they were smashing through the windows and kicking down the doors. . . . In the middle of the road lying face downwards was one of the officers of the bodyguard, sobbing out blood like a stuck pig he was quickly dying. Nobody gave him the slightest attention, nobody attempted to move him into a more comfortable position. Further away by the pumps and hydrant was a soldier also mutilated also quickly dying but nobody cared. Further away was a dead horse. By the pumps were signs of where a bomb had fallen. . . . In the shop, bombs were found and one was found unexploded in the road and was carried to the sidewalk and there placed under a basket guarded by soldiers. Troops and police quickly gathered. . . . There was much noise and confusion but prompt measures were taken to search the market and the neighbouring houses. In a short time one of the bomb throwers was captured and soon after another and later a third was brought along the street, a young man in a Chinese dress and Inverness cape with small mustache. He looked markedly Japanese but he was not. . . . Apparently I and a bible seller from Mongolia were the first there.

The bomb-throwers, whose home-made bombs were concealed in quarter-pound Three Castles cigarette tins, were underground members of the revolutionary party who had become impatient with Yuan's protracted peace negotiations. They were promptly shot. One of the soldiers killed was the chief of the guard who was riding just behind the carriage, but Yuan was uninjured and showed great equanimity, "remarking as he alighted, 'Bombs very near'. Tsai was standing there weeping."

Next morning, while Morrison was working in his library, Miss Robin, too, threw a bomb. She told him that she had become engaged to Herbert Phillips, assistant Chinese Secretary of the Consular Service—and a Jew! ("not popular among men nor as far as I have known among women, exceedingly mean and selfish but with good prospects of rising in the service . . . present salary about £600"):

> She has just in a cold-blooded entirely matter-of-fact businesslike way put love and romance to the winds. . . . He is very much in love, she quite calm like Toni in her workmanlike arrangement with men. . . . He is getting a treasure. She says she will not leave me *for ages*.

Miss Robin's engagement was followed by an unexplained breach with Bessie:

> *28 February*—"Before it was delightful having you here; now you are regular damned nuisance!" These were the uncourtly but true words which I spoke to Bessie tonight who is driving me mad with her jealousy and her nagging. . . . What a virago! I was quite upset and could do no work, driven into a fiery rage. Washington Irving says: "A sharp temper never mellows with age and a woman's tongue is the only edged instrument that grows keener with constant use." . . . it will be an immense burden lifted from my shoulders when Bessie departs for other clients. She is a champion sponger and bores me to a degree almost past endurance. . . . She was unclean in mouth and body. I could not get her to wash!

A Mr Bush, of the *Daily Mail*, with whom Bessie had also stayed, added his gallant tribute. "You're well out of it," he said. "You escaped cheap. . . . There's nothing she could ask for she did not ask for. She walked off with 50 Mexican dollars with scented soap and an enema syringe. She tried to entrap me and failed." But she succeeded in entrapping a young professor from the London School of Economics named Finlayson, who gave her two rings and considered himself engaged to her.

[V]

Moberly Bell wrote to Morrison on 20th March 1911: "I am dieting myself strictly and have reduced myself by 18½ lbs in 7 weeks. . . . I calculate that if I can continue at this rate, it will take me exactly a year and a half to vanish altogether. I hope *The Times* will last so long."

Morrison received the letter on 8th April. A week later, pen in hand, Moberly Bell died at his desk in Printing House Square. One of the barnacles had been removed.

Morrison's honeymoon with Northcliffe did not last long, nor were the promises that had been made to him fulfilled. Soon he was complaining again that his dispatches were not being published. "Lord Northcliffe does not appear to have great fixity of purpose," he wrote to Grigg on 15th August. "He has such a curious faculty of setting men against each other that I am fearful of writing to him." A few weeks later Morrison wrote to C. W. Campbell, who had retired and was living in England: "Northcliffe's methods are unsatisfactory. He would tell me, for example, the contemptuous things that Chirol had said of me; that I was currying favour with the Chinese with a view to ultimate employment. . . ."

Morrison's hatred of Chirol was undiminished. "Chirol who has stood in my way for so many years, has left London for six months' tour in the Middle East," he wrote. "I shall be glad if he took up his abode there permanently, either above or under ground." And to Mrs Moberly Bell: "Braham writes to me in a very pleasant way—quite different from the acrimonious letters which used to be consistently sent by Chirol." And he added: "I never hear from Lord Northcliffe. . . ."A few months later the disillusion had spread to Braham: "Wrote to Braham . . . who hardly deserves a letter. He never writes to me except the briefest scraps, and he gives me no information that can help me as a correspondent."

Morrison's discontent grew, nourished by ill-health and by worry about money. "My accounts are getting confused," the most methodical of men confessed to himself in August: "I am spending my capital fast." He was spending more than he could afford on his cottage and his library. "Am overdrawn £200 and owe the booksellers another £200. . . . the outlook is not reassuring." To Lionel James he wrote:

> It is impossible for me to live in Peking upon the income provided me by *The Times*, although I make no complaint of that. I mean to live in the style I have become accustomed to—keeping many servants, buying many books, travelling as a correspondent of *The Times* ought to travel. I am rebuilding my cottage in the country, for the simple reason that if I did not do so, I won't have a cottage to live in. The first structure, built by one of the most earnest Methodist deacons . . . of South Carolina, who pinched everything he could, was composed of sun-dried earthen clods instead of bricks, and common or garden earth, instead of lime. He will have his reward. My present contractor is also a Christian, or rather, he will become converted if the contracts which he is now carrying out for the London Mission be profitable.

He thought of selling some of his treasures, which he valued at £5000, and wrote to the Army and Navy Stores in London, asking if they could dispose of, for example:

A collection of flower paintings done by the late Empress Dowager. . . . a scroll which belonged to the Emperor Chien Lung, which contains 20 portraits of Chinese who were prominent at the time of the Conquest of Formosa, the description of each being written in the Emperor's own hand. This scroll came from the Winter Palace, and has been valued at £750 . . . an extremely fine specimen of Chinese wood carving, an Imperial sedan chair, certainly the best piece of carving I have seen in Peking.

"Since my return I have been making a serious effort to write my 'Reminiscences,'" he wrote to Grigg. "I have kept every scrap of paper that has been sent me for I should think thirty years past. I have been delving into these, and I have written a bald and unconvincing record of my life up to the 15 March 1897, about the time when I arrived in Peking. For the years 1897 and 1898, my records are not complete, but from 1 January 1899, I have kept a minute diary in which I have recorded every conversation that I ever had with anyone whose words were worth remembering. . . . I think that before the end of the year I should have the whole autobiography in fairly good shape. . . ."

Sir Robert Hart was "threatening" to return to Peking. "It will be a misfortune if the old dodger comes back and restores the corruption from which the Service is now free," Morrison wrote in his diary, and to Sir John Jordan, who, too, was still in England:

He is coming, or hoping to come, in the senile belief that his presence is needed "to save the Customs". . . . As a matter of fact the service has never been better run that it is at present, and it would be nothing less than a misfortune if Sir Robert, with his 76 years, with mind and body shattered after three strokes of paralysis, should return here. If he returns . . . there will be the same . . . corruption and nepotism. . . .

"The old rascal" squeezed another years' leave of absence out of the Chinese, and Morrison calculated that Hart since 1863 had been paid £426,000 plus a Boxer indemnity of £20,000. When Hart died in September, Morrison got a telegram from *The Times*: TELEGRAPH CHINESE FEELING HART'S DEATH. "What could I telegraph," he asked his diary. "Who can mourn him? Have they not amply rewarded him—perhaps more than a million sterling . . . divided among his family: Hart himself, his son, his brother James, Bredon and his brother Carl, the Edgars, two Mayers, and others. There was never a greater jobber than Sir Robert. And yet I have to telegraph home flapdoodle. There will not be the slightest sorrow at his death. . . . In the evening I squeezed out a poor telegram."

Several invitations to dinner reached Morrison on 3rd October. He refused them, "on the sentimental ground" that it was the anniversary of the day on which he was speared in New Guinea in 1883. "My God! How the time is fleeting!" he wrote.

A delicious interlude of solemn Oriental comedy enlivened the last few days of Manchu rule. The Empress Dowager replied to Yuan Shih-k'ai's request for her abdication by conferring on him the very rare honour of a marquisate, the second-highest rank of nobility that a Chinese could attain. "He is not permitted to decline," said the Imperial Decree. This astute move to convince the people of Yuan's loyalty to the Throne greatly embarrassed Yuan in his dealings with the Republicans. So, despite the unequivocal command, he refused it in a memorial which combined lyricism, self-abasement, and a calculated exaggeration of the revolutionary situation: "The dynasty is crumbling into dust, and the people's love is in fragments like a potsherd. The body politic is smitten with a murrain, and no cure for its distemper can be found. . . . The cup of my offences is daily filling and my desert is less than a grain of sand or a drop of water. . . . In the secrecy of my chamber I shed tears. . . ." The essence of Yuan's memorial, which burgeoned with about 2000 flowery words, was that the revolution could not be suppressed. He had been unable to accomplish the smallest result after many months, and if he accepted the high honour he would be casting a slur on the equitable bestowal by the Throne of rewards and punishments. "It remains to entreat Your Majesty to cancel your former mandate, and to allow my purity of intention to be manifested to the world, and my guilt to suffer no further aggravation. . . ."

The Throne ignored this moving entreaty and issued a second decree, which acknowledged Yuan's "modest sincerity" but tersely instructed him to refrain from further refusal. But Yuan refused a second time in another eloquent memorial, richly studded with historical allusions, and another decree was issued, acknowledging Yuan's historical erudition but pointing out that the present crisis was utterly unprecedented: "He is to pay due obedience and accept the title." Again Yuan circumspectly refused, and again was commanded to obey the decree. "Throne fears lose face. Yuan fears ill effect of acceptance of title from expiring and tottering throne," Morrison commented. In his fourth refusal Yuan pleaded that "the uneasiness of his conscience did not enhance the reverent reflection that the divine will is irrevocable." The final decree read: "Yuan Shih-k'ai has memorialized Us that he dares not persist in his refusal after our repeated expressions of favour. He asks that the acceptance of the patent may be postponed until the situation shall have improved. Rescript. Noted."

The Chinese Republic was proclaimed in a rhetorical edict which the Empress Dowager delivered from the throne in the presence of Yuan Shih-k'ai, and the boy-emperor, P'u Yi. Court officials prostrated themselves in fear and wonder, and tears streamed from the Empress's eyes as she read the death warrant of the dynasty:

By observing the nature of the people's aspirations, we learn the Will of Heaven. It is not fitting that We should withstand the desires of the nation merely for the sake of the glorification of Our House. We recognize the signs of the ages, and we have tested the trend of popular opinion; and We now, with the Emperor at Our side, invest the nation with sovereign power, and decree the establishment of a constitutional government on a republican basis. . . . We, the Empress Dowager and the Emperor, will retire into a life of leisure, free from public duties, spending our lives pleasantly and enjoying the courteous treatment accorded to us by the people, and watching with satisfaction the glorious establishment and consummation of the perfect Government.

Yuan Shih-k'ai became President of China three days later. He told Morrison that he believed the "true Chinese", such as Li Yuan-hung, whose act started the revolution, Chang Chieh, a man of quite exceptional ability who was optimus of his year, Wu Ting-fang, and others favoured him, but the "half-Chinese" men who know very little of their own country, such as Sun Yat-sen, did not seem to favour him. "He spoke with gratitude of the assistance given him by *The Times*, and I think he spoke sincerely for he has been in frequent, almost daily, communication with me since he returned to Peking."

"It is a curious feature of the present trouble," Morrison wrote to Rockhill at the end of January, "that the great majority of Englishmen in China are in favour of the revolutionaries, whereas the great majority of the Americans are in favour of a continuance of monarchical government—of course, a reformed government." What was the attitude of their respective Governments? Many historians say that only America was sympathetic to the Republic, that all the European powers were, in Professor C. P. Fitzgerald's words, "either covertly or actively hostile", and that Britain shared Japan's unconcealed hostility. "Britain, then the ally of Japan, believed that the reformation of the Empire, rather than its overthrow, was the true and proper pattern for Oriental progress," says Fitzgerald. But Morrison makes it clear that, whatever were Britain's beliefs, they were not reflected in her attitude towards Yuan's regime.

Everard Fraser in Shanghai was of great assistance to the revolutionaries, giving them advice, meeting-places, and protection. Sir John Jordan, briefed by Morrison, was able to counter Japanese opposition to the Republic, and to assure Yuan that Britain was not in any way pledged to support the continuance of the monarchy. He said that she had done her best to bring the contending factions together, but "cared not a damn whether there was a republic or a monarchy". Sir John was in a difficult position. Because of the alliance, he had to act in apparent concert with the Japanese while disagreeing with their policy. Morrison sent a telegram to *The Times* about Sir John's predicament, and the Foreign Office wired it back to Sir John, asking for an explanation, "My telegram did unquestionable good," Morrison wrote to Braham, "for as a result Sir John frankly exchanged views with Ijuin". As a result, when they were shown the abdication edict, Sir John approved it unreservedly and Ijuin guardedly agreed not to oppose it—though the Japanese Throne feared that a republic in China might stimulate the republican movement in Japan.

The Republic was established, but the wrangling went on. Sun Yat-sen faithfully surrendered his Presidency to Yuan, but protested that a republic could not be created by Imperial decree, and insisted that the capital should be shifted to Nanking, the ancient capital of the Mings. Two days after the birth of the Republic, Morrison wrote to Sir John Jordan:

> . . . Yuan Shih-k'ai is thoroughly well disgusted and will not cut off his queue. He has received a telegram from Sun Yat-sen virtually repudiating his promises, insisting that Yuan cannot hold any power from the Manchus, and demanding that he shall come at once to Nanking and there arrange matters. Apparently it is Sun Yat-sen and his callow young men who are thus insistent, for Wu Ting-fang has telegraphed his congratulations to Yuan Shih-k'ai and . . . Tang Shao-yi has also telegraphed his congratulations to Liang Shih-yi.

Yuan politely regretted that he could not move the capital to Nanking, because his presence in Peking was essential to maintain order and control the Northern Army. In fact, he had no intention of exchanging the security of Peking for the uncertainty of Nanking. Morrison supported him, pointing out the expense that a move would involve, the obligations to the legations, the unhealthiness of the city from which all foreign ministers would be exiled for four months of the year. . . . But to the revolutionaries Peking was a symbol of all that was most detested in the Manchu regime. "Weird carbuncles and chronic diseases of this sinful world are concentrated there," wrote Liang Chi-chao, a non-revolutionary and one of the 1898 Reformers. "If the political centre stays there, China will never see a single day of clean government." Both sides were obdurate, and again Morrison came forward with an ingenious proposal, which he submitted to Tsai Ting-kan:

> Li Yuan-hung has now telephoned that Wuchang should be the capital. I would suggest that telegrams should also be received from Tsinanfu, from Kaifengfu, from Honanfu, from Sianfu, from Chengtu, and from Canton, urging the advantages of each city to be the future seat of government. At least three of these have superior claims, for they have previously been capitals in earlier dynasties. When you have a dozen provinces claiming that their capital shall be the capital of the Empire, perhaps each one will put Peking as the second best capital.
>
> Before the battle of Marathon, one of the decisive battles of the world, when the question arose as to who was to have chief command, each of the Athenian generals voted for himself as the most deserving, and put the name of Miltiades second, because of this the casting vote was given to Miltiades. So it shall be with Peking.

"Thank you for the capital suggestion, which is capital," Tsai Ting-kan replied. "You should be styled in future The Australian Hero of the Chinese Reform Movement." And he gave Morrison, in return, some important intelligence: "It is agreed that *I* shall clip the President's top-knot and not a barber as he feels rather awkward. *This is your scoop.*"

The capital suggestion was not followed, and Sun Yat-sen sent a delegation to Peking to talk things over. A few days after its arrival Morrison was leaving his club just before 8 p.m. when he heard shots. "They are fighting in the Hatamen," someone said:

> Without waiting I at once ran off to my house running the whole way. My servants were in the gateway greatly excited. For nearly half an hour there had been the rattle of musketry. . . . Shots came nearer. Excited soldiers were seen in the street passing my house to the north. Then fire broke out in the warren of buildings north of my house on the west side of the street and the street became deserted except for the soldiers. All the police had run away. The soldiers of the 3rd division had mutinied had broken loose and were looting the city. Shots were flying but nobody seemed hit. It was some time before we realized that shots were being fired for intimidation only.

The 3rd Division was Yuan Shih-k'ai's most trusted force, the original division which he had created in 1895. It had been specially brought into Peking to preserve order during the crisis. Morrison's house was about half a mile outside the legation area. Next to him lived Willard Straight, who, after terms as American Vice-Consul at Seoul and Consul-General at Mukden, had married Dorothy Whitney and returned to Peking to represent a group of American capitalists, headed by E. H. Harriman, interested in Chinese railways. Dorothy Straight was dressing for dinner when the firing started. "The whole sky to the north of us seemed ablaze," Straight wrote to a friend, "while the firing continued unabated, the crack of rifles punctuated by the booming of field pieces somewhere in the distance and by the burr of machine guns nearby":

> Then came the crashing of glass, the rip-rip of planking and the shock of rifle butts on barred doors. The looters were at the silver shop, just across the alley—a very narrow one—from our gate. . . . In a moment there was a pounding . . . then came a voice, in Chinese, "Open the gate, Dr Morrison is here." I thought they were after him. The coolie fumbled with the key, so I pulled. Morrison pushed from outside, and the whole show came in on us. There was no trouble however. Morrison, with great kindness, came to say that he thought Dorothy would be better off in his place, where a number of foreigners were gathered. We . . . walked to Morrison's gate. The street was bright with the fire-glow. Luckily there was little wind, and that from the south, carrying flames away from, rather than towards us, otherwise we would have had a bad time. Parties of from two to a

dozen soldiers were walking or running along carrying bundles of loot. Every now and then they would stop and tie up their ill-gotten gains or smash in the doors of some shop which had up to that time escaped their attention. Some carried torches used to light them while they pillaged, which were then dropped on the floors to start another conflagration. The firing continued but we reached Morrison's seemingly unnoticed by the busy gentlemen in uniform. We stayed there until a guard of American Marines came out on the trot to rescue us.

Less fortunate in her knights-errant was Lady Bredon, who lived in the Tartar City, east of the Hatamen. The Danish Minister, Count Ahlenfeldt, led a party of Englishmen to her rescue. When they arrived they decided to consume all the provisions in the house rather than leave them for the looters. The cellar was well stocked with champagne, and by the time this was finished the rescuers had forgotten what they came for. They went home, leaving Lady Bredon, not only without protection, but without food or drink.

Morrison was busy with his telegrams to *The Times* when his house-guest, William Maxwell, of the *Daily Mail*, burst into his room excitedly. With him was Sidney Barton, Chinese Secretary to the British Legation, and a British guard. Barton formally ordered Morrison to leave, but Morrison refused. Two wounded shopkeepers shot through the lung had been brought in:

> They were made as comfortable as possible on stretchers. Air was coming through their wounds and I did not think they would live until morning. . . . Then I wrote a rotten bad message amid the excitement the noise of flames and people rushing in.

"Little sleep last night," Morrison noted next morning. "My house was so lit that I could see to read and the crackling of the burning buildings was quite sufficient to keep me awake."

From Tsai Ting-kan came a philosophic comment:

> Up all night with the President—Affair most unexpected. Tried to phone you last night without success. Felt for your life and then thought of your books—but eased in mind when told your premises intact.
>
> Sorry affair happened but since it took place I would not have missed it for anything. It adds another Chapter to life's experiences. Had a good study of Yuan under a sudden crisis like this.

This was followed by an official note:

> H.E. President Yuan has been informed that some natives were wounded on the night of Feb. 29th and that you benevolently took them into your house for treatment and nourishment and turned your premises into an improvised hospital—all of which kind and humane acts the President is deeply appreciative and desires to express, even inadequately in this letter, his thanks and admiration for

the noble deeds. He enclosed his card and hopes you are enjoying good health.

Morrison walked the smouldering streets and was shocked to see:

a good deal of shooting of alleged looters, who were almost invariably poor people, in one case a girl, a woman and an old woman who had picked up some scraps from the ruins of a burnt building. Another case, three poor women carrying some burnt wood and scrap iron, shot out of hand. A boy of 12 carrying charcoal. Three men trussed up waiting for execution. Eight beheaded bodies. . . . Altogether at this time you see the Chinese character, its brutality, at its worst. . . .

Another side of the Chinese character was displayed in the well-printed circulars, measuring about 12 inches by 10 inches, which were distributed with extraordinary celerity:

NOTICE

To all Foreign Missionaries, Merchants and Other Residents in Peking, greeting:

The unexpected disturbance last night on the part of a section of my soldiers has filled me with much sorrow. It is one of my chief duties to see to it that order is preserved in the Capital and until last night I was uniformly successful. To you, strangers in a strange land, I wish in particular to convey my sincere regret for the untoward incident and the very natural anxiety that you felt. Every measure and precaution is now taken to prevent the recurrence of such a disturbance.

(Signed) YUAN SHIH-K'AI.
Provisional President of the Republic of China.
Peking, March 1, 1912.

Yuan's measures and precautions were curiously ineffective. While old women and girls were being executed for gathering scraps, his picked men were looting treasures with impunity. Three days later Morrison wrote to Tsai Ting-kan:

Four Englishmen and myself rode out this morning to my cottage . . . and then across to Fengtai. . . .

Fengtai is a pitiful sight. . . . The whole place has been looted from end to end. I saw the train leave this morning filled with loot for Liang Hsing Hsien accompanied by a few Chinese of the 3rd Division.

Further in the country we saw almost the entire 12th Regiment, the men who had sacked Paotingfu. They were not carting any loot with them, because the whole of the loot had been sent on by train. It was a horrible thing to think that these men had systematically pillaged the town they were sent to protect and they are now going to pillage Changhsintien and Liang Hsing Hsien. . . . It is a terrible misfortune for China that these men should all have escaped punishment. The fact is, China has far too many soldiers. The country needs only a small body of men, highly trained, well paid, with good *esprit de corps*, each man being guaranteed by his family or by his village. . . .

I deeply sympathize with you all in the present distress, but good will, I hope, come out of ill.

Historians today are satisfied that Yuan himself engineered the "mutiny" to convince the delegation that he could not move to Nanking. The official explanation at the time was that the men had mutinied because they had not been paid, and Morrison, who seemed incapable of comprehending the depths of Yuan's duplicity, accepted this, as he had accepted Yuan's explanation of his Judas role in the 1898 coup. Others, including Colonel Bruce, Everard Fraser, and David Fraser, were more sceptical. "Have you made up your mind whether Yuan was responsible or not for the outbreak?" Bruce wrote. "It looks very like it." Everard Fraser wrote:

The suspicion of Yuan's double dealing is still strong and most thinking people appear to believe that Yuan himself was at the bottom of the trouble at Peking. The delegates just back from Peking do not think he was, but believe it was instigated by men immediately surrounding Yuan. They appear to have been got at by Yuan—blandished, not bought. But Yuan appears to have bought many of the Shanghai papers, and *some* members of the Assembly here, which accounts in some degree for the readiness to contemplate the retention of the capital at Peking.

Morrison commented testily in a letter to David Fraser:

Could anything conceivably be more preposterous than the suggestion that Y.S.K. inspired the mutiny in Peking in order to prevent his going to Nanking? Everard Fraser could not seriously believe such an absurdity. That mutiny, next to his dismissal, is the most serious blow that Y.S.K. has received during his lifetime. I believe myself that he is becoming heartily sick of the whole affair and could gladly retire. He is in bad health, is a bad colour, lives under insanitary conditions in over heated rooms, takes no exercise and clothes himself as if he were wintering in the Antarctic. It also seems to me preposterous to think that the Delegates have been got at by Yuan—no man ever seriously believed that he could leave Peking at this time, and for him to have brought about the mutiny and shattered his reputation throughout the world seems to be as unreasonable as to employ a steel hammer to crush a gooseberry. Everard Fraser is always getting hold of these cock-and-bull yarns, but surely he does not believe them, for he is far and away the best man in the Consular Service. . . .

David Fraser, who was living in a railway car about seven miles from

Nanking and working for *The Times*, was in close touch with the revolutionaries. He wrote:

> There are two ideas here, one that reactionaries stirred up the soldiers to break out, the other that Yuan engineered the affair . . . and lost control of his own squib. But whether either of these reasons is correct, or whether it was merely a question of pay . . . it remains that Yuan was not in sufficient touch with *his own* men to know there was something doing, nor was he able to check them once they had started. Their pardon, too, is a symptom of weakness hard to overlook.

Morrison, despite his faith in Yuan, did find this hard to overlook, and made efforts to have the men punished. He wrote to Major Menzies, who was still attached to Yuan's establishment:

> The barracks near my house of . . . Yuan's most trusted regiment were stacked with loot. . . . The soldiers commandeered carts . . . collared trains, and went off to Paotingfu, not a single man being punished. . . . Yesterday, there was a house to house visitation by Yuan Shih-k'ai's men, demanding money by menaces. I myself turned two out of a friend's house and four out of another. . . . I understand the police simply put off their uniforms and joined with the soldiers. It was all preconcerted. The whole future of China depends upon how this situation is handled. If there is to be conciliation, and the men are to be bribed to keep quiet, then the country is finished. . . .
>
> I hope you will use your great influence to induce the authorities to punish these soldiers with death, and not to promise them a few taels if they will be so kind as not to repeat the disturbances. . . .

Yuan told William Maxwell that he was afraid to punish the soldiers, but that they would be dealt with "in due course". Tsai Ting-kan offered Morrison similar reassurances: "The men will not escape," he wrote. "The *time* has not yet come." It never came.

Yuan's faithful men retained their heads and their loot, and Yuan retained Peking as his capital. The bodies were removed from the streets, and it was a tranquil city that witnessed, on 10th March, the inauguration of Yuan Shih-k'ai as the second provisional President of the Chinese Republic. At 2 p.m. Morrison hurried to the hall near the Imperial Palaces where the ceremony was to take place. In the Palace the Manchus were "watching with satisfaction the glorious establishment and consummation of the perfect Government", a patriotic satisfaction augmented by the fact that the perfect Government had guaranteed their persons, their pensions, and their properties.

Morrison's scribbled notes give a synoptic picture of the ceremony:

Tang Shao-yi—all the delegates in frock coats.

1. Ushers announced procedure.

2. Yuan came in wobbling like a duck looking fat and unhealthy, in Marshall's uniform loose flesh of his neck hanging down over his collar, hat too large for him, nervous and uncomfortable.

3. Was handed document in large letters which he read nervously—the oath—handing it then to Tsai who stepped forward. Band could be heard playing new National Anthem.

4. Tsai then made a speech of welcome.

5. Yuan read a reply self-depreciatory.

6. Then people in batches passed before him and bowed. The first to come were the two lamas, the first of whom handed a white and the second a blue hata then came two mongols (princes it was said) who handed images wrapped in silk.

7. Admirable order no confusion.

8. No more kowtowing
Now shake hands.
No more queues.
No more Chinese official dress—Chinese dressed most simply.

To Braham, Morrison wrote:

None of the foreign legations were represented except the American. It was arranged that no member of the diplomatic body should be present, but disregarding this agreement, the American Legation sent E. T. Williams, the first Secretary, C. D. Tenney, Chinese Secretary, and Reeves, Military Attaché, the latter in full uniform. A few foreign guests were present, and a considerable number of correspondents, among whom the Japanese largely predominated. Yuan seemed very nervous. . . . The revolt of his troops has been a severe blow to him. Probably no blow could have struck him harder. . . . The old Provincial troops have stood loyal, and the Manchu troops, who number in the neighbourhood of Peking and Peking itself some 25,000 . . . have kept good discipline. The police have also returned to duty and the occasional marching of foreign troops . . . has had a good effect . . . this was done by the desire of the Chinese themselves.

[VII]

"There is probably more suffering in China at the present moment than there is in the whole of the rest of the world put together," Morrison wrote to David Fraser on 26th March. "Reports from the interior are simply awful and most disheartening. China has created a force of armed brigands which she can no longer control. . . . The only tranquil part of the Empire . . . appears to be Manchuria and Mongolia." Yuan Shih-k'ai's inauguration had not inaugurated a Golden Age. He had about one million men under arms—twice as many as the Manchus had before the revolution—and the problem of demobilizing huge forces which he was unable to pay, clothe, or even feed, bedevilled him. Many of the soldiers solved their immediate problem by following the example of the 3rd Division. There was widespread mutiny, plundering, and violence. "I know one large town which to my certain knowledge has been looted clean seven times," F. W. Tuckey, a railway engineer in Shanghai, wrote. (No one pointed out that the Chinese had received some impressive lessons in the art of looting from the foreign powers during the Boxer uprising.) Morrison expressed his disillusion and his doubt to David Fraser:

> I have been much disappointed at the way things have gone on, and cannot see a very bright prospect for the future. The country is not bankrupt, but it is a defaulting country, and it may default in the payment of loan after loan. The payments of the Boxer indemnity have been postponed for a year. I doubt very much if the Powers will consent to any further postponement. . . . I do hope that Sun Yat-sen will travel in the interior before he goes abroad, and see for himself the condition of his country. . . .

Sir John Jordan, too, was "much depressed". The outlook was black indeed. Everard Fraser had wired him from Shanghai that there were 15,000 soldiers there who had not been paid. In Changsha the soldiers as an inducement to disband were promised life pensions of thirty dollars a year. China was defaulting all round. Yuan Shih-k'ai fully realized the danger of the situation. Tang Shao-yi did not; he was feather-brained and foolishly optimistic.

David Fraser was even more pessimistic. "The situation is pretty rotten," he wrote on 12th April:

> There are three major factors on the Yangtze, Li Yuan-hung, Huang Hsing and Ch'en Ch'i-mei, all independent of each other. Further south there is Canton, Swatow, and other places which completely ignore the Yangtze people. On the Yangtze itself are several minor commanders who fight and loot and rule independently of their brethren. . . . I guess this revolution is the biggest fluke on record. How it is all going to end beats me. But it is sure enough there is going to be a period of dreadful anarchy. . . .

Sir John Jordan was heartened by some flattering words spoken about him in the House of Lords, and Morrison noted bitterly that no word of commendation had come from *The Times* about his own work:

> No praise could be spared for me yet how I have kept poor old Sir John straight throughout this crisis. . . . But for me I believe that long before this he would have had a nervous breakdown. . . . Yuan had praised most highly the assistance Sir John had given him. "If I am president, it is largely due to your help," he said. (Yuan said the same to me substituting me for Sir John however.)

But soon after came emollient words from Buckle: ("Your work in this revolution continues to be of the most distinguished character") and news of changes in Printing House Square. Chirol had been knighted and was retiring. He was to be entertained at dinner to celebrate both events. "It would be a mockery to ask you to join the festivity," Buckle wrote, "but perhaps you would desire to send a message of appreciation —all the more as I know there has been at time friction between you." Morrison rose to the occasion with magnanimous hypocrisy. Congratulating the Jesuit-Jew on his knighthood, he added an unsolicited testimonial and an unconvincing apologia:

> You have, I think, the greatest brain of any man I have ever known, and if you will not mind my saying so, the kindest heart and the greatest capacity for friendship. There is nothing I regret more in my past career than that any cloud should ever have come over our friendship. It would be a mockery for me to pretend there was no cloud, but it was my fault, and it has long since passed away, and I hope you will forgive me and forget all about it. . . . I shall always be proud to remember that I was for so many years so closely associated with so great a master.

Chirol replied that Morrison's letter had given him genuine pleasure, "for the soreness I felt was, I confess, very keen. . . . So by all means let us be friends again as in the past". Morrison sent a letter to Buckle which was read out at the farewell dinner at the Savoy, and Chirol acknowledged it gratefully:

> . . . there was one point which touched me very much . . . namely, when you spoke of my capacity for friendship. . . .
>
> I have formed no plans as yet for the future. . . . But I don't know whether I shall be able to resist the temptation of running out perhaps in the Autumn . . . to see what a Chinese republic looks like at close quarters—if it endures so long, for I confess I am profoundly sceptical and I am very much afraid that the fall of the Manchus may only be the prologue to a drama almost as complicated and protracted as those which one has sampled on the Chinese stage.

"You have certainly distanced everybody throughout the whole of the long-drawn out crisis," Braham wrote to Morrison. "We put our trust in you and you did not fail us." But, like Chirol, he was not confident about China's future, and he voiced his doubts in a thoughtful editorial:

> Some of those who know China best cannot but doubt whether a form of Government so utterly alien to Oriental conceptions and to Oriental traditions as a Republic, can be suddenly substituted for a monarchy in a nation of four hundred millions of men, whom Kings with semi-divine attributes have ruled since the first dim twilight of history.

Another sceptic was Rockhill, who had been transferred to Constantinople: "You say most Americans in China are in favour of the monarchical principle," he wrote:

> I thoroughly concur in this opinion for I cannot see how China can stand without it, it is the keystone to the whole fabric ethically and politically—as well as from the point of view of the national cult. I cannot believe that a republican form of government will endure. It will be a provisional one leading to the founding of a new dynasty. Will it be Y.S.K. who will found it or will he simply be a king-maker? ...

Rockhill was thinking of leaving the diplomatic service, and wondered if Yuan Shih-k'ai would like him as adviser to the Chinese Legation in Washington. He would resign straightaway if he could see his way clear to an income of a thousand or fifteen hundred pounds a year. Soon after, Morrison had an opportunity of mentioning Rockhill to Dr Charles Eliot, of Harvard, the begetter of the famous Five Foot Bookshelf of Culture, who had been asked by the Chinese Government to recommend a prominent American as an adviser. Morrison lunched with Dr Eliot at the American Embassy ("fine-looking man, upright 6ft or more, 78 but looks much younger, clean cut face disfigured on right side by strawberry mark which extends from above the right eyebrow to the upper lip which in that side hangs down. Left side unusually handsome") and urged the claims of Rockhill ("linguist traveller knowing Chinese and Tibetan"). He reflected on the fickleness of fame when he found the learned professor was "wholly ignorant" of who Rockhill was. He also noted Dr Eliot's surprising lack of tact, "everywhere condemned", when the doctor gave a Unitarian address to an audience of Evangelical missionaries, embarrassing them by reference to "God the Father, Man the Brother, Christ the Teacher".

[VIII]

In the letter that Buckle read aloud at Chirol's farewell dinner Morrison had written that he owed much to Chirol: "for did he not write my obituary, which happily was published prematurely, and will not the eulogistic references he therein made to my character and capacity render it exceedingly difficult for *The Times* should they ever wish to disembarrass themselves of my services?"

But while he was writing this facetiously Morrison was thinking seriously of leaving *The Times* and returning to Australia. The thought had been in his mind for some time. He was tired of China, of his job—and of himself. He was fifty, in poor health—synovitis had been added to his complex of complaints—and, though he did not know it, was falling in love. Jennie Robin had broken off her engagement with Phillips, and Morrison was becoming more and more aware of her as a woman as well as a secretary.

He anatomized his discontent in letters to many of his friends; perhaps for the satisfaction of overhearing himself. To Lionel Pratt, a fellow-Australian who was editing the *Far Eastern Review* in Hong Kong, he wrote:

> I am tired of the incessant strain, the late hours, the irregular work, the difficulty of sifting truth from falsehood, the difficulty of understanding Chinese springs of action. I want to settle down quietly in a country village in Australia and rear . . . poultry and try and win prizes at the local horticultural show in competition with the village policeman. My idea is to buy a small place down in Gippsland, in the mountains overlooking the Southern Ocean, not too far from a rail-head, where I can get duck-shooting and reel-fishing and exercise in clearing off my selection. I once went down to Gippsland, and spent some delightful days there burning off the brush heaps. . . .

Recalling that Morrison had once talked of entering Federal politics, Pratt replied that it would be "ten thousand pities" if he wasted his unique knowledge of the Far East in a colonial legislature:

> The House of Commons is the place for you and the Unionist party would jump at the opportunity of giving you a seat. In Australia—though they have a hazy sort of idea that peril may threaten them from the Far East—they do not recognize the vital importance of the subject, and the result is that the Commonwealth Parliament expends all its energy in the little things that don't matter. . . . I feel sure that you, after so many years' intimate association with men and events of world importance, would become disgusted with the pettiness which characterizes Australian politics. . . . The type of man they want down there is the narrow minded politician whose mental horizon is bounded by Woolloomooloo or Fitzroy. . . .

As a "frantic Royalist", he added a gloomy assessment of the situation in China:

> I am hoping to see China recover from her Republican delirium and sweep all these mushroom "patriots" back into oblivion. The feeling among the Chinese here is decidedly pessimistic. What little popularity the Republic had appears to be waning and the utter incapacity of the scum that came to the top during the turmoil in regard to constructive work, is becoming more evident daily.

Morrison was surprised at Pratt's suggestion that he would be offered a Unionist seat in the House of Commons. "Certainly, I have concealed my politics. . . . I who am for Labour, Minimum Wage, Universal Suffrage, Home Rule for Everybody, Disestablishment of Everything, exclusion of aliens and a few other things which are not on the Unionist programme . . ." he wrote back. What were Morrison's politics? His admiration for Rudyard Kipling was undiminished. He shared Curzon's conviction of England's imperial destiny. One of his close friends in London was the fire-breathing Tory, Leo Maxe. But he wrote to Hutton at about the same time as he wrote to Pratt: "My sympathies were entirely with the strikers during the coal strike. I find that the older I get, the more sympathy I feel with the labouring classes":

> I would have left *The Times* two years ago, had I been able to leave it then with prestige, but owing to a difference of opinion between myself and the editorial staff, had I then left it might have been said that my resignation had been called for. . . . It takes a good deal to make me tired, but I have got weary of incessantly discussing loan questions, questions of Shanghai municipal extension, local questions of all kinds in which I have only an academic interest. I am only discussing things instead of doing things, and I intend . . . to do something before I am too old. . . . My present ambition is to get down to Australia as quickly as I can.

"I am simply getting mouldy," he wrote to C. W. Campbell. "Peking was at one time the centre of the world's interest. At present it is only a humdrum Far Eastern capital":

> When I returned to China it was my intention to leave Peking on 1 April and travel overland through Tibet to India, and so home. That scheme is no longer possible. It has always been my ambition to return to Australia sooner or later. . . .

The realization that he was in love came suddenly. One day he was complaining that Jennie was dancing all night and having her head turned by the attention shown her: "I was a fool to bring out one so young and fragile." Two weeks later he was writing: "My God how I do love her! I love her better than anything on earth":

> It is impossible for me to continue longer in Peking. I am discontented and unhappy. I am in love. If I stay here I will fret my heart out . . . all enthusiasm in my work has evaporated. I am—let the truth out—somewhat disgusted with my profession when I see the ranks filled by . . . reporters who may write well and will write to order but have no standing and no personality.

Among these he listed A. E. Wearne, the Reuter's representative, H. G. Woodhead, editor of the *Peking and Tientsin Times*, and J. K. Ohl, correspondent of the *New York Herald*.

[IX]

On a beautiful April day, as they were walking together along the Wall, Morrison told Jennie that he loved her, and Jennie told Morrison that she had consulted a fortune-teller in London who showed uncanny gifts. He had said that she would go abroad to a distant part of the world, that she would marry a famous man, be a widow, and would marry a second time, and would die at about forty-five:

> And her coming to me was most strange. Her mother was holding before the fire a sheet of the *Daily Telegraph* upon which was my advertisement. This caught here eye whereupon she showed it to her daughter and advised her to communicate with the writer XYZ. She did and I was struck by her and engaged her and there we are—she entwined round my heart and I'm going to sacrifice everything to have her come with me to Australia.

But he was consumed by doubts, and filled pages of his diary with self-searchings:

> My trouble is one of the heart am worried and perturbed, but hope 1. Because of kindness of heart. 2. Because of belief in prophecy that she was to marry a famous man I being the only one to which that term is applicable in sight. 3. Because of respect. But why the devil should any of these factors come into play? . . . Great capacity for affection. My unhappiness. Brooding and "When the inevitable comes?"—All this is somewhat incoherent but the bald fact remains that I am enmeshed as I have not been since 1882 and that my mode of life is now to change.
>
> Heartily sick and tired of my work unsettled because no hope of any advancement. I have today come to the determination:
> 1. To retire from *The Times*.
> 2. To sell my library.
> 3. To leave China and return to Australia.

He reviewed the prospects of selling his library. E. T. Williams wanted the United States to buy it. Willard Straight, who was planning the establishment of an Asiatic Association in America, asked for an option. The Japanese and Chinese were both interested. Morrison fixed the price at £40,000.

> Should it be purchased by the Chinese, I will present the Government with my freehold property in Peking, that is the fire-proof library building. . . . My own residence can be used upstairs as quarters for a Foreign Librarian until the library catalogue is completed and printed. Downstairs the rooms can be converted into a reading room. . . . I have determined to ask that the Library shall continue to be called after me.

"Why has this cruel fate been mine to fall in love, real sincere love for the second time in my life? I wonder does she care for me? I long to take her in my arms and tell her I love her," he wrote. Haunted by the "awful disparity" in their ages—fifty and twenty-three—he invoked, from some unrevealed source, a formula for marital harmony. The wife's age should be half the husband's age plus seven ("$(50 \div 2) + 7 = 32$"). By this equation Jennie was nine years too young.

In the midst of these curious speculations he received a letter from Hutton that offered, half-seriously, half-jocularly, singularly unwelcome advice: "Get married. Get married," Hutton wrote. "You are not fitted for single life. . . . But of all things don't marry a very young woman. I repeat. Not a young woman. Her tastes you would find too juvenile." Morrison should look around in Australia for a well-preserved woman between thirty and forty, "with an income of not less than £600 or £700 a year". Alternatively, Hutton offered an English candidate:

> I enclose her picture. I told her about you. She loves you already. She is the eldest daughter of our Vicar. Very well-educated. She was on the "batter" for a bit of a time—in Portsmouth. But you won't mind that I'm sure. . . . She is just the woman to suit you. Her father —the Vicar—is a very liberal-minded man—he says, "Tell Ernest he can have her for a week on trial!!"

Hutton, an omnivorous reader, supplemented this marriage counsel with a comment on contemporary fiction and faith: "Nearly all the successful books owe their prestige to the portrayals of fornication. . . . A great change has come over the world." At the same time the "ecclesiastical influence" was ebbing fast: "Men of all classes ridicule the superstitious dogmas of the church. I doubt if the Virgin Mary will live another ten years."

Morrison replied solemnly:

> As I understand it, I am to marry a woman of 38, with ossification of the joints, especially of the sacro-coccygeal joint, well domesticated, faddish, with rigid views about religion, spectacles, false uppers, but with six or seven hundred a year, the amount of the income to be in inverse proportion to the attractions of the subject. . . .

Jennie told Morrison that he would have to write to her father asking for her hand, mentioning all his physical defects and giving an assurance there was no madness in his family. Morrison wrote Mr Robin a "frank pleasant letter", saying that he was sending Jennie home by express so that she could consult both her parents before deciding to marry him:

> I spoke of the discrepancy in our ages. I younger than my years, she older than her years, thus making the disproportion less. . . . She has been with me now long enough to observe my good points which were few and bad points which were many. I assured her father that she was under no obligation to me, but in fact the obligation was all the other way and that the journey home might be regarded as a bonus for the admirable work she had done for me since I had the happiness of securing her assistance.

Rockhill was grateful for Morrison's suggestion that he might serve China as foreign adviser, but he thought the time had not yet come. He explained his doubts at length:

. . . It is unnecessary to say that, under proper conditions, I should be delighted to lend my poor assistance to the Government. . . . *But* many considerations require than any man of average sense and experience of public affairs—especially in China—should pause before committing himself to the desirability or even possibility of attempting to discharge such duties. Better than anyone you know the position of the present government of China; hardly yet established, not recognized by any of the Treaty Powers, up to its neck in financial troubles, in which the President and his Cabinet are ruled by an Advisory Council which seems to be the real governing body, with no men of real ability but lots of spectacled frock-coated young dreamers fresh from the United States, Japan or Great Britain, full of utopian dreams of individual and immediate reforms, etc., etc. What would be the role of a foreign adviser, subject to . . . strenuous opposition to his necessarily moderate and conciliatory suggestions? Draw his salary and compile a Chinese-English Dictionary, as did Walter Hillier? Such a role would not satisfy any man who has the reputation of a life time at stake. . . . until a permanent government is established and recognized, it seems useless to discuss the matter. . . .

Confucius said "the cautious seldom err" and if ever there was a case in which caution was necessary it seems to me to be this one. . . .

This was sound counsel. But within a week or so of receiving it, Morrison, despite Rockhill and Confucius, was himself considering an invitation to become foreign adviser to the Chinese Government. The offer was made in a letter from Tsai Ting-kan, which Morrison read with "great astonishment":

Immediately I went down to Sir John. I assured him that which required no assurance, that I had made no effort of my own to obtain or to encourage this offer. The Chinese knew that I was contemplating leaving China, and returning to Australia and they made me this offer hoping to retain my services in China. Sir John said he knew this well. I said that Yuan considered that I had been of constant help to him, that I was one of the mainstays of the Republic, that he wished me to remain with him and be his adviser as long as he was President.

[X]

In a letter to Buckle dated 17th May, Morrison modestly mentioned his services to *The Times*, and asked what recognition he could expect for these if he retired:

I joined *The Times* before November 1st, 1895. In the intervening years, I have been in every part of Eastern Asia, from Bangkok in the South to Blagovestchensk in the North, and from Japan and Korea in the East, across China to the ultimate limits of the Chinese dominions. During the earlier years of my connection with *The*

Times my salary was only £500 a year, my expenses being paid when I was away from Peking. Then for two years I was paid at the rate of £1000 per annum and expenses. Subsequently I compounded my expenses for a fixed amount of £200 per annum, and since the beginning of 1900 I have received £1200 per annum, from which I have paid, except on rare occasions such as my visit to the Portsmouth Conference, all my travelling and other expenses out of my own pocket. I find that the total expense *The Times* has incurred on account of my salary and expenses throughout the period from 1st November, 1895, to, say, the 1st May 1912, has been in round numbers £19,000. For a considerable period of this time my messages were sold to other papers, and the fees thus received reduced my cost to *The Times*. I do not think that anyone could ever suggest that I have been an expensive correspondent. Considering how well known I am, I think I can claim to have been an exceptionally inexpensive one. The opinion apparently is universally held that I am very much more highly paid than is the case. There was a time when I was offered £2000 per annum to join one of the other London papers, and twice I have been asked by Lord Northcliffe to join his staff. This, of course, was before he became head of *The Times*. On one of these occasions he said that he could give me a salary such as *The Times* could never dream of giving me.

I have never asked for an increase of salary. When Lord Northcliffe asked me in London whether I would care for an increase, I said that I thought my post was sufficiently well paid. Since this trouble began in October, the cost of living in Peking has risen to such a degree that I find it very difficult to live within my income. As a matter of fact, I cannot live in the position such as I have obtained on a salary of £1200 a year, and pay my own expenses. Recently the Manager has been good enough to make a certain allowance to me on account of the loss I am sustaining owing to the rise in exchange. Before the Revolution the sovereign was worth $11.15. Since the Revolution it is worth only $9.55

Now I have long thought that *The Times* is obtaining no special advantage from retaining me in Peking. Undeniably I am well known, and my position here as Correspondent is a good one—many would say a unique one. Many distinguished people who visit Peking, come to see me. . . . My relations both with our Legation and the foreign Legations and with the Chinese are, I think, more intimate than those of any other correspondent who has ever been in Peking. But I am thoroughly tired of being here. I am now fifty years of age, and I am not getting any further forward. I wish to give up this kind of work, which involves irregular hours, requires incessant attention, and for which I can now get very little credit. It is impossible for the paper to permit me to telegraph day by day, and it is more difficult for me to have to select my telegrams when they are sent only at intervals.

What I would like to ascertain from you is this: Can I, on leaving *The Times*, expect to receive a retiring allowance, and, if so, what amount? What steps should I take in order to secure this? These years of service that I have rendered to the paper have obviously absorbed much of my strength. I have more than once been seriously ill. I was wounded and invalided for some time. In Siam I suffered much from malarial fever which clung to me for nearly two years. All this has reduced my powers of earning.

It is my wish to leave China and return to Australia, and there, if opportunity should be given to me, to enter political life, for which in some degree my experiences in the Far East has fitted me. During the time I have been with you, I have been able to save very little money. At present, when all my debts are paid, I have a cash balance of less than £250. I have a collection of books on China. It is not fair that I should have to sell my library but I have no alternative. I have an inferior Chinese house in the city, which will soon have to be re-built, and I have a cottage in the country. These then are my assets upon which alone I have to retire.

What I would suggest is that I should arrange with you to leave *The Times* and be given some recognition of my work during all these years in the form of a sum of money which would enable me to leave China with content and to engage in a new sphere of activity. You would find an economy in this arrangement, because the correspondent in my stead would not require the income which is necessary for the maintenance of a position such as that which I have acquired in Peking—a position which I think I can claim, has added to the prestige of the paper. The Chinese are in the habit of believing that I am exceedingly well paid, and I have never disillusioned them in this regard.

I wish you would write to me frankly and tell me what you would suggest, or what is possible.

"What is to happen to me?" Morrison asked himself on 29th June. oney is my great lack." He tabulated his assets:

1. My library which is insured for £15,000 and for which I am asking £40,000!
2. My freehold city house which as it stands has cost me £2250.
3. My country cottage which all told has cost me £1250.
4. My household furniture and effects, curios and pictures worth in all perhaps £1000.

I have no reason to be discouraged! Will *The Times* give me anything?

His question was soon answered. Buckle's reply, a handwritten letter wo and a half foolscap pages, made it clear that the gratitude of *The* 𝑒s for Morrison's services was boundless, but not negotiable. He had ed the paper too old and was leaving it too young:

How the authorities of *The Times* have appreciated the remarkable work which you have done for it in the last fifteen years has been shown you, in letters and by word of mouth, again and again, by the late Mr Walter and Lord Northcliffe on behalf of the Proprietors, and by Moberly Bell and me for the Manager and Editor. In parting from you we shall be losing one of the greatest ornaments of *The Times*—a correspondent whose telegrams and letters, have in various periods of crisis in the Far East, been for the time the most distinctive and valued feature of the Paper; and one whose character and personality have maintained and enhanced its reputation on the other side of the world. I can only thank you very sincerely, and wish you all success in your new sphere of activity, which will be, I presume, politics in Australia. Sad as it is to lose you, I understand your wish to change your work while you may still look forward to many years of health and strength. You ask me a very delicate question when you request my private opinion as to whether on retirement you could look to receive from *The Times* any monetary payment. As you know, I have never specially concerned myself with the business side of the Paper, in which the initiative naturally rests with the Manager. But I will mention a few considerations which, it seems to me, must govern the matter.

Those who enter the service of the Paper young, and make it the work of their life, and those who, without entering its service young, yet serve it continuously till incapacitated by age or serious illness, have on retirement a special claim for consideration which is not shared by those who enter its service in middle life, and then after a certain number of years' service quit it of their own accord, while still in middle-life, to undertake work of another kind. The first two classes have usually, when their circumstances required it, received pensions from the Paper, but I don't know of any case in which a pension has been granted to a member of the third class, nor would it reasonable to expect it.

But, of course, where the service has been both of some duration, and of an exceptionally brilliant character, as yours has been, those responsible for the Paper might well desire to express, by the gift of a substantial sum at the close, their gratitude and appreciation—on one condition, that the financial position of the Paper was such as to afford it. Unfortunately, as you know, *The Times*, since the formation of the company, has never been able to pay a dividend on its ordinary shares, but only on its First Preference. In these circumstances it must rest entirely with the Proprietors, who are receiving no return on a large part of their capital, whether they will sanction extra expenditure of the kind suggested. At present they are, not unnaturally, urging upon us a policy of strict economy in every direction.

I am very sorry that you should feel anxious about money matters, though I note that you allow that the post of Peking Correspondent has been adequately paid, and that you declined Lord Northcliffe's suggestion that the salary should be increased. It is natural that you should be reluctant to sell your unique library; but, on the other hand, books have been the shape your savings have taken, and if you abandon Far Eastern Correspondence, you will have no special use for a valuable collection of Chinese works. You would have many excellent precedents for selling; for example, the late Lord Spencer and the Althorp library. But of course I realize what a wrench it would be for you. . . .

Morrison's reply to this remarkable document was admirably restrained, but he must have taken some satisfaction in letting Buckle know that the Chinese Government valued his services nearly four times as highly as *The Times* did:

Dear Mr Buckle,
I am indeed grateful to you for your kind and considerate letter of 20 June.

The considerations you have placed before me so delicately are entirely reasonable and convincing and in resigning my post I will ask for nothing further than my salary to the date of leaving and my passage fare home.

Before this letter reaches you it is possible that you will receive a cable from me regarding an offer made to me by the President Yuan Shih-k'ai. . . . Certain terms have been proposed to me. These I have communicated to my Minister and he has cabled them to the Foreign Office. . . . The terms proposed to me are an engagement of not less than three years beginning from the date that I leave *The Times*, my expenses from London to Peking when I take my engagement, my travelling expenses when in Chinese service, £250 a year house allowance and a salary of £3500. It is also proposed to allow me a secretary and a translator at Government expense.

I am told that it was the unanimous wish of both the Southern and Northern parties that I should be the first foreigner to be approached with a view to the securing of his services. . . .

To F. A. Mackenzie, a few months later, he wrote with more feeling: "*The Times* have treated me with characteristic generosity, having paid me £73 for my passage back from Peking to London after 17 years of service! . . . Their tendency now is . . . to pay their correspondents in an even more niggardly manner than they have done in the past."

Morrison summed up his seventeen years as a correspondent in a note intended for his "Reminiscences":

No doubt in my work in the Far East I made many mistakes and my judgement was often faulty but I can look back on the past and declare that I never sent a line to *The Times* that I did not believe to be the truth as I understood it at the time. Enemies of course I made—a correspondent if he is to be of any value to his paper must make enemies. . . . At no time throughout my services was I on friendly terms with all the Legations in Peking at the same time. . . .

[XI]

"Herewith the document," Tsai Ting-kan wrote on 2nd August, confirming Morrison's appointment. "It is neither an Agreement, nor yet a Contract nor yet a Compact. It is a free and spontaneous Invitation from the Government and People of the Chinese Republic to you who has kindly signified his consent and approval by the attachment of his signature. It is the most honourable invitation ever extended by China to any foreign gentleman and expressed in the most courteous language possible. . . ." When Morrison expressed his gratitude, Tsai wrote: "It is I and the Chinese Nation who should be *grateful* to *you*, I have assisted you because you were assisting us; therefore I am assisting myself."

[XII]

While he was waiting for Mr Robin's reply, Morrison fled from the unbearable heat of Peking in July to the sea at Peitaiho. Here he wrote a long letter to Hutton, "the wisest of my friends, the most far-seeing, the most philosophical":

> My life for a long time has been very lonely and I have felt the crying need of affection and sympathy. I want happiness. Of honours I have received a small share if it is an honour to be well-known and to be described as "famous". But I have little happiness. I am going to get married. . . .

He catalogued Jennie's qualities in detail: "a refined pure-minded English girl, highly educated . . . secretive and trustworthy . . . sings prettily and plays nicely . . . one of the best mimics I have ever known":

> Insensibly I have become attached to her and I have no shadow of doubt about her truly loving me. . . . Every Legation in Peking welcomes her. She had advantageous offers of marriage. . . . The Chinese talk of giving me employment and of never allowing me to leave China. The British Minister promises me but I need hardly say that I count nothing upon this that he will make every effort to obtain for me a knighthood. It is the least he can do, he says, for all I have done for him. But there can be no certainty about this. . . . It is also not certain that I would accept knighthood even if it were offered me. . . .

Mr Robin, from Lismore Road, South Croydon, proclaimed his parental approval ("as she expressed such love for you, we could not well oppose it") suggesting only that proper provision be made for Jennie "and a probable young family".

Morrison found a great heap of correspondence to deal with, without Jennie's expert assistance, when he returned to Peking. There was a letter from Sir Hiram Maxim, who described himself as "the greatest expert on fire-arms in the world" and expressed a strong desire to finish up his career "by serving China and the Chinese":

I took the personal Grand Prix in artillery at the last Paris Exposition.
    I am in a position to furnish China with the rifles she may require at extremely low prices. I could go to China myself and instruct the officials.
    I know the Rothchilds very well, and also many other great Capitalists and . . . could place a loan on very favourable terms. . . .

But the most interesting letters were about Sun Yat-sen. H. T. Foord, a railway engineer, wrote from Shanghai:

I made the acquaintance of Sun Yat-sen as I heard that he had a scheme for building extensive railways but the impression that I had formed of him from his short public life was strengthened at the interview as I found that he had not two ideas in his head. He is certainly not a dangerous man but only the figurehead of his party which by its Cantonese power of combination may cause trouble.

W. H. Donald, too, had discussed railways with Dr Sun, and was even less impressed with the doctor's ability:

He is a fool. . . . he told me that he had decided to devote himself entirely to railway development. He said he could not divulge his scheme for a couple of months, but I talked at him so much that eventually he . . . brought forth a large map. The map was about six feet square, and when Sun had spread it out upon the floor I saw evidence of a most convincing nature that Sun is not only as mad as a hatter, but that he is madder. He is absolutely unpractical, without commonsense and devoid of the most elementary ideas of the subject he professes to be now fathering. The map took in Tibet and Mongolia and the far western extremities of China. From time to time Sun had taken his brush and stick of ink and filled in every province and dependency with as many lines as he could cram there. He has double lines to indicate trunk railways sweeping round the coast from Shanghai to Canton, leading away across the precipitous mountains to Lhassa, and striking out due west to the western frontier, curling away into Sinkiang and out to Mongolia! He has another trunk line through from Shanghai to Szechwan and on to Lhassa. He has another off into Mongolia along the skirt of the Gobi desert. He has others running north and south, west and north-east. A myriad of smaller lines fills the provinces, and the map, as Sun has ornamented it, was nothing but a grotesque Chinese puzzle. Sun sat down on the floor to explain things to me, and as he sat there I thought that never could such a scene be drawn to depict the ineptitude of this, the first

President of the Chinese Republic. He is mad! And why, not because he drew the map, for with money and an abundance of time, every line he drew, and more, could be built, but Sun has the audacity to think that because He drew the thing the foreign capitalists would give him sufficient money to build the whole lot in from FIVE to TEN YEARS! . . . "Do you think the foreign capitalists will give the money?" he anxiously asked. "On what terms," I replied. "Oh", he answered, "if we give them the right to the lines for forty years, they to hand them back to China free of all cost and in good running condition at the end of that period!" I told him he had not the slightest hope of getting a cent of foreign money for even the most practical and promising line in the largest populated of the provinces unless there was a stable Government. And, amazing of amazing things, which only a man in the position of Sun could say to demonstrate his wisdom, his capacity and his acumen, he replied, "What matter if the Government is stable or not so long as the PROVINCES agree!!!" Doctor, the whole damned thing is impossible. . . . There was never a more grotesque position in any of Gilbert and Sullivan's comic-operas. . . . I would have given $100 to have had a picture of Sun sitting on the floor alongside of this map believing that in TEN years he could see the whole of China so covered. The little line from Laokay to Yunnan-sen cost something like £8,000,000. What in the name of goodness would a line from Yunnan to Lhassa cost? and what on earth would be the use of it unless to run summer excursions to the lid of the world, or be available when the D. Lama wants to escape?

"You must pardon the state of exasperation I am in," Donald concluded, "for my blood boils when I think of the fanatic who thinks he can preach anti-foreignism, socialism, and a dozen other isms in this benighted country and then think all the financiers of the world will pull open their purse-strings . . . because he, Sun Yat-sen, lifts his hand."

Now that Sun Yat-sen has had the unique distinction of a double canonization—by the Nationalists of Taipeh and the Communists of Peking—it is instructive to recall not only Donald's estimate of him but Li Yuan-hung's, made in July 1913:

The world has a false idea about Sun Yat-sen. He had nothing to do with the actual work of overthrowing the monarchy. The Revolution was finished when he reached China. I hardly had heard of him, except in a vague and general way, and did not know his political views, except that I had heard of his agitation. So far as I had thought about him at all, I had regarded him as a visionary. He arrived at Shanghai at a moment when the Southern, or Republican Party, had decided that some kind of a government should nominally be formed, with the capital at Nanking. This was done for moral effect in China and abroad. None of the real leaders of the Revolution, for various reasons, desired to take the position of Provisional President, which we felt would be of short duration. Sun Yat-sen, from being out of China for so long, was not associated with any faction here; his name was known abroad, and he seemed to suit the occasion. If he ever provided any tangible aid to the real Revolution, I did not know of it. His repute is largely founded on fiction. . . .

In Shanghai, Donald was exasperated by Dr Sun. In London, Alfred Hippisley was exasperated by the whole revolutionary movement. While "fully recognizing the utter corruption of the Manchu government", he could not believe a republic was suited to China:

> nor do I see the necessity for so violent a change. The edict of the 27 August 1908, when fixing the year 1917 for the granting of a Constitution, had issued a complete scheme of the reforms to be introduced in each intervening year to the end that by 1917 the political machine would be in full working order, and at least half the people sufficiently educated to understand both their duties and responsibilities. The Reform party had thus secured all they could have peacefully secured, the establishment of a Constitutional monarchy by orderly progressive stages. Instead, however . . . they have plunged the empire into anarchy and chaos by sweeping away the Throne, which alone exercised an authority generally respected . . . after destroying the existing government, they have practically no men with trained experience to take the places of the officials they have displaced. I confess I feel very pessimistic as to the future.

Morrison sprang to the defence of the Republic. He did not think it was a fair description of the country to speak of it as being "plunged into anarchy and chaos"; though he admitted that in removing the late Government "which stood for all that was unworthy and corrupt" officials had to be removed whom it was difficult to replace, he was still hopeful for the future. Hippisley was not convinced, and quoted an article in the *North China Daily News*, published on the date of Morrison's letter:

> From one quarter came . . . reports of agitation against financial reform; from another, of the danger of unemployed and underpaid soldiers; from a third, of actual mutiny and looting; from a fourth, of the multiplication of officials and of their jealousies and corruption, from a fifth, of the refusal of the people to pay taxes . . . in the face of such a showing it would be a sheer evasion of facts to pretend that the condition of China generally was aught but anarchical.

[XIII]

Before he left Peking, Morrison had a long talk with Yuan Shih-k'ai, who feared aggression by Russia and Japan while there was so much uncertainty in China. Morrison reassured him. They discussed banking problems, and the President told Morrison he was fond of gardening:

I spoke of the Russian difficulty, of getting labour in Siberia and of their fear of Chinese immigration being greater than Chinese fear of Russian aggression. Russia had an immense area unprotected. . . . I counselled placing smart young officers and men along the frontiers changing them frequently. . . . Literally Yuan *groaned* when I told him of the antiquated soldiers at Ulugchat.

Morrison combined medical with military advice: "You must get the President massaged," he told Tsai Ting-kan:

Half an hour daily of skilled massage would make an enormous difference to his bodily health . . . it would make him years younger. . . . But the massage must be done with skill. . . . While lying in bed before he gets up, he can have his body massaged from his toes up to the crown of his head and half an hour's treatment like this would be equal to two hours' exercise. I am a doctor, and I would strongly advise you to have this done.

I enclose a card of the Japanese masseur. He charges one dollar an hour and the treatment I should say in invaluable. You have no idea what a difference it makes to the circulation and to the general feeling of elation.

On the day of his departure Morrison received with the President's compliments and "heartiest congratulations" four rolls of silk for the future Mrs Morrison.

[XIV]

Consciously or unconsciously, Morrison continued to evade the facts, and almost his first act after he arrived in London on 19th Auugst— even before he ordered his wedding-suit—was to write a long letter over his own name in *The Times*, reassuring its readers about the stability of the new China. There was much scepticism in England about the future of the Republic; newspaper posters day after day proclaimed the imminence of civil war and collapse.

Morrison ridiculed the "gloomy" and "irresponsible" pessimists who foresaw "foreign intervention, universal anarchy, China split up into warring kingdoms, chaos, bankruptcy . . . the ruin of foreign bondholders . . . and the inevitable disruption of China". Life and property were equally safe in the Republic, he declared, confidently. McLeavy Brown wrote, "Your letter has made a considerable flutter in the journalistic world today and all the evening newspapers seem to comment on it." "My letter . . . has had an extraordinary effect in England," Morrison wrote to Tsai Ting-kan, who, by some unexplained legerdemain, had now become a colonel: "There has not been a single paragraph that I have seen adverse to China published since . . . England is ruled by public opinion as expressed through the newspapers. It is obvious then, that our first concern should be to have an erroneous impression removed from those papers and that has been the work that I have set myself to do."

He continued to operate successfully in that twilight world of adroit persuasion known today as "public relations". F. A. Mackenzie interviewed him for the *Daily Mail*, and began his column-length report:

There is a widespread impression in England that things are in a bad way in the young Chinese Republic. We have heard so much of internal strife . . . that the man in the street can almost see, in his mind's eye . . . the Republic at an end, and the most wonderful political and social experiment of our generation brought to ruin. A talk with Dr Morrison . . . is a good cure for such pessimism. Dr Morrison has a robust faith in the future of the commonwealth and a fund of indignation for the men who have been systematically spreading evil reports against it. . . . He left China steadily settling down, with the authority of the Central Government growing, with trade everywhere reviving, and with the unwieldy armies of the revolution being gradually disbanded and absorbed in the civil population.

Lovat Fraser invited Morrison to answer a set of questions in the *Pall Mall Gazette*, which, under J. L. Garvin's editorship, was consistently hostile to the new Chinese regime. "It is the paper of the moment," Fraser said. "Its circulation has *trebled* in the last six months." When Morrison returned the corrected proofs of the interview he admitted frankly that his primary loyalty was to Britain, not to China. But his attitude was curiously ambivalent. If he would not criticize Britain to the Chinese, he was as reluctant to criticize China to the British. "*To you I can speak my mind*," he wrote to Lovat Fraser:

But to the Chinese I am always (and I always will so continue . . .) championing the British action—always endeavouring to make them realize that we British are their best friends, that we are a phenomenon among the nations, acting with scrupulous fairness to our engagements among the nations, that where they, the Chinese, come into conflict with the British, it is they, the Chinese, are to blame. . . .

I will never do anything to depreciate my own Government in the sight of the Chinese—quite the contrary. Thus in all my communications I lay stress upon the friendly attitude of the official people and the sympathy felt in the Foreign Office for China and the Chinese and the desire of our Government to see China strong and united and to assist in the attainment of that end.

London streets on 16th September, to Morrison's great satisfaction, were prominently placarded with the bright yellow posters of the *Pall Mall Gazette*:

Dr Morrison on
THE NEW CHINA

Again he had made a special plea for the Republic that owed more to loyalty than to fact:

"People in England," said Dr Morrison, "have been saying that the

Republic does not yet show stability. I would rather ask: In what respect does it show increasing instability? Take trade. This will be a record year for trade in China, despite the enormous floods in Kiang-su and Anhui. Take the protection of foreigners. There never was a time when foreigners were so safe in China. . . . Take the troops recently under arms. They are being steadily disbanded and not turned adrift, without pay to prey on the people, as was often the case in the old days . . . the administration of President Yuan Shih-k'ai is not now seriously disputed anywhere. The very quietude of China today is proof of stability."

Yuan's only real difficulties were financial, and the suggestion that he aimed at dictatorial power was ridiculous. In all things he acted on constitutional lines, and the chief complaint now made against him was that he was far too anxious not to transgress constitutional limits:

"Then you are told," continued Dr Morrison, "that the Revolution was the work of hot-headed students and unpractical dreamers. It is preposterous. . . . The leaders of the movement were some of the most enlightened men in the country. Do you suppose that a few hot-headed students could have won immediate support in every part of the Empire, even in distant Kashgar? The leaders were serious thinking men. . . . Some of them are intellectually as well equipped as any leaders in the world's history. The Revolution was the work of reason rather than of force.". . .

"What about Dr Sun Yat-sen?" "There you touch on another Western delusion," remarked Dr Morrison. "It is said here that Sun Yat-sen is unpractical. But he is a man who had a very clear idea of what he wanted to do, and he has done it. What more can you ask? He gives unflinching support to the President. For the rest, he is carrying on his own work in his own way. He sees that the greatest need of China is industrial development and to that he now devotes all his energies."

"I read your interview with the *Pall Mall Gazette* with much interest, and have sent it to Sir Edward Grey," J. D. Gregory wrote from the Foreign Office. "I hope the interview correctly reflected your views!"

China's real condition was more honestly summed up in an undated note which Morrison made for his "Reminiscences":

At this time—I might say at all times—the pressing need in China was money. The Government was in desperate straits. . . . Remittances were coming in from the provinces but they were coming in the form of doles, voluntary remittances which the Provincial Governors made Peking clearly to understand were sent at their own pleasure and could be withheld at any time. Money was chiefly needed to pay the troops in Peking, the provincial authorities also found that the chief drain on their resources were the military forces. Governors wielded power because of their military whose loyalty was an uncertain factor or rather certain only in this respect, that the troops were more or less loyal to those that paid them. Rarely did the loyalty survive delay in payment. The soldiers in that case looted the property of the defenceless and paid themselves in kind. Disbandment was difficult for the military preferred a life of ease with the possibilities of plunder to a life of labour and the possibilities of being plundered. The provincial authorities always opposed disbandment because their power was derived from the military and without the military their authority disappeared.

"The President was desperately in need of money and was prepared to agree to any terms could he obtain it," Morrison wrote. "Yuan believed that with £5,000,000 he could safeguard his position and hold the military in check." He had telegraphed the Chinese Minister in London on 8th September, saying he was in desperate straits and asking how much could be sent him within a week. Morrison learned that negotiations for a loan of £10 million, secured upon the Salt Revenue of China, had been opened with a well-known English financier, Mr C. Birch Crisp. The Foreign Office disapproved of this. The curious policy of the British Government, which Morrison had often criticized in *The Times*, was to give a monopoly of loan transactions to one British bank in China, the Hong Kong and Shanghai Bank, though it was in partnership with German banking interests, and not to allow purely British Banks to make loans. Partly as a result of Morrison's efforts in the City, half of the Crisp loan was successfully negotiated, the remaining £5 million being abandoned later under pressure from the Foreign Office. Because of his work for the Crisp loan, Morrison's relations with the British Legation in Peking became strained. Morrison wrote to Sir John Jordan rather bitterly: "I am convinced that in giving support to an attempt to break down the monopoly, the highly injurious monopoly as I believe it to be, of the Hong Kong and Shanghai Bank, I was doing right. . . . I claim therefore that . . . however humble was the part I played in doing so, I was doing a service to the British, and therefore increasing the influence of the British Legation in China."

The *Pall Mall Gazette*, having allowed Morrison eight columns in which to extol the Republic, expressed its own reservations in a temperate leader, also written by Lovat Fraser. It was fascinated by Dr Morrison's suggestion that oil-lamps were "doing far more to enlighten China than the peripatetic crusades of Dr Sun Yat-sen and his followers", and Morrison's "courageous attempt" to convince his followers that a republic was not unsuited to Chinese traditions at least deserved "respectful attention":

> Where we really differ from DR MORRISON is with regard to his apparent assumption that representative government will suffice to hold China together. We doubt whether it will do so unless reinforced by a veiled autocracy, as in Japan. At the same time, we are bound to admit that DR MORRISON presents the Republic in a somewhat new

and distinctly more favourable light. He brings us nearer to comprehension of the springs of the revolutionary movement. It is not a movement which Great Britain should deliberately discourage. . . . There is only too much reason to fear that British policy is really preventing the leaders of the Republic from gaining the fair chance they desire. . . . Do we want to exploit China in the interests of particular financial groups, or are we to set our faces against delivering her bound hand and foot to usurers with political aims? There is little doubt about what the answer of the British nation will be, but the Foreign Office seems to have involved itself in entanglements which afford small present opportunity for escape. . . .

This was delicate scepticism. But there was nothing delicate about a rejoinder to Morrison's interview which Dr Emile Joseph Dillon contributed to the October issue of the *Nineteenth Century and After*. Dillon, who had been a special correspondent in Armenia, Spain, Crete, France (during the Dreyfus case), and China in 1900, was a man of formidable erudition, a Doctor of Oriental Languages and Literature, a Master of Classical Languages, and a Professor of Comparative Philology, whose universities included Innsbruck, Leipzig, Tübingen, Petrograd, Louvain, and Kharkov. In his article, "The Dismemberment of China", he described the "greatest Republic on earth" as "the biggest political fraud of modern times". It was an anarchy on the verge of disintegration. Morrison's way of looking at the formidable dangers that beset it was to shut his eyes to them. "Those who attack Yuan Shih-k'ai, alleging that he is aiming at a dictatorship, are ignoring the facts of his career," Morrison had written. Dillon replied that this was in a sense true because Yuan was already dictator of China, and many people suspected he was planning to found a dynasty of his own:

> That in pursuit of this aim he will not let trifles stand in his way is proven by another of the incidents of his career, which he himself often narrated with relish to my friend, the late Russian Minister Plenipotentiary in Pekin, Pokotiloff. It characterizes the man. Yuan Shih-k'ai, who was Governor of Shantung when the Boxer movement became aggressive, resolved for reasons of his own to root it out then and there. And he rooted it out. 'Yuan Shih-k'ai', remarked M. Pokotiloff, 'was the most cold-blooded human being I have ever encountered. He assured me many times—and I had no grounds to doubt his word—that he had had forty thousand Boxers put to death'. Yet Dr Morrison, with the filial piety of Noah's children who threw a veil over the paternal nakedness, dwells touchingly upon the man's reputed mildness.

Morrison was even more vulnerable in his justification of a recent, and better attested, example of Yuan's ruthlessness. In the middle of August, Yuan invited some important leaders of the revolutionary party to Peking, among them the Generals Chang Chen-wu and Fang Wei. Chang was a hero of the Wuchang rising, but he and Fang had fallen out with the military leader of the revolutionary army and Vice-President of the Republic, General Li Yuan-hung. To placate Li, his right-hand man, Yuan had the two difficult generals murdered—without trial and with great brutality. According to Peking reports, they were wined, dined, and toasted in a European hotel by the officer charged with their execution, immediately before it took place. Morrison's explanation in *The Times* was ingenuous. "Indisputable evidence was sent by the Vice-President to the President that those two arch-conspirators were plotting against the Government. They were endeavouring to sow dissension in the army," he wrote. "Undeniable evidence . . . justified the head of the Government in commanding the police to arrest them and execute them. . . ." Since he was travelling across Siberia when the "executions" took place, Morrison was scarcely in a position to assess the evidence as "indisputable" and "undeniable", even had it been disclosed. And the most dedicated apologist might have hesitated to describe Yuan's act as strictly constitutional.

Senators in Peking, not so easily satisfied as Morrison, demanded a convincing explanation of the murders, or the impeachment of Li. They got neither, and the unpleasant interlude was soon forgotten. Morrison's only comment in his diary was: "Dr E. J. Dillon is very violent against me in the *XIX Century*."

To a correspondent in Shanghai who had replied to Dillon in the *North China Daily News* Morrison wrote:

I thank you sincerely for so manfully standing up for me when I was debarred from taking any part in the fray myself. Dr Dillon in his article displays considerable personal bias. I have known him for many years. He is a disgruntled little man who is always foreseeing disaster. He was in China at the end of 1900. As far as I know that was his only visit here. He then stayed for a few days only and he saw China under conditions which apparently have left an indelible impression upon his memory.

[XV]

George Marvin, formerly American Vice-Consul at Mukden, gave his reminiscences in *Harper's Weekly* of "The Australian Doctor who is Piloting the Republic's Newly Launched Ship of State":

In late August it was the autumn snipe he came to meet on their annual pilgrimage from the Siberian solitudes of their summer exile. North of the city wall on the plains near the Pei-ling tombs, marshes and watery furrows made a famous caravansary for these migrating hosts, and Morrison's gun was often heard there. Later in the fall, in the wonderful Manchurian season of crystal sunlight and sparkling, frosty nights, he would only stop with us *en route* to the haunts of the wild Chinese pheasant which he rightly believed to be the most beautiful of all game birds. In the bracken fields of North Manchuria that glorious fowl was then still unsophisticated and it was Morrison's ambition to bag a clean hundred of them in one day by simply walking the birds up himself out of cover without beaters, a feat which he eventually accomplished.

But although he was an excellent shot, game birds were a small part of his bag on these apparently sporting trips into North China. How much more than snipe or pheasant he shot up would be indicated when, a month or so later, the London *Times* of that season appeared with those brief, crisply phrased, perfectly informed dispatches which made him famous as a foreign correspondent. Only the gist of it went into the telegrams: the rest, the background—the whole rich, shifting play of economics, politics and personalities, which have made the meeting of East and West in China since the Boxer time the world's most absorbing problem drama—you will find stored away in careful notes in his library at Peking.

* * * * *

It is characteristic of him that for many years he has preferred to live beyond the walls and the conveniences of the Legation quarter, but although he inhabits a Chinese house, he resides in it not as the Chinese do. It is a very spacious and comfortable residence; four buildings, or "chien", surrounding an open compound, all separated and hidden from the street by a high masonry wall through which a small postern door admits you to the interior. It was always a grateful, sharp change to step from the confusion, dust and noise of the crowded street across the threshold into Morrison's peaceful, sunny court, as clean as a hospital, and bright with flowers.

* * * * *

In a diplomatic society like that of Peking, where people take the matter of clothes with amusing seriousness, Morrison is a kind of Diogenes in simplicity of dress. He is most familiar to those who know him in a soft flannel shirt, plain linen or khaki suit, a pair of soft Russian leather boots on his feet. He is a very quiet man, as simple and direct in manner and speech as he is in appearance. He has none of the dourness of the Scot, but a Scots' dry, twinkling humour is his, and although he is generally taciturn and attentive, he possesses in a rare degree the great gift of speech.

[XVI]

Morrison's appointment produced a cascade of congratulations, and metaphors were invoked in gaudy profusion, the most popular being the troubled ship of state on which his firm hand now grasped the tiller, the wheel, or the helm. "I am quite sure you will steer a fine course through one of the most difficult seas a man can navigate," wrote Gwynne in a variant on this theme. Others substituted the "reins of affairs" for the "ship of state", and many agreed that though the task was not a light one, Morrison would be able to put his stamp on China for her lasting good. "Giants are scarce nowadays, and the Chinese Republic is . . . fortunate in having secured a real live one," George Kidston wrote from the British Embassy in Constantinople. Sir Cecil Clementi-Smith confessed that Morrison's appointment had made him feel more sanguine than he had done of the permanency of the new Chinese regime, and Sir John Jordan wrote:

> Your telegrams during the last fifteen years have come to be regarded as authoritative pronouncements. . . . They were a feature in *The Times* which can never, I am convinced, be reproduced. . . . Your new post will bring many anxieties and disappointments, but it will offer great opportunities and the best wish I can think of is that in future years your name will be as closely associated with the regeneration of China as it has been, the world over, with the reputation of *The Times*.

Sir Edward Grey asked Sir John to send Morrison his congratulations and to add that "in his efforts to assist China through her difficulties" he had all Sir Edward's sympathy and best wishes. "I congratulate you, ourselves, and the Chinese Government warmly," Beilby Alston wrote from the Foreign Office. "Everybody here is very pleased about it, from Sir Edward Grey down. . . ."

Willard Straight, who was in London wrestling with some tangled loan negotiations, thought the appointment of Morrison was "the first indication of intelligence" the Chinese had shown for a long time:

> If anyone can help them now, you can, for you enjoy their confidence as few others have ever done—and your position throughout the world is a unique one as regards all matters Chinese. . . . China . . . has, I fear, few friends who are willing to bear with her and take into account her point of view, after the events of the last year. She needs you very badly—and we are all very glad that you are going to serve her in her time of trial. . . .

"*The Times*' loss is China's gain," wrote Reginald Johnston, from Weihaiwei. "I am glad you are not going to throw yourself away on Australian politics." SORRY FOR PAPER AND MYSELF GLAD FOR YOU AND CHINA, Wickham Steed cabled, and in a following letter wrote: "Poor old Paper! Its mainstays are being removed one by one. . . . The foreign service is certainly in a critical state. . . . If the ship is destined to sink, I, at least, shall have done my best for it and shall hope to find a floating plank somewhere."

Buckle, the last of the Giant Tortoises, had retired in August, after twenty-eight years in the editorial chair. "I have given my best to the Paper," he said in a handsomely printed farewell message to his Dear Friends. "I pray that, as the years go on, *The Times* may be ever more and more indisputably recognized to be the greatest journal in the world." He and Chirol were more fortunate than Morrison. "Buckle, I understand, has a pension of £1000 a year, and Chirol, £500," Morrison wrote to Steed.

Morrison officially left *The Times* at the end of September. There is nothing in his diaries or letters about his last days in Printing House Square, but apparently Northcliffe, whose professions of friendship and admiration had been so ardent two years before, did not have time even to dictate a formal letter of farewell—or congratulations.

"Everyone wants a job," Morrison wrote to a friend in Peking early in September. "Apparently many think I have come to England to look for men willing to serve the Chinese Government at an extravagant salary, and to advise on everything from Christian Science to the building of battleships." Even with the help of two secretaries he had not answered one tenth of the letters. Many Englishmen, of course, were away for the grouse-shooting in Scotland, but others—generals, stockbrokers, bankers, arms-manufacturers, printers of postage stamps—were prepared, for China's sake, to give up this sacred ritual and pay their respects to Morrison. They had developed a burning zeal to assist in China's regeneration.

Lieutenant-General Sir Reginald Pole Carew, a veteran of the Afghan War, the March to Kandahar, and the South African War, invited Morrison to his castle in County Tipperary, and asked "whether by any chance" China wanted "a humble English soldier" to organize her Army so as to make it a match for both the Japanese and the Russians: "I would like to be allowed an English Cavalry officer, a Gunner and Infantryman and I have an eye on all three."

Colonel Alfred Woodrow Wingate, an old China hand, now A.Q.M.G. of the 9th Indian Division, wrote from Ootacamund: "Is there an opening for me? I would willingly chuck the Service [which he had entered in 1881] for a billet under the Chinese and might help them towards something *real* instead of the usual phantoms. . . ."; and Colonel Fredric Natusch Maud, author of *Cavalry, its Past and Future*, who had entered the Royal Engineers in 1873, offered not only his own services but those of a picked staff: "Perhaps you will allow the names of my friends Dr Sun Yat-sen and Homer Lea to serve as an introduction? When they left England last winter it was arranged that I should join them as soon as possible. . . ." Morrison replied that he had not yet had the honour of meeting Dr Sun or Mr Lea.

Less ambitious was Mr J. Murphy, a former Colour Sergeant of the Royal Marines, who had fought in the Boxer uprising and was now a messenger in the Admiralty. He was prepared to serve China "in the capacity of Head Messenger, Hall Porter or personal orderly".

Morrison was harassed not only by job-hunters but by people wanting all sorts of things. He was invited to address the Christian Literature for China Society in Glasgow and to write on the role of missionaries in China for the *International Review of Missions* and the *Home Messenger*, the organ of the Free Churches. Mr Osbert Burdett, assistant-editor of

The Hospital, asked for an article on Chinese hospitals. Mr H. J. Elwes sent five volumes of his *Trees of Great Britain and Ireland*, with a request that they be favourably reviewed in *The Times*, and Mrs L. E. Douglas, of Broadstone, Dorset, wanted Morrison to buy her a good Pekingese dog, "a red with a black mask, about 4-5 pounds, for about £10 or £15". These requests were punctiliously and apologetically declined.

Another correspondent disinterestedly urged Morrison to persuade the Australian Government to subsidize "half a dozen 27 knot vessels":

> The Australian is a clear-thinking man and knows what goes on in the world. His nearest neighbours are much too near. The power-fullest of Asian men not many hours sailing distant! There is only one defence . . . swift and still swifter communications between Britain and Australia—20 days now, and less later. These flying leviathans are powerful merchantmen, first of all! But also, they are armed cruisers of immeasurable strength . . . carrying one or two 10 mile guns. . . .

Among the requests for an interview which Morrison evaded by the technique of not answering the letter till the day before his departure was one from Mr Vincent C. Vickers, director of Vickers Ltd, who said he "would be happy to call . . . at any time convenient".

Amid the trumpetings of joy was one melancholy note, a letter from a sixty-seven-year-old cousin, Donald Morrison, who had been brought up in "the old family home, The Ardoch, Edinkillie" but was now re-siding in St Pancras Workhouse, Kings Road. Donald had driven Morrison's father to the station when he went out to Australia in 1858. "I would very much like to see your father's son," he wrote. "I have been unfor-tunate. . . ."

Congratulations on Morrison's appointment were soon followed by congratulations on his marriage. "It is the only secure haven in our voyage between the Eternities," Beatrice Brownrigg wrote, adding thoughtfully: "It is, of course, an artificial relationship because the fidelity which is expected in marriage is altogether unnatural."

When Dungate wrote that Morrison had beaten all records by marry-ing at fifty, Morrison replied:

> I have been collecting statistics and I find that this is by no means a record, the record is held by the Marquis of Donegal who married at 88 and had a son 6 months afterwards, but in the case of this noble peer, there were doubts about the fidelity of his wife. There are various other cases including the Most Noble, the Marquis of Nor-manby, but I do not think you know the peerage as well as I do or have the same veneration for it that I have.

In the midst of manifold social and political activities Morrison found time to see *Fanny's First Play* ("admirable . . . I laughed continuously");

Bunty Pulls the Strings ("amazingly stupid . . . home before the end of the second act"); the aviation at Hendon ("three foreigners in monoplanes and one in a biplane—no Britishers—an amazing spectacle"); the wax murderers at Madame Tussaud's; and to write to the Army and Navy Stores, strongly protesting against their "exorbitant charge" of thirty shillings for painting bands of red yellow and black, two inches wide, round five cases. "I could have done it myself for two and sixpence". It was "outrageous".

Even the unique experience of getting married did not interrupt Morrison's precise journalizing. On the day before the wedding he took the train to Haslemere and walked to Hindhead to engage a room for the honeymoon ("nice room . . . 13/6 a day each . . . beautifully situated small hotel in the most beautiful part of England that I have yet visited . . . drove back at a cost of 3/6 and sixpence tip, having, I suspect, been done in the eye"). On his wedding-day he was worried by nose-bleeding, and newspapermen to whom he had to be "quite rude". The ceremony took place at Emmanuel Church, South Croydon. The *Daily Chronicle*, in its front page report of the "Romantic Marriage", said:

> The bride . . . bore herself with winsome grace, arriving in her travelling dress in a motor-car which also brought her parents. . . . Dr Morrison's party included his mother and Sir John McLeavy Brown, but all told, there were only about a dozen people present. The bridegroom had not worried over dress. He was in a light grey check suit, with soft felt hat, and, as he alighted, carried a mackintosh over his arm. There were no bridesmaids nor bouquets, music or confetti. The vicar (the Rev. R. F. N. Phillips) took the service, which was without an address; nor was the Prayer Book substitute —the scriptural injunctions touching the duties of husband to wives and wives to husbands—read.

Morrison's diary, written that night in the hotel smoking-room ("am disturbed and disconcerted by two octogenarian croaks, one deaf and other loquacious"), supplemented the newspaper reports with characteristic detail:

> . . . The Rev. R. F. N. Phillips, M.A., good-looking man whose brother is in the C.M.S. at Foochow and has been there for 24 years . . . church endowed by Watney's the brewers and the stipend of the clergyman is £1000 a year. . . . Jennie and her father came in at 10 and the service . . . finished at 10.20. . . . at 10.30 started off in a motor for Hindhead. . . . At Guildford we stopped . . . and bought two *Robinson Crusoes* that I did not have and had a delightful lunch. . . . On in an hour. To Hotel. Then Jennie slept and I went for a lovely walk through the heather a glorious blaze of colour . . . afternoon tea at the Violet Tea Rooms dainty and good taste and then for a walk into Haslemere with Jennie. Long wait for dinner

at the White Horse Inn and so home in a brougham. Gave the vicar £5/5/- and a sovereign to the verger the worthy father of 10. He seemed overwhelmed.

Next day he and Jennie walked fourteen miles before breakfast, to Farnsham via Churt, and lunched by the pond in the open air. . . .

[XVII]

At midnight on 31st December 1912, after writing up his diary for the day, Morrison turned to a new page and set down his "Wishes for the New Year":

Health, Strength and Happiness for Jennie and for me. A healthy baby—one only—perfect in health to give joy to us both.

Health for myself strength and vigour, a clean tongue, pure breath, freedom from all ailments of the system stomach liver heart and kidneys—to be free from uric acid gout and rheumatism.

Great mental vigour and freedom from worry—and freedom from epistaxis. Let me have no bleeding from the nose.

Since I have been married I have been healthier than for many years.

Let my health get better throughout the coming year let me get stronger and more active spare of habit not portly but improve my figure. Let me have no impairment of sight or hearing.

A healthy scalp and the preservation of my hair.

Give me abundant means and great good fortune.

Personal distinction fame and honour.

To suffer no accident to wind or limb or brain no rupture.

To have no accident in my house no fire or damage to my house or books or things here or in transit.

To greatly increase my library and lose no books.

To have never any cause for anxiety about my health and all curious fears as to my bodily conditions to disappear e.g. this irritation in deglutition.

To let me be an unqualified success in my service to China, get authority and influence and make my power felt and myself feared and honoured.

In fine let this year just coming be the most successful and glorious of my life and incomparably the happiest with Jennie to have equal happiness and for us to have increasing delight in each other's company.

Set me on High because I have known Thy name.

Commit thy way unto the Lord; Trust also in Him and He shall bring it to pass!!

CHAPTER TEN

[I]

A YOUNG, attractive, and devoted wife; a handsome salary; a world-wide reputation; freedom from the goads and pinpricks of Printing House Square; serving a country whose interests he had very much at heart— for Morrison at the age of fifty these, surely, were the components if not of happiness at least of content. But less than three months after taking up his new appointment he wrote: "My job is becoming an impossible one. I am really heartily sick of it and will leave as soon as I am out of debt." He was enmeshed in "intrigues, lies and incompetence". The theme of dissatisfaction was often repeated. "Here am I paid nearly £4000 a year and kept in complete ignorance," he wrote in May: "It quickens my determination to be quit of the Country as soon as possible. And what revelations I will have to make of these ungrateful people! Not ingratitude to me but to others. Their pusillanimity. . . ."

He complained to Tsai Ting-kan: "One cannot build bricks without straw and I cannot get sufficient data from the Foreign Office. . . . I could, I know, render material help in the settlement of the Yunnan frontier question, but I am kept more in the dark now than when I was a Correspondent"; and in June he wrote: "This is a rotten damned country to be in and a putrid people to serve! Suspicious of me because I am friends with Donald. Unwilling to give me a pass into the Palace. . . . no work to do. . . . Donald thinks the crookedest man in China is Tsai Ting-kan!"

He was little consoled when Yuan Shih-k'ai conferred on him the Second Class Order of the Excellent Crop "for services that cannot be numbered"—which Morrison ungraciously described as "a decoration which I don't value a brass farthing":

> What I want is work and no work is being given me, that is to say no work is being entrusted to me. These suspicious Orientals suspicious of each other especially suspicious of the foreigner are impossible people to understand. Unwilling to learn the truth they have con-

fidence only in those base and servile foreigners who tell them what they find pleasing to hear. No post is worth holding under the Chinese that does not carry with it authority and executive power. And I have neither the one nor the other. Disgust of my appointment is increasing daily. Inactivity is becoming intolerable and yet I am chained to my post. Perhaps I will become callous as time goes on but it is the fear of this that worries. Jennie more than anything fears that I will lose all energy and ambition and think only of my salary. It isn't true that I have to think mainly of my salary, but if this inactivity continues I am bound to deteriorate bound to find my energy and ambition are sapping away. You cannot bustle the East. You cannot advise an Oriental like Yuan Shih-k'ai surrounded as he is by a cohort of upscrupulous Chinese jealous of the foreigner.

Morrison was not the only well-paid adviser of the Chinese Government who felt he was not earning his salary. When Morrison joined the Chinese service he induced the Government to engage many men of high standing to help in the task of reconstruction. They included Dr Nagao Ariga, Japan's greatest international jurist, as a constitutional adviser; George Padoux, a minister in the French diplomatic service, who had done valuable work in reforming the administration of Siam; and Dr Hirai, a Japanese graduate of Harvard and a member of the House of Peers, the permanent head of the railways in Japan. On army matters, the Chinese were advised by Lieutenant-Colonel Brissaud des Maillets, a brilliant French military attaché, and on problems of extra-territorial jurisdiction, by Henri de Codt, a Belgian with much experience in Egypt. As the result of Dr Eliot's visit, an American, Professor Frank Goodnow, had been nominated by the Carnegie Endowment for International Peace to assist in the drawing-up of a constitution. None of these experts had enough to do. They were seldom consulted. Goodnow worked only four hours a week. "They did not seek for sinecures," Morrison wrote. "The Chinese appoint a foreigner and never trust him."

The Sydney *Bulletin*, a widely read Australian weekly, carried a paragraph in its issue of 31st July:

Item from the Revelations of W. H. Donald, the well-known Australian pressman, representing the *New York Herald* in Peking, in a recent letter to a Sydney friend: "I see Dr Morrison daily, and he does not know whether to be tired of his job or not. He has a hard time of it. Advice is easy to give: the Chinaman listens to advice, but will do what he thinks he wants to do. Morrison feels that, frequently. During the Revolution, he asked me, in Shanghai, why I did not enter the service of the Government. They were then offering me £250 a month. My reply was that, once a man entered the paid service of a Chinese, his influence was gone. Morrison scoffed—now he admits it. Bitter proof. As *Times* correspondent he had twice the prestige and three times the influence."

Morrison was enraged, the more so, of course, as the Revelations were for the most part true. He recalled Psalm 41, verse 9, *"Yes, mine own familiar friend in whom I trusted which did eat of my bread hath lifted up his heel against me"*, and wrote to Tsai Ting-kan: "You can well imagine that such a statement written by one who says that he sees me every day—which is not true—has done me considerable injury in my own country." But the imminent breach between the two Australians—who had a great regard for each other—was averted when Donald explained very apologetically that he had never intended his casual observations to appear in print.

One expert whose offer of advice Morrison was able to have rejected was the tenacious Sir Hiram Maxim. When Tse Tsan-tai—a Sydney-born old boy of the Grafton High School, who had been a revolutionary since 1887—recommended Maxim's appointment, Morrison wrote: "Do you really think that such a man is needed in China at the present time?":

> What I, as a well-wisher of the country, desire to see is . . . the cessation of the insensate expenditure of money upon weapons of all kinds. China has been the dumping ground of rifles for the last 25 years. In no year during the last 25 years, even during the years following the Boxer troubles when the importation of arms was forbidden, has a less amount than 65,000 rifles per annum been imported. . . . Millions and millions of pounds sterling have been wasted upon arms. You can find every kind of rifle in the world in different sections of the Chinese territory. . . .
>
> Surely what China needs now is industrial development—building of railways, of roads, improving canals and waterways, the construction of telegraphs, the improvement of sanitation. Surely some effort should be made to stop the appalling destruction of life that takes place annually in the flood areas of the Hsui River, where famines are incessant and where this appalling destruction of life is preventable if river conservancy were to be taken in hand. . . .

[II]

Morrison exaggerated his inactivity, if not his frustration. There were endless disputes over loans and concessions, over opium and railways, over Tibet and Mongolia, in which he offered painstakingly documented counsel, even if it was ignored; and when he was not interviewing ministers, bankers, and businessmen he was writing telegrams on China's behalf for David Fraser of *The Times*, Wearne of Reuter's, and Donald of the *New York Herald*, as well as innumerable letters, including long background reports to Braham. And, of course, his diary was written up each day—at length and always with refreshing catholicity. Between scholarly annotations on urgent financial problems, he would record items of club humour such as "the difference between a diplomat and a virgin":

If a diplomat says Yes, he means Perhaps.
If a diplomat says Perhaps, he means No.
If a diplomat says No, he is no diplomat!
If a virgin says No, she means Perhaps.
If a virgin says Perhaps, she means Yes.
If a virgin says Yes, she is no virgin.

Nor was all his correspondence of international importance. He exchanged a great number of letters with a Mr William Ming, of Hillfield Avenue, Crouch End, London, who, though an Englishman, claimed to be heir to the throne of the Ming Emperors, the last of whom had ruled in 1643. "To claim the throne is not my idea," Mr Ming explained. He would be satisfied with the title of Marquis, and anything of value that could be recovered. His photograph, sent at Morrison's request, depicted a typical London shopkeeper, plump, moustached, obsequious.

A continuing claimant on Morrison's time was Dungate, whose frequent letters were as eccentric as his life. In one, rambling across fifteen handwritten pages, he asked: "Do you think I'm cranky? If so, tell me honestly." Cranky or not, he was an acute observer:

> Things are booming along in Old England, Lloyd George is just as much the leading actor as ever. . . . The well-to-do people detest him. . . . But these kind of people should really be very grateful to Lloyd George. Because if some such great leader of democracy had not come to the front—something bad must have happened. . . . In Australia, well known Labour leaders expressed to me their wonder at the inaction of the British working man. . . . They were muddled with beer and apathetic. . . . About 7 years ago when I came from Australia, and saw the conditions of the worker class in this country I was horrified. . . . The rich middle class upwards is incapable of feeling a real sympathy with those beneath them . . . they have no practical knowledge of what a worker likes.

Another tenacious correspondent was Mr Cordius Nielson, proprietor of the Shanghai *Cosmopolitan*, who sought a concession to show cinematograph films "throughout the vast country of China". He had two million Mexican dollars immediately available, and offered a royalty to town councils of five per cent of his gross earnings:

> . . . As long as obscenity and immorality are excluded from the repertoire there can be no doubt that these living pictures have a wholesome and educational effect on the people. . . . Morality could be served by films showing the evil effects of Opium Smoking. The evil effect of foot-binding. The evil effect of corruption. The evil effect of the indiscriminate use by many people of hot towels. The danger of indiscriminate expectoration which causes unnecessary disease. The result of Patriotism. The consequence of Treachery and many others.

Apart from the rather sombre didacticism of the programmes, Mr Nielson pointed out that "education and instruction should go hand in hand with innocent amusement": "When people laugh and enjoy themselves their frame of mind is in a much better condition of receptivity for absorbing that which really matters. . . . a living picture-show ought therefore to have at least 30% of light amusing pictures."

[III]

Fundamentally, Morrison's loyalty to Yuan, with whom he identified China's future, was unchanged, but he was not always uncritical. When he received from the President's office an article for publication in the foreign Press, denouncing the Kuomintang as a gang of desperadoes, assassins and extortionists, he returned it to Tsai Ting-kan with the curt scrawled comment: "Suppressed as wholly unworthy. I'd never be a party to the publication of such a foolish undignified diatribe. That it should emanate from the President's office is evidence itself of the evil influence with which the President is surrounded."

Was the President less evil than the influences surrounding him? Morrison had many opportunities to consider this question in the months that followed, but he seemed unwilling to reach a conclusion, even after another vivid demonstration of Yuan's ruthlessness.

The one powerful political organization in China was the Kuomintang, which had been formed in the South, after the revolution, from a fusion of Sun Yat-sen's old underground party, the Tungmenhui, with some smaller revolutionary parties. Its policies were often confused and impractical, and sometimes more partisan than patriotic, but basically it stood for a people's democracy, with power diffused among provincial governments, against the Northern Republican's emphasis on a strong Central Government controlled by the President. The Northerners supported Yuan unreservedly, the Southerners with caution. In the first elections for a Senate and House of Representatives, the Kuomintang easily won control of both chambers. It had been led to victory by an accomplished young man named Sung Chiao-jen, who had drafted its constitution. He had been Minister for Agriculture in the first Republican Cabinet, and was freely tipped as the next Prime Minister. Yuan feared Sung's growing popularity, and the growing power of the Kuomintang, which he saw as a challenge to his own ambitions.

As chairman of the Kuomintang's executive committee, Sung travelled often between Shanghai and Peking. On 20th March, as he was waiting for the train on a crowded platform in Shanghai, he was shot dead by a "short man in black". The murder roused the Southern Republicans to fury. The Kuomintang went into mourning; Sun Yat-sen, who was enjoy-a semi-private triumphal tour of Japan, hurried back to deliver an impassioned funeral oration; Yuan Shih-k'ai dutifully issued a warrant for the arrest of the assassin. On the day of the murder an antique-dealer walked into a Shanghai police station and made a remarkable statement. He said he had recently delivered some antiques to an old customer, Ying Kwei-shing, chief detective of Kiangsu Province. "He then showed me a photograph of a man and asked me to kill him at a certain place and a certain time," said the antique-dealer. "He also promised me a thousand dollars [about £95 sterling] for the job. I am, as you can see, merely a business-man, and have never killed anyone, so I refused. This morning I saw the same photograph in the papers. . . ."

The Shanghai police, who seemed to have a good knowledge of their colleague's habits, promptly arrested Ying in a private brothel in Shanghai. In his home they found a revolver with only two bullets, and many telegrams discussing the projected murder, exchanged between Ying and Premier Chao Ping-chun's confidential secretary, Hung Shu-tsu; and between Ying and a man named Wu Shih-ying. The last telegram from Ying to Hung, dated 21st March, read simply: "Bandit leader destroyed; no casualties. . . ." The telegrams were all in the Cabinet's secret code. Ying and Wu were tried by a court in the International Settlement. Wu took sole responsibility for the murder, and Ying pleaded not guilty. They were both still in custody after the trial when Wu was found dead in his cell, and Ying was released by Shanghai "gangsters" who broke into the jail.

Yuan Shih-k'ai was widely suspected of complicity in Sung Chiao-jen's murder. The London *Daily Telegraph*'s correspondent, "Putnam Weale", was often denounced by Morrison for his irresponsibility and sensationalism, but his telegram of 23rd March was factual and perceptive. There was "not the slightest doubt" that Sung Chiao-jen was shot by order, he wrote. By order of whom? Weale pointed out that the Kuomin-tang which with 368 out of a total of 546 members would control the coming Parliament, was devoted to two leading ideas, "a party Cabinet and Provincial rights, as opposed to Yuan Shih-k'ai's ideal of a Peking dictatorship". The murder must be looked at solely from the effect it would have on the forthcoming convocation of Parliament. The effect, of course, was to intimidate the Kuomintang, many of whose members, dis-couraged by their leader's fate, and encouraged by generous bribes, scuttled out of the party.

Morrison recorded the wholesale bribery that was taking place. An Australian-born Chinese barrister, Ah Ket, who was one of the six overseas Chinese delegates of the Kuomintang, said he had been offered $100 for his vote. Later the price went up considerably. According to some historians, it averaged about £1000 a head. "A cheerful and original way of forming a government," Morrison commented. But he offered no com-ment on the widely held belief that Yuan was responsible for Sung's mur-der. Yuan and Chao had a hard job to clear their names. First they in-vented an underground terrorist organization which convinced no one. Then Chao explained that he had certainly given Ying a copy of the Cabinet code, but for innocent reasons, and he knew nothing of the mes-sages between Hung and Ying. The court issued a warrant for Chao to give evidence, but he ignored it, though he resigned the Premiership and was consoled with the military governorship of Chihli.

An ingenious and imaginative explanation came nearly two months after the murder from the Premier's former secretary, Hung Shu-tsu, who had taken refuge in German Tsingtao. He confessed that he had fraudulently used the name of the Cabinet in order to carry out a patriotic project:

> Desirous to serve his country, he says, and knowing that Sung Chiao-jen had been guilty of forgery in Japan, where a warrant had been issued for his arrest by the Japanese police, he had been in telegraphic communication with Ying Kwei-shing . . . with a view to having this charge disclosed, "in order" he declares "that the world might know the true character of the leader". He asserts it was his intention only to expose Sung Chiao-jen's misdeeds and destroy his reputation and that he never contemplated his murder. . . . His confession was made voluntarily and has been cabled to the President, the Vice-President, and the high provincial authorities, everywhere causing a deep impression.

This farrago of nonsense was part of a telegram which Morrison gave Wearne for distribution through Reuter's. Morrison records only that he dictated the message. It is a pity he did not tell posterity what he thought about it.

What many Chinese thought about it is evident from a Cabinet memorandum which Morrison received two months later:

> Premier Chao Ping-chun has petitioned that from the time of the Sung Murder Case the public opinion has been so decided, he proposes to follow the example of European and American countries and request the President to appoint a Committee comprising of Chinese and Foreigners of high moral standing and well versed in law to thoroughly investigate into the case and to report the same. As Dr Wu Ting-fang and Dr Morrison are both well versed in Chinese and Foreign Law, I hereby appoint them to fully investigate into the case and report.
>
>   We are,
>   Yours sincerely,
>   (sgd) The Cabinet.

In his petition Chao Ping-chun observed blandly: "After the publication of the evidence although those of ordinary intelligence would be convinced that this was not sufficient to implicate the Government, still there are meddlesome people who would even use this as a means for stirring up trouble." For some arcane reason Morrison refused the assignment. As a person of more than ordinary intelligence, he could not have been satisfied with the assorted explanations of the murder that had been vouchsafed him. But he replied to Cabinet, "after consulting with H. E. Dr Wu Ting-fang", that as no charges worthy of consideration had been made against Chao, it was superogatory for him to refute them. As for the proposed Commission of Enquiry:

> I hope it will not be thought I desire to evade any work entrusted to me if I point out how undesirable it is in the interests of China that an enquiry of this delicate nature involving the character of one of its statesmen should be held in the official presence of a foreigner. These vague and intangible charges or rather suggestions and innuendoes are purely a domestic concern. . . . I believe I am right in saying that no instance has ever been known where a foreigner has been attached to such a commission.
>
> The fact that Mr Chao Ping-chun desires to have the case investigated by an impartial tribunal is the best possible evidence that he is innocent. I submit that for the dignity of the country and for the honour of the Chinese people it would be unwise to hold such an enquiry at the present time. . . .

The dignity of China and the honour of its people were upheld. There was no enquiry. Sung Chiao-jen's corpse, like the corpses of Chang Chen-wu and Fang Wei, became another stepping-stone on Yuan's path to dictatorship.

[IV]

Differences between South and North, exacerbated by the murder of Sung Chiao-jen, became even more acute when, on 27th April, the Peking Government signed a contract for a £25 million "Reconstruction loan" from five European banks. The act was unconstitutional. The contract was not submitted to Parliament, and Kuomintang leaders were refused admission to the bank where the negotiations were going on. They opposed the loan on the grounds that it placed China under foreign domination—and they feared that it might be used to strengthen Yuan Shih-k'ai in military action against the South. "It is the worst thing China ever did," Donald said to Morrison. "China has signed her death warrant." In Shanghai, Sun Yat-sen had told Sir Everard Fraser that if the loan were signed without being submitted to Parliament there would be civil war, and early in May he sent a manifesto—written not by Donald but by Chesney Duncan—to "the British Government, Parliament, Governments of Europe", and the Press, passionately appealing to them to stop the bankers from providing Yuan with the "sinews of war". It was clearly established, Dr Sun said, that the Peking Government was "seriously implicated" in the Sung murder:

> Consequently people are extremely indignant, and situation has become so serious that nation is on verge of most acute and dangerous

crisis yet experienced. Government conscious of its guilt and enormity of its offence . . . and perceiving that it is likely to lead to its downfall, suddenly and unconstitutionally concluded loan for £25,000,000 sterling.... This high-handed and unconstitutional action of Government instantly accentuated intense indignation which has been caused by foul murder of Sung Chiao-jen, so that at present time fury of people is worked up to white heat, and terrible convulsion appears almost inevitable. Indeed, so acute has crisis become that widespread smouldering embers may burst forth in devastating conflagration at any moment. I earnestly desire to preserve peace throughout Republic, but my efforts will be rendered ineffective if financiers will supply Peking Government with money that would, and probably will, be used in waging war against people.

If Peking Government is kept without funds there is prospect of compromise between it and people being effected, while immediate effect of liberal supply of money will probably be precipitation of terrible and disastrous conflict.

Morrison's comment on this outburst, which history has fully vindicated, was, "It had no effect whatever. The only person it damaged was Sun Yat-sen. I am assured that Sun Yat-sen now regrets it exceedingly." The loan was twelve times oversubscribed on the day of issue. Yuan had good reason to congratulate himself on the influence of his political adviser, even if he seldom took his advice.

By a happy fortuity, the day on which the contract was signed for this "infamous" loan, was the day set aside for Christian prayer on behalf of the Republic. After the Christian churches in Peking had held a united prayer service for "the Chinese nation and the National Assembly" Cabinet telegraphed all Chinese provincial governors and high officials:

Prayer is requested for the National Assembly now in session, for the newly established government, for the President yet to be elected, for the constitution of the Republic, that the Chinese Government may be recognized by the Powers, that peace may reign within our country, that strong virtuous men may be elected to office, and that the government may be established upon a strong foundation. Upon receipt of this telegram, you are requested to notify all Christian Churches in your province that April 27th has been set aside as a day of prayer for the nation. Let all take part.

In a telegram which he drafted for Reuter's about both these pious manifestations Morrison pointed out that it was the first time in history that a non-Christian nation had made such an appeal. The telegram, he noted, had an extraordinary effect in England, "even the Archbishop of Canterbury rejoicing over it". Dungate's reaction was more cynical:

Immediately I read it, I said, "That's Morrison . . . having a little joke!" I cannot help wondering at the childishness of men in believing that the Stupendous Power they name "God" could be influenced by kneeling and asking for something . . . surely even on the anthropomorphic basis this God of theirs is a better judge of the expediency of interfering than the Rector of Dorking—or even the Archbishop of Bungawallo.

There was some discussion about adequate allowances for members of the National Assembly, and the *Peking Daily News* sardonically suggested a budget based on "the present popular standard of living in society":

		$
1.	Hire of a rubber-tyred carriage	100
2.	House rent	100
3.	Salary of a Private Secretary (may be his wife's brother)	40
4.	Salary of an Accountant (may be his Concubine's brother)	50
5.	Salary of boy (may be his Mother's brother)	4
6.	Two door-keepers	8
7.	4 cooks and servants	16
8.	Two woman servants	10
9.	Hire of a new-fashion rubber-tyred carriage for 2nd wife	140
10.	Expenses for 2nd wife	100
11.	Dress and cumshaws for the driver of the carriage of 2nd wife	80
12.	Feasting the members in the hope of obtaining Speakership	200
13.	Bribery for the local press	100
14.	Feasts in the Singing House	100
15.	To buy presents for the prostitutes and their fees ..	300
16.	Cigarettes	80
17.	Whisky and other foreign wines	80
18.	Gambling	100
19.	Toilet	10
20.	Public bath, barber and other fees	30
21.	Medicines etc.	120
22.	Travelling expenses for an old uncle who went home ..	1.23
23.	Cumshaws for women servants etc.	21

$1899.23

Woodhead, of the *Peking Daily News*, had an intimate report on the senators, who had just voted themselves salaries of $6000 a year: "and who in large numbers spend most of their earnings in the brothels outside the Chien men. Every day, an 'Apostolic Bellringer' goes round the brothels and calls upon the Senators to rise and return to their duties!! This statement is announced gravely in the Native Press in praise of the Bellringer."

[V]

On 10th October 1913, Morrison stood in Peking's Hall of Great Harmony, where for centuries the Manchu Emperors had been enthroned, to see the short, wheezy, bullet-headed fifty-three-year-old Yuan Shih-k'ai installed on the Dragon Throne as first full President of the Republic of China. Yuan wore a field-marshal's uniform, with plume, knee-length boots, and sabre. Morrison wore his decoration, six feet of yellow silk ribbon embroidered with Chinese characters, and a new top-hat. Other guests wore dented billycocks. The soft hat had become a symbol of Republican fervour, and manufacturers from many countries had flooded Peking with cheap fedoras, homburgs, Borsalinos, and Stetsons:

> Raining miserable day. . . . Drove in the rain with Captain Tsao and wore my second class Chia ho but somewhat ashamed of it. At the function came across Alston acting the mountebank with Yamaza, the Japanese Minister, who is our most inveterate inebriate. Never since I came to China has the Legation been in charge of one more wholly lacking in dignity. Vast numbers were present, but no overcrowding the hall where the President read his inaugural address being one of the finest in the world. A grotesque element was the presence of Liang Shih-yi in a top hat which he retained on the back of his head throughout the ceremony.

Morrison did not philosophize on this memorable event. But Daniele Varè, the Italian chargé d'affaires, noted: "Yuan Shih-k'ai makes no mystery of his own conviction that the monarchic regime is the best for China", and in Hankow, the British Consul-General, Sir William Wilkinson, an old, informed China hand, wondered whether Yuan was to play the part of Napoleon III or of Washington?

At the march-past which followed the inauguration, Yuan Shih-k'ai invited Beilby Alston and Varè to stand in front of him. When Varè mentioned this act of courtesy to his wife she commented: "Yes, he was in mortal fear of someone throwing a bomb. You and Alston would have made a useful shield." The ceremony finished with a reception at which Yamaza was "very drunk indeed", too drunk perhaps, to appreciate "The Bill of Supper" as presented in English:

> *The food is made of swollow—The food is made of fine fish—The food is made of Shrimp—The boiling chickens—the spinach and fine meet—the cake is made of yellow hen's eggs—The boiling fish—The boiling duck—The vegetables—the canned fruit—The fruit—The Coffee*

[VI]

The Presidential election had been a farce—with tragic overtones. Voting went on all day. The first two ballots were inconclusive. The Parliament building was surrounded by thousands of armed men, variously described as "troops", members of a "Citizen's Association", and "Yuan's hired ruffians". Ostensibly their function was to keep order. Actually it was to prevent any member from leaving the building until Yuan had been declared President. Under this unusual persuasion, on the third weary ballot, Yuan was elected by 507 votes out of 759. Many members showed their contempt for the proceedings by recording votes for odd, unnominated candidates, such as the two murdered generals, and a popular Peking whore.

Once elected President, Yuan Shih-k'ai had no use for a National Assembly. On 4th November he declared the Kuomintang illegal. Police raided the houses of Kuomintang members of the Assembly and confiscated their party cards, thus expelling 438 elected representatives from Parliament. It is not surprising that Yuan Shih-k'ai was "very cheerful and confident" when Morrison saw him a few days later. "Parliament was an unworkable body," he explained. "800 men! 200 were good, 200 were passive, 400 were useless. What had they done? They had not even agreed on procedure."

[VII]

Morrison's first child, a son, was born on 31st May, and early in July was christened Ian Ernest McLeavy Morrison, though Jennie had suggested he might be called "Marco Polo". There was a small christening party ("only friends, all English except Varè") which included W. H. Donald. Ian was "as good as gold" during the ceremony, but when the Rev. Francis Norris added a homily, "the baby evidently in some mysterious way recognizing that this was not part of the service began to protest lustily". Donald was a "very depressing" guest:

> Outlook very bad. Country on the rocks. Recrimination. Distrust of the Kuomintang. Yuan doesn't employ the right men. Thinks to succeed by bribery and by forming a party consisting of the dregs of the three parties. He declares a Chinese came to him the other day and told him he had been given taels 9000 [£1125] to buy the votes of three members of the Kuomintang. . . . Donald counts among his best friends and the most loyal of the Kuomintang the three men.

A few days later Morrison talked with Yuan at length about the worsening situation, urging him to get in touch with the Kuomintang leaders and reason with them. Yuan said you could not reason with them. They were "bereft of shame". He could not understand the ingratitude of Sun Yat-sen and Huang Hsing: "Everything he could do he had done for these two men. Money. Sun 30,000 taels a month, Huang Hsing, 100,000. Former Director General of Railways, latter of Hukuang Railways. Yet they plot against him."

Nor could Yuan understand why Japan had asked him to give these two men "favourable treatment". Morrison himself had been puzzled by the reception Sun Yat-sen had been given by the Japanese in March. "No feature of Far Eastern affairs is more remarkable than the honour shown to this arch-Republican," Morrison wrote to Braham: "He has been entertained by Prince Katsura . . . by the Chief Bankers, high Court dignitaries, Cabinet Ministers, and has been treated with probably greater honour than has ever been shown before to the representative of any other country not of Princely rank. . . ."

[VIII]

Yuan had emasculated the National Assembly by murder, intimidation, and bribery. His next move against the Kuomintang was to replace the three Southern military governors who were still loyal to it by his own men. This sparked off a recrudescence of civil war. On 12th July fighting broke out again between Northern and Southern troops in Kiangsi, and the "Second Revolution" had begun. It lasted little more than two months. "The rebellion is now nearly finished," Yuan Shih-k'ai told Morrison on 13th August. Sun Yat-sen, Huang Hsing, and "other professional agitators" had fled to Japan, and Chang Hsun's pigtailed troops were driving swiftly on Nanking, which they captured and ruthlessly sacked early in September. With the fall of Nanking the second revolution collapsed.

Japan, hoping to strengthen its grip on a China progressively weakened by internal conflict, had aided the rebels in many ways. Tsai Ting-kan told Morrison the Japanese had supplied arms, fought beside the rebels, attempted to torpedo a Northern cruiser, and to bomb the Kin-siang arsenal from a balloon. Japanese papers headlined rebel "victories", violently abused the Northern leaders, and praised the rebels in terms that sometimes were a little extravagant. Thus Li Lieh-chun, one of the deposed military governors, was said to have "the voice of a bull, the beauty of a virgin, the appearance of an angel, and the wisdom of the ancient sages".

"I am sending home a message to the European papers regarding Japan, for it is only by the influence of public opinion . . . that Japan can be compelled to alter the policy upon which she is now embarking in China," Morrison wrote to Tsai Ting-kan on 28th September:

> The growth of feeling against Japan among all countries is really a marked feature. The Prime Minister of Australia in a public speech has declared that in the event of war between Japan and America, Australia would range herself on the side of America. Australians view with alarm the aggressive movement of Japan in China, for such movements interfere with trade and commerce in which British, and to an increasing extent the Australian section of the British people, are vitally interested.

In the telegram, which appeared in the London *Daily Telegraph* next day, Morrison said:

The Chinese believe that Japan is seeking a pretext for adventures on the mainland, with a view to diverting Japanese public opinion from internal affairs, which visitors from Japan state are becoming more serious, owing to the growth of a spirit of independence among the young Japanese, who desire a number of reforms, notably the extension of the present limited franchise.

The question deeply affects British interests, as the Japanese activities are directed principally to the Yangtze valley, where adventurous Japanese, during the recent rebellion, secured from the rebel leaders important contracts and concessions.

Japan is now increasing her troops at various points in China, particularly at Hankow, for which town 750 troops are now en route; and her general policy, bordering on aggression, bears out the Anglo-Chinese apprehensions.

When it was reported that Sun Yat-sen had left Japan for Hong Kong, Morrison wrote to Sir Edward Grey urging that the British Government should not allow Sun to land on British territory because he was engaged "in open rebellion against a country friendly to England". And when rewards of 100,000 taels each were offered by the Peking Government for Huang Hsing, Ch'en Ch'i-mei, and other Southern leaders, dead or alive, Morrison wrote to Tsai Ting-kan:

So far Sun Yat-sen's name has not been mentioned. You know nothing kills like ridicule. Would it not make Sun Yat-sen look ridiculous if a reward were offered for him not of a high amount, but of a very small amount, say $150 Mexican? Such an announcement would excite amusement all over the world and would show contempt which the Government have for this misguided man.

One can understand Morrison's contempt for the woolly minded Sun Yat-sen, whose windy inadequacies were apparent even to those who, like Donald, had actively supported his cause. One can understand also Morrison's confidence in the strong-minded Yuan Shih-k'ai as the only possible leader of a wobbly Republic, a confidence which most of Morrison's colleagues shared and which contemporary historians endorse. Dr Jerome Ch'en, for instance, in his uncompromisingly critical biography of Yuan says: "To be perfectly fair to Yuan, we must admit that at the beginning of 1912 there was no one else who had the slightest chance of holding the country together. . . . Upon assuming the Presidency his foremost duties were to maintain the unity of the nation and to strengthen his control over it."

Yuan had inherited from the Manchus and the revolution, chaos and bankruptcy. He could hope to obtain foreign recognition, and the foreign money which the country desperately needed, only by creating an integrated and disciplined China. "But," says Dr Ch'en, "he made grave mistakes in the process, in handling the opposition and in refusing to accept a limit to his personal power." And the incorruptible Morrison watched Yuan make these "mistakes", which involved the use of murder, intimidation, and bribery as political weapons, without comment. It would not perhaps be fair to say he condoned them. He certainly did not criticize them.

[IX]

Towards the end of the year Morrison again thought of selling his library. In a "private and confidential" letter to the Japanese Minister Ijuin he wrote:

> More than a year and a half ago Sir John Jordan told me that you had spoken to him with regard to the possibility of my library being acquired for Japan. . . . At that time my library was not catalogued. Since I entered the Chinese service, I have, with the assistance of three secretaries, worked incessantly at the index. It is now complete in 1600 typewritten pages. . . . In the library also are many MSS., as for example the MS. Journals of Lord Macartney's Embassy to China, and I have also catalogued my prints and engravings of personages and scenes and views in China, a collection which has been described as unique. . . .
>
> Although my library has been kept up to date, and I have continued to add to it almost daily, I find the work taxes my time and energies to a degree that I am no longer able to sustain. . . . I have been asked if I would prepare to sell . . . to an American institute and I have answered in the affirmative. But . . . I would prefer . . . to see my library permanently installed in the Far East. Asked by the American delegates what value I placed on it, I replied £40,000. . . . But if it were possible for the library to be retained in the Far East, where it would serve to some degree in recalling my association with the Far East, I would be prepared to part with it for a less sum. . . .

He noted in his diary that in fifteen months he had spent over £1500 on books. "From this date I cease this hobby; it is beyond my means."

Morrison finished his diary for 1913 with a New Year resolution to make friends of his enemies "Fraser—Bland—Chirol and others" and to complete his "Reminiscences", which had now reached 1898. His last note for the year was another gloomy reflection on life in China:

> China lightly taxed! No statement could be more misleading. Lightly taxed? What return do the taxpayers get for their money? Do they get effective police protection, a disciplined army, good roads and bridges, cheap railways and telegraphs, stable exchange or government notes that are redeemable? Are they provided with good sanitation, with drains, with protection from unhealthy occupations? Is slavery abolished? Judge China by the return given to the people for the taxes they pay and you will find it is the most heavily taxed

country in the world. Are broken locks repaired on the waterways, or embankments maintained? or rivers dredged or canals kept open? What a sight it is to see the herds of tax-gatherers at the *likin* barriers or at the locks on the canals, sitting idly but preying on the traffic which they do nothing to facilitate.

[X]

Many of Morrison's house-guests bored him profoundly. A notable exception was the feminist writer and traveller, Violet Markham, who arrived in Peking with an introduction from Mackenzie King. "I believe her to be one of the great women of England," he wrote, and Morrison, after meeting her, agreed. Miss Markham was a granddaughter of the architect of the Crystal Palace, Sir Joseph Paxton. "At the delightful house of the Morrisons one met everyone worth meeting in Peking," she wrote in a book of reminiscences published in 1943, and she recalled the condition of China thirty years before:

> The military governors of the provinces . . . each backed by a considerable provincial army constituted local problems of a formidable kind for the central government. Yuan Shih-k'ai, himself an autocrat in a precarious position, was naturally dependent on the goodwill of these minor rulers. Here was the germ of the desolating private armies which laid waste the unhappy country and terrorized its inhabitants. Yuan, like many men who have reached power by dubious methods, found himself weighed by the necessity of placating sinister interests and persons who contributed to the maintenance of an insecure position. . . . Corruption—it bored like a mole through the whole of Chinese life as I knew it. No one regarded it as a vice. Exploitation of a position of trust was to the Chinese a commonplace of everyday and conveyed no sense whatever of moral shortcomings. As for the corruption of the official class, it never entered a Chinaman's head to criticize the system of "squeeze" which permeates Far Eastern life from highest to lowest. This strange race is as paradoxical about honesty as about every other matter connected with them.

Her summing-up showed remarkable prescience:

> Little wonder that Communism has captured China. Every condition exists of poverty, want, and distress, conducive to that evil growth. But the Chinaman remains a sturdy and passionate individualist, and whatever home-grown variety of Communism he may adopt, he will, I think, be difficult to regiment from Moscow or any distant centre.

CHAPTER ELEVEN

[I]

YUAN SHIH-K'AI had disposed of Parliament, but he still had many problems. One was his old comrade-in-arms, General Chang Hsun. In 1900, Chang has efficiently carried out Yuan's orders to suppress the Boxers in Shantung and, as commander-in-chief in the Lower Yangtze, had just as efficiently crushed the second revolution, for which he was richly rewarded with the governorship of Kiangsu. He was a formidable brute with simple tastes; he liked killing, whoring, drinking, and making money. His army, which he regarded as a personal possession, was a considerable force of tough soldiers whose loyalty was solely to their general—as long as they were paid—and Chang's loyalty was not to Yuan but to the fallen Manchus. He had little sympathy with the Republic, a fact which he and his followers demonstrated by retaining their queues; they were known as "The Pigtailed Army". Yuan was afraid to disband them, though Morrison repeatedly urged him to do so, but under pressure from Japan, which was annoyed because some of the pigtailed warriors had carelessly killed three Japanese citizens in their rape of Nanking, Yuan transferred Chang to the Inspectorship of the Yangtze. Though this job had plenty of pickings, it was not as lucrative, or as exalted, as the governorship, and Chang was bitterly resentful.

When the Japanese were asking for Chang's removal, Morrison had written to Tsai Ting-kan:

> . . . Certainly to an outsider it would seem as though it would be of great benefit to China if Chang Hsun could be removed. He is the greatest danger at present existing in China. It is awful to think what suffering his savage followers have inflicted upon the innocent people of Nanking. The Legations view with anxiety the refusal of Chang Hsun to allow the Republican Flag to be hoisted. They fear that this is but a prelude to another outbreak of civil war. The reports from Nanking are simply harrowing.

"Things here are not doing well," Morrison told Ohl, who had returned to America. "What to do with the army is the most serious problem with which China is presented at the present time. All her earnings are being poured into the maw of the army. To keep these hordes would tax the resources of a rich State, while the burden in China is almost insupportable."

Yuan's financial problems had been little alleviated by the controversial £25 million loan. After meeting immediate liabilities, he was left with only £8.5 million—for which China was committed to repay, within forty-seven years, over £42 million.

"Occasionally I think I have some influence with the President," Morrison wrote to Henry Cockburn, who was then in retirement in England, at the end of January. "But I have many disappointments and I cannot see that the Chinese of the Republic are very different from the Chinese that we knew 15 years ago." In his diary he noted disgustedly that he had been kept in ignorance of many important government deals, including a prospecting concession to Standard Oil: "On no financial matter have I been consulted . . . nor are any inquiries addressed to me as to the standing of foreign concession hunters. My opinion in fact is not asked about anything more important than the shape of the President's hat." The last reference was not frivolous. A memorandum from Tsai Ting-kan addressed to Morrison reads: "Can you send your Russian hat over to be shown to the President's hatter as a sample? I shall see that it shall not be soiled in any way."

"Feeling much dispirited with everything and everybody", Morrison wrote early in March, and a few weeks later: "Am now weary of collecting books and would like to sell my library and be quit of it all! Oh God, let me sell it quickly! so that I may be independent and can go to Canada."

He gave no sign of this inner disquiet when he was interviewed by an Australian journalist, W. W. Rock, for the Melbourne magazine *Life*. Rock described him as a "tall-figured, fair-haired man . . . with a curious 'far-away' expression in his eyes":

> There is something typically Australian about Dr Morrison. A quiet man, somewhat reserved, he gives one the impression of a scholar rather than a statesman. He greets a roomful of visitors cordially, and relapses into silence. It is a mixed company—an American businessman, a railway engineer, a missionary, a war-correspondent. . . . They do the talking. . . . Beyond a question interposed here and there, Dr Morrison does not figure in the conversation.

Under Rock's questioning, Morrison discussed the Republic. Yuan Shih-k'ai, by general consent, was "the right man in the right place". There had been some mistakes and some failures under the new regime, but the second revolution—which Morrison referred to euphemistically as "the recent disturbances in Nanking"—was due to "professional agitators—men who have been associated for years with revolution and rebellion. . . ." Every conferable honour had been shown by Yuan to Sun Yat-sen, but recently Sun had opposed Yuan, and in a manifesto had called on him to resign. If Yuan resigned, the country would be thrown into anarchy. Yuan's party aimed at a Republic incorporating what was best in the American and French Republics, with some of the constitution of Switzerland and with the freedom provided by so many of the institutions of Great Britain. "The constitution is being drafted by a committee of both Houses, a distinguished American Professor, Mr Frank Goodnow, having been engaged by the Government to assist them in their deliberations," Morrison said. He did not say that Goodnow, like himself, was suffering acutely from frustration.

Early in April, Morrison briefly visited Shanghai, Canton, Hong Kong, and Hankow. In "the capital city of central China, one of the great cities of the world," Hankow, as he walked round to the Consul-General, he came across a dead body "lying uncared for in a scene of filth among stenches that were overpowering":

> Hovels with grass-thatched roofs inferior even to the sheds inhabited by the Lolo savages in Yunnan. No roads, no drainage. Nothing in China gives foreigners more ground for contempt of Chinese barbarity than the conditions here obtaining alongside beautiful clean healthy well-paved, well-drained, lit, foreign settlements . . . it is such sights as these which make it impossible for foreign countries to regard this country which permits such horrible scenes as on a level even with the lowest Western Civilization. To talk of the abolition of extra-territorial rights, of treatment on a footing of equality while such conditions exist, is mere waste of words. Remedy is at hand. Sanitation drainage lighting. . . . Until these conditions are removed there is daily danger that the filthy territory may be forcibly occupied by foreign troops. At any time it would be easy to find an excuse.

When he got back to Peking, Morrison told Yuan Shih-k'ai what he had seen in Hankow. The President "seemed shocked", and asked for a full report as soon as possible.

[II]

Change continued to sweep through Printing House Square. Northcliffe had reduced the price of *The Times* to a penny. Braham had quarrelled with the management and accepted the editorship of the Sydney *Daily Telegraph*. Wickham Steed had replaced him. Lionel James, too, had resigned: "You will remember N's promises in which you so bravely interested yourself," he wrote to Morrison in April. "Well, none of them showed any signs of materializing":

> . . . the state of the office became worse and worse, owing to the importation of N's 30/- a week men. . . . I delivered my ultimatum and walked out. I may speak with some bias about P.H. Square but I have reason. I have done about 11 campaigns for them and countless other missions and have never on one single occasion been beaten by a rival. . . . I am then told that "the paper cannot afford to pay me

a higher wage" or redeem Arthur Walter's pledge to me that I should qualify for a pension. Some dirty little fawning guttersnipe who lives upon N's love of adulation, whose origin was a cable clerk in the American Cable Company, told me that the policy of the NEW TIMES was "what men could do in the future, not what they had done in the past". This finished me, and I never darkened P.H. Sq.'s doorway again. Fortunately I was in the position of being independent of N. and the whole of the miserable set of puppets that are engaged in besmirching the old traditions of *The Times* with the cheap vulgarity of the *Daily Mail*.

"I was lucky I left the paper when I did," Morrison wrote back, "otherwise I might find myself at the present moment with a family to support and nothing to support them on."

Jennie had taken the baby to England for inspection by her parents, and Morrison wrote to Tsai Ting-kan at the end of May: "I think the time has come when I ought to go home to England in order to see what can be done to remove false impressions . . . with regard to China, and the policy of the President." It would be wise for him to travel simply as a private citizen bringing back his wife and child, not in any official capacity. On his way back he could study the Asiatic immigration question in Canada and British Columbia, and make discreet enquiries about the revolutionaries in Japan. In his formal request for the President's permission, Morrison dipped his spade deep into a pot of Oriental unction:

I make this application with the more confidence because the situation now seems to be better than it has ever been since I first came to China. Under Your Excellency's wise guidance, tranquillity has been established throughout the country, the financial position is one which enables the future to be faced without misgiving, railway and industrial development are being everywhere encouraged, while the relations of China with foreign countries are characterized by quite unusual friendliness.

Not to be outshone in civility, His Excellency replied:

Since the commencement of your duties you have within your power rendered valuable assistance and have eminently shown diligence and strenuous work. Such services are highly appreciated. . . . Your request is accordingly granted and you are hereby granted 3 months' leave, at the expiration of which you are expected to come back to China . . . so that you may continue to give me assistance and advice. . . .

[III]

"Arrived in London yesterday, same afternoon interviewed by *The Times*," Morrison wrote to Yuan Shih-k'ai on 26th June. "Many other correspondents sought interview with me. Immediate result of my interviews published in papers of estimated aggregate circulation of not less

297

than 3,500,000 has been a rise in all Chinese securities . . . amounting in all to some millions of dollars. Rise would have been more satisfactory had it not been for the disastrous news. . . . of the mutiny of the troops at Kalgan; the cruelty shown to women and children and the escape of the mutineers without punishment."

Once more Morrison's roseate picture of China ignored some of the more unpleasant realities, though he assured Yuan that he had said nothing except what he believed to be the truth. Unfortunately he had told *The Times* and other papers that tranquillity was firmly established throughout China—almost at the very moment when Kalgan was being looted by some of Yuan's regular troops. J. O. P. Bland was quick to point this out in an article in the *Observer* titled "The Chinese Paradox". He also compared Morrison's statement that the seventy members of Yuan's Council represented "every shade of opinion in China" including "the pick of the Young China party" with W. H. Donald's more accurate description of the Council, published in *The Times* a few days later, as "solely a Presidential organ . . . a regular mobilization of the Old Brigade", on which "Young China"—Sun Yat-sen's followers—had no representation at all.

Lovat Fraser, who was writing *The Times*' leaders on the Far East, showed Bland's article to his editor, and to Wickham Steed. They both agreed that "a steady but discriminating support" should continue to be given to Yuan Shih-k'ai. "Please understand quite clearly that *The Times* does not wish to attack the present administration in China, and does not care a straw about any deviations from the strict 'constitutional' path which the President may have found necessary," Lovat Fraser wrote to Morrison. "This attitude may not prevent occasional criticisms of particular acts or minor lapses of your Government, but the *general* support will, I am assured, continue to be given." Morrison elaborated the case for Yuan Shih-k'ai in an address to the London Chamber of Commerce. Many members of both Houses of Parliament were in the audience.

"The prevalent view held here seems to be that China . . . is at present in a state of anarchy, the country fast drifting to perdition under the regime of an autocratic dictator of unbridled ambition," Morrison said. "Such a view seems to me to be in direct conflict with all the evidence available to me." He presented the "evidence"—financial, economic, and diplomatic—at considerable length, and offered a carefully laundered picture of Yuan's smudgy exercises in republicanism:

There was a parliament in Peking, consisting of a Senate and a House of Representatives, largely composed of students who had no administrative experience (how could they have administrative experience under the Manchus?), who had an imperfect knowledge of their own country; but who had imbibed advanced ideas of government in Japan, America, and England. Then the trouble began. A committee of forty members selected by Parliament was chosen to draft a Constitution for China in place of the Provisional Constitution previously drawn up in Nanking. All advanced students, these men, with eager impetuosity, determined to leap from an archaic autocracy to the most advanced form of modern Parliamentary Government. They ignored the conditions of China. No one disputes their patriotism, but they did not realize that they were representatives not of the Chinese as they are, but of the Chinese as they might hope to become in the future. They devised a Constitution stripping the executive of all authority, and placing paramount power in the hands of Parliament. Although China had engaged the services of two great Constitutional jurists, Professor Ariga of Japan, and Professor Goodnow of Columbia University, these distinguished men were not even consulted by the Committee, whose deliberations they had been engaged to assist. It was enough that they had been engaged by the President, and, therefore, they were regarded as suspects. A climax was reached when, the Constitution nearing completion, the delegates of the President were even refused a hearing. Every kind of interference was devised to thwart the Executive. . . . A revolt, organized by the irreconcilables, broke out, and there was a definite policy to separate North from South.

But the President had acted with restraint and only struck when he was compelled to strike:

He dismissed the rebel party, suspended Parliament, and broke up the Provincial Assemblies. Then he summoned a body of seventy picked men to whom he submitted the Constitution as drawn up in Nanking, and subsequently modified in Peking, and called upon them, with the help of Professors Ariga and Goodnow, to amend it. That amended Constitution, consisting of sixty-eight articles, is the present Provisional Constitution of China. . . . By this Constitution the President holds office for five years. The President has pledged himself to this reformed Government. There is nothing in the past action of the President which should lead us to consider that he will not faithfully fulfil his pledges. Under this Constitution the powers given to the elected President are much the same as the powers given to the Emperor of Japan.

In his peroration Morrison referred to recent English Press comment on affairs in China. The "most disastrous incident" of Yuan's life, "the one which he recalled with the greatest regret", was the looting of Peking by his picked troops in February 1912:

This incident shook his prestige at home and abroad. Yet now I read in a high-class English magazine . . . that the general belief in England is that this mutiny was deliberately planned by Yuan Shih-k'ai to overawe the Southern delegates. This seems to me to be the limit of extravagant hypothesis.

Some of Morrison's listeners may have thought he had come pretty close to the limit of extravagant apologetics.

Mr C. Birch Crisp, his eye on more loans to China, not only congratulated Morrison on his "admirable address" to a "splendid audience" but paid for it to be published in full, as a news item, in the *Daily Telegraph*, which had a circulation of 200,000. "Your address will, of course, raise the question of what steps China will take to raise Funds to provide for the repayment of loans falling due this year, and next in connection with the Boxer indemnity," he wrote. Morrison tried to follow these steps, and found they led to utter confusion. There were about twenty-eight Chinese loan contracts being hawked about London, some, as Morrison pointed out in a letter to Yuan Shih-k'ai, at exorbitant rates of interest and by men of very dubious standing: a former clerk to the American consulate, a Tientsin dairyfarmer, a fourth engineer of the Shanghai municipality. "The British bankers think that China must be in desperate financial straits to resort to such extraordinary methods which brings ridicule upon the Government of China," Morrison wrote. Equally ridiculous was the fact that China had two representatives in London, a minister and a financial commissioner, neither of whom knew what the other was doing. "Such action conveys the impression that there is no united Government in China, and that one half of the people have no trust in the other half," Morrison told the President.

Pursuing financial phantoms, discussing loans with the Foreign Office, and Tibet with the India Office, giving interviews, and answering the usual crop of letters left Morrison little time for relaxation. "I am having no holiday whatever. In fact, I am working from early morning to night," he wrote to Tsai Ting-kan, who had now acquired the title of "Admiral" (China had thirty Admirals and five ships of war).

There was the usual queue of job- and concession-hunters: engineers, prospectors, former servicemen and civil servants, inventors, cranks and missionaries; a retired Chief Justice of Sierra Leone, a man with a sound-locating system for the minuscule Chinese Navy; another with a new system of wireless telegraphy. Morrison was asked to address the Ethological Society on the Chinese character, and to write an article for *Great Thoughts*. He attended many formal dinners. At one, given by Douglas Sladen, he met a number of popular writers: Jerome K. Jerome, "Miss Braddon" and her son, W. B. Maxwell; Elinor Mordaunt, "who wrote that magnificent Victorian novel *Lu of the Ranges*"; and Maxwell Gray, who wrote the Victorian best-seller, *The Silence of Dean Maitland*. At another, given by Lady St Helier, the guests included Kitchener, home on leave from Egypt, and Lord Charles Beresford, "very small and round, shrinking up". Lady Bryce invited him to breakfast at 8.45 a.m. at 3 Buckingham Gate, and the seventy-six-year-old Viscount Bryce, a former Regius Professor of Civil Law, Irish Secretary, and Ambassador to Washington, "ate ravenously", but discussed China's provisional constitution with perspicuity. He thought it right that the constitution should put stress on the executive rather than on the legislature, and said Yuan Shih-k'ai should be warned by the history of Diaz, who never provided for a successor. . . .

Morrison was asked to tea at the House of Commons by a fellow Australian, Colonel Arthur Lynch, the member for West Clare, who had known him at the Melbourne University ("I remember seeing you running in the mile race"). Lynch, a physician, electrical engineer, and poet, was perhaps the only Australian graduate ever indicted for high treason. During the South African war he had commanded an Irish Brigade on the Boer side. He was now secretary of a "China Group . . . established to watch the interests of the Young Republic. . . ." Mrs Sydney Webb invited Morrison to dine quietly with herself and her husband. "You will be amused to hear that we have embarked on a journalistic venture since we saw you!" she wrote. The venture was the *New Statesman*.

He entrusted an "extremely interesting" Chinese MS. to Laurence Binyon, assistant keeper in the British Museum, who promised to treat it "with due reverence". He went to the zoo and to the theatre, and between assorted commitments he found time to take five shooting lessons at the West London Shooting Grounds, Ealing W., at a cost of 25s. a lesson ("includes 100 cartridges and 100 birds each lesson, use of gun and motor to and from station").

[IV]

England in July 1914 was more interested in Ireland than in China. The Home Rule Bill had passed its third reading in May, and Ulster was threatening to revolt rather than accept Home Rule. The question everyone was asking when Morrison had lunch with J. B. Capper at Mrs Moberly Bell's on 15th July was whether the King would grant his assent to the Bill? Capper thought he must. Mrs Bell said, "To sign means civil war! It will mean the end of his Kingship." Preparations were being made in England to billet refugees from Ireland, and the assassination of the Archduke Francis Ferdinand, which had taken place on 28th June, did not seem very important.

Hutton, not long before, had made a characteristic comment on the Irish crisis:

> The Protestants in Ulster are very tough people. Fanatical anti-Roman Catholicism. If they had sufficient education, reading and insight, they would know that no religion is to be feared now. Religion in all western Europe is declining rapidly. Every week one could come into contact with printed references to scepticism, religious apathy, and suchlike. And parsons, bishops and church societies are still bickering about dogmas. Good Heavens! What better evidence could one demand than the shakiness of dogmas 1914 years after the birth of Christ? Shelley said, "If God has spoken, why is the world not convinced?" . . . . The Priest as a rule is a self-satisfied ignoramus.

But Ulster and Home Rule were both forgotten a few weeks later as war swept across Europe like a grass fire.

Morrison had lunch with Gwynne at the Bath Club on 27th July, the day when war between Austria and Serbia began. Gwynne said the British people did not realize that Britain was morally bound to go to the assistance of France—that she had committed herself much further than was generally known. He had frequently urged the Government to take the people into its confidence. "Can war be restricted?" Morrison asked in his diary. "I believe so despite the panic in the Bourses. Germany will scare off Russia. Russia does not want war. Whatever happens England must stand aside and be the honest broker."

Gwynne asked Morrison if it was true that Kitchener had been offered a position in the Chinese Army:

I said quite untrue. Gwynne told me Kitchener had endeavoured to induce him to make representation to the Government to secure his services, saying it would be a loss if they were to go to another country. Pressed for facts, Kitchener said China had asked him to reorganize the army. Gwynne says he always thought Kitchener was lying and was glad to have his impression confirmed.

Next day Morrison lunched with the Amerys, the Hon. Aubrey Herbert, and George Lloyd, of Lloyd's Bank. All agreed that Germany did not want war. Someone quoted Chirol as saying that Northcliffe was mad, but not sufficiently so to justify his being put under restraint.

On 1st August, Germany dismayed the prophets of the lunch-table by declaring war on Russia, and next day Morrison noted: "Papers selling like hot cakes. Mobilization of Fleet. Germany Siezes British Ships. 20,000 Germans Repulsed (this is a fake). Germany Invades France at 3 Points. Luxembourg Seized (and this is regarded as most serious)."

At this point the Great War disappears from Morrison's London diary. He does not mention Britain's declaration of war on 4th August, and his entry the following day consists of only one line: "Baron de Reuter says *The Times* is losing £10,000 a month." On 13th August, with Jennie and the baby, he sailed for Quebec.

Before leaving England he wrote to Lord Ronaldshay:

The President has telegraphed for me. . . . I am sorry that there will be no time for me to see you. . . . I am also sorry not to have seen Sir Edward Grey. . . . Serious alarm is naturally being felt by Yuan Shih-k'ai, and in view of the certain shrinkage of the Customs revenue, the financial outlook is black indeed. He fears specially Japan but I can see no reason for his fears. I will call at Japan on my way as it is his wish.

A prominent official in our Foreign Service tells me that Beilby Alston is to be our next Minister to Peking. I daresay you know him. He is a pleasant Society man, but . . . in my 17 years in China he is the British Official in charge of our Legation in Peking who has created the greatest feeling of discontent among the English community. He was wholly indifferent to his work, took no interest in it whatever. It was estimated in Peking that he spent 5 hours a day in the company of a lady and I believe it was the universal opinion, even among the Legation people, that he was the most incompetent noodle that had ever been given a post of responsibility. I have sometimes thought it would be a wise thing if the British Government were to appoint to the Legation a man of Indian experience. I do not know McMahon but I should have thought a man of that type, or Sir Francis Younghusband, who has a knowledge of the frontier question, might render important service in such an extremely difficult post as Peking will be for the next few years.

I believe that the British community in China . . . would regard the appointment of an amiable nonentity like Alston . . . as a calamity. . . .

What I think is chiefly to be feared in China is the scarcity of money, the inability to pay troops, and the consequent mutiny of those troops.

[V]

On 14th August there was a report on board Morrison's ship that the Germans had been caught between Liège and the French, and 125,000 slain. "I fear despite reports of German reverses that the Germans are steadily advancing to battle and that another and greater Waterloo will be fought near Waterloo," Morrison commented. "The Germans are prepared to sacrifice men by the hundreds of thousands. How long will Germany stand this?" All the passengers became prophets. "Belgium will receive Luxembourg." "France will be given Alsace and Lorraine." "There will be a Revolution in Germany and a Republic will be established." Jennie's soothsaying was succint: "It is the end of the Hohenzollerns," she said.

On 2nd September they picked up a message saying that Japan had declared war on Germany and that Tsingtao was blockaded. One of Morrison's fellow-passengers, Captain McCarthy, who had been in Port Arthur during the siege and was going to St Petersburg as naval attaché, was deeply suspicious of Japan's motives. He thought her intrusion "indefensible". It was indicative, he said, of what America could expect in the Philippines should she ever be in trouble. And what was to prevent the Japanese ousting the Germans from New Guinea and taking their place?

CHAPTER TWELVE

[I]

A WEEK after his return to Peking, Morrison was awarded the First Class Order of the Excellent Crop, and the Home Office, Whitehall, advised him that on payment of ten shillings, as required by the Stamp Act 1891 (54 and 55 Vict. c.39), His Majesty King George V would permit Dr Morrison to wear the appropriate insignia. No higher Chinese distinction could have been conferred on him—but he was still denied the confidence of the man who conferred it and whom he was paid to advise. Soon after Britain's declaration of war on 4th August, Yuan Shih-k'ai had approached Sir John Jordan, the doyen of the diplomatic corps, with an offer to provide 50,000 troops to assist in the capture of Tsingtao, Germany's headquarters in Shantung province. Sir John, with an irresponsibility explicable only in terms of senility, refused the offer without even consulting his colleagues in the French, Russian, and Japanese legations. (When the Allied ministers heard of it for the first time more than a year later they were, not surprisingly, outspokenly indignant.) Sir John advised Yuan to keep quiet and do nothing. It was a serious rebuff to the President, involving him in great "loss of face", and a gross diplomatic blunder. But Morrison was told nothing of the incident when he called on Yuan to report on his London mission. "China," he noted, "has gone mad about neutrality."

The Japanese Army was using its operations against Tsingtao as a cover for extending its grip on China. Despite Chinese protests, it had taken over the Shantung railway outside the German-leased territory on the grounds of "military necessity", and pushed on to Tsinanfu. Obata, the Counsellor of the Japanese Legation in Peking, told Morrison that the Japanese Government had not wished to occupy the railway, but that the military were too strong. "The scent of battle was in the air and the military could not be restrained," he said. Disquieting reports came from Shantung of Japanese atrocities ("maltreating Chinese, robbing them, raping women, burning furniture to warm their stoves"). But Yuan, "very wisely" in Morrison's opinion, said that though the Japanese wanted trouble, China would do nothing to irritate them. He professed "the most hearty and sincere distrust of Japan conceivable".

When Wellington Koo, the Chinese Minister in Washington, said Japanese action was a "humiliation to China", Morrison used his words as the text for a private homily on China's shortcomings—a homily somewhat at variance with the messianic sermons he had delivered a few months before in London, "Strain at a gnat and swallow a camel," he wrote. And:

It is a humiliation to have a German naval port in Shantung and a German controlled railway!

It is a humiliation to have foreigners protected by ex-territoriality no confidence being felt in Chinese administration of justice.

It is a humiliation to permit domestic slavery—the only country in the world where traffic is permitted in its own flesh and blood.

It is a humiliation to be unable to borrow money unless foreigners control the expenditure thereof.

It is a humiliation to have to get railways built under foreign supervision no trust being possible in China's good faith.

It is a humiliation to know that the only charitable medical work done in China is done by foreign missionaries.

It is a humiliation to know that in China no protection is given to the subject, no guarantee of law and order, no roads or railways but are foreign built, no protection is given to the worker in dangerous trades, no protection to child life, no hospitals for the insane.

It is a humiliation to have to extract evidence by torture.

[II]

Morrison was not surprised to learn that China's financial position was bad. Yuan told him that his revenue was $2 million a month—about £195,000 sterling—and his expenditure three times as much. Guy Hillier confirmed the fact that China was "desperately hard up". It was confirmed ever more convincingly for Morrison when his own salary fell into arrears. Yet Yuan, he noted, was squandering money on preparations for a celebration on 10th October, the anniversary of his election, and had recently added ten girls to his harem, bringing the total strength to twenty-four. It was reported that there was much quarrelling among the young ladies.

When he was asked to write an article on China's finances for the *Manchester Guardian*, Morrison refused, not because the pay was poor ("£2/2/- per thousand"), but because the new Minister for Finance, Chou Hsuei-hei, had reverted to "evil old mandarin methods" and was replacing competent officers with incompetent friends. "As I am in the service of the Chinese Government and render them all the help I can, it would be unseemly to attack them in an English newspaper." He spent "an evening of self-reproach" for his wasted time "in the service of this rotten people" and added a few more lines of condemnation:

> Extraordinary slovenliness of Chinese.
> Absence of discipline.
> Absence of pride in personal appearance.
> Universal slackness and inefficiency.
> Lack of restraint. Lack of patriotism more marked than before.
> Refusal to look facts in the face. Pusillanimity and fear of accepting responsibility.

Again and again he brooded on his "anomalous position" with the "rotten Government" to which he had bound himself for £3500 a year as "political Adviser without office":

> I have gained in health perhaps I am better in pocket I have greatly added to my library and brought it well up to date but I have lost in influence and in prestige and I fear sometimes in self-respect—though I am nowise deceived myself. Yuan now wants me to prepare the way for China's admission to the Conference after the war. . . . What case can she make out for herself? What claims has she got on the world's consideration? Has she zealously carried out her treaty obligations? Has she effected any reform in her administration?

China's expert advisers continued to gnaw their nails in frustration. George Padoux, who was being paid £4000 a year with "absolutely nothing to do", told Morrison he would have returned to France but for the war. He was an expert on matters such as extra-territoriality and neutrality, but his advice was never asked. Professor Goodnow had disgustedly left before the end of his contract and had been replaced by William Franklin Willoughby, a Princeton man "who closely resembled Woodrow Wilson".

[III]

The first week of January 1915 found Morrison in Newchang, Manchuria, at the Astor House Hotel, where English and Japanese hospitality blended harmoniously. The dining-room offered Barley Soup, Fried Fish, Jugged Hare, Braised Beef, Roast Mutton and Mint Sauce, and Steamed Bread and Currant Pudding; the bedroom, "a nice Japanese girl" who visited hotel guests for a fee of fifteen shillings a night.

On his way back to Peking, Morrison attended a performance of the Tientsin Amateur Dramatic Club, in aid of Belgian refugees. A tenor sang "Gunga Din", a baritone "Somewhere a Voice is Calling", and a conjurer manipulated cards and goldfish. . . . But the big event was the final pageant, "Song of the Allies", in which Miss Winsome Hunt, representing Japan, sang:

Japan as Britain's Ally
In keeping with her solemn vow,
Has so assisted the issue
By sweeping them out of Tsingtao.

Unfortunately, both the genuineness of the Japanese Alliance and the validity of the Japanese vow were soon to become suspect.

[IV]

When Morrison called on Yuan Shih-k'ai to discuss his report on Japanese trade in Manchuria—which consisted mainly of opium, gambling, pseudo-aphrodisiacs, and prostitution—he found the President "extraordinarily cheerful". Yuan discussed finance and collieries, and asked Morrison how England regarded the extension of Japanese influence in the Yangtze? The Japanese, he said, had swelled heads and caused him endless trouble. But he made no mention of the fact that two days before, Japan, an allegedly friendly power, had served on him a peremptory series of demands—virtually an ultimatum.

What Dr Ch'en calls "the most surreptitious diplomatic onslaught in history" took place at 3 p.m. on 18th January, when the Japanese Minister to Peking, Hioki, presented a document from his Government, not, as protocol required, to the Chinese Foreign Office, but to Yuan Shih-k'ai himself. This notorious document, which has become known as the "Twenty-one Demands", was on paper watermarked with dreadnoughts and machine-guns, a fact which to the Chinese had sinister significance.

The demands, which Morrison described as "worse than many presented by a victor to his vanquished enemy", would, in effect, have reduced China to a vassal state. They gave Japan control of Shantung, Southern Manchuria, and Inner Mongolia, and the exclusive right to establish naval bases and harbours in Fukien Province, dominating the mouth of the Yangtze. They established Japanese control of China's biggest arsenal and steel works. China was to entrust the training of her Army and Navy to Japan, to employ Japanese political and financial advisers, to place her principal police forces under joint Japanese control, to buy munitions from Japan, to allow Japanese schools and missionaries in China, and to grant Japan important railway rights. Hammering the table with his walking-stick, Hioki warned Yuan Shih-k'ai that the demands must be accepted immediately and that absolute secrecy about them must be maintained. Particularly, no disclosure was to be made to Britain—Japan's ally. Disclosure would be *casus belli*. "Secrecy is difficult to keep in Peking," Morrison wrote. "Almost immediately it had become known that the Japanese Minister, under threat of punishment . . . had made very serious demands on China. Disclosure was China's one safeguard and yet it was with the greatest difficulty that I could induce Yuan to reveal the text of the document."

Sir John Jordan was "doddering" and very much embarrassed when Morrison discussed the demands with him on 26th January. "China has brought it on herself," he said. "There is nothing that she cannot accept." In his dispatch to the Foreign Office that day Sir John said, "They [the Chinese] consulted me today and asked me if our Government had been consulted. I said I had no information but told them to be conciliatory and to run no risks." He called on Morrison three days later, "very lugubrious":

> The Japanese have kept him in entire ignorance of the demands have said nothing to him at all . . . and he knows nothing more than the man in the street. He presumes only that the F.O. may know something but he is not sure. He kept saying he wished the Japanese were not so secretive. Apparently in his shrinking way he has no influence over them and mighty little intercourse with them. Why cannot he talk to Hioki instead of relying on the newspaper rumour? He was in his lachrymose doddering state.

Morrison's assessment of his fellow-countrymen was not conspicuously charitable—or consistent. His protégé, Sir John Jordan, was now a "crushed worm", and David Fraser, another protégé, a "baboon-visaged fatuous ass". Lord ffrench was a "double-faced sneak and Jesuit", and Ronald Macleay's wife "a painted Jezebel".

On the day when he persuaded Yuan to reveal the text of the Twenty-one Demands, Morrison dined with the Minister for Foreign Affairs, Sun Pao-chi, and his wife. Sun said two interesting things, neither very relevant to the crisis: "Marco Polo saw coal for the first time in China used as fuel. . . . The Russians will not eat pigeons for some sacred reason."

[V]

Morrison celebrated his fifty-fourth birthday on 4th February with a melancholy reflection on the "years wasted in this degrading office which was so unfortunately thrust upon me and which I full of hope and enthusiasm so unhappily accepted". Yuan was in "a hell of a mess," he noted. "Prestige gone. How can he wriggle out?"

Though the demands were freely and fiercely discussed in the Chinese Press, sceptical English and American editors withheld mention of them for two weeks. Morrison concocted a "powerful message" for Donald, which was sent to *The Times* and, through Frederick Moore, to Associated Press in America. *The Times* replied: "Verify carefully. Reason believe reports from Peking wilfully exaggerated." Associated Press was even more discouraging; Moore received a bleak cable, "Disregarded intemperate message. Could not be published", and boldly wired back his resignation. Morrison advised Yuan Shih-k'ai to send photographs of the Japanese document to President Wilson and overseas editors. Yuan thought it an "excellent" idea. Sir John Jordan, "very shaken and wandering somewhat", kept repeating in a haze, "I feel very sorry for China . . . very sorry. . . ."

At first Japan strenuously denied that she had made any demands. Pressed by the other powers for nearly a month, she finally admitted to having made, not twenty-one, but only *eleven* demands, the text of which she solemnly released. There was an astonishing difference between the actual and the officially released texts. In the edited version some of the most outrageous demands were omitted entirely; others were watered down considerably. Even by the elastic standards of diplomacy, it was a monstrously dishonest act. "When these two documents are read side by side," Morrison wrote to Guy Hillier, "one can come only to one conclusion, that there has never been a more disgraceful case of diplomatic turpitude. . . ." Negotiations about the demands—based on the original version—went on till the beginning of May, the Chinese resisting, the Japanese insisting. Many people in Peking feared that Japan might impose her will by force. Tsai Ting-kan consulted Morrison about money in a Yokohama bank which he feared might be confiscated in the event of war, but Yuan Shih-k'ai never consulted his political adviser about the most acute political crisis in the history of the Republic. As the negotiations dragged on, Morrison had to find out what was happening from the American Legation, which received minutes of the conferences. "It is more than I have," he wrote bitterly on 7th May:

> "*the political adviser*" who not once since the crisis arose has been asked a single question by any Chinese official. So entirely am I kept in the dark that correspondents keen after news whose time is valuable don't waste time to come and see me. So it is with the Legation. Neither Sir John nor any one else take the trouble to come up my street and quite justifiably so for what information can I give unless I evolve "facts" as does Putnam Weale from his imagination. . . .
>
> Feeling somewhat ill these days—getting older and more dissatisfied with my false position as *Adviser*!

Despite his bitterness and disillusion, Morrison at the end of April renewed his contract with the Chinese Government for another term of three years. The *North-China Herald*, the most important British paper in Eastern Asia, congratulating him and China, said:

> There was a period, during the heated days of controversy surrounding the negotiation of the Reorganization Loan, when Dr Morrison was the subject of considerable criticism. Long ago has the bitterness of those days subsided and while opinions may still differ as to the wisdom of the particular loan to which Dr Morrison lent his advocacy, we frankly confess that the reasons, as regards China herself, which prompted him in the line he took have been largely justified. At a time when many people were utterly despondent about China's future, Dr Morrison retained all his old confidence in her

ability to weather these as other storms. No small part of the secret of his success had been his ability to distinguish the real, the solid, the permanent in China, from the pinchbeck and transient. This has enabled him to criticize without acerbity, and to retain the regard of the Chinese for himself in spite of the castigation which his pen occasionally inflicted. No people are quicker than the Chinese at summing up a character, and they have never failed to recognize in Dr Morrison a friend, even though at times he might be forced to become that obnoxious thing, the candid friend.

[VI]

China continued to protest that Japan's demands infringed her sovereignty and the treaty rights of other powers, but Hioki on 7th May delivered an ultimatum, threatening force if she did not comply within two days. One set of demands, however, the fifth and most vicious group, was withdrawn for the time being. Sir Edward Grey had played some part in persuading Japan to moderate her demands, and when Sir John Jordan advised Yuan Shih-k'ai to accept them in the modified form he had no alternative but to do so.

Hioki defined Japan's attitude candidly and picturesquely: "The present crisis throughout the world virtually forces my Government to take far-reaching action," he said. "When there is a fire in a jeweller's shop, the neighbours cannot be expected to refrain from helping themselves."

Two weeks after China had yielded to the Japanese ultimatum, Yuan Shih-k'ai sent for Morrison, who found him "well, but coughing, and spitting more than usual". There were many important matters that Morrison wished to discuss—the need for more liberal mining regulations to attract foreign capital, the "disastrous" monopoly of the Standard Oil Company, the antimony monopoly, some big English development projects—but Yuan showed no interest in any of them. He would talk only about Japan:

Japan is his obsession. Japan intriguing. Japan working against England, suffering from swelled head, trying to stir up strife in India etc. He is thoroughly scared of Japan. Fear of this active neighbour paralyses all his actions. Thus when I spoke to him of Revised Mining Regulations . . . he had no comment but to pinch in his eyes and say "Then Japan will come in take all our mines." I must confess my interview gave me great discouragement. The President had no continuity of policy, no constructive statecraft, his whole talk was—and this was to be kept most secret—the need of endeavouring to wean the powers from the Alliance or understanding or agreement with Japan and to contrive that among themselves they would come to an agreement guaranteeing the integrity of China for a period of 10 or 20 years during which time China could devote herself to the development of her resources. . . . He is hypnotized and paralysed by fear of Japan like a frog in the presence of a snake. He is doing no constructive work, not a single industrial enterprise is being carried out in the whole country.

[VII]

The Chinese people, from rickshaw boys to students, from merchants to coolies, reacted angrily to China's surrender. There were strikes, demonstrations, and boycotts. (In Tsinanfu, the Japanese Consul formally protested that the Chinese were boycotting the Japanese brothels.) Associations sprang up to preserve the memory of 7th May as a "National Disgrace Day" and to discourage housewives from buying Japanese goods. "The recent negotiations amply showed that the cunning Japanese want to destroy our National existence," C. L. Chang, a Chinese journalist, wrote to Morrison, explaining his part in promoting the boycott. Yuan did not welcome this upsurge of nationalism, and Morrison, though he disliked the writer intensely, "cordially agreed" with an "excellent article" in which Putnam Weale said:

> It is not through a process of Boxerism, it is not by negative boycott, that the road is to be built, but by constructive fiscal, financial and educational action. The primitive taxation, the pitiful currency, the absence of communications, the miserable mining-laws, the thirty-nine million boys and girls who run riot through the country wholly illiterate while a bare million are at school, the persistence of a personal government instead of government by principles, these are some of the things which invite 150,000 people to control four hundred millions. . . .
>
> The National Assembly must be assembled as soon as possible, the spirit of the deputies aroused and not crushed. . . . If regeneration is to come, if the old balance of power in Eastern Asia is to be re-established, the nation must at once share in the work of government.

But Yuan was moving swiftly towards a more dictatorial, not a more democratic, regime. His ambition to make himself Emperor, which some observers had discerned when he first accepted the Presidency, now became apparent.

[VIII]

Early in June, Morrison had the cathartic satisfaction of reviewing in his diary China's melancholy history since 1884. She had learned nothing, he wrote, from her war with France, or from her war with Japan, ten years later. She had failed to set her house in order after "the madness of the Boxer uprising". In 1904-5 she had the humiliation of witnessing a war waged between Russia and Japan on her own soil, and from that bitter experience she had sunk still lower:

The Revolution of 1911 was to witness the dawn of a new era when corruption would be swept away and the latent strength of the people would find expression. Has the strength been found? Since the Revolution, China has lost Outer Mongolia, Outer Tibet and her shadowy sovereignty in Manchuria and Eastern and Inner Mongolia has become still more nebulous. . . . How can a country become great and powerful ruled by Ministers of such matchless ignorance and corruption? How can a country become strong that has no Navy or Army, no strategic railways, whose territory is traversed by railways policed by the military of powerful neighbours, a country without industries, without . . . a currency, without a police service, without a single public work, whose cities have the most primitive form of government and taxation known, whose government enjoys so little confidence that no domestic loan is possible except by compulsory levy, who has no education system, who has no mining laws, whose Minister of Education is innocent of all knowledge either of administration or Western Education, whose Minister of Finance is ignorant of the rudiments of arithmetic, whose Minister of Communications is lethargic from much opium! . . .

Let China give an account of her stewardship. Compare what has been done in Korea. The blemish is the killing of 16,000 insurgents, but the number is insignificant compared with the hundreds of thousands killed by famine and insurrection in China.

Morrison expressed a similar disenchantment in a letter to Sir Cecil Clementi-Smith: ". . . things are not going well. Little if anything is accomplished. There is no constructive statesmanship, no continuity of purpose . . . all energy is devoted to the drawing up of interminable regulations. . . ." And he speculated on the future of the Anglo-Japanese alliance. Every Japanese soldier, he wrote, was imbued with the belief of German invincibility: "Japanese policy in China since the war began and her disregard of her treaty engagements with England are explicable if she believed that England would be defeated and would cease to be the great Power in the Far East."

Donald, too, was gloomy about the state of the nation. "China is continuing the Rake's Progress," he said:

Donald thinks there will be another Revolution. People getting to the limit of their patience. And I am disposed to agree with him. We are back to the old Manchu regime. Even to the method of dismissing high officials without warning or without giving them any opportunity of defence in order to find places for political supporters or old friends or fellow provincials.

Morrison decided to set down formally his criticism of China's policy —or lack of policy. Early in July he went to the seaside for a week and, though troubled with specks in his right eye ("can hardly be liver"), wrote a 6500-word letter to Liang Shih-yi, the Director-General of the Banks of Communications, and Yuan's close adviser. It was a powerful indictment of Chinese ineptitude, procrastination, and corruption. Liang said that after reading it he could not sleep for two nights. Morrison sent a copy to Sir John Jordan, with a covering note which said:

> . . . I am preparing also a detailed statement of what China has *not* done during the 3 years of my service. I prepare these papers so that I can subsequently defend myself—so that it cannot be said of me what it may be said of others in similar position, that an adviser is one who tells you that what you are doing is the proper thing to do. . . .

[IX]

When Morrison saw him on 17th August Yuan Shih-k'ai looked "puffy and ill with asthmatic breathing". Dr Jean Bussière, of the French Legation, thought he was suffering from syphilis. The wranglings and importunings of his polyglot harem may also have contributed to his *malaise*. Morrison again urged him to have massage:

> An entirely impractical unsatisfactory interview. Gives me despondency to hear such empty talk. Complained that he was much hampered by having to act constitutionally. . . . He spoke hot air. . . . He has a deadly fear of Japan and this fear hampers all his actions. . . . I could not get him to talk of anything practical.

Apart from his fear of the Japanese, Yuan now has one consuming thought, to make himself Emperor. In this he had the support of a coterie of opportunists and sycophants, one of whom, Yang Tu, the President's adviser, organized a "Planning for Peace" Society—the name implying that only a monarchy could bring peace to China. Another unexpected ally was Professor Frank Goodnow, whom Yuan had invited back to China to write a memorandum on systems of Government. Goodnow declared in his paper that he was in favour of a monarchical system, provided there was not strong opposition to it, domestic or foreign; that the line of succession was clearly defined by legislation; and that a form of constitutional government be developed under the Crown. His argument was based on the political immaturity of the Chinese people, and the danger of disorders in choosing a successor to Yuan.

Goodnow's paper caused an immense sensation, and he told Morrison dejectedly that he would have much to explain when he got back to the States. He told Associated Press that he had been "misrepresented", but Morrison thought his paper was "quite explicit": "But he must feel, I fancy, that he has been made a tool of—he has been brought over from America for this purpose and no other and he has been cleverly trapped."

The *China Press* a few days later carried a Reuter's message obviously written by Morrison:

Dr Morrison Opposes New
Monarchy Project: Thinks
It Inadvisable at Present

Peking, August 26—Reuter's Agency understand that Dr Goodnow is annoyed at the persistent misquotations . . . of his memorandum to President Yuan Shih-k'ai. Dr Goodnow never gave blank endorsement to a monarchy, but advised it under certain circumstances. Dr Goodnow's friends consider that the Government is making a tool of him.

Reuter's Agency learns that Dr Morrison opposes the monarchical project, considering that the present time is inadvisable.

"This monarchical agitation is great nonsense, and is, of course, a purely fictitious movement engineered by self-seekers," Sir John Jordan wrote to Morrison. But, nonsense or not, the agitation, methodically nourished, gathered force; telegrams from provincial generals and governors, commanded or inspired by Yuan, poured into Peking, exhorting him to save the country by becoming "Emperor of the Chinese Empire". Morrison sent a memorandum to Yuan, urging him to defer the monarchical question, and discussed it with Obata, the Japanese chargé d'affaires:

> I told him that I was opposed to the change at the present time, thinking the time most ill-chosen and unsettling to men's minds that energies ought to be devoted to work not to futile changes in the title of the ruler, that if only one in four was opposed to the change it ought not to be effected, that such a scheme engineered as it was believed to be by the President himself was most injurious to his prestige and to his honour for had he not affirmed in the eyes of all the world most solemnly that he would unhold the Republic, and would for ever be bound by the oath he had sworn in accepting the office as President. Obata said Yuan K'e-ting (the half-paralysed son of the President, half-witted) was the inspirer of the movement in his own interest that quite recently a plot was discovered having for its object the poisoning of Tuan Chi-jui possible aspirant to the office of Chief Executive. . . . Saw Dr A. H. Smith. What is all this talk? he asked excitedly. China is rushing to ruin. Why do you stick to the wreck? I said I thought wiser counsels would prevail and Yuan would not permit the propaganda to continue.

"Methuselah" Ariga, as Morrison called the venerable Japanese constitutional adviser, warned the President that the change would be "very disastrous". He told Morrison he knew of no constitutional way of changing a republic into a monarchy, but the Chinese were "so ingenious" they would probably invent a way. Yuan's latest stratagem moved Morrison to another outburst in his diary:

> CHINESE SERVICE. Fear I am steadily deteriorating. Surrounded by perfidy and rascality in an atmosphere of mendacity tempered by make-believe how could anyone maintain his self-respect? Which of Chinese foreign employees does any work commensurate with his working capacity? What incentive is there to work? What work is there that

you are permitted to do? Here am I political adviser kept in entire ignorance until the campaign has started of the intentions of the President to break all his promises and cast to the winds all his declarations, and engineer himself to the throne. Never would he accept the Imperial Yellow and yet under the influence of his son and his discarded first wife, he is manoeuvring himself to the throne. This is in accordance with the prophecy of the Japanese and of Sun Yat-sen. He makes himself, his country, and his advisers a byword and a derision.

Japan, England, and Russia, followed by France and Italy, in turn gave their "very proper and opportune advice" that the monarchy should be postponed. "More than once I had warned Yuan that such advice would be tendered," Morrison wrote.

[X]

Through the first weeks of November, while the addled monarchical egg was being hatched, Morrison worked hard on a personal project—to persuade China to break off diplomatic relations with Germany, on the grounds that Germans had constantly violated China's neutrality. "I am determined that China shall come into this war on the side of the Allies," he wrote to James Murray Allison, a fellow-Australian in London, who was Northcliffe's advertising manager. "Japan is the doubtful factor. It is quite clear that it is not to Japan's interest that this war should end quickly."

He unfolded his scheme to Tsai Ting-kan, who was enthusiastic, and to de Codt, to Basil Kroupensky (now Russian Minister in Peking), to Ronald Macleay (Counsellor to the British Embassy), to Jordan, and to the President himself. Sir John was unenthusiastic. He told Morrison that Japan was giving remarkable support to the Allies and the powers could therefore do nothing to ruffle her in any way. Japan regarded China as her future field and did not want to see a strong China. Morrison said that at the end of the war Japan would find the whole world arrayed against her. Sir John agreed, but in the meantime Japan was master. Despite this, Morrison urged him to take action to get China involved in the war. "I think I persuaded him a little bit," Morrison noted. Kroupensky and de Codt required no persuasion. They both wired their Governments suggesting that Sir John should be advised to encourage Chinese participation.

Morrison in a long interview with Yuan itemized some of the advantages China would derive from joining the Allies:

The main points emphasized were: stimulating effect upon the National character. China had only recently awakened to a consciousness of nationality and their newborn patriotism would be animated by the knowledge that their country was allied in a struggle for civilization with the great nations of the world: China would obtain a fair share of the profits to be obtained by the manufacture of arms for the Allies; her arsenals would be re-organized and equipped with modern machinery; China after the war would have a voice at the Peace Conference when her destinies would be involved. Hitherto it had been the rule when treaties have been signed regarding China between other countries, that China had not even been consulted; joining the Allies would facilitate the settlement of China's various frontier questions; China, without violating international law, could confiscate the German and Austrian share of the Boxer indemnities, amounting to £14,000,000 and suspend payment during the war of the service of various Railway and Reorganization loans obtained from German financiers, together with the service of the Boxer indemnity, a payment of £6000 a day; she would recover possession of the German and Austrian concessions in Tientsin and Hankow; she would be able to recover her Treaty independence and after the war could make treaties with Germany and Austria of reciprocal advantage . . . trade routes would be opened across the territory for the passage of goods, then contraband, and large numbers of Chinese could be employed in Russian territory, from which they were then excluded. On the other hand, should China remain neutral she would sink still lower. She would be exposed to outside menaces and be regarded with increasing mistrust. There was dissatisfaction among the Allies with the way in which China had failed to preserve her neutrality.

Yuan was convinced. He said he was determined to bring China into the war, though—and he whispered this—Japan had twice recently made secret overtures for a secret understanding. He also whispered that he had already supplied England with rifles and machine-guns, which he had offered free but which Britain had insisted on paying for. Yuan then disclosed how his offer of participation at the outbreak of war had been rebuffed by Sir John Jordan, and he made it clear that he would not be exposed to a second rebuff. China must be invited by each of the four powers—England, France, Russia, and Japan—to join the Alliance.

Morrison busied himself with bringing England, France, and Russia officially into line, and on 24th November their three Ambassadors in Tokyo had an audience with Viscount Ishi, who had succeeded Kato, and formally requested the Japanese Government to join them in inviting China to declare war. "The Ambassadors were not well informed," Morrison noted. "Not one of the three had any knowledge of China. The British Ambassador, Sir Conyngham Greene, was conspicuously impotent. His claim to this important embassy had been based not on knowledge but upon seniority." (Sir Conyngham had joined the Foreign Office in 1877, and ridden the diplomatic escalator from Athens to Teheran, from Pretoria to Switzerland.)

The three Ambassadors were unable to counter Japan's objections, one of which was that "Japan could not regard with equanimity the liberation of the activities of 400,000,000 Chinese". Japan confirmed her refusal in writing, and, Morrison wrote, "there began a vigorous campaign in the Japanese press, tolerated if not fostered by the Japanese Government, attacking Great Britain and the Alliance, which continued throughout the winter of 1915-16". The campaign had actually begun before this. An article in *The Far East*, published earlier in the year, had quoted a Mr Masani Oishi as saying: "The gilded dross of Great Britain has been exposed to us." Mr Oishi continued:

> Up to this day, she, as the strongest naval power in the world, was looked upon by others with a sense of terror, but the navy is no more than an armed transport in modern warfare. . . . Witness Britain's helplessness in defending her coast . . . in the present war. As to the British Army, it is cowardice itself. The English soldiers who participated in the campaign against Tsingtao . . . would not advance; they would only retreat, even when . . . struck on their backs by the rifle. . . .
>
> On the other hand, the tactics of Germany must be admired, though she is our enemy today. . . .

Japan left the door discreetly open for a painless reconciliation with a victorious Germany. "In the whole history of warfare no prisoners were ever coddled and pampered as the few thousand Germans who were captured at Tsingtao," said Carl Crow, an American journalist in Tokyo. "They were probably the only prisoners of war who, in addition to being comfortably if not luxuriously housed, fed and clothed, were provided with carefully selected Japanese prostitutes."

[XI]

Jennie Morrison had hoped that her second child would be a daughter. She gave it the provisional name of "Peggy". When on 24th August she gave birth to another son, Alistair Gwynne, many of the dozens of people who sent congratulations consoled her by pointing out that, because of the war, sons were more desirable than daughters. A typical letter from Violet Markham read:

> Oh my dear I am so *glad* that you had not followed the prevalent fashion for girls of whom a quite deplorable number are being born! Just now when our men are being killed like flies one does want to treasure the *boy* babies and it's strange that despite the superstition to the contrary such a large majority of girls are being born at this war time. . . . Peking seems to be the only quiet and restful place left in the world. . . . Things are about as bad as they can be—that's the truth. You will know the Russian news and how serious it is. The Russian armies have been really heroic but . . . it is gross corruption in the official world which is primarily responsible for this débâcle, owing to the failure to provide munitions. . . . Here our political situation is most unsatisfactory.

Beatrice Brownrigg, whose husband, Douglas, was now Chief Naval Censor, kept Morrison well posted on the home front. She wrote to him on 18th June, "conscious of the Censor looking over my shoulder all the time":

The Grand Fleet is sick of inaction, and aching for a big fight—but I don't think the German High Sea Fleet will come out of their safe retreat—their submarines are most galling, and most difficult to attack—we have been greatly hampered for want of destroyers—but now we are increasing their number with rapidity. . . . We have got a huge army in France—I don't understand our tactics *there*—we keep a swaying line—and we have enormous casualties, and the cry is always *"More shells—more men"*. My confidence in Sir John French is rather on the wane—but I am not in a position to criticize seriously. . . . In the meantime, except for the increasing expense of almost every necessary and the increase of taxation, life in England continues normal—everybody works and there is very little "play". . . . Douglas *loathes* the whole Northcliffe gang—Nobody has any regard for the *"Times"*—I know many people who have given up taking it—If I begin to discuss the ex-Government (Radical) I shall never end, every member of the Cabinet ought to have been shot—first for the unpreparedness of the country for war, and secondly for their blundering and corruption and pro-German bias during the months of war until the Coalition Government was made—You can't imagine the muddling and mistake, and even now *much more* could be done if we only had an Oliver Cromwell as a dictator, instead of that paltry old Rogue, Asquith! All the country should be under martial law . . . and there are "strikes" here, and "strikes" there—till it makes me sick with rage. . . . Winston Churchill never did a better thing than when he wrecked his Party and brought about his own downfall—he was too dangerous at the Admiralty—and really responsible for our terribly costly disaster at the Dardanelles —Lord Fisher, thank Heaven!, has also gone, and we have a very wise First Sea Lord in Sir Henry Jackson. . . .

From an old Peking Friend, Captain A. J. Shaw, who had built Morrison's country cottage, came news of the Australian troops in Egypt. Shaw's letter was headed "Union Club Alexandria, June 19, 1915":

I expect to be off to Gallipoli any day now. . . . I meet so many of your gallant companions—all of them of course know your name. . . . At first sight one is astonished at the appearance of the men in the streets: they go about dressed just as they would be in their up-country stations in Australia. Unkempt giants with long hair and hairy chests bared almost down to the plimsoll mark tanned a deep mahogany. The majority are fair complexioned under the tan for their eyes are light grey with that piercing all-embracing quality that colonials have. Individually they are magnificent fighters I hear from every officer who has seen them in battle. I am looking forward very much to seeing them in action. The lack of cohesion and discipline in their ranks caused them unnecessary loss after the landing. They wandered off after the Turks in small bands almost across the peninsula from Gaba Tepe and many of them were cut off of course. One of their officers told me yesterday that the Germans and Turks had perfect knowledge of their landing place, and as they approached the shore in the darkness the first sound he heard distinctly across the water was a derisive shout "Come along you —— Kangaroos." Well, they came and left their mark.

[XII]

Oscar King Davis, of the *Chicago Tribune*, who was staying with Morrison, had worked for Theodore Roosevelt for three years and was intimate with him. Roosevelt, he said, had been dismayed when in Berlin to find the Kaiser would talk of nothing but war and militarism, "armaments, operations, strategy". But he had been even more dismayed when William Bayard Hale in 1908 had his sensational interview with the Kaiser. Davis, who was on the *New York Times* when it took place, gave Morrison the inside story:

Hale interviewed Roosevelt and success great. Then conceived to interview in same way Kaiser. Wires were pulled and Hale went to Berlin. Kaiser yachting in Norway. Went to Bergen and kept appointment on yacht met him at ladder and walked him up and down the deck talking for 2 hours with the utmost vehemence and unrestraint. For 2 hours unburdened his soul about England denouncing her and all her works her rulers her ministers her people her newspapers. Thrillingly interesting but impossible to publish. Hale returned to shore and wrote out as completely as he could from memory the whole conversation and then cabled to the *New York Times* what had happened. Saw the F.O. in Berlin they were aghast. Steamer back to N.Y. Davis having received full text suggested he should take it to Roosevelt and this was done. Roosevelt horrified. You cannot publish this! Davis admitted impossible but explained he had brought it for Roosevelt's delectation. And it was never published. But an expurgated edition of it mild and innocuous was sold by Hale to *The Century Magazine* and featured. Knowledge of its intending publication reaching the German Government, the Ambassador was instructed to buy up the complete issue, and indemnify the Century Co for the loss incurred in bringing out a new edition. ... Now, why should the *New York Times* still keep this interview in its safe? The Managing Editor urges its publication, the Jew proprietor Adolph Ochs refuses to publish it!

At the end of November the 1993 members of the National Congress of Representatives—an organization created to rubberstamp Yuan's Imperial ambitions—voted unanimously for a monarchy. Yuan was expected decently to refuse the throne at least three times, as he had thrice refused the Empress Dowager's Dukedom—but after a second drilled chorus of supplication he reluctantly yielded to the voice of the nation, or of the 1993 well-trained voices speaking in its name. On the morning of 11th December, Morrison noted that Yuan had "with anger and determination" rejected the deputation's entreaty. "He expressed his surprise. It was all so unexpected that it came as a shock to him." But in the afternoon the farce was repeated, and Morrison wrote curtly: "Yuan Shih-k'ai today accepted the throne. *Quite a surprise!* Such is the silly make-believe."

Observers commented on the favourable auspices for the new regime. A Japanese-inspired outbreak in Shanghai had fizzled out. Snow had fallen on the exact day predicted by soothsayers. And, miraculous portent, the fossil of a "divine dragon" the symbol of Imperial rule, had been discovered in an Ichang cave. Unfortunately, after its discovery had been proclaimed in a special government announcement, the dragon proved to be a commonplace stalagmite. More unfortunately, a serious anti-monarchist rebellion broke out in the South. Yunnan, whose troops were perhaps the best-disciplined in China, declared its independence, and the revolt spread to other provinces. The rebel forces, commanded by General Tsai Ao, who had been Military Governor of Yunnan from 1911 to 1913, were successful on many fronts, and Yuan found he could not rely even on his most trusted commanders.

But when Morrison saw him on 13th January he was in good spirits ("though he is rushing headlong to perdition") and talked of the Yunnan trouble with contempt. It would be quelled in twenty days, he said. He was more interested in his enthronement, which was to take place that month, and in quelling the trouble in his harem, where with the approach of the coronation inter-wife conflict had become acute. Morrison reported an incident at a dress rehearsal held in the Palace of the Enthronement:

> Yuan Shih-k'ai sitting with his Crown; 3 thrones at his side for the 1st 2nd and 3rd wives on descending levels. First wife came in arrayed; kowtowed; took her proper seat. Long delay and 2nd wife the Korean wife, failed to come. Sent for peremptorily. She came in but refused to take her seat, saying Yuan had promised her a throne on the same level as the No. 1. Hearing this, No. 1 jumped down from the Throne and went for No. 2 with her fingers. The Master of the Ceremonies, Wang Kan-nien was supervising the Enthronement, but he could not lay impious hands on the struggling Empresses, where upon Yuan waddled down from the Throne and tried to separate the two combatants. Order was finally restored but the rehearsal was postponed....

Morrison left Yuan "more than ever impressed by the hopelessness of it all". Yuan was ignorant of conditions in Yunnan. He was surrounded by sycophants who never told him the truth. To find out the truth, Morrison went south, leaving with Tsai Ting-kan an improvised code:

The South needs machinery to develop its work	The Yunnanese or rebels lack guns and shells etc.
A gold mine is said to exist at Chaotung	Tsai Ao is said to be at Chaotung.
I shall investigate the gold mine..	I shall see Tsai Ao.
Iron mines are plentiful round Luchow	Rebel forces are at Luchow.
the cold wind has killed off a thousand promising plants	Government troops have killed 1000 rebels at ....
Iron mines have stopped my business	Rebels will not let me proceed.
the land of the leal	Yunnan.
the land of oil and honey	Szechwan.
The land of the limestone pinnacles	Kweichou.

When he returned to Peking at the beginning of February, having satisfied himself of the strength and resolution of the rebel forces, Morrison again urged Yuan to abandon his plans for a monarchy.

The revolution was not quelled in twenty days—or in sixty. The rebels suffered reverses, but they counter-attacked successfully, and it was apparent by the middle of March that they could not be crushed. There was a threat, too, of Japanese military action against China under the time-tested pretext of "maintaining peace". On 7th March, Morrison had a "curiously interesting" talk with Lieutenant-General Aoki, "Agent Militaire du Japon en Chine":

Yuan whom he saw yesterday lost greatly in prestige. Japs are opposed to him because he violates the teachings of Confucius. He was not faithful to his Empress he is not faithful to his people. To him was due the Second Revolution. I ventured to suggest that it was due to Japanese intrigue. . . . He said not at all. It was due to Yuan and the murder of Sung Chiao-jen whose death was decreed by Yuan.

Two days ago Li Yuan-hung said to him it was Yuan and Yuan alone who engineered the monarchy. I suggested that Yuan K'e-ting was a considerable force. He said not at all. Chinese custom would not permit the son to advise the father. . . . He discussed the retirement of Yuan as if it were inevitable, expressing his regret that his friend should have committed so grave a blunder. . . . He said that the Monarchy must be abandoned not postponed but Yuan could retain his power if he were to return to the Republic.

Three weeks later Yuan's dearly bought, pinchbeck Empire was no more. It had lasted eighty-three days. The preceding Empires had lasted 2137 years. On 22nd March, as President of the Republic, Yuan decreed the abolition of the Empire, as the Empress Dowager had decreed the establishment of the Republic three years before. In his proclamation he said:

> Ever since the establishment of the Republic, gentlemen . . . have urged on me the necessity of restoring the Imperial system, saying that only a constitutional monarchy can spare us the civil dissensions of Portugal and Mexico, which in turn will lead us along the road already travelled by Burma and Vietnam. . . . The volumes of our Chinese history are full of the disasters of emperors and princes. How could I dare to aspire to the throne from simple ambition? But the national representatives did not understand how sincerely I longed to decline the honour. Since then some people suspect that I have been moved by dreams of power. Truly, my lack of virtue is to be blamed for the compliance with the wishes of others which has brought this discord on the country. . . .

Morrison had nothing to do with the drafting of this ingenuous valediction. He was not consulted about Yuan's surrender of the throne, though he had repeatedly advised it, and had not seen him since 8th March, when the Emperor-elect attended a meeting of a newly formed Advisory Committee—another of the innumerable councils of experts who talked much and achieved nothing:

> Yuan came in clad in his old velvet coat that to my knowledge has been in use summer and winter since early 1912. It reaches down to near the ankles. Below were seen a pair of ill-fitting khaki pants and common Chinese slippers. . . . The President addressed us. We were to advise and recommend. The time had come for deeds not words. He might have quoted from my letters. . . . If we accomplished only one thing at each meeting that meant 50 in the course of a year. . . . Poppycock was the diet given us.

In a post-morten on the monarchist movement Tsai Ting-kan told Morrison that the real trouble was a "furious dispute" between Yang Tu, the founder of the monarchist-front "Planning for Peace" Society, and Liang Chi-chao, the former Minister for Justice, over a Tientsin prostitute, a highly educated Hupeh woman with large feet. Yang Tu, "having made a big fortune out of antimony", and probably also out of the diversion of funds from the "Planning for Peace" movement, had bought this desirable creature for $12,000. Liang Chi-chao, who was equally interested in her, was enraged, and determined to undo whatever Yang Tu supported. He had resigned from the ministry, quoting in his farewell letter to Yuan from a Chinese classic: "Rites, justice, incorruptibility and a sense of shame are the basic principles of an administration without which the government will perish." The harlot from Hupeh was not mentioned.

At the end of April, Morrison told Tsai Ting-kan that he was ashamed
to admit to the legation people that he had not seen Yuan Shih-k'ai for
nearly three months. It was "a shocking loss of face". Tsai assured him
it was nothing personal. The President, he said, was engrossed in "private
affairs". This may have meant the conciliation of his troublesome harem,
but the President's main preoccupation was the conciliation of his even
more troublesome army. One third of China's entire revenue was being
spent on the military, and the revenue had been greatly diminished by
the secession of the three rich southern provinces, Yunnan, Szechwan,
and Kwantung. Yuan had 30,000 troops in Peking and its environs, and a
bodyguard of 8000 which received double pay. The troops had been
promised two months' extra pay on the occasion of the coronation.
When the enthronement was abandoned they threatened to loot Peking
unless they got their bonus. "Soldiers are the curse of China," Morrison
reflected for the hundredth time. "To retain power Yuan has created
a vast military force. It is a Frankenstein." But despite his financial
difficulties Yuan had spent $30 million on preparations for the coronation,
and millions on bribing Japanese members of parliament not to oppose
the monarchy. "Was there ever such a Cabinet?" Morrison asked himself. "Liang Shih-yi is credibly believed to have $20,000,000. Yuan
Shih-k'ai has vast wealth, large sums invested abroad."

The day after he had complained to Tsai, Morrison was summoned
to the Palace, where Yuan received him in his "usual friendly way":

> Marked change since I saw him last. Has lost weight, his face some-
> what drawn. Is suffering from toothache and rubbed his teeth with
> alcohol using a chopstick covered with wool. . . . He said it was a
> long time since he had seen me, but he had been very busy, very
> much overworked and he was tired in the head and in the body.
> He would like to retire and have some rest. . . . But who could
> take up the responsibility of his post? . . . I asked if there was any-
> thing I could do to help him. Before, he said, I had saved China
> (meaning I had saved him) by obtaining the Crisp loan. There was
> no possibility of another loan, now, that he realized. Only in America
> it might be possible. . . .

Morrison asked Yuan what prospects there was of coming to an
agreement with the South? Yuan said none, because the South had no
leader. They were all in dispute among themselves. Should he retire
or not?—that was the question. A podgy Hamlet, Yuan returned to it
again and again:

> The South say, if Yuan retires order will be restored. The North
> declares, if Yuan retires, China will be broken up. If he retires,
> who will maintain order? I said to him, if order were not maintained
> in Peking, and if trouble should arise here from the mutiny of the
> soldiers, immediate Japanese armed intervention would be invited. . . .

Japan was all ready to send troops to Peking. . . . He knew this. I said surely the Southern leaders realize that continuation or extension of the present turmoil means Japanese intervention. He said they seemed rather to desire such intervention. . . . He asked me did I think the Japs would use military force to remove him from his post? I said no. Yet they were determined he should retire? I said they were but they would use other means. . . . He said their policy was to starve him in finances. . . .

Morrison pressed Yuan to disclose China's financial position. How much money did he require to pay the troops in Peking? Yuan said roughly $4 million. "And how much have you got for this month?" Morrison asked. Yuan said he did not know the actual position, but up till the previous day he had only $1 million. Many deposits had been withdrawn from the two Chinese banks, and money was a little scarce— "a euphemism", Morrison commented in his diary, "for saying that funds were not thus available for appropriation by the Government":

I gave him a survey of the present European situation . . . told him of the costly failure . . . of the German attempt to smash through at Verdun. Explained the obvious effect of such a failure upon military opinion in Japan. I told him Russia was no longer solely dependent upon Japan for munitions, and she was thus much more independent and would come to better terms with Japan. He interjected that Japan was furnishing munitions also to the rebels. Undoubtedly, I said and explained that Japan could not have reason to be well satisfied with her policy in the South for instead of having a united South looking to Japan for guidance, there was a South torn by hostile factions.

Morrison came away convinced that Yuan was preparing to abdicate, on the grounds not of increasing unpopularity but of increasing infirmity. On 11th May, when the Bank of China and the Bank of Communications suspended payment, and proclamations announced that government notes were inconvertible, it was apparent that Yuan could not defer his retirement much longer. China was bankrupt. Tsai Ting-kan called on Morrison to discuss the Moratorium:

Spoke with indignation, having veered with the prevailing wind, of Yuan Shih-k'ai, and of his policy in grabbing all the money he could and using it to his own ends. Money had been squandered in the Monarchical movement, and preparations for the Coronation. He had never dared to use his power against the military. That savage Chang Hsun has . . . robbed the taxes by millions, has purchased whole streets of houses in Peking and Tientsin. . . .

Morrison said he was thoroughly sick of it all and would clear out if he could sell his library to the Japanese. His chronic dissatisfaction had been exacerbated by a conversation the day before with Hioki, when the Japanese Minister had contrasted Morrison's present position as political adviser with the position he had enjoyed as correspondent of *The Times*. "The reference was made with complete politeness and apparent sympathy, but I winced under it. Nevertheless, the observation was a just one, the truth of which I am the first to admit," Morrison wrote in an undated "Memorandum" intended for his reminiscences. In it he distilled the bitterness of three disillusioned years:

> With what extravagant hopes I accepted the offer to enter the service of the Chinese Government! How quick and complete was my awakening! Others have entered the service of the Chinese before and after I did, and I do not know one whose experience has been different to mine. Where others had failed, I believed that I could succeed. Vain delusion! I was the greatest failure of all, for my hopes were higher than those of others. I honestly believed in the greatness of China's future, and I was anxious to be associated with her rise to power . . . taking part, perhaps a leading part, in the guidance of a semi-civilized country along the paths which alone can lead to success and honour. The measure of my disappointment is the measure of my hopes in joining the service of the Government in 1912. Not to warn other foreigners animated with equal hopes, but to warn the Chinese, do I submit this succinct account of my experiences. . . .

When Morrison told another caller, Hsu En-yuan, that he was "thoroughly disgusted" with his job, Hsu said he had no reason to be, that he did not know the value of the services he had rendered China. According to Hsu, it was Morrison's memorandum to Yuan which had brought about the abdication and the Chinese Minister to Japan, Lou, had told Hsu that if the President had not abdicated when he did, Japan would have taken action:

> He asked me if I had been consulted about the Moratorium? I told him no, that the rule was never to consult me until after the blunder had been committed. He said it was a grave mistake, that it meant the destruction of China, and prepared the way for the domination of Japan. Even Sun Pao-chi, the Minister for Finance, knew nothing about it till next day.

[XV]

The British community was about to celebrate the King's Birthday, on 3rd June, when news of the Battle of Jutland, fought three days before, reached Peking. Macleay spoke of the battle as the greatest disaster in the annals of the British Navy, and the birthday reception at the legation was marked by a "great absence of joviality, the news being very dampening". But the Germans celebrated boisterously and beerily, and in their drunken revelry set fire to their barracks. Morrison noted that "Austrians and Americans and *if you please*, Japanese assisted in putting out the flames".

[XVI]

At 3 a.m. on 6th June, Yuan, who had taken to his bed with what was popularly described as "fever of the belly", but which his three French doctors diagnosed as uraemia of the blood, died. "Thus Yuan himself has found the best solution of the crisis," Morrison wrote. Yuan was fifty-six, and his death was said to have been accelerated by a multiplicity of advisers. "Every member of his family recommended another doctor who recommended their decoctions. Between them recovery was rendered impossible," Morrison was told. A contemporary journalist named Fang gave a picturesque, if irreverent, account of the great man's last days:

> . . . Yuan's belly was rumbling fiercely and he was calling at the top of his voice to be helped out of bed to the privy. If he had been a southerner, this would have been simply a matter of going to a commode in a corner of the room, but . . . being a native of Honan he was . . . accustomed to squat on his haunches in an outhouse. He was supported to this place—not without difficulty for he was grossly corpulent—but as soon as he got there, he fell down head first, and when the servants raised him to his feet he was not an agreeable sight. Hearing the outcry, all the concubines came running, but they stopped short and covered their noses. . . .

On the day before his death Yuan was said to have uttered, with great effort, the word "constitution". His last intelligible words, spoken with great bitterness, were: "He destroyed me." It is not certain whether he was referring to his eldest son, as was generally believed, or to one of his doctors.

[XVII]

Historians are still wrangling over Yuan. Was he merely an unscrupulous opportunist, destroyed by greed and ambition? Or was he a frustrated statesman and patriot, destroyed by incapacity and circumstance, forced by political necessity into acts of treachery and violence? As Professor Ch'en reminds us, the question is whether one should judge a historical figure by contemporaneous or present-day standards. Morrison, who saw Yuan at very close range, would no doubt have agreed with Ch'en that critics of Yuan's mistakes need to point out "a better, wiser, and at the same time, more realistic alternative". This, of course, begs the moral issue. It ignores the problem of means and ends—one, which has become so much more meaningful in our time. The problem did not seem to bother Sir John Jordan, who wrote to Sir Walter Langley at the Foreign Office, defending Yuan's morally indefensible action in dismissing the National Assembly, and added: "I could go on indefinitely reciting acts to the credit of my dead friend—for simply as friend I shall always remember him. . . . He fell in an unequal struggle and to me he was greater in adversity than he had been even at the height of his power."

Morrison wrote to Tsai Ting-kan, who was writing a biography of Yuan:

> I recall vividly many of the endearing qualities of the famous ruler, his generosity, his kindness, his loyalty to his friends, his consideration for others, his invincible good humour and courage under difficulties. The most striking characteristics, as I observed them, of his relations with the foreigner was his caution, his unwillingness ever to give full confidence, his invariable withholding of the essential fact. Thus he could never be given a well-balanced judgment, because he never submitted the full facts of the case. During my four years intercourse . . . never once was I given complete information and this was specially striking in all financial questions . . . and in the case of the Japanese Demands, information regarding which first came to me from Donald. I fancy this will always be the difficulty in rendering effective service—this inveterate distrust of the foreigner. The same characteristic is very noticeable in Mr Liang Shih-yi, in Mr Lu Tseng-tsiang, and even in men of a younger generation like Alfred Sze and Wellington Koo.

Were the ghosts of the Emperor, of the Empress Dowager, of Sung Chiao-jen, Chang Chen-wu, and many others, grinning uneasily over Morrison's shoulder as he penned the words "kindness . . . loyalty . . . consideration"?

[XVIII]

Morrison found some satisfaction in his balance-sheet for 1915. He ended the year with a credit balance of £3648—an increase of £1770, and added to his litany of hopes for the following year a new theme: "That I may be guided wisely in my speculations and in my investment and that astonishing luck attend me."

CHAPTER THIRTEEN

[I]

On 9TH JUNE 1916, Morrison and some of the other advisers presented their compliments to the new President at his house in the Tung Chang Hutung. They were received in a pretty summer-house on the top of a rockery in a pleasant garden. President Li Yuan-hung, a heavily built man with a heavy moustache who, Morrison thought, bore a remarkable resemblance to Field-Marshal von Hindenburg, wore a black suit and a bowler hat, "Looking like a mute at a funeral". He was accompanied by his private secretary, Quo Tai-chi, "a very agreeable young Chinese goodlooking and sensible graduate University of Pennsylvania":

> I offered congratulations to the President. . . . He made a short speech his ignorance his inexperience his desire to rule by law and by constitution. The country's need, *education*. The military question. He wanted our assistance. . . . He invited discussion.

Morrison replied that the one wish of the advisers was to work and assist in China's development. But so far little opportunity had been given them. Rarely were they consulted, and still more rarely were they listened to. He spoke also of the pressing need of dealing with the military, who were absorbing "40% or 50% of the Revenue", and of settling China's boundary problems in Tibet, Yunnan, and Mongolia, so that she could be free to attend to affairs within her own border.

Morrison amplified his programme for a regenerated China in a letter to Tsai Ting-kan:

> What is to be the future? Actual work must take the place of . . . everlasting talk. . . . If we can . . . all strive together Chinese and foreign alike . . . we can recover much that now seems irretrievable, we can create a new and powerful China. . . .
>
> Again you will have seen that Roosevelt has denounced the policy of President Wilson, and the most opprobious terms he can find . . . in his denunciations are that "this college sissy is Chinafying America" reducing his country to impotence among the powers.

That reforms can be effected completely changing the attitude of the world towards China I have no doubt whatever, but such reforms can never be possible so long as their execution is entrusted to the hands of those who do not understand the foreigner and foreign method. China has every conceivable advantage . . . territorial extent, varied climate, fertile soil, abundant waterways, an intelligent and industrious people. But she lacks up-to-date government and up-to-date methods of administration. In her contest with the highly trained nations of the West, her strength is that of the bow and arrow fighting with the quickfirer.

Many things have to be accomplished. Working unitedly we can accomplish them.

When the new President moved into his Palace he was greeted by bare walls and empty floors. Yuan Shih-k'ai's sons had looted everything that could be removed, and the men of the Imperial Guard, charged with guarding the Imperial treasures, had sold even the glass from the windows.

[II]

Lionel Pratt thanked Morrison for the gift of *The Sentimental Bloke*, an epic in slang by the Australian versifier, C. J. Dennis, which was currently a best-seller in Australia. "It came as a little gleam of friendliness in an aspect that is d———dly dark," Pratt wrote with curious fastidiousness. He had been editing the *Far Eastern Review*, the monthly of which Donald was part-proprietor and titular editor, and had recently written with Morrison's help special articles on China for the *Manchester Guardian* and the *Quarterly Review*. Morrison had a considerable regard for Pratt as man and journalist, but when Pratt sought solace for domestic troubles in alcohol, Morrison's Calvinist upbringing asserted itself. In return for *The Sentimental Bloke* Pratt sent Morrison some of his poems, one of which he said read "like a wail of agony from a tortured soul —which it was", and a few months later made a desperate plea for a loan of £130, offering an insurance policy and furniture as security. Morrison coldly replied by telegram that he could not comply with the request, and amplified his refusal in a long and priggish homily, in which he said:

Your letter was quite disingenuous. . . As a journalist with a gift of lucid speech and with a reasoning faculty developed far above the ordinary you are prepared to sacrifice everything for beer. . . . You can escape from your present dilemma . . . by your own volition but apparently you prefer to remain down regardless of yourself, of your wife and of your child, so long as you may gratify your appetite for beer. It is simply horrible. . . . You must awake, arise or be for ever fallen.

When Pratt sent back the price of the telegram, Morrison apparently unconscious of the irony, wrote: "Many thanks for sending me the cost of the telegram. I did not expect you to repay me. Few men would be so punctilious." In his diary he wrote: "I am adamant about lending money."

[III]

Morrison was still determined to bring China into the war. Early in July he asked Li Yuan-hung for two months' leave, and crossed to Japan. From the Imperial Hotel in Tokyo he wrote to Viscount Kato, asking for a private interview: "I am still in the service of the Chinese," he wrote, "but it is not for that reason I would like so much to see your Excellency but as an Englishman who would like to help towards a better understanding of a question on which there has been much misunderstanding." Kato, though out of office, was the leader of the most powerful party in Japan. He had been Ambassador in London, where he had signed the Anglo-Japanese Treaty in July 1911, and Foreign Minister when the Twenty-one Demands were served on China. Morrison had known him intimately for seventeen years and regarded him as trustworthy and discreet.

The interview took place in Kato's residence, and Morrison immediately afterwards sent Sir Conyngham Greene a full report of it. He told Sir Conyngham that the Russian Minister, Kroupensky, had spoken to Kato without success about China joining the Allies, and Kroupensky could not understand Japan's policy except on the assumption that she believed Germany would win the war. But Kato had been impressed with Morrison's arguments, which, he said, had set forth the case in "a new and interesting light".

Morrison had spoken of the great American activity in China, of the railway and road concessions, the loans and reclamation schemes, of American industrial activity, of the eagerness of the Americans to lend money to China. He argued that this formidable trade activity could not be to the advantage of Japan. He then pointed out the advantages Japan could derive from China's joining the Alliance. He described German activity in China, and her plans to expand her commercial enterprise after the war. Looked at from the Japanese standpoint, it seemed certain that Japan must derive material advantage from the termination of Chinese relations with Germany, and all its consequences. China, in severing diplomatic relations with Germany, would confiscate Germany's share of the Boxer indemnity, amounting to £13 million, and with this sum as security China could raise £10 million from the Allied powers. America, a neutral country, could not lend this money without displaying unfriendliness to Germany. It seemed better that Japan should take a leading part in this transaction. Japan would fill many of the vacancies in the China administration now held by Germans. And then there was the Mohammedan question—of great importance to England and Russia.

There were from 15 to 20 million Moslems in China. The fact that China, a Mohammedan power, had joined the Alliance, would have a material effect upon Mohammedan feeling in India, Persia, and Mesopotamia. And surely China's defence of Turkey would cause far-reaching dismay throughout the Ottoman Empire?

Morrison's report to Sir Conyngham Greene occupied thirteen typewritten pages. Sir Conyngham's reply, "left furtively" at the Imperial Hotel while Morrison was out, occupied four handwritten lines. It was so noncommittal, Morrison commented, "that to be completely so, it ought to have been written in invisible ink". It read: "I had hoped to call at the Hotel today to thank you for your kind letter and its enclosure but heard you had gone to Enmote for the day. I beg therefore to send you my best thanks by letter instead."

Morrison left Tokyo with no increased regard for Sir Conyngham's diplomatic acumen, and continued his campaign in Peking. The Japanese Minister, Baron Hayashi, said he had received from Kato a report of Morrison's visit, and that he, Hayashi, was now in favour of China's joining the Alliance. Hostility to Yuan, he said, "unwillingness to do anything which might have helped him become Emperor", was no doubt the reason for the Japanese Government's opposition to the previous proposal. "Nothing however was done," Morrison commented. "Expressions of sympathy were not followed by action."

Morrison sent a long memorandum to the British Foreign Office, with a copy of his report to Sir Conyngham Greene. In the memorandum he said: "The Japanese have no intention of restoring the Marshall Islands to Australia though the Australians are nursing a belief that Japan undertook to do so." The islands had already been placed under Japanese civil administration and were referred to in Japan as "our South Sea Island possessions". The harbour of Jaluit was being fortified, and a powerful naval base was to be created there. "What will be the effect on Australia?" Morrison asked prophetically. "As regards Germany," he wrote, "Japan's attitude is one of neutrality. There is undisguised antagonism to the English Alliance":

> The Japanese boast . . . as to what they have accomplished during the present war for the Alliance. Apparently, they claim that they have shown the highest quality of "bushido". If "bushido" means that they have refrained from attacking their friends and allies, their claim is justified. By the help of the Allies, their financial equilibrium has been restored. From the verge of bankruptcy, they are now in a position of affluence, thanks to the supply of arms to the Allies at a vast profit to themselves. It is preposterous to speak of the services rendered by their navy. Did their navy save Craddock's fleet? Did their navy assist in the battle of the Falkland Islands? Have they no commerce of their own to protect? One would think when one reads of the wonderful services they have rendered in the Far Eastern Seas that they are doing this solely in the interest of British com-

merce. Did they check the depredations of the *Emden*? Or was a bargain struck that the activities of this raider would not be interfered with so long as they did not molest the Japanese flag? Whatever they boast, the fact remains, that the Japanese have not exchanged a single shot with any enemy ship.

Regarding Japan's attitude towards the admission of China into the Alliance, was it a friendly act or a service rendered to the Allies to prevent at a critical time in the history of the war, material help being given to the Allies? Will it ever be forgotten that when China was willing to give assistance to Great Britain, Japan forbade such assistance being given?

In the operations at Tsingtao, a fort of very inferior strength defended by 6000 Germans hastily gathered together, and containing a large percentage of clerks, pot-bellied cooks, and such like, was after a short siege reduced by a gigantic Japanese force whose casualties were quite insignificant. Ever since the incident, the Japanese Government had sedulously exaggerated the importance of the military operations which brought about the downfall of the heavily defended "fortress". In recognition of their services, they have created two baronies . . . have given 145,000 medals to the soldiers who took part, promoted many hundreds of officers, and decorated 380 nurses. Every cabinet minister has received high honours and gifts of gold ornaments, and every Member of Parliament similarly to a lesser degree. What is the object of doing all this? Is it not to impress the people with the mighty services rendered by Japan to the subjugation of mighty Germany?

In my memorandum of the talk with Viscount Kato, I did not note, because I was giving a copy to Sir Conyngham Greene, that Kato *said none of the three Ambassadors seemed to know much about the case.* He said it a little stronger than this, adding that the "Russian Ambassador seemed to know a little more than the British!"

To Lady Brownrigg, Morrison wrote on 14th October:

You no doubt know that Japan's attitude during this war has been open to much suspicion. German trade has gone on as usual in Japan. The German Bank in Japan was only closed down three weeks ago, and that was due, we believe, to a telegram in the *Daily Telegraph* [which Morrison had inspired]. It was certainly not due to any action taken by our Embassy, whose pusillanimity is astonishing. The explanation given is that the relations between the Germans and Mitsui firm are so intimate and so much was undisclosed of the Jap. naval scandal, that the Japanese dare not offend the Germans. Another explanation given, and widely credited, is that the Japanese and Germans have made a compact—the Germans to continue to trade in Japan and no opposition to be given to Germans in China, in return for the immunity of Japanese ships from German submarines. Only three Japanese ships have been sunk since the war began, and not a single shot has been exchanged by the Japanese fleet with a hostile ship. It is preposterous to talk about the great help Japan has rendered the Allies. . . . China is prepared to come in and ought to come in, and if the British Government will act with a little more resolution, Japan would be forced into compliance with our wishes. We have scrapped some of our useless generals, and yet we retain in this important post of Peking a doddering, muddle-headed Minister, whose timorousness is proverbial. He ought to be scrapped.

Lady Brownrigg, who sometimes followed Queen Victoria's practice of heavily underlining words and phrases, replied:

I entirely agree with what you say about the Japanese—but they are first and last—*opportunists*, and we can hardly expect them to feel as we do towards Germany. For them, as for America, the war has brought enormous wealth and prosperity. I don't suppose they care how long it goes on! They will certainly hold on to Kiao-Chao —and keep it a big naval base—a future menace to the Philippines! . . . I'm afraid the Foreign Office won't take any active interest in China till the war is over. It is overburdened with the complications of the nations in Europe. I don't know how successful Mr Balfour will be but he must be infinitely better than Sir Edward Grey— Lord Grey!—who was one of the *worst* Foreign Secretaries we have ever had in this country—since 1908/9 when he allowed Austria to annex Bosnia and Herzogovina his policy has been utterly rotten— he is a pacifist—a visionary—an idealist—a socialist—everything the Minister for Foreign Affairs should *not* be!—and thank Heaven—he has gone!!

M. de Cartier, who had just been appointed French Minister to Washington, had a similar opinion of Grey: "The most incompetent blunderer of all the Foreign Ministers," he said.

[IV]

Politically, China may have been stagnant, but Peking was still changing its face, as Morrison wrote to a friend in October 1916:

Peking you simply would not be able to recognize except by its monuments. Macadamized roads, electric light, great open spaces, museums, modern buildings of all kinds, one or two of them on a scale that would not be out of place in Whitehall, motor-cars (there are I think at least 200 in Peking) motor cycles more numerous than we care for, and bicycles literally by the thousand. New roads are being driven through the city, in many directions and the Imperial City Wall is now pierced in a dozen places. . . .

The social scene was changing, too—but remained the same. "Peking is a shocking place for gossip," Morrison wrote quite unselfconsciously.

333

Himself an avid collector of scabrous titbits, he nominated the chief scandalmongers: de Hoyer—"the homosexual opium-eating Russian who keeps a Japanese mistress as blind"; Madame Beelaerts, wife of the Dutch Minister, and Countess Ahlenfeldt, wife of the Danish Minister, who wore huge Gainsborough hats and was Peking's undisputed social leader. Other notable practitioners were Mlle Reine Everts, sister of the Belgian charge d'affaires, and Mrs Ronald Macleay. Mlle Everts, who used to receive Morrison in an unventilated drawing-room with an atmosphere so thick that if "I had thrown my hat in the air, it would have stuck", told him at a typical session that the Counsellor of the Belgian Legation, Baron Villenpagne, "an incredibly low-class dwarf", was a professional card-player and a masochistic pervert, and that the Italian Minister, Count Sforza, was sleeping with the handsome Madame de Gaiffier, whose husband was in the Banque Belge pour L'Étranger; because of her accessibility, Madame de Gaiffier was known as *La Blonde Belge pour L'Étranger*.

The diplomatic corps had many unconventional components. The Russian Minister, Basil Kroupensky, a tall, florid man, lived in a vast house where he entertained in the grand Imperial manner. Daniele Varè described the "champagne, the mounds of caviare in hollowed blocks of ice, the giant sturgeons from the Amur," which embellished his banqueting table. He was said to have two Cossacks travelling constantly between Siberia and Peking, solely to provide him with fresh butter. His *aide* at these Lucullan entertainments, ministering also to a more intimate appetite, was his bucktoothed English secretary, Leonard Huskisson, who when alone dressed in female costume and whom Morrison bluntly termed the minister's "catamite". But Kroupensky had a wandering eye; while still attached to Huskisson, he had an affair with Lieutenant Kelly, a chinless gunner from Hong Kong. The Portuguese Minister, de Freitas, who had dyed hair and moustaches, was "somewhat loathsome, with an evil record", Morrison noted: ". . . in Japan he lived on the prostitution of his wife who had been mistress of the King of Portugal who bore His Majesty a son de Freitas fathered. In the Tokyo legation he used to import cigars free of duty and sell them, so that the de Freitas cigars became a well-known brand on the market."

Morrison paid Madame de Gaiffier a generous tribute: "She is the liveliest and deadliest man-snarer in Peking, of remarkable adaptability," he wrote:

> Her bosom friend is Mrs Macleay who is the ruling spirit of a set comprising the de Martels, of the French Legation, Kroupensky, Raindre [a banker, and the father of Madame de Martel's child] and Huskisson, three men whose morals are a reproach even for Peking. . . . At present there is some estrangement among the friends. . . . One night last week Kroupensky had a picnic party to the hills, he and his two catamites, the de Martels, Sforza and Madame de Gaiffier. Mrs Macleay was piqued at not being asked. "What an easy party to entertain" was her comment. "They will want *only three*

beds!" Sforza heard the comment and was indignant and consulted Kroupensky. Such is modern society in Peking.

When the Count and Countess Sforza left Peking they conducted a sale of their effects, which included the Countess's stockings and under-clothing, and the Count's boots, shoes, and waistcoats. "A ludicrous sight," commented Morrison, who attended the sale with Jennie.

Mrs Macleay was an imaginative conversationalist. At one dinner party she discussed the relative advantages of polygamy and polyandry, and the possible result of crossing a man with a female orang-outang, and a female with a male orang-outang. She told Morrison how her friend Lady Carnegie, wife of the British Minister to Lisbon, a woman of unusual beauty had given herself in unusual circumstances, a week after her marriage, to the Duke of Alva, "a loathsome looking fellow with a tic. . . . According to Mrs Macleay, they got stuck in a lift, staying there all night!!!" And Percy Walsham reported that his cousin, the sixth Baron Abinger, had just married "the notorious French courtesan Madame Steinheil", in whose arms President Fauré had "expired in the first fatigues of an amorous interview". (Fauré, at a critical time in the Dreyfus affair, had been entertaining the handsome Marguerite Steinheil in the Presidential office when screams were heard and, as an unromantic historian put it, "the lady was patched up and sent off by a private side-door". M. Fauré died a few hours later and was given a splendid State funeral, with a service at Notre Dame.)

[V]

At the beginning of February 1917, Germany announced that her sub-marines would sink at sight all ships in the vicinity of the British Isles, no matter what flag they sailed under. On the evening of 3rd February, Captain Gaunt, British naval attaché at Washington, sent a code message to Admiral William Reginald Hall, head of British Naval Intelligence. It read "Bernstoff [the German Ambassador in Washington] has just been given his passports. I shall probably get drunk tonight!" The following day was a Sunday, and Dr P. S. Reinsch, the American Minister, recalls that he took advantage of Peking's "clear sunshine and mild air" to visit Dr Morrison at his country cottage:

> After lunch a message came from the Legation, bringing word that an important cablegram had arrived and was being decoded. I re-turned to the Legation. . . . The decoded message . . . said that the American Government had not only broken off diplomatic relations with Germany, but that she trusted the neutral powers would asso-ciate themselves with the American Government in this action. . . .

Morrison hurried back to Peking, and received a note from Donald:

My dear Doctor,
     Now that America has severed diplomatic relations with Ger-many, China should follow suit within 48 hours.

I am doing my best with Chinese I know to stir the Govt. up. *Confidential.* Reinsch went to Wai Wu Pu a few minutes ago on the same mission.

Could you not get at the President tonight?

Morrison found the President "weak, vacillating and tremulous, obsessed with the idea that Germany would be victorious". He thought the Germans would soon be in Odessa. "Bovine intelligence. Discouraging interviews," Morrison commented. Equally discouraging was his interview with Beilby Alston, to whom he reported his discussion with the President:

> He seemed little interested and only brightened up when happening to speak of Lloyd George he proceeded to tell me with much giggling and gesticulation and protrusion of the tongue of the Prime Minister's "rogering" powers declaring that when he went to open a Church bazaar he used always to "roger" the Baptist clergyman's wife!

"And this," Morrison commented, "from the Chief British authority in China at the most serious crisis!" Nor was Alston's colleague, Sidney Barton, of much more use. Wrestling with irresolute Chinese and irresponsible British, Morrison wrote to Lady Brownrigg of his difficulties:

> . . . we are doing everything we possibly can to induce China to accept the invitation. Unfortunately our Legation is not well served. By the system adopted in the Legation much responsibility is placed on the shoulders of the chief interpreter, who is called the Chinese Secretary. . . . At present our Chinese Secretary is a man named Barton, 40 years of age, a narrow-minded man who has had no experience outside of the consular service in China, and who is much dominated by his wife, a lady of high social pretensions. Her father was a bankrupt merchant who became head of Jardine's in Shanghai and realized a fortune. Barton is equally unpopular with the Chinese and with the British community. Thus through his unfitness for the post the Legation has very little influence with the Chinese. . . . The chargé d'affaires is a man from the Foreign Office named Alston, a pleasant fellow, 48 years of age, who is regarded by the Chinese rather as a buffoon.

Alston told Morrison that he had sent a wire to London, but had received no reply. The Foreign Office was closed because it was Sunday and everybody was out of town. But the American Legation was as active as the British Legation was inert. Dr Reinsch made tireless efforts to induce China to break with Germany. He was supported by Morrison, and Dr John Calvin Ferguson, who were close to the President, and by Donald and Roy Anderson, who were close to the Kuomintang. Another earnest crusader was the visiting American journalist, Sam Blythe. "These men," said Dr Reinsch, "made a spontaneous appeal based upon the fundamental justice of the policy resisting an intolerable practice, and on the beneficent effect which a great issue like this would have in pulling the Chinese nation together." It was a curious alliance. Donald and Anderson, despite their friendship with the Southern leaders, were both monarchists at heart. The "oily" American Ferguson, proprietor of the *Shanghai Times*, was an "unctuous adviser" of the Chinese Government, who, according to Morrison, had enriched himself "doing jackal work" for the Chinese and was "the most universally distrusted man in China".

Slowly, and with reservations, the Chinese yielded to their combined persuasion. After a six-hour discussion, Cabinet agreed on 8th February to make a protest to Germany "and to indicate that diplomatic relations will be broken off unless the present submarine warfare is abandoned". It was, as Reinsch pointed out, a historic decision. "China's first independent participation in world politics. She had stepped out of her age-long aloofness. . . ." The decision was celebrated at a dinner given by Sam Blythe at the Hotel des Wagons Lits the following evening. All the guests were Americans except Donald and Morrison, who noted: "Dr Reinsch has worked with his sleeves up and had a triumph." Dr Reinsch noted: "Greeting me, Dr Morrison said: 'This is the greatest thing ever accomplished in China. It means a new era. It will make the Chinese nationally self-conscious; and that, not for narrow, selfish purposes, but to vindicate human rights!' "

Once more, Morrison's optimism occluded his judgment. The decision of the Peking Government still had to be accepted in other parts of China, and President Li still had to be convinced that it was expedient for China to join the Allies. His fear of a victorious Germany persisted. On 27th February, Morrison recorded, "Last evening President said within four months England would be occupied by Germany and German submarines will be on their way to China." And the Foreign Minister, Dr Wu Ting-fang, whom Morrison described as "that senile mountebank", had threatened to resign if China broke her neutrality. Dr Wu was as much interested in spiritualism, longevity, and vegetarianism as in foreign affairs. During a discussion of the war he explained the international situation to Dr Reinsch: "There is an aura gradually spreading from Europe over the entire surface of the world. It enters the brains of people and penetrates them, making them warlike. . . ."

Another opponent of Chinese participation was Sun Yat-sen, who was quoted by the Japanese newspaper *Asahi* as saying that China and Japan must unite to drive the Europeans out of Asia. In a manifesto Sun warned Lloyd George that if China were brought into the war, anti-foreign disturbances would follow. Dr Reinsch, whom Morrison now regarded as an able man (though he spoke Yiddish to his family), thought the Machiavellian Japanese had inspired this manifesto, with the idea of so alarming Lloyd George that he would counsel China not to come into the war. Sir Richard Dane, chief of the Salt Revenue, agreed that Sun would never have dared to act as he was doing without Japanese encouragement. "All his debts are owing to Japan," he said. "The $2,600,000 he wants refunded by the Government is owing to the Japs."

Germany refused to modify her indiscriminate submarine warfare, and on 13th March, in spite of the opposition of Sun Yat-sen and Tang Shao-yi, China broke off diplomatic relations with Germany. Next day German ships were seized off Shanghai, and German concessions in China were occupied by the Chinese.

[VI]

Early in June, General Chang Hsun arrived in Tientsin with 5000 of his "pigtailed bandits". The General remained in his palatial residence in the German concession while 3000 of his ruffians moved on to Peking, where they swaggered arrogantly round the streets, terrorizing shopkeepers and even invading the sacrocant legation quarter. The city, Morrison reported, was in "mortal fear". Chang had been summoned by the President to mediate in a quarrel between himself and the northern militarists, whose representative was the Prime Minister, Yuan's tough commander-in-chief, Tuan Chi-jui. It was the old quarrel between New China and Old China, between those who believed in constitutional government and those who did not. When Tuan, backed by the *tuchuns*—the military governors —asked Li to dismiss Parliament, and threatened a military demonstration, Li responded by dismissing the Prime Minister.

Chang Hsun saw in the conflict an opportunity to realize his cherished project of restoring the Manchus. His first move, while he remained in Tientsin, was to back the *tuchuns'* demand for the dissolution of Parliament, and Li Yuan-hung summoned Morrison—whom he had not seen for nearly four months—and Ariga to discuss a constitutional dilemma. He had prepared the mandate for dissolving Parliament, he said, but none of his ministers would countersign it. What should he do? Morrison's answer was emphatic. "Tear it up!" he urged. Its proclamation would make Li's name detested and his memory dishonoured. But Ariga advised Li to get the mandate signed by the Chief of Staff, or the Chief of the Judiciary. It was obvious to Morrison that Li had made up his mind to yield to the militants, and he was not surprised to read in the *Peking Gazette* next morning that the mandate had been issued, countersigned, "not by the Acting Premier, Dr Wu Ting-fang, but by the Commander of the Peking Gendarmerie!" The report continued:

> The President is issuing forthwith a circular telegram to the country giving the reasons which have led him to take the fatal step. He takes upon himself all blame for the act, believing that in thus sacrificing his reputation and betraying the trust imposed upon him, he is saving the country from imminent bloodshed and disaster at the hands of the rebel *tuchuns*.
>
> The President's representatives were served by Chang Hsun yesterday with the warning that if the mandate was not issued THIS

MORNING he would not be answerable for the further acts of the "independent *tuchuns*".

Isolated, threatened and terrorized, the President has succumbed to the intrigues of the rebel gang at Tientsin. We learn that yesterday afternoon the President had another conference with his advisers Dr Morrison and Dr Ariga.

The Englishman emphasized the constitutional aspects of the issue and pointed out the course that duty and honour bound the President to follow despite all threats and intimidations from the militarists.

The Japanese with a more supple intellect, re-affirmed his previous advice that the President was justified in dissolving Parliament and could overcome Dr Wu Ting-fang's refusal to countersign the mandate by utilizing anyone else who was willing to do so.

Immediately the mandate was issued, Chang arrived in Peking in his huge motor-car, and was received with great ceremony. One of his first acts was to drive to the Forbidden City and kowtow before the little Emperor, the eleven-year-old P'u Yi.

[VII]

It was an intolerably oppressive summer—the hottest in Morrison's memory—and the Morrison family had moved to a seaside cottage at Peitaiho. On the first night of July, Morrison was dining with Dr Wu Ting-fang at Shanhaikwan when he received a telegram forwarded "by the intelligent Jennie" which read: EMPEROR RESTORED TWO O'CLOCK DONALD. Morrison showed it to Dr Wu, who said it was impossible. "Badness for China if true," he added. Morrison himself was incredulous. But there was no mistake. The previous night Chang Hsun and some of his officers had been entertained at a dinner and theatre party given by the Kiangsi guild, an association of Chang's fellow-provincials. Leaving the party early in the morning, heavily freighted with liquor, Chang had decided the time appropriate for the restoration of the Manchu dynasty. As dawn was breaking he and his associates, having struggled into court robes prepared for the occasion, made their way to the Forbidden City, and were admitted to the Imperial quarters. A contemporary newspaper gives an account, vivid if not entirely veracious, of what followed:

> Eunuchs in a cold sweat dashed in all directions. The Lustrous Concubine and the Grand Guardian came out in terror to see what was the matter. Chang Hsun announced in a loud voice, "There is to be a restoration today, and I have to ask the Young Master to come to the audience-hall without delay." "Whose idea is this?" stuttered the Grand Guardian. "It's old Chang Hsun's idea," said Chang with a grin, "so you see there's nothing for you to worry your head about."

"True, a restoration would be a very good thing," said the Grand Guardian, "but what will people say? Will they like it?" "Whether they like it or not," replied Chang, "I should be obliged if you would refrain from asking all these questions. Just go and request the Young Master to come to the audience-hall, then none of us will have any trouble." The Grand Guardian rolled his eyes piteously towards the Lustrous Concubine, who in her turn addressed herself to Chang. "This matter needs proper deliberations," she said gravely. "We must think carefully before we act.". . . The Lustrous Concubine by this time was in tears, and the Grand Guardian could not trust himself to say a word. Suddenly there came a hubbub of voices from the courtyard, as Chang's guards called for the Emperor. . . . In a few minutes the Grand Guardian appeared once more, escorting the eleven-year-old Emperor whom he assisted to mount the Dragon Throne. Chang at once flopped on his knees in a kowtow, imitated by his followers, some of whom seemed a little out of practice. There was a chorus of "May He reign for ten thousand years!"

The President, whose Palace was surrounded by Chang's men, sought refuge in the French Hospital, but Dr Bussière was out and the bewildered night-sister would not admit him. He then drove to the residence of General Saito, military attaché of the Japanese Legation, and was offered the hospitality of the military barracks, on condition that he did not engage in political activity. The President gave the required assurance, but before leaving his Palace he had sent a message to Tuan Chi-jui reappointing him Prime Minister and commanding him to lead the northern army against Chang. Tuan is said to have received the instruction with florid profanity, but he obeyed it promptly, and within two days 20,000 of his well-trained men were closing in on Peking. The monarchy lasted twelve days. The restoration ended as it had begun, with a flavour of *opéra bouffe*. There was some wild firing, but little fighting, and casualties, including a few curious foreigners, were negligible. An aeroplane dropped three bombs; one fell into a lake, one failed to explode. Most of Chang's ruffians fled. Those who were captured were disarmed, disbanded, and given three months' pay.

In a letter to W. W. Willoughby, Morrison wrote sardonically that he had witnessed "one of the most mighty combats that ever took place on earth":

Total casualties on both sides amounted to 25 killed, mostly by stray shots. I should imagine that not less than 50 million shots were exchanged. . . . A knowledge of ballistics is not an essential equipment as yet of the modern Chinese army. Now an American writer, Rodney Gilbert, is urging the restoration of the bow and arrow. His view is that a man with rifle, who does not know how to use it, is not nearly so dangerous as a man with a bow and arrow who does know how to use his weapon. A Chinese soldier with a rifle is not a great menace at more than 25 yards whereas a practised hand with a bow and arrow may be a real menace up to 300 yards. That is his contention. He thinks that if the bow and arrow could be re-introduced it would be impossible with bows and arrows for two forces to remain two miles apart and waste sufficient money to establish a university or hospital. He thinks that the introduction of the bow would help to stamp out rebellions, because rebellions would then be dangerous.

Chang had declared that he would fight to the end, the end came in the Dutch Legation, where he was interned when, in desperation, he asked the minister, Beelaerts, to mediate. "He is just an elderly Chinese who has seen better days," wrote David Fraser sympathetically to Morrison, but when he was released after an amnesty the following year Chang was able to retire to his Tientsin mansion with his huge fortune, amassed by extortion and theft, intact, and to pass the rest of his life, as Henry McAleavy puts it, "in that peculiarly brutal debauchery his nature craved". P'u Yi became an Emperor for the third time in 1934, when, as a Japanese puppet, he ascended the throne of Manchukuo; years later, after a redemptory term as gardener in Peking, he was miraculously transmogrified into a propaganda exhibit for the China of Mao Tse-tung.

[VIII]

China declared war on Germany on 14th August 1917, the anniversary of the relief of the Peking legations in 1900. A few days before, when Paul May, the new Belgian Minister, had wished to discuss the possibility of this declaration with Beilby Alston, the "incomparable nincompoop Alston" had said: "It is too hot to bother. Let us go to Peitaiho." And to the seaside he went.

From Windsor Castle came a telegram from King George V to the President of the Chinese Republic:

> I have learnt with great satisfaction of the entry of China into the war on the side of the Allies, and desire to offer you my cordial congratulations on the decision of the Great Republic over which you preside to associate herself with the countries which are combined against the aggressive policy of the Central Powers.

The Chinese received this message with less satisfaction. Morrison pointed out that they wanted to be described as a "Great Power" not as a "Great Republic".

Jennie wrote from Peitaiho:

> Dear Ernest: It was good of you to send me the telegram about China's Declaration of War. My dear, I *am* so glad. Your efforts of the last 2½ years have not been in vain. I always remember you saying to Sir John once "I am *determined* it shall go through," and I have often felt quite miserable that so far it *hadn't* gone through. I hope the Germans are not going to be allowed to run loose as in Japan. . . .

To think the declaration of war should have been made 3 years ago if it hadn't been for Sir John! What a list of blunders you will have to show the Prime Minister of Australia!—the delay in getting China in, the incapacity of our present representative—fancy being away at such a time—and one point you will have to insist on is the idiotic way you were treated by Conyngham Greene in Japan last year—Do you remember the chit he sent you—no address no beginning no ending and signed "CG"? It makes me furious to think of it. It's quite time a little more intelligence was introduced into the Diplomatic Service and a good beginning would be to have you in Peking. You have a jolly good case and I'm pretty sure it can be worked. England will do anything suggested now by her Colonial Statesmen, especially Australians. I am sending out powerful thought waves to the Rt Hon. Wm. Hughes, so as to pave the way for you when you go down to Australia!! I feel now, with the sale of the library our star is in the ascendant. . . .

To his brother Arthur, whom he had not seen for twenty-three years, Morrison wrote:

. . . Had I had more authority and had it not been for the weakness of the British Minister in Peking, and the gross incompetence of the British Ambassador in Tokyo, a poor amiable society lap-dog named Conyngham Greene, whose name is well-known in South Africa where his incompetence was not less clearly manifested than it has been in Japan, China would have entered the war in November 1915. Although I am well paid by the Chinese, my salary being £3500 a year, the cost of living has gone up so enormously and the price of silver has risen to such an unapproachable degree, that I have hardly enough to live on, a disgraceful statement to make, but my salary is just half what it was 2 years ago.

Two days later Morrison had more news to record: "Chinese Minister Petrograd wires that Revolution broken out and that military and navy are in it! no doubt anti-dynastic. Better that the throne should go. As Dane says, the monarchy is a mischievous anachronism—even ours."

There was no suggestion that the British monarchy was either mischievous or anachronistic in Morrison's reply to a letter from Master C. Kite, of Lyell Bay, South Australia, who signed himself "A scout boy, for King and Empire". Master Kite had read an interesting account of Morrison's adventures, and wrote: "That what interests me the most is that you were born on the same day as I was. I like to hear of great men like you who has been the means of bringing foreign countries into close touch with our great Empire. . . . Please excuse my writing to such a great man as yourself." Morrison wrote back punctiliously: "Dear Master Kite—I was glad to hear that I was born on the same day and in the same month as you were but in a somewhat earlier year. You will, I hope, grow up to be a loyal and stalwart son of the Empire, serving your King and Country with all your might."

Another of Morrison's correspondents, Mr F. E. Taylor, of the Inspectorate General of Customs, had no illusions about why his country was at war. "We English are fighting for England's interests and safety, and for nothing else . . . and quite good enough too," he wrote. "But we don't want it advertised that self-interest is at the bottom of our efforts and sacrifices, as it looks much better to say that we are fighting to save Belgium etc." However, England, "in the interests of Manchester, etc.", should not adopt the short-sighted policy of denying China the right to build up her own industries by increasing tariff protection:

> We ought to look 50 years ahead in these matters. . . . No doubt certain trades would suffer in competition with Chinese manufactures, but think of the enormous potential market presented by a China humming with industrial activity. Japan is an example. See how the imports into Japan have increased with the expansion of her industries. Help China to become wealthy and she will increase the wealth of the world. . . .

Taylor thought the Chinese had two "genuine grievances" against foreigners: the import tariff, which was fixed at five per cent, and having missionaries "shoved down their throats":

> The second is of course open to argument, but as I am convinced that the story of the synoptic gospels is a myth on a par with the fables about Attis, Adonis, Osiris, and Buddha, etc., I think it rough on the Chinese that an extra superstition should be forced on the ignorant populace under the threat of hell-fire, and against the will of the Government, especially as the presence of uneducated and tactless fanatics in the interior often causes serious embarrassment. But about the import tariff there can be no argument at all. . . .

[IX]

China's entry into the war did not cure Morrison's discontent. "A man joins the service as I did full of enthusiasm, believing he would succeed where others fail," he wrote to O. M. Green, editor of the *North China Daily News*, on 27th August. "The experience of us all is the same. The first year, enthusiasm. The second year, pessimism. The third year, indifference." Once more he decided to sell his library and, with his independence assured, to consider returning to Australia. Harvard and Yale alumni were anxious to secure the library for their respective universities, and the University of California made a firm offer of £35,000 for it, but Morrison felt bound to give the Japanese first refusal, and offered it to Baron Isawaki for the same price. "I have reason to believe I could have sold the library to an Eastern University for £40,000," Morrison wrote later. Baron Isawaki accepted the offer, and the 20,000 books, 4000 pamphlets and 2000 maps and engravings were shipped to Japan in fifty-seven cases, Morrison retaining the English section of 3000 volumes. The library was stored temporarily in Mitsubishi's Tokyo premises, where, to Morrison's great anger, about half of it was damaged by flood. The *Peking Daily News*, in an editorial headed "A Ha'p'orth of Tar", commented acridly:

> The books were sent from Peking by the buyer's agent in ordinary packing cases, were bundled into a godown in Tokyo as unceremoniously as if they had been hides, or cases of bully beef for an army, or soap, or candles, or dog-spikes, or any other quite unimportant or absolutely indestructible thing, and there when the floods came they were allowed to lie and be, irretrievably in all probability, damaged. The meticulous care with which they had for years been handled, the solicitude bestowed on their safe keeping, the constant vigilance that has preserved them from the hand of the spoiler, wilful or ignorant, all go for nothing. For an additional expenditure of some three hundred dollars the disaster might have been averted, and the collection, priceless as it is, would have remained as perfect as when it was housed in Peking.
>
> Surely a case of spoiling a ship for a ha'p'orth of tar! But it is not by any means unique. There is a score of enterprises begun in this part of the world that might well be placed in the same category. To take an example that will readily occur to the mind of our readers, we might refer to the declaration of war by the Government. There is a very strong feeling that the Government might well carry out more fully the obligations that it tacitly assumed when it entered the War. Why not adopt stricter measures towards the enemy in the land? Why not proceed more actively with the project of sending troops to Europe? Or, take the movement in the south. Why not give its suppression the ha'p'orth of tar that it needs? It is true that the tar will cost a ha'penny, but the tar would make all the difference.

"I have been criticized for selling my library," Morrison wrote to Paul King, of the Chinese Customs. "But how could I, at the age of 55, with a wife and three children, retain in my possession a hobby-horse worth £35,000? The sum provides me, not with a fortune, but with a competence, and makes me fairly independent." His present idea, he wrote, was to make all provision he could for the future, and then take leave in Australia. Whether he would go there permanently he would decide on his return. His wife would prefer to live in England where the children would get better education. "The library," he added candidly, "will remain a kind of monument, not to my learning, for my learning does not amount to a row of pins, but to my instinct as a collector."

When China's Finance Minister, Liang Chi-chao, gave a dinner to farewell Dr Morrison, and to welcome back Sir John Jordan, Morrison found Sir John little improved by his holiday. He was "tremulous, petulant and overburdened", his mind jumping unpredictably from subject to subject. Next day Morrison left Peking on six months' leave of absence. "The Chinese have treated me well as they always do," he wrote to Hutton. "My salary will be paid in full and they have given me in addition £20 a week for expenses." He was also given a portrait of the President for presentation to his mother.

The China that Morrison farewelled was still a torn and divided country. A National Council had been summoned in Peking, but the Southern leaders refused to recognize it, and what Morrison termed "a separate mock parliament" had been set up in Nanking, under the leadership of Sun Yat-sen, who had established his headquarters in a cement factory. "That enlightened warrior," Morrison wrote of Sun, "who once proposed to lead an army of three million men into Russia, and to reform the finances of China by the issue of an inconvertible paper currency, unsupported by bullion. His emergence as a Generalissimo provokes derisive laughter, but it is one of the most serious indications of the trend of Chinese politics."

A few days before his departure Morrison wrote to Arthur Balfour, an influential Sheffield steel manufacturer and a member of the Industrial Advisory Committee to the Treasury and of the Advisory Committee on War Munitions, that he was curious to learn what Australia's attitude was in regard to Japan:

> Censorship prevents anything being said about Japan and her action during the war, but in no sense can it be said that she has fulfilled her obligations as an ally, unless it is considered to be a very high qualification indeed that she did not join our enemies, although a considerable party in Japan would have had her do so. . . .
>
> Nothing is more astonishing than the action of Sir Edward Grey in sending to Peking, to be our chargé d'affaires during the absence of Sir John Jordan, a poor feeble creature from the Foreign Office, who is simply a society butterfly, who has no knowledge of the British Empire, who has no interest in his work, and who is looked upon by the Chinese, and by his fellow-countrymen here, as little better than a buffoon, and to think that Sir Edward Grey sent him here with the promise of succeeding Sir John in his pocket. . . . But for his incapacity, China would at the present time be making ships for Vickers—six standard ships which would have been of real service. . . . Sir Edward Grey appears to have made very bad appointments, and this is one of the worst. He sent his private secretary to Constantinople, and look at the unholy mess he made of things! Although he knew the record of Bax-Ironside as a swindling card-sharper, he had him in Bulgaria as Minister. Although the position in Peking is one of

enormous importance, for this must be the largest undeveloped market for British trade in the world, he sent here an amiable stuttering nincompoop. . . . It is nothing less than a scandal. It is toying with great British interests simply because of personal friendship. You are a powerful man. Surely you can help and have this post in Peking, after Sir J. Jordan leaves, given to someone who has British interests at heart, and not to a nonentity, such as we are likely to be saddled with. . . .

[XI]

In Canton, Morrison addressed the students of the Christian College after "an astonishingly bad lunch", and suggested that President Wilson should nominate an American intermediary to settle the differences between North and South. Dr Reinsch, he said, would be *persona grata* with all Chinese. He did not think that North and South were very far apart: "No great principle divided them, such as slavery versus anti-slavery, or Republic versus Monarchy." The only real difference was on the procedure for the re-establishment of republican government. In the present conflict both sides lost and only Japan gained.

[XII]

One of Morrison's fellow-passengers on the S.S. *Aki Maru* from Hong Kong, a Scottish hardware merchant named Soutar, who had spent some time in Melbourne, deplored the improvidence of the Australians:

No river harnessed. Millions of horsepower allowed to escape. Waste of tins, jam tins, kerosene tins. Fortunes lost in this. Tells me of the separation of Capital and Labour of the gulf between employer and employed. A policy of retaliation. No sympathy. Each exacting all he can each insisting on his rights. He emphasizes the general incompetence and unwillingness to learn.

There was much similar talk about Australia's inadequacies, and as the ship steamed towards the Queensland coast Morrison wrote to Donald:

What I have heard on board has not increased the cheerfulness of the prospect of revisiting my country after an absence of 15 years. I hear of nothing but loafing and slacking and the disloyalty of Archbishops preaching open sedition, and of men holding up their country at one of the most critical stages of the war. . . .

Equally dispiriting to the nostalgic exile was Morrison's first glimpse of his homeland when the *Aki Maru* berthed at Thursday Island on 30th November:

This is a horrid place, known as "Thirsty Island". . . . Men were more than usually drunk, most of the community from pilot downwards, this being St Andrew's Day. Officers loafed on ship all day

drinking with whoever could offer a drink. All houses were shut. . . .
A drunken constable trying to thumbprint the Jap crew. A humiliating experience. The fury of the captain watching the administration
of the law by a drunken policeman at the first port of entry. . . .

In the Queensland city of Townsville, "the rich and prosperous capital of the North", Morrison noted disapprovingly "large bodies of vigorous young men who ought to be serving their country loafing around the
pub bars". In the recruiting depot was a solitary citizen, sprawled on a
chair, "blissful and thirsty", a man of fifty-five who had mistaken the
depot for a pub and, having sat down, was too drunk to rise. Recruiting
was a lively issue in Australia, where the people were soon to vote for or
against conscription. In Brisbane, Morrison listened with displeasure to
speakers on both sides. The Federal Leader of the Opposition, "an ex-
hatter named F. G. Tudor", delivered a "blatant and unconvincing" anti-
conscription speech, suggesting that the real purpose of conscription was
to replace Australians with cheap Asiatic labour. The Federal Attorney-
General, Sir William Irvine, a nephew of the Irish rebel John Mitchel,
had none of the oratorical fire of his famous uncle. Morrison found his
arguments for conscription "heavy, dull, ponderous, and unconvincing"

The war news, too, was depressing:

Germans have driven us back near Cambrai 10 kilometres on a 4 mile
front. Appalling catastrophe in Halifax, Nova Scotia. Russian armistice. Roumania verging towards separate peace. Another Italian
defeat. Veritable catalogue of calamities. Air raid on London. Worst
shipping week for a long time.

Morrison continued his lamentations next day:

I am much depressed with the outlook. What a shocking condition is
Australia. Disloyalty. Governed by the unfit. Drunkenness. Prostitution. Came home late last night. Much drunkenness among soldiers in
uniform. They force their way when drunk into shops and refuse
to leave unless paid. There is no discipline. State police refuse to obey
the orders of Commonwealth officers. . . . I.W.W.'s, Sinn Feiners
and others against conscription. Irvine last night said, "Germany had
almost succeeded in getting Australia." He spoke of the 800,000 Germans who annually went abroad to live in other countries. . . . He
said nothing of the 680,000 of surplus population of Japan every year
—an annual surplus greater than the total population of Queensland.
Japan will prevent Germany coming to Australia, what price will we
have to pay for this protection? Japs would make short shrift with
the Labour Unions. Labour seems to be losing ground. The last elections were disastrous to the Labourites in every province. I am still
imperfectly informed and must preserve an open mind.

The Queensland Railways Commissioner, Colonel Charles Evans,
C.M.G., gave Morrison a free ticket to Sydney and a handsome mulga

walking-stick, and the Governor, Major Sir Hamilton Goold-Adams, G.C.M.G., a "white-haired livery warrior", gave him a "revolting luncheon":

> I suspect that it was cooked by the gardener. The Governor was helped first and wolfed most of the meagre fare provided. Conversation was equally flatulent and insipid. "Is this your first visit to Australia"? asked His Exc. "No", I replied, "I first came here on February 4, 1862." What did I do in China? Altogether the most uncomfortable lunch and I was glad to get away. . . .

In Sydney the Governor-General, Sir Ronald Munro-Ferguson ("dapper kindly-spoken Scotchman in Khaki with a somewhat squeaky voice suggesting arrested testicular development"), asked him to lunch at Admiralty House, and Lady Helena ("long-faced unprepossessing bony dame like Mrs Asquith") ingenuously asked him who he was and what he did? Sir Ronald spoke of the inferiority of the Australian civil service, and of the folly of admitting boys when they left school at the age of fourteen. The Lord Mayor, the Hon. R. D. Meagher, placed a car and chauffeur at Morrison's disposal and give him a civic reception. Meagher was a solicitor who, though struck off the roll for infamous behaviour in the famous Dean murder case, had been at the same time Lord Mayor and Speaker of the House. "What a laxity of public decency," Morrison reflected, "this appointment to two of the highest offices in the State of a disbarred solicitor and a public crook." The Lord Mayor elect, the Hon. J. Joynton Smith ("an ex-steward of the P. & O."), and "other men of note with streaky past" were among the guests. At a Millions Club lunch the Acting-Federal Treasurer, W. A. Watt, called for three cheers for Morrison, whom he compared with Cecil Rhodes. Morrison told the Sydney Press Club the truth about Japan, and appealed to thirty-two leading Chinese at the Chinese Chamber of Commerce not to support the southern movement in China, "a movement which was weakening the country and opening the way to Japanese aggression". The thirty-two Chinese drank nothing but champagne and applauded Morrison's twenty-minute speech lustily.

Morrison was given a free pass on the New South Wales railways; "I am being treated as a 'distinguished guest'," he noted. "It is all very surprising to me." Feeling that his wardrobe did not match his welcome, he slipped away from his hosts and bought a "respectable hat" from Richard Hunt & Co. "Its cost was 32/6," he noted. "An astonishing price for a hat." But he did not begrudge paying Hardy Brothers £200 for a diamond pendant, £54 for a diamond brooch, and £162 for a pearl necklet, for Jennie.

In Melbourne, Morrison was "greatly pleased" at being made an honorary member of the Melbourne Club ("an honour usually reserved for State Governors and distinguished visitors like Kitchener"). Here he met the State Governor, Sir Arthur Stanley ("little cock-sparrow"), and a generous assortment of Victoria's leading citizenry—legal, medical, and agricultural. Sir Arthur invited him to a dinner which began at 7 p.m. ("because after 8 no wine can be served at a Club, such being the law of the land"), and Morrison spoke for half an hour on the Far East. The dinner guests included Sir John Grice ("one of the most public-spirited men in Melbourne"), Hayden Starke ("barrister, large practice in common law"), and the club president, Edward Mitchell ("leader of the Victorian Bar, married my cousin Lizzie").

Morrison was greatly concerned over the conscription referendum. In his diary for Sunday 16th December he wrote:

> Thursday will be one of the fateful days in our history for on that day we will decide whether we as a nation are to follow the path of honour or the path of shame, whether we are to follow the ideals of Cardinal Mercier, the holy prelate who has been an eye-witness of the inhuman sufferings inflicted upon Catholic Belgium, whether we are to follow the ideals of the democratic President of the greatest of democracies, or the ideals of the Leninists and Maximalists, the Bolsheviks and the Anarchists, who in an incredibly few months have reduced to degraded impotence the mighty power that once was Russia.

This resonant passage was annotated: "Peroration to be got off sometime (if I can remember it)." In Melbourne four days later Morrison wrote:

> Referendum vote taken today and substantial majority against conscription assured. . . . What nation is there that would conscript itself? The wonder is not that conscription failed but that so many voted in its favour. Against conscription were most women, all slackers, all the disaffected, and the whole Catholic vote. As I was walking in William Street I heard a young Australian say to another "Have you heard of the revolution in New Zealand? The police have revolted and the prisoners have been liberated from gaol." Overhearing this, I apologized for intruding and asked what was the cause. He said "Conscription." I said one word only, the expressive word "Balls!" and walked on.
>
> Against conscription were the Labour leaders who feared the depletion of labour would give power to the Capitalist, and the Catholics led by Archbishop Mannix . . . who was sent to Australia to provoke Sectarian strife and Sinn Feinism and has been accepted as anti-conscription leader of Australia. . . . But most to blame are wholly misleading optimistic reports from England. . . . Daily we were doped with stories of Germany's disintegration.

Archbishop Mannix, a brilliant Irish theologian and a bitter Irish nationalist, was a tireless, witty, and deadly opponent of conscription, and the bogy-man of those who supported the hysterical conscription campaign of the Prime Minister, William Morris Hughes. Their attitude towards Mannix is well illustrated by a story which the New South Wales

Premier, William Holman—like Hughes a renegade from the Labour Party—told Morrison:

> Holman's favourite story of the woman who speaking of the new flush closets complained that the earthenware was so very cold to sit down on. "But there is a wooden covering?" she was asked. Oh, her husband had taken that away to use as a frame for a portrait of Archbishop Mannix.

Morrison saw the redoubtable Archbishop in action when he returned to Sydney by train. Dr Mannix ("the most aggressive Catholic prelate Australia has yet been cursed with") was a fellow-passenger:

> He had a welcome at every station the train drew into. I heard him speak. Very marked brogue. It seemed to me poor stuff vulgar and commonplace yet every sentence was received with cheers. The crowds mostly flippant schoolgirls seemed to regard it as a joke and there was not a trace of reverence only good humour the good lark of hearing the longhaired one speak.

[XIII]

Morrison did not get off his deliberated peroration, but on the last Sunday of December he spoke in Melbourne's Wesley Church at length and—for the first time—without notes or rehearsal. He was very nervous, and it was "another disagreeable experience":

> Rain fell heavily. The church was crowded. Not less than 2500—perhaps 3000. It was stiflingly hot. Before I was called upon there was a service of music and prayer and two songs. My thirst was unbearable, my lips parched and it was positive pain to move my tongue and the pattering of the rain added to my difficulty. . . . I did not pitch my voice properly and the effort of speaking was quite painful.

He had just begun when a man only two-thirds of the way down the hall stood up and disconcertingly said he could not hear the speaker. Morrison struggled on, feeling that his subject was over the heads of the audience, even if he could be heard, and that he was speaking vainly to "this crowd of artisans and spinsters". But he warned them croakingly that the Far Eastern problem "would sooner or later" compel the attention of all Australians. Blinded by prosperity, they were disregarding the signs and portents and the fact that outside their undefended borders other worlds were coming nearer and nearer. China had a population of 325 million and an annual increase of not less than 5 million. Australia had a population of 5 million and an undefended coastline. Prudence would suggest that she should bring her products to that thickly populated market. He described Australia as:

This favoured island still in swaddling clothes, nursed by the Mother Country, where 5 millions of people live in luxurious indolence, the largest undefended area in the world's surface today, the most defenceless of all countries, a country believed by the majority of its inhabitants to be not worth defending, the richest prey that can fall under the domination of an aggressive neighbour or a victorious enemy.

And he urged Australia carefully to consider the effect of anti-Asiatic legislation on China, on Japan, and, "a hundred times more carefully", on a combination of China and Japan:

> . . . one must carefully guard against a policy which effects or tends to effect such a combination. . . . Chinese superabundance of raw materials in men and material—wrought with efficiency by the high administrative genius of Japan, must evolve a combination of really formidable danger.

There were 135,000 Japanese in China, and only 8900 British. Japanese methods were entirely German, hence it was not unnatural that her avowed sympathy was not with Britain—to whom she owed her present position among nations—but with German militarism. There was a constant Japanese movement southwards and Japan was now a very great military and naval power. Her mercantile marine had been increasing during the war, and she had the largest dreadnought afloat. . . .

After the lecture two reporters waited urgently on Morrison, representatives of Melbourne's two leading papers, the *Argus* and the *Age*. The *Age* man confessed that he was deaf and had heard nothing. "The *Argus* man was in a worse predicament for he had not come to the lecture at all. Both were embarrassed because their orders were to send in 'half a column or more.'" Morrison felt that he had been snubbed, but he agreed to help them out, and dictated face- and job-saving reports to both of them.

"I was uncomfortable and spoke badly," he wrote to Donald, "but I did speak out for America, saying that if the policy of any Power in its relations with any other nation can be termed altruistic, that term can be applied to the policy of America in China. . . . I have had mighty little holiday. All the time I am talking or writing about the China question."

[XIV]

Among the many he talked to were Australia's leading politicians and defence authorities, including Prime Minister Hughes ("very keen and alert, fine diction though h's sometimes dropt"); the Minister for Defence, Senator Pearce ("simple, modest"); the Chief of the General Staff, Major-General J. G. Legge ("dull but honest"); and the First Member of the Naval Board, Rear-Admiral Sir William Creswell ("dotage, softening of the brain"). They listened politely when Morrison spoke of Japan's southward drive and of her duplicity as an ally, but apparently were neither interested nor convinced, and the naive belief that Japan had faithfully respected her treaty obligations unfortunately survived in Australia as late as 1941, when Japan was moving southward irresistibly towards Thailand. (When Hughes at an Advisory War Council meeting questioned Japanese integrity, Prime Minister Curtin cited as an indication of Japan's trustworthiness her respect for the Anglo-Japanese Alliance in World War I!)

Creswell ("this ancient mariner") spoke in strong terms of a former Australian Governor-General, "the disreputable" Earl of Dudley, who, though he owned 30,000 acres and large iron works in England, and big estates in Jamaica, was reluctant to spend money in Australia: "Licentious, unscrupulous, never paying his debts, having to be dunned by Dalgety's for payment for motor-car. At earlier date, had repudiated his debt at the Union Club, Sydney. . . ."

The Marshall Islands had become an obsession with Morrison, but few shared his interest in them. An exception was John Christian Watson, a former Labour Prime Minister, whom John Storey described as the "uncrowned King of Labour". Morrison found him "singularly modest and unassuming, the antithesis of the loud-voiced demagogue":

> I told him of the population of Japan and of Korea and of the rapidity of increase and the tendency to move *southwards*. He said that in the case of the Marshall Islands, Japan first intimated that the Islands would be handed over to the Australians and that arrangements were actually being made for this being done!
>
> 2. Then she asked for delay until other arrangements could be made.
>
> 3. She caused it to be known that the islands would be retained. . . . He spoke "with knowledge", he said, and "confidentially".

It was apparent from the letter Morrison received from the Director of Military Intelligence, Major E. L. Piesse, that Australia was not very well informed about her neighbours in Asia:

> I have to deal with a mass of information received from many sources as to affairs in the East. Much of this information is of great interest to us, but as none of the officers of the General Staff have been in the East we sometimes have difficulty in estimating what importance should be attached to it. For this reason, I take every opportunity that comes to meet men acquainted with Eastern affairs . . . if you could come to lunch, or perhaps to afternoon tea, with me some day, in one of the public gardens, we can talk over in pleasant surroundings the matters in which I am interested. Perhaps I should add that I am not specially interested in Chinese affairs, and that I do not think I should ask you any questions as to China which you might not be at liberty to answer. . . .

Morrison took tea with Major Piesse in Melbourne's "beautiful" botanical gardens ("among the finest in the world") and talked to him of

Japan's movement southward. Piesse produced reports of Japanese activity in the Dutch East Indies, and spoke of the misgiving caused by the visit there of the Japanese diplomat Count Otani.

W. M. Hughes told Morrison that he had suggested the line of the Equator be used to divide the Pacific, but he did not tell him that on 7th February that year he had told the British Government, in answer to a direct question, that Australia would not object to Japan's occupation of the islands north of the Equator. Britain had sought Australia's views before making a secret agreement with Japan about the disposal of these islands, and of Germany's rights in Shantung. Unaware of the *fait accompli*, Morrison continued to crusade against Japan retaining the islands.

[XV]

Morrison took his crusade to New Zealand, where he found a general reluctance to criticize Japan. The Attorney-General, Sir John Findlay, thought it "indiscreet at the present time" to refer to Japanese sympathies with German militarism. The Commander of the New Zealand Expeditionary Force, Major-General Sir Alexander Godley, however, agreed with Morrison that the Japanese were a menace. Many to whom Morrison talked thought that Sir Alexander was a menace. "Hated and loathed by New Zealanders. Wonder he hasn't been shot in the back," Morrison noted. A reporter on the *Auckland Herald* ("nice fellow, C. C. Nichol") who had served under Godley on Gallipoli said:

> Men hate him. Knowing that his men will never hesitate to take any risk takes advantage and sacrifices them needlessly in *posts of honour* are blown to bits. He told me what a bad effect upon the men had the announcement in Army orders one day that an Irishman had been executed for cowardice in leaving his trench. Men were unstrung by this. Any man might have had a panic. . . .

Morrison's tour through New Zealand was a dreary round of interviews, speeches, lunches, dinners, receptions. "Damn these civic receptions," he wrote after one in Wellington. "They are no good to anybody but the Mayor. In my speech I ought to have emphasized that the chief scenic beauties I have seen in New Zealand so far have been the Mayors and Town Councillors." (A witty friend suggested he was suffering from "mal de mayor".) But on another page, recording an invitation to speak to the Otago Expansion League, he wrote: "I will do so with pleasure. What an advance! Formerly nervous now delighted to speak and chagrined if not asked or if leading citizens not present."

He told the Otago audience, which included at least two leading citizens—the Minister for Defence, Sir James Allen, and the Chief Justice, Sir Robert Stout—that the Japanese military leaders "were rather with than against German military action in Europe", and that a year after the war began a vicious campaign was carried out in a Japanese newspaper

353

against the British. Though some of these observations appeared in the report in the *Auckland Herald*, they were cut out of the report in the *Otago Daily Times*, and the editor of the Auckland *Star* "bitterly cut" the report of another speech in which Morrison again denounced Japan:

> I spoke somewhat heatedly against the Japanese, against their treachery, their unscrupulousness, their failure to act up to the Alliance. Bell joined issue and seemed angry citing in their defence their escorting the New Zealand troops, the danger New Zealand was in from the "Scharnhorst" and "Gneisenau" at the outbreak of war and relief it was when the Jap cruisers appeared in Wellington. (But the Jap ships only arrived after the German ships were on their way to South America.) Apparently this act is the only one that can be cited in favour of the Japanese.

Next day Sir James Allen asked Morrison to explain what he meant by saying that the sympathy of the Japanese military was with the Germans. Sir Francis Bell, the leader of the Upper House, had reported Morrison's aggressively anti-Japanese speech to Cabinet. But Prime Minister Massey agreed with Morrison that Japan must not be left in possession of the Marshall Islands, and promised to bring the matter before the War Cabinet in London.

In Wellington, Morrison was taken to the "wonderful" private library of Alexander Horsburgh Turnbull (now the public Alexander Turnbull Library) of 55,000 volumes. He was more impressed with the collection ("one of the finest in the world") than with the collector:

> . . . a horrible-looking recluse . . . who is the worst of drug-takers. Archdeacon Herbert Williams, his greatest friend, tells me he has at times consumed £5 worth of cocaine *per week*. It seems incredible. Charges up to the firm, this was an excuse not unnaturally leading to his retirement from business. . . . Turnbull is an ill-favoured evil-smelling man who takes no exercise, lives on drugs. . . . I told him that I had the first edition of the second part of *Robinson Crusoe*. He told me he had the first *five editions*.

[XVI]

When Morrison returned to Melbourne the Prime Minister at lunch spoke to him "very confidentially" and "asked me to do certain things, offered to give me a code, and promised to recommend me for the K.C.M.G. He volunteered the promise asking me if it would be any help to me. I said emphatically it would be."

But Morrison's faith in the promise must have been shaken by Sir William Irvine, who had spoken of Hughes with "indignation and contempt"

> as one strongly opposed by one half of the people and cordially distrusted by the other half—unscrupulous and . . . regarded with grave

suspicion. "All for Hughes, Hughes first!" Could say nothing in his favour, slighting even his oratory. And broken all his pledges.

Theodore Fink, now chairman of directors of the Melbourne *Herald*, wanted to help Morrison to become British Minister in Peking. He thought he could influence Lloyd George and Bonar Law, through Keith Murdoch, the London correspondent of the *Herald*, "who is to marry the daughter of Bonar Law". But Murdoch did not marry Bonar Law's daughter and Morrison was not appointed Minister to Peking.

Sir Edmund Barton told Morrison that he had discussed the White Australia policy—which he claimed to have originated—with the Aga Khan, who had said that Indians did not take umbrage at the barring of coolies but at the refusal to admit Indian students and travellers. Morrison advocated the settlement of questions affecting Australia and China and Japan by direct intercourse between the countries: "negotiations in this way would lead to better results, the negotiations being conducted on the part of Australia by one who had a thorough knowledge of the conditions in Australia. . . . Barton expressed approval. . . ."

Morrison also urged Hughes and other Ministers to appoint an Australian High Commissioner to the Far East, with diplomatic rank and an adequate staff.

Inextinguishable Morrison optimism irradiated the "arresting address" he delivered to the Commercial Travellers Association in Melbourne. China was in a state of development, not of revolution, he said. The conflict they read about was a constitutional conflict as to the form of parliamentary government to be established. The restoration of parliamentary government was a question of months. It had taken eleven years to draft the constitution of the United States, and they must not be impatient if China had not accomplished more in the six years of the republic. He whetted the appetites of his listeners—described by one of them as "the pick of the brains of commercial Melbourne"—with an eloquent account of China's illimitable resources, and vast trade possibilities:

Its coal deposits in Shansi are sufficient to supply the world's need in coal for 2000 years. The modern coal mines, developed under British, Japanese, Belgian, and German auspices, are the finest in the world. The iron deposits of the country are considered equal to the iron deposits of Pennsylvania. China produces 70% of the world's output of antimony. The copper yield is shown by this fact. The common coin of China is the brass 'cash'. . . . It was possible since the war to purchase that brass cash at £31 a ton, and only one nation had the enterprise to develop that trade. Japan, in one year, purchased 65,000 tons. You can see what a profit was made. Quicksilver is there. Manganese is there. The Chinese produce in China and in Burma and in Siam the great bulk of the tin of the world. The vegetable resources of the country are infinite. The American Government for years has employed in China experts like Frank Myer to study the vegetable conditions of the country and to introduce into the markets Chinese products, alfalfa, pears, in varieties. He introduced 600 varieties of Persimmon alone. He found the Chinese jujube, which was eight times as large as any previously known. The flowers introduced into Great Britain have revolutionized the horticulture of that country. George Forrest has introduced into Great Britain from China a variety of flowers almost past belief. Scientific men for years have been cataloguing his discoveries. Then you have that country with its infinite possibilities of inland communication. No other country in the world possesses such means of inland water communication. It is possible for a man to get into a canoe in Peking and to travel by inland waterways right across China, and come out at Indo-China. . . .

China has, within quite recent years, followed along the lines of Western development. Her people are beginning to sleep in European beds, to dress in European clothes, to eat European food, to drink European wines, to consume European medicines. No importation into China has attained the development of that dealing with foreign drugs. You will find caravans proceeding from Western China to Lhassa, in Tibet, loaded up with 'pink pills for pale people'. (Laughter.) I have been told that the advertisement bill alone at that Company in China amounts to £40,000 sterling per annum, and the trade has been most profitable. Surely the time has come when some effort ought to be made to bring Australian traders into direct communications with the Chinese traders? Any foreigner going to China is under the jurisdiction of his own laws, and his trade is also under the protection of his own Minister or Consul. That condition, it is arranged by treaty, will continue until the administration of justice in China has reached the stage which the European Powers are willing to recognize as an adequate administration of justice. By China's entry into the war she has greatly raised her standing among the nations. (Hear, Hear.) She has expelled every German from her service. (Hear, Hear.) She has confiscated thirteen German ships. She has destroyed German trade. She has cancelled her treaties with Germany. Any treaty, then, made after this war by Germany must place Germany in a position of disadvantage compared with the position held by any one of the other trading nations in China. (Hear, Hear.)

Financially, China had never been more prosperous, Morrison assured the picked brains of commercial Melbourne:

The whole foreign debt of China is under £170,000,000 sterling. Of that, £33,000,000 sterling is due on account of war indemnity arising from the conflict between Japan and China of 1894-5. Of the balance, £67,500,000 sterling is due to the foreign Powers on account of the Boxer troubles of 1900-1. Of that sum, Germany's share of £12,500,000 sterling has been confiscated—(Hear, Hear)—and the Austrian share, amounting to £600,000 sterling, has been similarly dealt with. (Hear, Hear.) China has come into the war, and in recognition of the services she has rendered by declaring war on Germany and Austria, the Powers have unanimously agreed to the postponement of all payments in connection with the Boxer indemnity for five years. (Hear, Hear.) Of the remainder, £36,000,000 of her foreign debt is on account of railway loans and the railways of China are prosperous, some prosperous to a degree which will compare favourably with the prosperity even of the railways of your own country. (Laughter.)

Mr Warren Kerr, chairman of the Chamber of Commerce, who moved the vote of thanks, said apocalyptically: "We have had revealed to us a power of which most of us have scarcely dreamt, which in the ordinary course of things must develop and make its influence felt in the history of the world and its international intercourse." Mr York Syme, chairman of the Steamship Owners' Federation, said, botanically: "The seed Dr Morrison has planted today will . . . have every hope of attaining to a flourishing tree," and Mr D. G. Patterson, president of the C.T.A., said realistically: "It is now for us to act."

[XVII]

"I was rushed to death in Melbourne, and really was on the brink of a nervous breakdown," Morrison wrote. Rheumatism made his movements difficult, but he found time and energy to make a sentimental journey to Geelong, where he was given a civic reception; to Ballarat, where the town councillors wanted to show him the abattoirs; and to Queenscliff, "the seaside recreation ground of my boyhood", which he had not seen for thirty-five years, and where he felt "curiously lonely". The old family cottage now bore a notice: "Woodlands—First Class Accommodation". Though midsummer, it was wet and wintry, and he

> walked in the face of a pitiless wind down to the wharf to ask after Walter Shapter who was the Triton among minnows (whatever that may mean) among the fishermen . . . and when I was a boy used to take me to shoot gannets to bait his lobster-pots. Slouching along the pier was a monosyllabic fisher-lad . . . turned out to be a grandson of the man I was seeking who had died 6 years ago from "drink chiefly". . . . Then to Church . . . a poor divine was bleating reading a chapter of Genesis but bungling the words. . . . So, disgruntled, I came out. . . .

One Sunday in Melbourne, in the same ecumenical spirit that he had showed in his youth, Morrison, accompanied by Theodore Fink, a Jew, visited St Patrick's Cathedral ("only two thirds full"), the Scots Church ("still fewer"), and the Anglican Cathedral.

Morrison spent Christmas at Heronswood, Dromana, the bayside home of his brother-in-law, Justice Henry Bournes Higgins. It was another forgettable gastronomic experience, as his diary reveals:

357

Breakfast at 9.15, and this is the country . . . where one should breakfast at 7, a hearty hot meal. In this astonishing household we had a
breakfast of burnt porridge and lukewarm eggs and literally sour
bread with meagre helpings of tea doled out by my sister. . . .

Lunch was simply horrible. Remains of yesterday's cold beef
cut in thin unappetizing slices, potatoes in jackets and some dry
cheese. . . .

Christmas dinner: No wine was offered, and no whisky, and
there was found only one bottle of soda-water in this parsimonious
house—a shocking dinner . . . a most deplorable experience.

Last day of this infernal food. Rejoice at the prospect of going
tomorrow. . . . I am inadequately fed, and am offered food prepared
probably by the gardener. I am in a constant state of irritation. . . .
If the people were poor curates to whom threepence represented a
coin worth saving I would say nothing, but to be invited to a house
whose host is a Federal High Court Judge with ample earnings
£2000 or £3000 a year, and to find that he and his wife . . . are
always seeking to save *that* threepence, is quite nauseating.

Lunching with another distinguished member of the judiciary, the
Chief Justice, Sir Samuel Griffith, Morrison remembered how Griffith,
as Premier of Queensland, had described him during the kanaka controversy, in 1883, as "a very young man who does not bear a high reputation". Griffith, he noted, was now a very old man ("suffering hemiplegia,
very decrepit, can shake with right hand but writes with left, speech much
affected also, now 72") who refused to resign his high post because it
carried no pension.

There were many reminders of lost days. A letter from Mrs Agnes
Quodling, of Yass, New South Wales, recalled Morrison's canoe voyage
down the Murray, thirty-six years before:

Although our acquaintance was slight and happened a very long time
ago, still I never forget you. I was a small girl of five or six years of
age and lived of course with my parents in a place called Drik Drik
in the South West of Victoria and you arrived at our house one day
with a swag on your back and very sore foot. . . . You stayed with
us for a couple of days and my mother attended to your foot. When
I saw my mother for the last time some years ago, I told her what I
had been reading about you and she said "Well I'm not ashamed that
I washed his feet". You gave me some conversation lollies which delighted me very much but Mother made me save two for my teacher.
I could not resist licking the writing off them on the way to school.
. . . I am very proud of our slight acquaintance.

Morrison wrote back gratefully:

It must have been in February 1881. I had been on a canoe voyage
down the Murray and when walking out to my canoe at the mouth of
the Murray I trod on a broken glass bottle and cut my foot badly.
This injury I felt when carrying my swag back to Geelong and

Mount Gambier. It will give me much pleasure if you will tell me where Drik Drik was?

No greater compliment was ever paid to me than that paid by your Mother. . . . Any further particulars I would very much like to have. . . .

Mrs Quodling replied that Drik Drik was nine miles beyond Dartmoor, a small township on the Glenelg River, about twenty miles south-east of Mount Gambier.

Despite ill-health, Morrison's activity was prodigious. There were endless requests for photographs, autographs, articles, and money; for advice about jobs and trade; for opinions on anything from a frail book of poems to a fraudulent Chinese herbalist. Morrison patiently replied to them all. When Mr Meagher, of Bathurst, New South Wales, asked for information about Catholic literature in China, Morrison gave him a report of three typewritten pages. When Mr Burfitt, of Glebe Point, New South Wales, sent a copy of his history of the wool industry in Australia, Morrison told him that Ronald Macleay, the former British counsellor in Peking, was a direct descendant of John Macarthur, the father of Australian wool. "I often wonder why more attention is not given to the subject of the descendants of our great men," he wrote. Mr E. W. Cole, the eccentric Melbourne bookseller, sent a great bundle of his own publications, including a book on the better side of the Chinese character. Morrison acknowledged them gratefully and dropped them all in the wastepaper basket. He also solemnly acknowledged a letter from Mr Scott Brandon, of Wellington, N.Z., who had discovered two reasons for Chinese footbinding: "to keep the wife from gadding about and to assist callipygic development—the admiration of men of all ages".

From Oban Station, via Cloncurry, North Queensland, Mr Matt Langtree, who had been floodbound with Morrison in Northern Australia in 1882, wrote again:

I am glad to know you have made such progress and wish you all sorts of luck. . . . I am now 62 and owing to getting fever upon fever in the Kimberleys, Western Australia, coupled with sciatica and hard living, I am bending a bit now Dr., but suppose that's a natural consequence. I am just doing odd jobs here and have two years to go before I can get the pension—if ever I live long enough to get it. . . .

What changes since you and I met. Cattle then fat £3.10. to £7.10, now £17/-/- to £27/-/-.

Wages ordinary hands 25/- and 30/- now 50/- and 60/- a week. Drovers then "men", 35/- and 40/-, now 120/- and 140/- a week.

Wire cannot be procured, gal. iron ditto.

Material of all sort is hard to get and so are the *old time* men Dr. In those days men good Mates—generous to a fault—rough pebbles but honest and true as steel not so now—Rejects—Objects and the scum of the city are out here. . . . All my old Mates are gone—or like you migrated—and I know you have seen all sorts of men and—

God knows—are a man will help me a bit. Its a long way to send for it Doctor and it may be longer before I can repay you perhaps never —we waded in water together—weather-bound then—I am old-age bound now . . . for I am breaking up and have no one to help me now—

For boyhood's days.
and Old Time Sake.

Morrison posted back £10, which he hoped Langtree would accept "in memory of that time long ago".

[XVIII]

Another outbreak of plague was reported from China, and Morrison decided to cut short his "holiday". "My health has been bad," he wrote from Sydney at the end of March. "The rheumatism which I caught just before leaving Melbourne has stuck to me. I have not felt so rotten for years. I have no strength or energy and suffer from profound dejection. This gloom has now been intensified by the appalling news from the Western Front."

But he continued his journalizing, his discussions, and his letter-writing, with undiminished gusto. One letter to Sir William Irvine about Japanese policy in China—the first of several—occupied fifty typewritten pages. And no item of gossip was too small for his attention. He was particularly interested in the reiterated stories of corruption in Sydney public life. Again, the "humourless" Norman Pope was an unending source:

All stories told me by N.P. are stories of Universal Corruption among our politicians. . . . Holman the premier appears to be associated with every rascality. He is in the hands of Hugh D. McIntosh, a one-time steward in a small eating-house, rising to be proprietor of the Stadium and the Tivoli. Has financed Holman and in consequence is the Hon. H. D. McIntosh, M.L.C. Holman associated through McIntosh with Teasdale Smith a Scotch contractor from South Australia who by some of the most atrocious jobbery secured several million pounds sterling contracts for silos. Senator Pearce appears to be most hopelessly incompetent, perhaps a fool rather than a knave.

Holman's confidential secretary told Morrison—confidentially—that domestic infelicity had driven Holman to brandy and that under the "baleful influence" of McIntosh, he was encouraged to drink rather than restrained. Dudley Braham succinctly attributed Holman's collapse to "women and brandy".

In a farewell letter to Sir James Allen, Morrison wrote:

News from China in regard to the extension of the pneumonic plague is somewhat disquieting to me, the last report stating it had affected Paotingfu, only 80 miles from Peking. I am therefore expiditing my return. . . . Pneumonic plague is, I believe, the most serious epidemic in the world. It is the "black death" that spread over Europe in the Middle Ages. Defoe's account purporting to be written by an eye-witness is an accurate description. In Nov. 1910, the disease broke out in North Manchuria, having travelled from Russian Central Asia. . . . There was no known case of recovery though there were some cases of immunity. I saw one Chinese house set apart as a lazaretto in which 1400 patients were admitted and 1400 corpses taken out, whilst two caretakers, elderly men, living in contact with the stricken, both escaped infection. Naturally, therefore, I am anxious about the plague, for if once it were to take hold in China and Japan, the de-struction would be appalling.

Morrison enclosed a long critical report on Japanese activities: "Are we not justified in suspecting," he asked, "that Japanese protection to German trade in China and Japan, and Japan's immunity from German submarines, were in some way related? . . . The fact remains that it has been to Japan's commercial advantage, this destruction of British shipping. Every British ship sunk has increased the value of the Japanese mercan-tile marine. The few Japanese ships that have been sunk have in the majority of cases been under charter at the time to Allied countries. . . ." Allen, who was Acting Prime Minister of New Zealand, replied:

I think you know that I have not much faith in the Japanese and have had in mind for many years that ultimately we shall have to face them in the Pacific. I am surprised, therefore, at what happened to the Twenty one Demands . . . and think the Empire must be grateful to you that you secured their disclosure and ultimate modification.

You touch a very delicate subject when you allude to the attitude of Australia and New Zealand towards Japan at the present time. We have had our instructions as you know and must be very careful in any action we take which may prejudice the Imperial Govern-ment's relationship with Japan. I understand you think, however, that a broad policy which would indicate that the Empire would not allow certain things would have a greater effect than submission to circumstances as they exist today? You may be right, but from my point of view, when I tell a man he must do this, or he must do that, I want to have the power to make him do as I wish. . . .

The diary for 1918 ended on a bright financial note:

My Assets.
    War Loan £15,000 yielding £750   cost £14,233.
    Reorganization Loan £10,000 yielding £500 cost £8525.
    Railway Loan   £20,000 yielding £1000 cost £15,500
    Hongkong Bank   £2590 yielding £156 cost £2590
    Total £47,500   yielding £2406, cost £40,848.
    Credit A/c in London £2612.18.9.
    O/d, in Peking £2367.

At the back of his diary Morrison scribbled some random notes about Australia and Japan:

AUSTRALIA

No respect except among very restricted class for Gov.-General or Lieut. Gov. "Don't know 'im from a bar of soap" would be the comment. No discipline. On steamer I go into afternoon tea. Steward is sitting there reading newspaper with feet up on chair. He invites me to help myself. Stewards dine together in saloon. . . . It's a wonder the passengers don't have to wait on them.

Purity of public life! Higgins, one of the Justices of the High Court branding Hughes as a liar.

Striking difference between press of Jap and press of Aust. and N.Z. the one insolent and arrogant and the other obsequious and deferential.

Fuller, drunken Gov. of Victoria—known as "Fuller and Fuller".

Australians great unwillingness to walk. Always want a motor!

Norman Lindsay's excellent story of the Chinese elderly husband returning home found the door locked opened after some delay and shuffling in the corner he noticed a long bag that he had not seen before. "What in that bag?" he asked. No reply from his wife. "What in the bag?" he asked more insistently. Repeated. No reply. Feeble voice from the bag "Only rice."

People in N.Z. and Australia drink enormous quantities of tea. 7 a.m. 8.30 11 o'clock tea. Midday, afternoon tea and finally in the evening. Such habit must be very injurious and must account for the prevalence of anaemia and pallidity among the women.

Professor Baldwin Spencer giving dinner to some students who asked him if he would tell them what he had omitted from his lecture regarding the procreation of the seal owing to presence of ladies. He explained the male seal when desire comes seeks an icefloe and there reclines calling gently, "Koo Koo!". The female hearing responds with a similar cry "Koo Koo!!" Just then the door opened and Lady Spencer put her head in saying "Did you call, Baldwin dear?"

In Australia, dinner must be early to allow the servants time to go to the cinema!

Prevalence of the fly in Australia. No screening, no flytraps, only fly papers. As a retired Indian Med. Officer said, "You treat flies as domestic pets, not as pests."

Unchastity among women girls incontinent even at 16 open purchase of French letters and soluble pessaries.

Pilfering on the railways. Apparently universal pilfering at the stations and in the trains.

Apathy about the war. No enthusiasm over the return of war-tried veterans. . . . Even the workman carries his tools in a neat valise, or he goes on a bicycle. Shearers move from station to station on motor cycles.

Harrison Moore overheard one man ask another in reference to Hughes, "I wonder what the cow has up his sleeve?"

At Newcastle the miners work one shift of 6½ hours 3 days a week, surf, fish the other 4. Apparently no second shift is permitted in the coal-mining industry.

Waiters at the Hotel Australia are paid £2.13.6 a week for which 2/6d is deducted for food.

JAPAN

Japan while the Australian fleet was busy nipped in and seized the Marshall Islands enormously rich with phosphate.

What policing was it which permitted the preying of the German raider *Wolf* on British shipping for 15 months ending Jan. 25 1918?

Did the Japanese in the common cause do anything to facilitate the movement of Australian foodstuffs to the Allies?

The Marshall Islands surrendered to the British not to the Japanese. It was action of the Australian fleet in seizing Guam, etc. which enabled the capture of the Island. Japan slipping in behind our backs.

Sir William Irvine tells me March 1 1918 that Japan made a definite engagement that she would not retain possession of the Pacific Island. However does this tally with the documents published in the *Manchester Guardian* of Feb 7 1918?

In reply to a question Mr Balfour said at the time of the taking of the Marshall Islands the Japanese Government gave no undertaking to hand them over to the Commonwealth of Australia (House of Commons. 5/3/1918)

Burns Philp allowed only one steamer to visit Marshalls—this not once a month, rather once in 3 months. . . . Trade impossible under present conditions.

Japanese Warships convoyed through waters where there was no danger Australian troops going to fight in the trenches of France what Jap. troops had not dared to do the enemies of the Allies. What Jap. life has been lost in this peaceful service! Convoying Australians, 12,000 of whom had met their death fighting that Japs might carry on without danger the traffic of the seas.

CHAPTER FOURTEEN

[I]

"THINGS IN China are not going well. Japan has made enormous progress," Morrison wrote to Sir James Allen soon after his return to Peking in May 1918. In every direction Japan had strengthened her hold over China. She was ladling out concessions to the Chinese, who were inveterate borrowers, with both hands, and on disastrous terms to China. For a loan of 10 million yen, China might have to repay 20 million. "When I was in New Zealand," Morrison added, "I was taken to task for referring to certain pro-German sympathies in the Japanese Army. The correctness of the statement would never be questioned in the Far East."

The conflict between North and South remained unresolved, and Morrison, despite his contempt for Sun Yat-sen, and his job with the Peking Government, thought a suggestion by Herbert Goff, British Consul-General in Yunnan, that the Allies should support the South, was "excellent commonsense". Goff had recently talked to Roy Anderson, who had been in Yunnan "on some political stunt and also nosing around for contracts and concessions":

> He favours us and the Americans combining to support the South and this has long been my opinion; it is true at present there is not much to choose between the North and South, but I think the best brains of the country will go with the South especially if we support them. At any rate they stand for democratic principles which are the avowed aims of the Allies, whereas the northern *tuchuns* are mostly ex-bandits, are pro-German, stand for autocracy, and are busy handing the country over to the Japanese. A private letter from London tells me that Jordan was of this opinion at home and advocated this course but was overruled by . . . the Foreign Office. *This is of course confidential.* But it is a pity, I think. Our diplomacy went all wrong with the Young Turks and the Russian revolution, and it looks as though we were going to make the same mistakes with Young China, who will be forced to turn to Japan if other support fails.

365

"Things here are about as rotten as they can be," Morrison wrote to Samuel Couling in London. (Couling was a former Baptist missionary in Shantung, who, with Morrison's help, had compiled a scholarly *Encyclopaedia Sinica*). "I really do not know who is the Government. The whole country is torn with internecine strife. There are six *tuchuns* ravaging Chinese territory. Many parts of China are worse than Belgium."

He gave a more detailed report on China's troubles in a letter to Sir Herbert Dering, British Minister in Bangkok, an old friend from Boxer days:

> Conditions in China are in a parlous state. Elections for both Houses of Parliament have been proceeding for some time. The President has to be elected by 10 July and his inauguration will take place on 10 October. There are 3 candidates in the field. The one most likely to be elected is Hsu Shih-chang, who in your time in Peking was one of Yuan Shih-k'ai's staff at his camp near Tientsin. He rose under the Manchus to be first Viceroy of Manchuria. He has held many high posts and was one of "four Friends" of Yuan Shih-k'ai. To the foreigner, he appears to have every possible disqualification for such a post, and it is deplorable to think that the public should have such a President. The other 2 candidates are the Acting President, Feng Kuo-chang and Tuan Chi-jui, the present Prime Minister. Either of them would make a less unworthy President than Hsu. It is difficult to believe that with the reassembling of Parliament, strife will cease in China, for a large section of the people of China still regard the election as illegal.

The report on England which Morrison received from Mr Arthur Moore Bennett, an entrepreneur who knew Morrison and China well, was almost as dismal. Over two million had been killed and over six hundred thousand hopelessly maimed, though they never had any say in the determination of their own destinies, said Mr Moore Bennett. A debt averaging £200 on every life in Britain was being piled up. The Government was protected by "a bomb-proof censorship". The shibboleth of "Pro-German" was hurled against anyone who strove to pierce the veil of secrecy. Trade unions had been made to relinquish their hardly won privileges, and the Press its most cherished ideals of free speech. The health of the people was being seriously jeopardized. Young girls worked long hours with inadequate food, in unregulated factories. Immorality of every kind had crept into British public life. "Waste, wanton destruction, carelessness and ignorance seem to dance in one great orgy," Mr Moore Bennett wrote. "Chaos such as I believe never existed since the early 17th century now holds sway in Britain."

Mr Moore Bennett had tried to convince the Government and the trade unions—he had talked to "nearly everyone who matters"—that every worker in Britain was "an economic soldier", entitled to the best training, working and living conditions, and that there should be a board or ministry of commerce to co-ordinate all Britain's essential services from the welfare of workers to the development of export markets:

> An obvious corollary to this is the necessity for a more open diplomacy, but any examination into conditions will show the absolute illogic of permitting every other Government Department to have a ministry,—but TRADE and COMMERCE that pay the services of each and every Ministry is under the thumb of at least a dozen different departments helped by none, hindered by all.

The permanent officials were the real rulers of Britain. In the Foreign Office there was a state of "mental hand-to-mouth existence", no definite policy, no attempt to anticipate the future:

> The whole policy seems to be that China and the East generally with Australia are to be left to their fate. That Africa is to be made to take the place of China and that a great Union of Africas is to be made where the Rand crowd of magnates and goldfield owners will rule.

[II]

A group of well-wishers took camp cots, bedding, and mosquito nets to a temple in the Western Hills, a three-hour rickshaw ride from Peking, and settled down uncomfortably to examine China's *malaise*. The diagnosticians, included Dr Tenney, Mr Archibald Rose, the British traveller and consul, and Morrison, who opened the discussion with a talk on "Seven Years of the Chinese Republic, Signs of Progress, Present Conditions and Tendencies". Two of the speakers argued that it was too late to rally China to the active support of the Allied powers, and that she must be left as a passive and somewhat contemptible victim until her fate had been decided by others on the battlefields of Europe. But the majority claimed that a decisive and forward policy might still impel her to a more active participation in the conduct of a successful war, and the conclusion of a separate peace:

> The root of China's troubles was found to lie in the untrammelled activities of her military governors, each of whom was struggling merely for personal power, in the consequent pledging of her available resource to one country, Japan, in return for steady supplies of ready money on terms involving the alienation of her sources of real wealth, and in the ensuing negation of the policy of the open door. Suggested a real reorganization loan by America (and other powers as should be invited to join notably, Great Britain, France, and Japan) of 25 million pounds sterling, to be administered by Allied inspectors, first duty to be the disbandment of 700,000 out of 900,000 of her troops, and the immediate utilization of these men in productive enterprises—roadmaking, conservancy, food productions, and industrial development, remaining

200,000 to be formed into an effective gendarmerie, with certain supervising powers over provincial taxation. Inducements to be offered Central Government. Unification of various railway systems 2, promise to reconsider question of extra-territoriality.

Morrison was feeling "ill and nervous and weak and much depression" when on 23rd May he made his "annual sentimental pilgrimage" to the pine by the Princess's Temple where he and Jennie had made their vows six years before. His domestic life, at least, was serene. He had moved into a "fine big Chinese house" about a mile to the north of his old place, and he now had three sons; the third, Colin, was born in April 1917. But when Bernard Falk called on him early in June in his "lovely palace the glories of which no journalist in England could ever equal", he found there hung about Morrison "a listlessness and a melancholy which even the characteristic Northcliffe anecdotes which I recounted at his instance failed to dispel". Falk, the special correspondent of the *Daily Mail* in the Far East, described himself as Northcliffe's agent. Morrison described him as a "vulgar little bounder of great assurance . . . with a marked Manchester accent", and he reminded Jennie of a pawnbroker's assistant:

> Calls me "Morrison" with great familiarity and declares there are only two great men in England, Northcliffe and Lloyd George, Haig was hopeless. . . . Lunch with Falk, Beilby Alston, Sir Charles Eliot . . . an interesting experience! Falk talks with unblushing disrespect of the F.O. . . . Alston for many years in the F.O. present, Falk took the opportunity of telling us that the British Government had purchased the "Star and Garter" at Richmond as a home for incurables dug out of their holes at the F.O., and that any day now you may see these former officials walking out in column in the care of a keeper.

Falk, though a "bounder", was a welcome addition to the Peking gossip circles. As well as stories of Northcliffe, he told the story of Pemberton Billing's scabrous article about the dancer Maude Allan, titled "The Cult of the Clitoris". Billing, an eccentric M.P., claimed that the German Secret Service had a Black Book of 47,000 prominent people in Britain whose sexual oddities laid them open to blackmail. When Maude Allan took an unsuccessful libel action against him, a witness announced that Mr Asquith and Mr Justice Darling, the trial judge, were both in the Black Book. Bernard Falk assured his Peking audience that Mrs Asquith's relations with Miss Allan were the scandal of England:

> Here Beilby spoke: "On one occasion, Mrs Asquith received us at the Prime Minister's official residence, standing at the head of the stairs with her arm round Maude Allan's waist. Count Metternich, the German Ambassador, attended the reception, was on the steps, when seeing the spectacle, he turned round and left the hall, saying

that he would not permit himself to be received by Maude Allan, even though she was receiving with the wife of the Prime Minister."

Miss Allan was the daughter of a Montreal doctor named Durrant. There was some oddity in the family, according to a footnote of Morrison's which reads: "Maude Allan Durrant . . . is a sister of Theodore Durrant who was hanged for murder in California in 1908, having murdered two girls in a belfry and had carnal connection with them after death."

Morrison was perturbed to learn from Charles Denby, who had come to Peking to report to President Wilson and Secretary of State Lansing, that both had lost their distrust of Japan, and now believed in her good faith. Japan had won their sympathy by lending America transports on good terms, "and in other ways". The American Press, too, was more and more inclining towards Japan, Denby said. Morrison's dissatisfaction with this news was tempered by a report which appeared in the *Japan Advertiser*. Datelined "New York, June 1", it read:

Speaking at a Union Club dinner in New York last night, Mr W. M. Hughes . . . said he would ask the United States for a Monroe Doctrine in Australia at the coming Peace Conference. The United States, Australia, and New Zealand possess common interests in the Pacific, and he would expect the United States to support Australia at the Peace Conference as on the battlefield. For the existence of Australia as a confederacy of free people, it would be necessary for her to have a guarantee against enemy aggression, and this guarantee could only be obtained by the establishment of a Monroe Doctrine in the South Pacific. Mr Hughes said that to secure the safety of Australian territory, it would be necessary that the islands on the eastern and northern coasts of Australia should either be governed by Australia herself or be placed under the control of a friendly and civilized government. It is to the United States which Australia looks in this matter, he declared.

Morrison underlined the last few lines of the story, and commented: "this very important announcement. . . . A wise suggestion to which my visit to Australia has contributed not a little, for the reference to the Marshall Islands and placing them under the U.S.A."

[III]

Hsu Shih-chang, known as "Susie", was elected President in September: ". . . a man without a Republican idea in his head. An old-time Mandarin, formerly Minister for Communications, who when I was leaving Peking in January 1910 to cross over to Russia, gave me a farewell dinner!"

Morrison with an interpreter presented his compliments soon after the election:

We entered a picturesque pavilion. Susie was waiting dressed in old-time Chinese clothes. We shook hands. . . . For a few minutes we spoke some platitudes. I spoke in my own interest. Was anything prepared for the Peace Conference? Peace may come next year. Was any statement being compiled for the assistance of China's delegate at the conference? All such questions he parried. Never have I had a more footling interview.

The election of the sixty-five-year-old Susie did nothing to arrest China's distintegration. The period of warlord rule, which was to out-live Morrison, had begun: a period in which real power was in the hands of the military governors, who, as a first-hand observer, the French lawyer Jean Escarra, puts it, "made war and alliance between themselves and betrayed one another to their heart's content":

> Every now and then, one would get the better of the rest and set up in Peking a Government devoted to his interests. The foreign powers would back such and such a general regarded at the moment as the strong man likely to succeed. Over and over the struggle of the militarists, there were petty intrigues, and the intermittent pro-ceedings of a caricature of a government.

Conditions in the interior were appalling, Morrison noted: "anarchy, no government, chaos, brigandage, piracy, highway robbery, etc." Shantung, too, was in a state of brigandage:

> Postal inspectors are held for ransom, mailbags are seized. Robbers are the big-toothed comb, soldiers are the fine-toothed. At Yenchang, robbers raided the town. Soldiers were sent to drive them out. The robbers left the town before the soldiers came whereupon these valorous people systematically looted the town, pillaging and burning.

[IV]

The American chargé d'affaires, J. V. A. MacMurray, returned to Peking in the middle of September after six months' absence. Morrison told him that the time had come for President Wilson to propose arbitra-tion between the contending factions in China:

> Better still I suggested if the factions could be manoeuvered into requesting arbitration, I would speak to Hsu Shih-chang about this and suggest his inducing both North and South to approach the President. . . . I argued the time was opportune, the Japanese press were urging Japan to act as mediator, whereas America ought to be mediator. The President the most outstanding figure in the world today and America the first country to give recognition to China. Without loss of face could China ask for arbitration from this ally.

Morrison received a letter from Chao Shih-wu, "Minister for Foreign Affairs in the Military Government of the Republic of China" in Canton, urging the claims of the South to recognition by the Powers. It was not difficult for an impartial judge to decide which was the real Parliament of China, he wrote. The Southerners upheld the constitution and the Parliament, which had twice been illegally dissolved. The Northerners had a Parliament of their own creation composed of members "elected with bare-faced corruption and bribery". But because the Northerners happened to be in possession of the capital, the Powers continued to deal with them. The Southerners, besides their great asset of legality, were in full possession of five rich and strategic provinces and had armies in seven or eight others:

> With the disgusting incompetence of the Peking authorities, their absolute lack of patriotism, amounting in cases almost to treason, their revival of the dying opium traffic, their auction of the assets of their country bit by bit, their corruption open and rampant, it is really difficult to see what there is in them which can secure the continued support of the foreign governments. The only possible explanation so far as I can see is that they are nominally the Allies of the Entente Powers. . . . I have more than once wondered if the World War were to end today what figure China would cut at the Council Table tomorrow. Even in our present circumstances and with our resources, we should like to do something for the Allies' cause. We should like to do it for the highest interest of China as a whole, for the North as well as for the South, for the future diplomatic position of China among the States of the world.
>
> I am writing to you frankly and without reserve as friend to friend. While titularly you are adviser to the Peking Government I would rather consider you adviser to China. . . . I am sure you will exert to the utmost your good influence for China's greatest good. I am willing to do my best to collaborate with you. Between us I hope something can be done.

Without consulting anyone in Peking, Morrison took a trip to the South to talk to some of its leaders. In Nanking he lunched with the *tuchun* of Kiangsi, General Li Shun, and repeated the suggestion that America should be invited to mediate between North and South. There were many precedents, he pointed out, the most noteworthy being Japan's request for President Roosevelt's mediation in the Russo-Japanese war. Japanese intelligence officers were keenly interested in Morrison's mission. When they questioned General Li about his visit the General blandly denied that it had taken place.

In Shanghai, Morrison drove to the French concession and "with much difficulty" found the house of Sun Yat-sen. The diary report of the interview is curiously unrevealing, though it reflects a much more tolerant attitude towards Sun:

Sun Yat-sen gave me a very cordial welcome and I must say right here impressed me as I had not been impressed before by his sincerity and earnestness and by a certain magnetism which I previously did not notice. He was dressed in Chinese clothes, no signs of advancing age, and expressed himself forcibly and well. He reminded me that on my previous visit I had urged upon him the advantage of China's entering the war on the side of the Allied powers and that he was opposed to China's entry. His text was "Powers always support the wrong side as they did the Taipings and now the Northern Party." The Powers always intervene wrongly. He spoke of himself as an outlaw, and spoke with some bitterness of the way Englishmen attacked him, when he owed everything to England, and made acknowledgement. I spoke to him of my plans for China.

Morrison's southern journey ended in Hong Kong, where he was entertained by two eminent Englishmen. One was the Colonial Secretary —"Excellency the Officer administering the Government":

under which portentous title is concealed the Hon. Claude Severn C.M.G. the Buffoon of Hong Kong, a babyfaced stumpy man with a bulging tum, the last on earth you would expect to be selected for such an important post. His appointment . . . was one of the jokes of our time. Noted throughout the colony as a mountebank and retailer of risky after-dinner stories, he aspires to be admitted as a lay reader in the Church.

The other empire-builder was Major-General Francis Ventris, who was formerly in command at Tientsin some years before (1903-6).

He was then suffering from senile decay the progress of which has continued rapidly since. He is now suffering from softening of the brain and is almost paralytic in his decrepitude. No doubt because of his being in this mental state, he has been given command of a British force in China.

In a crowded Hong Kong street Morrison saw three little boys ("the ages of my own") following wistfully hand-in-hand a Chinaman of the artisan type. He was "curiously affected" on learning that they were slave children, being led by a slave-trader to market.

[V]

On the morning of 12th November, Reuter's in Peking released a message: THE PRESS BUREAU HAS ISSUED AN ANNOUNCEMENT FROM THE MINISTER SAYING THAT AN ARMISTICE HAS BEEN SIGNED FOR A PERIOD OF FIVE MONTHS FROM THE 11TH INSTANT AND THAT HOSTILITIES CEASE ON ALL FRONTS AT NOON TODAY THE 11TH INSTANT.

"For a period of five months" was amended in a later message to "5 o'clock in the morning". Next day, after a pleasant lunch, Morrison went along to see the Ketteler monument being pulled down. He had dictated a paragraph for a Peking paper the night before, urging that this should be done:

> The work had already been taken in hand. . . . French soldiers, mostly inebriated, had begun the work late last night. . . . Relieved by Chinese coolies. Huge blocks in construction, no blocks so large are to be found in Peking. As far as possible they will be preserved and re-erected in the Palace grounds in memory of the Allied victory to which the Chinese contributed so overwhelmingly. They were in fact the determining cause of the Allied success, for they only ratified the declaration of war on November 5 and hostilities ceased on November 11.

A flattering letter, written two days after the Armistice, from Sun Johnson, "sole proprietor and editor" of the *Chinese Australian Herald*, Sydney, read:

> My reason for writing you this is to convey to you my own and the thanks of my Countrymen here in Australia for the able way in which you have guided China through these years of War.
>
> I must confess that at times I experienced many feelings of dread that she may have allowed herself to be guided by less able counsel, but, thanks to your firmness, political foresight and tact, the Nation has emerged honorably from the gloom.
>
> It is a blessing that at last Peace is practically assured for the World, but unfortunately your troubles are increased by the disruption between North and South of China.
>
> My sympathy goes out to you in the very strenuous times you have been passing through and we here all know what your brain must suffer.
>
> Allow me to give you a message of comfort.
>
> Deep down in the hearts of every Chinese today is a feeling of loving gratitude to you, and we ask you to accept our many thanks for the great services you have rendered China.

[VI]

There was an indecorous scramble to join the Chinese delegation to the Peace Conference. "All are crowding to go," an official told Morrison. "Difficulty is the expense." Inexplicably, Morrison was not invited, and understandable rancour creeps into his comments on some of the chosen:

> I praise them highly, especially de Codt, who was an honest man who knew nothing about China and was never afraid to say so. I . . . thought he would be a most dignified assistant, especially as he was deaf, and his favourite words were "I know nothing"—truthful words. I also highly praised Denis who equally had the advantage

of knowing nothing about China, and as for that oily scoundrel Dr J. C. Ferguson, I thought China would be well advised to secure his services. I could think of no more fitting representative.

Morrison's friends were put out because he had been excluded. Wearne said, "We are determined you shall go", and without consulting Morrison wired London that the Japanese opposed Morrison's going. "What an unfortunate telegram," Morrison wrote in his diary. "I will be blamed for having inspired it." A few days later Lu Tseng-tsiang, one of China's senior delegates, told Morrison that the President wanted him to go, but had not officially invited him because he did not want to have to ask Ariga or Padoux, who would expect to be present also. "Therefore apparently the fiction was that I was to go on *congé* and turn up accidentally as it were at this interesting gathering," Morrison commented.

He expressed neither surprise nor satisfaction at this devious decision. He was feeling very ill and was much worried about himself. Not long before he had observed that his "meagre medical knowledge", just sufficient to cause him to exaggerate all ailments, had almost since his graduation been a source of anxiety to him. "It would have been better had I never studied medicine," he wrote. Now he made a melancholy recapitulation of some of his anxieties:

> At different times of recent years I have feared epithitonia of the tongue, carcinoma of the rectum, impotence, albuminuria, prostatic enlargement, trachoma, arterio-sclerosis, and now glycosuria. . . . Have malaise and depression and much thirst. Have indeed to carry an overpowering burden and yet am such a poltroon that I cannot summon sufficient courage to go and see the doctor for if anything is wrong I dread that Jennie should know it.

[VII]

Yoshizara, the Japanese chargé d'affaires at Peking, called on Morrison informally at the end of December "to have a frank talk". He said he would speak with a candour that would not be expected from a member of the diplomatic body, and begged Morrison also to speak without reserve. Morrison did; he began by citing a number of assaults by Japanese soldiers on British citizens in China for which no redress could be obtained, and moved from these to the broad political scene:

> I said there was no Englishmen who knew his facts who did not consider that Japan had failed to fulfil her obligations as an ally and I spoke of the bitterness felt by her failure. I spoke of the anxiety we Englishmen felt right up to the last April as to what Japan might do. We knew that the Japanese military were in a large degree sympathetic with Germany, I spoke of her naval failure, her failure to check the raiders, and now of the change of attitude, not due to

the Alliance, but to the collapse of Germany. I told him what was the truth regarding the extraordinary care taken by the British Government to prevent any criticism that could in any way be regarded as adverse from appearing in any English paper, in Great Britain, or her overseas dominions etc., and I spoke of the indignation which we feel against Japan for taking advantage of this friendly act on our part and in not making any compensatory effort to control the hostilities of the Japanese press!

He made a speech thanking me for all this quoting the proverb about the unpleasantness of good medicine, and gave the explanation, which I believe to be true, that the Japanese military were undoubtedly sympathetic with Germany and secondly that Japan was still in an imperfect state of development, that there were still gaps in her civilization to be filled in, and that the Diplomatic service had wider knowledge than that possessed by the Military. He spoke of the difficulty with the military. . . . A very interesting experience. I have given the skeleton only of what I said.

Morrison spent the last day of 1918 in Yokohama, on his way to Europe. Peace, "so early and unexpected", had thrown the economic life of Japan into confusion, he noted. He was met by the librarian of the Morrison library, Mikinosuke Ishida, who showed him the new bindings replacing the old destroyed bindings of his "beautiful library", and in the cabin of his ship, the *Fushimi Maru*, was a huge basket of flowers with red silk streamers, "a gift to George Ernest Morrison from the Dr George Ernest Morrison library".

His diary ended with his annual prayer for health and happiness— it occupied a page and a half—to which he now added:

May my sons have inherited all that is good in the father and none of the much that is evil and weak. . . .

I pray that I be given the K.C.M.G. for it was promised me, and that the Lord will set me on high and make me the British Minister to Peking. . . .

I pray that my outstanding fear of glycosuria may prove groundless. . . .

Among the odd notes at the end of the diary is: "Asquith is known as 'The Old Champagner'—very obvious and excellent."

[VIII]

When he left Yokohama, Morrison carried a letter of introduction from an old friend, Henry Bonar, former British Consul-General in Korea, to Commander Serrocold, R.N.V.R., London. This enclosed an introduction to the Director of the Intelligence Division at the Admiralty, Admiral Sir Reginald Hall, and a sealed envelope addressed to Hall. To Serrocold, Bonar wrote:

Greetings, Please give enclosed to Admiral Hall. It is about Morrison. His revelations—I hope he will make them to you too—about our diplomacy *vis a vis* of the Chinese at the commencement of the war are appalling. I think it will be most useful for the D.I.D. to hear fully what Morrison has to say, for being an Australian with very strong views as to the admission of Japanese to the Southern regions of the Pacific and full of historical and chronological remembrances of the doings of the J's—coupled with his position as Adviser to the Chinese Government opposed to all Japanese ambition—his opinions are more than valuable—essential. Being rather shy he requires to be drawn but he speaks plainly. It was most refreshing to hear his views of our diplomatic representatives over there.

The introduction to Hall described Morrison as "certainly one of the wise men of the East . . . full of information if only he will dispense it". The letter in the sealed envelope read:

Apart from the introduction I have given Dr Morrison, may I suggest that you give him every opportunity of talking?

I took him into my confidence about the Japanese Secret Service Bonds. His accurate chronological sense of events in those years—1904-5 and his own version of the Port Arthur surrender, give those documents a curiously interesting aspect. He agrees with me that they must be genuine. He thinks the British Government should use this knowledge and take advantage of it.

But of course it is hopeless to interest the F.O. in a matter of this sort.

At this stage, the knowledge of the incident might prove a powerful weapon.

If you think it expedient and like to hear his views you might invite him to discuss the subject. Which otherwise he is bound to keep secret.

Morrison inspected photo-copies of the bonds, which told an astonishing story: that the Russian commander Stoessel had been bribed by the Japanese to surrender Port Arthur—a surrender described by Morrison as "the most discreditable in history":

On 7 July 1904, Japan . . . having suffered severe losses to her fleet and her transports . . . entered into a contract with three prominent Russians . . . including among them probably Stoessel himself. . . . It was arranged that when peace was secured three promissory notes of 46,000,000 yen each were to be issued by Japan to the Russian signatories, and to be payable on 22 March 1915.

Why this day?

. . . After the signature of peace, the three promissory notes were signed in Tokyo . . . by Prince Yamagata, Grand Councillor of State. These documents are known to be in existence . . . for a sum of

£15,000 they can be acquired. . . . Photos of the whole dossier . . . have been shown to Eyre Crowe. [Assistant Under-Secretary for Foreign Affairs] who advised they should not be shown to Conyngham Greene who would "have a fit" if he knew, added Crowe.

[IX]

Morrison's cabin mate on the *Fushimi Maru* was W. R. Betcher, head of the silk department in Marshall Fields, the great Chicago department store. Mr Betcher was an uninhibited conversationalist. He had known Morrison only a few hours when he revealed that Marshall Field II had been shot in a brothel by a "flash American harlot" and had died in hospital, nothing having crept into the papers. Marshall Field's sister, Ethel, was married to Sir David Beatty.

Within a day or two Morrison had charted the more interesting fellow-passengers: Baron Kondo, a member of the Japanese House of Peers, and president of the N.Y.K. line, on his way to Europe to claim compensation for five steamers lost by enemy action; Dr Manuel Quezon, "a striking-looking Filipino, clean-shaven, well-formed hooked nose, clear piercing eyes", on his way to America to redeem President Wilson's promise of independence for the Philippines; Mrs M. Kline, a "physically splendid animal elaborately dressed", who cast the "glad eye", played poker, swilled cocktails, and was heard to say late one night, "Is it the steamer rolling or is it me?"; Miss E. Gleason, president of a bank in Rochester, N.Y., a "sprightly spinster of 60 with a man's voice who dances politely, her head downward, and her buttocks outward, leaving the furthest gap possible between her pubic region and her partners." A fellow delegate to the Peace Conference, V. K. Ting, told Morrison that his allowance for expenses was $7000, that Lu Tseng-tsiang, had $60,000, and "the greatest humbug of all", Lieutenant-General Liang Shan-tung, who had no military training of any kind, had an allowance of $30,000. "Not a soul knows what is to be done," Morrison wrote. "The Delegation is farcical. . . . I must admit that I feel somewhat ashamed to be attached to it."

Jennie wrote soon after his departure:

President Roosevelt's death . . . was a great shock to me. He was such a fine big generous figure. . . . I have always had such an admiration for him and I know you had too. I am getting tired to death of Wilson, and so is everyone else—he talks too much!

. . . I hope you will see Northcliffe when you are home. I often think (tho' my intuition tells me you will do so) that if you can't pull off the job I want for you so much in Peking, I would like you to take up journalistic work again in Peking. It seems to me imperative that there should be somebody here who will be able to give the world trustworthy information about China. Northcliffe might be only too glad to get you back and at a high salary too! I feel your present position here is intolerable, and as you know it has been a grief to me for years. I saw how hopeless it was. . . .

Jennie disliked the Americans as well as the Japanese. In another letter she wrote: "You'd think they had won the War altogether instead of having made millions out of it for the first three years and only coming in when it was nearly over. I hope Wilson will be taken down a peg or two in Europe. . . ."

[X]

The sea trip did not improve Morrison's health. After being interviewed by three "amazingly ignorant" reporters in Toronto he was thoroughly worn out and almost speechless. "Why should I break down in this way?" he asked himself. "Yet I remember being weary in the same way far back in the 80's. My power of recuperation must be weaker now." In Montreal he hired a buffalo-robed sleigh and drove round the town. Passing a house in Cadieux Street, his driver, a French Canadian, said it was staffed by thirty-one young French Canadian girls. "He seemed quite proud of the success of his fellow-provincials who had a monopoly of the high-class prostitution in Montreal."

Morrison could not stand the "infernal racket and bustle" in New York and, after buying nine *Robinson Crusoe*s at Putnam's, was glad to get away to Washington, where a talk in the State Department convinced him that America was playing a double game, "supporting Japan in her attitude towards China, while inveigling China into looking to America for support against Japan". He talked to Debuchi, the Counsellor at the Japanese Embassy, who admitted that Japan in 1914 did not want China to enter the war ("the first admission I had received that Sir John . . . was not acting alone!") and visited the Chinese Legation, where "a dirty foreign porter with fly unbuttoned opened the door—a shabby place, indeed". Yet the Minister, Wellington Koo, he reflected, had a salary of $1800 a month, an entertainment allowance of $2400, and "a fair share of the pickings from Cuba, where the Consul-General gathers $100,000 a year".

He arrived in Liverpool on an icy-cold wet night early in February, and went to bed supperless and without a fire after reading that F. E. Smith, "a hard-drinking a-whoring irresponsible politician of the worst type", had been appointed Lord Chancellor.

At the Langham Hotel in London, Morrison's maid, "a very pretty girl", told him she was paid ten shillings a week and averaged five shillings a week from tips ("horrible food, hours 6 a.m. to 10 p.m."). But she was better off than girls at the Frederick Hotel, who were paid only £14 a year. One of his first appointments was with Hutton ("a loyal friend for 33 years"), who was "comfortably installed with £440 a year and everything found, in charge of a lunatic baron". They dined at Hackett's, and Morrison felt rather ashamed "for he eats rather horribly".

Morrison had an interesting talk with Lady Stanley and Mrs Moberly Bell. Lady Stanley was most indignant against President Wilson "and his hatred of Great Britain":

> His policy was deliberately designed to prolong the peace, to the detriment of Great Britain and to involve her more and more in the financial toils of America. England will get no indemnity, that was her conviction. President Wilson has to conspire for the German vote and Irish vote. He hates the English, she said again and again, and greatly embarrasses Marshal Foch.

Mrs Moberly Bell said *The Times* was paying well. She had been given 5000 shares which had paid no dividends for years, but were now paying six per cent.

The Times announced the resignation of the editor, Geoffrey Dawson, and his succession by Wickham Steed. No reason was given, but other papers published a letter from Dawson to John Walter, chairman of *The Times*, which showed that Dawson had had a disagreement with Northcliffe, and Morrison recalled maliciously that Northcliffe used to say of Dawson, "At last *The Times* has an editor who knows his mind!"

Morrison sent a letter of congratulations to Chirol on winning a libel case (in which Sir Edward Carson had defended him for a brief of 2000 guineas, and a refresher of 250 guineas a day), but he did not seek out any of his former colleagues of Printing House Square. He inserted an advertisement in *The Times*—"Dr G. E. Morrison has arrived in London from Peking on his way to Paris and is staying at the Langham Hotel"— and brooded over the fact that whereas once such an announcement would have been published free, as an item of public interest, now it cost him twenty-one shillings.

Jennie and the children were on their way to England, and Morrison rented from his brother-in-law, Lance Gaunt, for £9 a week, a country house in Forrest Row, Sussex, "with a dear little pony, a dog, and beautiful views". Gaunt, who had a law business in Singapore, contributed his meed of gossip:

> Earl Percy was undoubtedly killed in a duel in Paris. Often said Winston Churchill was present. Mrs Asquith, Elizabeth Asquith, and Lady Diana Manners are all in some way connected with the Billie Carleton case where a young prostitute died from an overdose of some dope.

Morrison lunched with Brigadier-General Charles Snodgrass Ryan, a leading Melbourne surgeon, and a former Consul-General for Turkey in Australia, who had served as a medical officer with the Australians on Gallipoli, and had a remarkable story of the campaign:

> Informal armistice for burial of dead. Wearing all his ribbons, he strolled across No Man's Land and entered the Turkish trenches.

379

Officers and men surrounded him. An officer seeing his decorations said, "But you have the Turkish medal?" Yes, fought with the Turks against the Russians. . . . "And you also have the Plevna medal"? Ryan explained that he had been in Plevna during the siege and added that for 20 years, he had been Consul-General in Australia. The officer much excited said, "But my officers are the sons of officers who fought at Plevna" and then and there, gave orders, and summoning his officers made them pass one by one before Ryan, and give him the salute. It was a striking scene.

[XI]

A "majestic double room, 20ft x 19, with bathroom and pantry attached" had been reserved for Morrison in Paris, in the MacMahon Palais Hotel, near the Place de l'Étoile, for forty-five francs (about thirty-four shillings) a day, "without nourishment". Here he was met by "the wonderful Sir John McLeavy Brown, aged 83". Brown told him that the Chinese delegation was at sixes and sevens. "Self before country is their motto. All intriguing for each other's advancement. Like being in a circus." But the other powers had their circuses, too.

Watching the "Big Three"—Wilson, Lloyd George, and Clemenceau —at work with a map, Harold Nicolson, as a young diplomat attached to the British Delegation, wrote: "Isn't it appalling that these ignorant and irresponsible men should be cutting Asia Minor to bits as if they were dividing a cake. . . . Isn't it terrible, the happiness of millions being decided in this way? . . ." Foch was equally unhappy about the work of the Big Three. He protested strongly that he had not seen the terms of the Peace Treaty dealing with the military defences of the Rhine frontier. He thought the defences quite inadequate. "Fancy the politicians drafting military clauses relating to the safeguarding of France without reference to the highest military authority," Morrison commented.

Of the three cake-cutters, Lloyd George was perhaps the most ignorant. "Our Prime Minister seems woefully ill-equipped for settling these important questions," Morrison wrote, when the fate of Shantung was being decided. If Lloyd George knew little about foreign affairs generally, he knew nothing at all about China. In an important discussion with President Wilson he admitted that he had never heard of the Twenty-one Demands, and when Wilson read him extracts from them he declared with a triumphant air of discovery: "This means the Japanization of China!" Wilson curtly suggested that he should study a case before discussing it. The veteran American journalist Melville Stone, of Associated Press, observed: "Lloyd George has a startling indifference to, if not ignorance of, the larger affairs of nations." He had expressed surprise when told that in America the war-making power was invested in Congress, not in the President, and at one session had asked: "What is this place Roumania is so anxious to get—Transylvania?" Nor, according to Sir

Charles Addis, a leading London banker, was Arthur Balfour much better fitted for his important post. Sir Charles, a director of the Bank of England, and the London Manager of the Hong Kong and Shanghai bank, said to Morrison: "Balfour is a brilliantly clever man but he ought never to have been Foreign Secretary. He is very lazy, comes to the Foreign Office at 6 p.m. after sitting with his heels on the mantelpiece, leaves at 8. Quite frankly he admits that he knows nothing about China. His appointment has been a misfortune."

Morrison lunched at the Hotel Majestic with W. M. Hughes and other members of the Australian delegation, including the Minister for the Navy, Sir Joseph Cook ("very good-looking man") and "a banal man", Lieutenant-Commander John Latham. "There was considerable banter at the table, the men baiting Mr Hughes, who showed the most vigorous hostility to President Wilson and the Americans." He also showed that despite his reputation for wit, his sense of humour was often as immature as Morrison's:

> He had read in the paper that Mr Wilson was unwell. He knew what it meant when a woman was unwell, but what did it mean in the case of a man? He appealed to me. . . . It was later reported that Mr Wilson had walked vigorously round the deck five miles. "Ah", said Mr Hughes, "now I know what will happen. He strained his heart doing so, he will drop dead suddenly and will be buried at sea wrapped in the Flag of the League of Nations!"
>
> Of the Americans who are talking so big, strutting over the world as though they had won the war . . . he spoke gleefully of the recent riot in Charing Cross when 50 London policemen had put to rout, 1000 Americans. He repeated the figures and declared his intention when he went to London of going to the Bow Street Police Station and saluting the station.

Morrison does not report whether the distinguished company was convulsed by these coruscating sallies. A. J. Fraser, of the Australian Press Agency, told him another of the Prime Minister's *bon mots*: "When Billy Hughes was in Sheffield he received so many and ample gifts that he said to the correspondent who was reporting the gifts to Australia, 'Tone it down, Jack, or they'll think I've been looting the bloody town!' "

President Wilson heartily reciprocated Prime Minister Hughes's dislike of him. "What can you do with a man," he once remarked in exasperation, "who won't read and can't hear?"

Morrison walked down the Bois de Boulogne with the Australian correspondent, Keith Murdoch, who had been on Gallipoli, where he was involved in a breach of faith with the Commander-in-Chief, General Sir Ian Hamilton. He did not impress Morrison:

> Murdoch is a rather common ugly man, apparently on good terms with Lloyd George and Hughes, but despite his boastfulness, on terms

381

less familiar than he had led Theodore Fink to believe. . . . He told me that he worked with Adam of *The Times* and that he gave Adam two very important documents. He conveyed to me that he saw all documents, that he studied the highly confidential documents on British *desiderata* etc. His pay is £1500, plus £200 for his share in the Sydney *Sun*, and much more of the same sort of talk. He spoke of the bitterness of the Australians against the British officers, especially the junior officers, and of the injustice done to the Australians in giving them the hardest fighting and in putting them under British officers. Godley . . . was another butcher sending his men to needless slaughter. Sir Hubert Gough was the worst of all, yet Haig did his best to retain him and it was only Lloyd George himself who removed him. . . . The great trouble all through was jobbery and cliquism, and Haig's refusal to remove incompetent generals.

Referring to the "Battle of the Wazir", when Australian troops burnt down brothels in Cairo, Murdoch said they were quite right to act as they did:

The finest men in Australia were brought to that infected spot. They begged to the British to have the infected women removed. The British refused whereupon, after a time, the Australians raided the quarter and set fire to it. And repeated this when the house was rebuilt.

Jennie arrived in Paris, having left the children in Sussex, and Morrison took her to dinner at the Restaurant Larue ("the most expensive restaurant in Paris, said to be the favourite of Marshal Foch"): "We had pea-soup, mackerel, too salt, oily and tough, asparagus with the taste of turnip, large coarse and freakish, and Jennie had coffee which was really chicory." This repast, without wine, cost fifty shillings. In Peking, he noted disenchantedly, it would have cost not more than five shillings.

Murdoch and Sir Arthur Willert, *The Times* Washington correspondent, who had been secretary of the British War Mission in America, discussed the difficulty of finding a suitable British Ambassador to Washington. Lord Crewe? Morrison said he was a hemiplegic. Winston Churchill? Willert recalled that Roosevelt had said Churchill was an Anglo-American who combined the worst qualities of both countries. Other nominees were Lord Willington, Munro-Ferguson, and Robert Cecil—whom Northcliffe favoured except for the fact that his wife was deaf—and Northcliffe himself, whom several American diplomats favoured. "There is an astonishing poverty of talent in the diplomatic service," Morrison reflected. Willert spoke strongly of President Wilson: "His opportunism, his unscrupulousness, his insincerity." Willert was glad that the view he had held of Wilson for years was the view that now generally prevailed.

Morrison's health, a recurring anxiety, had become alarmingly worse. On 2nd April he was "much disconcerted" to find that his weight was 158lb, four pounds less than it had been five weeks before. He was feeling "ill and worn" and so tired that he carried his bag with difficulty. On 16th April he wrote, "Bad health—I'm as near jaundice as can be", and a few days later, "Feeling very ill, as yellow as parchment. I am really worried": "Masseur came but I am really no better and am much worried. I am quite unfit to go about, and this is especially unfortunate for Jennie. Work is impossible for me for I look really ill. My skin is like old parchment. . . . I have never been like this before. . . ."

A Chinese doctor diagnosed colo-cystitis—a catarrhal condition of the bile-duct—and prescribed two grains of calomel and saline purgatives. An English doctor diagnosed infective catarrhal jaundice, and prescribed calomel, salines, and abundance of water, tea, and to Morrison's surprise, coffee, which he characterized as one of the best of the diuretics. He thought Morrison would be all right in five or six days.

[XIII]

The Peace Conference, formally opened on 18th January, did not seriously get down to business till more than nine weeks after the signing of the Armistice. Wilson was determined that the Covenant of the League be inserted in the Peace Treaty, no matter how long this delayed the signing of the Treaty. "The whole world wants peace. The President wants his League. I think the world will have to wait," Lansing wrote in his diary on 20th March. The world waited, and ultimately the President got his League—sacrificing China on its altar. "I am glad I am not there. They are all out for loot," wrote Sir Edward Grey, as he heard in retirement of the wranglings and intrigues of the men of Versailles. The loot that Japan wanted was Shantung and the Northern Pacific Islands. No one except Morrison was particularly interested in the islands, but the Chinese were vitally interested in Shantung. They did not know till the conference began that, by a secret agreement made on 16th February 1917, England and France had agreed to recognize Japan's claim to both Shantung and the islands. Defending this monstrous agreement, Lloyd George said: "At that time the submarine menace was very formidable. Most of our destroyers were in the North Sea. There was a shortage in the Mediterranean. We asked the assistance of Japan and hard-pressed as we were, agreed to her proposals." He added. "It was a hard bargain!" He did not add "for China".

Ronald Macleay admitted to Morrison that Balfour had not consulted Sir John Jordan when the agreement was made. He said Balfour was pressed into acquiescence by the Admiralty, and this was the blackmail England had to pay. Speaking of the Japanese expedition against

Tsingtao, Macleay said emphatically, "It was that brute Winston impetuously butting in without consulting others." He also spoke strongly against Lansing, whom he called a "poisonous brute".

In failing health, Morrison fought strenuously against Japan's demands. He hoped that America and the British dominions would support China in resisting them, and at first it seemed clear that President Wilson's lofty words in his Adriatic declaration, with its denunciation of secret treaties, would apply to China as much as to Yugoslavia. "Peace should be founded on . . . a new order of right and justice," he said. What could be more right or just than to restore to China the territory that Germany had filched from her? The Chinese delegates were convinced that Wilson was on their side, and certainly Australia, if not her sister dominions, might have been expected to support a friendly China against an aggressive Japan. But Hughes, through vanity, demagogy, and stupidity, proved to be Japan's most valuable ally.

When Japan made a quite reasonable plea, that recognition of national and racial equality should be written into the Covenant of the League—a plea supported by China and an overwhelming majority of the powers—President Wilson allowed himself to be manoeuvred by Britain into rejecting it on a flimsy technicality. Britain may have feared the effect of such recognition on her "inferior" Indian subjects, but the immutable stumbling-block was Billy Hughes, who, with a keen eye on the voters in "White Australia", pretended to believe that "racial equality" really meant "unrestricted immigration" of black, brown, and yellow men, the Great Australian Bogy. He threatened to walk out if the slightest concession were made on the racial question. The obduracy of this posturing demagogue, well described by Patrick Gallagher, an American observer, as "physically, politically and intellectually stone deaf", played right into Japan's hands. Baron Makino let it be known that Japan would suffer only one rebuff. If she were rebuffed again over Shantung, she would boycott the League. To win her adherence, Wilson handed over one of China's most valuable provinces. Wilson was satisfied. His cherished League was preserved. Hughes was satisfied. Shantung was not worth many votes in Australia. And China should have been satisfied. In exchange for Shantung, she was given the booby prize of the peace settlement; the ancient astronomical instruments stolen from the Peking observatory by the Germans in 1900 were returned to her.

Wilson wielded a big enough stick to have overruled the Anglo-French secret agreement on Shantung. He had once threatened that if his views did not prevail he would return to America with his staff and call in the £800 million, mostly on short loan, owed by Great Britain to America.

When the Japanese Ambassador, Matsui, reproachfully spoke to Morrison of the assistance Japan had given to Australia in convoying her ships he got the well-rehearsed reply:

I observed that the convoying was through peaceful waters where there was no enemy. He said there was the *Emden* whereat I said with some brutality that the *Emden* did not molest Japanese ships. I went on to say that the feeling in Australia represented the Japanese as having done little in the war. He contested this view saying that Japanese at the great distance of Japan from the seat of war could not be blamed for not having done more, that public opinion in Japan naturally did not have the same feeling towards the war that would be felt in Europe. And I spoke to him about Japan's action in keeping China out of the war. . . .

"There is no shadow of a doubt that President Wilson has played with the Chinese for his own political ends, has befooled them callously," Morrison wrote. At his "urgent request", Colonel Stephen Bonsal, an adviser with the American delegation, called on him. They had known each other during the Boxer troubles, when Bonsal was a correspondent of the *New York Herald*. Bonsal, whom Morrison described as "a loud-voiced, noisy American", noted in his diary:

He is ill with the jaundice and is evidently in a serious condition, but he hopes to leave for England in a few days. He said he did not wish to express his personal opinion, but he thought we ought to know that the members of the Chinese delegation were more furious with Wilson than they were with Balfour, whom they regard as his cat's paw. Koo and all of them insist Wilson said, "You can rely on me." "We did so and now we are betrayed in the house of our only friend." He feels confident that the Chinese would not sign and the American interests would suffer greatly as the result of what the Chinese were united in regarding as a base betrayal.

[XIV]

"A lovely day," Harold Nicolson wrote in his diary on 7th May. "Great chestnut trees drinking gulps of sunlight." On this lovely day the bulky document of the Peace Treaty, impregnated with the seeds of another world war, was presented to the German delegates at the Trianon Palace Hotel. "It is strange," reflected Colonel House, the American delegate, "that the presentation of the treaty . . . should occur on the anniversary of the sinking of the *Lusitania*." Morrison, an assiduous collector of coincidences, overlooked this historic specimen. On this lovely day, "appallingly ill", he was travelling to England to consult more doctors. He was "the colour of deepest yellow, emaciated and ghastly", and he wondered dispiritedly how anyone could travel in the same compartment with him. But he was amused by a paragraph in *The Times* which he read as the train sped through the hopfields of Kent. In Paris someone had recently lamented that it was impossible to widen the doors of the British diplomatic service. Now Morrison read that the doors had been widened, if only slightly. A new set of temporary regulations for recruitment to the service had been promulgated: "The loss of limb will not in itself be regarded as a disqualification," it said. "But the loss of sight, deafness or bad stammer will be so regarded." Appreciatively, Morrison underlined this sentence.

In London, struggling against depression and debility, Morrison saw innumerable people and conducted a huge correspondence. The day after his arrival he wrote to Gwynne:

> The Chinese lost their case entirely. They were spurred on by the Americans to put their trust in the President, and they were left in the lurch, just as from the beginning I warned them they would be. President Wilson completely befooled the Chinese. In order to . . . buy off Japan's opposition to a League of Nations which did not include words stipulating for national equality, he made a bargain, and in return for Japan's not pressing her claim, he undertook to support in their entirety all Japan's claims in regard to China. The result has been that Japan has obtained in China far more than ever she could have hoped for, and more than she would have accepted as adequate. Now the President is endeavouring to cajole China into believing that he was their champion throughout, but that the opposition of Mr Lloyd George, and the French, was such that in order to save his precious League of Nations, he had to yield.

Expressing regret that he could not attend a meeting of the Royal Colonial Institute to hear a lecture on "Railway Development in Australia", Morrison wrote:

> I hope the day will come when the Trans-Continental Railway in Australia, from Adelaide to Darwin, will be completed, and that I may live to travel by it. Such a railway would bring Adelaide, in the south of Australia, within twelve days of Peking, in the north of China, and as in normal times, Peking is within twelve days of London, and may be brought within ten days when the Siberian railway is reorganized and again open, it is not inconceivable that within measurable time letters from London may be sent to Australia *via* Siberia. . . . I see no reason why Hong Kong should not be brought within three days of Peking and Hong Kong—with an efficient service of mail steamers—brought within five days of Darwin. . . . Such improvement of communication opens up infinite possibilities of trade development between Australia and the thickly-populated regions of Eastern Asia. . . .

"You asked me the other day the economic consequences of the Japanese victory," V. K. Ting wrote from Paris. "Well, I think they are more important than many people can imagine":

> Japan in spite of her organization, is a country without resources. Nothing made her realize her impotence more than when America prohibited the export of steel on entering the War. As you well

know, in recent years great efforts have been made to secure her needs at the expense of China. The Peace Conference has given her 30-40,000,000 tons of good iron ore, and more than one billion tons of good coal, all near to the railway, the extension of which will traverse three more coalfields, containing billions of tons of coking coal. Thus Japan has secured her monopoly of Chinese iron industry. There can be no doubt that in the near future Japan will be able to build as many ships as she likes with her own steel. Then she will assume a different attitude towards such questions as racial equality. . . .

I wonder how many Englishmen understand the mental attitude of the Japanese towards India? I remember vividly that in 1903, the Indian students in Tokyo organized an evening party. . . . There many prominent Japanese spoke openly against England, told the Indians that *as soon as Japan was strong enough* India would be cleared of Englishmen. And they were prolongedly applauded. . . . Now so far Japan has remained passive (apparently at least) because she is fully aware of her weakness in resources, but when she can produce 5,000,000 tons of steel instead of 500,000, she will only wait for a favourable opportunity to become your enemy instead of your ally, and not only India, but even Australia, will not be safe without a large navy.

In thinking over these things, I cannot help becoming a fatalist. It seems that fate is with Japan in her effort to dominate Asia, for at the Paris Conference, Great Britain, who of all nations, should have opposed Japan in her own interest, vigorously supported her claims. Is it Fate that has whispered to Lloyd George in favour of her protégé, or is it simply ignorance?

Hutton wrote from The Priory, Roehampton, that he had just bought his third lute—a Panormo in wonderful condition, dated 1838, for £21 —and he deplored the neglect of this "beautiful instrument" which gave him so much pleasure. He had returned from a holiday at Dorking, convinced that England was going to have much trouble:

Take this example of ill-usage of employees. Overlooking Dorking— just on the hill, is Lord Ashcombe's house. Flaunting a flag when his lordship is in residence. I have chatted with an honest fellow who keeps the carriage drive in repair and order. He had been employed for years at the sum of 16/- a week. He kept a wife and 4 children on this. Even after the war began, the wages were the same. No cottage was provided for him. And my Lord had his shooting parties, and entertained, and all over the place, *Trespassers will be prosecuted*. Can you blame the working classes if they are inexorable in their class antagonism? This Lord Ashcombe has done nothing for the people. . . . My forecast is that the producers will not be content until they have effected such change as would astonish us, if we could see not many years ahead. . . .

And from W. R. Strickland, Foreign Chief Inspector of the Salt Administration in China, came another forecast of social change:

> If only our Legations could take an interest in the broader issues of humanity . . . foreigners would be able to produce beneficial results and could check the undoubted increase of anti-foreign sentiment among the very poor population of the country who will one day direct the policy of the country. At the present time they have the one "right" quoted by Hobbes in the *Leviathan*—"the right of revolution." This they will exercise sooner or later and we shall call it Bolshevism. Their present existence is again (if I remember correctly) rightly described by Hobbes as "nasty, solitary, poor, brutish and short." What is called the "people of China" in the Press, does not include in its connotation these "starving millions who live merely to create others in their own likeness and then die". . . . What can be said of an Administration under which a pound of salt in a tropical country costs far more than a man's daily wage?

The "people of China" were responding vigorously to the Shantung betrayal. A delayed dispatch from Peking, sent on 18th May and published in *The Times* on 28th May, read:

> Thoughtful Chinese are suffering from a keen sense of injustice, and, while deploring the deficiencies of their own Government, which through weakness or corruptibility, has, in their view, signed away the future of their country, feel that they have been badly let down. Apart from the limited official circle, the whole articulate population of the country is furious at the turn of events in Paris, and feeling is strong. Public bodies everywhere have been telegraphing, and protesting, while demonstrations and mass meetings have been held in innumerable cities and towns. Japanese bank-notes have become unnegotiable, in several centres, and lively efforts are being made to promote a universal boycott of Japanese goods. Some Chinese papers refuse to insert Japanese ads. Travellers decline to patronize Japanese steamers, and even ricksha coolies are barring Japanese passengers.

"The most significant event of the week is the Chinese boycott . . ." said the *Nation*. "It has long been foreseen, and it is China's only answer to the crime which her allies have contrived against her."

But even this bitter national crisis could not bring North and South together. The North was not prepared to make concessions to the South, and the South itself was divided. There was little unity between the Young China element and the Southern military leaders, whose aims were very similar to those of the northern *tuchuns*. They preferred to remain in power, grabbing their share of the plunder, rather than see established a united, representative government. Morrison's dream was as far from realization as ever.

[XV]

Dr Oscar Leyton, a German (" 'Late Hun', as he is styled by his rivals, his pre-war name being Grunbaum"), confirmed the diagnosis of acute catarrhal jaundice, but Morrison, finding him "cold and unsympathetic", turned to the "kind and garrulous" Dr Fegan, a Barts man, who was "fairly confident" that he had obstructive jaundice due to gallstones. X-rays were negative, and Morrison was referred to another Barts man, the eminent bacteriologist and cancer expert, Sir Thomas Jeeves Horder, whose verdict was "either malign disease of the pancreas or gall-bladder obstruction". Sir W. H. Clayton-Greene, one of England's leading surgeons, concurred, and a fortnight later operated on Morrison, whose weight when he entered the nursing home on 1st June was 123lb 2oz. "My temperature normal, my pulse 86," he wrote just before the operation. "Feel in no way agitated, despondent or depressed. . . . Afraid to give me chloroform or ether . . . oxygen and gas." Mrs Moberly Bell sat with Jennie during the operation, and they rejoiced greatly when the surgeon found no evidence of malignancy. He reported "extensive inflammatory adhesions, involving pancreas, left lobe liver, diaphragm, gall-bladder which enlarged inspissated biliary secretion." A week after the operation Morrison paid his bills: "nursing home £13/13/0; anaesthetist, £10/10/-; Assistant at operation, £5/5/-; Clayton-Greene, £105."

Visitors called in great numbers. Lady Stanley, Mrs Macleay, Mackenzie King, Brigadier-General Pereira, Colonel Bruce, Chirol, Hutton, McLeavy Brown, Gwynne, and Alfred Sze, the Chinese Minister, who announced that the Chief Clerk of the Foreign office, J. A. C. Tilley, had been given charge of Far Eastern affairs, "his special recommendation presumably being that he has never been in the Far East". A welcome caller was the proprietress of the nursing-home, Miss Clapperton, with her store of intimate society gossip. One of her more aristocratic patients, she revealed, was the Princess de Monaco, "a gutteral Hun", who had an elderly lover, a well-known pianist named Isidore de Lara. "He professes unbounded attachment and sympathy. Feels all the pains of flatulence when his ladylove has wind . . ."

[XVI]

Morrison left hospital on 21st June, and was driven down to Forrest Row, "somewhat battered, frail and weak, but determined to get well". He weighed 118lb 12 oz. Mackenzie King, over from Paris and about to leave London for Canada, regretted that a change in liner sailings prevented him from paying a visit. He sent Morrison a copy of his book *Industry and Humanity* as a "most inadequate expression of" his "very great admiration and affection". No Australian statesman sent even a telegram. Morrison noted on 28th June that the Peace Treaty had been signed on the anniversary of the Sarajevo murders in 1914—and that he had lost nearly a pound weight since leaving hospital.

A few weeks later, "feeling much better", he went to London to see Dr Ernest Young, whom he had consulted in 1910: "Gives me much confidence. Diagnosis chronic pancreatitis. Would not call me diabetic. He spoke with cheerfulness and intelligence. What a damned fool I was not to go to him before." Walking down St James's Street, he passed J. O. P. Bland, "portly, pompous", on his way to the Thatched House Club, and reflected on the contrast: "He healthful and self-satisfied and well-nourished and I nervous, shaken, and emaciated, woe-begone." Back home, Morrison contributed five guineas to the Forrest Row Peace Celebrations, which offered a spirited three-point programme:

1. Procession of decorated vehicles, carts, cars, perambulators, cycles, etc.
2. Tea (plain) to be provided for all demobilized men, men on leave, and all children under 14 years.
3. Sports of all descriptions.

Chirol wrote from Chelsea:

The rain is spoiling the fireworks tonight but we have had a very fair day especially for the procession of which we got quite a good birds' eye-view from the top of the Athenaeum. I can't say I feel much attuned to these peace celebrations, when there is still so little peace in the world and not much even at home. But I cheered Foch and Beatty and Haig for all I was worth, and the fine fellows who stood for so much heroism, and made such appalling sacrifices. . . . Is it conceivable that we should muddle away the fruits of it all?

Another pessimistic correspondent was Marcel van Lerberge, a French journalist who had known Morrison well in Peking and was now back in France. "The peace has been signed at last," he wrote. "A very poor peace which leaves France in a pitiful condition. . . . I have jumped on my typewriter to send you this short letter":

The life here is awfully expensive . . . and we do not see anything in the future to bring about a better state of conditions. . . . On the contrary, the salary of the workmen having been increased and the duration of the working day shortened, it is absolutely certain that the future will be impossible for everyone except the working classes. . . . Besides that the financial position of France is somewhat critical. . . . I do not see any hope of a normal state of affairs in the near future, I simply wish that the catastrophe started in Russia will not happen here, but it is only a wish. God knows what tomorrow reserves for us! The damned Germans have really ruined the world and put everything upside down. A revolution seems to me very probable in all the old Europe. . . . Actually already, a workman, the worst, is earning bigger wages than a magistrate, a lawyer, a judge, a prefect and still the workmen are not satisfied. What they want, it seems, is no work at all, and a perpetual strike with plenty of money.

You should get pale to see what everyone is able to see. The "bourgeois" are starving, having scarcely enough to bring up their children. They dare not buy a pair of shoes, nor a suit, they look just like beggars. During that time, the workmen without work buy the dearest things. . . . They are dressed in silk with varnish shoes and in the evening they never miss the balls which are numerous. It looks like a "sarabande" everybody running joyfully to the end of everything.

And the peace has changed absolutely nothing. On the contrary the prices are increasing considerably. . . .

And it makes me laugh when I read the beautiful speeches about the end of every war in the future. Do you remember what I told you a few years ago about Japan? Do you see now clearly the big conflict between Japan on one side and United States, China and Britain on the other side? The conflict will burst soon, believe me, and there will be no pact of nations to prevent it. We may see by that time Japan allied to Germany and Russia. That is the show of tomorrow. You will see it as I told you often.

But there is nothing to do. There is a fatal power which the humanity is not able to fight against.

William R. Giles, of the *Chicago Daily News*, sent a first-hand report on Japanese rule in Korea:

The cruelties and atrocities committed are beyond the imagination of the people in Europe and America. Useless murder and brutalities, rape and torture, have occurred in all parts of Korea. . . . The Prisons are crowded in the most awful manner. I saw in the Prison from thirty to forty crowded into a room twelve feet by six. . . . Prisoners were unable to sleep as there was only room for them to sit crammed in together. The worst tortures, however, take place in the police stations where they are first examined after arrest. The Japanese treat men and young school girls alike. In fact the Japanese are acting in Korea worse than the Germans did in Belgium. . . . All the demonstrations have been pacific, and the only time that the Koreans have turned around on the mob has been when the Japanese were shooting and beating a crowd of women. . . . The Koreans are the most oppressed people in the world today.

And Morrison's eighty-five-year-old mother reported gloomily from Melbourne on the influenza epidemic and the labour scene: "What a time of unrest this is! Strikes abound. Domestic servants are almost unobtainable and demand enormous wages. Consequently many are giving up their homes." The servant problem was not quite so acute in England; Morrison had taken over from his sister a staff of six, whose wages were tabulated by her:

Maud's wages,   £48 a year.
Cook's wages,   £40 a year.
Fred's wages,   15/- a week.
Olive's wages,   15/- a week.
    Mr & Mrs Standee, 30/- a week.

[XVII]

The graph of Morrison's health was now a jagged scrabble of ups and downs. On one visit to London, Clayton-Greene was "very satisfied, delighted in fact". Another visit, to Dr Young was "unsatisfactory" and Morrison wrote in his diary: "I find these perfunctory examinations unscientific and wanting in accuracy. Medicine is a very inexact science. I am making no progress." Dissatisfied now with Young, he consulted Dr Easter, whose report was "discouraging".

On 7th August he noted: "Today, 35 years ago, I left the Royal Infirmary after my 80 days stay during which I was operated on for the spearhead. Would that I had the same bodily health that I had then!" And he wrote to Dr Young: "I am going to discontinue all medicaments, all fancy treatments, and try and heal myself with gentle exercise in the pure fresh air and attention to diet."

The anniversary may have turned his thoughts towards Scotland; in the middle of August he was in Edinburgh, consulting Professor Francis Caird, Regius Professor of Clinical Surgery, who recommended Emeritus Professor William Russell, Professor of Clinical Medicine at Edinburgh University. Morrison found Russell "a prosy conscientious dull Scotch churchman with *paralysis agitans*":

> The only acute remark he made to me followed my telling him that my normal weight was round about 12 stone. Gazing with shaking head at me under his shaggy eyebrows, he nodded at me sagely and said "You're not that now". He had been reading the letter I had sent to Caird, he said, and as was his custom, had been thinking over my case in his sleep. As a matter of fact he was still sleeping. He gave me little help. His mind was addled but he advised me to go to Duff House, Banff and put myself in the care of Dr Spriggs. On seeing this poor prosy old dodderer who until recently was instructing a new generation of medical students in the art of Medicine, I can well understand how grievously Edinburgh University Medical School has fallen from its high esteem.

Morrison's experience in Russell's outpatients' ward reinforced this judgment:

> Such incompetence, such inefficiency, and absence of all that inspired confidence in the sick! None of the apparatus was in effective running order. The fine syringe was blocked, the high power of the microscope wouldn't work, the reagents were stale, even the weighing

machine was out of order, there was general slovenliness. The attempt
to obtain an adequate specimen of my blood from the lobe of my
right ear took more than an hour and then counting was almost
oriental in its approximation. . . . It looks as if I will have to depend
upon myself for examination, diagnosis and treatment until I get
to Duff House.

While waiting for a vacancy Morrison saw the Senior Physician of
Duff House, Dr Edmund Spriggs, was sure that he had pancreatitis, not
diabetes, and said he would get better and be able to continue his work.
He counselled Morrison not to "get the hump". But how was it possible
to bear up, Morrison asked himself, when his weight was "oozing
away"? His appetite, however, was good and, "bewildered by conflicting
instructions, all guessing and experimental", he decided to adopt a "normal
diet". He recorded typical meals:

Breakfast. Porridge, milk and cream, toast and butter, haddock, bacon
    sausage, tea and milk.
Lunch. Lentil soup, fried whiting, stewed mutton, vegetable marrow,
    plum tart, oatmeal biscuits, 2 pints stout, no potatoes.
Dinner. Soup, boiled turbot, Chicken stewed, cauliflower, strawberry
    mousse, oatmeal biscuit, pint stout.

"Am feeling somewhat stronger, having disregarded all advice, the
conflicting nature of which made rational conduct impossible," he noted
after a few days of "normal" meals.

But soon he was "very dejected" again, and still losing weight. On
the seventh anniversary of his marriage—26th August—he wrote: "What
a poor wreck of a husband, sunken-cheeked, mirthless, cadaverous, without a spark of energy, a future of the gravest misgiving; And Jennie so
robust and vigorous and fresh and handsome. . . ."

The Episcopal Church offered little consolation:

Nothing more uninspiring could be imagined than the sermon of the
Rev. Mr Muirhead who gabbled through the service at the torrential
rate of 225 words a minute, for I timed him. His sermon was a feeble
attempt to attack the teachings of science and to condemn the folly
of the abandonment of the teaching of the Classics. Education had
raised the masses from freedom to serfdom and was now—such was
his logic—conducting them from freedom to ruffiandom. No wonder
the church is losing its grip when it licenses such irresponsible dun-
derheads to minister to the intelligent.

[XVIII]

Duff House was a fashionably expensive institution with a distinguished
clientele. Just a year before Morrison entered it the American wartime
Ambassador to London, Walter H. Page, also suffering from a wasting
disease, had been a patient—or "guest" as customers were euphemistically

termed. Morrison's fellow-guests included a melancholy collection of jaundiced colonial administrators, malarial Indian Army officers, and diabetic tea-planters. Within a few days he had filled three diary pages with tabloid biographies of most of them—from Lieutenant-Colonel Manners Smith, who had won the Victoria Cross on the Gilgit frontier and been badly mauled by a panther in Rajputana, to Mr Francis Pixley, a London barrister interested in heraldry and accountancy, who as Receiver-General of the Order of St John of Jerusalem, signed all the cheques of the Order, and who assured Morrison that Mrs George Keppel's daughter was "undoubtedly begotten by King Edward VII".

The guests of Duff House dressed for dinner, though gastronomically it was not a notable event. Dr Edmund Spriggs, former Dean of the Medical School at St George's Hospital, London, as a member of the wartime Committee on Rationing had written a booklet on *Food and How to Save it* for the Ministry of Food. There was certainly no waste of food at Duff House. Morrison lugubriously copied out the Spriggs diet, which he described as "very trying":

7 a.m. 150 grammes milk.

Breakfast. 1 egg, 3 slices brown bread, 3 pats butter, basin porridge, 250 grammes milk.

Lunch. Basin porridge, piece brown bread, minced meat, dish mashed potatoes, 250 grammes milk.

Afternoon Tea. 1 egg, 2 pieces brown bread, little butter, 150 grammes milk.

Dinner. Two plates porridge, minced meat, dish mashed potatoes, 250 grammes milk, 1 slice brown bread.

10 p.m. 250 grammes milk—in 24 hours 1300 grammes milk = 46·4 ozs.

"There is nothing to tempt my appetite," he wrote:

Insipid tasteless soup the nature of which I cannot even guess. Cooking is simply abominable. Not once since I have been here have I been given a beefsteak, not once kidneys, tripe or kipper or anything in fact that I could eat with appetite. . . . No reason why we shouldn't get fish nicely cooked appetisingly with anchovy sauce. Excellent fresh whiting are available but they do not appear at our table. Only meat at dinner yesterday was dried overcooked stewed rabbit . . . never cold ox-tongue or brawn or corned meat. . . . Even if I were in strong health, I would lose weight with such insipid undesired food.

When he complained to the "ginger-topped, pallid" Diet Sister she told him confidently that in his condition loss of weight was quite a minor consideration. "I blurted out that if Jesus Christ Himself told me so I would disbelieve Him." Food had become a gnawing obsession. "All my waking thoughts are food, especially suet pudding and jam roll," he wrote:

At one period of my life—perhaps at most periods—I desired and wished I should be flat-stomached. I looked especially since my marriage with misgiving upon my developing into portly age with a *Bulging Tum*. Now my ambition in life would be achieved if I were to grow like the sugar-broker in "Bab Ballads."

His weight was down to 97½ lb—15 lb less than when he arrived in Banff —and he was "heartily sick of being surrounded by patients whose topics of conversation are the stomach-pump—intestinal douches—sugar excretion—diet and duodenal ulcers. Appendicitis is their most cheerful topic . . ." And Dr Spriggs was as cautious with fuel as with food. The weather was "bitterly cold, bleak and raining", but the temperature in Morrison's room was never higher than 60 degrees Fahrenheit. Jennie wrote from Sussex where she was enjoying a "glorious Indian summer": "You are being starved on the Duff House regime. Your fellow patients seem to be getting on your nerves and the sooner you say good-bye to them the better." She enclosed a cutting from the *Daily Express*. "This paragraph will amuse," she wrote. "I should think for pure inaccuracy it would take the cake anywhere":

Mr Beilby Francis Alston C.B., who has just been appointed British Minister in Japan, has a brilliant diplomatic past, and is a comparatively young man, for whom his friends predict an even more brilliant future. The younger son of Sir Francis Alston, who was one of the great figures of Queen Victoria's reign, as a boy he met at his father's house in Eccleston Square, most of the leading diplomats of the time. Mr Alston was educated on the Continent and is a distinguished linguist. His Eastern experience is invaluable at this moment—hence his promotion.

Morrison was not amused. "So after all, the F.O. have perpetrated this outrage," he wrote in his diary. "A really shameful appointment of an impossible mountebank."

Morrison wrote to Jennie, urging that they return to Peking as soon as possible, by way of Canada and British Columbia, and Jennie wired back that the only passages available were on the *Mauretania* and the *Korea Maru* leaving San Francisco on 30th December. Passages were hard to get, and Morrison wired an acceptance. "Fares from London to Shanghai for our large party of 6½ adult fares [it included a valet, a governess and a nurse] comes to £806," he noted. "It seems highly probable that it will cost at least £1250 to land us all in Peking—a ruinous charge, but my one wish is to get to Peking away from the unrest in England. Better to die there than in England. In Peking I have most of my interests. If I die there, the Chinese Government would probably give Jennie a handsome present of $10,000."

On 8th October Morrison said good-bye to the optimistic Dr Spriggs, to the ginger-topped Sister, to the overcooked stewed rabbit, to the valetudinarians and the hypochondriacs, and to the rice "served like finger poultices". In his diary he scribbled an eloquent testimonial to Duff House:

"My stay must always be the most loathsome of all the recollections of my lifetime. Much worse than when I came. . . . Thankful to escape. Surroundings horrifying." Jennie was shocked to see him so thin, emaciated and feeble, and one of the children said to her: "I won't be wuff with Daddy, I pwomise, because he might bweak in pieces."

[XIX]

The unavailing struggle continued. "Am in a bad way but must strive on," he wrote on 5th November. A week later another specialist, Dr A. White Robinson, inspired hope. He thought Morrison was suffering from a "bacterial intestinal invasion" and instructed him to eat grapes with their skins on to "*raft* down the streptococci". Morrison's mother-in-law, from whose unsolicited counsel he had already suffered much, now categorically diagnosed his illness as "biliousness". Her kindly intervention was not appreciated: "Her lugubrious speech is more depressing than a London fog. She does not talk, she whines like Rab the Grinder and no degree of ignorance can prevent her from volunteering advice."

Dr John Matthews took a Wassermann test, and Dr Ernest Young called, "excited and enthusiastic", to report colonies of streptococci. "All my hopes are in the discovery of the invading bug, now being rafted down to the bottle and the laboratory." Dr Young gave Morrison a prescription containing morphia ("a drug which I think I ought to have tried in my case some months ago") and sent him to Dr Charles Clark to have his teeth X-rayed. Dr John Matthews, a pathologist, discovered the micro-organism *bacillus asiaticus* in Morrison's intestine, and Dr Young gave him anti-toxin injections. Morrison's dentist, Mr H. E. Cribb, who had a poor opinion of Dr Young urged him to consult Sir Hugh Rigby, Surgeon to the King's Household, and someone else urged him to consult Dr Arthur Beddard, of Guy's. Lady Stanley urged him to put a teaspoonful of Plasmon powder in his tea, coffee, or soup. Lady Cromer said she had no faith in English doctors. "In the multitude of doctors there is much confusion," he wrote. But none was doing him any good. He was getting "uninterruptedly weaker every day".

On 12th December he entered Mrs Bateman's nursing-home in Queen Anne Street, and put himself in the hands of Dr Beddard: "Good reasoning, good horse sense. Instructions: plenty of butter, milk, raw pancreas 2/3 hours after each meal. Ditto holodin, 2 capsules. Calcium lactate any time."

A few days later he wrote:

> I cannot go on like this drifting on the rocks. Starving in the midst of food which I cannot eat with relish but which acts a little later like a purge, scouring my poor frame now shrunk and emaciated. . . .
> I wish more eagerly for life to be continued for so much has to be accomplished and so much is awaiting accomplishment. "O my God leave me not nor forsake me!" What hope is there for me?

The attempt to supply the deficiency of pancreatic secretion by means of raw pig's pancreas had failed. He was getting "perceptibly thinner". But there were brief remissions. A fortnight later he was feeling "undoubtedly better and stronger. More cheerful and hopeful."

[XX]

"Thus I begin the New Year—in a Nursing Home—gravely ill," he wrote:

> Pancreatitis of the most serious kind. The problem is now being solved. It has narrowed itself to this issue. Can I check the wastage? ... If I can put on weight, then is the outlook hopeful. Shall the wastage continue, then I am doomed.... Last Sunday I weighed 7st. 10lb. At the same hour and under the same conditions I will weigh myself next Sunday and will observe the result with courage and equanimity. It will be my sentence.

"I now wish Dr Beddard to take full charge of my case," he wrote to Dr Young:

> If you think ... I am making a mistake, you must attribute my error of judgement to my distressing illness and to the obscuration of my better judgement. ... Since last July, I have been given much attention by you, and I am really grateful to you. ... But the fact remains that I am drifting, the tide is ebbing, and the experimental treatment—I might almost call it haphazard—to which I am being treated is to say the least not successful. ... You are now, I understand, going to experiment with cinnamon oil, a reputed intestinal antiseptic. No treatment which you have given me has had any of the results anticipated ... while the multiplicity of drugs I have taken, from Kaolin, which was to cause me constipation, in two days, to activated Trypsin, in homeopathic doses, would be amusing in any other case but one of such extreme gravity as my own. No proof has yet been established of the efficacy of detoxicated vaccines except on the word of that noisy braggart whose name I forget just now....
>
> I should like to settle up all accounts. I owe fees to Mr Matthews for the blood test and for his discovery of the *bacillus asiaticus, subspecies Sinesis, sub-sub-species Pekingensis*. As for the other pathologist, I have been advised that the elaborate report he made to me contains one trifling error, namely the assumption that a streptococcus which can be found in any intestine has any pathogenic significance.
>
> Please make all allowances for my letter. I repeat how grateful I am for all you have done for me....

Dr Young replied urbanely, without "the slightest ill-feeling", that a patient had a perfect right to consult any doctor he pleased. "Regarding the question of fees, I prefer that my services should be gratuitous."

XXI

Morrison wasted little time brooding over his condition. When he was not talking to visitors, who called in great numbers, he was writing letters, advising others about articles, and reading omnivorously:

> *1st January*—Engrossed in the fascinating volume "Memoirs of William Hickey". Read McCarthy's "George I", "Press Platform and Parliament," a feeble book of reminiscences by Spencer Leigh Hughes. Glanced at "The Unseen Hand in English History", by Ian D. Colvin. "My Japanese Year", by T. Sanders (amiable slush). "The War Lords", by A. G. Gardiner (brilliant), "The Roman Mischief-maker", by Hugh E. M. Stutfield, (promising).
>
> *3rd January.*—Read most of the day. Asquith's "Occasional Addresses". A bulky volume on Java, ill-arranged and ill-assorted, by Donald MacCaine Campbell. F. A. Mackenzie's "Korea's Fight for Freedom".

He spent a pleasant hour or two with the life of that "eccentric egotist of genius, Ouida", who had been Curzon's lover, and noted that Curzon had written the inscription on her memorial at Bury St Edmunds. C. J. Dennis's two books of verse, *Digger Smith* and *Backblock Ballads* were haunting—"the most national, most original and most penetrating of our Australian poets"—and Scawen Blunt's *Diaries 1888-1914* of "absorbing interest", but his revolutionary views were "detestable and repellent". Kingsley's *At Last* was "one of the most vivid and picturesque books in the language . . . the work of a cultured, independent thinker, a scholar, and gentleman".

When he read in the honours list that Dick Richards, "the Rt Honourable, Lord Mayor of Sydney", had been knighted he commented in his diary: "A wonderful recovery—never could such a thing happen in any other country than in New South Wales. He used to be fished out of the gutter putrid drunk and yet he has come out on top as he declared always he would." But Morrison's own knighthood, promised by Sir John Jordan and W. M. Hughes, had been forgotten. "So after a brave fight for the Chinese, you have to fight for yourself and fight alone," Dungate wrote, when the New Year honours were announced. "The Chinese will at least give you honour. The noble Briton is a past participle fool with no conscience at all when it is a question of giving honour to men who richly deserve it. . . ." Sir Edmund Barton died in January, and Morrison noted that the London papers had overlooked the fact that he was "the author and most uncompromising defender of the White Australia policy . . . the most vital and most national policy in Australia . . . which finds support from every section of the Australian people."

The visitors to Queen Anne Street included Sir Douglas Brownrigg, who had just published his *Indiscretions of a Naval Censor*, and Morrison wrote to Lady Brownrigg, urging her to write a memoir of her father, Sir Cecil Clementi-Smith:

You possess an unusual gift of literary expression. Your father had a career of exceptional distinction—he was one of the great personages of his time, equally trusted by both the Colonial Office and the Foreign Office, a man who by sheer merit rose to be Governor of the Straits Settlement . . . a man who was able to refuse the post of Minister to Peking, and who declined a baronetcy, and who did work of international importance at the Opium Conference in Shanghai. . . .

Lady Brownrigg replied that her father did not wish a memoir to be written and had kept no papers. But she agreed with all that Morrison had said about him: "He was really a great man. I know no other man who had higher ideals and lived up to them . . . both in private and public life. . . ."

A few days later "the bluff hearty healthy" G. E. Buckle called:

It was a great pleasure to see him, the embodiment of bluff British rude vigorous health. And to think that in October 1907 . . . he had suffered a grave operation for cancer of the tongue when he was given a possible tenure of life, if all went for the best, of one year and nine months. Now 70, without a trace of illness . . . playing golf for the last few days. . . .

Another remarkable visitor was Lord Bryce, who at eighty-two climbed the steep stairs to Morrison's room without faltering and questioned him keenly about Kashgar, Mongolia, China, Japan, and Bolshevism in Chinese Turkestan—"the keenest, the greatest intellect I have yet had the opportunity of meeting". Wickham Steed came, "very buoyant and friendly", and jubilant at the success of *The Times*. He discussed the Washington post. The Chief Justice, the Earl of Reading, wanted the appointment, and Northcliffe admitted that he had done well as a special envoy to Washington during the war, but Reading wanted the promise of Paris later, and then the Foreign Office. "And," said Steed, echoing his master, "we don't want Jew influence there too strong!"

Northcliffe, who had not written a word to Morrison when he left *The Times*, or since, paid an unannounced visit towards the end of January. (He was still not recovered from an operation for adenoma of the thyroid performed six months before):

He declared that he had pancreatitis himself the year King Edward VII died that he was worse than me as regards weakness that he could not even digest water that he recovered by his own will after seeing many doctors and being in many nursing homes. He puts hope in the Spring, the fresh air, and the sunshine. Sugar no importance. Everyone had sugar. He is restricted as to starches. . . . Much wild talk. . . .

Jennie was greatly encouraged by what Northcliffe had said, and was disappointed to find that Morrison "could in no way accept Northcliffe's story that he suffered from pancreatitis and completely recovered":

I cannot believe that the conditions were the same. He was 44 and I am nearly 58. He was 14 stone and reduced to 11 stone. I am reduced to 8 stone from well above 11 stone whereas he is now 14 stone again, fat and puffy.

A week later, as he was lying in bed "much dejected", Morrison was "greatly touched" to receive a "kindly message from the great Lord Northcliffe", written in lead pencil:

My dear Morrison,

I have thought much and deeply about you since our meeting. Are you trying all the resources of medical skill? Are not our best men often narrow and ill-informed of what has been discovered elsewhere, in the United States for example?

In October last I said adieu to Lord Grey on his departure for the U.S. He was very nearly a totally blind man. Last week I saw an entirely different Grey *and he saw me*. Why? Because Wilmer the great American occulist at once discovered that Grey's trouble was not eyes, but *teeth*. Grey is younger by 10 years. Our eye men are very angry about this damnably convincing proof of their ignorance. It is a miracle.

Have you been out? Have outings had ill effect upon you? Are there methods of feeding by skin absorption? If you continue to debilitate, are there not other treatments or men? I don't know your men so have no feelings about that.

What I do feel is that there is plenty of time for you to get well and that your recovery *may be brought about by your own action*, in taking your case in hand while you have the strength to travel, if travel is necessary.

It may seem to you an impertinence on my part. It is meant only as a demonstration of affection and interest, my dear fellow.

"Kindly acts of this kind it is which binds men to him with hooks of steel," Morrison commented in his diary—"inspiring a devotion rarely given to a great Captain of Industry".

He wrote back to Northcliffe:

My wife and I were touched by your kind letter . . . and we have given it much attention. What you say about absorption of fat through the skin I have already tried, but in a perfunctory way. Dugong oil, which is used in massage in Australia, I have been unable to get in London.

I am determined to follow the suggestion made to me by you, to go across to America when the warmer weather comes round. . . . I wish to get well, for never have I felt a keener interest in what is going on around me, nor have I ever felt a keener desire to keep myself in touch with the Far East, especially the Chinese, who, ever since I was taken ill, have treated my wife and myself with extraordinary kindness and consideration.

XXII

F. Ashton Gwatkin of the Foreign Office ("Eton scholar and Newdegate Prize winner, married to a brainless little affected ballet dancer") showed Morrison a letter from Major-General Sir Dudley Ridout ("the highly competent military commander of Singapore") expressing much anxiety about Japanese activities and Japanese ambitions; Major Piesse had been in Singapore for a month studying Japan's activity on behalf of Australia. Morrison revised an "excellent and important" article Gwatkin had written on "Japan and the War", and suggested he send it to G. W. Prothero. It was published in the *Quarterly Review* of October 1920. One paragraph read:

> Four years of the European war have made an immense change in the Far East. The influence of the white nations seems to be tottering into bankruptcy. Their hold over China, which they have often so shamefully abused, is seriously shaken. . . . Japan has asserted her right to prior consultation in all matters concerning China; and no Power as yet has taken up the challenge. The Chinese people have seen their railways, mines, industries and territories mortgaged to Japan by a gang of corrupt statesmen. They have seen the White Powers unable or unwilling to protect China's rights at the Peace Conference. They have concluded that, in spite of any Wilsonian idealism . . . Might is still Right, and Might is on the side of Japan. This is a critical moment in Eastern Asia. The Chinese nightingale is dumb. . . .

On another visit, Gwatkin asked if Morrison could make suggestions about the renewal or modification of the Anglo-Japanese alliance. Unless notice of determination were given before 13th July it would remain in force for another ten years. Gwatkin put forward the arguments for renewal:

1. If not renewed Hong Kong must be put in a state of defence at a cost of millions sterling.
2. If not renewed Japan at a later date might enter into an alliance with Russia and Germany.
3. If renewed England is in a position to exercise a restraining influence over the activities and aggressiveness of Japan, for example in her China policy.

Morrison did not agree. He submitted:

1. That if there is to be a League of Nations, an Anglo-Jap alliance is an anachronism.
2. Japan has been a treacherous ally throughout the war. She has been our enemy not our friend in Asia. See her failures to act in the Pacific. Witness her policy in Siberia. Look at the way she blackmailed England, kept China out of the war, and refused us help when most needed.

3. Allied to us, she had a secret understanding with Germany! Her ships were immune while ours were being sunk.

4. Suppose she did seize Hong Kong. The possibility or the power are not denied her. Australia too would be at her mercy for a time, but her prosperity depends upon her ocean-borne commerce, and within a week or two of hostilities, it would disappear from the seas.

5. How can our rapprochement with America be developed as long as our alliance with Japan bars the way?

6. Cast Japan aside and the act will be welcomed in the U.S.A., in Canada and Australia, in China above all and throughout Asia!

But he confided to his diary: "The Alliance will be renewed, of that I am convinced, for both the Admiralty and War Office *are dead in favour* of renewal—in revised shape, of course. Only the verdict of the Colonial Office is awaited, and the C.O. are waiting for the views of the Overseas Dominions." (The Alliance was replaced in 1921 by a Four Power Pacific Pact between Great Britain, Japan, America, and France.)

Morrison's masseur, Arthur Robertson, was a handyman to Lord Carmichael, who had been Governor of Victoria from 1908 to 1911. His Lordship, though he possessed "immensely valuable art treatures", had no baronial robe, and Mr Robertson was trying to pick up a secondhand one for about £30. Meanwhile Carmichael had been forced to borrow a robe from Lord Colebrooke, Captain Gentleman-at-Arms. Mr Robertson, who was a great gossip, told Morrison that G. F. Vernon, one of the Ivo Bligh team of cricketers, had a son, a man of violent temper, who in a fit of jealousy had murdered a white companion on a Queensland station, smashing his head with a cricket bat. "By dexterous defence," said Mr Robertson, "the blame was affixed to an Australian blackfellow who was found guilty by a prejudiced jury and hanged. Subsequently, Vernon came to England, confessed his crime to *John Bull*, and blew out his brains!"

Morrison continued his book-hunting, concentrating on *Robinson Crusoe*s. One day he managed to get as far as Francis Edwardes' in High Street, Marylebone. To his "great content", he bought the first edition of the First Part of *Robinson Crusoe* from Basil Blackwood of Oxford for £75. Another day he had sufficient energy to call on Alfred Sze at the Chinese Legation, and Sze described the attitudes of three Foreign Secretaries to Foreign Ministers—"Grey, sympathetic and cordial; Balfour, philosophic and detached, Curzon haughty and arrogant". Morrison went to the Playhouse and laughed till he was sore at Gladys Cooper and Charles Hawtrey in Somerset Maugham's farce, *Home and Beauty*, and at the Yiddish Theatre in the East End he saw Maurice Moscovitch act marvellously in *The Merchant of Venice*. He noted amusedly that his old Edinburgh colleague, Ernest Titbold Badcock, a medical equipment maker, had changed his name to "Ernest Greville".

Early in January, Jennie went to the Chinese Legation Ball and met, in Morrison's words, "the vulgar Sir James and Lady Cantlie". Sir James, an energetic Scottish surgeon, writer, and traveller, was Sun Yat-sen's old professor and champion, who had saved Sun's life in 1896 when Sun was kidnapped and held prisoner by the Chinese Legation in London. There is no other mention of Cantlie in Morrison's scrupulously detailed diaries, but in a biography of Sir James by Nevil Cantlie and George Seaver this paragraph occurs:

> Morrison had always been bitterly hostile to Sun and the new regime, but just before he died in London, he asked Cantlie to come and see him. "If I had appreciated the character of Sun Yat-sen years ago as I do now, the history of China would have been different, and I would like you to make that known. . . ."

No more credence need be given to this dramatic story than to the statement that Morrison "died in London".

[XXIII]

Morrison found the paste of minced pig's pancreas—"as supplied formerly to H.R.H. Princess Beatrice!!"—nauseating, and without telling anyone, he stopped taking it. A fortnight later he wrote:

> I have felt more cheerful today, more hopeful and with a feeling of restraint . . . which I experience for the first time since coming here. This is . . . clear evidence of improvement, attributable by me to the discarding of all the horrible medicines that were poured into me as into a sink, and attributed by the Dr to my taking raw pig's offal (I paid for this filth £5/2/6, hoping thus to save the faces of the Matron and of the Dr) the very name of which gives me a spasm of nausea, and not a grain of which have I taken since my decision was come to on February 12.

At the beginning of March, feeling "somewhat more vigorous and more hopeful", Morrison managed to get to the Langham, to the Oriental Club, and again to Francis Edwardes'. He continued the quest for *Robinson Crusoe*s and shipped 1400 books to China. On 9th March he wrote: "Dr Beddard has quite dropped me, I am thankful to say, the Matron having disclosed to him my failure to take his muck. He has *lost face*, a much more serious matter than his patient losing his life!"

He cabled Peking: DOCTORS CONSIDER ME PROGRESSING FAVOURABLY THEREFORE HAVE TAKEN PASSAGE SELF FAMILY EMPRESS RUSSIA LEAVING VANCOUVER JULY 29 PLEASE SEE READY FOR OCCUPATION. Colonel G. F. Browne, the former military attaché in Peking, invited him to come down to Lynsted, "a second-rate country-town . . . with no attractions beyond a beautiful country . . . and no bother about rations of milk, butter or eggs". But Jennie had discovered a furnished house, Devoran, on the Esplanade at Sidmouth, Devon, and on 18th March the Morrisons moved into it. The rent was fourteen guineas a week, "plus fires, etc.". A typical week's bill shows what was meant by "etc.":

Apartments etc.	£14.14.0
Sitting-room fire	14.0
Kitchen do.	7.0
Bedroom do.	1.1.0
Sitting-room gas	6.0
Bedroom candles	3.6
Paid for breakages, plate	1.3
Housekeeping	12.10.8
Laundry	15.10
7 bottles wine	1.9.6
Pkt Bromo	2.0
Soda water	5.6
	£32.10.3

[XXIV]

Sir John Jordan left Peking in March, and Morrison read with amusement David Fraser's panegyric on him in *The Times*. He commented in his diary:

> Curiously unbalanced for if he were such an immense authority on China, why did he accomplish so little? His policy of Anglo-German co-operation, which was first broken down by the Crisp loan, was singularly unwise and shortsighted. His pusillanimity kept China out of the War for two years. His apathy kept the Deutsch-Asiatische Bank going full swing ahead until the exposure in *The Times* of October 1918, and now he withdraws from China, having settled nothing except the Opium Agreement. . . .

Soon after he reached England, Sir John sent a sympathetic note to Morrison. "Very little interest seems to be taken in the Far East in this country," he wrote. "The affairs of places like Teschen attract far more attention in the press than China does. But China will come into her own sooner or later." Morrison replied, in a letter dated 6th May:

> Although I have definitely decided to return to China, I am in such a state of emaciation and weakness that I am often despondent as to whether I shall ever be able to get there . . . there is no use blinking the fact that I am living on the very verge of death.

[XXV]

The news from China followed a familiar pattern: "Hsu Shih-chang is not showing himself a strong leader, Parliament is a farce and its opening has been postponed," Dr Gray wrote from Peking on 14th March. But the students were trying to organize a big national strike, "as evidence of their country's deep feeling over the Shantung question". "The Government is infinitely worse than it has been since I came to

China in 1908," wrote W. R. Strickland, from the Central Salt Administration. "There is a general breakdown of the communications of the country."

Colonel Bruce, just back in Peking, was a little less pessimistic:

The change in Peking is most marked. . . . Since I last was here, they have made good motor roads everywhere, which seems very well policed, and the number of cars is surprising.

Of the atmosphere it is difficult to speak, but here also I feel a distinct change. They are more corrupt than ever I should dare to say and no one seems to think of anything but filling his own and his friends' pockets, but there seems above and outside such common delinquencies a certain public articulate opinion, which I do not remember ever before, and which if carefully nursed and handled by us and the Americans could do a great deal to set the old country going.

Harold Porter, of the British Consular Service, wrote:

I suppose it is indiscreet to say so and still more to write it, but I haven't much faith in China and a man like you will be needed to oil the wheels a bit. I wish I had as much belief in my own service, but I have long been of the opinion that we are more or less anachronisms. . . . So long as our functions *vis-à-vis* the Chinese Authorities are practically limited to efforts to maintain by diplomacy, rights which were exacted at the point of the sword and many of which are palpably unfair to the Chinese, we merely retard progress by fostering an attitude of mutual hostility. The Chinese know we are futile, and will never fight them again and the time has long since come in my opinion when we ought to revise our whole attitude and try to meet them on common ground and give them a fair deal. Apart from the 1900 business, China has never done us any harm and we have lived and traded there on extraordinarily favourable terms . . .

"Far Eastern things are in great confusion," wrote David Fraser, who had been reporting on Japanese activities in Siberia. "*The Times* suppressed nearly all of my messages about the Shantung question, and jumped on me for being, practically, anti-Japanese. That will explain why you see so little in the paper on that subject." *The Times* was also behaving with traditional generosity. Fraser had told them he would go bankrupt unless they did "something substantial" for him. He was only kept afloat by imposing on his relatives. "*The Times* have no possible excuse for not indemnifying you most handsomely," Morrison replied. "They are enormously prosperous—they are simply rolling in wealth." Northcliffe had told him it was the most prosperous paper in the world.

Since Morrison's departure the Chinese Ministry of Finance had become more and more dilatory in paying his salary. In March, when he had not been paid for three months, a friend in Peking who was looking after his affairs wrote to Mr J. H. Ju, of the Department of the Grand Master of Ceremonies, appealing for his help. Mr Ju replied that the ministry was in a "very stringent position", adding sadly that his own salary was in arrears. "P.S.," he wrote, "you may be surprised to know that the Ministry of Finance has not paid into the President's Treasury for about half a year!"

"I would say that the political and financial situation—and the international situation—could not be worse . . ." Forsythe Sherfessee, American forestry adviser to the Chinese Government, wrote on 12th May. "The *tuchuns* have ceased to exact money from Peking—knowing its hopelessness, for Peking had been sucked dry—and support themselves and their troops from the unlucky provinces they govern in true feudal-baron style, and Peking on its side received not a cent from any province except a pittance from Shantung. . . . Its prestige is as low as its finances."

[XXVI]

"After months and months in nursing homes, attended by many physicians, each of whom disagreed with . . . his fellows, I have followed a suggestion made to me by Lord Northcliffe, have thrown physic to the dogs, and have come down to the seaside in the hope that a balmier air . . . may enable me to recover sufficient strength to return to China," Morrison wrote to Guy Hillier at the end of April. But "Sunny Sidmouth" belied its name. In twenty-three days, only three had been sunny. The air was far from balmy, and the atmosphere almost as depressing as that of Duff House. Along the rainswept, windy, tempestuously cold esplanade hobbled a sombre procession of "the maimed, the crocks, the paralytics, the octogenarians".

Among the octogenarians Morrison met the eighty-five-year-old General Sir John Dunne, one of the last survivors of the British force that captured Peking in 1860. The General told Morrison how he had discovered among some womens' draperies in the Imperial Palace a little sleeve-dog which he christened "Looty" and later presented to Queen Victoria. "Looty" was one of the first two Pekingeses brought to England, and the Queen had commissioned Landseer's only pupil, F. W. Keyl, to paint two portraits of it. One was exhibited in the Royal Academy of 1863, and the other was given to the General.

Morrison dosed himself with charcoal and chlorodyne, and continued to lose weight. He consulted a local physician, Dr Pollard, who told him he did not have sprue, though Morrison's inhospitable brother-in-law, Mr Justice Higgins, was convinced he was suffering from this "obscure germ disease peculiar to the East". Higgins was perturbed about public affairs. "Things are very perplexing all over the world," he wrote:

. . . Wilson seems to have failed in his efforts to make the world "safe for democracy." The treaty of peace—and the separate treaties—creates incitement to future wars. I confess that I had hoped for better things—hoped that the sacrifice (including the sacrifice of my boy) would not be in vain. But our leaders are swayed by selfish national and other interests.

We have our labour troubles here, but not nearly as bad as in Britain and in America. It is found to be a great advantage to have in Australia recognized tribunals for industrial contests. But the machinery is as yet very defective; and our Government led by Hughes, acts very unwisely. Hughes is vain, with swollen head. . . .

[XXVII]

Lying in bed one afternoon in May, Morrison tried to think if he could recall "a single instance of feeling gaiety of heart" since he was taken ill in Paris fourteen months before:

It has been one long drawn out suffering, the one long deferred hope that wrings my heart and then gives place to hopeless despair. My one hope now is to get back to China. I do not wish to die but if I have to die, let it be in Peking among the Chinese who have treated me with such consideration for so many years.

He was pleased to get a letter from Lionel Pratt, who wrote from Winchester:

The general run of people in England harbour a profound lack of knowledge about China. . . . One thing they all seem to believe implicitly, *i.e.*, that Japan played the part of a gallant and chivalrous ally during the war. It is impossible to withhold . . . admiration from the Japs for their propaganda work. . . .

Morrison replied that though the weather was very trying he felt somewhat better and had been able to walk nearly a mile. He was definitely leaving England on 18th June, and proposed to go to London on Saturday 5th June, to get ready.

In the middle of May he caught a severe chill which left him very weak and shaken. But he insisted that Jennie, against her better judgment, go up to London to arrange for passports and a governess. She booked a room overlooking Cavendish Square, and on Sunday 23rd May wrote to him:

I went to High Mass at Westminster Cathedral this morning and was much moved by the beautiful service. You have been in my thoughts all day, my dearest loved one, and that wonderful day eight years ago when you first told me you loved me—blessed day which I shall always remember. Darling, I offered up such loving prayers for you today from the depths of my heart that your health and our happiness may be restored to us, and I feel they must be answered. I felt comforted and helped after leaving the Cathedral and am confident there are happy years before us yet. . . . I hate leaving you alone. . . .

The day before, Morrison had written in his diary: "The day of our engagement 1912. Seven years of happiness for Jennie and one year of tribulation borne with exemplary patience and devotion." Under this he wrote, with undiminished exactitude:

Had a visit from Bray, son of Sir Edward Bray the County Court Judge. Age 44, 23 years in the Hubbard's business in St Petersburg driven out by the Bolsheviks. A good-looking tall, clean-cut Englishman, sympathetic and prepossessing. He hold me what others had told me that Sir George Buchanan had said to him: "For seven years, I have been in Russia as Ambassador and I must have acquired some knowledge. Yet the F.O. will not accept my suggestions they will not even give me a hearing on the ground that my judgment is warped and that I have been so long in Russia I have lost my sense of perspective!"—These were the words. How characteristic of the F.O. . . . It is true they have a Russian committee, but not one of the members can speak Russian and with one exception not a member has ever been in Russia and that exception is the case of a man who has been in Warsaw!

This was the last entry in his big diary. In a small notebook, four days later, Morrison entered, as usual, clinical details of his condition, and wrote: "Pollard discussed lucid balanced statement for and against operation." The final entry was on Friday, 27th May:

Almost can believe death struggle began. . . . Temperature 95.4 10 a.m. Almost collapsing. If to die better die now so that arrangements can be made for Jennie in good time.

It was forty-two years since the schoolboy at Geelong College had begun his "rum sort of diary".

On the same day Jennie got a telegram that brought her back to Sidmouth by the first train. "I then saw that my dear One would not be long with me," she later wrote to Dr Gray, "and I never left him until he died on Sunday afternoon. . . . He died as he lived, nobly and with supreme courage."

At the end of his diary, in the place which he usually filled with miscellaneous notes, Morrison had written:

> Not heaven itself upon the past has power
> But what has been has been and I have had my hour.
>
> —Dryden quoted by Earl Russell.

The entry was dated "21/1/20". Perhaps he intended it for his epitaph.

Morrison was buried "on a glorious day of sunshine," Jennie wrote to his mother, "in the peaceful little Sidmouth cemetery, right on the top of the hill, looking over Salcombe Hill and the Valley." The Vicar of Sidmouth, who conducted the service, paid tribute to Dr Morrison's life from a religious aspect, declaring that "he was, for the last eight years, an enthusiastic supporter of the foreign missions of the Church as the power for uplifting and instructing other races", a statement that would have surprised Morrison. Among those at the funeral were Mrs Moberly Bell, Dr Sze, Sir John Jordan, Sir John McLeavy Brown, Lord ffrench, General Sir John and Lady Dunne, Sir Pelham Warner, Sir Richard Dane, Mr Henry Cockburn, Vice-Admiral Sir Ernest Gaunt, Rear-Admiral Sir Douglas Brownrigg, and Sir Ernest Satow. Mr John Walter represented *The Times*, and Mr Ashton Gwatkin the Foreign Office. The Australian High Commissioner, apparently too busy to attend, was represented by Major A. W. Arkill. The flowers included a wreath of orchids from the President of the Chinese Republic, with a card "In sorrow and gratitude". Other wreaths were from Sir John Jordan, Viscount Northcliffe, Sir Valentine Chirol, Sir John Dunne, Sir Francis and Lady Aglen, Mrs Moberly Bell, and *The Times*. There was no wreath from the Commonwealth of Australia.

A characteristic letter from Hutton arrived too late:

So you were reading Buckle. . . . What a pity he was carried off so young. Consumption! What a fine research man he was . . . a real investigator. There is no doubt that Free Will is all bosh. . . . The great failure of modern times is Religion. The highly educated admit this. The average person just leaves the question alone and follows the crowd. . . .

"As a medical man, he had known his fate for months and quietly warned friends of what must be expected," said *The Times* in a special article:

But even in the months which daily sapped his physical strength, his enthusiasm for China was undiminished, and even grew. It was a strange experience to see the wasted, ascetic figure propped in a chair or in bed, and to hear the dying man planning for the future of China with a skill of analysis, a breadth of vision in constructive statesmanship, and altogether a mental vigour such as one associates with only a few men in the world, and these in the enjoyment of bodily health. It was then one realized how inadequate to the breadth of the man was even the proud title, "Morrison of Peking". His passion was that Great Britain might play her part in China's development, and even the smallest opportunity became a great opportunity to him if it offered the winning of interest in this theme. China never had a more devoted servant.

"An Old China Hand", writing in *The Times*, quoted Meredith's lines:

> *The tender humour, the fire of sense*
> *In your good eyes: how full of heart for all*
> *And chiefly for the weaker by the wall.*

"Tenderness and humour, indeed were of his very fibre," said the Old China Hand:

> Tenderness that took its health from humour; humour mellowed by tenderness. Both are needed if a man is to understand China. . . . When Morrison spoke of the land to which he gave the best years of his life, it was with a compassionate clearness of comprehension. . . .
>
> It became clear, though he would never put it in words, that his love for China and the Chinese people was the great fact, the all-absorbing passion, of his mature life.

"To pretend that you knew Morrison was to affect the impossible," wrote Lionel James in the *Nineteenth Century*. "Even those who imagined that they were intimate would suddenly discover that there was still a Morrison altogether incomprehensible to them":

> It was my great good fortune to be intimately associated with Morrison for some months. . . . During this period the writer came under the spell of his many-sided greatness: he was inspired by his seriousness: elevated by his humour: impressed by his infinite capacity for taking pains: chastened by his manly dignity: delighted by his kindliness of character and love for children: terrified by his unerring memory: appalled by his cold judgment on men and matters: enticed by his peculiar vanity: and overwhelmed by his pride in Australia and himself as an Australian.

It was a perceptive summing-up. Morrison never forgot Australia, even though Australia forgot him. In his last letter to Jennie, written a few days before his death, he said:

> I leave to you, to your absolute discretion, all my papers, and letters and diaries. These would form the basis of a life of me, should such a life be worth recording. You should carefully go through these and then, at your discretion, you should present them to the Mitchell Library, Sydney. They are an interesting contemporary record of Far Eastern history, intimately written, of value to the historian, and their proper resting place is in the Mitchell Library.

In the same letter he expressed the wish that a collection of his Chinese curiosities should be presented to the Melbourne Museum. The Melbourne *Age*, the paper on which Morrison made his start as a journalist, devoted one-third of a column to his obituary. Unfortunately for Morrison it was a day of big news in Melbourne; the Prince of Wales had shaken the hands of 800 invalid soldiers, and watched 10,000 school-children spell out OUR PRINCE in letters of pink, yellow, green, mauve, and blue.

POSTSCRIPT

[I]

SOON AFTER Morrison's death many London publishers approached Mrs Morrison about producing a biography. "It is a book that must be written," said Mr Jonathan Cape. And Mr John Murray advised her that it should be in one volume of about 80,000 to 100,000 words. "The public have become tired of two-volume biographies," he said. Mrs Morrison decided to have the diaries edited before the biography was written, and asked Buckle to suggest an editor. He recommended J. B. Capper, who had retired from *The Times*, after thirty-eight and a half years of night work, on a "modest, not lavish" pension, and Capper, when he had carefully assayed the material, accepted. "The progress cannot be rapid," he warned Mrs Morrison, "as the writing in the earlier years is very small, cramped and hurried." But he was "greatly interested and much attached to the work", which he began at the end of 1922. Six months later, on 20th June 1923, Mrs Morrison died, and it was not till 1925 that the first two volumes, comprising the diaries from 1899 to 1901, were completed. The manuscript was accepted for publication by Constable and Company, but the trustees of the estate withdrew it on the grounds that "sufficient time had not elapsed since the events etc. described". It is strange that they did not make this decision before Capper had devoted three years to his punctilious editing.

[II]

"George Ernest Morrison never ceased to prophesy the danger of the rapid expansion of Japanese military policy," Beatrice Brownrigg wrote to *The Times* in December 1937, when Japanese forces had captured Shanghai and were striking at the heart of China. "When he finally left China in 1919, he was aware of the grave personal risk he took in removing his diaries from Peking, because it was important to Japan's international reputation that his peculiar knowledge of her machinations should not become history.

411

"Dr Morrison asked me to edit his diaries for publication and honoured though I was, I felt unequal to that prodigious task. . . . It is to be hoped that before much time elapses someone will realize the immense value of their contribution to the history of the Far East in the 20th century. . . ."

The diaries were deposited in the Mitchell Library, Sydney, together with a huge mass of miscellaneous material: letters, telegrams, cuttings, cards, photographs, even pawn-tickets and hotel bills, which Morrison indiscriminately preserved. When his mother died in 1932 her collection of letters was added to his. The whole consists of 255 boxes, volumes, and packets. Mrs Morrison in her will said that she wished the diaries and papers to be kept from the public for twenty-five years. I had some difficulty in getting access to them after forty years. I am grateful to the staff of the Mitchell Library, however, for its amiable co-operation once I had broached the wall arbitrarily flung up by the trustees. I wish also to record my gratitude to the late Miss Edith Moberly Bell; to Mr Harry Nunn, Senior Archivist, and Mr Phillip Garrett, former Senior Research Officer of the State Library of Victoria; to Dr Lo Hui-min, Department of Far Eastern History, the Australian National University; to Mr P. Henchy, Keeper of Printed Books, National Library of Dublin; to Dr Leon Shirlaw, of Romford, Essex, and to Dr George Shaw and Miss Sue Aland, of Melbourne. The Commonwealth Literary Fund helped me with a research grant, and the then editor of *The Times*, Sir William Haley, hindered me by curtly refusing me access to its archives. I travelled to London specifically to see the private letters which Morrison had written to Moberly Bell, and which Miss Moberly Bell had entrusted to *The Times* for safe-keeping, but despite the fact that they were her property, and despite her gracious intervention on my behalf, Sir William, who showed not the slightest interest in Morrison, remained obdurate.

[III]

The Morrison library was given a permanent home in 1923, when a building to house it was erected in the Hongo quarter of Toyko, where the Imperial University is situated. "Each volume . . . will bear Morrison's bookplate, in which, in memory of his Australian birth, a kangaroo figures prominently," said *The Times*. The bookplate has more zoological than artistic value, though Morrison was very proud of it. "The design is not quite original," he explained to Ashton Gwatkin. "It was drawn for me by one who was said to be a Royal Academician in the service of the Army and Navy Stores. . . . It is based upon two drawings in that great work in three volumes . . . 'Pictorial Australasia' [*the Picturesque Atlas of Australasia*]".

The Times listed some of the more interesting items in the library:

The Morrison collection includes over four hundred early manuscript dictionaries and grammars, some twenty thousand printed
volumes, four thousand pamphlets, and two thousand maps and
engravings. Among the treasures are five beautiful examples of the
rare books printed on rice paper at Macao in the latter part of the
17th century, a Chinese-Latin manuscript dictionary finished in
1724, a Latin translation of the Nestorian tablet, published in 1685,
forty-one editions of Marco Polo, including the first edition of 1496
in Italian, and the first English, French and German editions, the
MS. dictionary used by Sir John Barrow in 1793, together with the
log book of the Lion frigate which took Lord Macartney and
Barrow to China. The books in the collection are in over twenty
different languages; they include the most complete collection known
of missionary literature and other special subjects, that relating to
ornithology being particularly fine.

A feature of the collection is the section devoted to pamphlets,
reports and Blue-books; the pamphlets alone fill several hundred
cases. The maps, which date from 1565, are very valuable; in one of
them Korea is shown as an island.

Dr Mikinosuke Ishida, an accomplished Chinese historian and linguist,
who as a young graduate had supervised the removal of the library from
Peking, remained in charge of it until 1934. When I saw him in 1964 he
told me, over a cup of lemon tea, a huge banana, and a paper towel, how
the library had been moved during World War II to a remote village
in the North of Japan, and had escaped damage. But in January 1949
The Times reported that the books, which were still in the north, were
"merely tied up with straw ropes, inadequately protected against the rain
and snow". The Japanese were afraid that the library might have been
claimed as war reparations, and took the view "that they would rather
see the collection perish than allow it to fall into alien hands". The
Australian Minister for External Affairs, Dr Herbert Evatt, is said to
have demanded it for Australia and to have been rebuked by General
MacArthur for making such an undemocratic proposal.

The "Morrison Library", as its creator wished it to remain and to be
known for all times, no longer exists. In contempt of Morrison's wishes,
the books have been distributed through the library of the Toyo Bunko
—the Tokyo Institute of Oriental Studies—and can be identified only by
the sad and reproachful kangaroo that looks out from the bookplate.

SELECT BIBLIOGRAPHY

The following is a select list only. It does not include books of marginal importance or references to the many newspapers and periodicals, from England, Australia, the United States, and the East, that have obviously been consulted. For an account of other research, see Postscript.

ALLEN, Roland: *The Siege of the Peking Legations*. London, 1901.

AMERY, Leopold: *My Political Life*. London, 1953.

BLAND, J. O. P. and BACKHOUSE, E.: *China Under the Empress Dowager*. London, 1910.

BONSAL, Stephen: *Suitors and Supplicants*. New York, 1916.

CH'EN, Jerome: *Yuan Shih-k'ai*. London, 1961.

CHIROL, Sir Valentine: *Fifty Years in a Changing World*. London, 1927.

COWAN, James: *Suwarran Gold*. London, 1936.

CROW, Carl: *I Speak for the Chinese*. London, 1938.

CURZON, George: *Problems of the Far East*. London, 1894.

DICKINSON, G. Lowes: *The International Anarchy*. London, 1926.

DOUGLAS, Robert K.: *Society in China*. London, 1901.

DUNBABIN, Thomas: *Slavers of the South Seas*. Sydney, 1935.

ESCARRA, Jean: *Le Droit Chinois*. Peking, 1936.

FITZGERALD, C. P.: *Revolution in China*. London, 1952.

FLEMING, Peter: *The Siege at Peking*. London, 1959.

GAMMIE, Alexander: *Dr George H. Morrison: His Life and Work*. London, 1928.

GREEN, O. M.: *The Story of China's Revolution*. London, 1945.

History of the Times, The, 4 vols. London, 1935-52.

HOOKER, Mary: *Behind the Scenes in Peking*. London, 1910.

JAMES, Lionel: *Times of Stress*. London, 1929.

KITCHEN, F. H.: *Moberly Bell and his Times*. London, 1925.

LANDOR, Arnold Henry Savage: *China and the Allies*. London, 1901.

LANSING, George: *Old Forces in China*. Shanghai, 1912.

MAGNUS, Phillip: *Kitchener: Portrait of an Imperialist*. London, 1958.

McALEAVY, Henry: *A Dream of Tartary*. London, 1963.

MOOREHEAD, Alan: *Cooper's Creek*. London, 1963.

MORRISON, G. E.: *An Australian in China*. London, 1895.

NICHOLSON, Harold: *Peacemaking, 1919*. London, 1933.

PURCELL, Victor: *The Boxer Uprising*. Cambridge, 1963.

REED, S. W.: *The Making of New Guinea*. Philadelphia, 1943.

REINSCH, P. S.: *An American Diplomat in China*. London, 1922.

SMITH, Arthur H.: *China in Convulsion*, 2 vols. New York, 1901.

TAN, Chester, C.: *The Boxer Catastrophe*. New York, 1955.

TREVELYAN, G. M.: *Grey of Fallodon*. London, 1937.

VARÉ, D.: *Laughing Diplomat*. London, 1938.

WALDERSEE, Count Alfred, von: *A Field-Marshal's Memoirs*. London, 1924.

WARD, J. M.: *British Policy in the South Pacific (1786-1893)*. Sydney, 1948.

WEALE, B. L. P.: *Indiscreet Letters from Peking*. New York, 1922.

WEALE, B. L. P.: *The Fight for the Republic in China*. London, 1918.

WHYTE, W. Farmer: *William Morris Hughes, His Life and Times*. Sydney, 1957.

WINGFIELD-STRATFORD, E. C.: *The Victorian Aftermath, 1901-1914*. London, 1933.

WITTE, Count S. G.: *Memoirs*, ed. by A. Yarmolinsky. New York, 1921.

WRIGHT, M. C.: *The Last Stand of Chinese Conservatism*. Palo Alto, 1962.

INDEX

418

Morrison, *Dr* George Ernest—continued
87; and Russian demands on China,
88, 96-7; and reform movement in
China, 90, 92; visits Siam, 93-4; and
British Foreign Office, 96-8, 99, 102,
106, 109, 143, 165, 171, 218, 225, 242,
261, 273, 291; in England, 1899, 100-4;
voyage to Australia, 1899-1900, 103-5;
visits Japan and Korea, 105; warmongering of, 105, 143-5, 147, 154;
relations with Chirol of *The Times*, 105-
6, 139-40, 143, 181, 194-7, 205, 215, 218-
19, 221, 239, 251, 252; and Boxer uprising, 107, 108-28, 131-2, 133; defence
of Chinese Christians, 113-14, 116;
wounded during Peking siege, 124-5,
127, 133-4; *The Times* acknowledges,
126, 128; "obituary", 126, 127, 252;
books projected by, 128, 138-9, 209,
240; on Manchu Court's return to
Peking after Boxer uprising, 135-8;
1902 holiday in Australia, 141-2; appetite for scandal, 141-2, 158-62, 174-6,
210-11, 333-5, 360, 379, 402; on Manchuria, 143-5, 192-3, 194; and Russo-
Japanese war, 145-8, 376-7; recognition in Japan, 146, 147, 170, 193; at
Portsmouth conference, 151-5, 158;
meets Theodore Roosevelt, 156-7;
London-Europe visit, 158-71; recognition of work, 162-3, 164, 170; returns to Peking, 1906, 173-4; travels
from Peking to Hanoi, 179-81; discus-
ses his future with *The Times*, 182-4,
187-8; addresses China Association,
185-6; meets Dalai Lama, 188-9; and
Yuan Shih-k'ai, 190, 242, 247-9, 326;
on the Empress Dowager's funeral,
190-2; disillusionment with Japan,
192-5, 205, 219, 220, 290-1, 307 (*see
also* Japan); and Lord Kitchener,
198-200; journey through far western
China to Moscow, 200-3, 219; and reorganization of *The Times*, 203-5;
1910-11 visit to London, 205-15, 222;
in Europe, 217; and Northcliffe, 218-
20, 221, 239, 399-400; in St Petersburg, 221-2; travels to Harbin, 222-3;
returns to Peking, 1911, 223-5; and
1911 revolution, 228-34, 235-8, 241-
50, 251; in financial difficulties, 239-
40, 258-61; "Hero of the Chinese Reform Movement", 244; on army
"mutiny" in Peking, 244-8, 249; resignation from *The Times*, 252-4, 255,
257-62, 273, 274, 297; politics of, 253-
4; adviser to Yuan Shih-k'ai's Gov-

ernment, 257, 261, 262, 265-6, 272-3,
274-5, 278-80, 282-3, 286, 287-92, 294-
6, 297-300, 305-6, 307-10, 312-17, 323-
5, 327; 1912 visit to London, 266; on
the New China, 266-71; marriage of,
275, 276-7; Chinese honours conferred
on, 278, 304; and Sung murder case,
284-5; and Reconstruction loan, 285-6,
309-10; 1914 visit to London, 297-303;
criticism of Chinese, 306, 311-13; and
Twenty-one Demands, 307-9; opposes
re-establishment of Chinese monarchy, 313-15, 320-2, 325; and China's
entry into First World War, 315-17,
330-3, 335-8, 341-2, 404; adviser to
Li Yuan-hung's Government, 328-9,
336, 338-9, 341-2, 345, 346, 355-7, 365-
6, 367; 1916 visit to Japan, 330-1; 1917
visit to Australia, 345-53, 354-63; visit
to New Zealand, 353-4, 365; returns to
Peking, 1918, 365-6; adviser to Hsu
Shih-chang's Government, 369-72,
373-4, 400, 403, 405-6, 409; and Chinese in Australia, 373; and First World
War peace conference, 373-4, 377, 380,
383-5, 386; talk with Yoshizara, on
Anglo-Japanese relations, 374-5; Can-
ada/United States visit, 378; arrives in
London, 1918, 378-80; fatal illness of,
389-90, 392-7, 399-400, 403, 404, 406,
407; desire to return to Peking, 395,
403, 406, 407; death of, 408-9; articles
written on his death, 409-10; his
diaries, 410, 411-12; fate of his library,
412-13 (*see also* Library)
Morrison, Hugh, 2
Morrison, Ian Ernest McLeavy, son, 289,
297, 302
Morrison, *Reverend* James, uncle, 1, 2
Morrison, Jennie, wife, 276-7, 297, 302,
303, 317, 339, 341-2, 348, 368, 374,
377-8, 379, 382, 389, 393, 395, 396, 399,
400, 402, 403, 407-8, 409, 410, 411, 412.
See also Robin, Jennie Wark
Morrison, Kenneth, 2
Morrison, *Mrs* Rebecca, mother, 20, 21,
30, 49, 64, 68, 391, 409, 412. *See also*
Greenwood, Rebecca
Morrison, Robert, uncle, 2
Morrison, Thomas, uncle, 2
Morrison, *Dr* W. A., cousin, 4
Mount, —, 9, 18-19
Muirhead, *Reverend*, 393
Mukden, fall of, 147, 151
Munro-Ferguson, *Lady* Helena, 348
Munro-Ferguson, *Sir* Ronald, 348, 382
Murdoch, Keith, 381-2

427